WOMEN AND AMBITION

A BIBLIOGRAPHY

by
Patricia Spencer Faunce

The Scarecrow Press, Inc.
Metuchen, N.J., & London
1980

Library of Congress Cataloging in Publication Data

Faunce, Patricia Spencer, 1937-
  Women and ambition.

  Includes index.
  1. Women--Psychology--Bibliography. 2. Achievement motivation--Bibliography. 3. Success--Bibliography.
4. Ambition--Bibliography. I. Title.
Z7961.F38 [HQ1206]   016.30141'2   79-18347
ISBN 0-8108-1242-8

Copyright © 1980 by Patricia Spencer Faunce

Manufactured in the United States of America

ACKNOWLEDGMENTS

The monumental task of developing this bibliography required the efforts and commitment of many people, and would not have been possible without their assistance.

First, I offer my deepest appreciation and gratitude to Melinda Monteith Sonderling for her dedication, energy, enthusiasm, zest for excellence, shared expertise, and splendid humor during the long and tedious process as we proofread together, edited, and finalized the manuscript.

My sincere and heartfelt thanks to Robin Cooper, Dana Fox, Nicki Davidson, and Anne Nevaldine who extended their gracious efforts, wholehearted assistance, and willing persistence in the hand search of references.

Janice Bobrowske and Nora Page certainly are deserving of laudatory acknowledgment for their incredible detective work in sleuthing and tracking references in the libraries.

Special thanks also are due to Anne and to Phyllis Dozier for the painstaking and laborious hours they spent checking and alphabetizing the numerous references.

Kathy Cummings and Vivian Nordgren should be commended for devoting their fine skills to typing the manuscript.

Paula Fladeboe, Jennifer Kinnee, Wendy Seikkula, and Laura Parham are also deserving of extra special mention. They all assisted in a variety of ways including typing and xeroxing.

While many persons have assisted on the project, I alone assume responsibility for any errors in or omissions from this bibliography.

Patricia Spencer Faunce
April 11, 1978

CONTENTS

Acknowledgments		iii
Introduction		vii
Overview: Women and Ambition		xv
I.	BACKGROUND ON WOMEN AND AMBITION	1
II.	SOCIETAL FORCES AND WOMEN'S AMBITION	5
	A. Society, Culture, Socialization	5
	B. Sex Roles	
	1. General	42
	2. Ambition, and ambition-related behavior	79
	C. Family Background, Parental Influence, Role Models	146
III.	SOCIAL-PSYCHOLOGICAL FORCES AND WOMEN'S AMBITION	174
	A. Self-Concept, Self-Esteem	174
	B. Personality Characteristics	192
	C. Interests, Values	213
	D. Fear of Success, Fear of Failure	220
	E. Expectations, Control, and Attributed Causes of Success/Failure	
	1. Expectations of success/failure	238
	2. Internal-external control of success/failure	242
	3. Attributed causes of success/failure	255
IV.	COUNSELING FORCES AND WOMEN'S AMBITION	264
V.	EDUCATIONAL FORCES AND WOMEN'S AMBITION	303
	A. General	303
	B. Students	338
	C. Faculty	368
	D. Administrators	384
VI.	OCCUPATIONAL FORCES AND WOMEN'S AMBITION	397
	A. General	397
	B. Specific	

1.	Business, management, industry	451
2.	Sciences, engineering, mathematics	467
3.	Health sciences	474
4.	Social and behavioral sciences	480
5.	Law and law enforcement	486
6.	Government and politics	487
7.	Arts, music, media	490
8.	Religion	493
9.	Athletics	496
10.	Military	497
11.	Professional	498

VII. CAREER DEVELOPMENT, ORIENTATION, CONTINGENCIES 500

    A. Career Development and Orientation 500
    B. Career Contingencies 518

VIII. MINORITY WOMEN AND AMBITION 541

    A. Minority Women--General 541
    B. Black Women
        1. Societal forces 551
        2. Social-psychological forces 576
        3. Counseling, educational, occupational forces 586
        4. Career development, orientation, contingencies 601
    C. Latin Women
        1. Societal forces 603
        2. Social-psychological forces 617
        3. Counseling, educational, occupational forces 619
        4. Career development, orientation, contingencies 623
    D. Native-American Women 624

Author and Coauthor Index 629

INTRODUCTION

This bibliography is about women's achievement motivation; that is, women's ambition. As we grow older, one of the recurring questions most of us seek to answer is "What shall I do with my life?" This quest begins when we are very young. Adults are fond of asking children "What do you want to be when you grow up?" What they really want to know is "What will you achieve?" Boys expressing the desire to be doctors or lawyers or astronauts are assumed to reflect a concern with achievement and success in the marketplace. Girls also set goals, but their goals are usually more "modest"; they want to be nurses or teachers or mommies. Success as a teacher or nurse is not considered comparable to success as a doctor or attorney. Therefore, it has been easy to conclude that women and girls are not as interested in achievement as men and boys.

Achievement--its nature, level, and experience--is one of the most significant facets of the lives of people in industrialized societies. A major indicator of the current status of any definable group, collective achievement profoundly affects the lives of the group's members. American society emphasizes ambition, striving, accomplishment--in a word, success. Women as a group constitute over half of the population. Why have they not pursued occupational goals earmarked by this American sense of success?

Until recently it was generally agreed that discriminatory hiring practices were responsible for the underrepresentation of women in positions of power and prestige. But times are changing. The federal Pay Act of 1963 and Title VII of the federal Civil Rights Act of 1964 have provided women with increased opportunities for occupational advancement. Yet, this increase in opportunity has been accompanied by a decline in the proportion of women seeking every level of higher education and achievement.

In 1940, 45 per cent of the technical and professional positions in this country were held by women; by 1968 the proportion of women in technical and professional occupations had declined to 35 per cent. Even among those women who do hold professional-level jobs, most are employed in fields traditionally considered appropriate for the female sex role. For example, 97 per cent of all registered nurses, 92 per cent of all dieticians, 85 per cent of all elementary school teachers, and 70 per cent of all health technicians are women. In contrast, only 2 per cent of the engineers, 5 per cent of the attorneys, and 9 per cent of all physicians in this country are women.

Recently, considerable attention has been focused on changing patterns of women's achievements. The diverse collection of references in this bibliography reflects this attention. The arrangement chosen attempts to place the problem and issues of women's achievement within a broad social and psychological context.

A variety of explanations have been proposed to account for why women do not set and strive for those goals inherent in the American dream of success. These explanations, related to women's ambition and the lack of it, include societal forces (culture, socialization, sex roles, family background, parental influence, role models); social-psychological forces (self-concept, personality characteristics, interests, fear of success, expectations, control, and attributed causes of success or failure); counseling, educational, and occupational forces; and women's career development and contingencies. This bibliography presents these explanations in the form of theoretical, research, and general-literature references.

The comprehensiveness of this bibliography is indicative of current interest and research in women and their achievement. Not all of this material has been published, but, as interest sky-rockets, especially so since the early 70's, more and more is being published.

To put the bibliography into perspective, an overview on women's ambition is first presented.

Section I then presents references to background studies on

Introduction / ix

the state of affairs regarding women's ambition. A book on women's achievement is more than a book about women; it deals with the achievement motive in all people, both women and men. Much of the recent research on women has made it apparent that our behavior and social sciences have applied largely to men only. In 1953, David McClelland, who has contributed much to our understanding of human motivation in general and of the achievement motive in particular, wrote that his efforts to study women were "totally puzzling." Since his theory of human behavior cannot, then, be applied to over half the human population, it is inadequate. The new research on women's achievement is forcing us to revise existing theories regarding all people's achievement; such revision can only enrich the discipline. The themes of this bibliography move us in that direction.

The study of women and achievement is incomplete if told only in the context of one discipline, one culture, and one time perspective. Thus, Section II presents works on women's ambition as influenced by societal forces. The citations in this section provide the broader perspective needed to assess and comprehend the social determinants of women's status and attainments, past and present, and prospects for change. Each sub-section focuses on a particular facet of the many issues involved, including the impact of culture, and socialization; the problem of stereotypic sex-role behavior, attitudes, and traits in general, as well as those specifically related to achievement practices; and family and role-model considerations.

To provide a complete picture, other crucial aspects of women's achievement motivation must be considered. Section III documents references on the social-psychological forces influencing the ambition of women. Self-concept and self-esteem, personality characteristics, interests and values are covered as well as fear of success, expectations, control, and attributed causes of success or failure. All these dimensions are influential in women's achievement behavior.

Up to this point, the stress has been on writings about personal and internal forces affecting each women's ambition, but women's ambition is also affected by external forces found in counseling, education, and the work world.

The effect of counseling forces such as biases in counseling/therapy and testing, and special programs such as assertiveness training, are presented in Section IV.

Educational forces which affect women's ambition are referenced in Section V. A general overview is followed by the experience of women in academic life as students, as faculty, and as administrators. Higher education has historically been a major avenue for upward mobility in the United States. It has also become a necessary preliminary or adjunct to careers in many professional fields. Therefore sex biases in composition or treatment of students, faculty, and administrators significantly effect the achievement opportunities of large numbers of women.

When women move from the educational world into the work world, they continue to face issues/problems regarding their achievement. The impact of these occupational forces on women's ambition is dealt with in Section VI; first in general, and then in specific occupational fields.

Works about women's career development and orientation and their career contingencies are catalogued in Section VII. In the latter, such contingencies or factors as role conflict, husband's attitudes and dual-career families are covered.

Section VIII has special interest because it focuses on minority women and their achievement. While not as much has been researched or written about the achievement motivation of minority women, studies in this area are increasing. The story of women and achievement would be incomplete if told only in the context of the majority white culture. First, general references are presented. These are followed by references for black women and Latin women, with each sub-section similarily classified parallel to the overall bibliography. The scarcity of material on native-American women did not permit a similar classification.

For each section and sub-section, the references are alphabetized by the author's last name, or, where there is no name, by title of the book, article or paper. Within one author's listings, the arrangement is chronological, from the earliest writing to the latest. The references in Sections I through VII are cross-referenced, with the exception of those in III D and III E, Fear of Success (and of failure), and Expectations, Control, and Attributed causes of Success or Failure. References for Section VIII, Minority Women, are cross referenced only within that section.

The research and literature references are to works published in the years 1960 through 1976 and some of 1977. The search was conducted during the summer and early fall of 1977.

Computer searches were made for ERIC, Comprehensive Dissertation Index, Sociological Abstracts, and ABI/INFORM. Hand searches were made for Psychological Abstracts, Education Index, Reader's Guide to Periodical Research, part of the Sociological Abstracts, and some of the more recently published magazines and journals about women, e. g., New Women, Women at Work, SIGNS: Journal of Women in Culture and Society, Sex Roles: A Journal of Research, and Psychology of Women Quarterly. ERIC contains citations to unpublished research reports indexed in Resources in Education since 1966, and to journal articles indexed in Current Index to Journals in Education since 1969. Although the loading dates for ERIC were 1966 and 1969, information before these dates can be found in ERIC. Sociological Abstracts began in 1963, so, in addition to the computer search, a hand search was completed for 1960 through 1962. ABI/INFORM, which began in 1971, contains information from major periodicals, magazines, and journals in business and management.

Some problems were encountered in compiling this volume. In some cases only incomplete references were available; for example, the volume or page number could not be found because the actual article or book itself could not be located. If reasonable information was available, these references were included. The reader may track them down should she/he desire to do so. Contradictory references, that is, ostensibly identical references but with contradictory information, also were a problem. In some cases, the original sources could be located and the problem resolved; in other cases, this was not true and the references were omitted. There is always the problem of completeness; that is, was every reference that should be included found in the searches? The answer is probably no. However, the user of this bibliography can assume that the vast majority of references for the years noted have been included, and that the bibliography is quite complete.

Several factors provided the impetus for this bibliography. First is the new feminism, which is increasing women's thinking about their roles and the consequences of being born female. Another is consideration of women's conflicting ambitions, or the dilemma of trying to achieve both as women and as workers--goals that seem totally incompatible much of the time. A final factor is my personal involvement combined with the awareness of growing interest and research in this area on the part of a number of colleagues, mostly women. It followed quite naturally that pulling together much of this work would be useful.

The basic goal of this bibliography has been to compile a variety of references that reflect thinking, research and theoretical concerns which will provide a useful frame of reference for further work. Thus, this bibliography will be useful to a wide variety of persons in a wide variety of areas; the social and behavioral sciences, education, librarianship, business and management, counseling, social work, minority studies, and women's studies, to mention only a few. Hopefully, Women and Ambition: A Bibliography will become a cornerstone for future research in this area.

"Look at My Life"

a song by Meredith Tax

I was first a daughter, and then a wife
Belongin' to somebody else all my life
I never learned what I needed to know
And I started to die when I started to grow.

    Look at my life, what have I done?
    I learned to walk, but not to run,
    I learned to walk, but not to fly,
    When they tied my wings I began to die.

Look at the mirror upon the wall
Is that a toy, girl, is that a doll?
Is there anybody there behind the mask?
What's the answer? Are you scared to ask?

    (Chorus)

Oh, when I die and go to hell
They'll keep me doin' the things I learned to do well
I'll be cookin' and sewin', standin' by the sink
Have to die at least twice to get time to think.

    (Chorus)

1970.

Reprinted by permission of the poet.

OVERVIEW: WOMEN AND AMBITION

> I'm looking toward the day when all barriers get broken so that there's no longer a first female anything and we can get on with our work. --Lynn Sherr.*

The American Dream of Success is deeply rooted in our history and our culture. This same dream based on achievement and ambition often restrains potential Einsteins, Salks, or Lincolns from fulfilling their highest potential ... if they are born female.

Not many years ago, families took it for granted that a son would be sent to college but a daughter would not. However, in the last thirty to forty years large numbers of women have had opportunities for higher education opened to them. This period is long enough that the results may be appraised. Such an appraisal is disappointing to those who had hoped that equal opportunities for women would yield equal intellectual achievements.

Women are still conspicuous for their absence in the arts, sciences, medicine, law, higher education, and business.

Why is this so?

We are beginning to uncover some deep barriers to women's success. They are rooted in her socialization, role expectations, education, and her relation to the world of masculine ambition and success.

The pressures on American women not to achieve are stronger and more complex than most people realize. Evidence exists regarding important differences in the experiences of female and male

---

*Quoted in Kazickas, J., and Sherr, L., The Woman's Calendar for 1978 (New York: Universe Books, 1977). Lynn Sherr became the nation's first female anchor of a national prime-time network news show as host of PBS's "USA: People and Politics," August 19, 1976.

xvi / Overview

children. This evidence indicates that the sexes have been differentially socialized with different training practices, for different goals, and with different results. Girls are taught to be passive, dependent, and compliant, and are rewarded for such behaviors, while boys are expected to be independent, aggressive, and self-sufficient. Empirical data suggest that parental expectations center on their daughters' being "pretty, nice, affectionate, and well-liked." In contrast, the same parents expect their sons to be "responsible, to show initiative, and to stand up for themselves." Relationships have been found among child-rearing practices, independence and mastery training in particular; and achievement-motivation scores of individuals tested, actual achievement of individuals, and, indeed, the economic growth of whole societies. These findings leave no doubt as to why the historical achievement of women has been low. In fact, with the dependence training women receive so early in life, the wonder is that they have achieved so much.

In the human drama, the general orientation of girls, young women, and older women is usually "other directed." Children are taught sexual stereotypes early, as well as the appropriate behavior for a sex-determined role in life. To ask a little boy, "What do you want to be when you grow up?" implies to him unlimited possibilities in his future. But to ask the little girl, "Where did you get your pretty dress?" suggests that her importance lies in her prettiness. If she is asked what she wants to be when she grows up, her response is likely to be sex-role conditioned, "a mother," or at most "a mother and a teacher."

Throughout childhood and on into adulthood, females are constantly urged to consider, "Am I doing the right thing?" and "What can I be or do in order to please others?" Occupational success almost never emerges as the answer to these questions. Pleasing others and doing the right thing usually means repressing strong ambition and career commitment.

Ironically, black women, who are traditionally strong and ambitious, are recently being subjected to a dose of the more traditional orientation as an outgrowth of the black political movement.

They are asked to weigh from the perspective of black men rather than their own, the choices they will make toward a richer life or a wider set of options.

The effects of low-status expectations on the development of self-esteem are also striking and harmful to the creation of healthy adult personalities. Women, given tasks which are not rewarded financially, socially, or psychologically, traditionally accept society's negative stereotypes. They believe themselves and other women to be less ambitious, less intellectually capable, less important, and less able to make decisions than men.

Thus, women from childhood on are rewarded for the development of personality traits which are inimical to competitiveness and strong self-motivation. This occurs because achievement is considered, on the one hand, detrimental to their femininity and, on the other hand, unnecessary to the performance of their allotted adult roles--a self-fulfilling prophecy. Her original assignment to low-status roles, her weak identity formation, her low self-esteem, and the negative emphasis on achievement make it unlikely that an adult woman will be motivated or successful in roles other than her traditional feminine one.

This mixed bag of myths about women, assertions about her incapabilities or special strengths, models of (hu)man nature as opposed to the nature of woman, all contribute to assign and resign women to supporting roles in the human drama. They are rarely experienced by society at large as ambitious and successful; that is, they are rarely heroes.

Self-identity for females derives from a prevailing concept of femininity focusing almost exclusively on the fulfillment of wife/mother roles. Unlike men, whose sense of identity stems from an assessment of their own abilities, talents, and aspirations for achievement in occupational roles, women's status and identity is determined not by her own achievements or accomplishments but by those of her husband.

Young women are oriented to a future which they determine only indirectly--by marrying a suitable man whose ideas, aspirations, and identity will determine their own. That same future depends on an irrational process of "falling in love," with the male taking the initiative and making the advances. As a result, clear ideas or plans for the future are rarely found in adolescent and even college-age American women. This assignment of women to roles that involve being cared for and dependent on another for status identity and prestige relieves a young woman of the responsibility for discovering who she is and what she may accomplish as an adult. At the same time, her failure to develop a strong positive sense of identity reinforces the conformity and dependency encouraged during her earlier socialization. Significantly, that young woman is under no pressure to carefully think about and plan for gainful employment.

The social-psychological measure of success is self-realization or identity formation. However, these concepts have been given exclusively masculine interpretations. Sociologists, for example, view adult identity as "primarily a function of career movements within occupations and work organizations." Psychoanalysts write that personality integration is usually achieved "preparatory to or coincidentally with occupation choice." Does this mean that if a woman chooses never to take a job, she cannot hope to become a well-integrated adult? If she defers career plans until she raises a family, is she spending an extra decade as a psychological adolescent? Conversely, if she follows the prescription for career development, is she becoming a man?

Many women, some more overtly than others, regard their choice as marriage versus a career, or more basically, femininity versus masculinity. Unfortunately, the "feminine-masculine" dichotomy carries an overload of attached meanings and values that has distorted the biological concepts implicit in the words "female-male."

Thus, the institutions of family and work collaborate to deter women from achieving occupation success. Family demands keep a woman out of real competition in the job market: reciprocally, the lack of positive reinforcement a woman faces in her occupation sends her back to the home to seek rewards there.

To add to the confusion, women are deterred from success

by the fact that they, in order to be considered "really" successful, must demonstrate competence in a range of roles, "female" roles as well as occupational roles. The "ideal" woman is a perfectly balanced person who does a little of everything--a little writing and research, a little gourmet cooking, a little loving, a little mothering. But nowhere is the ideal woman encouraged to rise to the top of her profession. And even if she does, occupational excellence is not sufficient for a woman to be considered really successful, that is, ideal.

What standards are used in assessing women's accomplishments in this society? The dominant standard in our culture is the occupational criterion. In American society it is a double standard: one for males, a contingent standard for females.

A knowledge of problems of female personality development and sex-role stereotyping are important to an understanding of women's achievement motivation. The assignment of women to low-status roles is significant. Anticipation of their adult roles influences the psychological, behavioral, and intellectual development of female children and adolescents. The relative importance of her future role is particularly crucial in accounting for the limited development of achievement motivation, strong positive identity, and self-esteem in an adolescent girl.

Negative self-concepts result in negative efforts. It is another self-fulfilling prophecy. Women stifle motivation and channel energies into those areas in which they are more likely to find positive social rewards as opposed to occupational or intellectual rewards. Today, women are condemned for not striving for the highest rewards society has to offer. This situation clearly puts women in the classic double bind; a woman can be feminine but incompetent; or competent but unfeminine.

The American female is formed in the "feminine" image from childhood. By the time she is going steady at twelve her future is so clearly determined that only exceptional will and courage on her part can change it. To change her future she must risk loss of popularity and, in turn, loss of femininity, which to her has come to mean a manner of dress, make-up, attitude, and talk that mark her as desirable. Clearly undesirable in this social lexicon of femininity are independence of mind, intellectual ambition, and occupational ambition. Cultural forces persuade a woman these qualities are also undesirable investments of her time and energy. If gainful employment is not anticipated as a lifelong obligation, no motive to develop an occupational ambition is likely to occur.

College years add a dimension of reality that challenges both a woman's sense of self and her fears about her future. In high school her academic achievement has been rewarded, if only by admission to an elite college. When this achievement forces her to consider a serious commitment to a career, it begins to loom as a threat to her stereotyped view of femininity. It is not surprising to learn from recent studies that women undergraduates, unlike their male peers, become less happy over the four years. As seniors they are less career-oriented than they were as freshmen. One can say that as the young man comes closer to graduation, his perceptions of himself in a work role are strengthened; the young woman more often becomes ambivalent. Even the uncommitted young man knows that at a certain time he will have to make a commitment to some sort of work, while the young woman translates ambivalence into the need to make her commitment to a man.

Although today more women enter college with career plans, these plans slowly assume tentative, vague outlines. A young woman must resolve her sexual identity and her career identity at the same time. Occupational future fades under the burden of immediate pressures to find a man. Because of socialization, in the most stereotyped sense, her feminine identity is thus established.

Most women perceive their choice to be between the affective and the intellectual, as if the two were mutually exclusive. Undergraduate women often find it difficult to understand fully that reading a book or writing a paper (which they often see as intellectual) is just as feminine as setting one's hair or buying a dress. The difficulty arises because both of these types of activities are expected from a young woman simultaneously. She must be attractive, and she must also understand the book. For the male students of the same age, reading the book is seen as part of a unifying process that leads to male adulthood. For the female the process is often divisive. At this age, academic success begins to conflict with the wish to love, to be loved, and in time, to be married. Women undergraduates discover, after many years of being rewarded for high academic achievement, that top grades and specific career goals coupled with overt competition for awards and scholarships threaten their male peers and undermine their own developing sense of womanliness. It is not unusual to hear a gifted student say that she consciously refrains from speaking up in class lest she sound aggressive--masculine. Thus the pattern of women to view achievement and femininity as incompatible persists to the present day.

The young woman in this free country has, in truth, little choice. She is taught that security is the goal and that she must achieve it as soon as possible. Marry the man right away, get the house right away, have the brood right away. No time for self-searching, no time for experiments in love and life, no time for internal growth, no time for the great world outside. Her problems are not so much inherent in her nature as in her relationship to a society which accepts her only on traditionally masculine conditions.

If she tries to think, she will only become anxious. Some anxiety is beneficial to creative thinking but high or sustained anxiety levels are damaging. Anxiety narrows her search for solutions, interferes with breaking undesirable or outgrown behavioral habits, and prevents experiencing the whole range of perceptions. Such anxiety is particularly manifest in college women who experience the most conflict between their current intellectual activities and expectations about behavior in their future unintellectual careers.

It is clear that women pay a high price for intellectual success--anxiety. Able women deny their ambition. They perform at lower levels in mixed-sex competitive situations. Many who do succeed downgrade their own performance in the presence of males. They lower their career aspirations and narrow their opportunities. Finally, faced with the conflict between their feminine image and the development of their abilities and interests, many women simply remove themselves from competition. Women become like Sally in the "Peanuts" cartoon, who at the early age of five says: "I never said I wanted to be someone. All I want to do when I grow up is to be a good wife and mother. So ... why should I have to go to kindergarten?" Achievement in the outside world is not a viable option for many women because of their internal psychological barriers.

Women are not encouraged to succeed in a profession. Rather, a woman with high achievement orientation is often asked to explain why she wants to be something or somebody. Men also face the problems of making important life decisions and experience anxiety about competition and the drive for success. However, they have the firm approval of a society that says, "Yes, you are a person, a potential contributor to society; you are on the right course, aim high, be something!" Women do not hear these insistent voices saying they must achieve. Women are not challenged to face their fears and to conquer them as are men. Thus, women remain self-doubting. They lack support and encouragement to do their best, to enjoy achieving. Most of those who could "make it" do not.

The dynamics of the achievement motivation process in women remain unclear, although the process in men has been studied extensively. It has barely been looked at in women until recently. Clearly women do have ambition, but its direction differs from that of men. In fact, the achievement orientation of both sexes goes precisely where it is socially directed--educational and occupational achievement for males and marriage achievement for females. One might postulate that both marital and educational/occupational success might be possible for a woman. In reality, the two are more often perceived as contradictory; success in one is viewed as precluding success in the other.

The dynamics of achievement motivation in women must be analyzed in terms of the most recent data on expectancies and attribution for success and failure as well as the motive to avoid success. Findings document that in tasks involving intellectual mastery, females are less optimistic about their future performances than are males, often in spite of superior previous performances. Women's expectancies for success are lower than men's. Research on casual attributions for performance, that is, on the ways in which people assign causes for their own behavior and that of others, indicate that men generally attribute success to the stable, internal factor of ability and failure to the unstable, external factor of luck. Women, on the other hand, tend to attribute their success to luck and their failure to lack of effort or ability. This suggests a "low expectation cycle"; the hypothesized pattern is as follows: Feminine socialization involves learning modest, non-competitive behavior. This results in a lack of self-esteem and a devaluation of feminine ability. Low expectations follow. Should success occur, it is unpredicted and causes uneasiness. When women attribute success to the external and unstable factor of luck, no increase in self-confidence occurs with its attainment, and the cycle of low expectations continues. Should failure occur, this is an expected outcome; this reduces self-confidence and perpetuates the cycle of low expectations.

A woman may choose to avoid success when confronted with certain situational factors. These factors determine the nature of her expectations in a specific situation, the likely consequences of her actions, and the value of those consequences to her. These, in turn, influence her actions. For example, a woman may deliberately perform a task poorly in a situation because if she outperforms a male competitor, she fears rejection by him. In the fear-of-success concept we see the familiar double bind in operation. Often women are outwardly encouraged to seek success in the conventional masculine values of our society; but if they achieve success they risk rejection from the same society. They can fail and be popular, or succeed and be rejected--familiar no-win options.

From another analytical perspective, the low incidence of success among women is the result of a state of structural imbalance in society. The vast increase in women's labor force participation has not been accompanied by any significant change in the distribution of women workers. The infinitesimal degree of women's success relative to their potential makes it apparent that a large investment must be made on women's behalf to create even a modest ratio of input to payoff. Now, the few women who have been successful are destined to be regarded as exceptions. All women--outside as well as inside the professions and other occupations--are regarded as second-class citizens. They are incompetents, dependent on males to make the important decisions.

The male gatekeepers of the channels of success commonly voice the opinion that standards of performance would be diminished by the presence of women. Ironically, these same gatekeepers believe that bringing in women poses unfair competition first, psychologically, because men's frail egos would be damaged if they were to be "outdone" by a woman; and second, economically, because men are the providers for their family. Male gatekeepers can structure success for other men they judge will become competent. No one will ask them about their hormones or whether or not they have lovers, spouses, or children. A man with flashes of insight and emotion often is said to have a creative nature or an interesting mind. He is told that great things are expected from him, and he is protected from the mundane routines. In contrast, the woman who is similarly unusual is labeled a muddleheaded deviate.

"The creation of competence," a result of on-the-job training, is given only when these important gatekeepers decide that a person not only has talent but also will continue to work and to perform well. Thus, competence is created by exposing a new professional to the tasks and providing the opportunity to learn the new techniques and avoid the pitfalls. The new professional is given access to persons who can help, and to information about the important people in the system. The accepted newcomer learns by observing and performing. Important colleagues will watch how the newcomer does and provide feedback vital for improvement as a professional. Women rarely have this opportunity.

The phenomenon of success is often explained in terms of the charisma of the leader and not the charisma of the office. The person who is given a role with high status finds that she (or he) has the charisma of office. She is more successful in effecting changes than the person who has a low-ranking position. Success breeds success. Once the mantle of success is cast on a person, the wheels are set in motion for greater authority. Women have long been denied this charisma of office, the halo effect of place. A man may not listen to the wise comments of the female co-worker, but if she is made chairperson, his hearing will become more acute. Given the taste of success, women not only do not fear it any longer, they actively seek and enjoy it.

Ambition and occupational success are developing phenomena for women. Those women who have had any success in their profession find that, in fact, it is more pleasant to succeed than to fail. Women who fear jobs with authority find, when given the opportunity to exercise authority, that people will listen to them, and that they can be effective leaders and administrators.

The reasons for this dichotomy of expectation and reality is evident. Traditionally, women have been defined as passive creatures--sexually, physically, and mentally. The roles they have been trained for from birth are dependent, auxiliary, nonaggressive ones. However, active qualities are necessary for success in this society. Achievement orientation, intellectual strength, and analytic ability all are commonly thought to require a certain amount of independence and aggression. These qualities inherent in a capacity for mastering intellectual problems, attacking difficulties, and making final decisions are considered incompatible with femininity. This view is reinforced by the psychologists and sociologists who have assumed over the years that it is "good" to rear women to be "feminine." Awareness is growing that stereotypic femininity is limiting and even maladaptive. However, women have internalized the traditional female image. This image exerts psychological pressures, of which they are frequently unaware, on their own behavior.

Today, more young women are planning careers; admissions of women to law schools and medical schools have risen. For an increasing number, marriage is not an immediate goal; meanwhile, temporary alliances are not as frowned on by society. In some instances, new arrangements in lifestyles and work patterns are being achieved in partnership with young men who are eager to expand their own horizons. It is too early to tell what the professional lives of these young women will be like. They are a minority, albeit a vocal and much publicized one.

Nevertheless, the undergraduate woman will continue to have the same psychological conflicts and reality problems to resolve as have her counterparts in the past. In the next decade or two we may unwittingly be preparing many gifted young women for "Great Disappointments" if we and they do not thoroughly understand the kinds of personal role dilemmas they must still face. Work toward providing the structural changes that will make it possible for women to follow careers is vital.

The percentage of women who achieve in academic and other professions and disciplines will, one hopes, increase in the coming years through efforts, for instance, of the Department of Health, Education and Welfare, and a growing number of professional women's groups. With this increase, more young women, seeing older women who have achieved success in professional roles, will begin to take their own career ambitions and aspirations seriously. The presence of an increased, albeit small, number of professional women in universities and business organizations will hopefully aid in deenergizing the feminine-masculine, dependent-independent, emotional-rational, compliant-competitive, passive-active dichotomies that have impaired both female and male functioning. In order to diminish sex-stereotyping, personality traits need to be viewed on a spectrum rather than as polarities.

Clearly, it is time to eradicate the misconceptions and timidities, and to open the door in the suffocating space of women's social patterning. One important task, among many, is to alter young women's time perspective. Beginning in the early school years, she must learn the importance of recognizing the future as long term and internalize those aspirations which led her to study in an educational institution. She must confront those demands which call for excellence and achievement. The young women who have begun successful careers have recognized this in themselves. Many more women must be able to accept the achievement-oriented part of themselves without feeling that their futures as women, married or single, are impaired. Of course not all women want careers, and a similar mold for aspirations must not be imposed on all women. However, an environment must be created in which all choices become <u>autonomous</u> <u>choices</u> rather than responses to social patterns of outmoded feminine-masculine stereotypes.

I

BACKGROUND ON WOMEN AND AMBITION

> There is no female mind. The brain is not an organ of sex. As well speak of a female liver. --Charlotte Perkins Gilman, 1898.

Alper, T. G. Achievement Motivation in College Women: A Now-You-See-It-Now-You-Don't Phenomenon. American Psychologist, 1974, March, 29(3), 194-203.

_____. Where Are We Now? Psychology of Women Quarterly, 1977, Spring, 1(3), 294-303.

Bardwick, J. M. The Motive to Achieve. In Psychology of Women: A Study of Bio-Cultural Conflicts. New York: Harper & Row, 1971, 167-187.

Bart, P. B. Sexism and Social Science: From the Gilded Cage to the Iron Cage or the Perils of Pauline. Journal of Marriage and the Family, 1971, November, 33(4), 734-745. Also a reprint from KNOW, Inc., P.O. Box 86031, Pittsburgh, PA 15221.

Bernard, J. Sex Differences: An Overview. Reprint from MSS Information Corp., 655 Madison Ave., New York, NY 10021.

Darmofall, S. H., and McCarbery, R. J. Achievement Orientation in Females: A Social Psychological Perspective. Paper presented at the American Psychological Association Convention, San Francisco, 1977.

Deaux, K. Striving for Achievement: Who's Afraid of Success? In The Behavior of Women and Men. Belmont, CA: Wadsworth, 1976, 45-56.

Denmark, F. The Psychology of Women: An Overview of an Emerging Field. Personality and Social Psychology Bulletin, 1977, Summer, 3(3), 356-367.

Doherty, M. A. Sexual Bias in Personality Theory. The Counseling Psychologist, 1973, 4(1), 67-74.

2 / Background

Donelson, E., and Gullahorn, J. E. (eds.). Individual and Interpersonal Achievement. In Women: A Psychological Perspective. New York: John Wiley, 1977, 168-183.

Epstein, C. F. Mind, Matter, and Mentors: The Making of a Sociologist. In Judith Stiehm (ed.), The Frontiers of Knowledge. University Park, CA: University of Southern California Press, 1976, 23-36.

Giele, J. Z. Introductory Essay for the American Edition: New Developments in Research on Women. In V. Klein, The Feminine Character: History of an Ideology. Urbana: University of Illinois Press, 1972, xix-lvi.

Huber, J. Sociology: Review Essay. SIGNS: Journal of Women in Culture and Society, 1976, Spring, 1(3), 685-697.

Hyde, J. S., and Rosenberg, B. G. Abilities, Achievement, and Motivation. In The Psychology of Women: Half the Human Experience. Lexington, MA: D. C. Heath, 1976, 81-106.

Jacobs, S. L. Achievement Motivation and Relevant Achievement Contexts: A Revised Methodology. Unpublished doctoral dissertation, University of Nebraska. Dissertation Abstracts International, 1971, November, 32(5-A), 2798-2799.

Lopata, H. Z. Sociology: Review Essay. SIGNS: Journal of Women in Culture and Society, 1976, Spring, 2(1), 165-176.

McCarbery, R. J., and Darmofall, S. H. Achievement Orientation in Females: Social Psychological Perspective. Paper presented at the American Psychological Association Convention, San Francisco, 1977.

Mednick, M. T. S. Psychology of Women--An Overview. Symposium presentation at the American Psychological Association Convention, San Francisco, 1977.

_____, and Tangri, S. S. New Social Psychological Perspectives on Women. Journal of Social Issues, 1972, 28(2), 1-16.

_____, _____, and Hoffman, L. W. (eds.). Women and Achievement: Social and Motivational Analyses. New York: Halsted Press, 1975.

_____, and Weissman, H. J. The Psychology of Women--Selected Topics. Annual Review of Psychology, 1975, 26, 1-18.

O'Leary, V. E. Female Achievement. In Toward Understanding Women. Monterey, CA: Brooks/Cole, 1977, 77-105.

Parlee, M. B. Psychology: Review Essay. SIGNS: Journal of Women in Culture and Society, 1975, Autumn, 1(1), 119-138.

Shields, S. A. The Variability Hypothesis, and Sex Differences in Intelligence. Unpublished manuscript, Department of Psychology, Pennsylvania State University, State College, Pennsylvania, 1974.

_____. Functionalism, Darwinism, and the Psychology of Women: A Study in Social Myth. American Psychologist, 1975, 30, 739-754.

Silveira, J. The Effects of Sexism on Thought: How Male Bias Hurts Psychology and Some Hopes for a Woman's Psychology. n. d. Reprint from KNOW, Inc., P.O. Box 86031, Pittsburgh, PA 15221.

Stein, A. H., and Bailey, M. M. The Socialization of Achievement Orientation in Females. Psychological Bulletin, 1973, November, 80, 345-366. Also in F. L. Denmark (ed.), Women--Volume I: A PDI Research Reference Work. New York: Psychological Dimensions, 1976, 77-98.

Stillion, J. M. Different but Equal: A Look at the Current State of the Psychology of Women. Western Carolina University Journal of Education, 1974, Fall, 6(2), 9-15.

Vaughter, R. M. Psychology: Review Essay. SIGNS: Journal of Women in Culture and Society, 1976, Spring, 2(1), 120-146.

Veroff, J. Process Versus Impact in Men's and Women's Achievement Motivation. Psychology of Women Quarterly, 1977, 1(3), 283-293.

_____, McClelland, L., and Ruhland, D. Varieties of Achievement Motivation. In M. T. S. Mednick et al. (eds.), Woman and Achievement: Social and Motivational Analyses. New York: Halsted Press, 1975, 172-205.

Weisstein, N. Kinder, Kuche and Kirche as Scientific Law: Psychology Constructs the Female. Motive, 1969, March/April, 78, 55. Also in R. Morgan (ed.), Sisterhood Is Powerful. New York: Random House, 1970, 205-220.

_____. Psychology Constructs the Female; or the Fantasy Life of the Male Psychologist (with some Attention to the Fantasies of His Friends, the Male Biologist and the Male Anthropologist). Social Education, 1971, 35, 362-373. Also in V. Gornick and B. K. Moran (eds.), Woman in Sexist Society. New York: Basic Books, 1971, 207-224; and in A. Koedt et al. (eds.), Radical Feminism. New York: Quadrangle/The New York Times Co., 1973, 178-197. Also a reprint from MSS Information Corp., 665 Madison Ave., New York, NY 10021.

_____. Stimulus/Response: Woman as Nigger. Psychology Today, 1969, October, 3(5), 20-22+. Also in C. Tavris (ed.), The Female Experience, from the editors of Psychology Today, Del

4 / Background

    Mar, CA: Communications/Research/Machines, 1973, 67-70.

Wortis, R. P. The Acceptance of the Maternal Role by Behavioral Scientists: Its Effects on Women. American Journal of Orthopsychiatry, 1971, 41(5), 733-746.

_____. The Acceptance of the Concept of the Maternal Role by Behavioral Scientists: Its Effects on Women. In H. Wortis and C. Rabinowitz (eds.), The Women's Movement: Social and Psychological Perspectives. New York: John Wiley, 1972, 32-51.

II

SOCIETAL FORCES AND WOMEN'S AMBITION

It is not easy for a girl to make up her mind about what she's going to do with her life. Too often, other people are trying to make it up for her. --Pat Ross, 1972.

A. SOCIETY, CULTURE, SOCIALIZATION

Acker, J. Women and Social Stratification: A Case of Intellectual Sexism. American Journal of Sociology, 1973, January, 78, 963-945.

Ahammer, I. M. Desirability Judgments as a Function of Item Content, Instructional Set, and Sex: A Life-Span Developmental Study. Human Development, 1971, 14(3), 195-207.

Albrecht, S. L. Social Class and Sex-Stereotyping of Occupations. Journal of Vocational Behavior, 1976, December, 9(3), 321-328.

Aldous, J. Family Background Factors and Originality in Children. Gifted Child Quarterly, 1973, August, 17(3), 183-192.

Allgeier, E. R. Beyond Sowing and Growing: The Relationship of Sex Typing to Socialization, Family Plans, and Future Orientation. Journal of Applied Social Psychology, 1975, 5, 217-226.

Allison, R. B. A Guide to Parents: How to Raise Your Daughter to Have Multiple Personalities. Family Therapy, 1974, 1 (1), 83-88

Anderson, R., Manoogian, S. T., and Reznick, J. S. The Undermining and Enhancing of Intrinsic Motivation in Preschool Children. Journal of Personality and Social Psychology, 1976, 34, 915-922

Andreas, C. Sex and Caste in America. Englewood Cliffs, NJ: Prentice-Hall, 1971.

Annerblom, M. L. Sex Roles in a Nursery School. Special Issue, Pedagogisk-Psykologiska Problem, 1976, November, (306).

6 / Society, Culture

Armanda, A., DeGarma, E.G., Langer, M., and Rascovsky, A. Psychology of the Woman. Revista de Psicoanálisis, 1966, 23(1), 37-49

Aronoff, J., and Crano, W. D. A Re-Examination of the Cross-Cultural Principles of Task Segregation and Sex Role Differentiation in the Family. American Sociological Review, 1975, 40, 12-20

Astin, H. S. Young Women and Their Roles. In R. J. Havighurst (ed.), Youth (Part I). Chicago: University of Chicago Press, 1975, 419-434.

Atkinson, J., and Endsley, R. C. Influence of Sex of Child and Parent on Parental Reactions to Hypothetical Parent-Child Situations. Genetic Psychology Monographs, 1976, August, 94 (1), 131-147.

Bakan, D. The Duality of Human Existence. Chicago: Rand McNally, 1966

Baltes, P. B., and Nesselroade, J. R. Cultural Change and Adolescent Personality Development. Developmental Psychology, 1972, 7, 244-256.

Bardwick, J. M., and Douvan, E. Ambivalence: The Socialization of Women. In V. Gornick and B. K. Moran (eds.), Woman in Sexist Society. New York: Basic Books, 1971, 147-159. Also in J. M. Bardwick (ed.), Readings on the Psychology of Women. New York: Harper & Row, 1972, 52-57.

―――, Horner, M. S., Douvan, E., and Guttman, D. Feminine Personality and Conflict. Monterey, CA: Brooks/Cole, 1970.

Barnett, R. C. Vocational Planning of College Women: A Psycho-Social Study. Proceedings of the 75th Annual Convention of the American Psychological Association, 1967, 2, 345-346.

Barrett, C. A New Theory of the Development of Women's Identity. Symposium presentation at the American Psychological Association Convention, San Francisco, 1977.

Barry, H., III, Josephson, L., Lauer, E. M., and Marshall, C. Traits Inculcated in Early and Later Boyhood and Girlhood. Paper presented at the Society for Cross-Cultural Research meeting, Chicago, 1975.

Baruch, G., and Barnett, R. Implications and Applications of Recent Research on Feminine Development. Psychiatry, 1975, November, 38, 318-327.

Battle-Sister, A. Conjectures on the Female Culture Question. Journal of Marriage and the Family, 1971, August, 33(3), 411-420.

Baumrind, D. Socialization and Instrumental Competence in Young Children. Young Children, 1970, December, 26(2), 104-119.

_____. Current Patterns of Parental Authority. Developmental Psychology Monograph, 1971, January, 4(1, 2), 1-101.

_____. From Each According to Her Ability. School Review, 1972, February, 80(2), 161-197.

_____, and Black, A. E. Socialization Practices Associated with Dimensions of Competence in Preschool Boys and Girls. Child Development, 1967, 38, 291-327.

Beardslee, C. Acquisition of Appropriate Sex-Role Behavior: A Review of the Literature. Maternal-Child Nursing Journal, 1974, Summer, 3(2), 139-153.

Becker, W. C. Consequences of Different Kinds of Parental Discipline. In M. L. Hoffman and L. W. Hoffman (eds.), Review of Child Development Research (Vol. 1). New York: Russell Sage Foundation, 1964, 169-208.

Bem, S. L., and Bem, D. J. Homogenizing the American Woman: The Power of an Unconscious Ideology. 1972. Reprint from KNOW, Inc., P. O. Box 86031, Pittsburgh, PA 15221.

_____, and _____. Training the Woman to Know Her Place: The Power of a Nonconscious Ideology. In D. J. Bem (ed.), Beliefs, Attitudes and Human Affairs. Monterey, CA: Brooks/Cole, 1970. Also in D. Gersoni-Stavn, Sexism and Youth. New York: R. R. Bowker, 1974, 10-22; and a Reprint from KNOW, Inc., P. O. Box 86031, Pittsburgh, PA 15221

_____, and _____. Training the Woman to Know Her Place: The Social Antecedents of Women in the World of Work. Unpublished Manuscript, Stanford University, 1971. Also available from ERIC (ED082098), 1974.

_____, and _____. Case Study of a Nonconscious Ideology: Training the Woman to Know Her Place. In S. Cox (ed.), Female Psychology: The Emerging Self. Chicago: Science Research Associates, 1976, 180-191.

Berens, A. E. The Socialization of Achievement Motives in Boys and Girls. Unpublished doctoral dissertation, York University, Toronto, Ontario, 1972.

_____. The Socialization of Need for Achievement in Boys and Girls. Proceedings of the 80th Annual Convention of the American Psychological Association, 1972, 7(Pt. 1), 273-274. Paper also available from ERIC (ED071734), 1973.

Berger, G. The Socialization of American Females as a Dysfunctional Process: Selected Research. Journal of Research and Development in Education, 1977, 10(4), 4-11.

Bernard, J. Second Sex and the Cichlid Effect. The Journal of the National Association of Women Deans and Counselors, 1967, Fall, 31, 8-17

_____. Status of Women in Modern Patterns of Culture. Annals of American Academy of Political and Social Science, 1968, January, 375, 3-14.

_____. A Developmental Paradox. In Women, Wives, Mothers: Values and Options. Chicago: Aldine, 1975, 33-42.

_____. Adolescence and Socialization for Motherhood. In S. E. Dragastin and G. H. Elder (eds.), Adolescence in the Life Cycle: Psychological Change and Social Context. Washington, D. C.: Hemisphere Publishing Corp., 1975, 227-254.

Bernstein, J. The Elementary School: Training Ground for Sex Role Stereotypes. Personnel and Guidance Journal, 1972, October, 51(2), 97-104.

Biber, H., Miller, L. B., and Dyer, J. L. Feminization in Preschool. Developmental Psychology, 1972, 7(1), 86.

Biller, H. B. Father, Child and Sex Role. Lexington, MA: Lexington Books, 1971.

_____, and Weiss, S. D. The Father-Daughter Relationship and the Personality Development of the Female. Journal of Genetic Psychology, 1970, 116(1), 79-93.

_____, and Zung, B. Perceived Maternal Control, Anxiety, and Opposite Sex Role Preference among Elementary School Girls. Journal of Psychology, 1972, May, 81(1), 85-88.

Bing, E. Effect of Child-Rearing Practices on Development of Differential Cognitive Abilities. Child Development, 1963, 34, 631-648.

Birnbaum, J. A. Life Patterns and Self-Esteem in Gifted Family Oriented and Career Committed Women. In M. T. S. Mednick, et al. (eds.), Women and Achievement: Social and Motivational Analyses. New York: Halsted Press, 1975, 396-419.

Birns, B. The Emergence and Socialization of Sex Differences in the Earliest Years. Merrill-Palmer Quarterly, 1976, July, 22(3), 229-254.

Blake, J. The Changing Status of Women in Developed Countries. Scientific American, 1974, September, 231, 136-147.

Blaubergs, M. S. Overcoming the Sexist Barriers to Gifted

Women's Achievement. In B. Johnson (ed.), Advantage/Disadvantage Gifted. Ventura, CA: Ventura County Superintendent of Schools Office, 1979.

Bledsoe, J. C., and Wiggins, R. G. Self-Concepts and Academic Aspirations of "Understood" and "Misunderstood" Boys and Girls in Ninth Grade. Psychological Reports, 1974, August, 35(1, Pt 1), 57-58.

Block, J., von der Lippe, A., and Block, J. H. Sex-Role and Socialization Patterns: Some Personality Concomitants and Environmental Antecedents. Journal of Consulting and Clinical Psychology, 1973, 41, 321-341.

Block, J. H. Conceptions of Sex Role: Some Cross-Cultural and Longitudinal Perspectives. American Psychologist, 1973, 28(6), 512-526.

Blumberg, R. L. Structural Factors Affecting Women's Status: A Cross Cultural Paradigm. Paper presented at the International Sociological Association meeting, Toronto, Ontario, Canada, 1974.

Boyle, R. P. Community Influence on College Aspirations: An Empirical Evaluation of Explanatory Factors. Rural Sociology, 1966, 31(3), 277-292.

Brabant, S., and Garbin, A. P. Sex of Student as Defined by Sex-Typical Experiences and Persistence in Higher Education. Journal of College Student Personnel, 1976, January, 17(1), 28-33.

Breytspraak, C. H. The Relationship of Parental Identification to Sex-Role Acceptance in Married, Single, Career and Noncareer Women. Unpublished doctoral dissertation, Columbia University, 1964.

Brogan, C. L. Changing Perspectives on the Role of Women. Smith College Studies in Social Work, 1972, February, 42(2), 155-173.

Broverman, D. M., Klaiber, E. L., Kobayashi, Y., and Vogel, W. Roles of Activation and Inhibition in Sex Differences in Cognitive Abilities. Psychological Review, 1968, 75, 23-50.

Broverman, I. K. Sexual Stereotypes Start Early. Saturday Review, 1971, October 16, 76-82+.

Bryant, B. E. American Women Today and Tomorrow. Washington, D. C.: National Commission on the Observance of International Women's Year, 1977.

Bullough, V. L., and Bullough, B. The Subordinate Sex. Urbana: University of Illinois Press, 1973.

Burton, G. I'm Running Away from Home, But I'm Not Allowed to Cross the Street. New York: Avon Books, 1975.

Campbell, P. B. Feminine Intellectual Decline During Adolescence. Available from ERIC (ED091620), 1974.

──── . Adolescent Intellectual Decline. Adolescence, 1976. Winter, 11(44), 629-635.

──── , and McKain, A. E. Intellectual Decline and the Adolescent Woman. Paper presented at the American Psychological Association Convention, Montreal, 1974.

Carney, R. E., and McKeachie, W. J. Religion, Sex, Social Class, Probability of Success, and Student Personality. Journal for the Scientific Study of Religion, 1963, 3, 32-42.

Carter, D. Developmental Stages of Feminism. Unpublished manuscript, University of Iowa, 1974.

Cater, L. A., Scott, A. F., and Martyna, W. (eds.). Discussions: Sex Roles and Cultural Symbolism. In Women and Men: Changing Roles, Relationships, and Perceptions. New York: Praeger, 1977, 43-54.

Chafe, W. H. Women and Equality: Changing Patterns in American Culture. New York: Oxford University, 1977.

Chasen, B. Sex-Role Stereotyping and Prekindergarten Teachers. In P. M. Insel and L. F. Jacobson (eds.), What Do You Expect? An Inquiry Into Self-Fulfilling Prophecies. Reading, MA: Cummings, 1975, 164-178.

Cherniss, C. Personality and Ideology: A Personological Study of Women's Liberation. Psychiatry, 1972, 35, 109-125.

Chodorow, N. Being and Doing: A Cross-Cultural Examination of the Socialization of Males and Females. In V. Gornick and B. K. Moran (eds.), Woman in Sexist Society. New York: Basic Books, 1971, 259-291,

──── . Family Structure and Feminine Personality. In M. Z. Rosaldo, and L. Lamphere (eds.), Woman, Culture, and Society. Stanford, CA: Stanford University Press, 1974, 43-66.

Chombart de Lauwe, M. J. and Henry, P., Huguet, M., Perroy, E., and Bisseret, N. La Femme dans la société: son image dans different milieux sociaux [Woman in Society: Her Image in Different Social Environments]. Paris: Centre National de la Recherche Scientifique, 1963, xviii.

Clock, J. H. Another Look at Sex Differentiation in the Socialization Behaviors of Mothers and Fathers. In F. Denmark, and

J. Sherman (eds.), Psychology of Women: Future Directions of Research. New York: Psychological Dimensions, in press.

Coates, S., Lord, M., and Jakabovics, E. Field Dependence--Independence, Social--Non-Social Play and Sex Differences in Preschool Children. Perceptual and Motor Skills, 1975, February, 40(1), 195-202.

Cohen, L., and Batcock, A. Female University Students and Social Influence; Great Britain. Educational Review, 1969, June, 21, 234-241.

Coker, D. R. Development of Gender Concepts in Preschool Children. Symposium presentation at the American Psychological Association Convention, San Francisco, 1977.

Coleman, J. S. The Adolescent Society. Glencoe, IL: The Free Press, 1961.

———. The Adolescent Subculture and Academic Achievement. In M. Kornrich (ed.), Underachievement. Springfield, IL: Charles C. Thomas, 1965, 49-64.

———. The Adolescent Culture. In J. Pottker and A. Fishel (eds.), Sex Bias In the Schools--The Research Evidence. Madison, NJ: Fairleigh Dickinson University Press, 1977, 69-77.

Conway, J., and O'Neil, W. L. Women Reformers and American Culture, 1870-1930. Journal of Social History, 1971-72, Winter, 5(2), 164-177.

Cramer, B. Some Sex Differences in Children Between Three and Seven. Psychosocial Process, 1970, 1(2), 60-76.

Crandall, V. C., and Battle, E. S. The Antecedents and Adult Correlates of Academic and Intellectual Achievement Effort. In J. P. Hill (ed.), Minnesota Symposia on Child Psychology. Minneapolis: University of Minnesota Press, 1970, 4, 36-93.

Crandall, V. J., Katkovsky, W., and Preston, A. A Conceptual Formulation for Some Research on Children's Achievement Development. Child Development, 1960, 31, 787-797.

———, ———, and ———. Motivation and Ability Determinants of Young Children's Intellectual Achievement Behaviors. Child Development, 1962, 33(3), 643-661.

Crown, D. P., Conn, L. K., Marlowe, D., and Edwards, C. N. Some Developmental Antecedents of Level of Aspiration. Journal of Personality, 1969, 37, 73-92.

Dahlstrom, E. The Changing Roles of Men and Women. Boston: Beacon Press, 1971.

Damico, S. B. The Effects of Clique Membership upon Academic Achievement. Adolescence, 1975, Spring, 10(37), 93-100.

_____. Clique Membership and its Relationship to Academic Achievement and Attitudes Toward School. Journal of Research and Development in Education, 1976, Summer, 9, 29-35.

D'Andrade, R. G. Sex Differences in Cultural Institutions. In E. E. Maccoby (ed.), The Development of Sex Differences. Stanford, CA: Stanford University Press, 1966, 174-204.

_____. Sex Differences and Cultural Institutions. In R. A. LeVine (ed.), Culture and Personality Readings. Chicago: Aldine, 1974.

Daniels, A. K. Socialization and the Educational System. A Survey of Research Concerns on Women's Issues. Washington, D. C. : Association of American Colleges, May, 1975, 7-17.

Davis, W. L., and Phares, E. J. Parental Antecedents of Internal-External Control of Reinforcement. Psychological Reports, 1969, 24, 427-436.

Dean, D. G., Powers, E. A., Braito, R., and Bruton, B. Cultural Contradictions and Sex Roles Revisited: A Replication and a Reassessment. The Sociological Quarterly, 1975, 16(2), 207-215.

DeCrow, K. Home and Family Life: What You Learn at Home About Being a Woman. In The Young Woman's Guide to Liberation. New York: Bobbs-Merrill, 1971, 90-99.

_____. The Young Woman's Guide to Liberation. New York: Bobbs-Merrill, 1971.

Dellas, M., and Gaier, E. L. The Self and Adolescent Identity in Women: Options and Implications. Adolescence, 1975, Fall, 10(39), 399-407.

Dixit, R. C., and Mathur, M. B. Loving and Punishing Parental Behaviour and Masculinity-Femininity Development in School Girls. Journal of Psychological Researches, 1973, May, 17(2), 47-49.

Domash, L., and Balter, L. Sex and Psychological Differentiation in Preschoolers. Journal of Genetic Psychology, 1976, March, 128 (1st half), 77-84.

Domingues, P. M. Self Concept and Socio-Economic Background of the Mature Female Undergraduate Student. Unpublished doctoral dissertation, Northwestern University. Dissertation Abstracts International, 1971, December, 32(6-A), 3085.

Donelson, E. Development of Sex-Typed Behavior and Self-Concept. In E. Donelson and J. E. Gullahorn (eds.), Women: A Psychological Perspective. New York: John Wiley, 1977, 119-139.

Dorman, L. Assertive Behavior and Cognitive Performance in Preschool Children. Unpublished doctoral dissertation, Boston University, 1969.

Douvan, E. Sex Differences in Adolescent Character Process. Merrill-Palmer Quarterly, 1960, 6, 203-211.

_____. New Sources of Conflict in Females at Adolescence and Early Adulthood. In J. M. Bardwick et al. (eds.), Feminine Personality and Conflict. Monterey, CA: Brooks/Cole, 1970, 31-43.

_____. Higher Education and Feminine Socialization. New Directions for Higher Education, 1975, Spring, 9, 37-50.

_____. Sex Differences in the Opportunities, Demands, and Developments of Youth. National Society for the Study of Education Yearbook, 1975, 74(1), 27-45.

_____, and Adelson, J. The Adolescent Experience. New York: John Wiley, 1966.

_____, and _____. The Adolescent Experience: Integrating Themes. In E. Lasky (ed.), Humanness: An Exploration into the Mythologies About Women and Men. New York: MSS Informational Corp., 1975, 179-192.

Draper, P. Cultural Pressure on Sex Differences. American Ethnologist, 1975, November, 2(4), 602-616.

Dreifus, C. (ed.). Little Girl/Big Girl--Childhood Training for Sex Roles. In Woman's Fate: Raps from a Feminist Consciousness-Raising Group. New York: Bantam Books, 1973, 55-73.

DuBrin, A. J. Women in Transition. Springfield, IL: Charles C. Thomas, 1972.

Duquin, M. E. Perceptions of Sport and Psychological Well-Being. Symposium presentation at the American Psychological Association Convention, Washington, D. C., 1976.

_____. Three Cultural Perceptions of Sport. Unpublished manuscript, University of Pittsburgh, n. d.

Easton, B. Industrialization and Femininity: A Case Study of Nineteenth Century New England. Social Problems, 1976, April, 23(4), 389-401.

Ehrensaft, D. R. Sex Role Socialization in a Preschool Setting. Unpublished doctoral dissertation, University of Michigan. Dissertation Abstracts International, 1975, January, 35(7-B), 3646.

Elliott, E. D. Effects of Female Role Models on Occupational Aspiration Levels of College Freshman Women. Unpublished doctoral dissertation, University of Missouri-Columbia, 1972.

Ellis, L. J., and Bentler, P. M. Traditional Sex-Determined Role Standards and Sex Stereotypes. Journal of Personality and Social Psychology, 1973, 25, 28-34.

Ellman, M. Thinking About Women. New York: Harcourt Brace Jovanovich, 1968.

Emmerich, W. Socialization and Sex-Role Development. In P. B. Baltes and K. W. Schaie (eds.), Life-Span Developmental Psychology: Personality and Socialization. New York: Academic Press, 1973, 123-144.

Epstein, C. F. The Socialization Process and Its Consequences: Roads to Careers and Dead Ends. In Woman's Place: Options and Limits in Professional Careers. Berkeley: University of California Press, 1970, 50-85.

_____. Structuring Success for Women: Guidelines for Gatekeepers. Journal of the National Association for Women Deans, Administrators, and Counselors, 1973, Fall, 37(1), 34-42.

Epstein, R., and Liverant, S. Verbal Conditioning and Sex Role Identification in Children. Child Development, 1963, 34, 99-106.

Erickson, V. L. Women in Young Adulthood: Longitudinal Growth Study. Symposium presentation at the American Psychological Association Convention, San Francisco, 1977.

Etaugh, C. Effects of Maternal Employment on Children: A Review of Recent Research. Merrill-Palmer Quarterly, 1974, April, 20(2), 71-98.

_____. Biographical Predictors of College Students' Attitudes Toward Women. Journal of College Student Personnel, 1975, 16(4), 273-275.

_____. Differential Socialization of Girls and Boys by Parents and Teachers. Symposium presentation at the American Psychological Association Convention, San Francisco, 1977.

_____, Collins, G., and Gerson, A. Reinforcement of Sex-Typed Behaviors of Two-Year-Old Children in a Nursery School Setting. Developmental Psychology, 1975, March, 11(2), 255.

Fagot, B. I. Sex Determined Reinforcing Contingencies in Toddler

Children. Paper presented at the Society for Research in Child Development meeting, New Orleans, 1971.

_____, and Littman, I. Stability of Sex Role and Play Interests from Preschool to Elementary School. Journal of Psychology, 1975, March, 89(2), 285-292.

_____, and _____. Relation of Preschool Sex-Typing to Intellectual Performance in Elementary School. Psychological Reports, 1976, December, 39(3, Pt 1), 699-704.

_____, and Patterson, G. R. An In Vivo Analysis of Reinforcing Contingencies for Sex-Role Behaviors in the Preschool Child. Developmental Psychology, 1969, 1(5), 563-568.

Fakouri, M. E., and Mehryar, A. H. A Cross-Cultural Study of Achievement Motivation. Psychology, 1972, November, 9(4), 31-32.

Farmer, H. S. What Inhibits Achievement and Career Motivation in Women? The Counseling Psychologist, 1976, 6(2), 12-15.

Farrell, W. The Resocialization of Men's Attitudes Toward Women's Role in Society. Unpublished paper, available from author, 100 Bleecker St., apt. 3-B, New York, NY 10012.

Faunce, P. S. The Psychological Environment of Women. Syllabus/study guide for an independent study course. Minneapolis: University of Minnesota, 1974.

_____. Woman's Studies 1-301; The Psychological Environment of Woman: The Implementation and Evaluation of an Experimental Course (Spring 1974). Minneapolis: University of Minnesota, 1975.

Fay, T. L. Culture and Sex Differences in Concepts of Sex Role and Self. Unpublished doctoral dissertation, Dissertation Abstracts International, 1971, 31, 6239.

_____. Ideal and Typical Males and Females: Stereotypes in Three Cultures. Symposium presentation at the American Psychological Association Convention, Chicago, 1975.

Fein, G., Johnson, D., Kosson, N., Stork, L., and Wasserman, L. Sex Stereotypes and Preferences in the Toy Choices of 20-Month-Old Boys and Girls. Developmental Psychology, 1975, July, 11(4), 527-528.

Fein, L. G. (ed.). International Understanding: Culture Differences in the Development of Cognitive Processes (1972): Women in National and International Psychology (1973). International Council of Psychologists, New York: MSS Information Corp., 1974.

Fennema, E. Sex Differences in Mathematics-Learning: Why???
Elementary School Journal, 1974, December, 75(3), 183-190.

———, and Sherman, J. Sex-Related Differences in Mathematics
Achievement, Spatial Visualization and Affective Factors. American Educational Research, 1977, Winter, 14, 51-71.

Fenwick-Naditch, S. Sex Differences in Field Dependence: The
Role of Social Influences. Symposium presentation at the
American Psychological Association Convention, Washington,
D. C., 1976.

Ferdman, J. Differential Sex Learning in Early Childhood. Journal of Asthma Research, 1974, June, 11(4), 151-158.

Figes, E. Patriarchal Attitudes. New York: Fawcett World Library, 1970.

Firestone, S. The Dialectic of Sex. New York: William Morrow, 1970.

Fischer, P. L., and Torney, J. V. Influence of Children's Stories
on Dependency, a Sex-Typed Behavior. Developmental Psychology, 1976, September, 12(5), 489-490.

Fitzgerald, H. E. Infants and Caregivers: Sex Differences as Determinants of Socialization. In E. Donelson and J. E. Gullahorn (eds.), Women: A Psychological Perspective. New York:
John Wiley, 1977, 101-118.

Flammer, D. P. Self-Esteem, Parent Identification, and Sex-Role
Development in Preschool Age Boys and Girls. Child Study
Journal, 1971, 2, 39-45.

Fling, S., and Manosevitz, M. Sex Typing in Nursery School
Children's Play Interests. Developmental Psychology, 1972,
7, 146-152.

Fontana, G. L. An Investigation into the Dynamics of Achievement
Motivation in Women. Unpublished doctoral dissertation, University of Michigan. Dissertation Abstracts International, 1971,
September, 32(3-B), 1821-1822.

Francis, B. R. Effect of Maternal Employment on the Socialization
of Sex Role and Achievement in New Zealand. Unpublished doctoral dissertation, Cornell University. Dissertations Abstracts
International, 1975, 36(4-A), 2452.

Franzini, L. R., Litrownik, A. J., and Blanchard, F. Modeling
Sex-Typed Behaviors: Effects on Boys Versus Girls. Paper
presented at the American Psychological Association Convention, Washington, D. C., 1976.

Freeman, J. Building the Gilded Cage. Reprint from KNOW, Inc., P.O. Box 86031, Pittsburgh, PA 15221.

_____. Growing Up Girlish. Transaction, 1970, November/December, 8(1 & 2), 36-43.

_____. The Social Construction of the Second Sex. In M. H. Garskof (ed.), Roles Women Play. Monterey, CA: Brooks/Cole, 1971, 123-141. Also in D. Gersoni-Stavn (ed.), Sexism and Youth. New York: R. R. Bowker Co., 1974, 23-41; and a reprint from KNOW, Inc., P.O. Box 86031, Pittsburgh, PA 15221.

Freiberg, P. Modeling and Assertive Training: The Effect of Sex and Status of Model on Female College Students. Unpublished doctoral dissertation, University of Maryland, 1974.

Freidl, E. Women and Men: An Anthropologist's View. New York: Holt, Rinehart & Winston, 1975.

Fricker, S. K., and Werner, E. E. Achievement Orientation of Adolescent Women of Hawaiian-, Japanese-, and Philipino-American Descent. JSAS Catalog of Selected Documents in Psychology, 1976, August, (7), 69.

Friedan, B. The Feminine Mystique. New York: W. W. Norton, 1963.

Friedlander, F. Emergent and Contemporary Life Styles: An Inter-Generational Issue. Human Relations, 1975, May, 28(4), 329-347.

Friedman, J. S. On Ideology and Achievement: Determinants of Career Orientation Among American Women. Paper presented at the Gerontological Society meeting, Louisville, Kentucky, 1975. Also available from ERIC (ED123537), 1976.

Froschl, M. It's Never Too Early: Sex-Role Stereotyping in the Preschool Years. Colloquy, 1973, 6(9), 16-18.

Frueh, T., and McGhee, P. E. Traditional Sex Role Development and Amount of Time Spent Watching Television. Developmental Psychology, 1975, January, 11(1), 109.

Fujitomi, I., and Wong, D. The New Asian-American Women. In S. Cox (ed.), Female Psychology: The Emerging Self. Chicago: Science Research Associates, 1976, 236-248.

Gallimore, R. Affiliation Motivation and Hawaiian-American Achievement. Journal of Cross-Cultural Psychology, 1974, December, 5(4), 481-491.

Garrett, C. S. The Effects of Modeling on the Development of Sex

Role Behaviors in Children. Unpublished manuscript, Iowa State University, n. d.

Gersoni-Stavn, D. (ed.). Sexism and Youth. New York: R. R. Bowker, 1974.

Ghei, S. N. Needs of Indian and American College Females. Journal of Social Psychology, 1966, 69(1), 3-11.

Giele, J. Z. Changes in the Modern Family: Their Impact on Sex Roles. American Journal of Orthopsychiatry, 1971, 41, 757-766.

Glidewell, J. C., Kantor, M. B., Smith, L. M., and Stinger, L. A. Socialization and Social Structure in the Classroom. In M. L. Hoffman and L. W. Hoffman, (eds.), Review of Child Development (Vol. 2). New York: Russell Sage Foundation, 1966, 221-256.

Gold, D., and Andres, D. Maternal Employment and Child Development at Three Age Levels. Journal of Research and Development in Education, 1977, 10(4), 21-29.

Gold, M. Achievement Motivation and the Child's Social Environment. Paper presented at the National Institute of Child Health and Human Development, Bethesda, MD, n. d.

Goldberg, S. and Lewis, M. Play Behavior in the Year-Old Infant: Early Sex Differences. Child Development, 1969, 40, 21-31.

Gordon, F. E., and Hall, D. T. Self-Image and Stereotypes of Femininity: Their Relationship to Women's Role Conflicts and Coping. Journal of Applied Psychology, 1974, 59, 241-243.

Gough, H. G. Cross-cultural Study of Achievement Motivation. Journal of Applied Psychology, 1964, June, 48, 191-196.

Gove, W. R., and Herb, T. R. Stress and Mental Illness Among the Young: A Comparison of the Sexes. Social Forces, 1974, December, 53(2), 256-265.

Greendorfer, S. L. A Social Learning Approach to Female Sport Involvement. Paper presented at the American Psychological Association Convention, Washington, D. C., 1976.

Greenstein, M., Miller, R. H., and Weldon, D. E. Attitudinal and Normative Beliefs as Antecedents of Female Occupational Choice. Paper presented at the American Psychological Association Convention, San Francisco, 1977.

Grigg, C. M., and Middleton, R. Community of Orientation and Occupational Aspirations of Ninth Grade Students. Social Forces, 1960, May, 38(4), 303-308.

Grossman, M. L. Early Child Development in the Context of Mothering Experiences. Child Psychiatry and Human Development, 1975, Summer, 5(4), 216-223.

Grusec, J. E., and Brinker, D. B., Jr. Reinforcement for Imitation as a Social Learning Determinant with Implications for Sex-Role Development. Journal of Personality and Social Psychology, 1972, 21, 149-158.

Guber, S. A Cross-Cultural Study of the Perceived Feminine Role and Self-Concept of College Women in the United States and Israel. Unpublished doctoral dissertation, New York University. Dissertation Abstracts, 1966, 27(2-B), 609.

Gurwitz, S. B., and Dodge, K. A. Adults' Evaluations of a Child as a Function of Sex of Adult and Sex of Child. Journal of Personality and Social Psychology, 1975, 32, 822-828.

Gutmann, D. Female Ego Styles and Generational Conflict. In J. M. Bardwick et al. (eds.), Feminine Personality and Conflict. Monterey, CA: Brooks/Cole, 1970, 77-96.

Halas, C. M. Sex-Role Stereotypes: Perceived Childhood Socialization Experiences and the Attitudes and Behavior of Adult Women. Journal of Psychology, 1974, November, 88(2), 261-275.

Halperin, M. S. Sex Differences in Children's Responses to Adult Pressure for Achievement. Journal of Educational Psychology, 1977, April, 69(2), 96-100.

Halpin, G., Scott, O., and Halpin, G. Biographical Factors Related to Academic Achievement. Psychological Reports, 1973, August, 33(1), 321-322.

Hansson, R. O., Chernovetz, M. E., and Jones, W. H. Maternal Employment and Androgyny. Psychology of Women Quarterly, 1977, Fall, 2(1), 76-78.

Hartley, R. E. Some Implications of Current Changes in Sex Role. Merrill-Palmer Quarterly, 1960, April, 6(3), 153-164.

———. A Developmental View of Female Sex-Role Definition and Identification. Merrill-Palmer Quarterly, 1964, January, 10(1), 3-16.

———. Role Models and Role Outcomes. Paper presented at Radcliffe Institute Conference on Women: Resource for Changing World, Cambridge, MA, 1972.

Hartup, W. W. Early Pressures in Child Development. Young Children, 1965, May, 20, 270-283.

Hatfield, J. S., Ferguson, L. R., and Alpert, R. Mother-Child

Interaction and the Socialization Process. Child Development, 1967, 38, 365-414.

Heilbrun, A. B. Sex-role Identity in Adolescent Females: A Theoretical Paradox. Adolescence, 1968, 3(9), 79-88.

_____, Kleemeier, C., and Piccola, G. Developmental and Situational Correlates of Achievement Behavior in College Females. Journal of Personality, 1974, 42, 420-436.

_____, and Orr, H. K. Maternal Childrearing Control History and Subsequent Cognitive and Personality Functioning of the Offspring. Psychological Reports, 1965, 17, 259-272.

Helson, R. Childhood Interest Clusters Related to Creativity in Women. Journal of Consulting Psychology, 1965, 29(4), 352-361.

Hess, R. D. Social Class and Ethnic Influences Upon Socialization. in P. H. Mussen (ed.), Carmichael's Manual of Child Psychology (Vol. 2). New York: John Wiley, 1970, 457-557.

Hetherington, E. M. A Developmental Study of the Effects of Sex of the Dominant Parent on Sex Role Preference, Identification, and Imitation in Children. Journal of Personality and Social Psychology, 1965, 2, 188-194.

_____. Effects of Father Absence on Personality Development in Adolescent Daughters. Developmental Psychology, 1972, 7, 313-326.

Hoffman, L. W. Early Childhood Experiences and Women's Achievement Motives. Journal of Social Issues, 1972, 28(2), 129-155. Also in M. T. S. Mednick et al. (eds.), Women and Achievement: Social and Motivational Analyses, New York: Halsted Press, 1975, 129-150; and in E. Lasky (ed.), Humanness: An Exploration into the Mythologies About Women and Men, New York: MSS Informational Corp., 1975, 152-178.

_____. Changes in Family Roles, Socialization, and Sex Differences. American Psychologist, 1977, August, 32(8), 644-657.

Hoffman, M. L. Sex Differences in Moral Internalization and Values. Journal of Personality and Social Psychology, 1975, 32(4), 720-729.

Hoffman, R. L., and Maier, R. P. Social Factors Influencing Problem Solving in Women. Journal of Personality and Social Psychology, 1966, 4(4), 382-390.

Hollender, J. Sex Differences in Sources of Social Self-Esteem. Journal of Consulting and Clinical Psychology, 1972, June, 38(3), 343-347.

Holter, H. Sex Roles and Social Change. In C. Safilios-Rothschild (ed.), Toward a Sociology of Women. Lexington, MA: Xerox College Publishing, 1972, 331-343.

Hong, L. K. The Role of Women in the People's Republic of China: Legacy and Change. Social Problems, 1976, June, 23(5), 545-557.

Howe, F. Sexual Stereotypes Start Early. Saturday Review, 1971, October 16, 76-82+. Also in E. S. Maccia et al. (eds.), Women and Education, Springfield, IL: Charles C. Thomas, 1975, 8-21; and in J. A. Dyal et al. (eds.), Readings in Psychology: The Search for Alternatives, New York: McGraw-Hill, 1975, 135-141.

Huber, J. (ed.). Changing Women in a Changing Society. Special Issue. American Journal of Sociology, 1973, January, 78(4).

Hunter, J. E. Images of Woman. Journal of Social Issues, 1976, 32(3), 7-17.

Hyde, J. S., and Rosenberg, B. G. Cross-Cultural Perspectives on the Female Role. In The Psychology of Women: Half the Human Experience. Lexington, MA: D. C. Heath, 1976, 239-256.

_____, _____, and Behrman, J. Tomboyism: Implications for Theories of Female Development. Paper presented at the Western Psychological Association meeting, 1974.

_____, and Schuck, J. R. Development of Sex Differences in Aggression: Revised Model. Paper presented at the American Psychological Association Convention, San Francisco, 1977.

Jackson, D. W. Stage Factors Relating Alienation and Self-Role Diffusion. Journal of Vocational Behavior, 1974, October, 5(2), 269-274.

Jackson, J. The Underdeveloped Sex. New Society, 1965, April 24, 131(1).

Jacobs, J. C. Evaluation of Mother Teaching Style in High Ability Families. Gifted Child Quarterly, 1971, Spring, 15, 32-35.

Jacobs, S. E. Women in Perspective: A Guide for Cross-Cultural Studies. Urbana: University of Illinois Press, 1974.

Janeway, E. Man's World, Woman's Place: A Study in Social Mythology. New York: William Morrow, 1971.

_____. Between Myth and Morning: Women Awakening. New York: William Morrow, 1974.

Jankowska, H. Wplyw Srodowiska na Plany Zyciowe Dziewcząt [Influence of Environment on Girls' Plans for the Future]. Psychologia Wychowawcza, 1968, 11(3), 396-403.

Jennings, S. A. Effects of Sex Typing in Children's Stories on Preference and Recall. Child Development, 1975, March, 46(1), 220-223.

Joffe, C. Sex Role Socialization and the Nursery School: As the Twig Is Bent. Journal of Marriage and the Family, 1971, August 33(3), 467-475. Also in J. Pottker and A. Fishel (eds.), Sex Bias in the Schools--The Research Evidence. Madison, NJ: Fairleigh Dickinson University Press, 1977, 25-39.

Johnson, B. L., and Kilmann, P. R. The Relationship between Recalled Parental Attitudes and Internal-External Control. Journal of Clinical Psychology, 1975, January 31(1), 40-42.

Johnson, M. M. Sex Role Learning in the Nuclear Family. Child Development, 1963, June, 34(2), 319-333.

───── . Fathers, Mothers and Sex Typing. Sociological Review, 1975, 45, 15-26.

Jorgensen, E. C., and Howell, R. J. Changes in Self, Ideal-Self Correlations from Ages 8 Through 18. Journal of Social Psychology, 1969, October, 79, 63-67.

Journal of Marriage and the Family. 1971, August, 33(3). Contains research on sex-role socialization.

Kagan, J. Acquisition and Significance of Sex-Typing and Sex-Role Identity. In M. L. Hoffman and L. W. Hoffman (eds.), Review of Child Development Research (Vol. 1). New York: Russell Sage Foundation, 1964, 137-165.

───── . The Child's Sex Role Classification of School Objects. Child Development, 1964, December, 35, 1051-1056. Also in D. L. Schaeffer (ed.), Sex Differences in Personality: Readings. Monterey, CA: Brooks/Cole, 1971, 50-55.

───── , and Freeman, M. Relation of Childhood Intelligence, Maternal Behaviors, and Social Class to Behavior During Adolescence. Child Development, 1963, 34, 899-911.

───── , and Moss, H. A. The Stability of Passive and Dependent Behavior from Childhood through Adulthood. Child Development, 1960, 31, 577-591.

Kammeyer, K. Birth Order and the Feminine Sex Role among College Women. American Sociological Review, 1966, August, 31(4), 508-515.

───── . Sibling Position and the Feminine Role. Journal of Marriage and the Family, 1967, August, 29(3), 494-499.

Karman, F. J. Women: Personal and Environmental Factors in Role Identification and Career Choices. Unpublished doctoral dissertation, University of California, Los Angeles. Dissertation Abstracts International, 1972, October, 33(4-A), 1440. Also available from ERIC (ED084383), 1973.

Kellogg, R. L. A Direct Approach to Sex-Role Identification of School-Related Objects. Psychological Reports, 1969, June, 24, 839-841.

Kelly, J. A., and Worell, L. The Relation of Sex Role Categories to Dimensions of Parental Behavior. Paper presented at the American Psychological Association Convention, Chicago, 1975.

_____, and _____. Parent Behaviors Related to Masculine, Feminine, and Androgynous Sex Role Orientations. Journal of Consulting and Clinical Psychology, 1976, October, 44(5), 843-851.

Kemper, T. D. Reference Groups, Socialization and Achievement. American Sociological Review, 1968, 33(1), 31-45.

Kent, M. Higher Education and Gender Role Socialization. Paper presented at the American Association of University Women Symposium on Graduate and Professional Education of Women, Washington, D. C., 1974.

Kimball, M. M. Socialization of Women--A Study in Conflict. Unpublished manuscript, University of British Columbia, 1973.

King, M. E. Parental Self-Actualization and Child's Self-Concept. Unpublished doctoral dissertation, Iowa State University. Dissertation Abstracts International, 1974, July, 35(1-B), 366-367.

Kinsolving, D. L., and Bone, R. N. Firstborns, Only Children, Sex, and Field Independence. Psychological Reports, 1971, 29, 126.

Kipnis, D. M. Inner Direction, Other Direction and Achievement Motivation. Human Development, 1974, 17(5), 321-343.

Klein, E. B., and Gould, L. J. Alienation and Identification in College Women. Journal of Personality, 1969, 37(3), 468-480.

Klemmack, D. L., and Edwards, J. N. Women's Acquisition of Stereotyped Occupational Aspirations. Sociology and Social Research, 1973, July, 57, 510-525.

Kline, C. The Socialization Process of Women. In H. Peters and J. C. Hansen (eds.), Vocational Guidance and Career Development, 3d ed. New York: Macmillan, 1977, 443-453.

Kohlberg, L. A. A Cognitive-Developmental Analysis of Children's Sex-Role Concepts and Attitudes. In E. E. Maccoby (ed.), The

Development of Sex Differences. Stanford, CA: Stanford University Press, 1966, 82-173.

Komarovsky, M. Learning the Feminine Role. In E. M. Schur (ed.), The Family and the Sexual Revolution: Selected Readings. Bloomington: Indiana University Press, 1964, 213-223.

———. Cultural Contradictions and Sex Roles. In J. M. Bardwick (ed.), Readings on the Psychology of Women. New York: Harper & Row, 1972, 58-62.

Koral, A. Are You a Daddy's Girl? Seventeen, 1977, March, 36, 53.

Krieger, W. G. Infant Influences and the Parent Sex X Child Sex Interaction in the Socialization Process. JSAS Catalog of Selected Documents in Psychology, 1976, May, 6, 36-37.

Kundsin, R. B. (ed.). Women and Success: The Anatomy of Achievement. New York: William Morrow, 1974.

Landisberg, S. Changing the World of Women. Symposium presentation at the American Psychological Association Convention, Chicago, 1975.

Lansky, L. M. The Family Structure Also Affects the Model: Sex-Role Attitudes in Parents of Pre-School Children. Merrill-Palmer Quarterly, 1967, April, 13(2), 139-150.

Laosa, L. M., and Brophy, J. E. Effects of Sex and Birth Order on Sex-Role Development and Intelligence among Kindergarten Children. Developmental Psychology, 1972, 6, 409-415.

Lapidus, D. Differential Socialization of Male and Female Preschoolers: Competition Versus Cooperation. Psychology honors thesis for Dr. Eleanor Maccoby, Stanford University, 1972.

Lawrence, George L. Behaviors and Attitudes of College Females Differing in Parent Identification. Unpublished doctoral dissertation, George Peabody College for Teachers. Dissertation Abstracts International, 1969, 30(3-B), 1362.

Laws, J. L. Social Psychology of Women: Shibboleths and Lacunae. Symposium presentation at the American Psychological Association Convention, Washington, D. C., 1969. Also a reprint from KNOW, Inc., P. O. Box 86031, Pittsburgh, PA 15221.

Lefkowitz, M. M. Some Relationships between Sex-Role Preference in Children and Other Parent and Child Variables. Psychological Reports, 1962, 10, 43-53.

Lever, J. R. Games Children Play: Sex-Differences and the Development of Role Skills. Dissertation Abstracts International, 1975, July, 36(1-A), 553-554.

_____. Sex Differences in the Games Children Play. Social Problems, 1976, April, 23(4), 478-487.

Levine, A. Educational and Occupational Choice: A Synthesis of Literature from Sociology and Psychology. Journal of Consumer Research, 1976, March, 2(4), 276-289.

Levine, S. Sex-Role Identification and Parental Perceptions of Social Competence. American Journal of Mental Deficiency, 1966, May, 70, 822-824.

Levitt, E. S. A Study of Four Career Patterns and Associated Life History Characteristics Among Female Professional Librarians. Unpublished doctoral dissertation, New York University. Dissertation Abstracts International, 1971, January, 31(7-B), 4381.

Levy, B. Sex Role Socialization in Schools. In Sex Role Stereotyping in the Schools. Washington, D. C.: National Education Association, 1973, 1-7.

Lewis, E. C. Developing Woman's Potential. Ames: Iowa State University Press, 1968.

Lewis, H. B. How Do Other Cultures Train the Sexes? In Psychic War in Men and Women. New York: New York University Press, 1976, 52-60.

Lewis, M. Culture and Gender Roles: There Is NO Unisex in the Nursery. Psychology Today, 1972, 5(12), 54-57. Also in C. Tavris (ed.), The Female Experience, from the editors of Psychology Today, Del Mar, CA: Communications/Research/Machines, 1973, 46-49.

_____. Parents and Children: Sex-Role Development. School Review, 1972, 80(2), 229-240.

Lipman-Blumen, J. How Ideology Shapes Women's Lives. Scientific American, 1972, January, 226(1), 34-42. Also in E. S. Maccia et al. (eds.), Women and Education. Springfield, IL: Charles C. Thomas, 1975, 37-49.

_____. The Development and Impact of Female Role Ideology. Paper presented at the Radcliffe Institute Conference, Cambridge, MA, April 1972.

_____. The Implications for Family Structure of Changing Sex Roles. Social Casework, 1976, February, 57(2), 67-79.

_____, and Leavitt, H. J. Vicarious and Direct Achievement Patterns in Adulthood. Counseling Psychologist, 1976, June, 6(1), 26-31.

Lippman, M. Z., and Grote, B. H. Social-Emotional Effects of Day

Care. Final Report. Washington, D.C.: Office of Child Development, 1974. Also available from ERIC (ED110164), 1976.

Liversidge, W. Life Chances. Sociological Review, 1962, March, 10(1), 17-34.

Lorber, J. Beyond Equality of the Sexes: The Question of the Children. Family Coordinator, 1975, October, 24(4), 465-472.

Loring, R. and Wells, T. Our Sex-Role Culture. In Breakthrough: Women Into Management. New York: Van Nostrand-Reinhold, 1972, 89-108.

Lower, D., and Krain, M. The Relation of Women's Career Commitment and Their Attitudes Regarding the Socialization of Children into Sex Roles, Marital Role Relations and Marital Adjustment. Unpublished manuscript, available from first author, Department of Sociology, University of Iowa, Iowa City, IA 52240.

Lyell, R.G. Adolescent and Adult Self-Esteem as Related to Cultural Values. Adolescence, 1973, Spring, 8(29), 85-92.

Lynn, D.B. The Process of Learning Parental and Sex-Role Identification. Journal of Marriage and the Family, 1966, 28(4), 466-470. Also in D.L. Schaeffer (ed.), Sex Differences in Personality: Readings. Monterey, CA: Brooks/Cole, 1971. 41-49.

_____. Parental and Sex-Role Identification. Berkeley, CA: McCuthan, 1969.

_____. Determinants of Intellectual Growth in Women. School Review, 1972, 80(2), 241-260.

_____, and Sawrey, W.L. Sex Differences in the Personality Development of Norwegian Children. Journal of Genetic Psychology, 1962, 101, 367-374.

McArthur, L.Z., and Eisen, S.V. Achievements of Male and Female Storybook Characters as Determinants of Achievement Behavior by Boys and Girls. Journal of Personality and Social Psychology, 1976, 33(4), 467-473.

McBride, K.D. Inner Direction, Other Direction and Achievement Motivation. Human Development, 1974, 17(5), 321-343.

McCandless, B.R., Bush, C., and Carden, A.I. Reinforcing Contingencies for Sex-Role Behaviors in Preschool Children. Contemporary Educational Psychology, 1976, 1, 241-246.

McCarbery, R.J., and Darmofall, S.H. Achievement Orientation in Females: Social Psychological Perspective. Paper presented at the American Psychological Association Convention, San Francisco, 1977.

Maccoby, E. E. Feminine Intellect and the Demands of Society. Impact of Science on Society, 1970, 20(1), 13-20.

_____, and Jacklin, C. N. Differential Socialization of Boys and Girls. In The Psychology of Sex Differences. Stanford, CA: Stanford University Press, 1974, 303-348.

MacDonald, A. P., Jr. Internal-External Locus of Control: Parental Antecedents. Journal of Consulting and Clinical Psychology, 1971, 37(1), 141-147.

McFadden, J. R. Sex Role Stereotyping: The Socialization of Youth. A Conference on Youth. University of Minnesota, September, 1976.

McGinnies, E., Nordholm, L. A., Ward, C. D., and Bhanthumnavin, D. L. Sex and Cultural Differences in Perceived Locus of Control Among Students in Five Countries. Journal of Consulting and Clinical Psychology, 1974, 42, 451-455.

Maehr, M. L. Culture and Achievement Motivation. American Psychologist, 1974, 29(12), 887-896.

_____. Sociocultural Origins of Achievement. Monterey, CA: Brooks/Cole, 1974.

Mandel, S. L. Nurturance, Persistence and Distraction in Pre-School Children. Unpublished doctoral dissertation, University of Cincinnati. Dissertation Abstracts, 1968, 29(B), 1845.

Mandle, J. D. Women's Liberation: Humanizing Rather than Polarizing. The Annals of the American Academy of Political and Social Science, 1971, September, 397, 119-128.

Mannes, M. Women Are Equal, But. McCall's, 1965, September, 92, 18+.

Margolin, G., and Patterson, G. R. Differential Consequences Provided by Mothers and Fathers for Their Sons and Daughters. Developmental Psychology, 1975, July, 11(4), 537-538.

Marmor, J. Women in Medicine: Importance of the Formative Years. Journal of the American Medical Women's Association, 1968, July, 23(7), 621-625.

Matthews, E. E. Adolescence and Young Adulthood. In E. E. Matthews et al. (eds.), Counseling Girls and Women Over the Life Span. Washington, D. C.: National Vocational Guidance Association, 1972, 23-33.

_____. Infancy, Childhood, and Pre-Adolescence. In E. E. Matthews et al. (eds.), Counseling Girls and Women Over the Life Span. Washington, D.C.: National Vocational Guidance Association, 1972, 17-22.

———. Life Stages and the Development of Sex Differences in Girls and Women. In E. E. Matthews et al. (eds.), Counseling Girls and Women Over the Life Span. Washington, D.C.: National Vocational Guidance Association, 1972, 9-16.

May, R. A Method for Studying the Development of Gender Identity. Developmental Psychology, 1971, 5, 484-487.

Meade, R. D., and Barnard, W. A. Group Pressure Effects on American and Chinese Females. Journal of Social Psychology, 1975, June, 96(1), 137-138.

Meda, R., Hefner, R. and Oleshansky, B. A Dialectic Model of Sex-Role Socialization. Symposium presentation at the American Psychological Association Convention, Chicago, 1975.

Mednick, M. T. S., Tangri, S. S., and Hoffman, L. W. (eds.). Women and Achievement: Social and Motivational Analyses. New York: Halsted Press, 1975.

Meier, H. C. Mother-Centeredness and College Youths' Attitudes Toward Social Equality for Women: Some Empirical Findings. Journal of Marriage and the Family, 1972, 34(1), 115-121.

Meixal, C. A. Effects of Social Structural, Social Psychological, and Sex Role Factors on Female and Male Adolescents' Status Expectations. Unpublished doctoral dissertation, Cornell University. Dissertation Abstracts International, 1976, 37(11-A), 7351. Available from ERIC (AD677-11003), 1976.

Meyer, J. W., and Sobieszek, B. I. Effect of a Child's Sex on Adult Interpretations of Its Behavior. Developmental Psychology, 1972, 6, 42-48.

Miles, B. Harmful Lessons Little Girls Learn in School. Redbook, 1971, March, 136(86), 168-169.

Miller, S. M. Effects of Maternal Employment on Sex Role Perception, Interests, and Self-Esteem in Kindergarten Girls. Developmental Psychology, 1975, May, 11(3), 405-406.

Miller, S. R. An Investigation of the Relationship between Mothers' General Fearfulness, Their Daughters' Locus of Control and General Fearfulness in the Daughter. Unpublished doctoral dissertation, New York University. Dissertation Abstracts International, 1974, November, 35(5-B), 2281.

Miller, T. W. Effects of Maternal Age, Education, and Employment Status on the Self-Esteem of the Child. Journal of Social Psychology, 1975, 95, 141-142.

Millman, M., and Kanter, R. M. Another Voice: Feminist Perspectives on Social Life and Social Science. Garden City, NY: Anchor Press/Doubleday, 1975.

Mintz, E. The Prejudice of Parents. In F. L. Denmark (ed.), Who Discriminates Against Women? (Issue 15). Beverly Hills, CA: Sage Publications, Inc., 1974, 9-13; also in International Journal of Group Tensions, 1974, March, 4(1), 6-20; and a reprint from KNOW, Inc., P. O. Box 86031, Pittsburgh, PA 15221.

Minuchin, P. Sex-Role Concepts and Sex Typing in Childhood as a Function of School and Home Environments. Child Development, 1965, December, 36, 1033-1048. Also in A. G. Kaplan and J. P. Bean (eds.), Beyond Sex-Role Stereotypes: Readings Toward a Psychology of Androgyny. Boston: Little, Brown, 1976, 206-222.

Mischel, W. A Social Learning View of Sex Differences in Behavior. In E. E. Maccoby (ed.), The Development of Sex Differences. Stanford, CA: Stanford University Press, 1966, 56-81.

―――. Sex-Typing and Socialization. In P. H. Mussen (ed.), Carmichael's Manual of Child Psychology (Vol. 2). New York: John Wiley, 1970, 3-72.

Mishler, S. A. Barriers to the Career Development of Women. In S. H. Osipow (ed.), Emerging Women: Career Analysis and Outlooks. Columbus, OH: Charles E. Merrill, 1975, 117-146.

Mitchell, E. The Learning of Sex Roles Through Toys and Books: A Woman's View. Young Children, 1973, 28(4), 226-231.

Mitchell, J. Woman's Estate. New York: Random House, 1973.

Mohr, D., and Clementson, J. Sex-Role Socialization: A Need for New Research Models. Symposium presentation at the American Psychological Association Convention, San Francisco, 1977.

Money, J. Developmental Differentiation of Femininity and Masculinity Compared. In S. M. Farber and R. H. L. Wilson, (eds.), The Potential of Woman: Proceedings of Symposium. New York: McGraw-Hill, 1963, 51-65.

―――, and Ehrhardt, A. A. Man and Woman, Boy and Girl. Baltimore: Johns Hopkins Press, 1972.

Morris, L. D. A Socio-Psychological Study of Highly Skilled Women Field Hockey Players. International Journal of Sport Psychology, 1975, 6(3), 134-147.

Moss, H. A. Sex, Age, and State as Determinants of Mother-Infant Interaction. Merrill-Palmer Quarterly, 1967, 13, 19-36.

_____, and Kagan, J. Stability of Achievement and Recognition Seeking Behaviors from Early Childhood Through Adulthood. Journal of Abnormal and Social Psychology, 1961, 62(3), 504-513.

Moulton, R. W., Burnstein, E., Liberty, P. G., and Altucher, N. Patterning of Parental Affection and Disciplinary Dominance as a Determinant of Guilt and Sex-Typing. Journal of Personality and Social Psychology, 1966, 4, 356-363.

Munger, M. O. Sex Differentiation in Pre-School Children: Sex-Typical Toy Preferences. Unpublished doctoral dissertation, 1971.

Mussen, P. H. Early Sex-Role Development. In D. Goslin (ed.), Handbook of Socialization Theory and Research. New York: Russell Sage Foundation, 1969, 707-731.

_____ (ed.), Sex-Typing and Socialization. In Carmichael's Manual of Child Psychology (Vol. 2). New York: John Wiley, 1972, 3-72.

_____, and Parker, A. Mother Nurturance and Girls' Incidental Imitative Learning. Journal of Personality and Social Psychology, 1965, 2, 94-97.

_____, and Rutherford, E. Parent-Child Relations and Parental Personality in Relation to Young Children's Sex-Role Preference. Child Development, 1963, 34, 589-607. Also in E. Lasky (ed.), Humanness: An Exploration into the Mythologies About Women and Men. New York: MSS Informational Corporation, 1975, 133-151.

Naffziger, C. C., and Naffziger, K. Development of Sex Role Stereotypes. Family Coordinator, 1974, July, 23(3), 251-258.

Nakamura, C. Y., and Rogers, M. M. Parents' Expectations of Autonomous Behavior and Children's Autonomy. Developmental Psychology, 1969, 1, 613-617.

Nelson, D. D. Study of Personality Adjustment Among Adolescent Children with Working and Non-Working Mothers. Journal of Educational Research, 1971, March, 64, 328-330.

Nordlie, D. A. The Socialization of Achievement Values. Unpublished doctoral dissertation, University of Nebraska. Dissertation Abstracts International, 1971, November, 32(5-A), 2811.

Norman, R. D. Sex Differences in Preferences for Sex of Children: A Replication After 20 Years. Journal of Psychology, 1974, November, 88(2), 229-239.

Nowicki, S., and Segal, W. Perceived Parental Characteristics, Locus of Control Orientation, and Behavioral Correlates of

Locus of Control. *Developmental Psychology*, 1974, January, 10(1), 33-37.

Nurkhart, M. Q. Vocational Decision-Making: A Comparison of the Rates of Development for Men and Women. *Dissertation Abstracts International*, 1973, 34(A), 1605.

O'Connell, A. A. Determinants of Women's Life Styles and Sense of Identity: Personality, Attitudes, Significant Others, and Demographic Characteristics. Unpublished doctoral dissertation, Rutgers University. *Dissertation Abstracts International*, 1974, December, 35(6-B), 2996-2997.

Ollison, L. Socialization: Women, Worth, and Work. Unpublished manuscript, San Diego State University, 1975.

Orum, A. M., Cohen, R. S., Grasmuck, S., and Orum, A. W. Sex, Socialization and Politics. In M. Githens and J. L. Prestage (eds.), *A Portrait of Marginality*. New York: David McKay, 1977, 11-37.

Osofsky, J. D. The Socialization and Education of American Women. In A. F. Scott (ed.), *What Is Happening to American Women*. Atlanta: Southern Newspaper Publishers Association Foundation, 1970, 3.

Parsons, J. The Development of Achievement Expectancies in Girls and Boys. Paper presented at the Eastern Psychological Association meeting, 1974.

Parsons, T. The School Class as a Social System: Some of Its Functions in American Society. In *Socialization and Schools*. Cambridge, MA: President and Fellows of Harvard College, 1968, 69-90.

Patai, R. *Women in the Modern World*. New York: Free Press, 1967.

Patton, R. G., and Gardner, L. I. Influence of Family Environment on Growth: The Syndrome of "Maternal Deprivation." *Pediatrician*, 1962, 30, 957-962.

Perrucci, C. C., and Targ, D. B. *Marriage and the Family: A Critical Analysis and Proposals for Change*. New York: David McKay, 1974.

Perry, D. G., and Perry, L. C. Observational Learning in Children: Effects of Sex of Model and Subject's Sex Role Behavior. *Journal of Personality and Social Psychology*, 1975, 31, 1083-1088.

Peters, A. An Investigation of the Relationship Between the Inability of Some Women in Psychotherapy to Accept their Female Role and Their Perception of Their Mothers' Attitudes

Toward the Female Role. Unpublished doctoral dissertation, New York University. Dissertation Abstracts, 1961, 21(12), 3856-3857.

Peterson, C. C., and Peterson, J. L. Preferences for Sex of Offspring as a Measure of Change in Sex Attitudes. Psychology, 1973, 10, 3-5.

Peterson, E. T. The Impact of Maternal Employment on the Mother-Daughter Relationship. Marriage and Family Living, 1961, November, 23(4), 355-361.

Poffenberger, T., and Norton, D. Sex Differences in Achievement Motive in Mathematics as Related to Cultural Change. Journal of Genetic Psychology, 1963, 103, 341-350.

Polk, B. B. Male Power and the Women's Movement. Journal of Applied Behavioral Science, 1974, 10(3), 415-431.

Potter, N. D. Mathematical and Verbal Ability Patterns in Women: Personality and Environmental Correlates. Unpublished doctoral dissertation, University of Missouri, Columbia. Dissertation Abstracts International, 1975, July, 36(1-B), 426.

Poznanski, E., Maxey, A., and Marsden, G. Clinical Implications of Maternal Employment: A Review of Research. Journal of the American Academy of Child Psychiatry, 1970, October, 9(4), 741-761.

Rebecca, M., Hefner, R., and Oleshansky, B. A Model of Sex-Role Transcendence. Journal of Social Issues, 1976, 32(3), 197-206.

Reeves, N. Womankind: Beyond the Stereotypes. Chicago: Aldine, 1971.

Reiter, R. (ed.). Toward an Anthropology of Women. New York: Monthly Review Press, 1975.

Rheingold, H. L., and Cook, K. V. The Content of Boys' and Girls' Rooms as an Index of Parents' Behavior. Child Development, 1975, 46(2), 459-463.

Ribal, J. E. Learning Sex Roles: American and Scandanavian Contrasts. San Francisco: Canfield Press, 1973.

Ridgeway, C. L., and Seater, B. B. Role Models, Significant Others, and the Importance of Male Influence on College Women. Sociological Symposium, 1976, Spring, 15, 49-64.

Riesche, D. L. Women and Society. New York: H. W. Wilson, 1972.

Rohner, R. P. Sex Differences in Aggression: Phylogenetic and Enculturation Perspectives. Ethos, 1976, Spring, 4(1), 57-72.

Rosaldo, M. Z. Woman, Culture, and Society: A Theoretical Overview. In M. Z. Rosaldo and L. Lamphere (eds.), Woman, Culture, and Society. Stanford, CA: Stanford University Press, 1974, 17-42.

Rosen, B. C., and Aneshensel, C. S. The Chameleon Syndrome: A Social Psychological Dimension of the Female Sex Role. Journal of Marriage and the Family, 1976, November, 38(4), 605-617.

_____, et al. (eds.). American Women and American Values. In Achievement in American Society. Cambridge, MA: Schenkman, 1969.

Rosenberg, B. G., and Sutton-Smith, B. Family Interaction Effects on Masculinity-Femininity. Journal of Personality and Social Psychology, 1968, 8, 117-120.

_____ and _____. Family Structure and Sex-Role Variations. Nebraska Symposium on Motivation, 1973, 21, 195-220.

Rosenfeld, E. F. The Relationship of Sex-Typed Toys to the Development of Competency and Sex-Role Identification in Children. Paper presented at the Society for Research in Child Development meeting, Denver, 1975.

Rosenhan, D., and Greenwald, J. A. The Effects of Age, Sex, and Socioeconomic Class on Responsiveness to Two Classes of Verbal Reinforcement. Journal of Personality, 1965, March, 33(1), 108-121.

Rossi, A. S. Equality Between the Sexes: An Immodest Proposal. Daedalus, 1964, Spring, 93(2), 607-652. Also in C. C. Perrucci and D. B. Targ (eds.), Marriage and the Family: A Critical Analysis and Proposals for Change. New York: David McKay, 1974, 178-182.

_____. Changing Sex Roles and Family Development. Paper presented at the American Psychological Association Convention, Washington, D. C., 1971.

_____. The Roots of Ambivalence in American Women. In J. M. Bardwick (ed.), Readings on the Psychology of Women. New York: Harper & Row, 1972, 125-127.

Rothbart, M. K., and Maccoby, E. E. Parents' Differential Reactions to Sons and Daughters. Journal of Personality and Social Psychology, 1966, 4(3), 237-243. Also in R. K. Unger and F. L. Denmark (eds.), Woman: Dependent or Independent Variable? New York: Psychological Dimensions, 1975, 247-262.

Rowbotham, S. Woman's Consciousness, Man's World. New York: Penguin, 1973.

Rubin, J. Z., Provenzano, F. J., and Luria, Z. The Eye of the Beholder: Parents' Views on Sex of Newborns. American Journal of Orthopsychiatry, 1974, 44(4), 512-519.

Russo, N. F. The Motherhood Mandate. Journal of Social Issues, 1976, 32(3), 143-153.

Rychlak, J., and Legerski, A. A Sociocultural Theory of Appropriate Sexual Role Identification and Level of Personal Adjustment. Journal of Personality, 1967, 35(1), 31-49.

Safilios-Rothschild, C. A Cross-Cultural Examination of Women's Marital, Educational and Occupational Options. ACTA Sociologia, 1971, 14, 96-113.

———. Toward a Sociology of Women. Lexington, MA: Xerox College, 1972.

———. Social Policy to Liberate Women. In Women and Social Policy. Englewood Cliffs, NJ: Prentice-Hall, 1974, 17-71.

Sanday, P. R. Toward a Theory of the Status of Women. American Anthropologist, 1973, 75, 1682-1700.

Sandis, E. E. The Transmission of Mothers' Educational Ambitions, as Related to Specific Socialization Techniques. Journal of Marriage and the Family, 1970, 32(2), 204-211.

Santrock, J. Paternal Absence, Sex Typing, and Identification. Developmental Psychology, 1970, 2, 264-272.

Scanzoni, J. Socialization, n Achievement, and Achievement Values. American Sociological Review, 1967, June, 32(3), 449-456.

Scheck, D. C., Emerick, R., and El-Assal, M. M. Adolescent's Perceptions of Parent-Child Relations and the Development of Internal-External Control Orientation. Journal of Marriage and the Family, 1973, 35, 634-654.

Schlacter, G., and Belli, D. The Changing Role of Women in America: A Selected Annotated Bibliography of Reference Sources. Monticello, IL: Council of Planning Librarians, December, 1975.

Schmuck, R. Sex of Sibling, Birth Order Position, and Female Dispositions to Conform in Two-Child Families. Child Development, 1963, December, 34, 913-918.

Scott, A. F. (ed.). What Is Happening to American Women? Atlanta: Southern Newspaper Publishers Association Foundation, 1970.

Sears, R. R. Relation of Early Socialization Experiences to Aggression in Middle Childhood. Journal of Abnormal Social Psychology, 1961, 63, 466-492.

──────. Relation of Early Socialization Experiences to Self-Concepts and Gender Role in Middle Childhood. Child Development, 1970, 41, 267-289.

──────, Rau, L., and Alpert, R. Identification and Child Rearing. Stanford, CA: Stanford University Press, 1965.

Seavey, C. A., Katz, P. A., and Zalk, S. R. Baby X: The Effect of Gender Labels on Adult Responses to Infants. Sex Roles: A Journal of Research, 1975, 1(2), 103-109.

Seiden, A. M. Overview: Research on the Psychology of Women: II. Women in Families, Work, and Psychotherapy. American Journal of Psychiatry, 1976, October, 133(10), 1111-1123.

Selcer, R. J., and Hilton, I. R. Cultural Differences in the Acquisition of Sex-Roles. Proceedings of the Annual Convention of the American Psychological Association, 1972, 7(Pt. 1), 91-92.

Senders, V. What Sets the Limits to a Woman's Growth. Counseling Girls Toward New Perspectives: A Report of the Mid-Atlantic Regional Pilot Conference. Washington, D. C.: U. S. Government Printing Office, 1966.

Serbin, L. A. Sex Differences in the Preschool Classroom: Patterns of Social Reinforcement. Unpublished doctoral dissertation, State University of New York at Stoney Brook, 1972.

Seward, D. Women Around the World: An Overview. Journal of the National Association of Women Deans, and Counselors, 1970, Fall, 34(1), 2-6.

Seward, G. H. Psychological Complications of Women's Roles. International Understanding, 1964-65, 2, 1-4.

──────, and Williamson, R. C. A Cross-National Study of Adolescent Professional Goals. Human Development, 1969, 12(4), 248-254.

Sex and the Contemporary Scene. The Annals of the American Academy of Political and Social Science, 1968, March. Special Issue.

Sexton, P. Socialization, Sex Roles, Discrimination. In Women in Education. Bloomington, IN: Phi Delta Kappa Educational Foundation, 1976, 61-74.

Sherman, J. A. Socializing for Female Competence. Paper Presented at the American Association for the Advancement of Science meeting, Washington, D. C., 1972.

_____. Social Values, Femininity, and the Development of Female Competence. Journal of Social Issues, 1976, 32(3), 181-195.

Sherwood, E. B. The Antecedents of Career Choice for Women in Two Professions. Unpublished doctoral dissertation, University of Maryland. Dissertation Abstracts International, 1976, 36 (10-A), 6995.

_____. The Antecedents of Career Choice for Women in Two Professions. Unpublished doctoral dissertation, University of Maryland, 1975. Available from ERIC (ADG76-08436), 1975.

Shuval, J. T. Occupational Interests and Sex-Role Congruence. Human Relations, 1963, 16(2), 171-183.

Smith, D. The Early Socialization of Women. Unpublished manuscript, Michigan State University, East Lansing, n. d.

Smith, P. K., and Green, M. Aggressive Behavior in English Nurseries and Play Groups: Sex Differences and Response of Adults. Child Development, 1975, 46, 211-214.

Snyder, E. E., and Spreitzer, E. Correlates of Sport Participation Among Adolescent Girls. Research Quarterly, 1976, December, 47(4), 804-809.

Socialization and Schools. Cambridge, MA: President and Fellows of Harvard College, 1968.

Spencer, A. G. Why Are There No Woman Geniuses? In J. Stacey et al. (eds.), And Jill Came Tumbling After: Sexism In American Education. New York: Dell, 1974, 33-36.

The Spocks: Bittersweet Recognition in a Revised Classic. New York Times, 1975, March 19, 28.

Stake, J. E. Effects of Contrived Information of Female and Male Performance on the Achievement Behavior of Preschool Girls and Boys. Journal of Applied Social Psychology, 1976, 6(1), 85-93.

Standley, K., and Soule, B. Women in Professions: Historic Antecedents and Current Lifestyles. In R. E. Hardy and J. G. Cull (eds.), Career Guidance for Young Women: Considerations in Planning Professional Careers. Springfield, IL: Charles C. Thomas, 1974, 3-16.

_____, and _____. Women in Male-Dominated Professions: Contrasts in Their Personal and Vocational Histories. Journal of Vocational Behavior, 1974, April, 4(2), 245-258.

Stefic, E. C., and Lorr, M. Age and Sex Differences in Personality During Adolescence. Psychological Reports, 1974, December, 35(3), 1123-1126.

Stein, A. H. The Effects of Sex-Role Standards for Achievement and Sex-Role Preference on Three Determinants of Achievement Motivation. Developmental Psychology, 1971, March, 4(2), 219-231.

———. The Effects of Maternal Employment and Educational Attainment on the Sex-Typed Attributes of College Females. Social Behavior and Personality, 1973, 1(2), 111-114.

———, and Bailey, M. M. The Socialization of Achievement Orientation in Females. Psychological Bulletin, 1973, 30(3), 345-366. Also in A. G. Kaplan and J. P. Bean (eds.), Beyond Sex-Role Stereotypes: Readings Toward a Psychology of Androgyny. Boston: Little, Brown, 1976, 239-261.

Steinmann, A. Male-Female Concepts of Sex Roles: Twenty Years of Cross-Cultural Research. Symposium presentation at the American Psychological Association Convention, Chicago, 1975.

Stevenson, M. Women in Canada. Toronto: New Press, 1973.

Stewart, A. J., and Winter, D. G. Self-Definition and Social Definition in Women. Journal of Personality, 1974, 42(2), 238-259.

Stiehm, J. (ed.). The Frontiers of Knowledge. In The Frontiers of Knowledge. Los Angeles: University of Southern California Press, 1976, 1-7.

Stimpson, C. R. Sex, Gender, and American Culture. In L. A. Cater et al. (eds.), Women and Men: Changing Roles, Relationships, and Perceptions. New York: Praeger, 1977, 201-244.

Stinnett, N., Farris, J. A., and Walters, J. Parent-Child Relationships of Male and Female High School Students. Journal of Genetic Psychology, 1974, September, 125(1), 99-106.

Stockard, A. J. The Development of Sex-Role Related Attitudes and Behaviors of Young Women. Dissertation Abstracts International, 1975, February, 35(8-A), 5539.

Stoller, R. J. Sex and Gender: On the Development of Masculinity and Femininity. New York: Jason Aronson, 1968.

Suber, C. J.. The Effect of Certain Social Variables on Sex-Role Preference and Gender Identification in Preschool Age Girls.

Unpublished doctoral dissertation, University of Maryland. Dissertation Abstracts International, 1976, April, 36(10-B), 5287.

Sullerot, E. Women, Society and Change. New York: McGraw-Hill, 1971.

Sybouts, W. Employed Mothers and Adolescent Behavior. School and Community, 1968, October, 55, 20-21.

Symonds, A. The Psychology of the Women's Liberation Movement. Medical Aspects of Human Sexuality, 1971, 5(4), 24-29.

_____, Moulton, R., and Badaracco, M. R. The Myth of Femininity: A Panel. American Journal of Psychoanalysis, 1973, 33(1), 42-55.

Szal, J. A. Sex Differences in the Cooperative and Competitive Behaviors of Nursery School Children. Unpublished master's thesis, Stanford University, 1972.

Tangri, S. S. Determinants of Occupational Role Innovation Among College Women. Journal of Social Issues, 1972, 28(2), 177-199. Also in M. T. S. Mednick et al. (eds.), Women and Achievement: Social and Motivational Analysis. New York: Halsted Press, 1975, 255-273.

_____. Effects of Background, Personality, College and Post-College Experiences on Women's Post-Graduate Employment. Final Report. Washington, D. C.: U. S. Commission on Civil Rights, Manpower Administration, 1974. Also available from ERIC (ED101223), 1975.

Tavris, C., and Offir, C. Getting the Message: The Learning Perspective. In The Longest War: Sex Differences in Perspective. New York: Harcourt Brace Jovanovich, 1977, 161-198.

Thomas, P. J. Sub-cultural Differences in Sex Role Preference Patterns. Unpublished doctoral dissertation, Western Reserve University. Dissertation Abstracts, 1966, 26(11), 6894-6895.

Thorne, B., and Henley, N. (eds.). Difference and Dominance: An Overview of Language, Gender, and Society. In Language and Sex: Difference and Dominance. Rowley, MA: Newbury House, 1975, 5-42.

Thurnher, M. Resisting Socialization to Become an Old Woman. Symposium presentation at the American Psychological Association Convention, San Francisco, 1977.

Toyama, J. S., and Barfield, V. M. Childhood Games Played by Successful Women: A Pilot Study. Paper presented at Research Council Free Papers: Sport Sociology, American Alliance for Health, Physical Education and Recreation, Seattle, Washington, March 1977.

Trigg, L. J., and Perlman, D. Social Influences on Women's Pursuit of a Nontraditional Career. Psychology of Women Quarterly, 1976, 1(2), 138-150.

Trilling, B. A. Factors Related to Women's Prejudice Against Women. Unpublished doctoral dissertation, Fordham University, 1975.

Trilling, D. Daughters of the Middle Class: Excerpt from We Must March My Darlings. Harper's Magazine, 1977, April, 254, 31-36.

Troll, L. E., Neugarten, B. L., and Kraines, R. J. Similarities in Values and Other Personality Characteristics in College Students and Their Parents. Merrill-Palmer Quarterly, 1969, 15, 323-336.

Trumbo, S. S. A Woman's Place Is in the Oven. The New York Times, 1971, October 10.

Tyler, L. E. The Development of Career Interests in Girls. Genetic Psychology Monographs, 1964, 70, 203-212.

Ullian, D. Z. The Development of Conceptions of Masculinity and Femininity. In B. B. Lloyd and J. Archer (eds.), Exploring Sex Differences. New York: Academic Press, 1976, 25-47.

Unger, R. K. Male Is Greater Than Female: The Socialization of Status Inequality. Counseling Psychologist, 1976, 6(2), 2-9.

―――――, and Denmark, F. L. Woman: Dependent or Independent Variable? New York: Psychological Dimensions, 1975.

Van Dijk-den Bandt, M. L. Akademisch Gevormde Vrouwen en hun Mogelijkheden [Academically Formed Women and Their Possibilities]. Mens en Onderneming, 1972, May, 26(3), 181-193.

Van Dusen, R. A., and Sheldon, E. B. The Changing Status of American Women: A Life Cycle Perspective. American Psychologist, 1976, February, 31(2), 106-116. Also in H. J. Peters and J. C. Hansen (eds.), Vocational Guidance and Career Development. New York: Macmillan, 1977.

Vener, A. M., and Snyder, C. A. The Preschool Child's Awareness and Anticipation of Adult Sex-Roles. Sociometry, 1966, 29(2), 159-168.

Verheyden-Hilliard, M. E. Kindergarten: The Training Ground for Women in Administration. Journal of the National Association for Women Deans, Administrators, and Counselors, 1975, Summer, 38, 151-155.

Veroff, J. Social Comparison and Development of Achievement Motivation. In C. P. Smith (ed.), Achievement-Related Motives in Children. New York: Russell Sage Foundation, 1969, 46-101.

Vogel, S. R., Broverman, I. K., Broverman, D. M., Clarkson, F. E., and Rosenkrantz, P. S. Maternal Employment and Perception of Sex Roles Among College Students. Developmental Psychology, 1970, 3(3), 384-391.

Vroegh, K. Masculinity and Femininity in the Elementary and Junior High School Years. Developmental Psychology, 1971, 4(2), 254-261.

Waldman, E., and Gover, R. Children of Women in the Labor Force. Monthly Labor Review, 1971, 94, 19-25.

Wallston, B. S. The Effects of Maternal Employment on Children. Journal of Child Psychology and Psychiatry and Allied Disciplines, 1973, June, 14(2), 81-95.

_____, and Citron, M. The Myth of the Working Mother. Reprint from KNOW, Inc., P. O. Box 86031, Pittsburgh, PA 15221, 1973.

Ward, W. D. Process of Sex-Role Development. Developmental Psychology, 1969, 1, 1963-1968.

_____. Patterns of Culturally Defined Sex-Role Preference and Parental Imitation. Journal of Genetic Psychology, 1973, 122, 337-343.

Weaver, F. J. Selected Aspects of Father-Daughter Interaction and Daughter's Instrumentalness in Late Adolescence. Unpublished doctoral dissertation, Pennsylvania State University. Dissertation Abstracts, 1969, 29(10-A), 3690-3691.

Weisstein, N. Stimulus/Response: Woman as Nigger. Psychology Today, 1969, 3(5), 20-22+.

Weitz, S. The Psychological Maintenance System: The Family. In Sex Roles: Biological, Psychological, and Social Foundations. New York: Oxford University Press, 1977, 58-113.

Weitzman, L. J. Sex-Role Socialization. In J. Freeman (ed.), Women: A Feminist Perspective. Palo Alto, CA: Mayfield, 1975, 105-144.

Werner, E. E. Sex Differences in Correlations Between Children's I. Q.'s and Measures of Parental Ability and Environmental Ratings. Developmental Psychology, 1969, 1, 280-285.

Westervelt, E. M. Woman as a Compleat Human Being. Journal

of the National Association of Women Deans and Counselors, 1966, Summer, 29(4), 150-155.

_____. The Feminine Agenda: Influences of Biology, Society and Culture on the Lives of Women. Paper presented at workshop: Counseling Girls and Women over the Life Span, University of Oregon, July 1970.

Whiting, B. B., and Edwards, C. P. A Cross-Cultural Analysis of Sex Differences in the Behavior of Children Aged Three Through Eleven. Journal of Social Psychology, 1973, 91, 171-188.

Williams, J. H. Growing Up Female. In J. M. Bardwick (ed.), Psychology of Women: Behavior in a Biosocial Context. New York: W. W. Norton, 1977, 158-195.

Wilson, A., Bolt, M., and Larsen, W. Woman's Biology--Mankind's Destiny: The Population Explosion and Women's Changing Roles. In J. Freeman (ed.), Women: A Feminist Perspective. Palo Alto: Mayfield, 1975, 3-15.

Woelfel, J. Significant Others and Their Role Relationships to Students in a High School Population. Rural Sociology, 1972, March, 37(1), 86-97.

Women and the Law: Symposium Issue. Valparaiso University Law Review, 1971, 5(2).

Woods, M. M. The Relation of Sex Role Categories to Autobiographical Factors. Symposium presentation at the American Psychological Association Convention, Chicago, 1975.

Worell, L., and Kelly, J. A. Parent Behaviors Related to Masculine, Feminine, and Androgynous Sex Role Orientations. Journal of Consulting and Clinical Psychology, 1976, 44(5), 843-851.

Wortis, R. P. The Acceptance of the Maternal Role by Behavioral Scientists: Its Effects on Women. American Journal of Orthopsychiatry, 1971, 41(5), 733-746.

_____. The Acceptance of the Concept of the Maternal Role by Behavioral Scientists: Its Effects on Women. In H. Wortis and C. Rabinowitz (eds.), The Women's Movement: Social and Psychological Perspectives. New York: John Wiley, 1972, 32-51.

Wright, B., and Tuska, S. The Nature and Origin of Feeling Feminine. British Journal of Social and Clinical Psychology, 1966, 5(2), 140-149.

Yarrow, M. R. Maternal Employment and Child Rearing. Children, 1961, November, 8, 223-228.

Yudkin, S., and Holme, A. Working Mothers and Their Children. London: Sphere Books, 1969.

Zecca, G. M., and Muzio, N. R. Determinanti Principali del Sentimenti d'Inferiorita in un Gruppo di Giovana Adulte [Main Determinants of Feelings of Inferiority in a Group of Young Adult Women]. Neuropsichiatria, 1968, January, 24(1), 1-7.

Ziebarth, C. A. Feminine Role Conflict: The Influence of Models and Expectations of Others. Unpublished doctoral dissertation, University of Colorado. Dissertation Abstracts International, 1971, August, 32(2-A), 1076.

B. SEX ROLES

1. GENERAL

Adams, E., and Briscoe, M. L. Up Against the Wall, Mother. Beverly Hills, CA: Glencoe Press, 1971.

Adams, M. The Compassion Trap, Women Only. Psychology Today, 1971, November, 70-72+.

Ahammer, I. M. Desirability Judgments as a Function of Item Content, Instructional Set, and Sex: A Life-Span Developmental Study. Human Development, 1971, 14(3), 195-207.

Alberti, J. M. Alternatives for Women. Educational Horizons, 1975, Spring, 53(3), 95-97.

Albrecht, S. L. Social Class and Sex-Stereotyping of Occupations. Journal of Vocational Behavior, 1976, December, 9(3), 321-328.

Albright, D., and Chang, A. An Examination of How One's Attitudes Toward Women Are Reflected in One's Defensiveness and Self-Esteem. Sex Roles: A Journal of Research, 1976, 2, 195-198.

Alexander, A. Who's Come a Long Way, Baby? Johns Hopkins Alumni Magazine, 1970, Spring.

Alpert, J. L., and Richardson, M. S. Conflict and Women's Roles: An Empirical Investigation of Women's Perceptions. Paper presented at the American Psychological Association Convention, Chicago, 1975.

_____, and _____. Conflict, Outcome, and Perception of Women's Roles. Paper presented at the American Psychological Association Convention, Chicago, 1975.

_____, _____, Perlmutter, B., and Shutzer, F. Women's and Men's Perceptions of Single and Multiple Roles. Paper presented at the American Psychological Association Convention, Washington, D.C., 1976.

The American Woman: Special Issue. Time, 1972, March 20, 99(1).

Amundsen, K. The Silenced Majority: Women and American Democracy. Englewood Cliffs, NJ: Prentice-Hall, 1971.

Anderson, C., and Jacobson, L. Construction of a Scale Measuring Beliefs about Equal Rights for Men and Women. Paper presented at the Southeastern Psychological Association meeting, Hollywood, FL, 1974.

Angrist, S.S. The Study of Sex Roles. Journal of Social Issues, 1969, January, 25(1), 215-232. Also in J.M. Bardwick (ed.), Readings on the Psychology of Women. New York: Harper and Row, 1972, 101-107; and in C.C. Perrucci and D.B. Targ (eds.), Marriage and the Family: A Critical Analysis and Proposals for Change. New York: David McKay, 1974, 182-188.

Anthony, S.B. The Status of Woman, Past, Present and Future. In F.C. Griffin (ed.), Woman as Revolutionary. New York: Mentor Books, 1973.

Archer, J., and Lloyd, B.B. Sex Roles: Biological and Social Interactions. New Scientist, 1974, November, 21, 582-584.

Astin, H.S., Parelman, A., and Fisher, A. Sex Roles: A Research Bibliography. Rockville, MD: National Institute of Mental Health, 1975.

Aulette, J.R., and Doherty, E.G. Sex Role Stereotypes of Normal Children by School Social Workers. Paper presented at the Midwestern Sociological Meeting, Minneapolis, April 1977.

Badaracco, M.R., Gould, R.E., and Landman, L. Recent Trends Toward Unisex: A Panel Discussion. American Journal of Psychoanalysis, 1974, 34(1), 17-31.

Bakan, D. The Duality of Human Existence. Chicago: Rand McNally, 1966.

Baker, B.J. Acceptance Versus Rejection of the Traditional Feminine Role: Consideration of Women's Liberation. Unpublished doctoral dissertation. Dissertation Abstracts International, 1972, November, 33(5-A), 2157-2158.

Banikiotes, P.G., and Banikiotes, F.G. Male and Female Perceptions of Liberated Versus Conventional Sex Roles. Psychonomic Science, 1972, October, 29(2), 111-112.

Bardwick, J. M. Androgyny and Humanistic Goals or Goodby, Cardboard People. In M. L. McBee and K. A. Blake (eds.), The American Woman: Who Will She Be? Beverly Hills, CA: Glencoe Press, 1974, 49-64.

_____, Douvan, E., Horner, M., and Gutman, N. D. Feminine Personality and Conflict. Monterey, CA: Brooks/Cole, 1970.

Barry, K. View from the Doll Corner. Women: A Journal of Liberation, 1969, Fall, 1(1).

Bart, P. Why Women See the Future Differently from Men. In A. Toffler (ed.), Learning for Tomorrow: The Role of the Future in Education. New York: Random House, 1974, 33-55.

Bar-Tal, D., and Saxe, L. Physical Attractiveness and Its Relationship to Sex-Role Stereotyping. Sex Roles: A Journal of Research, 1976, 2(2), 123-133.

Baruch, G. K. Sex-Role Attitudes of Fifth-Grade Girls. In J. Stacey et al. (eds.), And Jill Came Tumbling After: Sexism in American Education. New York: Dell, 1974, 199-210.

Baumrind, D. Early Socialization and Adolescent Competence. In S. E. Dragastin and G. H. Elder, Jr. (eds.), Adolescence in the Life Cycle; Psychological Change and Social Context. New York: Halsted Press, 1975, 117-143.

Bayer, A. E. Sexist Students in American Colleges: A Descriptive Note. Journal of Marriage and the Family, 1975, May, 37(2), 391-397.

Beaven, M. Responses of Adolescents to Feminine Characters in Literature. Research in the Teaching of English, 1972, Spring, 6(1), 48-68.

Below, H. I. Life Styles and Roles of Women as Perceived by High School Girls. Unpublished manuscript, Indiana University, 1970.

Bem, S. L. Psychology Looks at the Sex Roles: Where Have all the Androgynous People Gone? Paper presented at the University of California at Los Angeles, Symposium on Women, 1972.

_____. The Measurement of Psychological Androgyny. Journal of Consulting and Clinical Psychology, 1974, 42(2), 155-162.

_____. Sex-Role Adaptability: One Consequence of Psychological Androgyny. Journal of Personality and Social Psychology, 1975, April, 31(4), 634-643.

_____. Androgyny Versus the Tight Little Lives of Fluffy Women and Chesty Men. Psychology Today, 1975, September, 9(4), 58-62.

_____. Probing the Promise of Androgyny. In A. G. Kaplan and J. P. Bean (eds.), Beyond Sex-Role Stereotypes: Readings Toward a Psychology of Androgyny. Boston: Little, Brown, 1976, 47-62.

_____. On the Utility of Alternative Procedures for Assessing Psychological Androgyny. Journal of Consulting and Clinical Psychology, 1977, 45(2), 196-205.

_____. Psychological Androgyny. In A. G. Sargent (ed.), Beyond Sex Roles. St. Paul, MN: West, 1977, 319-324.

_____. Beyond Androgyny: Some Presumptuous Prescriptions for a Liberated Sexual Identity. In J. Sherman and F. Denmark (eds.), Psychology of Women: Future Direction of Research. New York: Psychological Dimensions, 1978.

_____, and Bem, D. J. We're All Nonconscious Sexists. Psychology Today, 1970, November, 4(6), 22-26+. Also in D. J. Bem (ed.), Beliefs, Attitudes and Human Affairs. Monterey, CA: Brooks/Cole, 1970.

_____, and _____. Training the Woman to Know Her Place: The Power of a Nonconscious Ideology. In D. Gersoni-Stavn (ed.), Sexism and Youth. New York: R. R. Bowker, 1974, 10-22.

_____, and _____. Case Study of a Nonconscious Ideology: Training the Woman to Know Her Place. In S. Cox (ed.), Female Psychology: The Emerging Self. Chicago: Science Research Associates, 1976, 180-190.

_____, and Lenney, E. Sex Typing and the Avoidance of Cross-Sex Behavior. Journal of Personality and Social Psychology, 1976, 33(1), 48-54.

_____, Martyna, W., and Watson, C. Sex Typing and Androgyny: Further Explorations of the Expressive Domain. Journal of Personality and Social Psychology, 1976, 34(5), 1016-1023.

Berger, S. E., Jordan, E. P., Ham, M. H., and Gaines, S. Some Psychological Effects on Women of Sex Role Discrimination. Unpublished manuscript, University of Southern California, Los Angeles, 1973.

Bernard, J. S. Second Sex and the Cichlid Effect. Journal of the National Association of Women Deans and Counselors, 1967, Fall, 31, 8-17.

_____. The Sex Game. New York: Atheneum, 1973.

_____. Sex Differences: An Overview. Reprint from MSS Information Corp., 655 Madison Ave., New York, NY, 10021, 1974.

_____. The Future of Motherhood. New York: Penguin, 1974.

_____. The Bitter Fruits of Extreme Sex-Role Specialization. In Women, Wives, Mothers: Values and Options, Chicago: Aldine, 1975, 217-239.

_____. Research on Sex Differences: An Overview of the State of the Art. In Women, Wives, Mothers: Values and Options. Chicago: Aldine, 1975, 7-29.

_____. Sex-Role Transcendence and Sex-Role Transcenders. In Women, Wives, Mothers: Values and Options. Chicago: Aldine, 1975, 43-68.

_____. Women, Wives, Mothers; Values and Options. Chicago: Aldine, 1975.

_____. Change and Stability in Sex-Role Norms and Behavior. Journal of Social Issues, 1976, 32(3), 207-223.

Berscheid, E. and Walster, E. Beauty and the Best. Psychology Today, 1972, March, 5(10), 42-46+.

Berzins, J. I. New Perspectives on Sex Roles and Personality Dimensions. Paper presented at the American Psychological Association Convention, Chicago, 1975.

_____, and Welling, M. A. The PRF ANDRO Scale: A Measure of Psychological Androgyny Derived from the Personality Research Form. Unpublished manuscript, University of Kentucky, 1974.

_____, _____, and Wetter, R. E. Androgynous Versus Traditional Sex Roles and the Interpersonal Behavior Circle. Paper presented at the American Psychological Association Convention, Washington, D. C., 1976.

Bieliauskas, V. J. Recent Advances in the Psychology of Masculinity and Femininity. Journal of Psychology, 1965, 60, 255-263.

_____. A New Look at "Masculine Protest." Journal of Individual Psychology, 1974, May, 30(1), 92-97.

Biggar, J. C. Bibliography on the Sociology of Sex Roles. Department of Sociology, University of Virginia, Charlottesville, VA, n. d.

Biller, H. B. Adults' Conceptions of Masculinity and Femininity in Children. Unpublished study, Emma Pendleton Bradley Hospital, Riverside, RI, 1966.

Billings, V. Equality Isn't What You Need. In The Womansbook. Los Angeles: Wollstonecraft, 1974, 29-47.

_____. The Unnatural Order. In The Womansbook. Los Angeles: Wollstonecraft, 1974, 49-83.

Bird, C. Born Female: The High Cost of Keeping Women Down. New York: David McKay, 1971.

Blakey, W. A. Everybody Makes the Revolution: Some Thoughts on Racism and Sexism. Civil Rights Digest, 1974, Spring, 6(3), 11-19.

Blimline, C. A. The Emerging Woman: A Profile. Journal of the National Association for Women Deans, Administrators, and Counselors, 1974, Fall, 38(1), 38-40.

Block, J. H. Conceptions of Sex-Role: Some Cross-Cultural and Longitudinal Perspectives. American Psychologist, 1973, 28(6), 512-526.

_____. Debatable Conclusions about Sex Differences. Contemporary Psychology, 1976, 21, 517-522.

Bloom, L. Z., Coburn, K., and Pearlman, J. The New Assertive Woman. New York: Delacourt, 1975.

Bohannon, W. E., and Mills, C. J. Statistical and Conceptual Analysis of Two Measures of Masculinity/Femininity. Paper presented at the American Psychological Association Convention, San Francisco, 1977.

Boulding, E. Women in the 20th Century World. New York: John Wiley, 1977.

Boyd, M. Equality Between the Sexes: The Results of the Canadian Gallup Polls, 1953, 1973. Paper presented at the Canadian Sociology and Anthropology Association meeting, Toronto, 1974.

_____. English-Canadian and French-Canadian Attitudes Toward Women. Journal of Comparative Family Studies, 1975, 11(2), 153-169.

Bozeman, B., Thornton, S., and McKinney, M. Continuity and Change in Opinions about Sex Roles. In M. Githens and J. L. Prestage (eds.), A Portrait of Marginality. New York: David McKay, 1977.

Brannon, R. Measuring Attitudes (Toward Women, and Otherwise): A Methodological Critique. In J. Sherman and F. Denmark (eds.), Psychology of Women: Future Directions of Research. New York: Psychological Dimensions, 1978.

Brogan, D., and Kutner, N. G. Measuring Sex-Role Orientation: A Normative Approach. Journal of Marriage and the Family, 1976, February, 38(1), 31-40.

48 / Sex Roles--General

Brophy, B. Speaking Out; Women Are Prisoners of Their Sex. Saturday Evening Post, 1963, November 2, 236, 10+.

Broverman, I. K., Vogel, S. R., Broverman, D. M., Clarkson, F. E., and Rosenkrantz, P. S. Sex-Role Stereotypes: A Current Appraisal. Journal of Social Issues, 1972, 28(2), 59-78. Also in E. Lasky (ed.), Humanness: An Exploration into the Mythologies about Women and Men. New York: MSS Information Corporation, 1975, 29-48; and in M. T. S. Mednick et al. (eds.), Women and Achievement: Social and Motivational Analyses. New York: Halsted Press, 1975, 32-47.

Brown, B. A., Emerson, T. I., Falk, G., and Freedman, A. E. The Equal Rights Amendment: A Constitutional Basis for Equal Rights for Women. The Yale Law Journal, 1971, April, 80(5), 871-985.

Brown, F. Changes in Sexual Identification and Role Over a Decade and Their Implications. Journal of Psychology, 1971, 77, 229-251.

Brown, L. S. Sex-Role Consciousness Raising Through a Psychology of Women Course. Symposium presentation at the American Psychological Association Convention, Washington, D. C., 1976.

_____. Sex-Role Stereotype Asymmetry and Favorability. Symposium presentation at the American Psychological Association Convention, San Francisco, 1977.

Bruckman, I. R. The Relationship Between Achievement Motivation and Sex, Age, Social Class, School Stream and Intelligence. British Journal of Social and Clinical Psychology, 1966, 5(3), 211-220.

Bruemmer, L. Condition of Women in Society Today. Journal of the National Association of Women Deans and Counselors, 1969-70, Fall-Winter, 33, 18-22.

Bullough, V. L., and Bullough, B. The Subordinate Sex. Urbana: University of Illinois Press, 1973.

Bunker, G. L., and Bitton, D. Some Antecedents of Psychology and the Legitimization of Stereotypes. Paper presented at the American Psychological Association Convention, San Francisco, 1977.

Burhenne, D. P. Female and Male Evaluations of Sex-Appropriate and Sex-Inappropriate Sex-Role Stereotypes. Unpublished doctoral dissertation, Ohio State University, 1972.

Burton, G. I'm Running Away from Home But I'm Not Allowed to Cross the Street: A Primer of Woman's Liberation. New York: Avon Books, 1972.

Cadden, V. How Women See Themselves. Redbook, 1965, May, 125, 46-47+.

Caldwell, T. Speaking Out; Women Get a Dirty Deal. Saturday Evening Post, 1963, May 25, 236(20), 8+.

Campbell, R. R. Women's Life Styles in the '70's. Address, Stanford Alumni Day, Stanford University, Stanford, CA, May 22, 1971.

Can a Woman Be a Fellow? Intellect, 1973, April, 101, 420+.

Canary, B. Surviving as a Woman. Chicago: Henry Regnery, 1970.

Carlson, R. Understanding Women: Implications for Personality Theory and Research. Journal of Social Issues, 1972, 28(2), 17-32. Also in M. T. S. Mednick et al. (eds.), Women and Achievement: Social and Motivational Analyses. New York: Halsted Press, 1975, 20-31.

Carpenter, M. Today's Tensions; Women, the Problem or the Answer; Address, November 9, 1963. Vital Speeches of the Day, 1964, January 1, 30(6), 184-186.

Cassara, B. American Women: The Changing Image. Boston: Beacon, 1962.

Cater, L. A., Scott, A. F., and Martyna, W. (eds.). Women and Men: Changing Roles, Relationships, and Perceptions. New York: Praeger, 1977.

Centers, R. Authoritarianism and Misogyny. Journal of Social Psychology, 1963, October, 61, 81-85.

Chafe, W. H. The American Woman: Her Changing Social, Economic, and Political Role, 1920-1970. New York: Oxford University, 1972.

Chafetz, J. S. Masculine/Feminine or Human?: An Overview of the Sociology of Sex Roles. Itasca, IL: F. T. Peacock, 1974.

Chayes, A. H. Outer and Inner Status of Women. Educational Record, 1965, Fall, 46(4), 435-438.

Cherniss, C. Personality and Ideology: A Personological Study of Women's Liberation. Psychiatry, 1972, 35, 109-125.

Clautour, S. E., and Moore, T. W. Attitudes of Twelve-Year-Old Children to Present and Future Life Roles. Human Development, 1969, 12(4), 221-238.

Clifton, A. K., and Fiorenzo, B. Is the Affective Component of

Prejudice Toward Women Pervasive and Highly Consensual? Paper presented at the Illinois Sociological Association Meeting, Macomb, Illinois, October 1973.

____, McGrath, D., and Wick, B. Stereotypes of Woman. A Single Category? Sex Roles: A Journal of Research, 1976, 2, 135-148.

Cochran, D. The Stereotypes of Maleness and Femaleness. International Journal of Offender Therapy and Comparative Criminology, 1976, 20(2), 174-177.

Cohen, M. B. Personal Identity and Sexual Identity. Psychiatry, 1966, February, 29, 1-14.

____. You've Come a Long Way, Baby ... or Have You? Sexual Behavior, 1972, June, 2(6), 48-51.

Constantinople, A. Masculinity-Femininity: An Exception to a Famous Dictum? Psychological Bulletin, 1973, 80(5), 389-407.

Cosentino, F., and Heilbrun, A. B., Jr. Anxiety Correlates of Sex-Role Identity in College Students. Psychological Reports, 1964, 14, 729-730.

Costrich, N., Feinstein, J., Kidder, L., Marecek, J., and Pascale, L. When Stereotypes Hurt: Three Studies of Penalties for Sex-Role Reversals. Journal of Experimental Social Psychology, 1975, November, 11(6), 529-530.

Craik, M. Measuring Attitudes Towards Women's Roles. Symposium presentation at the American Psychological Association Convention, San Francisco, 1977.

Dahlstrom, E. (ed.). Analysis of the Debate on Sex Roles. In The Changing Roles of Men and Women. Boston: Beacon, 1971, 179-205.

____, (ed.). The Changing Roles of Men and Women. Boston: Beacon, 1971.

Davis, E. C. Women in Non-Traditional Roles: Hurdles, Challenges, Rewards. Educational Horizons, 1975, Spring, 53(3), 98-101.

Davis, N. J., and Bumpass, L. L. Dialog. What Is Sex-Role Stereotyping? Teacher, 1974, March, 6-10.

Dean, D. G., Powers, E. A., Braito, R., and Bruton, B. Cultural Contradictions and Sex Roles Revisited: A Replication and a Reassessment. The Sociological Quarterly, 1975, 16(2), 207-215.

Deaux, K. To Err Is Humanizing, But Sex Makes a Difference. Representative Research in Social Psychology, 1972, 3, 20-28.

Deckard, B. S. The Women's Movement: Political, Socioeconomic, and Psychological Issues. New York: Harper & Row, 1975.

Decter, M. The Liberated Woman and Other Americans. New York: Coward, McCann, and Geoghegan, 1971.

Degler, C. N. Revolution Without Ideology: The Changing Place of Women in America. Daedalus, 1964, Spring, 93(2), 653-670.

Delworth, U. Raising Consciousness about Sexism. Personnel and Guidance Journal, 1973, 51(9), 672-674.

Dermer, M. When Beauty Fails. Unpublished doctoral dissertation. Dissertation Abstracts International, 1973, 34(67A), 4402.

Dion, K., Berscheid, E., and Walster, E. What Is Beautiful Is Good. Journal of Personality and Social Psychology, 1972, 24(3), 285-290.

Dixon, R. B. Measuring Equality Between the Sexes. Journal of Social Issues, 1976, 32(3), 19-32.

Dorros, K., and Follet, J. Prejudice Towards Women as Revealed by Male College Students. Unpublished manuscript, Connecticut College, 1969.

Douvan, E. New Sources of Conflict in Females at Adolescence and Early Adulthood. In J. M. Bardwick et al. (eds.), Feminine Personality and Conflict. Monterey, CA: Brooks/Cole, 1970, 31-43.

Doyle, J. A. Pseudoliberalism Toward Women's Roles Among College Males. Paper presented at the Association for Women in Psychology meeting, St. Louis, Missouri, February 1977.

DuBrin, A. J. Women in Transition. Springfield, IL: Charles C. Thomas, 1972.

Dudar, H. Women's Lib! The War on 'Sexism.' Newsweek, 1970. March 23, 75(12), 71-76+.

Dufresne, M. J. Differential Reactions of Males to Three Different Female Sex Roles. Unpublished doctoral dissertation, University of Connecticut. Dissertation Abstracts International, 1972, May, 32(11-B), 6642-6643.

Dworkin, A. Woman Hating. New York: E. P. Dutton, 1974.

Dyer, W. W. One Small Step Toward Self-Love. New Woman, 1977, May-June, 7(3), 89-91.

Ellis, L. J., and Bentler, P. M. Traditional Sex-Determined Role Standards and Sex Stereotypes. Journal of Personality and Social Psychology, 1973, 25(1), 28-34.

Ellman, M. Thinking About Women. New York: Harcourt Brace Jovanovich, 1968.

Epstein, C. F. (ed.) Ideals, Images, and Ideology of Women and Women's Roles in American Society. In Woman's Place: Options and Limits in Professional Careers. Berkeley: University of California Press, 1970, 18-49.

_____, (ed.). Reconciliation of Women's Roles: Paths and Obstacles. In Woman's Place: Options and Limits in Professional Careers. Berkeley: University of California Press, 1970, 86-150.

_____, and Bronzaft, A. L. Female Freshmen View Their Roles as Women. Journal of Marriage and the Family, 1972, 34(4), 671-672.

_____, and Goode, W. J. (eds.). The Other Half: Roads to Women's Equality. Englewood Cliffs, NJ: Prentice-Hall, 1971.

Erickson, V. L. Beyond Cinderella: Ego Maturity and Attitudes Toward the Rights and Roles of Women. The Counseling Psychologist. 1977, 7(1), 83-88.

Erikson, E. Inner and Outer Space: Reflections of Womanhood. Daedalus, 1964, 93(2), 582-606.

Erskine, C. G. The Effects of Consciousness-Raising Groups on Sex-Role Stereotyping Among College Students. Unpublished doctoral dissertation. Dissertation Abstracts International, 1974, October, 35(4-A), 1977.

Etaugh, C. Biographical Predictors of College Students' Attitudes Toward Women. Journal of College Student Personnel, 1975, 16, 273-276.

_____. Stability of College Students' Attitudes Toward Women During One School Year. Psychological Reports, 1975, February, 36(1), 125-126.

_____, and Bowen, L. Attitudes Toward Women: Comparison of Enrolled and Nonenrolled College Students. Psychological Reports, 1976, 38(1), 229-230.

_____, and Gerson, A. Attitudes Toward Women: Some Biographical Correlates. Psychological Reports, 1974, 35, 701-702.

Evans, C. Conflicting Views of Men and Women: By the New

Biologists, the New Feminists and as Human Beings. Unpublished doctoral dissertation, U. S. International University. Dissertation Abstracts International, 1975, September, 36(3-B), 1404.

Facos, T. Double Standard Denies Girls Equal Freedom with Boys. Seventeen, 1976, December, 35, 76.

Fairlie, H. On The Humanity of Women. The Public Interest, 1971, Spring, 23, 16-32.

Farber, S. M., and Wilson, R. H. L. (eds.). The Potential of Woman. New York: McGraw-Hill, 1963.

_____, and _____ (eds.). The Challenge to Women. New York: Basic Books, 1966.

Faunce, P. S. The Psychological Environment of Women. Syllabus/study guide for an independent study course. Minneapolis: University of Minnesota, 1974.

_____. Women's Studies 1-301; The Psychological Environment of Women: The Implementation and Evaluation of an Experimental Course (Spring 1974). Minneapolis: University of Minnesota, 1975.

_____, and Phipps-Sanger, S. Personality Theories of Women. Implementation and Evaluation of an Experimental Course (Psychology 8-970): Spring, 1976. Minneapolis: University of Minnesota.

Fay, T. L. Ideal and Typical Males and Females: Stereotypes in Three Cultures. Symposium Presentation at the American Psychological Association Convention, Chicago, 1975.

Feinman, S. Approval of Cross-Sex-Role Behavior. Psychological Reports, 1974, August, 35(1, Pt 2), 643-648.

Feldman, M., and Feldman, H. Beyond Sex Role Differentiation: Dangerous or Desirable. Paper presented at a Conference on Sex Roles in American Society--The Psychological Perspective, Russell Sage College, New York, May 1976.

Fibel, B. Transcendence of Sex Roles: Parallel Cultural and Psychotherapeutic Change Processes. Symposium presentation at the American Psychological Association Convention, Washington, D. C., 1976.

Figes, E. The Largest Minority. Britannica Yearbook, 1971, Special Report. Chicago: Encyclopaedia Britannica, 1971, 672.

Filene, P. G. Him/Her/Self: Sex Roles in Modern America. New York: New American Library, 1974.

Firestone, S. The Dialectic of Sex. New York: William Morrow, 1970.

Flerx, V. C., Fidler, D. S., and Rogers, R. W. Sex Role Stereotypes: Developmental Aspects and Early Intervention. Child Development, 1976, December, 47(4), 998-1007.

Fontana, G. L. An Investigation into the Dynamics of Achievement Motivation in Women. Unpublished doctoral dissertation. Dissertation Abstracts International, 1971, September, 32(3-B), 1821-1822.

Foster, N. J. Women: Locus of Control and Attitudes Toward Femininity and Masculinity. Unpublished doctoral dissertation. Dissertation Abstracts International, 1975, April, 35(10-B), 5109.

Fowler, M. G., and Van de Riet, H. K. Women Today and Yesterday: An Examination of the Feminist Personality. Journal of Psychology, 1972, November, 82(2), 269-276.

Fox, G. L. Nice Girl: Social Control of Women Through a Value Construct. SIGNS: A Journal of Research, 1977, Summer, 2(4), 805-817.

Freedman, M. B. The Role of the Educated Woman: An Empirical Study of the Attitudes of a Group of College Women. Journal of College Student Personnel, 1965, 6(2), 145-155.

Freeman, J. Growing Up Girlish. Transaction, 1970, November/December, 8, 36-43.

_____. The Legal Basis of the Sexual Caste System. Valparaiso University Law Review, 1971, 5, 203-236.

Friedman, J. S. On Ideology and Achievement: Determinants of Career Orientation Among American Women. Paper presented at the Gerontological Society meeting, Louisville, KY, October 1975.

Frieze, I. H. Changing Self-Images and Sex-Role Stereotypes in College Women. Paper presented at the American Psychological Association Convention, New Orleans, 1974.

_____, Parsons, J. E., Johnson, P., Ruble, D. N., and Zellman, G. Women and Sex Roles: A Social Perspective. New York: W. W. Norton, 1978.

_____, and Ramsey, S. J. Nonverbal Maintenance of Transitional Sex Roles. Journal of Social Issues, 1976, 32(3), 133-141.

Fullmer, D. W. Male-Order Female--The Symbol and the Substance. Counseling Girls Toward New Perspectives. Report of the Mid-

Atlantic Regional Pilot Conference. Washington, D. C.: U. S. Government Printing Office, 1966, 18-20.

Gardiner, H. W., Singh, U. P., and D'Orazio, D. E. The Liberated Woman in Three Cultures: Marital-Role Preferences in Thailand, India, and the United States. Human Organization, 1974, Winter, 33(4), 413-415.

Garskof, M. H. (ed.). Roles Women Play: Readings Toward Women's Liberation. Monterey, CA: Brooks/Cole, 1971.

Gaudreau, P. A. Bem Sex-Role Inventory Validation Study. Symposium presentation at the American Psychological Association Convention, Chicago, 1975.

Gerber, G. L., and Balkin, J. Sex-Role Stereotypes as a Function of Marital Status and Role. Journal of Psychology, 1977, January, 95(1), 9-16.

Gerson, M. Women in the Kibbutz. American Journal of Orthopsychiatry, 1971, July, 41(4), 566-573.

Getz, S. K., and Herman, J. B. Sex Differences in Judgments of Male and Female Role Stereotypes. Paper presented at the Midwestern Psychological Association meeting, 1974. Also available from ERIC (ED099711), 1975.

Gilbert, D. Changing Female Role. Nation's Business, 1972, December, 60, 39.

Gilbert, L. A., and Strahan, R. F. Clarification of the Bem Sex-role Inventory. Paper presented at the American Psychological Association Convention, Washington, D. C., 1976.

Ginn, R. O. Male and Female Estimates of Personal Problems of Men and Women. Journal of Counseling Psychology, 1975, 22(6), 518-522.

Glazer-Malbin, N., and Waehrer, H. Y. (eds.). Woman in a Man-Made World. Chicago: Rand McNally, 1972.

Glenn, H. M., and Walters, J. Feminine Stress in the Twentieth Century. Journal of Home Economics, 1966, November, 58(9), 703-707.

Goldberg, P. A. Are Women Prejudiced Against Women? Transaction, 1968, 5, 28-30.

_____. Prejudice Toward Women--Measure of Misogynous Attitudes. Paper presented at the American Psychological Association Convention, Honolulu, 1972.

_____, Gottesdiener, M., and Abramson, P. R. Another Put-Down of Women? Perceived Attractiveness as a Function of Support for the Feminist Movement. Journal of Personality and Social Psychology, 1975, July, 32(1), 113-115.

Goldberg, S. The Inevitability of Patriarchy. New York: William Morrow, 1973.

Goodman, W. Women's Prejudices Against Women. Redbook, 1965, February, 124, 46-47+.

Goodstein, L. D., and Sargent, A. G. Psychological Theories of Sex Differences. In A. G. Sargent (ed.), Beyond Sex Roles. St. Paul, MN: West, 1977, 168-177.

Gove, W. R. The Relationship Between Sex Roles, Marital Status, and Mental Illness. Social Forces, 1972, 51(1), 282-292. Also in A. G. Kaplan and J. B. Bean (eds.), Beyond Sex-Role Stereotypes: Readings Toward a Psychology of Androgyny. Boston: Little, Brown, 1976, 281-292.

Grambs, J. D., and Waetjen, W. B. Being Equally Different: A New Right for Boys and Girls. The National Elementary Principal, 1966, November, 46, 59-67. Also in The Education Digest, 1967, March, 32, 8-11.

Grant (West), A. Women's Liberation or Exploding the Fairy Princess Myth. Scholastic Teacher, 1971, November. Supplement to the Nov. 1, 1971, Teacher's Editions of Sr. Scholastic, Jr. Scholastic, World Week, Scholastic Voice, Scholastic Scope, and Science World, 6-11.

Greenberg, R. P., and Zeldow, P. B. Effect of Attitudes Toward Women on Sex Attribution. Psychological Reports, 1976, December, 39(3, Pt. 1), 807-813.

Greenberg, S. Attitudes Toward Increased Social, Economic, and Political Participation by Women as Reported by Elementary and Secondary Students. In J. Pottker and A. Fishel (eds.), Sex Bias in the Schools--The Research Evidence. Madison, NJ: Fairleigh Dickinson University Press, 1977, 200-206.

Greenhouse, P., and Rosenthal, E. Attitudes Toward Women's Right to Self-Determination. Journal of Family Counseling, 1974, Fall, 2(2), 64-70.

Greer, G. The Female Eunuch. New York: McGraw-Hill, 1971.

Guber, S. A Cross-Cultural Study of the Perceived Feminine Role and Self-Concept of College Women in the United States and Israel. Unpublished doctoral dissertation, New York University, 1965.

Gullahorn, J. E. Equality and Social Structure. In E. Donelson and J. E. Gullahorn (eds.), Women: A Psychological Perspective. New York: John Wiley, 1977, 266-281.

Gump, J. P. Sex-Role Attitudes and Psychological Well-Being. In M. T. S. Mednick et al. (eds.), Women and Achievement: Social and Motivational Analyses. New York: Halsted Press, 1975, 274-284.

Gumperz, E. Women: The Last Minority? Columbia University Forum, 1967, 11, 30-34.

Gunderson, B. B. The Implication of Rivalry. In S. M. Farber and R. H. L. Wilson (eds.), The Potential of Woman. New York: McGraw-Hill, 1963, 165-187.

Guttentag, M., and Tavris, C. It's Tough to Nip Sexism in the Bud. Psychology Today, 1975, December, 9(7), 58+.

Haan, N., and Livson, N. Sex Differences in the Eyes of Expert Personality Assessors: Blind Spots. Unpublished research, Institute of Human Development, University of California, Berkeley, CA, 1972.

Hacker, H. M. Women as a Minority Group. In B. Roszak and T. Roszak (eds.), Masculine/Feminine: Readings in Sexual Mythology and the Liberation of Women. New York: Harper & Row, 1969, 130-147. Also in N. Glazer-Malbin and H. Y. Waehrer (eds.), Woman in a Man-Made World. Chicago: Rand McNally, 1972, 39-44; and in J. Freeman (ed.), Women: A Feminist Perspective. Palo Alto, CA: Mayfield, 1975, 402-416.

Hall, E. R. Behavioral-Situational Approach to Sex-Role Ideals. Paper presented at the American Psychological Association Convention, San Francisco, 1977.

Hanisch, C. Male Psychology: A Myth to Keep Women in Their Place. Woman's World, 1971, 19, 2.

Harford, T. C., Willis, C. H., and Deabler, H. L. Personality Correlates of Masculinity-Femininity. Psychological Reports, 1967, 21, 881-884.

Harris, J. The Prime of Ms. America: The American Woman at Forty. New York: G. P. Putnam, 1975.

Harris, L. H., and Lucas, M. E. Sex-Role Stereotyping. Social Work, 1976, September, 21(5), 390-395.

Harrison, J. A Critical Evaluation of Research on Masculinity/Femininity and a Proposal for an Alternate Paradigm for Research on Psychological Differences and Similarities Between the Sexes. Unpublished doctoral dissertation, department of Psychology, New York University, 1975.

Sex Roles--General

Hartley, R. E. Children's Concepts of Male and Female Roles. Merrill-Palmer Quarterly, 1960, January, 6(2), 83-91.

_____. Some Implications of Current Changes in Sex Role Patterns. Merrill-Palmer Quarterly, 1960, 6(3), 153-164.

_____, and Hardesty, F. P. Children's Perception of Sex-Roles in Childhood. Journal of Genetic Psychology, 1964, 105, 43-51.

_____, _____, and Gorfein, D. Children's Perception and Expression of Sex-Preferences. Child Development, 1962, 33, 221-227.

Hartup, W. W., and Moore, S. G. Avoidance of Inappropriate Sex-Typing by Young Children. Journal of Consulting Psychology, 1963, 27, 467-473.

Hefner, R., Rebecca, M., and Oleshansky, B. The Development of Sex-Role Transcendence. Human Development, 1975, 18, 143-158. Also in K. Riegel (ed.), Development of Dialectical Operations. Basel, Switzerland: Karger, 1975.

Heilbrun, A. B., Jr. Influence of Observer and Target Sex in Judgments of Sex-Typed Attributes. Perceptual and Motor Skills, 1968, 27, 1194.

_____. Sex-Role Identity in Adolescent Females: A Theoretical Paradox. Adolescence, 1968, 3, 79-88.

_____. Measurement of Masculine and Feminine Sex Role Identities as Independent Dimensions. Journal of Consulting and Clinical Psychology, 1976, 44(2), 183-190.

Herman, M. H., and Sedlacek, W. E. Measuring Sexist Attitudes of Males. Proceedings of the 81st Annual Convention of the American Psychological Association, Montreal, Canada, 1973, 8, 341-342.

_____, and _____. Sexist Attitudes among Male University Students. Journal of College Students Personnel, 1973, 14(6), 544-548.

Herschberger, R. Adam's Rib: A Defense of Modern Woman. New York: Harper & Row, 1970.

Hipple, J. L. Perceptual Differences Between Married and Single College Men for Concepts of Ideal Woman. Adolescence, 1976, Winter, 11, 579-583.

Hochreich, D. J. Sex-Role Stereotypes for Internal-External Control and Interpersonal Trust. Journal of Consulting and Clinical Psychology, 1975, April, 43(2), 273.

Hochschild, A. R. The American Woman: Another Idol of Social Science. Transaction, 1970, November-December, 8, 13-14.

_____. A Review of Sex Role Research. American Journal of Sociology, 1973, 78, 1011-1029. Also in J. Huber (ed.), Changing Women in a Changing Society. Chicago: University of Chicago Press, 1973, 249-267; and in H. H. Frank (ed.), Women in the Organization. Philadelphia: University of Pennsylvania Press, 1977, 197-217.

Hoffman, D., and Fidell, L. Characteristics of Androgynous, Undifferentiated, Masculine, and Feminine Middle-Class Women. Paper presented at the American Psychological Association Convention, San Francisco, 1977.

Hole, J., and Levine, E. Feminist Social Critique. In Rebirth of Feminism. New York: Quandrangle Books, 1971, 194-225.

Holstrom, E., and Bernard, J. Sex Role Transcendence and Sex Role Transcenders. In J. Bernard (ed.), Women, Wives, Mothers: Values and Options. Chicago: Aldine, 1975, 43-68.

Holter, H. Sex Roles and Social Change. Acta Sociologica, 1971, 14(1&2), 2-12. Also in C. Safilios-Rothschild (ed.), Toward a Sociology of Women. Lexington, MA: Xerox College, 1972, 331-343.

Hough, K. S., and Allen, B. P. Is the "Women's Movement" Erasing the Mark of Oppression from the Female Psyche? Journal of Psychology, 1975, March, 89(2), 249-258.

How Women's Role in U. S. is Changing. U. S. News & World Report, May 30, 1966, 60, 58-60.

Huber, J. (ed.). Changing Women in a Changing Society. Chicago: University of Chicago Press, 1973.

Hunter, E. Women of the 60's: How Different? Symposium presentation at the American Psychological Association Convention, San Francisco, 1977.

Hunter, J. E. Images of Woman. Journal of Social Issues, 1976, 32(3), 7-17.

Huyck, M. Age and Sex Similarities in Personal and Perceived Sex Role Norms. Presented at the Scientific Meeting of the Gerontological Society, Portland, Oregon, October 1974.

Hyde, J. S., Rosenberg, B. G., and Behrman, J. A. Tomboyism. Psychology of Women Quarterly, 1977, Fall, 2(1), 73-75.

Iglitzin, L. B. A Child's Eye View of Sex Roles. Today's Education, 1973, 61, 23-25. Also in Sex Role Stereotyping in the

Schools. Washington, D. C.: National Education Association, 1973, 23-30.

_____. Sex-Typing and Politicization in Children's Attitudes. In J. Pottker and A. Fishel (eds.), Sex Bias in the Schools--The Research Evidence. Madison, NJ: Fairleigh Dickinson University Press, 1977, 178-198.

Insel, P. M., and Jacobson, L. (eds.). What Do You Expect? An Inquiry into Self-Fulfilling Prophecies. Menlo Park, CA: Cummings, 1975.

Jenkin, N., and Breogh, H. Contemporary Concepts of Masculinity and Femininity. Psychological Reports, 1969, 25, 679-697.

Joesting, J. Comparison of Women's Liberation Members with Their Nonmember Peers. Psychological Reports, 1971, 29(3), 1291-1294.

Jordan-Viola, E., Fassberg, S., and Viola, M. T. Feminism, Androgyny, and Anxiety. Journal of Consulting and Clinical Psychology, 1976, October, 44(5), 870-871.

Kagan, J. The Emergence of Sex Differences. School Review, 1972, 80, 217-227.

_____. Check One: Male, Female. In C. Tavris (ed.), The Female Experience from the Editors of Psychology Today. Del Mar, CA: Communications/Research/Machines, 1973, 51-53.

Kahn, D. Fairy Tale Heroines, Role Models, and Ideal Self-Concepts of Women with Contrasting Sex Role Orientations. Symposium presentation at the American Psychological Association Convention, San Francisco, 1977.

Kahoe, R. D. The Psychology and Theology of Sexism. Journal of Psychology and Theology, 1974, Fall, 2(4), 284-290.

_____, and Meadow, M. J. Three Dimensions of Sexist Attitudes: Differential Relationships with Personality Variables. Paper presented at the American Psychological Association Convention, San Francisco, 1977.

Kalka, B. S. A Comparative Study of Feminine Role Concepts of a Selected Group of College Women. Unpublished doctoral dissertation, Oklahoma State University. Dissertation Abstracts, 1968, 28(12-A), 4822.

Kaplan, A. G., and Bean, J. P. (eds.). Beyond Sex-Role Stereotypes: Readings Toward a Psychology of Androgyny. Boston: Little, Brown, 1976.

Kaplan, R. M., and Goldman, R. D. Stereotypes of College Students

Toward the Average Man's and Woman's Attitudes Toward Women. Journal of Counseling Psychology, 1973, 20(5), 459-462.

Katz, P. A., and Weiss, J. Sex Bias in Children. Paper presented at the American Psychological Association Convention, Washington, D. C., 1976.

Kelly, J. A., Caudill, M. S., Hathorn, S., and O'Brien, C. G. Socially Undesirable Sex-Correlated Characteristics: Implications for Androgyny and Adjustment. Journal of Consulting and Clinical Psychology, 1977, 45(6), 1185-1186.

_____, and Worell, J. New Formulations of Sex Roles and Androgyny: A Critical Review. Journal of Consulting and Clinical Psychology, 1977, 45(6), 1101-1115.

Keniston, K. Themes and Conflicts in 'Liberated' Young Women. Nineteenth Annual Karen Horney Memorial Lecture, presented at the annual meeting of the Association for the Advancement of Psychoanalysis, New York, March 1971.

Kessler, S. Female Equals Not Male. Symposium presentation at the American Psychological Association Convention, San Francisco, 1977.

Kiesler, S. B. Actuarial Prejudice Toward Women and Its Implications. Unpublished manuscript, University of Kansas, 1976.

King, M. C. The Politics of Sexual Stereotypes. In M. Githens and J. L. Prestage (eds.), A Portrait of Marginality. New York: David McKay, 1977, 346-365. Also in A. G. Kaplan and J. P. Bean (eds.), Beyond Sex-Role Stereotypes: Readings Toward a Psychology of Androgyny. Boston: Little, Brown, 1977, 338-351.

Kinsell-Rainey, L. W. Working with the BSRI: The New Views on Androgyny. Paper presented at the American Psychological Association Convention, Washington, D. C., 1976.

Kirschner, B. F. Introducing Students to Women's Place in Society. American Journal of Sociology, 1973, 78, 1051-1054.

Klein, E. A. Role Conflict in Feminist and Non-Feminist Women. Unpublished doctoral dissertation, U. S. International University. Dissertation Abstracts International, 1975, September, 36(3-B), 1410.

Koeske, G. F., and Koeske, R. K. Sex Stereotypes and Self-Perception: A New Look at Female Devaluation. Paper presented at the American Psychological Association Convention, Chicago, 1975.

Kohlberg, L. and Zigler, E. The Impact of Cognitive Maturity on the Development of Sex-Role Attitudes in the Years 4-8. Genetic Psychology Monographs, 1967, 75, 89-165.

Komisar, L. Where Feminism Will Lead: An Impetus for Social Change. Civil Rights Digest, 1974, 6, 2-9.

Kotzin, M., and Soehngen, S. Women, Like Blacks and Orientals, Are All Different. Media and Methods--Exploration in Education, 1972, March, 8(7), 18-26.

Kravetz, D. F. Sex Role Concepts of Women. Journal of Consulting and Clinical Psychology, 1976, June, 44(3), 437-443.

Krech, H. S. Identity of Modern Woman. Nation, 1965, September 20, 201, 125-128.

Kurth, S. A Process of Identity Transformation for the Never Married Woman. Impact, 1974, 3(6), 3-9+.

Kutner, N. G., and Brogan, D. An Investigation of Sex-Related Slang Vocabulary and Sex-Role Orientation Among Male and Female University Students. Journal of Marriage and the Family, 1974, August, 36(3), 474-484.

Lambert, R. D. Sex Role Imagery in Children: Social Origins of Mind. Studies of the Royal Commission on the Status of Women in Canada. Ottawa: Information Canada, 1969.

Lansky, L. M., and McKay, G. Sex Role Preference of Kindergarten Boys and Girls: Some Contradictory Results. Psychological Reports, 1963, 13, 415-421.

Lederer, W. The Fear of Women. New York: Harcourt Brace Jovanovich, 1968.

Leidig, M. S. A Comparative Study of Feminists and Anti-Feminists with Regard to Current Life Styles and Attitudes. A paper presented at the Colorado Mental Health Association meeting, Colorado Springs, September 1976.

Lerner, G. Women's Rights and American Feminism. The American Scholar, 1971, 40(2), 235-248.

Lerner, H. E. Early Origins of Envy and Devaluation of Women: Implications for Sex Role Stereotypes. Bulletin of the Menninger Clinic, 1974, November, 38(6), 538-553.

Lifton, R. J. (ed.). The Woman in America. Boston: Beacon, 1965.

Linnér, B. What Does Equality Between the Sexes Imply? American Journal of Orthopsychiatry, 1971, October, 41(5), 747-756.

Lipman-Blumen, J. Toward a Homosocial Theory of Sex Roles: An Explanation of the Sex Segregation of Social Institutions. In B. B. Reagan and M. Blaxall (eds.), Women and the Workplace: The Implications of Occupational Segregation. Chicago: University of Chicago Press, 1976, 15-31.

_____, and Lickamyer, A. R. Sex Roles in Transition: A Ten-Year Perspective. Annual Review of Sociology, 1975, 1, 297-337.

Lloyd, B. B. Social Responsibility and Research on Sex Differences. In B. B. Lloyd and J. Archer (eds.), Exploring Sex Differences. New York: Academic Press, 1976, 1-23.

Losco, J., and Epstein, S. Humor Preference as a Subtle Measure of Attitudes Toward the Same and the Opposite Sex. Journal of Personality, 1975, June, 43(2), 321-334.

Lozoff, M. Changing Life Style and Role Perceptions of Men and Women Students. Paper presented at Radcliffe Institute Conference, Women: Resource for a Changing World, Cambridge, MA, April 1972.

Lundy, M. A. W. Myths That Tell Us Who We Are. Illinois Teacher of Home Economics, 1975, May/June, 18(5), 276-279.

Lunneborg, P. W. Stereotypic Aspects in Masculinity-Femininity Measurement. Journal of Consulting and Clinical Psychology, 1970, 34, 113-118.

_____. Validity of Attitudes Toward Women Scale. Psychological Reports, 1974, June, 34(3, Pt 2), 1281-1282.

MacBrayer, C. T. Differences in Perception of the Opposite Sex by Males and Females. Journal of Social Psychology, 1960, 52, 309-314. Also in D. L. Schaeffer (ed.), Sex Differences in Personality: Readings. Monterey, CA: Brooks/Cole, 1971, 56-61.

McCelland, D. C. Wanted: A New Self-Image for Women. In R. J. Lifton (ed.), The Woman in America. Boston: Beacon, 1965, 173-192.

Maccoby, E. E. The Meaning of Being Female. (Review of J. M. Bardwick's Psychology of Women: A Study of Bio-Cultural Conflicts), Contemporary Psychology, 1972, 17, 369-372.

_____, and Jacklin, C. N. Sex Differences and Their Implications for Sex Roles. Paper presented at the American Psychological Association Convention, Washington, D. C. 1971.

McComb, A. Role of Anger in Differentiating From Traditional Sex Roles. Symposium presentation at the American Psychological Association Convention, San Francisco, 1977.

MacDonald, A. P. Identification and Measurement of Multidimensional Attitudes Toward Equality Between the Sexes. Journal of Homosexuality, 1974, Winter, 1(2), 165-182.

McFarlane, L., Schallberger, B., and Rothbart, M. Sex-Role Stereotypes and Non-Traditional Women. Symposium presentation at the American Psychological Association Convention, San Francisco, 1977.

McManus, M. L. Sex Differences in Rating Female/Male Voiced Political Announcements. Paper presented at the American Psychological Association Convention, Washington, D. C., 1976.

Mahoney, J. An Analysis of the Axiological Structures of Traditional and Proliberation Men and Women. Journal of Psychology, 1975, May, 90(1), 31-39.

Mai-Dalton, R., and Feldman-Summers, S. Are Angry Women More Acceptable Than Angry Men? Symposium presentation at the American Psychological Association Convention, San Francisco, 1977.

Maides, S. On the Relative Contribution of Masculinity and Femininity. Symposium presentation at the American Psychological Association Convention, San Francisco, 1977.

Malmaud, R. K. Moving Toward Androgyny: Illustrations from One Group's Process. Symposium presentation at the American Psychological Association Convention, Washington, D. C., 1976.

Mandle, J. D. Undergraduate Activists in the Woman's Movement and their Public: Attitudes towards Marriage and the Family. Sociological Focus, 1975, August, 8(3), 257-269.

Manning, T. T. Sex-Typed and Androgynous Males and Females: Personality and Ego Development Differences. Symposium presentation at the American Psychological Association Convention, San Francisco, 1977.

Marecek, J. Androgyny and the Politics of Personal and Social Change. Symposium presentation at the American Psychological Association Convention, Washington, D. C., 1976.

Marke, S., and Gottfries, I. Measurement of Masculinity-Femininity. Psychological Research Bulletin, Lund U. (Sweden), 1967, 7(4).

_____, and _____. Measurement of Sex Role Perception and Its Relation to Psychological Masculinity-Femininity. Psychological Research Bulletin, Lund U. (Sweden), 1970, 10(5).

Marmor, J. Changing Patterns of Femininity and Masculinity. In N. Glazer-Malbin and H. Y. Waehrer (eds.), Woman in a Man-Made World: A Socioeconomic Handbook. Chicago: Rand McNally, 1972, 68-73.

Mason, K. O., and Bumpass, L. L. Women's Sex Role Attitudes in the United States, 1970. Unpublished Paper, University of Wisconsin-Madison, 1973. Also a paper presented at the American Sociological Association meeting, New York, August 1973.

_____, and _____. U. S. Women's Sex-Role Ideology, 1970. American Journal of Sociology, 1975, March, 85, 1212-1219.

_____, Czajka, J., and Arber, S. Changes in U. S. Women's Sex-Role Attitudes, 1964-74. American Sociological Review, 1976, 41(4), 573-596.

Mead, M., and Kaplan, F. (eds.). American Women. New York: Scribner's, 1965.

Mednick, M. T. S., and Tangri, S. S. New Social Psychological Perspectives on Women. Journal of Social Issues, 1972, 28(2), 1-16.

_____, _____, and Hoffman, L. W. Women and Achievement: Social and Motivational Analyses. New York: Halsted Press, 1975.

Meyer, M. I., Sr. Explorations of Feminine Role Concepts Among Catholic College Women and Men. Unpublished doctoral dissertation, St. Louis University. Dissertation Abstracts, 1966, 27, (4-A), 1111.

Michaelson, E. J., and Aaland, L. M. Masculinity, Femininity, and Androgyny. Ethos, 1976, Summer, 4(2), 251-270.

Miller, T. W. Male Self-Esteem and Attitudes Toward Women's Roles. Journal of College Student Personnel, 1973, 14, 402-406.

_____. Male Attitudes Toward Women's Rights as a Function of Their Level of Self-Esteem. In F. Denmark (ed.), Who Discriminates Against Women? (Issue 15). Beverly Hills, CA: Sage, 1974, 37-46.

Millett, K. Sexual Politics. New York: Doubleday, 1970.

Millman, M. Observations on Sex Role Research. Journal of Marriage and the Family, 1971, November, 33(4), 772-776.

Minnigerode, F. A. Attitudes toward Women, Sex-Role-Stereotyping and Locus of Control. Psychological Reports, 1976, June, 38(3, Pt. 2), 1301-1302.

Mitchell, J. S. Women, the Longest Revolution. New Left Review, 1966, November/December, 40, 11-37. Also in N. Glazer-Malbin and H. Y. Waehrer (eds.), Woman in a Man-Made World. Chicago: Rand McNally, 1972, 45-52.

_____, (ed.). Other Choices for Becoming a Woman. Pittsburgh: KNOW, Inc., 1974.

Mitchell, L. H. Dominance and Femininity as Factors in the Sex Role Adjustment of Parents and Children. Unpublished doctoral dissertation, University of California. Dissertation Abstracts, 1965, 26(12), 7440.

Money, J. Biology = ♂/♀ Destiny: A Woman's View (a review of C. Hutt's Males and Females). Contemporary Psychology, 1973, 18, 603-604.

_____. Destereotyping Sex Roles. Society, 1977, July, 14, 25-28.

_____, and Ehrhardt, A. A. Man and Woman, Boy and Girl. Baltimore: Johns Hopkins Press, 1972.

Moreland, J. R. A Humanistic Approach to Facilitating College Students Learning About Sex Roles. Counseling Psychologist, 1976, 6(3), 61-64.

Mowder, B. Children's Views of Gender Traits. Symposium presentation at the American Psychological Association Convention, San Francisco, 1977.

Murray, P. The Rights of Women. In N. Dorsen (ed.), The Rights of Americans: What They Are and What They Should Be. New York: Random House, 1971, 521-545.

Myrdal, A., and Klein, V. Women's Two Roles. London: Routledge and Kegan Paul, 1968.

Nevill, D., and Damico, S. The Development of a Role Conflict Questionnaire for Women: Some Preliminary Findings. Journal of Consulting and Clinical Psychology, 1974, October, 42(5), 743.

Nicoll, T. L., and Bryson, J. B. Intersex and Intrasex Stereotyping on the Bem Sex Role Inventory. Paper presented at the American Psychological Association Convention, San Francisco, 1977.

Norman, R. Anti-Feminism and the Negative Imperative in the Male. Symposium presentation at the American Psychological Association Convention, San Francisco, 1977.

O'Leary, V. E. Psychological Differences Between Females and Males. In Toward Understanding Women. Monterey, CA: Brooks/Cole, 1977, 53-75.

_____. Stereotypes and Conceptions of the Female Role. In Toward Understanding Women. Monterey, CA: Brooks/Cole, 1977, 107-130.

_____. Androgynous Man: The "Best of Both Worlds"? Symposium presentation at the American Psychological Association Convention, San Francisco, 1977.

_____, and Depner, C. E. College Males' Ideal Female: Changes in Sex-Role Stereotypes. Journal of Social Psychology, 1975, February, 95(1), 139-140.

_____, and _____. Alternative Gender Roles Among Women: Masculine, Feminine, Androgynous. Intellect, 1976, January, 104, 313-315.

Ortner, S. B. Is Female to Male as Nature Is to Culture? Feminist Studies, 1972, Fall, 1, 5-31.

Oslooper, T., and Hayes, M. The Femininity Game. New York: Stein & Day, 1973.

Osmond, M. W., and Martin, P. Y. Sex and Sexism: A Comparison of Male and Female Sex-Role Attitudes. Journal of Marriage and the Family, 1975, November, 37(4), 744-758.

Osofsky, J. D., and Osofsky, H. J. Androgyny as a Life Style. In C. C. Perrucci and D. B. Targ (eds.), Marriage and the Family: A Critical Analysis and Proposals for Change. New York: David McKay, 1974, 141-155.

Parelius, A. P. Emerging Sex-Role Attitudes, Expectations, and Strains Among College Women. Journal of Marriage and the Family, 1975, February, 37(1), 146-153.

Parsons, J. E., Frieze, I. H., and Ruble, D. N. Sex Roles: Persistence and Change. Journal of Social Issues, 1976, January, 32(3), 1-5.

Pate, B. Changing Roles of Women. Social Studies: 0425. Available from ERIC (ED079227), 1973.

Penman, R. Women's Current and Future Role Conceptions. Australian Psychologist, 1975, July, 10(2), 193-201.

Penn, L. Current Sex Role Identification, Sex Role Stereotypes, and Role Conflict in University Women. Unpublished doctoral dissertation, Adelphi University. Dissertation Abstracts International, 1975, July, 36(1-B), 425-426.

Pepe, E. A., Wyly, M. V., and Hulicka, I. M. Age and Sex as Determinants of Sex-Role Identity. Paper presented at the American Psychological Association Convention, Washington, D. C., 1976.

Peplau, L. A., Rubin, Z., and Hill, C. T. The Sexual Balance of Power. Psychology Today, 1976, November, 10, 142.

Peters, J., Schell, A., Barr, M., and Patigalia, S. Variables Affecting Sex-Role Stereotyping. Unpublished manuscript. Occidental College, 1973.

Peterson, M. J. The Asymmetry of Sex-Role Perceptions. Sex Roles: A Journal of Research, 1975, January, 1(3), 110-115.

Phillips, F. L. The Changed Status of Women. Education, 1966, December, 87(4), 246-247.

Pleck, J. My Male Sex Role--And Ours. Reprint from KNOW, Inc., P. O. Box 86031, Pittsburgh, PA 15221, 1974.

_____. Masculinity-Femininity: Current and Alternate Paradigms. Sex Roles: A Journal of Research, 1975, 1, 161-178.

_____. Men's Reactions to the Changing Consciousness of Women. In E. Zuckerman (ed.), Women and Men: Changing Roles, Attitudes, and Power Relationships. New York: Radcliffe Club of New York, 1975.

_____. The Psychology of Sex Roles: Traditional and New Views. In L. A. Cater and A. F. Scott (eds.), Women and Men: Changing Roles, Relationships, and Perceptions. New York: Praeger, 1977, 181-200.

Poffenberger, T., and Norton, D. Sex Differences in Achievement Motivation in Mathematics as Related to Cultural Change. Journal of Genetic Psychology, 1963, 103, 341-350.

Polk, B. B. Male Power and the Women's Movement. Journal of Applied Behavioral Science, 1974, 10(3), 415-431.

_____. Women's Liberation: Movement for Equality. In C. Safilios-Rothschild (ed.), Toward a Sociology of Women. Lexington, MA: Xerox College, 1972, 321-330.

Quinn, S. What Is Sexy, Feminine, Assertive? New Woman, 1977, May-June, 7(3), 41-43.

Radl, S. Mother's Day Is Over. New York: Charterhouse, 1973.

Rapaport, A. F., Payne, D., and Steinmann, A. Perceptual Differences Between Married and Single College Women for the Concepts of Self, Ideal Woman, and Man's Ideal Woman. Journal of Marriage and the Family, 1970, 32(3), 441-442.

Rebecca, M., Hefner, R., and Oleshansky, B. A Model of Sex-Role Transcendence. Journal of Social Issues, 1976, 32(3), 197-206.

Reeves, N. Womankind: Beyond the Stereotypes. Chicago: Aldine, 1971.

Reid, P. T. Sex-Role Preferences of Females. Symposium presentation at the American Psychological Association Convention, San Francisco, 1977.

Richards, C. V. Discontinuities in Role Expectations of Girls. National Society for the Study of Education Yearbook, 1966, 65 (Pt. 1), 164-188.

Richardson, M. S., and Alpert, J. L. Factor-Analytic Study of Male and Female Role Perceptions. Paper presented at the American Psychological Association Convention, Washington, D. C., 1976.

_____, and _____. Role Perceptions: Variations by Sex and Roles. Paper presented at the American Psychological Association Convention, Washington, D. C., 1976.

Roberts, D. F., and Roberts, G. Techniques for Confronting Sex Role Stereotypes. School Psychology Digest, 1975, 2(3), 47-54.

Romano, N. C. Relationships Among Identity Confusion and Resolution, Self Esteem, and Sex Role Perceptions in Freshman Women at Rutgers University. Unpublished doctoral dissertation, Rutgers University. Dissertation Abstracts International, 1976, April, 36(10-A), 6487.

Roper, Inc. The Virginia Slims American Women's Opinion Poll. New York: The Roper Organization, 1974.

Rose, C. Women's Sex-Role Attitudes: A Historical Perspective. New Directions for Higher Education, 1975, Autumn, 11, 1-31.

Rosen, B., and Jerdee, T. H. The Psychological Basis for Sex Role Stereotypes. Organizational Behavior and Human Performance, 1975, 14, 151-153.

Rosenkrantz, P., Vogel, S., Bee, H., Broverman, D. M., and Broverman, I. Sex-Role Stereotypes and Self-Concepts in College Students. Journal of Consulting and Clinical Psychology, 1968, 32(3), 287-295.

Rossi, A. S. Sex Equality: The Beginnings of Ideology. The Humanist, 1969, September-October, 29(5), 3-6+. Also in B. Roszak and T. Roszak (eds.), Masculine/Feminine: Readings in Sexual Mythology and the Liberation of Women. New York: Harper & Row, 1969, 173-185; and in C. Safilios-Rothschild (ed.), Toward a Sociology of Women. Lexington, MA: Xerox College, 1972, 344-353.

_____. The Use and Misuse of Science in the Study of Gender Roles. Paper presented to the Society for the Scientific Study of Sex, New York, November 1973.

Rozsnafszky, J., and Hendel, D. D. Measuring Attitudes Toward Women: The Need to Use a Standardized Scale. Unpublished manuscript, University of Minnesota, 1975.

Rubin, G. Woman as Nigger. In B. Roszak and T. Roszak (eds.), Masculine/Feminine: Readings in Sexual Mythology and the Liberation of Women. New York: Harper & Row, 1969, 230-240.

Ruble, D. N., Croke, J. A., Frieze, I., and Parsons, J. E. A Field Study of Sex-Role Attitude Change in College Women. Journal of Applied Social Psychology, 1975, 5(2), 110-117.

Rudy, A. J. Sex-Role Perceptions in Early Adolescence. Unpublished doctoral dissertation, Columbia University. Dissertation Abstracts, 1966, 26(10), 6174-6175.

Ruth, S., and Richards, R. Intellect vs. Femininity, or Men Seldom Make Passes at Girls Who Wear Glasses. Gifted Child Quarterly, 1974, Autumn, 18, 182-187.

Ryan, S. M., and Castleman, J. Children's Knowledge and Use of Sex Stereotypes. Paper presented at the American Psychological Association Convention, San Francisco, 1977.

Saarni, C. I., Taber, R., and Shaw-Hamilton, L. The Vicissitudes of Sex-Role Assessment. Paper presented at the Western Psychological Association meeting, Anaheim, CA, April 1973.

Sacks, K. State Bias and Women's Status. American Anthropologist, 1976, 78(3), 565-570.

Salzman-Webb, M. Woman as Secretary, Sexpot, Spender, Sow, Civic, Actor, Sickie. In M. H. Garskof (ed.), Roles Women Play: Readings Toward Women's Liberation. Monterey, CA: Brooks/Cole, 1971, 7-24.

Sanders, M. K. Proposition for Women. Harper's Magazine, 1960, September, 221(1324), 41-48. Discussion: 1960, November, 221(1326), 6+. More discussion in K. M. Bryne, E. Harback, and P. McGinley. The Redundant Housewife. America, 1961, March 25, 104, 812-814. Continued discussion in State of the Question, America, 1961, April 29, 105, 218-219.

Sargent, A. G. (ed.). Beyond Sex Roles. St. Paul, MN: West, 1977.

Sarup, G. Gender, Authoritarianism, and Attitudes Towards Feminism. Social Behavior and Personality, 1976, 4(1), 57-64.

Scarf, M. He and She: The Sex Hormones and Behavior. New York Times Magazine, 1972, May 7.

Schell, R. E., and Silber, J. W. Sex-Role Discrimination Among

Young Children. Perceptual and Motor Skills, 1968, 27, 379-389.

Scott, A. F. (ed.). What Is Happening to American Women? Atlanta: Southern Newspaper, 1970.

Scott, H. Does Socialism Liberate Women? Boston: Beacon, 1974.

Seaman, B. Free and Female. New York: Fawcett World Library, 1973.

Sears, R. R. Relation of Early Socialization Experience to Self-Concepts and Gender Role in Middle Childhood. Child Development, 1970, 41, 267-289.

_____, Rau, L., and Alpert, R. Sex Typing and Gender Role. In Identification and Child Rearing. Stanford: Stanford University Press, 1965, 170-198.

Sedlacek, W. E., Brooks, G. C., Jr., Christensen, K. C., Harway, M., and Merritt, M. S. Racism and Sexism: A Comparison and Contrast. Journal of the National Association for Women Deans, Administrators, and Counselors, 1976, Spring, 39(3), 120-127.

Sedney, M. A. Process of Sex-Role Development During Life Crises in Middle-Aged Women. Symposium presentation at the American Psychological Association Convention, San Francisco, 1977.

Sells, L. Current Research on Sex Roles. Berkeley: Research Committee, Sociologists for Women in Society, August 1971.

Seward, D. Women Around the World: An Overview. Journal of the National Association for Women Deans, Administrators, and Counselors, 1970, Fall, 34(1), 2-6.

Seward, G. H., and Larson, W. R. Adolescent Concepts of Social Sex Roles in the United States and the Two Germanies. Human Development, 1968, 11, 217-248.

Sharma, P. C. A Special Bicentennial Focus on Women: Their Progress, Problems, Concerns in 1976. American Association of University Women Journal, 1976, April, 69, 1-27.

Shelly, A. C. Can We Find More Diverse Adult Sex Roles? Educational Leadership, 1973, 31(2), 114-118.

Shively, M. G., Rudolph, J. R., and DeCecco, J. P. The Identification of the Social Sex-Role Stereotypes. Center for Homosexual Education, Evaluation and Research, San Francisco State University, 1977.

Sigall, H., and Page, R. Current Stereotypes: A Little Fading, A Little Faking. Journal of Personality and Social Psychology, 1971, 18, 247-255.

Smith, D. How I Stopped Being the Little Woman. McCalls, 1977, April, 104, 70+.

Smith, S. A. Women are People. In L. C. Muller and O. G. Muller (eds.), New Horizons for College Women. Washington, D. C.: Public Affairs Press, 1960, 25-26.

Smith, S. D., and Carlson, H. Sex-Role Attitudes and Androgyny in Religious Women. Symposium presentation at the American Psychological Association Convention, San Francisco, 1977.

Snider, A. J. Crises in Being Female. Science Digest, 1970, May, 67, 70-71.

──── . Are Women Kept in Psychological Cages? Science Digest, 1972, February, 71, 55.

Soysa, N. Self-Concept and Role Conflict: A Study of Some Aspects of Women's Self-Perception and Self-Evaluation in Relation to Their Attitudes Towards Their Sex-Role. Unpublished doctoral dissertation, Cornell University. Dissertation Abstracts, 1962, 22(8), 2898.

Spence, J. T. Traits, Roles and the Concept of Androgyny. Paper presented at the Conference on Perspectives on the Psychology of Women, Michigan State University, May 1977.

────, and Helmreich, R. The Attitudes Toward Women Scale: An Objective Instrument to Measure Attitudes Toward the Rights and Roles of Women in Contemporary Society. JSAS Catalogue of Selected Documents in Psychology, 1972, Spring, 2, 66.

────, ────, and Stapp, J. A Short Version of the Attitudes Toward Women Scale (AWS). Bulletin of the Psychonomic Society, 1973, 2, 219-220.

────, ────, and ────. The Personal Attributes Questionnaire: A Measure of Sex Role Stereotypes and Masculinity-Femininity. JSAS Catalogue of Selected Documents in Psychology, 1974, Spring, 4, 43-44.

────, ────, and ────. Ratings of Self and Peers on Sex Role Attributes and Their Relation to Self-Esteem and Conceptions of Masculinity and Femininity. Journal of Personality and Social Psychology, 1975, July, 32(1), 29-39.

Spiegal, J. Sex Role Concepts: How Women and Men See Themselves and Each Other; A Selected Annotated Bibliography. Washington, D. C.: Business and Professional Women's Foundation, 1969.

Stanley, G., Boots, M., and Johnson, C. Some Australian Data on the Short Version of the Attitudes to Women Scale (AWS). Australian Psychologist, 1975, December, 10(3), 319-323.

Steinem, G. What It Would Be Like if Women Win. In W. Martin (ed.), The American Sisterhood. New York: Harper & Row, 1972, 183-195.

Steinmann, A. Bibliography on Male-Female Role Research. New York: Maferr Foundation, 1971.

_____. Female and Male Concepts of Sex Roles: An Overview of Twenty Years of Cross-Cultural Research. International Mental Health Research Newsletter, 1975, Winter 17(4).

_____. Role Change Cover-Up: Woman, Man, and Work. Symposium presentation at the American Psychological Association Convention, Washington, D.C., 1976.

_____, and Alshan, L.M. Role Change: Liberating Fact and Fiction. Symposium presentation at the American Psychological Association Convention, Washington, D.C., 1976.

_____, and Fox, D.J. Male-Female Perceptions of the Female Role in the United States. Journal of Psychology, 1966, 42(2), 265-276.

Stericker, A.B., and Johnson, J.E. Sex-Role Identification and Self-Esteem in College Students: Do Men and Women Differ? Sex Roles: A Journal of Research, 1977, 3(1), 19-26.

Stoller, R.J. Sex and Gender. New York: Science House, 1968.

_____. The Sense of Femaleness. In J.B. Miller (ed.), Psychoanalysis and Women. New York: Brunner/Mazel, 1973, 260-272.

Strauss, M.D. Women About Women: A Descriptive Study of the Psychological Impact of the Feminine Sex-Role Stereotype. Unpublished doctoral dissertation, University of Texas. Dissertation Abstracts International, 1972, July, 33(1-A), 401.

Sullerot, E. Women, Society and Change. New York: McGraw-Hill, 1971.

Suziedelis, A. Differentiation of "Masculine" and "Feminine" Among Adolescent Girls. Symposium presentation at the American Psychological Association Convention, San Francisco, 1977.

Symonds, A. The Liberated Woman: Healthy and Neurotic. American Journal of Psychoanalysis, 1974, Fall, 34(3), 177-183.

_____, Moulton, R., and Badaracco, M.R. The Myth of Femininity: A Panel. American Journal of Psychoanalysis, 1973, 33(1), 42-55.

Taleporos, E. Women's Liberationists and Pseudo-Women's Liberationists: Their Beliefs About Sex-Role Socialization, Opinions About Social Issues, and Perceptions of Male-Female Relations. Unpublished doctoral dissertation, New York University. Dissertation Abstracts International, 1975, April, 35(10-A), 6521.

Tavris, C. Women and Man. Psychology Today, 1972, March, 5, 57+.

―――――. Male Supremacy Is on the Way Out .... Psychology Today, 1975, January, 8(8), 61-63.

Tennov, D. The Reactions of Women to the Inferior Status of Women. Unpublished manuscript, University of Bridgeport, Bridgeport, CT, 1973. Also a reprint from KNOW, Inc., P. O. Box 86031, Pittsburgh, PA 15221, 1973.

Tetenbaum, T. B., and Pedhazur, E. J. Masculinity and Femininity: Separate But Equal? Paper presented at the American Psychological Association Convention, San Francisco, 1977.

Thompson, C. M. On Women. New York: New American Library, 1971.

Thorne, F. C. The Measurement of Femininity. Journal of Clinical Psychology, 1977, January, 33(1), 5-10.

Tibbetts, S. L. The "Enemy" Is Us. Reprint from KNOW, Inc., P. O. Box 86031, Pittsburgh, PA 15221, 1973.

―――――. Sex-Role Stereotyping in Lower Grades: Part of the Solution. Journal of Vocational Behavior, 1975, April, 6(2), 255-261.

Toews, L. K. Self-Hatred in College Women: Sex Role Stereotypes and Same-Sex Affiliation. Unpublished doctoral dissertation, University of Alberta, Edmonton, Alberta, 1974.

Tolor, A., Kelly, B. R., and Stebbins, C. A. Assertiveness, Sex-Role Stereotyping, and Self-Concept. Journal of Psychology, 1976, 93, 157-164.

Tonesk, X. Refinement of the Meaning of "Femininity" for Males. Symposium presentation at the American Psychological Association Convention, San Francisco, 1977.

Touhey, J. C. Masculinity-Femininity and Accuracy of Sex Role Ascription. Social Behavior and Personality, 1974, 2(1), 40-42.

Tremaine, L. S. Cognitive and Social-Learning Approaches to Sex-Role Development: Theory and Methods. Paper presented at the American Psychological Association Convention, San Francisco, 1977.

Tresemer, D. Assumptions Made About Gender Roles. In M. Millman and R. M. Kanter (eds.), <u>Another Voice: Feminist Perspectives on Social Life and Social Science.</u> New York: Doubleday, 1975, 308-339.

_____, and Pleck, J. Maintaining and Changing Sex-Role Boundaries in Men (And Women). Paper presented at the Women: Resource for a Changing World Conference, Radcliffe Institute, Cambridge, MA, 1972.

_____, and _____. Sex-Role Boundaries and Resistance to Sex-Role Change. <u>Women's Studies</u>, 1974, 2, 61-78.

Turner, S. A. Male and Female Attitudes Toward Sex-Role Concepts. <u>Psychology,</u> 1975, February, 12(1), 27-29.

Turnipseed, D. <u>Playboy</u>'s Stereotype of the American Woman. Unpublished undergraduate research paper, Illinois State University, 1973.

Ullian, D. Z. The Development of Conceptions of Masculinity and Femininity. In B. Lloyd and J. Archer (eds.), <u>Exploring Sex Differences.</u> New York: Academic Press, Inc., 1976, 25-47.

_____. A Developmental Study of Conceptions of Masculinity and Femininity. Unpublished doctoral dissertation, Harvard University, 1976.

Unger, R. K. (ed.). The Politics of Gender: A Review of Relavant Literature. In <u>Sex-Role Stereotypes Revisited: Psychological Approaches to Women's Studies.</u> New York: Harper & Row, 1975.

_____. Status, Power and Gender: An Examination of Parallelisms. Paper presented at the conference "New Directions for Research on Women," Madison, WI, May 1975.

_____, Raymond, B. J., and Levine, S. M. Women as a 'Functional' Minority Group. Paper presented at the American Psychological Association Convention, Honolulu, 1972.

_____, _____, and _____. Are Women a 'Minority' Group? Sometimes! <u>International Journal of Group Tensions</u>, 1974, March, 4(1), 71-81. Also in F. L. Denmark (ed.), <u>Women: A PDI Research Reference Work.</u> (Vol. 1). New York: Psychological Dimensions, 1976, 431-446.

_____, and Siiter, R. Sex-Role Stereotypes: The Weight of a

'Grain of Truth.' In R. K. Unger (ed.), Sex-Role Stereotypes Revisited: Psychological Approaches to Women's Studies. New York: Harper & Row, 1975.

Van Gelder, L. Countdown to Houston: Memo for the First National Women's Convention. Ms., 1977, November, 6(5), 60-62+.

Van Vuuren, N. The Subversion of Women. Philadelphia: Westminster Press, 1973.

Vedovato, S. Children and Androgyny. Symposium presentation at the American Psychological Association Convention, San Francisco, 1977.

The Victorian Woman: A Special Issue. Victorian Studies, 1970, September, 14(1).

Vroegh, K. Masculinity and Femininity in the Elementary and Junior High School Years. Developmental Psychology, 1971, 4, 254-261.

_____. Young Children's Sex Role and Knowledge of Sex Stereotypes. Paper presented at the American Psychological Association Convention, Chicago, 1975.

_____, Jenkin, N., Black, M., and Handrich, M. Discriminant Analyses of Preschool Masculinity and Femininity. Multivariate Behavioral Research, 1967, 2, 299-313.

Wagner, E., and Fay, T. L. Components of Sex-Role Stereotyping and Attitudes Toward Traditional Sex Roles. Paper presented at the Canadian Psychological Association Convention, Quebec City, June, 1975.

Wakefield, J. A., Jr., Sasek, J., Friedman, A. F., and Bowden, J. D. Androgyny and Other Measures of Masculinity-Femininity. Journal of Consulting and Clinical Psychology, 1976, October, 44(5), 766-770.

Walstedt, J. J. Antecedents of Female Powerlessness. Symposium presentation at the American Psychological Association Convention, Washington, D. C., 1976.

Ward, W. D. Variance of Sex-Role Preference among Boys and Girls. Psychological Reports, 1968, 23, 467-470.

Warnes, H., and Hill, G. Gender Identity and the Wish to be a Woman. Psychosomatics, 1974, 15(1), 25-29.

Webb, A. P. Sex-Role Preferences and Adjustment in Early Adolescents. Child Development, 1963, 34, 609-618.

Weisstein, N. Woman as Nigger. In H. H. Frank (ed.), Women

in the Organization. Philadelphia: University of Pennsylvania Press, 1977, 234-240.

Welling, M. A. A New Androgyny Measure Derived from the Personality Research Form. Symposium presentation at the American Psychological Association Convention, Chicago, 1975.

West, A. G. Women's Liberation or, Exploding the Fairy Princess Myth. Scholastic Teacher, Junior High Edition, 1971, November, 10, 6-13.

Westervelt, E. M. A Tide in the Affairs of Women: The Psychological Impact of Feminism on Educated Women. The Counseling Psychologist, 1973, 4, 3-26.

Where the Sex Roles Converge. The Times (London) Educational Supplement, 1966, November 11, 2686, 1148.

Whyte, M. K. Lowered Status of Women. Intellect, 1976, February, 104(2372), 347-348.

Williams, J. E., and Bennett, S. M. The Definition of Sex Stereotypes via the Adjective Check List. Sex Roles: A Journal of Research, 1975, 1(4), 327-338.

_____, _____, and Best, D. L. Awareness and Expression of Sex Stereotypes in Young Children. Developmental Psychology, 1975, 11(5), 635-642.

_____, and Best, D. L. Sex Stereotypes and Trait Favorability on the Adjective Check List. Educational and Psychological Measurement, 1977, Spring, 37(1), 101-110.

Williams, J. H. Sexual Role Identification/Personality Functioning in Girls. Journal of Personality, 1973, 41(1), 1-8.

_____. Growing Up Female. In Psychology of Women: Behavior in a Biosocial Context. New York: W. W. Norton, 1977, 158-195.

Willis, E. Whatever Happened to Women? NOTHING--That's the Trouble. Mademoiselle, 1969, September, 69(5), 150+.

Winick, C. The Beige Epoch: Depolarization of Sex Roles in America. Medical Aspects of Human Sexuality, 1969, 3, 73-74+.

Wish, C. W. Self Perception of Sex Role Among Older Women. Symposium presentation at the American Psychological Association Convention, San Francisco, 1977.

Wolman, B. B. On Men Who Discriminate Against Women. In F. Denmark (ed.), Who Discriminates Against Women? (Issue 15). Beverly Hills, CA: Sage, 1974, 47-53.

Woman's Place. The Atlantic, 1970, March, 225(3), 81-126.

Women and the Law: Symposium Issue. Valparaiso University Law Review, 1971, 5(2).

Women Around the World. Special Issue. The Annals of the American Academy of Political and Social Science, 1968, January.

Women: Nine Reports on Role, Image, and Message; Symposium. Journal of Communications, 1974, Spring, 24, 103-155.

The Women's Movement. Special Section. American Journal of Orthopsychiatry, 1971, October, 41(5), 708-792.

Worell, J. Issues in the Measurement and Development of Sex-Role Styles. Paper presented at the American Psychological Association Convention, Chicago, 1975.

Wortis, R. P. The Acceptance of the Maternal Role by Behavioral Scientists: Its Effects on Women. American Journal of Orthopsychiatry, 1971, 41(5), 733-746.

——. The Acceptance of the Concept of the Maternal Role by Behavioral Scientists: Its Effects on Women. In H. Wortis and C. Rabinowitz (eds.), The Women's Movement: Social and Psychological Perspectives. New York: John Wiley, 1972, 32-51.

Yates, G. G. An Androgynous View. Unpublished manuscript, Bethel College and Seminary, St. Paul, MN, n.d.

Yockey, J. M., Severy, L. J., and Shaw, M. E. Sex Role Perceptions and Behavior. Unpublished manuscript, Stanislaus, CA, California State College, n.d. Also paper presented at the American Psychological Association Convention, Washington, D. C., 1976.

Yonge, G. D. A Dynamic Image of Masculine and of Feminine Movement. Journal of Phenomenological Psychology, 1976, Spring, 6(2), 199-208.

Yorburg, B. Sexual Identity: Sex Roles and Social Change. New York: John Wiley, 1974.

Zalk, S. R., Katz, P. A., and Weiss, J. Sex Biases in Children. Paper presented at the American Psychological Association Convention, Washington, D. C., 1976.

Zanna, M. P., and Pack, S. J. On the Self-Fulfilling Nature of Apparent Sex Differences in Behavior. Journal of Experimental Social Psychology, 1975, 11, 583-591.

Zaro, J. S. An Experimental Study of Role Conflict in Women. Unpublished doctoral dissertation, University of Connecticut. Dissertation Abstracts International, 1972, 33(B), 2828B.

Zeldow, P. B. Psychological Androgyny and Attitudes Toward Feminism. Journal of Consulting and Clinical Psychology, 1976, 44(1), 150.

B. SEX ROLES (continued)

2. AMBITION AND AMBITION-RELATED BEHAVIOR

Akhtar, S., Pestonjee, D., and Farooqi, F. Attitudes Towards Working Women. Indian Journal of Social Work, 1969, 30(1), 93-97.

Alberti, J. M. Alternatives for Women. Educational Horizons, 1975, Spring, 53(3), 95-97.

Albino, J. E. Sex Differences on Factor Dimensions Related to Withdrawing from College. Paper presented at the American Educational Research Association Meeting, New Orleans, 1973. Also available from ERIC (ED080926), 1974.

_____, and Shuell, T. J. Contextual Determinants of Achievement Responses in Men and Women. Paper presented at the American Psychological Association Convention, San Francisco, 1977.

Albjerg, M. H. Why Do Bright Girls Not Take Stiff Courses? The Educational Forum, 1961, January, 25, 141-144.

Albrecht, S. L. Social Class and Sex-Stereotyping of Occupations. Journal of Vocational Behavior, 1976, December, 9(3), 321-327.

Alexander, K. L., and Eckland, B. K. Sex Differences in the Educational Attainment Process. American Sociological Review, 1974, October, 39(5), 668-682.

Almquist, E. M. Sex Stereotypes in Occupational Choice: The Case for College Women. Journal of Vocational Behavior, 1974, 5, 13-21.

_____. Attitudes of College Men Toward Working Wives. Vocational Guidance Quarterly, 1974, December, 23(2), 115-121.

Alpaugh, P. K., and Birren, J. E. Are There Sex Differences in Creativity Across the Adult Life Span. Human Development, 1975, 18(6), 461-465.

Alper, T. G. The Relationship Between Role Orientation and Achievement Motivation in College Women. Journal of Personality, 1973, March, 41(1), 9-31.

_____. Achievement Motivation in College Women: A Now-You-See-It-Now-You-Don't Phenomenon. American Psychologist, 1974, March, 29(3), 194-203.

_____. Achievement Motivation in College Women. Unpublished Manuscript, Department of Psychology, Wellesley College, Wellesley, MA, 1974.

_____, and Eister, D. Z. Succeed Bright Woman Say College Males, But Do They Really Mean It? Unpublished Manuscript, Wellesley College, Wellesley, MA, 1971.

_____, and Greenberger, E. Relationship of Picture Structure to Achievement Motivation in College Women. Journal of Personality and Social Psychology, 1967, 7(4), 362-371.

Alpert, J. L., Richardson, M. S., Perlmutter, B., and Shutzer, F. Perceptions of Major Roles by Young Adults. Unpublished Manuscript, Department of Educational Psychology, New York University. Also, paper presented at the American Psychological Association Convention, Washington, D. C., 1976.

Altschule, M. D. The Liberation of Women--From What? Psychiatric Opinion, 1972, June, 9(3), 13-22.

American Women Today and Tomorrow. Washington, D. C.: U. S. Government Printing Office, 1977.

Amidjaja, I. R., and Vinacke, W. E. Achievement, Nurturance, and Competition in Male and Female Triads. Journal of Personality and Social Psychology, 1965, 2(3), 447-451.

Anastasi, A. Sex Differences in Vocational Choices. National Catholic Guidance Conference Journal, 1969, 13(4), 63-76.

Angrist, S. S. Role Conception as a Predictor of Adult Female Roles. Sociology and Social Research, 1966, 50(4), 448-459.

Antwisle, D. R., and Greenberger, E. A Survey of Cognitive Style in Maryland Ninth-Graders: I. Achievement Motivation, Productivity. Report No. 60. Washington, D. C.: Office of Education, 1970. Also available from ERIC (ED035952), 1970.

Appleton, H. L. Sex Roles and Helping Behavior. Unpublished Master's thesis, Northwestern University, Chicago, 1972.

_____, and Gurwitz, S. B. Willingness to Help as Determined by the Sex-Role Appropriateness of the Help-Seeker's Career Goals. Sex Roles: A Journal of Research, 1976, December, 2(4), 321-329.

Appley, D. The Changing Place of Work for Women and Men. In A. G. Sargent (ed.), Beyond Sex Roles. St. Paul, MN: West, 1977, 300-318.

Arbuthnot, J. Level of Moral Judgment as a Function of Sex and Sex Role Identity. Journal of Social Psychology, 1975, 97, 297-298.

Are Girls Getting Too Aggressive? Symposium, with Study-Discussion Program by C. Smallenburg and H. Smallenburg. PTA Magazine, 1966, September, 61, 4-7+.

Astin, H. S. Sex Differences in Mathematical and Scientific Precocity. In H. Blumberg (ed.), Symposium on Research and Early Childhood Education. Baltimore: Johns Hopkins University, 1973, 73-86.

Baefsky, P. M., and Berger, S. E. Self-Sacrifice, Cooperation, and Aggression in Women of Varying Sex-Role Orientations. Personality and Social Psychology Bulletin, 1974, 1(1), 296-298.

Bailey, R. C., and Bailey, K. G. Perceived Ability in Male and Female College Students. Perception and Motor Skills, 1971, 32, 293-294.

_____, Zinser, O., and Edgar, R. Perceived Intelligence, Motivation, and Achievement in Male and Female College Students. The Journal of Genetic Psychology, 1975, 127, 125-129.

Baird, J. E. Sex Differences in Group Communication: A Review of Relevant Research. Quarterly Journal of Speech, 1976, April, 62(2), 179-192.

Baird, L. L. Men and Women College Seniors' Images of Five Careers. Paper presented at the American Psychological Association Convention, San Francisco, 1977.

Baker, C. C. Sex Differences in Achievement-Related Behaviors in Upper-Elementary School Children. Unpublished doctoral dissertation, Florida State University, 1973. Dissertation Abstracts International, 1973, 34(04-B), 1618. Also available from ERIC (ADG73-25112), 1973.

Banerjee, D., and Pareek, U. Development of Co-operative and Competitive Behaviour in Children of Some Sub-Cultures. Indian Journal of Psychology, 1974, 49(3), 237-256.

Bardwick, J. M., and Arbuckle, D. S. Study of the Relationship Between Parental Acceptance and the Academic Achievement of Adolescents. The Journal of Educational Research, 1962, November, 56, 148-151.

Barnes, W. F., and Jones, E. B. Differences in Male and Female Quitting. Journal of Human Resources, 1974, 9, 439-451.

Barnett, M. A., and Andrews, J. A. Sex Differences in Children's

Reward Allocation Under Competitive and Cooperative Instructional Sets. Developmental Psychology, 1977, January, 13(1), 85-86.

Barnett, R. C. The Relationship Between Occupational Preference and Occupational Prestige: A Study of Sex Differences and Age Trends. Paper presented at the American Psychological Association Convention, Montreal, 1973.

_____. Johnnie Will Be an Executive and Janie Will Be a ... . Harvard Business Review, 1974, May, 52, 7-8.

_____. Sex Differences and Age Trends in Occupational Preference and Occupational Prestige. Journal of Counseling Psychology, 1975, January, 22(1), 35-38.

_____, and Baruch, G. K. Empirical Literature on Occupational and Educational Aspirations and Expectations: A Review (1975). Paper presented at the American Psychological Association Convention, Washington, D. C. , 1976.

_____, and Faguiri, R. What Young People Think About Managers. Harvard Business Review, 1973, May-June, 51(3), 106-118.

Bart, P. B. Why Women See the Future Differently from Men. In A. Toffler (ed.), Learning for Tomorrow: The Role of the Future in Education. New York: Random House, 1974, 33-55.

Bartol, K. M. The Effect of Male Versus Female Leaders on Satisfaction, Performance, and Perception of Leader Behavior in Small Work Groups. Unpublished doctoral dissertation, University of Massachusetts. Dissertation Abstracts International, 1973, 33(09-A), 4597.

_____. Male Versus Female Leaders: The Effect of Leader Need for Dominance on Follower Satisfaction. Academy of Management Journal, 1974, June, 17(2), 225-233. Also in Journal of Business Research, 1975, January, 3, 33-42.

_____. Relationship of Sex and Professional Training Area to Job Orientation. Journal of Applied Psychology, 1976, June, 61, 368-370.

_____, and Butterfield, D. A. Sex Effects in Evaluating Leaders. Journal of Applied Psychology, 1976, August, 61(4), 446-454.

_____, and Wortman, M. S. Sex Effects in Leader Behavior Self-Descriptions and Job Satisfaction. Journal of Psychology, 1976, November, 94(2), 177-183.

Baruch, R. W. and Nagy, J. Declaring a College Major: Sex, Motivations, Expectations, and Other Influences. A symposium at the American Psychological Association Convention, San Francisco, 1977.

Battle, E. S. Motivational Determinants of Academic Competence. Journal of Personality and Social Psychology, 1966, 4, 634-642.

Bayer, A. E. Marriage Plans and Educational Aspirations. American Journal of Sociology, 1969, 75(2), 239-244.

Beck, B. H. A Comparison of the Achievement Level of College Men and Women Enrolled in Engineering Drawing. Unpublished doctoral dissertation, University of Missouri. Dissertation Abstracts, 1968, 28(12-A), 4943.

Becker, G. Sex Role Identification and the Needs for Self and Social Approval. Journal of Psychology, 1968, May, 69(1), 11-15.

Bedell, J., and Sistrunk, F. Power, Opportunity Costs, and Sex in a Mixed-Motive Game. Journal of Personality and Social Psychology, 1973, 25, 219-226.

Bem, S. L. Sex Role Adaptability: One Consequence of Psychological Androgyny. Journal of Personality and Social Psychology, 1975, 31, 634-643.

_____, and Bem, D. J. On Liberating the Female Student. School Psychology Digest, 1973, Summer, 2(3), 10-18.

Benton, A. A. Reactions to Demands to Win from an Opposite-Sex Opponent. Journal of Personality, 1973, 41, 430-442.

Bentzen, F. Sex Roles in Learning and Behavior Disorders. American Journal of Orthopsychiatry, 1963, 33, 92-98.

Berens, A. E. Sex-Role Stereotypes and the Development of Achievement Motivation. Ontario Psychologist, 1973, 5(2), 30-35.

Berger, G., and Blum, S. H. Vocational Desires of Urban High School Seniors: A Study of Sex Differences. Unpublished manuscript, 1976.

Berman, G. S., and Haug, M. R. Occupational and Educational Goals and Expectations: The Effects of Race and Sex. Social Problems, 1975, December, 23(2), 166-181.

Berman, V. A. Effects of Success and Failure on Gender Identity. Paper presented at the American Psychological Association Convention, Chicago, 1975.

Bernard, J. The Sex Game. New York: Atheneum, 1973.

Bert, C. V. Educational and Occupational Aspirations and Expectations of Adolescent Girls in Florida. Unpublished doctoral dissertation, Florida State University, 1967. Dissertation Abstracts International, 28, (7B), 2920. Also available from ERIC (ADG68-00337), 1967.

Betz, N. E. Math Anxiety: What is It? Symposium presentation at the American Psychological Association Convention, San Francisco, 1977.

Beuf, A. Doctor, Lawyer, Household Drudge. Journal of Communication, 1974, Spring, 24(2), 142-145.

Bickman, L. Sex and Helping Behavior. Journal of Social Psychology, 1974, 93, 43-53.

Bingham, G. Young Children's Perceptions of Occupational Roles. In E. House and M. E. Katzell (eds.), Facilitating Career Development for Girls and Women. Washington, D. C.: National Vocational Guidance Association, 1975, 55-66.

Bingham, S. Brightest Girls in the Class. Harper's Bazaar, 1972, July, 105, 84.

Binyon, M. Girls Shun Engineering. The Times (London) Educational Supplement, 1969, March 28, 2810, 1015.

Bird, A. M. Cross Sex Effects of Subject and Audiences During Motor Performance. Research Quarterly, 1975, October, 46(3), 379-384.

Bird, C. Born Female: The High Cost of Keeping Women Down. New York: David McKay, 1974.

──────. What Do Women Want? Address. Vital Speeches of the Day, 1977, July 15, 43(19), 598-602.

Black, T. E., and Higbee, K. L. Effects of Power, Threat, and Sex on Exploitation. Journal of Personality and Social Psychology, 1973, 27, 382-388.

Blaubergs, M. S. Overcoming the Sexist Barriers to Gifted Women's Achievement. In B. Johnson (ed.), Advantage/Disadvantage Gifted. Ventura, CA: Ventura County Superintendent of Schools Office, 1979.

Bledsoe, J. C., and Wiggins, R. G. Academic Aspirations and Vocational Maturity of Ninth Grade Boys and Girls. Psychological Reports, 1973, April, 32(2), 674.

Blimline, C. A. The Emerging Women: A Profile. Journal of the National Association for Women Deans, Administrators, and Counselors, 1974, 38(1), 38-44.

Bloom, A. R. Achievement Motivation and Occupational Choice: A Study of Adolescent Girls. Unpublished doctoral dissertation, Bryn Mawr College. Dissertation Abstracts International, 1972, July, 33(1-B), 417.

Blumen, J. L. The Structuring of Inequality: Female Role Ideology and Education Aspiration. Paper presented at the American Sociological Association meeting, Denver, 1971.

Bobbe, C. N. Sex-Role Preference and Academic Achievement. Unpublished doctoral dissertation, Yeshiva University. Dissertation Abstracts International, 1971, September, 32(3-B), 1818-1819.

Bogie, D. W. Occupational Aspiration-Expectation Discrepancies Among High School Seniors. Vocational Guidance Quarterly, 1976, 24(3), 250-255.

Bond, J. R., and Vinacke, W. E. Coalitions in Mixed-Sex Triads. Sociometry, 1961, 24, 61-75.

Borchert, J., and Masendorf, F. Social Status, Educational Styles of Mothers and Teachers, and Students' Anxiety and Achievement. Psychologie in Erziehung and Unterricht, 1975, 22(3), 137-147.

Borich, G. D., and Peck, R. F. Achievement and Aptitude as a Function of Grade, Ethnicity, and Sex. Paper presented at the American Psychological Association Convention, Washington, D. C., 1976.

Bose, C. E. Jobs and Gender: Sex and Occupational Prestige. Baltimore: Johns Hopkins University, Center for Metropolitan Planning and Research, 1973.

──────. Women and Jobs: Sexual Influences on Occupational Prestige. Unpublished doctoral dissertation, Johns Hopkins University, 1973. Dissertation Abstracts International, 1973, 34, (11-A), 7338. Also available from ERIC (ADG74-10394), 1973.

Boss, D. L. Ramifications of Sex-Role Stereotypes for the Self-Concepts of Males and Females. Unpublished manuscript, Purdue University, 1974.

Bott, Margaret M. Measuring the Mystique. Personnel and Guidance Journal, 1968, 46(10), 967-970.

Bouchard, T. J. Jr., Barsaloux, J., and Drauden, G. Brainstorming Procedure, Group Size, and Sex as Determinants of the Problem-Solving Effectiveness of Groups and Individuals. Journal of Applied Psychology, 1974, April, 59, 135-138.

Boulding, K., Leavitt, H. J., Mason, K. O., and Tangri, S. S. The Social Institutions of Occupational Change. SIGNS: A Journal of Women in Culture and Society, 1976, Spring, 1(3), 75-86.

Bower, W. S. Boyer, J. L., and Scheirer, E. A. Research Related to Academic Achievement Motivation: An Illustrative Review. Theory into Practice, 1970, February, 9, 33-46.

Brabant, S., and Garbin, A. P. Sex of Student as Defined by Sex-Typical Experiences and Persistence in Higher Education. Journal of College Student Personnel, 1976, January, 17(1), 28-33.

Bradley, R. H. Sex, Race, Socioeconomic Status, Locus of Control, and Classroom Behavior Among Junior High School Students. Unpublished doctoral dissertation, University of North Carolina. Dissertation Abstracts International, 1974, December, 35(6-A), 3505-3506.

Brager, G., and Michael, J. A. The Sex Distribution in Social Work: Causes and Consequences. Social Casework, 1969, 50(10), 595-601.

Brannigan, G. G., and Tolor, A. Sex Differences in Adaptive Styles. Journal of Genetic Psychology, 1971, 119, 143-149.

Brehony, K. A., Augustine, M., Barachie, D., Miller, B., and Woodhouse, W. Psychological Androgyny and Social Conformity. Paper presented at the American Psychological Association Convention, San Francisco, 1977.

Brierley, J. Sex Differences and Education. Trends in Education, 1975, February, 1, 17-24.

Brinkerhoff, M. B., and Kunz, P. R. Some Notes on the Measurement of Perceived Barriers to Occupational Aspirations. Rural Sociology, 1972, September, 37(3), 436-444.

Britton, G. E. Sex Stereotyping and Career Roles. In P. M. Insel and L. F. Jacobson (eds.), What Do You Expect? An Inquiry into Self-Fulfilling Prophecies. Menlo Park, CA: Cummings, 1975, 127-136.

Brook, J., Whiteman, M., Peisach, E., and Deutsch, M. Aspiration Levels Of and For Children: Age, Sex, Race, and Socioeconomic Correlates. Journal of Genetic Psychology, 1974, 124, 3-16.

Brooke, M. J. Status Incongruence and Support for Change in Sex-Role Ideology: A Study of Women in Various Professions. Unpublished doctoral dissertation, Loyola University. Dissertation Abstracts International, 1976, May, 36(11-B), 5858-5859.

Brooks, L. P. The Sex-Role Stereotyping of Occupational Perceptions by Sixth Grade Students. Dissertation Abstracts International, 1974, January, 34(7-A), 3862.

Broverman, D. M., Klaiber, E. L., Kobayashi, Y., and Vogel, W. Roles of Activation and Inhibition in Sex Differences in Cognitive Abilities. Psychological Review, 1968, 75(1), 23-50.

Bruce, P. Reactions of Preadolescent Girls to Science Tasks. Journal of Psychology, 1974, 86, 303-308.

Bruch, C. B. Sex Role Images Influencing Creative Productivity and Non-Productivity in Women. Symposium presentation at the Southeastern Psychological Association meeting, Atlanta, 1972.

———, and Morse, J. A. Initial Study of Creative (Productive) Women under the Bruch-Morse Model. Gifted Child Quarterly, 1972, Winter, 16(4), 282-289.

Buchanan, H T., Blankenbaker, J., and Cotten, D. Academic and Athletic Ability as Popularity Factors in Elementary School Children. Research Quarterly, 1976, October, 47(3), 320-325.

Bucher, C. H. The Impact of a Non-Stereotyped Sex-Role Occupational Unit on Elementary School Children's Occupational Knowledge, Vocational Aspirations, and Expressed Occupational Attitudes. Unpublished doctoral dissertation, University of Virginia. Dissertation Abstracts International, 1974, November 35(5-A), 2672-2673.

Buescher, R. M. The Relationship Between Selected Noncognitive Variables and Academic Achievement of College Women in Various Fields of Study. Unpublished doctoral dissertation, Fordham University. Dissertation Abstracts International, 1969, 30(5-A), 1858-1859.

Burghardt, N. R. Sex Differences in the Development of Achievement-Related Motives, Sex Role Identity, and Performance in Competitive and Noncompetitive Conditions. Unpublished doctoral dissertation, University of Michigan. Dissertation Abstracts International, 1975, 35(7-B), 3549.

Burke, R. J. Differences in Perceptions of Desired Job Characteristics in the Same Sex and the Opposite Sex. Journal of Genetic Psychology, 1966, September, 109, 37-46.

Burlin, F. D. Sex-Role Stereotyping: Occupational Aspirations of Female High School Students. School Counselor, 1976, November, 24, 102-108.

Butcher, H. J., and Pont, H. B. Opinions about Careers among Scottish Secondary School Children of High Ability. British Journal of Education Psychology, 1968, 38(3), 272-279.

Butterfield, D. A. Evaluations of Leadership Behavior: Do Sex or Androgyny Matter? Symposium presentation at the American Psychological Association Convention, San Francisco, 1977.

Caldwell, M. D. Communication and Sex Effects in a Five-Person Prisoner's Dilemma Game. Journal of Personality and Social Psychology, 1976, 33(3), 273-280.

Campbell, D. P. The Clash Between Beautiful Women and Science.

Paper presented at the American Psychological Association Convention, San Francisco, 1978.

Campbell, P. B. Adolescent Intellectual Decline. Adolescence, 1976, Winter, 11, 629-635.

Canavan, D. Field Dependence in Children as a Function of Grade, Sex, and Ethnic Group Membership. Paper presented at the American Psychological Association Convention, Washington, D. C., 1969.

Canter, R. J. An Analysis of Achievement-Related Expectations and Aspirations in College Women. Unpublished doctoral dissertation, University of Colorado. Dissertation Abstracts International, 1976, May, 36(11-B), 5860.

Caplan, P. J. Sex Differences in Determinants of Antisocial Behavior. Paper presented at the American Psychological Association Convention, Montreal, 1973. Also available from ERIC (ED087566), 1974.

Cardi, M. W. The Relationship Between Sex-Role Stereotype and Trust Among Women, as Measured by Cooperation/Competition. Unpublished doctoral dissertation, Ohio State University. Dissertation Abstracts International, 1972, October, 33, 1784.

Carment, D. W. Effects of Sex Role in a Maximizing Difference Game. Journal of Conflict Resolution, 1974, September, 18(3), 461-472.

Carmody, J. F., Fenske, R. H., and Scott, C. S. Changes in Goals, Plans, and Background Characteristics of College Bound High School Students. American College Testing Research Report #52, Iowa City, IA, 1972.

Carrigan, W. C., and Julian, J. W. Sex and Birth-Order Differences in Conformity as a Function of Need Affiliation Arousal. Journal of Personality and Social Psychology, 1966, 3, 479-483.

Carroll, J. S., and Gersick, K. E. Sex Role Stereotyping and Cognitive Style. Unpublished Manuscript, Harvard University, 1975.

Carter, N. The Effects of Sex and Marital Status on a Social-Psychological Model of Occupational Status Attainment. Unpublished master's thesis, University of Wisconsin, n. d.

Cartwright, L. K. Conscious Factors Entering into Decisions of Women to Study Medicine. Journal of Social Issues, 1972, 28(2), 201-215.

Cecil, E. A., Paul, R. J., and Olins, R. A. Perceived Importance of Selected Variables Used to Evaluate Male and Female Job Applicants. Personnel Psychology, 1973, Fall, 26(3), 397-404.

Cegelka, P. T., Omvig, C., and Larimore, D. L. Effects of Aptitude and Sex on Vocational Interests. Measurement and Evaluation in Guidance, 1974, July, 7(2), 106-111.

Centers, R. Authoritarianism and Misogyny. Journal of Social Psychology, 1963, 61, 81-85.

Chambers, J. L., and Surma, M. B. Motivation Concepts and Sexual Identity. Journal of Research and Personality, 1976, 10, 228-236.

Chobot, D. S., Goldberg, P. A., Abramson, L. M., and Abramson, P. R. Prejudice Against Women: A Replication and Extension. Psychological Reports, 1974, August, 35(1, Part 2), 478.

Christensen, H. T. Lifetime Family and Occupational Role Projections of High School Students. Marriage and Family Living, 1961, 23, 181-183.

Clark, E. T. Influence of Sex and Social Class on Occupational Preference and Perception. Personnel and Guidance Journal, 1967, 45(5), 440-444.

Coates, T. J., and Southern, M. L. Differential Educational Aspiration Levels of Men and Women Undergraduate Students. Journal of Psychology, 1972, May, 81(1), 125-128.

Cole, D., Jacobs, S., Zubok, B., Fagot, B., and Hunter, E. The Relation of Achievement Imagery Scores to Academic Performance. Journal of Abnormal and Social Psychology, 1962, 65(3), 208-211.

Coleman, J. S. The Adolescent Subculture and Academic Achievement. In M. Kornrich (ed.), Underachievement. Springfield, IL: Charles C. Thomas, 1965, 49-64.

Coleman, M., McElroy, D. K., and Whitehurst, C. A. Sex Differences in the Perception of Leadership in Small Groups. Paper presented at the Pacific Sociological Association meeting, Scottsdale, AZ, 1973.

Colker, R., and Widom, C. S. Sex-Roles and Female Athletic Participation. Symposium presentation at the American Psychological Association Convention, San Francisco, 1977.

Collier, H. V. An Investigation of the Career Choice Patterns of Female Two-Year College Students from 1969 to 1973. Unpublished doctoral dissertation, University of Toledo. Dissertation Abstracts International, 1974, December, 35(6-A), 3420-3421.

Collins, J. A. A Reflective Examination of the Feminine Role: Teaching Strategies. High School Journal, 1975, March, 28, 259-273.

Comer, N. A. From Honey to Ms. to Doctor. Mademoiselle, 1974, April, 78, 204-205+.

Connell, D. M., and Johnson, J. E. Relationship Between Sex-Role Identification and Self-Esteem in Early Adolescents. Developmental Psychology, 1970, 3, 268.

Cope, R. G. Sex-Related Factors and Attrition Among College Women. Journal of the National Association of Women Deans and Counselors, 1970, Spring, 33, 118-124.

Cosentino, F., and Heilburn, A. B., Jr., Anxiety Correlates of Sex-Role Identity in College Students. Psychological Reports, 1964, 14, 729-730.

Cotier, S., and Palmer, R. J. Relationships Among Sex, Sociometric, Self, and Test Anxiety Factors and the Academic Achievement of Elementary School Children. Psychology in the Schools, 1970, July, 7, 211-216.

Cottle, T. J. Family Perceptions, Sex Role Identity and the Prediction of School Performance. Educational and Psychological Measurement, 1968, 28, 861-886.

Cowan, G., and Moore, L. Female Identity and Occupational Commitment. Paper presented at the American Psychological Association Convention, Denver, 1971.

Crandall, V. C. Achievement Behavior in Young Children. Young Children, 1964, 20, 77-90. Also in W. W. Hartup and N. L. Smothergill (eds.), The Young Child: Reviews of Research. Washington, D. C.: National Association for the Education of Young Children, 1967, 165-185.

_____. Personality Characteristics and Social and Achievement Behaviors Associated with Children's Social Desirability Response Tendencies. Journal of Personality and Social Psychology, 1966, 4, 477-486.

_____, Crandall, V. J., and Katkovsky, W. A Children's Social Desirability Questionnaire. Journal of Consulting Psychology, 1965, 29, 27-36.

Crandall, V. J., Katkovsky, W., and Preston, A. Motivational and Ability Determinants of Young Children's Intellectual Achievement Behaviors. Child Development, 1962, September, 33(3), 643-661.

_____, and Rabson, A. Children's Repetition Choices in an Intellectual Achievement Situation Following Success and Failure. Journal of Genetic Psychology, 1960, 97, 161-168.

Crano, W. D. Effects of Sex, Response Order, and Expertise in

Conformity: A Dispositional Approach. <u>Sociometry</u>, 1970, 33, 239-252.

Crawford, J. D. A Comparative Study of Feminine Role Perception, Selected Personality Characteristics, and Career Development. Unpublished doctoral dissertation, Texas Technical University. <u>Dissertation Abstracts International</u>, 1976, May, 36(11-B), 5756-5757.

Cristall, L., and Dean, R. S. Relationship of Sex-Role Stereotypes and Self-Actualization. <u>Psychological Reports</u>, 1976, December, 39(3, Part 1), 842.

Cropley, A. J., and Field, T. W. Achievement in Science and Intellectual Style. <u>Journal of Applied Psychology</u>, 1969, 53(2, Part 1), 132-135.

Crouch, J. G. The Role of Sex, Anxiety, and Independence as Moderator Variables in the Achievement of College Freshmen. <u>Dissertation Abstracts</u>, 1968, 29(11-A), 3827.

The Daring Young Girls: Symposium. <u>Seventeen</u>, 1969, January, 28(4), 92-95+.

Dauw, D. C. Career Choices of High and Low Creative Thinkers. <u>Vocational Guidance Quarterly</u>, 1966, 15(2), 135-140.

Davidson, L. R. Sex Roles, Affects, and the Woman Physician: A Comparative Study of the Impact of Latent Social Identity upon the Role of Women and Men Professionals. Unpublished doctoral dissertation, New York University, 1975. <u>Dissertation Abstracts International</u>, 1975, 36(6-A), 4035. Also available from ERIC (AOG75-28518), 1975.

Davis, D. A., Hagan, N., and Strouf, J. Occupational Choice of Twelve-Year-Olds. <u>Personnel and Guidance Journal</u>, 1962, 40(7), 628-629.

Davis, E. C. Women in Non-Traditional Roles: Hurdles, Challenges, Rewards. <u>Educational Horizons</u>, 1975, Spring, 53(3), 98-101.

Davis, J. A. <u>Great Aspirations: The Graduate School Plans of America's College Seniors.</u> Chicago: Aldine, 1964.

_____. <u>Undergraduate Career Decisions: Correlates of Occupational Choice.</u> Chicago: Aldine, 1965.

Davis, L. S., and Spiegler, M. D. Bright and Ambitious: Kiss of Death for Women? Paper presented at the American Psychological Association Convention, New Orleans, 1974.

Day, D. R., and Stogdill, R. M. Leader Behavior of Male and Female Supervisors: A Comparative Study. Personnel Psychology, 1972, Summer, 25(2), 353-360.

Dearden, J. Sex Linked Differences of Political Behavior: An Investigation of Their Possibly Innate Origins. Social Science Information, 1974, April, 13(2), 19-45.

Deaux, K. (ed.). Strategies of Interaction: Compliance, Cooperation, Competition, and Congeniality. In The Behavior of Women and Men. Belmont, CA: Wadsworth, 1976, 93-106.

_____, and Taynor, J. Evaluation of Male and Female Ability: Bias Works Two Ways. Psychological Reports, 1973, February, 32(1), 261-262.

Defabaugh, G. L. Attitudes of Potential Professional Women Toward Women's Unconventional Occupations. Unpublished doctoral dissertation, University of Rochester. Dissertation Abstracts International, 1975, July, 36(1-B), 468.

Dellas, M., and Gaier, E. L. The Self and Adolescent Identity in Women: Options and Implications. Adolescence, 1975, Fall 10(39), 399-407.

Denise, Sister Mary. Role of the Intellectual Girl. America, 1961, April 22, 105(4), 191-192.

Denmark, F. L., and Diggory, J. C. Sex Differences in Attitudes Toward Leaders' Display of Authoritarian Behavior. Psychological Reports, 1966, 18, 863-872.

Depner, C. A Multidimensional Investigation of Sex Differences in Achievement Motivation. Unpublished manuscript, 1975.

Deutsch, C. J., and Gilbert, L. A. Sex Role Stereotypes: Effect on Perceptions of Self and Others and on Personal Adjustment. Journal of Counseling Psychology, 1976, July, 23, 373-379.

DeWolf, V. A. High School Mathematics Preparation and Sex Differences in Quantitative Abilities. Paper presented at the American Psychological Association Convention, San Francisco, 1977.

Diamond, E. E. Relationship Between Occupational Level and Masculine and Feminine Interests. Proceedings of the Annual Convention of the American Psychological Association, 1970, 5 (Part 1), 177-178.

Dias, S. L. A Study of Personal, Perceptual, and Motivational Factors Influential in Predicting the Aspiration Level of Women and Men Toward the Administrative Roles in Education. Unpublished doctoral dissertation, Boston University. Dissertation Abstracts International, 1975, September, 36(3-A), 1202.

Dickstein, L. S., and Brown, N. Effects of Role Orientation and Instructions Regarding Competition on Cognitive Performance of College Females. Psychological Reports, 1974, 34, 291-297.

Dion, K. L. Women's Reactions to Discrimination from Members of the Same or Opposite Sex. Journal of Research in Personality, 1975, December, 9(4), 294-306.

Dipboye, R. L., Fromkin, H. L., and Wiback, K. Relative Importance of Applicant Sex, Attractiveness, and Scholastic Standing in Evaluation of Job Applicant Resumes. Journal of Applied Psychology, 1975, February, 60(1), 39-43.

DiSabatino, M. Psychological Factors Inhibiting Women's Occupational Aspirations and Vocational Choices: Implications for Counseling. Vocational Guidance Quarterly, 1976, September, 25(1), 43-49.

Dixon, R. B. Measuring Equality Between the Sexes. Journal of Social Issues, 1976, 32(3), 19-32.

Doherty, E. G., and Culver, C. Sex Role Identification, Ability, and Achievement among High School Girls. Sociology of Education, 1976, 49(1), 1-3.

Dole, A. A. Sex as a Factor in the Determination of Educational Choice. Journal of General Psychology, 1964, 71(2), 267-278.

Douvan, E. Internal Barriers to Achievement in Women: An Introduction. Women on Campus: 1970. Ann Arbor: University of Michigan Press, 1970, 2-3.

_____, and Kaye, C. Motivational Factors in College Entrance. In N. Sanford (ed.), The American College. New York: John Wiley, 1962, 199-224.

Drew, D., and Patterson, M. Noah's Ark in the Frog Pond: The Educational Aspirations of Male and Female Undergraduates. Unpublished manuscript, National Research Council, Washington, D. C. 1974.

Droege, R. C. Sex Differences in Aptitude Maturation During High School. Journal of Counseling Psychology, 1967, September, 14(5), 407-411.

Ducker, D. G. The Effects of Two Sources of Role Strain on Women Physicians. Unpublished doctoral dissertation, City University of New York. Dissertation Abstracts International, 1975, January, 35(7-B), 3552.

Duffly, P. R. Differences Between the Sexes in Competitiveness and Orientation to Power as Manifested in Coalition-Formation Game.

Unpublished doctoral dissertation, University of Connecticut. Dissertation Abstracts International, 1974, August, 35(2-B), 1103.

Dukes, R. L., and Seidner, C. J. Self-Roles Incongruence and Role Enactment in Simulation Games. Simulation and Games, 1973, June, 4(2), 159-173.

Dunbar, D. S. Sex-Role Identification and Achievement Motivation in College Women. Unpublished doctoral dissertation, Ohio State University. Dissertation Abstracts, 1960, April, 20, 4161-4162.

Duncan, B., and Evers, M. Measuring Change in Attitudes Toward Women's Work. In K. S. Land and S. Spilerman (eds.), Social Indicator Models. New York: Russell Sage, 1975, 129-155.

Dunlap, S. M., and Magelsdorff, A. D. Male-Female Co-Leadership: Testing the Adam and Eve Myth. Paper presented at the Southwestern Psychological Association Meeting, Houston, 1975.

Dutton, R. E. Sex as a Factor in Occupational Choice. Personnel Journal, 1967, 46(8), 510-513.

Dweck, C. S. Sex Differences in the Meaning of Negative Evaluation in Achievement Situations: Determinants and Consequences. Paper presented at the Society for Research in Child Development meeting, Denver, 1975.

_____, and Gilliard, D. Learned Helplessness and Reinforcement Responsibility in Children. Journal of Personality and Social Psychology, 1973, 25(1), 109-116.

Dwyer, C. A. Children's Sex Role Standards and Sex Role Identification and Their Relationship to Achievement. Unpublished doctoral dissertation, University of California, Berkeley, 1973.

_____. Influence of Children's Sex Role Standards on Reading and Arithmetic Achievement. Journal of Educational Psychology, 1974, December, 66(6), 811-816.

Edwards, C. N. Cultural Values and Role Decisions: A Study of Educated Women. Journal of Counseling Psychology, 1969, 16(1), 36-40.

_____. The Student Nurse: A Study in Sex Role Transition. Psychological Reports, 1969, 25(3), 975-990.

Ein, P. L. Effects of Role-Reversed Stories on Children's Stereotyping of Occupations. Symposium presentation at the American Psychological Association Convention, San Francisco, 1977.

Eisenman, R., and Platt, J. J. Birth Order and Sex Differences in

Academic Achievement and Internal-External Control. Journal of General Psychology, 1968, April, 78(second half), 279-285.

Elder, G. H., Jr. Achievement Orientations and Career Patterns of Rural Youth. Sociology of Education, 1963, Fall, 37, 30-58.

Ellis, J. R., and Peterson, J. L. Effects of Same Sex Class Organization on Junior High School Students' Academic Achievement, Self-Discipline, Self-Concept, Sex Role Identification, and Attitude Toward School. Journal of Educational Research, 1971, 64(10), 455-464.

Elman, J. B., Press, A., and Rosenkrantz, P. S. Sex-Roles and Self-Concepts: Real and Ideal. Paper presented at the American Psychological Association Convention, Miami, FL, 1970.

Elton, C. F., and Rose, H. A. Traditional Sex Attitudes and Discrepant Ability Measures in College Women. Journal of Counseling Psychology, 1967, November, 14(6), 538-548.

Entwisle, D. R. To Dispel Fantasies About Fantasy-Based Measures of Achievement Motivation. Psychological Bulletin, 1972, 77, 377-391.

_____, and Greenberger, E. A Survey of Cognitive Styles in Maryland Ninth Graders: IV. Views of Women's Roles. Center for the Study of Social Organization of Schools Report, Johns Hopkins University, 1970, November, No. 89. Also available from ERIC (ED043918), 1971.

_____, and _____. Adolescents' Views of Women's Work Role. American Journal of Orthopsychiatry, 1972, July, 42(4), 648-656. Also in J. Pottker and A. Fishel (eds.), Sex Bias in the Schools--the Research Evidence. Madison, NJ: Fairleigh Dickinson University Press, 1977, 207-216.

Epstein, C. F. Separate and Unequal: Notes on Women's Achievement. Social Policy, 1976, March-April, 6(5), 17-23.

_____, and Bronzaft, A. L. Female Modesty in Aspiration Level. Journal of Counseling Psychology, 1974, January, 21(1), 57-60.

Equality for Uglies. Time, 1972, February 21, 99, 8.

Erb, E. D. Conformity and Achievement in College. Personnel and Guidance Journal, 1961, 39, 361-366.

Erickson, L. G., and Nordin, M. L. Sex-Role Ideologies and Career Salience of College Women: A Preliminary Report. Center for Student Development, Kansas State University, Manhattan, KA: 1974. Also available from ERIC (ED0955449), 1975.

Erickson, V. L. Beyond Cinderella: Ego Maturity and Attitudes

Towards the Rights and Roles of Women. The Counseling Psychologist, 1977, 7(1), 83-88.

Ernest, J. Mathematics and Sex. Mathematics Department, University of California, Santa Barbara, 1976. A preprint of an article to appear in the American Mathematical Monthly.

Eskilson, A., and Wiley, M. G. Sex Composition and Leadership in Small Groups. Sociometry, 1976, September, 39(3), 183-194.

Etaugh, C., and Rose, S. Adolescents' Sex Bias in the Evaluation of Performance. Developmental Psychology, 1975, 11, 663-664.

_____, and Sanders, S. Evaluation of Performance as a Function of Status and Sex Variables. Journal of Social Psychology, 1974, December, 94(2), 237-241.

Exline, R. V. Effects of Need for Affiliation, Sex, and the Sight of Others Upon Initial Communications in Problem-Solving Groups. Journal of Personality, 1962, 30, 541-556.

_____. Exploration in the Process of Person Perception: Visual Interaction in Relation to Competition, Sex, and the Need for Affiliation. Journal of Personality, 1963, 31, 1-20.

Falbo, T. The Effects of Sex and "Masculinity" on Person and Space Related Perception. Sex Roles: A Journal of Research, 1975, 1(3), 283-295.

_____. Sex Roles and Sex in the Use of Social Power. Symposium presentation at the American Psychological Association Convention, Chicago, 1975.

_____. Relationships Between Sex, Sex Role, and Social Influence. Psychology of Women Quarterly, 1977, Fall, 2(1), 62-72.

Fallon, B. J., and Hollander, E. P. Sex-Role Stereotyping in Leadership: A Study of Undergraduate Discussion Groups. Paper presented at the American Psychological Association Convention, Washington, D. C., 1976.

Farber, S. M., and Wilson, R. H. L. (eds.). The Potential of Woman. New York: McGraw-Hill, 1963.

_____, and _____ (eds.). The Challenge to Women. New York: Basic Books, 1966.

Farmer, H. S. What Inhibits Achievement and Career Motivation in Women? The Counseling Psychologist, 1976, 6(2), 12-15.

_____. Why Women Contribute Less to the Arts, Sciences, and

Humanities. Paper presented at the American Educational Research Association meeting, San Francisco, 1976. Also available from ERIC (ED0123178), 1976.

Faunce, P. S. The Psychological Environment of Women. Syllabus/ study guide for an independent study course. Minneapolis: University of Minnesota, 1974.

_____. Women's Studies 1-301: The Psychological Environment of Women: The Implementation and Evaluation of an Experimental Course (Spring 1974). Minneapolis: University of Minnesota, 1975.

_____. Psychological Barriers to Occupational Success for Women. Journal of the National Association for Women Deans, Administrators, and Counselors, 1977, 40(4), 140-145. Also in Contact, Journal of the Minnesota College Personnel Association, 1977, Spring, 8(2), 8-15.

_____. Women and Achievement: A Lost Potential? Humboldt Journal of Social Relations, 1977, Spring-Summer, 4(2), 74-89.

_____, and Phipps-Sanger, S. Women's Studies 5-910: Achievement Motivation in Women: Psychological and Sociological Perspectives. Implementation and Evaluation of an Experimental Course (Spring 1975). Minneapolis, University of Minnesota, 1975.

_____, and _____. Achievement Motivation and Women: Psychological and Sociological Perspectives, Evaluation of a Course (Psychology 8-970): Fall 1975. Minneapolis, University of Minnesota, 1976.

Feather, N. T. Level of Aspiration and Performance Variability. Journal of Personality and Social Psychology, 1967, 6(1), 37-46.

_____. Positive and Negative Reactions to Male and Female Success and Failure in Relation to the Perceived Status and Sex-typed Appropriateness of Occupations. Journal of Personality and Social Psychology, 1975, March, 31(3), 536-548.

_____, and Simon, J. G. Stereotypes About Male and Female Success and Failure at Sex-Linked Occupations. Journal of Personality, 1976, March, 44(1), 16-37.

Feij, J. A. Field Independence, Impulsiveness, High School Training, and Academic Achievement. Journal of Educational Psychology, 1976, December, 68(6), 793-799.

Feinman, S., and Rogers, J. D. Sex Differences in Psychological Rigidity. Perceptual and Motor Skills, 1974, December, 39(3), 1337-1338.

Feldhusen, J., et al. Prediction of Achievement with Measures of Learning, Social Behavior, Sex and Intelligence. Psychology in the Schools, 1974, January, 11, 59-65.

Fennema, E. Mathematics Learning and the Sexes: A Review. Journal for Research in Mathematics Education, 1974, 5, 126-139.

_____. Sex Differences in Mathematics Learning: Why? The Elementary School Journal, 1974, 75, 183-190.

_____. What Difference Does it Make? (If Boys Learn Math Better than Girls.) Wisconson Teacher of Mathematics, 1974, 25, 6-7.

_____, and Sherman, J. A. Sex Related Differences in Mathematics Learning: Myths, Realities and Related Factors. Symposium presentation at the American Association for the Advancement of Science Convention, Boston, 1976.

_____, and _____. Selected Cognitive and Affective Factors Related to Mathematics Achievement by Males and Females. Paper presented at the American Association for the Advancement of Science, Boston, 1976.

_____, and _____. Sex-Related Differences in Mathematics Achievement, Spatial Visualization, and Affective Factors. American Educational Research Journal, 1977, 14(1), 51-71.

_____, and _____. Sexual Stereotyping and Mathematics Learning. The Arithmetic Teacher, 1977, May, 24(5), 369-372.

Field, T. W., and Cropley, A. J. Cognitive Style and Science Achievement. Journal of Research in Science Teaching, 1969, 6(1), 2-10.

Fink, A., and Kosecoff, J. Girls' and Boys' Changing Attitudes Toward School. Psychology of Women Quarterly, 1977, Fall, 2(1), 44-49.

Fisher, J. E., O'Neal, E. C., and McDonald, P. J. Female Competitiveness as a Function of Prior Performance Outcome, Competitor's Evaluation, and Sex of Competitor. Paper presented at the Midwestern Psychological Association meeting, Chicago, 1974.

Fitzgerald, B. J., and Pasewark, R. A. Sex Differences on the Edwards Personal Preference Schedule. Psychological Reports, 1971, December, 29(3, Pt. 1), 892.

Fitzgerald, L. F. Sex, Occupational Membership, and the Measurement of Psychological Androgyny. Paper presented at the American Psychological Association Convention, Washington, D. C., 1976.

Fitzgerald, N. M. Verbal Competency in a Sex-Stereotyping Dilemma. Paper presented at the American Psychological Association Convention, Washington, D.C., 1976.

Fitzpatrick, J. L. Academic Underachievement, Other-Direction, and Women's Role in Bright Adolescent Females. Paper presented at the American Psychological Association Convention, San Francisco, 1977.

Forisha, B. Women and Creativity. Symposium presentation at the American Psychological Association Convention, San Francisco, 1977.

Forslund, M. A., and Hull, R. E. Sex-Role Identification and Achievement at Preadolescence. Rocky Mountain Science Journal, 1972, January, 9(1), 105-110.

Fortner, M. L. Vocational Choices of High School Girls: Can They Be Predicted? Vocational Guidance Quarterly, 1970, 18, 203-206.

Fox, L. H. Facilitating the Development of Mathematical Talent in Young Women. Unpublished doctoral dissertation. Dissertation Abstracts International, 1974, 35(7-B), 3553.

──────. Career Interests and Mathematical Acceleration for Girls. Paper presented at the American Psychological Association Convention, Chicago, 1975.

──────. Sex Differences in Mathematical Talent: Bridging the Gap. In D. P. Keating (ed.), Intellectual Talent: Research and Development. Baltimore: Johns Hopkins University Press, 1976.

──────. Women and the Career Relevance of Mathematics. Special Issue on Career Education. School Science and Mathematics, 1976, April, 76(4), 347-353.

──────, Pasternak, S., and Peiser, N. Career Related Interests of Adolescent Boys and Girls. In D. P. Keating (ed.), Intellectual Talent: Research and Development. Baltimore: Johns Hopkins University Press, 1976.

Fox, R. B. The Relationship of Achievement Motivation to Sex Achievement, Intelligence, Socioeconomic Status, and Level of Educational Aspiration for an Eighth-Grade Group. Unpublished doctoral dissertation, University of Kentucky. Dissertation Abstracts International, 1969, 30(4-A), 1331-1332.

Frankel, P. M. Sex-Role Attitudes and the Development of Achievement Need in Women. Journal of College Student Personnel, 1974, March, 15(2), 114-119.

Frankel, P. S. The Relationship of Self Concept, Sex Role Attitudes, and the Development of Achievement Need in Women. Unpublished manuscript, Northwestern University, 1970.

Franken, R. E., and Morphy, D. R. Effects of Fortuitous Success on Goal-Setting Behavior of Individuals High and Low in Achievement Motivation. Perceptual and Motor Skills, 1970, 30(3), 855-864.

Freedman, B. E. Task Performance as a Function of Task Sex-Typing. Unpublished doctoral dissertation, Syracuse University. Dissertation Abstracts International, 1975, July, 36(1-B), 440.

French, E., and Lesser, G. S. Some Characteristics of the Achievement Motive in Women. Journal of Abnormal and Social Psychology, 1964, 68, 119-128.

Friedan, B. Woman: the Fourth Dimension. Ladies Home Journal, 1964, June, 81(5), 48-55.

Friedrich, L. K. Achievement Motivation in College Women Revisited: Implications for Women, Men, and the Gathering of Coconuts. Sex Roles: A Journal of Research, 1976, 2(1), 47-61.

_____, and Harding, J. Achievement Motivation and Academic Performance in Women. Final report. Washington, D. C.: National Institute of Mental Health, 1968.

Friedrichs, A. G., Hertz, T. W., Moynahan, E. D., Simpson, W. E., Arnold, M. R., Christy, M. D., Cooper, C. R., and Stevenson, H. W. Interrelations among Learning and Performance at the Preschool Level. Developmental Psychology, 1971, 4, 164-72.

Fruen, M. A., Rothman, A. I., and Steiner, J. W. Comparison of Characteristics of Male and Female Medical School Applicants. Journal of Medical Education, 1974, February, 49(2), 137-145.

Fry, P. S. Effects of Male and Female Endorsement of Beliefs on the Problem Solving Choices of High and Low Dogmatic Women. Journal of Social Psychology, 1975, June, 96(1), 65-77.

Gadzella, B. M., and Fournet, G. P. Sex Differences in Self-Perceptions as Students of Excellence and Academic Performance. Perceptual and Motor Skills, 1976, December, 43(3), 1092-1094.

Gallagher, J. J. Sex Differences in Expressive Thought of Gifted Children in the Classroom. Personnel and Guidance Journal, 1966, November, 45(3), 248-253.

Gardiner, H. W., Singh, U. P., and D'Orazio, D. E. The Liberated Woman in Three Cultures: Marital-Role Preferences in Thailand, India, and the United States. Human Organization, 1974, Winter, 33(4), 413-415.

Garland, H. Sometimes Nothing Succeeds like Success: Reactions to Success and Failure in Sex-Linked Occupations. Psychology of Women Quarterly, 1977, Fall, 2(1), 50-61.

Gaskell, J. S. The Influence of the Feminine Role on the Aspirations of High School Girls. Unpublished doctoral dissertation, Harvard University, 1973. Dissertation Abstracts International, 1974, May, 34(11-A), 7359. Also available from ERIC (ADG74-11322), 1973.

Gickling, E. E. From a Dawdling to a Doing Daughter: Modifying the Occasional Problems of Average Children. Education, 1975, Summer, 95, 381-385.

Gill, M. K. Psychological Femininity of College Women as it Relates to Self-Actualization, Feminine Role Attitudes, and Selected Background Variables. Unpublished doctoral dissertation, St. John's University. Dissertation Abstracts International, 1976, May, 36(11-A), 7206-7207.

Gilmore, B. To Achieve or Not to Achieve: The Question of Women. Paper presented at the Gerontological Society meeting, Louisville, KY, 1975. Also available from ERIC (ED 624855), 1969.

Ginn, R. O. Psychological Androgyny and Self-Actualization. Psychological Reports, 1975, December, 37(3, part I), 886.

Gitter, A. G., Altavela, J., and Mostofsky, D. I. Effect of Sex, Religion, and Ethnicity on Occupational Status Perception. Journal of Applied Psychology, 1974, February, 59, 96-98.

Gjesme, T. Achievement-Related Motives and School Performance for Girls. Journal of Personality and Social Psychology, 1973, 26, 131-136.

──────. Sex Differences in the Connection between Need for Achievement and School Performance. Journal of Applied Psychology, 1973, October, 58(2), 270-272.

Glasser, K. J. Sex-Role Orientation of the Task and Expectancy of Success as Variables Affecting the Achievement Behavior of Male and Female College Students. Unpublished doctoral dissertation, Princeton University. Dissertation Abstracts International, 1975, March, 35(9-B), 4707.

Gold, A. R. Reactions to Work by Authors Differing in Sex and Achievement. Unpublished doctoral dissertation, Columbia University. Dissertation Abstracts International, 1972, December, 33(6-B), 2790.

Goldberg, C. Sex Roles, Task Competence, and Conformity. Journal of Psychology, 1974, January, 86(1), 157-164.

———. Conformity to Majority Type as a Function of Task and Acceptance of Sex-Related Stereotypes. Journal of Psychology, 1975, January, 89(1), 25-37.

Goldberg, P. A. Are Women Prejudiced Against Women? Transaction, 1968, May, 5, 28-30; Also in D. L. Schaeffer (ed.), Sex Differences in Personality: Readings. Monterey, CA: Brooks/Cole, 1971, 62-66; and in C. Safilios-Rothschild (ed.), Toward a Sociology of Women. Lexington, MA: Xerox College, 1972, 10-13.

———. Prejudice Toward Women: Some Personality Correlates. In F. Denmark (ed.), Who Discriminates Against Women? Issue 15, Beverly Hills: Sage, 1974, 55-65. Also in International Journal of Group Tensions, 1974, March, 4(1), 53-63.

———. The Sexist Woman: The Psychology of Self Hatred and the Politics of Liberation. Paper presented at the Adelphi University Conference on Women and Politics, September 1975.

Goldberg, R. E. Sex Role Stereotypes and Career Versus Homemaking Orientations of Women. In S. H. Osipow (ed.), Emerging Woman: Career Analysis and Outlooks. Columbus, OH: Charles E. Merrill, 1975.

Golden, G. A. The Relationship of Social and Academic Success in High School Girls. Paper presented at the Association for Women in Psychology Conference, Saint Louis, MO, February 1977.

Goldman, R. D., Kaplan, R. M., and Platt, B. B. Sex Differences in the Relationship of Attitudes Toward Technology to Choice of Field of Study. Journal of Counseling Psychology, 1973, September, 20, 412-418.

———, and Hewitt, B. N. The Scholastic Aptitude Test "Explains" Why College Men Major in Science More Often Than College Women. Journal of Counseling Psychology, 1976, 23(1), 50-54.

Goodman, J., and Schlossberg, N. K. A Woman's Place; Children's Sex Stereotyping of Occupations. Vocational Guidance Quarterly, 1972, 20, 226-270.

Gordon, F. E. Where Happiness Lies: Self-Image, Stereotypes, Work Status, and Happiness. Working paper, Department of Administrative Sciences, Yale University, 1971.

———, and Hall, D. T. Self-Image and Stereotypes of Femininity: Their Relationship to Women's Role Conflicts and Coping. Journal of Applied Psychology, 1974, April, 59, 241-243.

Gosswiller, R. Girl Becomes a Doctor. Today's Health, 1969, June, 47, 29-33.

Gottfredson, G. D., and Holland, J. L. Some Normative Self-Report Data on Activities, Competencies, Occupational Preferences, and Ability Ratings for High School and College Students, and Employed Men and Women. JSAS Catalog of Selected Documents in Psychology, 1975, Winter, 5, 192.

_____, and _____. Vocational Choices of Men and Women: A Comparison of Predictors from the Self-Directed Search. Journal of Counseling Psychology, 1975, January, 22(1), 28-34.

Gould, J. S., and Pagano, A. Sex Discrimination and Achievement. Journal of the National Association of Women Deans and Counselors, 1972, Winter, 35, 74-82.

Gove, W. R. The Relationship Between Sex Roles, Marital Status, and Mental Illness. Social Forces, 1972, 51, 34-44.

Grabe, M. Grade and Sex Differences in the Impact of Academic Achievement. Paper presented at the American Psychological Association Convention, Chicago, 1975. Also available from ERIC (ED115534), 1976.

Grainger, B., Kostich, B., and Stanley, Y. A Study of Achievement Motivation of Females in Two Southern, Non-Coeducational Colleges. Unpublished manuscript, 1970.

Gray, B. Women in Transition: From Insurance Policies to Lifelong Career Planning. In D. Wark and E. G. Joselyn (eds.), Student Counseling Bureau Review: Women in Transition. Minneapolis: Student Counseling Bureau, University of Minnesota, 1975, September, 26(1), 36-41.

Green, E. Unreasoning Prejudice Hinders Attainment of Women's Dreams. Delta Kappa Gamma Bulletin, 1970, Fall, 37, 8-17.

Greendorfer, S. L. A Social Learning Approach to Female Sport Involvement. Symposium presentation at the American Psychological Association Convention, Washington, D. C., 1976.

Greenwald, E. R. Perceptual Style in Relation to Role Choices and Motivational Variables. Unpublished doctoral dissertation, Yeshiva University. Dissertation Abstracts International, 1968, 29(06-B), 2192.

Grenell, G., Berger, S. E., and Ingram, B. Sex of Experimenter as a Cue for Women's Aggression. Paper presented at the American Psychological Association Convention, San Francisco, 1977.

Groome, A. J. Interaction Effects in Life Career Simulation: Sex and Ability of Role and Participants. Simulation and Games, 1975, September, 6(3), 312-319.

Gross, W., and Crovitz, E. A Comparison of Medical Students' Attitudes Toward Women and Women Medical Students. Journal of Medical Education, 1975, April, 50(4), 392-394.

Groszko, M., and Morgenstern, R. Institutional Discrimination: The Cast of Achievement-Oriented Women in Higher Education. International Journal of Group Tensions, 1974, 4(1), 82-92.

Groth, N. J. Success and Creativity in Male and Female Professors. Gifted Child Quarterly, 1975, 19(4), 328-335.

──────. College Student Perception of Sex-Role Stereotypes Ramifications for Female Creativity. Gifted Child Quarterly, 1976, Fall, 20(3), 327-335.

Group for the Advancement of Psychiatry, Committee on the College Student. The Educated Women: Prospects and Problems. New York: Charles Scribner's, 1975.

Gruder, C. L., and Cook, T. D. Sex, Dependency, and Helping. Journal of Personality and Social Psychology, 1971, 19, 290-294.

Gullahorn, J. E. Equality and Social Structure. In E. Donelson and J. E. Gullahorn (eds.), Women: A Psychological Perspective. New York: John Wiley, 1977, 266-281.

Gumbach, D. A Woman's Place. Commonweal, 1961, April 28, 74(5), 119-121. Discussion. 1961, May 19, 74(8), 207-209.

Gump, J. P. Sex-Role Attitudes and Psychological Well-Being. Journal of Social Issues, 1972, 28(2), 79-92. Also in M. T. S. Mednick et al. (eds.), Women and Achievement: Social and Motivational Analyses. New York: Halsted, 1975, 274-284.

Gunderson, B. B. The Implication of Rivalry. In S. M. Farber and R. H. L. Wilson (eds.), The Potential of Woman. New York: McGraw-Hill, 1963, 165-187.

Gupta, A. K. Status Values of Professions and Vocational Preferences: Studying Vocational Development Among 11+ Pupils in an Indian School. Adolescence, 1974, Fall, 9(35), 443-459.

Gupta, V. P. Some Correlates of Occupational Choices. Manas, 1973, 20(1), 33-40.

Gurwitz, S. B., and Dodge, K. A. Adults' Evaluations of a Child as a Function of Sex of Adult and Sex of Child. Journal of Personality and Social Psychology, 1975, 32(5), 822-828.

Haavio-Mannila, E. Sex Differentiation in Role Expectations and

Performance. *Journal of Marriage and the Family*, 1967, 29(3), 568-578.

Hagen, R. L., and Kahn, A. Discrimination Against Competent Women. *Journal of Applied Social Psychology*, 1975, October-December, 5(4), 362-376.

Hales, L. W., and Fenner, B. J. Sex and Social Class Differences in Work Values. *Elementary School Guidance and Counseling*, 1973, October, 8, 26-32.

Hall, D. T. A Model of Coping with Role Conflict, The Role Behavior of College Educated Women. *Administrative Science Quarterly*, 1972, 471-485.

Hall, K. P. Sex Differences in Initiation and Influence in Decision-Making Among Prospective Teachers. Unpublished doctoral dissertation, Stanford University. *Dissertation Abstracts International*, 1972, 33(8-A), 3952.

Halperin, M. S. Sex Differences in Children's Responses to Adult Pressure for Achievement. *Journal of Educational Psychology*, 1977, 69(2), 96-100.

Hanley, M. A. Factors of Achievement and Femininity as Predictors of Career Commitment in College Senior Women. Unpublished doctoral dissertation, Boston University. *Dissertation Abstracts International*, 1974, October, 35(4-A), 2050-2051.

Hansen, P. Sex Differences and Supervision. Paper presented at the American Psychological Association Convention, New Orleans, 1974.

Hansen, R. A., and Neujahr, J. L. A Comparison of Career Development between Males and Females Gifted in Science. *Proceedings of the 81st Annual Convention of the American Psychological Association, Montreal, Canada*, 1973, 8, 669-670.

_____, and _____. Career Development of Males and Females Gifted in Science. *Journal of Educational Research*, 1974, September, 68, 43-45.

Hanson, D. E. Social Role Expectation: Motivation Variable in Girls. *Journal of Home Economics*, 1964, May, 56, 312-316.

Harper, J. Educated Women in Niugini. *Australian and New Zealand Journal of Sociology*, 1974, June, 10(2), 90-95.

Harris, M. J. Sex-Typing of In-School Movement Behaviors: Perceptions and Rationales of Sixth Grade Boys and Girls. Unpublished doctoral dissertation, University of Oregon. *Dissertation Abstracts International*, 1975, February, 35(8-A), 4983.

Harter, S. Developmental Differences in the Manifestation of Mastery Motivation on Problem-Solving Tasks. Child Development, 1975, June, 46(2), 370-378.

Hartman, E. A. Degree of Cooperation in a Prisoner's Dilemma as a Function of Sex Roles, Responsiveness, and the Exploitativeness of the Simulated Other. Personality and Social Psychology Bulletin, 1974, 1(1), 287-289.

Harvey, A. L. Goal-Setting Behavior in High School Girls. Unpublished doctoral dissertation, Cornell University. Dissertation Abstracts International, 1971, June, 31(12-A), 6403-6404.

Haug, M. R. Sex Role Variations in Occupational Prestige Ratings. Sociological Focus, 1975, 8, 47-56.

Haven, E. W. Factors Associated with the Selection of Advanced Academic Mathematics Courses by Girls in High School. Research Bulletin of the Educational Testing Service, 1972, 72 (12).

Hawley, M. J. The Relationship of Women's Perceptions of Men's Views of the Feminine Ideal to Career Choice. Unpublished doctoral dissertation, Claremont Graduate School. Dissertation Abstracts, 1969, 29(8-A), 2523, 629.

_____. What Women Think Men Think: Does it Affect Their Career Choice? Journal of Counseling Psychology, 1971, May, 18(3), 193-199.

_____. Perceptions of Male Models of Femininity Related to Career Choice, Journal of Counseling Psychology, 1972, 19(4), 308-313.

Heilbrun, A. B., Jr. Sex-Role Identity and Achievement Motivation. Psychological Reports, 1963, 12(2), 483-490.

_____. Sex-Role Instrumental-Expressive Behavior, and Psychopathology in Females. Journal of Abnormal Psychology, 1968, 73(2), 131-136.

_____, Piccola, G, and Kleemeier, C. Male Sex-Gender Identification: A Source of Achievement Deficit in College Females. Journal of Personality, 1975, December, 43(4), 678-692.

Heinsohn, A. L. Work/Career Expectations of Female College Seniors Having Traditional and Non-Traditional Sex Role Equality Attitudes. Unpublished doctoral dissertation, Pennsylvania State University, 1974. Dissertation Abstracts International, 1974, 36(3-A), 1845. Also available from ERIC (ADG75-19913), 1974.

Helson, R. Sex Differences in Creative Style. Journal of Personality, 1967, 35, 214-233.

_____. Generality of Sex Differences in Creative Style. Journal of Personality, 1968, March, 36, 33-48.

_____. The Changing Image of the Career Woman. Journal of Social Issues, 1972, 28(2), 33-46. Also in M. T. S. Mednick et al. (eds.), Women and Achievement: Social and Motivational Analyses. New York: Halsted, 1975, 420-431.

_____. Inner Reality of Women. Arts in Society, 1974, Spring-Summer, 11(1), 25-36.

Henken, V., Unger, R. K., and Aronew, E. Preference for Group Leaders: Gender Versus Sex Role. Paper presented at the American Psychological Association Convention, Washington, D. C., 1976.

Henley, N. M. Power, Sex and Nonverbal Communication. Berkeley Journal of Sociology, 1973, 18, 1-26.

Heppner, P. P., and Pew, S. Effects of Diplomas, Awards, and Counselor Sex on Perceived Expertness. Journal of Counseling Psychology, 1977, March, 24, 147-149.

Hewer, V. H., and Neubeck, G. Attitudes of College Students Toward Employment Among Married Women. Personnel and Guidance Journal, 1964, 42(6), 587-592.

Hewitt, B. N., and Goldman, R. D. Occam's Razor Slices Through the Myth that College Women Overachieve. Journal of Educational Psychology, 1975, April, 67(2), 325-330.

Hewitt, L. S. Age and Sex Differences in the Vocational Aspirations of Elementary School Children. Journal of Social Psychology, 1975, 96, 173-177.

Hill, K. T., and Dusek, J. B. Children's Achievement Expectations as a Function of Social Reinforcement, Sex of Subject and Test Anxiety. Child Development, 1969, 40(2), 547-558.

Hilpert, F. P., Kramer, C., and Clark, R. A. Participant's Perceptions of Self and Partner in Mixed-Sex Dyads. Central States Speech Journal, 1975, 26, 52-56.

Hilton, T. L., and Berglund, G. W. Sex Differences in Mathematics Achievement--a Longitudinal Study. Research Bulletin, Princeton, NJ: Educational Testing Service, 1971, 50-54. Also in Journal of Educational Research, 1974, January, 67, 231-237.

Hipple, J. L. Perceptual Differences in Concepts of the Ideal Woman. School Counselor, 1975, January, 22(3), 180-186.

Hjelle, L. A., and Butterfield, R. Self-Actualization and Women's

Attitudes Toward Their Roles in Contemporary Society. Journal of Psychology, 1974, July, 87(2), 225-230.

Hoffman, D. S., and Hoeflin, R. Freshman and Sophomore Women: What do They Want Most in the Future? Journal of College Student Personnel, 1972, November, 13(6), 490-493.

Hoffman, L. R., and Maier, N. R. F. Sex Differences, Sex Composition, and Group Problem Solving. Journal of Abnormal Social Psychology, 1961, 63(2), 453-456.

_____, and _____. Social Factors Influencing Problem Solving in Women. Journal of Personality and Social Psychology, 1966, 4, 382-390.

Holmes, D. S. Leadership and Women in Organizations. JSAS Catalogue of Selected Documents in Psychology, 1976, 6(4), 1.

Hottes, J. H., and Kahn, A. Sex Differences in a Mixed-Motive Conflict Situation. Journal of Personality, 1974, June, 42(2), 260-275.

Houts, P. S. and Entwisle, D. R. Academic Achievement Effort Among Females: Achievement Attitudes and Sex-Role Orientation. Journal of Counseling Psychology, 1968, 15, 284-285.

Howe, F. Sexism and the Aspirations of Women. Phi Delta Kappan, 1973, October, 55(2), 99-104.

Howe, K. G., and Zanna, M. P. Sex Appropriateness of the Task and Achievement Behavior. Paper presented at the Eastern Psychological Association meeting, New York, 1975.

Howell, M. C. Professional Women and Feminist Movement. Journal of the National Association for Women Deans, Administrators, and Counselors, 1974, Winter, 37(2), 84-87.

Hulbert, T. Sex, Psyche, and Behavior. The UCLA Monthly, 1973, 2.

Hull, R. E. Sex-Role Identification and Achievement. Unpublished doctoral dissertation, University of New Mexico. Dissertation Abstracts International, 1970, July, 31(1-A), 104.

Hunt, J. G., and Hunt, L. L. The Sexual Mystique: A Common Dimension of Racial and Sexual Stratification. Sociology and Social Research, 1975, 59(3), 231-242.

Hurwitz, R. E., and Bryant, N. D. Effect of Sex of Participants on Small-Group Decision Making. Paper presented at the American Psychological Association Convention, San Francisco, 1977.

Husén, T., Fägerlind, I., and Liljefois, R., Sex Differences in Science Achievement and Attitudes: A Swedish Analysis by Grade Level. <u>Comparative Education Review</u>, 1974, June, 18 (2), 292-304.

Ingram, B., and Harnsberger, S. Sex-Role Orientation, Defensiveness, and Interpersonal Behavior of Women. Symposium presentation at the American Psychological Association Convention, Washington, D. C., 1976.

Isaacs, A. F. Role Expectancy and Its Effect on Performance and Achievement Among Gifted Students. <u>The High School Journal</u>, 1964, November, 48, 107-116.

Jacklin, C. N., and Maccoby, E. E. Mathematics, Intellectual Ability and the Sexes. Unpublished manuscript, Department of Psychology, Stanford University, 1974.

_____, and _____. Sex Differences and Their Implications for Management. In G. E. Gordon and H. M. Strober (eds.), <u>Bringing Women into Management.</u> New York: McGraw-Hill, <u>1975</u>, 23-38.

Jackson-White, R., Fraser, S. C., and Colman, D. Assessment of Stereotyped Male and Female Modes of Influence. Paper presented at the American Psychological Association Convention, Chicago, 1975.

_____, Renee, A., Condelli, L., Ritschel, S., and Fraser, S. C. Sex-Role Stereotypes in Interpersonal Judgments. Paper presented at the American Psychological Association Convention, San Francisco, 1977.

Jacobs, J. E. A Comparison of the Relationships Between the Level of Acceptance of Sex-Role Stereotyping and Achievement and Attitudes Towards Mathematics of Seventh Graders and Eleventh Graders in a Suburban Metropolitan New York Community. Available from ERIC (ED107502), 1974.

_____, and Alberti, J. M. (eds.). Realizing Human Potential: Alternatives for Women; Symposium. <u>Educational Horizons</u>, 1975, Spring, 53(3), 94-148.

Jacobson, M. B., and Effertz, J. Sex Roles and Leadership: Perceptions of the Leaders and the Led. <u>Organizational Behavior and Human Performance</u>, 1974, 12(3), 383-396.

Jain, K. C. Vocational Choices of Ninth Class Students. <u>Rajasthan University Studies</u>, 1964-1965, 6, 55-63.

James, R. J. Traits Associated with the Initial and Persistent Interest in the Study of College Science. <u>Journal of Research in Science Teaching</u>, 1972, 9(3), 231-234.

Janeway, E. Realizing Human Potential. <u>Between Myth and Morn-</u>

ing: Women Awakening. New York: William Morrow, 1974, 129-146.

Jardine, L. L., and Wurster, S. R. A Study of Attitudes of Twelfth Grade Students Toward High-Success-Oriented College/Career Goals of Females. Available from ERIC (ED087969), 1974.

Jellison, J. M., Jackson-White, R., Bruder, R. A., and Martyna, W. Achievement Behavior: A Situational Interpretation. Sex Roles: A Journal of Research, 1975, 1(4), 369-384.

Joesting, J. The Influence of Sex Roles on Creativity in Women. Gifted Child Quarterly, 1975, 19(4), 336-339.

———. Personality Correlates of Sexism and Anti-Sexism in College Students. College Student Journal, 1976, Fall, 10(3), 194-196.

———, and Joesting, R. Future Problems of Gifted Girls. Gifted Child Quarterly, 1970, Summer, 14(2), 82-90.

———, and ———. Sex Differences in Group Belongingness as Influenced by Instructor's Sex. Psychological Reports, 1972, December, 31(3), 717-718.

———, and ———. Sex Differences in Equalitarianism and Anxiety in Ninth Grade Students. Adolescence, 1975, Spring, 10, 59-61.

Johnson, P. B. Social Power and Sex Role Stereotypes. Paper presented at the Western Psychological Association meeting San Francisco, May, 1974.

———. Social Power and Sex Role Stereotyping. Unpublished doctoral dissertation, University of California, Los Angeles. Dissertation Abstracts International, 1974, November, 35(5-B), 2406.

———. Women and Power: Toward A Theory of Effectiveness. Journal of Social Issues, 1976, 32(3), 99-110.

Johnson, R. W., and MacDonnell, J. The Relationship Between Conformity and Male and Female Attitudes Toward Women. Journal of Social Psychology, 1974, October, 94(1), 155-156.

Johnson, T. J., and Smith, L. M. Achievement, Affiliation, and Power Motivation in Adolescents. Psychological Reports, 1965, 16(3, Pt. 2), 1249-1252.

Johnston, H. S. Male Authoritarianism: The Attitudes of Male Graduate Students in Professional Schools Toward Women. Unpublished doctoral dissertation, Cornell University. Dissertation Abstracts International, 1975, January, 35(7-A), 4159.

Jones, R. H. Sex Prejudice: Effects on the Inferential Process of Judging Hireability. Unpublished doctoral dissertation. Dissertation Abstracts International, 1970, 31(3-A), 1013.

Jongeward, D., and Scott, D. (eds.). Women's Lack of Achievement: Then and Now. In Affirmative Action for Women: A Practical Guide. Reading, MA: Addison-Wesley, 1973, 15-38.

Juran, S. H. Sex Differences in Negative Achievement Motivation. Unpublished master's thesis, Brooklyn College, 1972.

Kagan, J. Why Women Fail at Math. McCalls, 1974, December, 102, 39.

Kahn, A., Hottes, J., and Davis, W. L. Cooperation and Optimal Responding in the Prisoner's Dilemma Game: Effects of Sex and Physical Attractiveness. Journal of Personality and Social Psychology, 1971, 17, 267-279.

_____, Larum, H., and Nelson, R. E. Preferences for an Equal or Equitable Allocator. Journal of Personality and Social Psychology, 1977, 35(11), 837-844.

Kanareff, V. T., and Lanzetta, J. T. Effect of Success-Failure Experience and Probability of Reinforcement Upon the Acquisition and Extinction of an Imitative Response. Psychological Reports, 1960, 7, 151-166.

Kane, R. D., et al. A Study of the Factors Influencing the Participation of Women in Non-Traditional Occupations in Postsecondary Area Vocational Training Schools. Washington, D. C.: Bureau of Occupational and Adult Education, 1977.

Kanekar, S., and Ahluwalia, R. B. Academic Aspirations in Relation to Sex and Physical Attractiveness. Psychological Reports, 1975, June, 36(3), 834.

Kangas, J., and Bradway, K. Intelligence at Middle Age: A Thirty-Eight Year Follow-Up. Developmental Psychology, 1971, September, 5(2), 333-337.

Karabenick, S. A. The Effect of Sex of Competitor on the Performance of Females Following Success. Paper presented at the American Psychological Association Convention, Honolulu, 1972.

Karmel, B. Education and Employment Aspirations of Students: A Probabilistic Approach. Journal of Educational Psychology, 1975, 67(1), 57-63.

Keating, D. P. (ed.). Discovering Quantitative Precocity. In Intellectual Talent: Research and Development. Baltimore: Johns Hopkins University Press, 1976.

Keller, S. The Future Role of Women. The Annals of the American Academy of Political and Social Science, 1973, 408, 1-12.

Kerr, B. A., and Dell, D. M. Perceived Interviewer Expertness and Attractiveness: Effects of Interviewer Behavior and Attire and Interview Setting. Journal of Counseling Psychology, 1976, November, 23, 553-556.

Kidd, T. R., and Woodman, W. F. Sex and Orientations Toward Winning in Sport. Research Quarterly, 1975, December, 46(4), 476-483.

Kidder, L. H., and Belletterie, G. Secret Ambitions and Public Performances: The Effects of Anonymity on Reward Allocations by Men and Women. Paper presented at the American Psychological Association Convention, Chicago, 1975.

_____, _____, and Cohn, E. S. Secret Ambitions and Public Performances: The Effects of Anonymity on Reward Allocations Made by Men and Women. Journal of Experimental Social Psychology, 1977, January, 13(1), 70-80.

Kinsell-Rainey, L. W., and Deichmann, J. Sex Differences: An Obsolete Distinction in the Analysis of Classroom Task Approach Patterns. Paper presented at the American Educational Research Association meeting, San Francisco, 1977.

Kipnis, D. M. Sex Roles, Sex Differences, Incentives and Anxiety: Who Will Achieve? Unpublished manuscript, 1973.

_____. Inner Direction, Other Direction, and Achievement Motivation. Human Development, 1974, 17, 321-343.

_____. Intelligence, Occupational Status and Achievement Orientation. In B. B. Lloyd and J. Archer (eds.), Exploring Sex Differences. New York: Academic Press, 1976, 95-122.

Kirk, B. A. Young Women's Attitudes Toward Science and Math Careers: Research Study. Symposium presentation at the American Psychological Association Convention, San Francisco, 1977.

Knudsen, D. D. The Declining Status of Women: Popular Myths and the Failure of Functionalist Thought. Social Forces, 1969, December, 48(2), 183-193.

Koehler, V. The Theory of Achievement Motivation, and Grades and Occupational Aspirations. Unpublished doctoral dissertation, Syracuse University. Dissertation Abstracts International, 1974, August, 35(2-B), 1083.

Koenig, F., and Seaman, J. Comparison of Cognitive Complexity of Male and Female Subjects Responding to Male and Female Stimuli. Perceptual and Motor Skills, 1974, June, 38(3, Pt. 2), 1345-1346.

Kogan, N. Creativity and Sex Differences. *Journal of Creative Behavior,* 1975, 8(1), 1-14.

Kristal, J., Sanders, D., Spence, J. T., and Helmreich, R. Inferences About the Femininity of Competent Women and Their Implications for Likability. *Sex Roles: A Journal of Research,* 1975, 1(1), 33-40.

Kundsin, R. B. (ed.). *Women and Success: The Anatomy of Achievement.* New York: William Morrow, 1974.

Kuvlesky, W. P., and Reynolds, D. H. *Educational Aspirations and Expectations of Youth: A Bibliography of Research Literature.* (Vol. II). Departmental Information Report No. 70-5. College Station, TX: Texas A & M University, Department of Agricultural Economics and Rural Sociology, 1970.

Lancaster, J. B. In Praise of the Achieving Female Monkey. In C. Tavris (ed.), *The Female Experience,* from the editors of *Psychology Today,* Del Mar, CA: Communications/Research/Machines, 1973, 5-9.

Landers, D. A. Psychological Femininity and the Prospective Female Physical Educator. *Research Quarterly,* 1970, 41, 164-170.

Lando, H. A. Sex Differences in Response to Differing Patterns of Attack. *Personality and Social Psychology Bulletin,* 1976, Summer, 2(3), 286-289.

Langsam, I. The Effect of Sex and Social Settings in Help-Seeking Behavior in a Problem-Solving Situation. Unpublished doctoral dissertation, University of Michigan. *Dissertation Abstracts International,* 1973, (34-A), 5313.

Lao, R. C., Upchurch, W. H., Corwin, B. J., and Grossnickle, W. F. Biased Attitudes Toward Females as Indicated by Ratings of Intelligence and Likeability. *Psychological Reports,* 1975, December, 37(3, Pt. 2), 1315-1320.

Larwood, L. Sex Role as a Mediator of Achievement in Task Performance. *Sex Roles: A Journal of Research,* 1977, 3, 109-114.

Latorre, R. A., Endman, M., and Gossmann, I. Androgyny and Need Achievement in Male and Female Psychiatric Inpatients. *Journal of Clinical Psychology,* 1976, April, 32(2), 233-235.

Lawlis, G. F., and Crawford, J. D. Cognitive Differentiation in Women and Pioneer-Traditional Vocational Choices. *Journal of Vocational Behavior,* 1975, 6, 263-267.

Leder, G. C. Sex Differences in Mathematics Problem Appeal as a Function of Problem Context. Journal of Educational Research, 1974, April, 67, 351-353.

Legoux, Y. Attitudes de Jeunes Filles Devant une Profession Technique. [Attitudes of Young Girls Towards a Technical Profession.] Sociological Traveler, 1962, June-September, 4, 3, 243-261.

Leland, C. Women-Men-Work: Women's Career Aspirations as Affected by the Male Environment. Unpublished doctoral dissertation, Stanford University, 1965.

Lenning, O. T. An Exploratory Study of Factors Differentiating Freshmen Educational Growth. Paper presented at the American College Personnel Association Convention, St. Louis, MO, March 1970. Also available from ERIC (ED039574), 1970.

Leo, E. S., and Chow, E. N. L. "Men's" Work and "Women's" Work: Attitudes and Aspirations of University Undergraduates. Unpublished manuscript, American University, 1975.

Leonard, M. Increasing Achievement Motivation in Females. Symposium presentation at the American Psychological Association Convention, Washington, D. C., 1976.

Lerner, G. Women's Rights and American Feminism. American Scholar, 1971, 40(2), 235-248.

Lerner, R. M., Benson, P., and Vincent, S. Development of Societal and Personal Vocational Role Perception in Males and Females. Journal of Genetic Psychology, 1976, September, 129(1), 167-168.

Leserman, J. P. Boys and Girls in White: Professional Orientation of the Student Physician. Unpublished doctoral dissertation, Duke University. Dissertation Abstracts International, 1976, 37(12-A), 7981. Also available from ERIC (ADG77-11832), 1976.

Lesser, G. S., Packard, R., and Krawitz, R. N. Experimental Arousal of Achievement Motivation in Adolescent Girls. Journal of Abnormal and Social Psychology, 1963, January, 66(1), 59-66.

Levenson, H., Burford, B., Bonno, B., and Davis, L. Are Women Still Prejudiced Against Women? A Replication and Extension of Goldberg's Study. Journal of Psychology, 1975, 89(1), 67-71.

Leventhal, D. B., and Shemberg, K. M. Sex Role Adjustment and Nonsanctioned Aggression. Journal of Experimental Research in Personality, 1969, 3, 283-286.

_____, _____, and van Schoelandt, S. K. Effects of Sex Role

Adjustment Upon the Expression of Aggression. Journal of Personality and Social Psychology, 1968, 8, 393-396.

Leventhal, G. S. Reward Allocation by Males and Females. Paper presented at the American Psychological Association Convention, Montreal, 1973.

_____, and Anderson, D. Self-Interest and Maintenance of Equity. Journal of Personality and Social Psychology, 1970, 15(1), 57-62.

_____, and Lane, D. W. Sex, Age, and Equity Behavior. Journal of Personality and Social Psychology, 1970, 15, 312-316.

_____, and Popp, A. L. Equity or Equality in Children's Allocation of Reward to Other Persons? Child Development, 1973, 44(4), 753-763.

Levine, A. Forging a "Feminine Identity": Women in Four Professional Schools. American Journal of Psychoanalysis, 1975, 35, 63-67.

Lewis, H. B. Intellectual Functioning: The Importance of Things Over People. In Psychic War in Men and Women. New York: New York University Press, 1976, 90-106.

Lewis, J. Undergraduate Ability-Achievement and the Earning of Graduate Degress. Educational and Psychological Measurement, 1974, Summer, 34(2), 383-385.

Lewis, R. O. Consistent Career Preferences, Personality and Women's Perceptions of Male Views of Femininity. Dissertation Abstracts International, 1975, May, 35(11-A), 7062.

Lifton, R. J. (ed.). The Woman in America. Boston: Beacon Press, 1965.

Lipinski, B. Sex Role Conflict and Achievement Motivation in College Women. Unpublished doctoral dissertation, University of Cincinnati. Dissertation Abstracts, 1966, 26(7), 4077.

Lipman-Blumen, J. The Vicarious Achievement Ethic and Nontraditional Roles for Women. Paper presented at the Eastern Sociological Society meeting, New York, April 1973.

_____. Toward a Homosocial Theory of Sex Roles: An Explanation of the Sex Segregation of Social Institutions. In B. B. Reagan, and M. Blaxall (eds.), Women and the Workplace: The Implications of Occupational Segregation. Chicago: University of Chicago Press, 1976, 15-31.

_____, and Leavitt, H. J. Vicarious and Direct Achievement Patterns in Adulthood. The Counseling Psychologist, 1976, 6(1), 26-32.

Lipsitt, P. D., and Strodtbeck, F. L. Defensiveness in Decision Making as a Function of Sex-Role Identification. Journal of Personality and Social Psychology, 1967, 6, 10-15.

Lirtzman, S. I., and Wahba, M. A. Determinant of Coalitional Behavior of Men and Women: Sex Roles or Situational Requirements? Journal of Applied Psychology, 1972, October, 56(5), 406-411.

Liss-Levinson, N., and Karmens, L. Effect of Sex Role on Career Development and Aspirations. Symposium presentation at the American Psychological Association Convention, Chicago, 1975.

Littig, L. W., and Yeracaris, C. A. Academic Achievement Correlates of Achievement and Affiliation Motivations. Journal of Psychology, 1963, 55(1), 115-119.

Lloyd-Jones, E. M. The Self-Actualized Woman. In M. L. McBee and K. A. Blake (eds.), The American Woman: Who Will She Be? Beverly Hills: Glencoe Press, 1974, 37-47.

Locke, E. A. Some Correlates of Classroom and Out-Of-Class Achievement in Gifted Science Students. Journal of Educational Psychology, 1963, 54, 238-248.

Lockheed-Katz, M. E. Final Report: Modification of Female Leadership Behaviors in the Presence of Males. Princeton, NJ: Educational Testing Service, 1974. Also available from ERIC (ED106742), 1975.

_____ (ed.). Research on Women's Acquisition of Professional and Leadership Roles. Princeton, NJ: Educational Testing Service, 1975.

_____. Cognitive Style Effects on Sex Status in Student Work Groups. Princeton, NJ: Educational Testing Service, 1976.

_____, and Hall, K. P. Sex as a Status Characteristic: The Role of Formal Theory in Developing Leadership Training Strategies. Princeton, NJ: Educational Testing Service, 1975.

_____, and _____. Conceptualizing Sex as a Status Characteristic: Applications to Leadership Training Strategies. Journal of Social Issues, 1976, 32(3), 111-124.

Long, C. K. Achievement Motives, Extrinsic Personal Motives and the Choice of Credit/Nocredit Courses by Female College Students. Unpublished doctoral dissertation, University of Pittsburgh. Dissertation Abstracts International, 1975, October, 36(4-A), 2105.

Looft, W. R. Sex Differences in the Expression of Vocational Aspirations by Elementary School Children. Developmental Psychology, 1971, 5, 366.

―――. Vocational Aspirations of Second-Grade Girls. Psychological Reports, 1971, February, 28(1), 241-242.

Loring, R., and Wells, T. Our Sex-Role Culture. In Breakthrough: Women Into Management. New York: Van Nostrand Reinhold, 1972, 89-108.

Lubetkin, B. S., and Lubetkin, A. I. Achievement Motivation in a Competitive Situation: The Older Female Graduate Student. Journal of Clinical Psychology, 1971, April, 27(2), 269-271.

Lunneborg, C. E., and Lunneborg, P. W. Deviation from Predicted Growth of Abilities for Male and Female College Students. Journal of Educational Measurement, 1969, 6, 165-172.

Lunneborg, P. W. Sex Differences in Aptitude Maturation During College. Journal of Counseling Psychology, 1969, September, 16, 463.

―――. Sex Differences in Career Decision-Making Stages and Styles. Poster Session presented at the American Psychological Association Convention, San Francisco, 1977.

―――, and Rosenwood, L. M. Need Affiliation and Achievement: Declining Sex Differences. Psychological Reports, 1972, 31(3), 795-798.

Lutzker, D. R. Sex Role, Cooperation and Competition in a Two-Person, Non-Zero-Sum Game. Journal of Conflict Resolution, 1961, 5, 366-368.

McArthur, L. Z., and Eisen, S. V. Achievements of Male and Female Storybook Characters as Determinants of Achievement Behavior by Boys and Girls. Journal of Personality and Social Psychology, 1976, 33(4), 467-473.

McClintock, C. G., and Moskowitz, J. M. Children's Preferences for Individualistic, Cooperative, and Competitive Outcomes. Journal of Personality and Social Psychology, 1976, October, 34(4), 543-555.

Maccoby, E. E. Woman's Intellect. In S. M. Farber and R. H. L. Wilson (eds.), The Potential of Woman. New York: McGraw-Hill, 1963, 24-39. Also in K. O. Doyle, Jr. (ed.), Interaction: Readings in Human Psychology. Lexington, MA: D. C. Heath, 1970, 280-292.

――― (ed.). Sex Differences in Intellectual Functioning. In The Development of Sex Differences. Stanford: Stanford University Press, 1966, 25-55. Also in J. M. Bardwick (ed.), Readings on the Psychology of Women. New York: Harper & Row, 1972, 34-43.

_____. Feminine Intellect and the Demands of Society. Impact of Science on Society, 1970, 20(1), 13-20.

_____, and Jacklin, C. N. Sex Differences in Intellectual Functioning. Proceedings of the Invitational Conference on Testing Problems, 1972, 37-55.

_____, and _____. The Psychology of Sex Differences. Stanford: Stanford University Press, 1974.

_____, and _____. Myth, Reality and Shades of Gray: What We Know and Don't Know About Sex Differences. Psychology Today, 1974, December, 8(7), 109-112.

McConnell, W. A. Sex Differences in a Noncompetitive Group Task. Unpublished doctoral dissertation, Colorado State University. Dissertation Abstracts International, 1971, 32(5-B), 3049.

McDermott, M., and Lichtenstein, P. A Longitudinal Study of the Status of Hofstra Freshman Classes Five Years After Entry. Report No. 108. Available from ERIC (ED0100211), 1975.

McFarland, W. J. Are Girls Really Smarter? The Elementary School Journal, 1969, October, 70(1), 14-19.

McGovern, L. P., Ditzian, J. L., and Taylor, S. P. Sex and Perceptions of Dependency in a Helping Situation. Bulletin of Psychonomic Society, 1975, 5, 336-338.

McGuire, J. M., and Thomas, M. H. Effects of Sex, Competence, and Competition on Sharing Behavior in Children. Journal of Personality and Social Psychology, 1975, 32(3), 490-494.

Mack, D., Auburn, P. N., and Knight, G. F. Sex Role Identification and Behavior in a Reiterated Prisoner's Dilemma Game. Psychonomic Science, 1971, 24, 280-281.

McKay, B. J. An Empirical Study of Feminine Attitudes Toward Feminine Achievement. Unpublished doctoral dissertation, Northwestern University. Dissertation Abstracts International, 1975, February, 35(8-B), 4148.

McKeachie, W. J., Isaacson, R. L., Milholland, J. E., and Lin, Y. G. Student Achievement Motives, Achievement Cues, and Academic Achievement. Journal of Consulting and Clinical Psychology, 1968, February, 32(1), 26-29.

McKenzie, S. P. A Comparative Study of Feminine Role Perceptions, Selected Personality Characteristics, and Traditional Attitudes of Professional Women and Housewives. Unpublished doctoral dissertation, University of Housten. Dissertation Abstracts International, 1972, April, 32(10-A), 5615-5616.

McMahan, I. D. Sex-Role Stereotypes of Cognitive Task Performance. JSAS Catalog of Selected Documents in Psychology, 1976, May, 6, 39.

McMillan, M. R. Attitudes of College Men Toward Career Involvement of Married Women. Vocational Guidance Quarterly, 1972, 21, 8-11.

McNeel, S. P., McClintock, C. G., and Nuttin, J. M., Jr. Effects of Sex Role in a Two-Person Mixed-Motive Game. Journal of Personality and Social Psychology, 1972, 24(3), 372-380.

Macy, J. W., Jr. Unless We Begin Now: Womanpower Address, July 25, 1966. Vital Speeches of the Day, 1966, September, 32(22), 678-682.

Maier, N. R. Male Vs. Female Discussion Leaders. Personnel Psychology, 1970, 23, 455-461.

Manaster, G. J., Friedman, S. T., and Larson, D. Premedical Students' Survivability and Specialization: A Social and Psychological Study. Psychological Reports, 1976, August, 39(1), 35-45.

Mannes, M. The Problems of Creative Women. In S. M. Farber and R. H. L. Wilson (eds.). The Potential of Woman. New York: McGraw-Hill, 1963, 116-130. Also in E. Adams and M. L. Briscoe (eds.), Up Against the Wall, Mother. Beverly Hills: Glencoe Press, 1971, 402-415.

Marecek, J. When Stereotypes Hurt: Response to Dependent and Aggressive Communications. Paper presented at the Eastern Psychological Association meeting, Philadelphia, April 1974.

Marjoribanks, K. School Attitudes, Cognitive Ability, and Academic Achievement. Journal of Educational Psychology, 1976, December, 68(6), 653-660.

Martin, D. Relative Expectations of Women Engineering Students Concerning Their Future Professional Life. Psychologie Francaise, 1975, November, 20(3), 133-145.

Martin, J. C. Competitive and Noncompetitive Behavior of Children in Beanbag Toss Game. Unpublished manuscript, University of California, 1973.

Marwell, G., Schmitt, D. R., and Shotola, R. Sex Differences in a Cooperative Task. Behavioral Science, 1970, 15, 184-186.

Masih, L. K. Career Saliency and Its Relation to Certain Needs,

Interests, and Job Values. Personnel and Guidance Journal, 1967, 45(7), 653-658.

Matteson, M. T. Attitudes Toward Women as Managers: Sex or Role-Differences? Psychological Reports, 1976, August, 39(1), 166.

_____, McMahon, J. T., and McMahon, M. Sex Differences and Job Attitudes: Some Unexpected Findings. Psychological Reports, 1974, December, 35(3), 1333-1334.

Maxted, M. C. Self Realization for Women. Delta Kappa Gamma Society Bulletin, 1975, Spring, 41, 43-46.

Maxwell, P. G., and Gonzalez, A. E. Traditional and Non-Traditional Role Choice and Need for Failure Among College Women. Psychological Reports, 1972, October, 31(2), 545-546.

Mead, M., and Kaplan, F. (eds.), American Women. New York: Scribner's, 1965.

Mednick, M. T. S., Tangri, S. S., and Hoffman, L. W. (eds.). Women and Achievement: Social and Motivational Analyses. New York: Halsted Press, 1975.

Medvene, A. M., and Collins, A. Occupational Prestige and Its Traditional and Nontraditional Views of Women's Roles. Psychology, 1974, 21(2), 139-143.

_____, and _____. Occupational Prestige and Appropriateness: The Views of Mental Health Specialists. Journal of Vocational Behavior, 1976, August, 9(1), 63-71.

Meeker, B. F., and Weitzel-O'Neill, P. A. Sex Roles and Interpersonal Behavior in Task-Oriented Groups. American Sociological Review, 1977, February, 42(1), 91-105.

Megargee, E. I. Influence of Sex Role on the Manifestation of Leadership. Journal of Applied Psychology, 1969, 53(5), 377-382.

Mendelsohn, G. A., and Covington, M. V. Internal Processes and Perceptual Factors in Verbal Problem Solving: A Study of Sex and Individual Differences in Cognition. Journal of Personality, 1972, September, 40, 451-471.

Mental Abilities: Sex or Maturation Rate. Science News, 1976, May, 109, 292-293.

Messe, L. A., and Callahan, C. Sex and Message Effects in Reward Allocation Behavior. Paper presented at the American Psychological Association Convention, Chicago, 1975.

Meyer, M. M. Patterns of Perceptions and Attitudes Toward Traditionally Masculine and Feminine Occupations Throughout Childhood and Adolescence. Unpublished doctoral dissertation, Michigan State University, 1970.

Michaelson, B. L. Vocational Interests, Self-Concepts, and Attitudes Toward Feminine Roles as Related to the Educational and Vocational Choices of College Women. Unpublished doctoral dissertation, Temple University. Dissertation Abstracts International, 1974, December, 35(6-B), 2994.

Mikula, G. Nationality, Performance, and Sex as Determinants of Reward Allocation. Journal of Personality and Social Psychology, 1974, 29, 435-440.

Miller, B. S. Sex Differences in Attitudes Toward Achievement in Adolescence. Unpublished honors thesis, University of Michigan, 1972.

Miller, G. R., and McReynolds, M. Male Chauvinism and Source Competence: A Research Note. Speech Monographs, 1973, 40(2), 154-155.

Miller, R. L. What's Good Is Beautiful but What's Superior Depends Upon Sex. Paper presented at the American Psychological Association Convention, Washington, D. C., 1976.

Millett, K. Sexual Politics. New York: Doubleday, 1970.

Millman, M., and Kanter, R. M. (eds.). Another Voice: Feminist Perspectives on Social Life and Social Science. Garden City, NY: Anchor Press/Doubleday, 1975.

Miner, J. B. Motivation to Manage Among Women: Studies of College Students. Journal of Vocational Behavior, 1974, October, 5(2), 241-250. Also in J. B. Miner, Motivation to Manage: A Ten-Year Update on the "Studies in Management Education" Research. Atlanta, GA: Organizational Measurement Systems Press, 1977, 159-166.

Mintz, R. S., and Patterson, C. H. Marriage and Career Attitudes of Women in Selected College Curriculums. Vocational Guidance Quarterly, 1969, March, 17(3), 213-217.

Minuchin, P. Sex Differences in Children: Research Findings in an Educational Context. National Elementary Principal, 1966, November, 46(2), 45-48.

Mishel, H. Sex Bias in the Evaluation of Professional Achievements. Journal of Educational Psychology, 1974, 66, 157-166.

Montagu, A. The Natural Superiority of Women. New York: Macmillan, 1968.

Montanelli, D. S., and Hill, K. T. Children's Achievement Expectations and Performance as a Function of Two Consecutive Reinforcement Experiences, Sex of Subject, and Sex of Experimenter. Journal of Personality and Social Psychology, 1969, 13, 115-128.

Montemayor, R. Children's Performance On and Attraction To an Activity as a Function of Masculine, Feminine or Neutral Lables and Sex-Role Preference. Paper presented at the Eastern Psychological Association meeting, April 1972.

──────. Children's Performance in a Game and Their Attraction to It as a Function of Sex-Typed Labels Child Development, 1974, 45, 152-156.

Morse, J. A., and Bruch, C. R. Gifted Women: More Issues Than Answers. Educational Horizons, 1971, Fall, 49(1), 25-32.

Mukherjee, B. N. Multivariate Relationships Among Measures of Achievement Motive and Achievement Values. Indian Journal of Psychology, 1972, September, 47(3), 293-317.

Murphy-Berman, V. Effects of Success and Failure on Perceptions of Gender Identity. Sex Roles: A Journal of Research. 1976, December, 2(4), 367-374.

Murray, S. R. Achievement Evaluation: Variations Related to Causal Attribution, Sex, Sex Role, and Outcome. Unpublished manuscript, Howard University, 1976.

Nash, S. C. Conceptions and Concomitants of Sex-Role Stereotyping. Unpublished doctoral dissertation, Columbia University, 1973.

──────. The Relationship Among Sex-Role Stereotyping, Sex-Role Preference, and the Sex Difference in Spatial Visualization. Sex Roles: A Journal of Research, 1975, 1(1), 15-32.

Nelson, H. Y., and Goldman, P. R. Attitudes of High School Students and Young Adults Toward the Gainful Employment of Married Women. Family Coordinator, 1969, 18(3), 251-255.

Nemeth, C., Endicott, J., and Wachtler, J. From the '50s to the '70s: Women in Jury Deliberations. Sociometry, 1976, December, 39(4), 293-304.

Nevin, M. Sex Differences in Participation Rates in Mathematics and Science at Irish Schools and Universities. International Review of Education, 1973, 19(1), 88-91.

Notman, M. T., and Nadelson, C. C. Medicine: A Career Conflict for Women. American Journal of Psychiatry, 1973, October, 130(10), 1123-1127.

Nuthall, G. A. Research Note: Sex in Differences in Ratings of the Occupational Status of Teaching. New Zealand Journal of Educational Studies, 1969, November, 4(2), 170-176.

Nuttall, R. L. Do the Factors Affecting Academic Achievement Differ by the Socioeconomic Status or Sex of the Student? JSAS Catalog of Selected Documents in Psychology, 1972, Summer, 2, 122-123.

O'Carroll, M., and Logan, J. Sex Role as a Mediator of Achievement in Task Performance. Sex Roles: A Journal of Research, 1977, 3, 109-114.

O'Connell, A. N. Relationship Between Life Style and Identity Synthesis and Resynthesis in Traditional, Neotraditional, and Nontraditional Women. Journal of Personality, 1976, December, 44, 675-688.

Oetzel, R. The Relationship Between Sex Role Acceptance and Cognitive Abilities. Unpublished master's thesis, Stanford University, 1961.

Offir, C. Sex of Author Changes Credibility, Study by Harriet Mischel. Psychology Today, 1974, October, 8, 32-3.

O'Hara, R. The Roots of Careers. Elementary School Journal, 1962, February, 62(5), 277-280.

O'Leary, J. A. The Relationship of Sex Role Stereotyping to Self Reinforcement and Reinforcement of Others. Unpublished doctoral dissertation, Ohio University. Dissertation Abstracts International, 1976, April, 36(10-A), 6481-6482.

O'Leary, V. E. Some Attitudinal Barriers to Occupational Aspirations in Women. Psychological Bulletin, 1974, 81(11), 809-826.

Olive, H. Sex Differences in Adolescent Vocational Preferences. Vocational Guidance Quarterly, 1972, 21, 199-201.

Orso, D. P. Comparison of Achievement and Affiliation Arousal on nAch. Journal of Projective Techniques and Personality Assessment, 1969, 33(3), 230-233.

Osawa, M. Sex Differences in Intellectual Abilities. Japanese Psychological Review, 1975, 18(1), 25-38.

Osen, L. The Feminine Math-Tique. Reprint from KNOW, Inc., P. O. Box 86031, Pittsburgh, PA 15221, 1971.

Osipow, S. H. (ed.). Perspective and Issues. In Emerging Woman: Career Analysis and Outlooks. Columbus, OH: Charles E. Merrill, 1975, 147-158.

Otto, L. B., Haller, A. O., and Meier, R. P. High School Students'

Levels of Occupational Aspiration: Variations by Sex, Socioeconomic Status, and Grade in School. Paper presented at the Rural Sociological Society meeting, Maryland, August 1973.

Page, R. H., and Orton, J. Why Do Women Perform Better with Women Than with Men? Paper presented at the American Psychological Association Convention, San Francisco, 1977.

Painter, E. G. Women: The Last of the Discriminated. Journal of the National Association of Women Deans and Counselors, 1971, Winter, 34(2), 59-63.

Panek, P. E., Rush, M. C., and Greenawalt, J. P. Current Sex Stereotypes of 25 Occupations. Psychological Reports, 1977, February, 40(1), 212-214.

Papalia, D. E., and Tennent, S. S. Vocational Aspirations in Preschoolers: A Manifestation of Early Sex Role Stereotyping. Sex Roles: A Journal of Research, 1975, 1(2), 197-199.

Park, C. C. As We Like It: How a Girl Can Be Smart and Still Popular. The American Scholar, 1973, Spring, 42(2), 262-278.

Parlee, M. B. Comments on Roles of Activation and Inhibition in Sex Differences in Cognitive Abilities, by D. M. Broverman, E. L. Klaiber, Y. Kobayashi, and W. Vogel. Psychological Review, 1972, 79, 180-184.

Parsley, K. M., Jr., Powell, M., O'Connor, H. A., and Deutsch, M. Are There Really Sex Differences in Achievement? Journal of Educational Research, 1973, December, 57, 210-212.

Parsons, J. E., Ruble, D. N., Hodges, K. L., and Small, A. W. Cognitive-Developmental Factors in Emerging Sex Differences in Achievement Related Expectancies. Journal of Social Issues, 1976, 32(3), 47-61.

Pavalko, R. M. Aspirants to Teaching: Some Differences Between High School Senior Boys and Girls Planning on a Career of Teaching. Sociology and Social Research, 1965, October, 50(1), 47-62.

Payne, D. A., Wells, R. A., and Clarke, R. R. Another Contribution to Estimating Success in Graduate School: A Search for Sex Differences and Comparison Between Three Degree Types. Educational and Psychological Measurement, 1971, Summer, 31, 497-503.

Peden, I. C. Missing Half of Our Technical Potential: Can We Motivate the Girls? The Mathematics Teacher, 1965, January, 58, 2-13.

Peele, S., and Morse, S. J. The Thrill of Chase: A Study of Achievement Motivation and Dating Behavior. Irish Journal of Psychology, 1973, 2, 65-77.

Peltier, G. L. Sex Differences in the School: Problem and Proposed Solution. Phi Delta Kappan, 1968, 50(3), 182-185.

Pengelly, R. S. A Comparative Study of Academic Self-Estimates, Academic Values and Academic Aspirations of Adolescent Males and Females. Unpublished doctoral dissertation, University of Minnesota. Dissertation Abstracts International, 1974, December, 35(6-A), 3433.

Penn, J. R., and Gabriel, M. E. Role Constraints Influencing the Lives of Women. The School Counselor, 1976, 23, 252-256.

Peplau, L. A., Rubin, Z., and Hill, C. T. The Sexual Balance of Power. Psychology Today, 1976, November, 10, 142.

Peretti, P. O. Sex, Aspiration Level, and Perceptual Discrimination. Social Behavior and Personality, 1974, 2(1), 4-9.

Perney, L. R. The Relationship of Field Dependence-Field Independence with Academic Achievement. Unpublished doctoral dissertation, Case Western Reserve University. Dissertation Abstracts International, 1971, September, 32(3-A), 1342.

Perrone, P. A. Factors Influencing High School Seniors Occupational Preference. Personnel and Guidance Journal, 1964, 42(10), 976-980.

Peterson, R. E. Peer-Conformity and Achievement Motivation as Functions of Sex, Intellectual Ability, and Family Social Status. Unpublished doctoral dissertation, University of California, Berkeley. Dissertation Abstracts, 1963, 24(3), 1272-1273.

Pheterson, G. J., Kiesler, S. B., and Goldberg, P. A. Evaluation of the Performance of Women as a Function of Their Sex, Achievement and Personal History. Journal of Personality and Social Psychology, 1971, 19, 114-118.

Phillips, W. E. The Motive to Achieve in Women as Related to the Perception of Sex Roles in Society. Unpublished doctoral dissertation, University of Maryland. Dissertation Abstracts International, 1975, March, 35(9-A), 5934.

Piacente, B. S., Penner, L. A., Hawkins, H. L., and Cohen, S. L. Evaluation of the Performance of Experimenters as a Function of Their Sex and Competence. Journal of Applied Social Psychology, 1974, October-December, 4(4), 321-329.

Pierce, J. V. Sex Differences in Achievement Motivation of Able High School Students. Cooperative Research Project, No. 1097. December 1961. Also available from ERIC (ED003041), 1966.

_____, and Bowman, P. H. Motivation Patterns of Superior High School Students. Cooperative Research Monograph, 1960, (2), 33-36.

Piliavin, J. A., and Martin, R. R. Playing Dumb and Stroking: The Effects of Opposite Sex on Group Participation. Unpublished manuscript, 1974.

Plant, W. T., and Southern, M. L. Meaningfulness of Sex Differences in Selected Interest-Values Test Scores. Paper presented at the American Psychological Association Convention, San Francisco, 1977.

Pleck, J. H. Male Threat from Female Competence. Journal of Consulting and Clinical Psychology, 1976, August, 44(4), 608-613.

Poffenberger, T., and Norton, D. Sex Differences in Achievement Motive in Mathematics as Related to Cultural Change. Journal of Genetic Psychology, 1963, 103, 341-350.

Pogrebin, L. C. So You Want to Be a Doctor! Seventeen, 1975, June, 34, 110-111+.

Pollis, N. P., and Doyle, D. C. Sex-Role Status and Perceived Competence Among First Graders. Perceptual and Motor Skills, 1972, 34, 235-238.

Porter, J. Sex-Role Concepts, Their Relationship to Psychological Well-Being and to Future Plans in Female College Seniors. Unpublished doctoral dissertation, University of Rochester. Dissertation Abstracts, 1967, 28(5-A), 1903.

Powell, M., and Bloom, V. Development of and Reasons for Vocational Choices of Adolescents Through the High School Years. Journal of Educational Research, 1962, 56, 126-133.

Prather, J. Why Can't Women Be More Like Men? A Summary of the Sociopsychological Factors Hindering Women's Advancement in the Professions. American Behavioral Scientist, 1971, November, 15(2), 172-182.

Pratt, A. B. Exploring Stereotypes of Popular and Unpopular Occupations Among Women-In-General. Journal of Vocational Behavior, 1975, 6(2), 145-164.

Prenter, I. L., and Stewart, R. A. Educational and Vocational Aspirations of New Zealand Adolescent Girls, in Relation to Achievement and Motivation. New Zealand Journal of Educational Studies, 1972, May, 7(1), 38-44.

Profant, P. M. Sex Differences and Sex Role Stereotypes as Related to Professional Career Goals. Unpublished doctoral dissertation, Ohio State University. Dissertation Abstracts International, 1969, 30(1-B), 388-389.

Rand, L. Masculinity or Femininity? Differentiating Career-Oriented and Homemaking-Oriented College Freshmen Women. Journal of Counseling Psychology, 1968, 15(5), 444-450. Also in A. Theodore (ed.), The Professional Woman. Cambridge, MA: Schenkman, 1971, 156-166.

Rapoport, A., and Chammah, A. M. Sex Differences in Factors Contributing to the Level of Cooperation in the Prisoner's Dilemma Game. Journal of Personality and Social Psychology, 1965, 2(6), 831-838.

Rapoport, R., and Rapoport, R. N. Men, Women, and Equity. The Family Coordinator, 1975, October, 24, 421-432.

Rebecca, M., Oleshansky, B., Hefner, R., and Nordin, V. D. Polarized Sex Roles as a Model of the Process of Sex Discrimination: Transcending Sex Roles as a Model of the Future. Final Report. Washington, D.C.: National Institute of Education, 1976.

Red, S. B., McCary, J. L., and Johnson, B. A Study of the Relationship between Aspirational Levels and Academic Achievement. Journal of Educational Research, 1962, 55, 159-163.

Reid, I., and Cohen, L. Male and Female Achievement Orientation and Intellectual Responsibility: A British Validation Study. Educational and Psychological Measurement, 1974, Summer, 34(2), 379-382.

Reiter, R. G. Sex and the Single Field. Measurement and Evaluation in Guidance, 1975, April, 8(1), 51-54.

Reschly, D. J. Consistency of Self-Reinforcement Rates Over Different Tasks; and Sex, Task Success, and Ability as Determinants of Rates of Self-Reinforcement. The Psychological Record, 1973, 23, 237-242.

Rey, L. D. Sex and the Aspiration Formation Process. Unpublished doctoral dissertation, University of Notre Dame. Dissertation Abstracts International, 1976, May, 36(11-A), 7675.

Rice, R. W. Sex Role Definition--Attitudes toward Marriage and Careers of Teacher-Trainees as Compared to Married Couples. Unpublished doctoral dissertation, Indiana University. Dissertation Abstracts International, 1973, 34(9-A), 6142. Also available from ERIC (ADG74-07015), 1973.

Rich, N. A. Effects of Competition on Impressions of Same and Opposite Sex Workers. Dissertation Abstracts International, 1971, 32(2-B), 1256.

Richards, J. M., Jr. Life Goals of American College Freshmen. Journal of Counseling Psychology, 1966, Spring, 13, 12-20.

Richardson, M. S., and Alpert, J. L. Role Perceptions of Educated

Adult Women: An Exploratory Study. Educational Gerontology, 1976, April-June, 1(2), 171-185.

Rodin, J. Menstruation, Reattribution, and Competence. Journal of Personality and Social Psychology, 1976, 33(3), 345-353.

Rohlen, J. M., and Yoesting, D. R. Congruency between Occupational Aspirations and Attainments of Iowa Young People. Rural Sociology, 1968, 33(2), 207-213.

Rose, H. A., and Elton, C. F. Sex and Occupational Choice. Journal of Counseling Psychology, 1971, 18(5), 456-461.

Rosen, B., and Jerdee, T. H. The Influence of Sex-Role Stereotypes on Evaluations of Male and Female Supervisory Behavior. Journal of Applied Psychology, 1973, February, 57(1), 44-48.

_____, and _____. Influence of Sex-Role Stereotypes on Personnel Decisions. Journal of Applied Psychology, 1974, 59, 9-14.

_____, and _____. Effects of Applicant's Sex and Difficulty of Job on Evaluations of Candidates for Managerial Positions. Journal of Applied Psychology, 1974, August, 59(4), 511-512.

Rosen, J. Why Haven't Women Become Great Composers? Hi Fi, 1973, February, 22, 46-53.

Rosen, R. A. Occupational Role Innovators and Sex Role Attitudes. Journal of Medical Education, 1974, June, 49(6), 554-561.

Rossi, A. S. Ambivalence in Women: Should We Plan for the Real or the Ideal? Adult Leadership, 1967, September, 16(3), 100-103.

_____. Barriers to the Career Choice of Engineering, Medicine, or Science among American Women. In J. M. Bardwick (ed.), Readings on the Psychology of Women. New York: Harper & Row, 1972, 72-82.

Ruble, D. N., Frieze, I. H., and Parsons, J. E. (eds.). Sex Roles: Persistence and Change. Special Issue. Journal of Social Issues, 1976, 32(3).

_____, and Higgins, E. T. Effects of Group Sex Composition on Self-Presentation and Sex-Typing. Journal of Social Issues, 1976, 32(3), 125-132.

_____, and Nakamura, C. Y. Task Orientation Versus Social Orientation in Young Children and Their Attention to Relevant Social Cues. Child Development, 1972, 43, 471-480.

Rutledge, C., and Andreasen, V. K. Socio-Demographic Variables and Women's Issues. Unpublished manuscript, Louisiana State University, Baton Rouge, 1977.

Sacks, S. R., and Eisenstein, H. Feminism and Psychological Autonomy: A Study in Decision-Making. Symposium presentation at the American Psychological Association Convention, Washington, D. C., 1976.

Sader, M., and Specht, H. Leistung, Motivation und Leistungsmotivation: Korrelationsstatistische Untersuchungen zur Leistungsmotivmessung nach Heckhausen. [Achievement, Motivation and Achievement Motivation: A Statistical Correlational Investigation of the Measurement of Achievement Motivation According to Heckhausen.] Archiv für die Gesamte Psychologie, 1967, 119(1-2), 90-130.

Saegert, S., and Hart, R. The Development of Sex Differences in the Environmental Competence of Children. In P. Burnett (ed.), Women in Society. Chicago: Maaroufa Press, 1976.

Safilios-Rothschild, C. A Cross-Cultural Examination of Women's Marital, Familial, Educational and Occupational Options. Acta Sociologica, 1971, Spring, (14$\frac{1}{2}$), 96-113.

St. Peter, S. Jack Went Up the Hill but Where Was Jill? Paper presented at the Society for Research in Child Development meeting, New Orleans, 1977.

Saleh, S. D., and Lalljee, M. Sex and Job Orientation. Personnel Psychology, 1969, 22(4), 465-471.

Saltzstein, H. D., and Ast, S. The Influence of Males and Females on the Psychophysical Judgments of Females. Journal of Psychology, 1975, July, 90(2), 259-268.

Sampson, E. E. Achievement in Conflict. Journal of Personality, 1963, 31(4), 510-516.

Sanders, E. B. What Do Young Women Want? In D. Gottlieb (ed.), Youth in Contemporary Society. Beverly Hills: Sage, 1973.

Sanders, M. K. Proposition for Women. Harper's Magazine, 1960, September, 221(1324), 41-48. Discussion. 1960, November, 221(1326), 6+. More discussion in K. M. Bryne, E. Harback, and P. McGinley. The Redundant Housewife. America, 1961, March 25, 104, 812-814. Continued discussion. State of the Question. America, 1961, April 29, 105, 218-219.

Sandidge, S., and Friedland, S. J. Sex Role-Taking and Aggressive Behavior in Children. Paper presented at the Society for Research in Child Development meeting, Philadelphia, March 1973.

Sashkin, M., and Maier, N. R. F. Sex Effects in Delegation. Personnel Psychology, 1971, Autumn, 24(3), 471-476.

Saunders, T. R., and Gravitz, M. A. Sex Differences in the Endorsement of MMPI Critical Items. Journal of Clinical Psychology, 1974, October, 30(4), 557-558.

Schaeffer, D. L., and Eisenberg, J. Cognitive Conflict and Compromise between Males and Females. In D. L. Schaeffer (ed.), Sex Differences in Personality: Readings. Monterey: Brooks/Cole, 1971, 104-115.

Schearer, M. Aspirations and Work Choices of Urban Working Class Men and Women. Symposium presentation at the American Psychological Association Convention, San Francisco, 1977.

Schein, V. E. The Woman Industrial Psychologist: Illusion or Reality? American Psychologist, 1971, August, 26(8), 708-712.

_____. The Relationship between Sex Role Stereotypes and Requisite Management Characteristics. Journal of Applied Psychology, 1973, 59(2), 95-100. Also in F. L. Denmark (ed.), Women--Volume I: A PDI Research Reference Work. New York: Psychological Dimensions, 1976, 393-398.

_____. Relationships between Sex Role Stereotypes and Requisite Management Characteristics Among Female Managers. Journal of Applied Psychology, 1975, June, 60(3), 340-344.

Schell, D. M., Veroff, J., and Schell, R. E. Achievement Motivation and Performance among Second-Grade Boys and Girls. Journal of Experimental Education, 1967, Summer, 35(4), 66-73.

Schersky, R. The Gender Factor in Six- to Ten-Year-Old Children's Views of Occupational Roles. Psychological Reports, 1976, June, 38(3, Pt. 2), 1207-1210.

Schlossberg, N. On the Brink: Your Own Career Decision. Journal of the National Association of Women Deans and Counselors, 1976, Fall, 40(1), 22-26.

_____, and Goodman, J. A Woman's Place: Children's Sex-Stereotyping of Occupations. Vocational Guidance Quarterly, 1972, 20, 266-270. Also in J. Pottker and A. Fishel (eds.), Sex Bias in the Schools--The Research Evidence. Madison, NJ: Fairleigh Dickinson University Press, 1977, 167-172.

Schmidt, L. C. Sex-Roles and Life Styles of Professional Women. Unpublished doctoral dissertation, University of Alberta, 1974.

_____. Sex-Role Attitudes and Differing Life-Styles of Professional Married Women. Canadian Counsellor, 1974, June, 8(3), 197-206.

Schmidt-Relenberg, N. Die Berufstaetigkeit Der Frau in Den Leitbildern Von Abiturientinnen. [The Images of Female High School Graduates Regarding Professional Work for Women.] Soz. Welt, 1965, 16(2), 133-150.

Schmuck, R., and Van Egmond, E. Sex Differences in the Relationship of Interpersonal Perceptions to Academic Performance. Psychology in the Schools, 1965, 2, 32-40.

Schomburg, T. E. A Correlative Study of Body Concept, Academic Achievement, Level of Aspiration, Race and Sex. Unpublished doctoral dissertation, American University. Dissertation Abstracts International, 1975, June, 35(12-A, Pt. 1), 7662.

Schopler, J. An Investigation of Sex Differences in the Influence of Dependence. Sociometry, 1967, March, 30(1), 50-63.

Schroeder, C. C. Sex Differences and Growth Toward Self-Actualization During the Freshman Year. Psychological Reports, 1973, April, 32(2), 416-418.

Schuldt, W. J., and Smee, P. G. Personal Needs of Graduate Students in Psychology. Psychological Reports, 1968, 23(3, Pt. 1), 916.

Schwartz, J. Medicine as a Vocational Choice Among Undergraduate Women. Journal of the National Association of Women Deans and Counselors, 1969, Fall, 33, 7-12.

Scott, A. Sex Differences in Graduate School Survival. Paper presented at the American Sociological Association Convention, New York, 1973.

Scott, C. S., Fenske, R. H., and Maxey, E. J. Change in Vocational Choice as a Function of Initial Career Choice, Interests, Abilities, and Sex. Journal of Vocational Behavior, 1974, October, 5(2), 285-292.

Seaburg, D. Sex Role Stereotype and Occupational Choice. Unpublished manuscript, University of Minnesota, Psychology department, Spring 1974.

Seiden, A. M. Overview: Research on the Psychology of Women: II. Women in Families, Work, and Psychotherapy. American Journal of Psychiatry, 1976, October, 133(10), 1111-1123.

Setzman, E. J. Cooperation and Competition between Men and Women in a Dyadic Game-Playing Situation. Unpublished doctoral dissertation, New York University. Dissertation Abstracts International, 1974, August, 35(2-B), 1109-1110.

Seward, G. H., and Williamson, R. C. A Cross-National Study of Adolescent Professional Goals. Human Development, 1969, 12(4), 248-254.

Sewel, C. Why Waste Our Gifted Women. Coronet, 1961, June, 50, 102-107.

Shaffer, D. R., and Wegley, C. Success Orientation and Sex-Role Congruence as Determinants of the Attractiveness of Competent Women. Journal of Personality, 1974, December, 42(4), 586-600.

Shaw, M. C., and McCuen, J. R. The Onset of Academic Underachievement in Bright Children. Journal of Educational Psychology, 1960, 51(3), 103-108.

Sheehan, T. J. Patterns of Sex Differences in Learning Mathematical Problem Solving. Journal of Experimental Education, 1968, 36, 84-87.

Shepard, W. O., and Hess, D. T. Attitudes in Four Age Groups toward Sex Role Division in Adult Occupations and Activities. Journal of Vocational Behavior, 1975, February, 6(1), 27-39.

Sherman, J. A. Problems of Sex Differences in Space Perception and Aspects of Intellectual Functioning. Psychological Review, 1967, 74, 290-299.

──────. Psychological Sex Differences. In On the Psychology of Women: A Survey of Empirical Studies. Springfield, IL: Charles C. Thomas, 1971, 12-42.

──────. Field Articulation, Sex, Spatial Visualization, Dependency, Practice, Laterality of the Brain, and Birth Order. Perceptual and Motor Skills, 1974, 38(3), part 2, 1223-1235.

──────, and Fennema, E. The Study of Mathematics by High School Girls and Boys: Related Variables. American Educational Research Journal, 1977, Spring, 1(2), 51-71.

Sherman, R. C., and Smith, F. Sex Differences in Cue-Dependency as a Function of Socialization Environment. Perceptual and Motor Skills, 1967, 24, 599-602.

Shields, S. A. Functionalism, Darwinism, and the Psychology of Women. American Psychologist, 1975, 30, 739-754.

Shinar, E. H. Sexual Stereotypes of Occupations. Journal of Vocational Behavior, 1975, 7, 99-111.

Shrigley, R. L. Sex Difference and Its Implications on Attitude and Achievement in Elementary School Science. School Science and Mathematics, 1972, December, 72, 789-793.

Shuval, J. T. Occupational Interests and Sex-Role Congruence. Human Relations, 1963, 16(2), 171-183.

Siegel, C. L. F. Sex Differences in the Occupational Choices of Second Graders. Journal of Vocational Behavior, 1973, 3, 15-19. Also in J. Pottker and A. Fishel (eds.), Sex Bias in the Schools--The Research Evidence. Madison, NJ: Fairleigh Dickinson University Press, 1977, 173-177.

Sigel, I. Sex Differences in Cognitive Functioning Re-Examined: A Functional Point of View. Paper presented at the Society for Research in Child Development meeting, Berkeley, CA, 1964.

Siggins, L. D. Women University Students and Careers. Australian and New Zealand Journal of Psychiatry, 1973, September, 7(3), 142-145.

Singer, J. N. Sex and College Class Differences in Attitudes toward Autonomy in Work. Human Relations, 1974, May, 27(5), 493-499.

_____. Sex Differences-Similarities in Job Preference Factors. Journal of Vocational Behavior, 1974, December, 5(3), 357-365.

Singer, S. L., and Stefflre, B. Sex Differences in Job Values and Desires. In D. L. Schaeffer (ed.), Sex Differences in Personality: Readings. Monterey: CA: Brooks/Cole, 1971, 116-119.

Singleton, D. Sex as a Determinant of Responses to Patient Management Problems by Physicians and Medical Students. Symposium presentation at the American Psychological Association Convention, San Francisco, 1977.

Sinha, S. P. A Study of the Effect of Achievement and Sex on the Direction of Aggression and Reaction-Type. Journal of Psychological Researches, 1973, May, 17(2), 50-53.

Sistrunk, F., and McDavid, J. W. Sex Variable in Conforming Behavior. Journal of Personality and Social Psychology, 1971, 17, 200-207.

Skotko, V., Langmeyer, D., and Lundgren, D. Sex Differences as Artifact in the Prisoner's Dilemma Game. Journal of Conflict Resolution, 1974, December, 18(4), 707-713.

Slee, F. W. The Feminine Image Factor in Girl's Attitudes to School Subjects. British Journal of Educational Psychology, 1968, 38(2), 212-214.

Slocum, W. L., and Bowles, R. T. Attractiveness of Occupations to High School Students. Personnel and Guidance Journal, 1968, April, 46, 754-761.

Slovic, P. Risk-Taking in Children: Age and Sex Differences. Child Development, 1966, 37, 169-176.

Smith, A. D., Kilpatrick, D. G., Sutker, P. B., and Marcotte, D. B. Male Student Professionals: Their Attitudes toward Women, Sex, and Change. Psychological Reports, 1976, August, 39(1), 143-148.

Smith, C. P. (ed.), Achievement Related Motives in Children. New York: Russell Sage, 1969.

_____, and Smith, C. H. Why Don't Women Succeed? New Society, 1972, October, 22, 577-579.

Smith, M. E. The Values Most Highly Esteemed by Men and Women in Who's Who Suggested as One Reason for the Great Difference in Representation of the Two Sexes in Those Books. Journal of Social Psychology, 1962, 58(2), 339-344.

Smith, N. S., Vernon, C. R., and Tarte, R. D. Random Strategies and Sex Differences in the Prisoner's Dilemma Game. Journal of Conflict Resolution, 1975, December, 19(4), 643-658.

Snyder, E. E., and Kivlin, J. E. Perceptions of the Sex Role Among Female Athletes and Non-Athletes. Adolescence, 1977, Spring 12, 23-29.

_____, and Spreitzer, E. Participation in Sport as Related to Educational Expectations Among High School Girls. Sociology of Education, 1977, January, 50, 47-55.

Snyder-Ott, J. Female Experience and Artistic Creativity. Art Education, 1974, September, 27, 15-18.

Solomon, L. Z. Perception of a Successful Person of the Same Sex or the Opposite Sex. Journal of Social Psychology, 1975, 95, 133-134.

Sommers, T., and Curacar, G. The Not-So-Helpless Female. New York: David McKay, 1973.

Sorenson, T. C. A Parade Poll: What Does a Woman Want? Parade, Washington Post, 1973, April 15, 9-11.

Spence, J. T., and Helmreich, R. Who Likes Competent Women? Competence, Sex-Role Congruence of Interests, and Subjects' Attitudes toward Women as Determinants of Interpersonal Attraction. Journal of Applied Social Psychology, 1972, 2, 197-213. Also in Mental Health Digest, 1973, 5(2).

_____, _____, and Stapp, J. Likability, Sex-Role Congruence of Interest, and Competence: It All Depends on How You Ask. Journal of Applied Social Psychology, 1975, 5(2), 93-109.

Spencer, A. G. Why Are There No Woman Geniuses? In J. Stacey, et al. (eds.), <u>And Jill Came Tumbling After: Sexism in American Education</u>. New York: Dell, 1974, 33-36.

Spock, B. Should Girls Expect to Have Careers? <u>Redbook</u>, 1972, March, 138, 50.

Stake, J. E. Effects of Contrived Information of Female and Male Performance on the Achievement Behavior of Preschool Girls and Boys. <u>Journal of Applied Social Psychology</u>, 1976, 6(1), 85-93.

_____, and Stake, M. Performance Self-Esteem and Dominance in Mixed-Sex Dyads. Paper presented at the American Psychological Association Convention, San Francisco, 1977.

Stanford, B. (ed.). What Girls Can Really Be. In <u>On Being Female</u>. New York: Washington Square Press, 1974, 137-151.

Stapp, J., and Pines, A. Career or Family? The Influence of Goals on Liking for a Competent Woman. Paper presented at the Western Psychological Association meeting, Los Angeles, 1976.

Stasz, C., Weinberg, S., and McDonald, F. J. The Influence of Sex of Student and Sex of Teacher on Student's Achievement and Evaluation of the Teacher. JSAS <u>Catalog of Selected Documents in Psychology</u>, 1974, 4, 54.

Stein, A. H. The Influence of Social Reinforcement on the Achievement Behavior of Fourth Grade Boys and Girls. <u>Child Development</u>, 1969, 40, 727-736.

_____. The Effects of Sex-Role Standards for Achievement and Sex-Role Preference on Three Determinants of Achievement Motivation. <u>Developmental Psychology</u>, 1971, 4(2), 219-231.

_____, Pohly, S. R., and Mueller, E. Sex-Typing of Achievement Areas as a Determinant of Children's Motivation and Effort. Paper presented at the Society for Research in Child Development meeting, Santa Monica, CA, March 1969.

_____, and Smithells, J. Age and Sex Differences in Children's Sex Role Standards About Achievement. <u>Developmental Psychology</u>, 1969, 1, 252-259.

Steinbacher, R., and Gilroy, F. D. Persuasibility and Persuasiveness as a Function of Sex. <u>Journal of Social Psychology</u>, 1976, December, 100(2), 299-306.

Steinberg, B., and Amidon, A. Who Wants to Play Doctor: Sex-Role Stereotyping Among Preschoolers. Paper presented at the American Psychological Association Convention, Washington, D. C., 1976.

Steinmann, A., and Fox, D. J. Specific Areas of Agreement and Conflict in Women's Self-Perception and Their Perception of Men's Ideal Woman in Two South American Urban Communities and an Urban Community in the United States. Journal of Marriage and the Family, 1969, 31(2), 281-289.

_____, and Rappaport, A. Self-Achieving Versus Family Orientation of "Professional-Liberated" Women. Paper presented at the American Psychological Association Convention, Miami, FL, 1970.

Stericker, A. B., and Johnson, J. E. Sex-Role Identification and Self-Esteem in College Students: Do Men and Women Differ? Sex Roles: A Journal of Research, 1977, 3(1), 19-26.

Stewart, A. J. Power Arousal and Thematic Apperception in Women. Symposium presentation at the American Psychological Association Convention, Chicago, 1975.

_____, and Winter, D. G. Arousal of the Power Motive in Women. Journal of Consulting and Clinical Psychology, 1976, 44, 495-496.

Stillion, J. M. Different but Equal: A Look at the Current State of the Psychology of Women. Western Carolina University Journal of Education, 1974, Fall, 6(2), 9-15.

Stingle, S. F. Age and Sex Differences in the Cooperative and Competitive Behavior of Children. Unpublished doctoral dissertation, Columbia University, 1973.

Strainchamps, E. Plight of the Intellectual Girl. Saturday Review. 1960, November 19, 43, 63-64+.

Stringer, P. Masculinity-Femininity as a Possible Factor Underlying the Personality Responses of Male and Female Art Students. British Journal of Social and Clinical Psychology, 1967, 6(3), 186-194.

Suchner, R. W., and More, D. M. Stereotypes of Males and Females in Two Occupations. Journal of Vocational Behavior, 1975, 6(1), 1-8.

Suls, J., and Gastorf, J. W. Comparison Choices of Adolescents Evaluating Sex- and Age-Related Abilities. Symposium presentation at the American Psychological Association Convention, San Francisco, 1977.

Sundheim, B. J. M. The Relationships Among "N" Achievement, "N" Affiliation, Sex-Role Concepts, Academic Grades, and Curricular Choice. Unpublished doctoral dissertation, Columbia University. Dissertation Abstracts, 1963, 23(9), 3471.

Suter, B. A. Masculinity-Femininity in Creative Women. Unpublished doctoral dissertation, Fordham University. *Dissertation Abstracts International*, 1971, October, 32(4-B), 2411.

_____, and Domino, G. Masculinity-Femininity in Creative College Women. *Journal of Personality Assessment*, 1975, August, 39(4), 414-420.

Sutton-Smith, B., and Savasta, M. Sex Differences in Play and Power. Paper presented at the Eastern Psychological Association meeting, Boston, 1972.

Swanson, M. A., and Tjosvold, D. W. Effects of Sex and Unequal Competence on Performance and Self-Presentation. Paper presented at the American Psychological Association Convention, San Francisco, 1977.

Synge, J. Scottish Regional and Sex Differences in School Achievement and Entry to Further Education. *Sociology*, 1973, January, 7(1), 107-116.

Tamir, P. The Relationship between Achievement in Biology and Cognitive Preference Styles in High School Students. *British Journal of Educational Psychology*, 1976, February, 46(1), 57-67.

Tangri, S. S. Role-Innovation in Occupational Choice among College Women. Unpublished doctoral dissertation, University of Michigan. *Dissertation Abstracts International*, 1970, 30(9-A), 4021.

_____. Implied Demands Character of the Wife's Future and Role-Innovation: Patterns of Achievement Orientation among Women. JSAS *Catalog of Selected Documents in Psychology*, 1974, 4, 12. Also in M. T. S. Mednick, et al. (eds.), *Women and Achievement: Social and Motivational Analyses.* New York: Halsted Press, 1975, 239-254.

Tavris, C., and Offir, C. Sex Differences, Real and Imagined. In *The Longest War: Sex Differences in Perspective.* New York: Harcourt Brace Jovanovich, 1977, 29-56.

_____, and _____. *The Longest War: Sex Differences in Perspective.* New York: Harcourt Brace Jovanovich, 1977.

Taylor, P. L. The Role of Sex-Stereotypes in Matching Self-Concepts and Job Concepts. Unpublished doctoral dissertation, Catholic University of America. *Dissertation Abstracts International*, 1975, June, 35(12-B), 6118-6119.

Taylor, S. E. College Women's Evaluation of Other Women as a Function of Congruence of Intellectual or Social Role Motives. *Connecticut College Psychology Journal*, 1967, 4, 25-32.

Taylor, S. P., and Epstein, S. Aggression as a Function of the Interaction of the Sex of the Aggressor and the Sex of the Victim. Journal of Personality, 1967, 35, 474-486.

_____, and Smith, I. Aggression as a Function of Sex of Victim and Male Subject's Attitude toward Women. Psychological Reports, 1974, December, 35(3), 1095-1098.

Taynor, J., and Deaux, K. When Women Are More Deserving than Men: Equity, Attribution and Perceived Sex Differences. Journal of Personality and Social Psychology, 1973, 28, 360-367.

_____, and _____. Equity and Perceived Sex Differences: Role Behavior as Defined by the Task, the Mode, and the Actor. Journal of Personality and Social Psychology, 1975, 32, 381-390.

Tedeschi, J. T., Lindskold, S., Horai, J., and Gahagan, J. P. Social Power and the Credibility of Promises. Journal of Personality and Social Psychology, 1969, 13, 253-261.

TenElshof, A., and Mehl, D. Academic Achievement in College Women. Journal of the National Association for Women Deans, Administrators, and Counselors, 1976, February, 40(1), 7-10.

Thagaard, S. T. Sex Differences in Academic Behavior. Acta Sociologica, 1971, 14(1-2), 59-67.

Thomas, G. P., and Garvin, A. D. Sex Differences in Risk-Taking on Essay Tests. Journal of the Student Personnel Association for Teacher Education, 1973, September, 12(1), 32-36.

Thomas, H. B. The Effects of Sex, Occupational Choice and Career Development Responsibility on the Career Maturity of Ninth Grade Students. Paper presented at the American Education Research Association meeting, Chicago, 1974. Also available from ERIC (ED092819), 1974.

Thompson, E. G. An Experimental Study of Aggression Habit Patterns and Sex-Role. Dissertation Abstracts, 1965, 26(10), 6161.

Thurber, S. The Achievement Motivation-Performance Relationship as Moderated by Sex-Role Attitudes. Educational and Psychological Measurement, 1976, Winter, 36(4), 1075-1077.

Tittle, C. K., and Chitayat, D. Sex-Role Factors in Career Decision Making. Symposium presentation at the American Psychological Association Convention, San Francisco, 1977.

Tobias, S. Math Anxiety: What It Is and What Can Be Done About It. MS., 1976, September, 5(3), 56-59+.

Todd, F. J., Terrell, G., and Frank, C. E. Differences between Normal and Underachievers of Superior Ability. In M. Kornrich (ed.), Underachievement. Springfield, IL: Charles C. Thomas, 1965, 399-414.

Tomlinson-Keasey, C. Role Variables: Their Influence on Female Motivational Constructs. Journal of Counseling Psychology, 1974, 21(3), 232-237.

Torrance, E. P. Changing Reactions of Preadolescent Girls to Tasks Requiring Creative Scientific Thinking. Journal of Genetic Psychology, 1963, 102, 217-223.

_____. Creative Young Women in Today's World. Exceptional Children, 1972, April, 38, 597-603.

Touhey, J. C. Effects of Additional Women Professionals on Ratings of Occupational Prestige and Desirability. Journal of Personality and Social Psychology, 1974, 29, 86-89.

_____. Effects of Additional Men on Prestige and Desirability of Occupations Typically Performed by Women. Journal of Applied Social Psychology, 1974, October-December, 4(4), 330-335.

Trembly, D. Age and Sex Differences in Creative Thinking Potential. Paper presented at the American Psychological Association Convention, 1964.

Trent, J. W., and Medsker, L. L. Beyond High School: A Psychosociological Study of 10,000 High School Graduates. San Francisco: Jossey-Bass, 1968.

Tresemer, D. Measuring 'Sex Differences.' Sociological Inquiry, 1975, 45, 29-32.

Tucker, B. Z. Feminine Sex-Role and Occupational Choice: A Study of Self and Intergroup Perceptions of Three Groups of Women. Unpublished doctoral dissertation, Temple University. Dissertation Abstracts International, 1971, May, 31(11-A), 5783-5784.

Tukey, R. S. Intellectually-Oriented and Socially-Oriented Superior College Girls. Journal of the National Association for Women Deans, Administrators, and Counselors, 1964, Spring, 27, 120-127.

Turner, R. H. Some Aspects of Women's Ambition. American Journal of Sociology, 1964, 70(3), 271-285.

Turnure, C. Cognitive Development and Role-Taking Ability in Boys and Girls from 7-12. Developmental Psychology, 1975, March, 11(2), 202-209.

Tyler, L. Sex Differences in Vocational Interests and Motivation

Related to Occupations. Testimony before the Federal Commerce Commission, Washington, D.C., August 1972.

Uesugi, T. T., and Vinacke, W. E. Strategy in a Feminine Game. Sociometry, 1963, 26, 75-88.

Unger, R. K., and Denmark, F. L. (eds.). Woman: Dependent or Independent Variable? New York: Psychological Dimensions, 1975.

_____, and Krooth, D. M. Female Role Perception and Attitudes toward Competence as Related to Activism in Housewives. Paper presented at the American Psychological Association Convention, New Orleans, 1974.

_____, Raymond, B. J., and Levine, S. M. Are Women a "Minority" Group? Sometimes! International Journal of Group Tensions, 1974, March, 4(1), 71-81. Also in F. L. Denmark, (ed.), Women: Volume I: A PDI Research Reference Work. New York: Psychological Dimensions, 1976, 431-446.

Unkel, E. A Study of the Interaction of Socioeconomic Groups and Sex Factors with the Discrepancy between Anticipated Achievement and Actual Achievement in Elementary School Mathematics. Arithmetic Teacher, 1966, 13, 662-670.

Valentine, D., Ellinger, N., and Williams, M. Sex-Role Attitudes and the Career Choices of Male and Female Graduate Students. Vocational Guidance Quarterly, 1975, 24(1), 48-53.

Valle, V. A., and Koeske, G. F. Sex Differences in the Relationship of POI Self-Actualization to Other Adjustment and Maturity Measures. Paper presented at the American Psychological Association Convention, New Orleans, 1974.

Vaughter, R. M., Ginorio, A. B., and Trilling, B. A. The Failure of Trait Theories to Predict Success. SIGNS: Journal of Women in Culture and Society, 1977, 2(3), 664-674.

_____, Gubernick, D., Matossian, J., and Haslett, B. Sex Differences in Academic Expectations and Achievement. Paper presented at the American Psychological Association Convention, New Orleans, 1974.

Veldman, D. J. Effects of Sex, Aptitudes and Attitudes on the Academic Achievement of College Freshmen. Journal of Educational Measurement, 1968, 5, 245-249.

_____. Correlates of Visual Acuity in College Freshmen. Journal of Perceptual and Motor Skills, 1970, April, 30(2), 551-558.

Veroff, J. Measuring the Achievement Motive in Young Boys and Girls. Unpublished manuscript, University of Michigan, 1966.

_____. Process Versus Impact in Men's and Women's Achievement Motivation. Psychology of Women Quarterly, 1977, Spring, 1(3), 283-293.

_____, Feld, S., and Crockett, H. Explorations into the Effects of Picture Cues on Thematic Apperceptive Expression of Achievement Motivation. Journal of Personality and Social Psychology, 1966, 3(2), 171-181.

Vetter, L. B. A Factor Analytic Study of the Attitudes toward Work of High School Senior Girls. Unpublished doctoral dissertation, Ohio State University. Dissertation Abstracts International, 1969, 30(1-A), 143.

Vinacke, W. E., and Bond, J. R. Coalitions in Mixed-Sex Triads. Sociometry, 1961, 24, 61-75.

Vogel, S. R., and Rosenkratz, P. S. Sex-Role Self-Concepts and Life Style Plans of Young Women. Journal of Consulting and Clinical Psychology, 1975, 43, 427.

Wagman, M. Sex and Age Differences in Occupational Values. Personnel and Guidance Journal, 1965, November, 44, 258-262.

Wahrman, R., and Pugh, M. D. Sex, Nonconformity, and Influence. Sociometry, 1974, 37(1), 137-147.

Walberg, H. J. Physics, Femininity, and Creativity. Developmental Psychology, 1969, 1(1), 47-54.

Wallston, B. S. The Effects of Sex-Role Ideology, Self-Esteem, and Expected Future Interactions with an Audience on Male Help Seeking. Sex Roles: A Journal of Research, 1976, 2(4), 353-365.

Walsh, D. K. Sex-Role Differentiation in Problem-Solving Groups. Unpublished doctoral dissertation, New York University. Dissertation Abstracts International, 1975, January, 35(7-B), 3569.

Walster, E., and Pate, M. A. Why Are Women So Hard on Women? In S. Cox (ed.), Female Psychology: The Emerging Self. Chicago: Science Research Associates, 1976, 394-399.

Ware, C. K. Cooperation and Competition in Children: A Developmental Study of Behavior in Prisoner's Dilemma and Maximizing Differences Games. Unpublished manuscript, Yale University, New Haven, 1969.

Warrior, B. Sex Roles and Their Consequences: Research in Female and Male Differences. No More Fun and Games: A Journal of Female Liberation, 1969, February, 2, 21-31.

Weinberg, E., and Rooney, J. F. The Academic Performance of

Women Students in Medical School. *Journal of Medical Education*, 1973, March, 48, 240-247.

Weinberg, J. R. The Effects of Degree and Personalization of Failure on Performance. *Personnel Journal*, 1960, 28, 266-278.

Weiner, B. Effects of Unsatisfied Achievement-Related Motivation on Persistence and Subsequent Performance. Unpublished doctoral dissertation, University of Michigan. *Dissertation Abstracts*, 1964, 24(12), 5581-5582.

_____. Achievement Motivation and Task Recall in Competitive Situations. *Journal of Personality and Social Psychology*, 1966, June, 3(6), 693-696.

_____, Johnson, P. B., and Mehrabian, A. Achievement Motivation and the Recall of Incompleted and Completed Exam Questions; Zeigarnik Effect and Interrupted Learning. *Journal of Educational Psychology*, 1968, June, 59(3), 181-185.

Weisman, C. S., Morlock, L. L., Sack, D. G., and Levine, D. M. Sex Differences in Response to a Blocked Career Pathway among Unaccepted Medical School Applicants. *Sociology of Work and Occupations*, 1976, May, 3(2), 187-208.

Weiss, P. Some Aspects of Femininity. Unpublished doctoral dissertation, University of Colorado. *Dissertation Abstracts*, 1962, 23, 1083.

Weissman, E. I. The Relationship between the Marital Status, Feminine Identity Conflict, and Self-Actualization of Women Doctoral Students. Unpublished doctoral dissertation, Boston University. *Dissertation Abstracts International*, 1974, December, 35(6-A), 3441.

Weisstein, N. Woman as Nigger. In H. H. Frank (ed.), *Women in the Organization*. Philadelphia: University of Pennsylvania Press, 1977, 234-240.

Weitzenkorn, S. D. An Adjusted Measure of Achievement Motivation for Males and Females and Effects of Future Orientation on Level of Performance. *Journal of Research in Personality*, 1974, 8, 361-377.

Welsh, G. S. On the Relationship of the California Psychological Inventory's Femininity Measure and Intelligence. *Journal of Counseling Psychology*, 1973, May, 20, 269-271.

Werts, C. E. Sex Differences in College Attendance. *Research Reports*, Vol. 2, No. 6. Evanston, IL: National Merit Scholarship, 1966.

_____. A Comparison of Male Versus Female College Attendance

Probabilities. Sociology of Education, 1968, Winter, 41, 103-110.

West, S. D., Jr. Attitudes of High School Teachers, Principals, Guidance Counselors, Librarians, and Teacher Educators Toward the Social, Educational, and Economic Roles of Women. Unpublished doctoral dissertation, University of Florida, 1975.

Wexley, K, and Hunt, P. Male and Female Leaders: Comparison of Performance and Behavior Patterns. Psychological Reports, 1974, 35, 867-872.

What Should a Girl Do about College? Changing Times, 1962, April, 16, 35-38.

White, K. Male Reactions to Success and Failure in Sex-Linked Careers. Symposium presentation at the American Psychological Association Convention, San Francisco, 1977.

White, R. F. Female Identity and Work Roles: The Case of Nursing. Unpublished doctoral dissertation, University of Chicago, 1964. Also available from ERIC (AD602-58237), 1964.

―――. Female Identity and Career Choice: The Nursing Case. In A. Theodore (ed.), The Professional Woman. Cambridge, MA: Schenkman, 1971, 275-289.

White, W. F., and McConnell, J. Affective Responses and School Achievement Among 8th Grade Boys and Girls. Journal of Perceptual and Motor Skills, 1974, June, 38(3, Pt. 2), 1295-1301.

Whiteside, M. What Happens to the Gifted Girl? PTA Magazine, 1974, February, 68, 20-21.

Wiegers, R. M., and Frieze, I. H. Gender, Female Traditionality, Achievement Level and Cognitions of Success and Failure, Psychology of Women Quarterly, 1977, Winter, 2(2), 125-137.

Wiley, M. G. Sex Roles in Games. Sociometry, 1973, 36, 526-541.

Williams, C. Does Different Equal Less? A High School Woman Speaks Out. In D. Gersoni-Stavn (ed.), Sexism and Youth. New York: R. R. Bowker, 1974, 83-87.

Williams, J. A. Sex Role Conflict and Academic Achievement: A Study of Superior Women Students. Unpublished doctoral dissertation, University of Illinois. Dissertation Abstracts International, 1971, June, 31(12-A), 6419-6420.

Williams, T. H. Educational Aspirations: Longitudinal Evidence on Their Development in Canadian Youth. Sociology of Education, 1972, Spring, 45(2), 107-133.

Wills, B. S. Personality Variables which Discriminate Between Groups Differing in Level of Self-Actualization. Journal of Counseling Psychology, 1974, May, 21(3), 222-226.

Wilson, B. O., Lee, D., and Quisenberry, D. Measures of Stereotype toward College Women Physical Education Majors. Physical Educator, 1974, October, 31(3), 140-142.

Wilson, D. W., and Kahn, A. Rewards, Costs, and Sex Differences in Helping Behavior. Psychological Reports, 1975, February, 36(1), 31-34.

Wilson, K. M. Today's Women Students: New Outlooks and New Challenges. Journal of College Student Personnel, 1975, September, 16(5), 376-381.

Wilson, V. An Analysis of Femininity in Nursing. American Behavioral Scientist, 1971, 15(2), 213-220.

Winsberg, S., and Ste-Marie, L. Correlation of Motivation and Academic Achievement in Physics: Merritt College Motivation Inventory. Journal of Research in Science Teaching, 1976, July, 13, 325-329.

Winter, D. G. Power Motives and Power Behavior in Women. Symposium presentation at the American Psychological Association Convention, Chicago, 1975.

Wisenthal, M. Sex Differences in Attitudes and Attainment in Junior Schools. British Journal of Educational Psychology, 1965, 35, 79-85.

Witkin, M. H. The Relationship between Personality Factors and Attitudes toward Women's Roles and the Career Aspirations of Female College Students. Dissertation Abstracts International, 1973, 34(A), 1664-1665.

Wittig, M. A. Sex Differences in Intellectual Functioning: How Much of a Difference Do Genes Make? Sex Roles: A Journal of Research, 1976, 2(1), 63-74.

Witty, P. A. Study of Pupils' Interests, Grades 9, 10, 11, 12. Education, 1961, 82, 169-174.

Wolfgang, M. What Price Women's 'Equality?' Dissent, 1971, June, 18(3), 265-266+.

Wolman, C., and Frank, H. No Place for a Woman. Behavior Today, 1972, 3(48), 2.

Women Are Their Own Worst Friends. Science Digest, 1976, August, 80(2), 8-9.

Wozencraft, M. Are Boys Better Than Girls in Arithmetic? The Arithmetic Teacher, 1963, 10, 486-490.

Wyer, R. S., Jr. Behavioral Correlates of Academic Achievement: Conformity under Achievement- and Affiliation-Incentive Conditions. Journal of Personality and Social Psychology, 1967, 6(3), 255-263

_____, Henninger, M., and Wolfson, M. Informational Determinants of Females' Self-Attributions and Observers' Judgments of Them in an Achievement Situation. Journal of Personality and Social Psychology, 1975, September, 32(3), 556-570.

_____, and Malinowski, C. Effects of Sex and Achievement Level upon Individualism and Competitiveness in Social Interaction. Journal of Experimental Social Psychology, 1972, 8, 303-314.

_____, and Terrell, G. Social Role and Academic Achievement. Journal of Personality and Social Psychology, 1965, 2(1), 117-121.

_____, Weatherley, D. A., and Terrell, G. Social Role, Aggression, and Academic Achievement. Journal of Personality and Social Psychology, 1965, 1(6), 645-649.

Wylie, R. C., and Hutchins, E. B. Schoolwork Ability Estimates and Aspirations as a Function of Socioeconomic Level, Race, and Sex. Psychological Reports, 1967, Monographic Supplement 3-V21.

Yasinski, L. Achievement Motivation in College Women; You Can't See the Forest for the Trees. Unpublished master's thesis, Wake Forest University, Winston-Salem, NC, 1975.

Yerby, J. Attitude, Task, and Sex Composition as Variables Affecting Female Leadership in Small Problem-Solving Groups. Speech Monographs, 1975, June, 42(2), 160-168.

Yonge, G. D. The Use of Masculinity-Femininity Measures to Account for Sex Differences in Problem Solving. California Journal of Education Research, 1961, 12, 208-212.

_____. Sex Differences in Cognitive Functioning as a Result of Experimentally Induced Frustration. Journal of Experimental Education, 1964, 32, 275-280.

Young, D. M., Beier, E. G., Beier, P., and Barton, C. Is Chivalry Dead? Sex-Role' Preferences and the Display of Aggressive Behavior between the Sexes. Journal of Communication, 1975, Winter, 25(1), 57-64.

Young, R. K., Williams, M., and Wrather, N. Competence and Sex as Attitudinal Determinants. Paper presented at the American Psychological Association Convention, San Francisco, 1977.

Zanna, M. P. Intellectual Competition and the Female Student. Final Report. Washington, D. C.: U S. Department of Health, Education, and Welfare, 1973 Also available from ERIC (ED 072389), 1973.

_____, Goethals, G. P., and Hill, J. F. Evaluating a Sex Related Ability: Social Comparison with Similar Others and Standard Setters. Journal of Experimental Social Psychology, 1975, January, 11(1), 86-93.

Zellman, G. L. The Role of Structural Factors in Limiting Women's Institutional Participation. Journal of Social Issues, 1976, 32(3), 33-46.

Zimmerman, J., and Levin, P. Intellectual Performance of Women in Direct Competition with Men. Symposium presentation at the American Psychological Association Convention, Washington, D. C., 1976.

Zuckerman, D. M. Self-Concept, Family Background, and Personal Traits which Predict the Life Goals and Sex-Role Attitudes of Technical College and University Women. Unpublished doctoral dissertation, Ohio State University, 1977.

Zunich, M. Children's Reactions to Failure. Journal of Genetic Psychology, 1964, 104, 19-24.

C. FAMILY BACKGROUND, PARENTAL INFLUENCE, ROLE MODELS

Abel, H., and Gingles, R. Life Goals of Parents for Children. Journal of Home Economics, 1965, November, 57, 734-735.

Adams, B. N., and Meidam, M. T. Economics, Family Structure, and College Attendance. American Journal of Sociology, 1968, 74(3), 230-239.

Adams, E. B., and Sarason, I. G. Relation between Anxiety in Children and Their Parents. Child Development, 1963, 34, 237-246.

Adams, R. L., and Phillips, B. N. Motivational and Achievement Differences Among Children of Various Ordinal Birth Positions. Child Development, 1972, March, 43, 155-164.

Adilman, P. H. Mary Ann and Mother: An Adolescent's Turmoil to Individuate. Adolescence, 1974, Summer, 9, 199-220.

Almquist, E. M., and Angrist, S. S. Career Salience and Atypicality of Occupational Choice Among College Women. Journal of Marriage and the Family, 1970, May, 32(2), 242-249.

_____, and _____. Role Model Influences on College Women's Career Aspirations. Merrill-Palmer Quarterly, 1971, July, 17(3), 263-279.

Alper, T. G., and Greenberger, E. Relationship of Picture Structure to Achievement Motivation to College Women. Journal of Personality and Social Psychology, 1967, 7(4, Pt. 1), 362-371.

Altman, S. L. Women's Career Plans and Maternal Employment. Unpublished doctoral dissertation, Boston University. Dissertation Abstracts International, 1975, January, 35(7-B), 3569.

Anastasi, A., and Schaefer, C. E. Biographical Correlates of Artistic and Literary Creativity in Adolescent Girls. Journal of Applied Psychology, 1969, 53(4), 267-278.

Anderson, R. C., Mawby, R. G., Miller, J. A., and Olson, A. L. Parental Aspirations: A Key to the Educational and Occupational Achievements of Youth. Adult Leadership, 1965, May, 14(1), 8-10.

Angrist, S. S. Sources of Influence on Women's Career Aspirations: Family, College, and Self. Paper prepared for the School of Urban and Public Affairs, Carnegie-Mellon University, Pittsburgh, 1970.

_____. Variations in Women's Adult Aspirations During College. Journal of Marriage and the Family, 1972, 34(3), 465-468.

_____, and Almquist, E. M. Women Use Role Models for Adult Life. In Careers and Contingencies. New York: Dunellen, 1975, 147-168.

Astin, A. W. Personal and Environmental Factors Associated with College Dropouts Among High Aptitude Students. Journal of Educational Psychology, 1964, 55, 219-227.

_____. Socio-economic Factors in the Achievements and Aspirations of the Merit Scholar. Personnel and Guidance Journal, 1964, 42, 581-586.

Astin, H. S. Personal and Environmental Factors in Career Decisions of Young Women. Washington, D. C.: Bureau of Social Science Research, 1970.

_____. Sex Differences in Mathematical and Scientific Precocity. In J. C. Stanley, et al. (eds.), Mathematical Talent: Discovery, Description and Development. Baltimore: Johns Hopkins University Press, 1974, 70-87. Also in Journal of Special Education, 1975, Spring, 9(1), 79-91.

Balazs, E. K. Psycho-Social Study of Outstanding Female Athletes. Research Quarterly, 1975, October, 46(3), 267-273. Also in

E. K. Balazs, Quest of Excellence: A Psycho-Social Study of Female Olympic Champions. Waldwick, NJ: Hoctor Products for Education, 1975.

Bancke, L. L. Background Antecedents of Aggressiveness and Assertiveness Found in Academically Achieving Women. Unpublished doctoral dissertation, University of Cincinnati. Dissertation Abstracts International, 1972, 33(6-B), 2800.

Banducci, R. The Effect of Mother's Employment on the Achievement Aspirations, and Expectations of the Child. Personnel and Guidance Journal, 1967, 46(3), 263-267.

Banker, J. Attitudes and Parental Role Orientations of Married Professional Women and the Self-Concept of Their Children. Unpublished manuscript, University of Michigan, Ann Arbor, 1974.

Baruch, G K. Maternal Influences Upon College Women's Attitudes Toward Women and Work. Developmental Psychology, 1972, January, 6(1), 32-37.

_____. Maternal Role Pattern as Related to Self-Esteem and Parental Identification in College Women. Paper presented at the Eastern Psychological Association Meeting, Boston, 1972.

_____. Feminine Self-Esteem, Self-Ratings of Competence, and Maternal Career Commitment. Journal of Counseling Psychology, 1973, September, 20(5), 487-488.

_____. Correlates of Girls' Evaluation of Their Competence. Unpublished manuscript, Worchester Foundation for Experimental Biology, Shrewsbury, MA, 1974.

_____. Maternal Career-Orientation as Related to Parental Identification in College Women. Journal of Vocational Behavior, 1974, April, 4(2), 173-180.

_____. Maternal Influences Upon Girls' Evaluation of Their Competence. Unpublished manuscript, Worchester Foundation for Experimental Biology, Shrewsbury, MA, 1974.

_____. Girls Who Perceive Themselves as Competent: Some Antecedents and Correlates. Psychology of Women Quarterly, 1976, 1, 38-49.

Baumrind, D. The Development of Instrumental Competence Through Socialization. In A. D. Pick (ed.), Minnesota Symposia on Child Psychology: (VII). Minneapolis: University of Minnesota Press, 1973, 3-46.

_____, and Black, A. E. Socialization Practices Associated

with Dimensions of Competence in Preschool Boys and Girls. Child Development, 1967, 38, 291-327.

Bayer, A. E. The College Drop-Out: Factors Affecting Senior College Completion. Sociology of Education, 1968, Summer, 41(3), 305-316.

Bennett, W. S., and Gist, N. P. Class and Family Influences on Student Aspirations. Social Forces, 1964, 43, 167-173.

Berman, G., and Eisenberg, M. Psycho-Social Aspects of Academic Achievement. American Journal of Orthopsychiatry, 1971, April, 41(3), 406-415.

Bernstein, B. E., and Grambs, J. Sex and Academic Field in Relation to Birth Order and Achievement. Psychological Reports, 1976, October, 39(2), 659-663.

Bertsch, D. P. Parental Influence in College Selection. Student Personnel Association for Teacher Education, 1968, 7(1), 9-14.

Besdine, M. Mrs. Oedipus Has Daughters, Too. Psychology Today, 1971, March, 4(10), 62-65.

_____. The Jocasta Complex, Mothering and Women Geniuses. Psychoanalytic Review, 1971, Spring, 58(1), 51-74.

Bieri, J. Paternal Identification, Acceptance of Authority, and Within-Sex Differences in Cognitive Behavior. Journal of Abnormal and Social Psychology, 1960, 60, 76-79.

Biller, H. B. Paternal and Sex-Role Factors in Cognitive and Academic Functioning. Nebraska Symposium on Motivation, 1973, 21, 83-123.

Bing, E. Effect of Childrearing Practices on Development of Differential Cognitive Abilities. Child Development, 1963, 34, 631-648.

Blau, Z. S. Maternal Aspirations, Socialization, and Achievement of Boys and Girls in the White Working Class. Journal of Youth and Adolescence, 1972, March, 1(1), 35-57.

Blaubergs, M. S. Overcoming the Sexist Barriers to Gifted Women's Achievement. In B. Johnson (ed.), Advantage/Disadvantage Gifted. Ventura, CA: Ventura County Superintendent of Schools Office, 1979.

Bledsoe, J. C. Comparison of Interests of Urban Disadvantaged Boys and Girls. Psychological Reports, 1975, June, 36(3), 932-934.

Bloom, A. R. Achievement Motivation and Occupational Choice:

A Study of Adolescent Girls. Unpublished doctoral dissertation, Bryn Mawr College, 1971.

Bordua, D. J. Educational Aspirations and Parental Stress on College. Social Forces, 1960, 38, 262-269.

Bragg, B. W. E. Academic Primogeniture and Sex-Role Contrast of the Second-Born. Journal of Individual Psychology, 1970, 26(2), 196-199.

Brogan, D., and Kutner, N. G. Measuring Sex-Role Orientation: A Normative Approach. Journal of Marriage and the Family, 1976, February, 38(1), 31-40.

Brook, J. S., Whiteman, M., Peisach, E., and Deutsch, M. Aspiration Levels of and for Children: Age, Sex, Race, and Socioeconomic Correlates. Journal of Genetic Psychology, 1974, March, 124(1), 3-16.

Bruce, J. A. The Role of Mothers in the Social Placement of Daughters: Marriage or Work. Journal of Marriage and the Family, 1974, August, 36(3), 492-497.

Bryan, W. E. A Comparison of the Career Orientation of College Women in Contrasting Majors. Unpublished doctoral dissertation, Wayne State University, Detroit, MI, 1968.

Burlin, F. D. Occupational Aspirations of Adolescent Females. Paper presented at the Association of Women in Psychology meeting, February 1976. Also available from ERIC (ED124838), 1969.

_____. The Relationship of Parental Education and Maternal Work and Occupational Status to Occupational Aspiration in Adolescent Females. Journal of Vocational Behavior, 1976, August, 9(1), 99-104.

Butler, R. R., and Baird, A. W. Status Projections of Lower Social Strata Pre-Adolescents: A Focus on Some Intervening Social Psychological Factors. Paper presented at the Association of Southern Agricultural Workers meeting, Atlanta, February 1973. Also available from ERIC (ED071796), 1976.

Callard, E. D. Achievement Motive of Four-Year-Olds and Maternal Achievement Expectancies. The Journal of Experimental Education, 1968, Summer, 36, 14-23.

Carlson, N. L. Occupational Choice and Achievement of Women Graduate Students in Psychology as a Function of Early Parent-Child Interactions and Achievement as Related to Birth Order and Family Size. Unpublished doctoral dissertation, University of Kansas. Dissertation Abstracts International, 1970, December, 31(6-A), 2679.

Carney, R. E., and McKeachie, W. J. Religion, Sex, Social Class, Probability of Success and Student Personality. Journal of Science and the Study of Religion, 1963, October, 3(1), 32-42.

Carrigan, W. C., and Julian, J. W. Sex and Birth Order Differences in Conformity as a Function of Need Affiliation Arousal. Journal of Personality and Social Psychology, 1966, 3, 479-483.

Cartwright, L. K. Women in Medical School. Unpublished doctoral dissertation, University of California, Berkeley. Dissertation Abstracts International, 1971, April, 31(10-B), 6237.

Chance, J. E. Mother-Child Relations and Children's Achievement. United States Public Health Terminal Report, Washington, D. C., 1968.

Chodorow, N. Family Structure and Feminine Personality. In M. Z. Rosaldo and L. Lamphere (eds.), Woman, Culture and Society. Stanford: Stanford University Press, 1974, 43-66.

Christopher, S. A. Parental Relationship and Value Orientation as Factors in Academic Achievement. Personnel and Guidance Journal, 1967, 45(9), 921-925.

Clark, E. T. Culturally Disadvantaged Boys' and Girls' Aspirations to and Knowledge of White-Collar and Professional Occupations. Urban Education, 1965, 1(3), 164-174.

_____. Status Level of Occupations Chosen and Rejected by Middle and Lower Class Boys and Girls. Psychological Reports, 1965, 17(1), 301-302.

_____. Influence of Sex and Social Class on Occupational Preference and Perception. Personnel and Guidance Journal, 1967, 45(5), 440-444.

Constantinople, A. Analytical Ability and Perceived Similarity to Parents. Psychological Reports, 1974, December, 35(3), 1335-1345.

Cook, B. I. Role Aspirations as Evidenced in Senior Women. Unpublished doctoral dissertation, Purdue University. Dissertation Abstracts, 1968, 28(6-A), 2067.

Cottle, T. J. Family Perceptions, Sex Role Identity and the Prediction of School Performance. Educational and Psychological Measurement, 1968, 28(3), 861-886.

_____. Of Parents, Children, and Higher Education. In College-Reward and Betrayal. Chicago: University of Chicago Press, 1977, 15-35.

Crandall, V. J., Dewey, R., Katkovsky, W., and Preston, A. Parents' Attitudes and Behaviors and Grade-School Children's Academic Achievements. Journal of Genetic Psychology, 1964, 104, 53-66.

_____, Katkovsky, W., and Preston, A. A Conceptual Formulation for Some Research on Children's Achievement Development. Child Development, 1960, 31, 787-797.

_____, Preston, A., and Rabson, A. Maternal Reactions and the Development of Independence and Achievement Behavior in Young Children. Child Development, 1960, 31, 243-251.

Crescimbeni, J. Broken Homes Affect Academic Achievement. Education, 1964, 84, 440-441.

Cristo, M. G. Factors Influencing Career Mobility and Career Attainment of Women in the Field of Education. Unpublished doctoral dissertation, University of Virginia. Dissertation Abstracts International, 1975, 36(6-A), 4034.

Crowne, D. P. Family Orientation, Level of Aspiration, and Interpersonal Bargaining. Journal of Personality and Social Psychology, 1966, 3, 641-645.

_____, Conn, L. K., Marlowe, D., and Edwards, C. N. Some Developmental Antecedents of Level of Aspiration. Journal of Personality, 1969, 37(1), 73-92.

Davis, J. A. Undergraduate Career Decisions. Chicago: Aldine, 1965.

DePree, S. The Influence of Parental Achievement Expectations and Role Definitions on Achievement Motive Development in Girls. Unpublished Honors thesis, University of Michigan, Ann Arbor, 1962.

Dixon, P. W., Fukuda, N. K., and Ignacio, R. Prediction of Post-High School Destination Choice from Curriculum, Financial Need, and Students' Rating of Parents' Wishes for Post-High School Occupation. Journal of Experimental Education, 1972, Winter, 41, 18-22.

Dodson, E. A. The Effects of Female Role Models on Occupational Exploration and Attitudes of Adolescents. Unpublished doctoral dissertation. Dissertation Abstracts International, 1974, June, 34(12-A), 7535.

Doss, C. Parental Influence on Career Ambitions of Fourth Grade Pupils. Education, 1975, Winter, 96, 165-167.

Douvan, E. The Role of Models in Women's Professional Development. Psychology of Women Quarterly, 1976, 1, 5-20.

Eisenman, R., and Platt, J. J. Birth Order and Sex Differences in Academic Achievement and Internal-External Control. Journal of General Psychology, 1968, 78(2), 279-285.

Elder, G. H., Jr. Family Structure and Educational Attainment. A Cross-National Analysis. American Sociological Review, 1965, 30, 81-96.

Eliasberg, A. Are You Hurting Your Daughter Without Knowing It? Family Circle, 1971, February, 38+. Also in W. Martin (ed.), The American Sisterhood. New York: Harper & Row, 1972, 308-312.

Elliott, E. D. Effects of Female Role Models on Occupational Aspiration Levels of College Freshman Women. Unpublished doctoral dissertation, University of Missouri-Columbia. Dissertation Abstracts International, 1973, 34(3-A), 1075.

Entwisle, D. R., and Hayduk, L. A. Academic Expectations and the School Attainment of Young Children. Unpublished manuscript, Johns Hopkins University, Department of Social Relations, Baltimore, 1977.

Epstein, A. S., and Radin, N. Motivational Components Related to Father Behavior and Cognitive Functioning in Preschoolers. Child Development, 1976, December, 46(4), 831-839.

Eyde, L. D. Work Values and Background Factors as Predictors of Women's Desire to Work. Doctoral dissertation, Ohio State University. Dissertation Abstracts, 1960, March, 20, 3829. Published as Bureau of Business Research Monograph, no. 8 Columbus: Bureau of Business Research, College of Commerce and Administration, Ohio State University, 1962.

Farley, F. H., Smart, K. L., and Brittain, C. V. Implications of Birth Order for Motivational and Achievement-Related Characteristics of Adults Enrolled in Non-Traditional Instruction. Journal of Experimental Education, 1974, Spring, 42(3), 21-24.

Farley, J. Maternal Employment and Child Behavior. Cornell Journal of Social Relations, 1968, 3(2), 58-71.

Farmer, H. S. Why Women Contribute Less to the Arts, Sciences, and Humanities. Paper presented at the American Educational Research Association meeting, San Francisco, 1976.

Ferdinand, W. [On the Marks of Children of Working Mothers (And Two Supplementary Observations).] Psychologie in Erziehung und Unterricht, 1975, 22(3), 190-194.

Finlayson, D. S. Parental Aspirations and the Educational Achievement of Children. Educational Research, 1971, November, 14 61-64.

Fischer, A. The Importance of Sibling Position in the Choice of a

Career in Pediatric Nursing. Journal of Health and Human Behavior, 1962, 3(4), 283-288.

Fischer, E. H., Wells, C. F., and Cohen, S. L. Birth Order and Expressed Interest in Becoming a College Professor. Journal of Counseling Psychology, 1968, 15(2), 111-116.

Fontana, G. L. An Investigation into the Dynamics of Achievement Motivation of Women. Unpublished doctoral dissertation, University of Michigan. Dissertation Abstracts International, 1971, 32(3-B), 1821.

Foster, A. Home Environment and Performance in School; Premise and Home Environment Health Survey. School and Society, 1972, April, 100, 236-237.

Fox, R. B. The Relationship of Achievement Motivation to Sex, Achievement, Intelligence, Socioeconomic Status, and Level of Educational Aspiration for an Eighth-Grade Group. Dissertation Abstracts International, 1969, 30(4-A), 1331-1332.

Francis, B. R. Effect of Maternal Employment on the Socialization of Sex-Role and Achievement in New Zealand. Dissertation Abstracts International, 1975, 35(4-A), 2452.

Frerking, R A. Occupational Status of the Mother as a Determinant of Achievement Motivation in Women. Unpublished doctoral dissertation, University of Alabama. Dissertation Abstracts International, 1975, May, 35(11-B), 5616.

Gadbois, C. [Career Orientation: Family and Professional Plans Among Young Girls During Their Training.] Bulletin de Psychologie, 1973-1974, 27(10-12), 622-628.

Ginn, F W. Career Motivation and Role Perception of Women as Related to Parental Role Expectation and Parental Status Discrepancy. Unpublished doctoral dissertation, Catholic University of America. Dissertation Abstracts, 1969, 29(12-B), 4845.

Ginzberg, E., Berg, I. E., Brown, C. A., Herma, J. L., Yohalem, A. M., and Gorelick, S. Life Styles of Educated Women. New York: Columbia University Press, 1966.

_____, and Yohalem, A. M. Educated American Women: Life Styles and Self-Portraits. New York: Columbia University Press, 1966.

Gitter, A. G., Altavela, J., and Mastofsky, D. I. Effect of Sex, Religion, and Ethnicity on Occupational Status Perception. Journal of Applied Psychology, 1974, February, 59, 96-98.

Goldstein, R. L. Effects of Reinforcement and Female Career Role Models on the Vocational Attitudes of High School Girls. Unpublished doctoral dissertation, Boston University. *Dissertation Abstracts International*, 1975, September, 36(3-A), 1304.

Goodale, J. G., and Hall, D. T. Inheriting a Career: The Influence of Sex, Values, and Parents. *Journal of Vocational Behavior*, 1976, February, 8(1), 19-30.

Grandy, T. G., and Stahmann, R. F. Family Influence on College Students' Vocational Choice: Predicting Holland's Personality Types. *Journal of College Student Personnel*, 1974, September, 15(5), 404-409.

_____, and _____. Types Produce Types: An Examination of Personality Development Using Holland's Theory. *Journal of Vocational Behavior*, 1974, October, 5(2), 231-239.

Grebow, H. The Relationship of Some Parental Variables to Achievement and Values in College Women. *Journal of Educational Research*, 1973, January, 66(5), 203-209.

Green, L. B., and Parker, H. J. Parental Influences Upon Adolescents' Occupational Choice: A Test of an Aspect of Roe's Theory. *Journal of Counseling Psychology*, 1965, 12(4), 379-383.

Groth, N. J. Differences in Parental Environment Needed for Degree Achievement for Gifted Men and Women. *Gifted Child Quarterly*, 1971, Winter, 15(4), 256-261.

Gurman, A. S. Role of the Family in Underachievement. *Journal of School Psychology*, 1969, September, 16, 385-389.

Gysbers, N. C., Johnston, J. A., and Gust, T. Characteristics of Homemaker and Career-Oriented Women. *Journal of Counseling Psychology*, 1968, 15(6), 541-546.

Haas, M. B., and Britton, J. H. Competition in Children as Related to Maternal Acceptance. *Journal of Home Economics*, 1961, March, 53, 179-184.

Halpin, G., Scott, O., and Halpin, G. Biographical Factors Related to Academic Achievement. *Psychological Reports*, 1973, August, 33(1), 321-322.

Hansen, A. H. The Relationship of Personality Factors to Academic Achievement in College. Unpublished doctoral dissertation, Brigham Young University. *Dissertation Abstracts International*, 1970, 30(8-A), 3277-3278.

Hanson, J. T. Ninth Grade Girls' Vocational Choices and Their Parents' Occupational Level. *Vocational Guidance Quarterly*, 1965, 13(4), 261-264.

Harmon, L. W. Variables Related to Women's Persistence in Educational Plans. *Journal of Vocational Behavior*, 1972, April, 2(2), 143-153.

Harrison, F. Aspirations as Related to School Performance and Socioeconomic Status. *Sociometry*, 1968, 32(1), 70-79.

Haven, E. W. Selected Community, School, Teacher, and Personal Factors Associated with Girls Electing to Take Advanced Academic Mathematics Courses in High School. Unpublished doctoral dissertation, University of Pennsylvania. *Dissertation Abstracts International*, 1971, 32(A), 1747.

Healey, R. E. Parental Behavior as Related to Children's Academic Achievement. Unpublished doctoral dissertation, Catholic University of America. *Dissertation Abstracts International*, 1974, August, 35(2-B), 1020.

Heilbrun, A. B., Jr. Parental Identification and the Patterning of Vocational Interests in College Males and Females *Journal of Counseling Psychology*, 1969, 16(4), 342-347.

_____, and Gillard, B. J. Perceived Maternal Child-rearing History and Motivational Effects of Social Reinforcements in Females. *Perceptual and Motor Skills*, 1966, 23(2), 439-446.

_____, Harrell, S. N., and Gillard, B. J. Perceived Child-Rearing Attitudes of Fathers and Cognitive Control in Daughters. *Journal of Genetic Psychology*, 1967, 111, 29-40.

_____, _____, and _____. Perceived Maternal Child-Rearing Patterns and the Effects of Social Nonreaction Upon Achievement Motivation. *Child Development*, 1967, 38(1), 267-281.

_____, Kleemeier, C., and Piccola, G. Developmental and Situational Correlates of Achievement Behavior in College Females. *Journal of Personality*, 1974, September, 42(3), 420-436.

_____, and Waters, D. B. Underachievement as Related to Perceived Maternal Child Rearing and Academic Conditions of Reinforcement. *Child Development*, 1968, 39(3), 913-921.

Helson, R. Personality Characteristics and Developmental History of Creative College Women. *Genetic Psychology Monographs*, 1967, 76, 205-256.

_____. Effects of Sibling Characteristics and Parental Values on Creative Interest and Achievement. *Journal of Personality*, 1968, 36(4), 589-607.

_____. Women Mathematicians and the Creative Personality. *Journal of Counseling and Clinical Psychology*, 1971, 36(2), 210-220. Also in J. M. Bardwick (ed.), *Readings on the Psychology of Women*. New York: Harper & Row, 1972, 93-101.

Hennig, M. Family Dynamics for Developing Positive Achievement Motivation in Women: The Successful Woman Executive. In R. B. Kundsin (ed.), Women and Success: The Anatomy of Achievement. New York: William Morrow, 1974, 88-93.

Heretick, D M. L., Vorwerk, K. E., Feldman, R. S., and Plovsky, G. Modeling Effects in Male and Female Performance and Expectations. Paper presented at the American Psychological Association Convention, San Francisco, 1977.

Hermans, H. J. M., ter Laak, J. J. F., and Maes, P. C. J. M. Achievement Motivation and Fear of Failure in Family and School. Developmental Psychology, 1972, 6(3), 520-528.

Hess, R. D., and Shipman, V. C. Maternal Influences Upon Early Learning. In R. D. Hess and R. M. Baer (eds.), Early Education. Chicago: Aldine, 1968, 91-103.

Hetherington, M. A Developmental Study of the Effects of Sex of the Dominant Parent on Sex-Role Preference, Identification, and Imitation in Children. Journal of Personality and Social Psychology, 1965, 2, 188-194.

Hill, A. H. Autobiographical Correlates of Achievement Motivation in Men and Women. Psychological Reports, 1966, 18(3), 811-817.

Hilton, T. L, and Berglund, G. W. Sex Differences in Mathematics Achievement--a Longitudinal Study. Educational Testing Service Research Bulletin, 1971.

Hjelle, L. A., and Smith, G. Self-Actualization and Retrospective Reports of Parent-Child Relationships Among College Females. Psychological Reports, 1975, June, 36(3), 755-761.

Hoffman, L. W. Effects of Maternal Employment on the Child. Child Development, 1961, March, 32, 187-197.

──────. Mother's Enjoyment of Work and Effects on the Child. In F. I. Nye and L. W. Hoffman (eds.), The Employed Mother in America. Chicago: Rand McNally, 1963.

──────. Early Childhood Experiences and Women's Achievement Motives. Journal of Social Issues, 1972, 28(2), 129-155. Also in School Psychology Digest, 1973, Summer, 2(3), 18-23; and in R. K. Unger and F. L. Denmark (eds.), Woman: Dependent or Independent Variable? New York: Psychological Dimensions, 1975, 723-750.

──────. Effects of Maternal Employment on the Child: A Review of the Research. Developmental Psychology, 1974, 10, 204-228. Also in A. G. Kaplan and J. P. Bean (eds.), Beyond Sex-Role Stereotypes: Readings Toward a Psychology of Androgyny. Boston: Little, Brown, 1976, 293-318.

Hohman, D. W., Rounds, J. B., Jr., Dawis, R. V., and Lofquist, L. H. Biographical Factors Related to Vocational Needs: Sex Differences. Poster Session presented at the American Psychological Association Convention, San Francisco, 1977.

Holder, R. L. Sex, Social Class and Student Performance. University Quarterly, 1970, Spring, 24, 166-172.

Hollenbeck, G. P. Conditions and Outcomes in the Student-Parent Relationship. Journal of Consulting Psychology, 1965, 29, 237-241.

Honzik, M. P. Environmental Correlates of Mental Growth: Prediction from the Family Setting at 21 Months. Child Development, 1967, June, 38, 337-364.

House, G. F. Orientations to Achievement: Autonomous, Social Comparison, and External. Unpublished doctoral dissertation, University of Michigan. Dissertation Abstracts International, 1973, 34(A), 2027.

Husen, T. Ability, Opportunity and Career; a 26 Year Follow-Up. Educational Research, 1968, June, 10(3), 170-184. Also in School Review, 1968, June, 76, 190-209.

Hutner, F. C. Mother's Education and Working: Effect on the School Child. Journal of Psychology, 1972, 82, 27-37.

Jackson, P. W. On Middle-Class Children's Feelings and Concepts Regarding School and the Motives Behind Their School Achievement. In Life in Classrooms. New York: Holt, Rinehart and Winston, 1968, 41-81.

Jain, D. C. Vocational Choices of Ninth Class Students. Rajasthan University Studies, 1964-1965, 6, 55-63.

Janes, G. D. Student Perceptions, Parent Perceptions, and Teacher Perceptions of Student Abilities, Aspirations, Expectations, and Motivations: Their Relationship to Under- and Over-Achievement. Unpublished doctoral dissertation, University of Iowa. Dissertation Abstracts International, 1971, March, 31(9-A), 4548-4549.

Johanson, A. J. Factors Related to Career Choice by Women Physical Education Majors and Implications for Early Recruitment. Dissertation Abstracts, 1968, 28(10-A), 3986-3987.

Johnson, B. L., and Kilmann, P. R. The Relationship between Recalled Parental Attitudes and Internal-External Control. Journal of Clinical Psychology, 1975, January, 31(1), 40-42.

Johnson, R. W. Parental Identification and Vocational Interests of College Women. Measurement and Evaluation in Guidance, 1970, 3(3), 147-151.

Johnson, Z. C. Parental Childrearing Attitudes and the Development of Achievement Motivation in Daughters. Unpublished doctoral dissertation, Boston University. Dissertation Abstracts International, 1974, August, 35(2-B), 1051.

Johnston, J. R. Family Interaction Patterns and Career Orientation in Late Adolescent Females. Unpublished doctoral dissertation, Boston University. Dissertation Abstracts International, 1974, July, 35(1-B), 509.

Jones, J. B., Lundsteen, S. W., and Michael, W. B. The Relationship of the Professional Employment Status of Mothers to Reading Achievement of Six-Grade Children. California Journal of Educational Research, 1967, 18(2), 102-108.

Kaminski, D. M., et al. Why Females Don't Like Mathematics: The Effect of Parental Expectations. Paper presented at the American Sociological Association meeting, New York, 1976. Also available from ERIC (ED134530), 1977.

Kane, R. D. et al. A Study of the Factors Influencing the Participation of Women in Non-Traditional Occupations in Postsecondary Area Vocational Training Schools. Washington, D C.: Bureau of Occupational and Adult Education, 1977.

Kandel, D. B., and Lesser, G. S. Parental and Peer Influences on Educational Plans of Adolescents. American Sociological Review, 1969, 34, 213-223.

Karman, F. J. Women: Personal and Environmental Factors in Role Identification and Career Choice. Unpublished doctoral dissertation, University of California, Los Angeles. Dissertation Abstracts International, 1972, October, 33(4-A), 1440. Also available from ERIC (ED084383), 1973.

Katkovsky, W., Crandall, V. C, and Good, S. Parental Antecedents of Children's Beliefs in Internal-External Control of Reinforcements in Intellectual Achievement Situations. Child Development, 1967, 38(3), 765-776.

_____, Preston, A., and Crandall, V. J. Parents Attitudes Toward Their Personal Achievements and Toward the Achievement Behaviors of Their Children. Journal of Genetic Psychology, 1964, 104(1), 67-82.

Keil, W., and Keil-Specht, H. Leistungsmotivation und Erziehungstile: Eine Familienuntersuchung [Achievement Motivation and Educational Styles: An Investigation of Families]. Zeitschrift für Entwicklungspsychologie und Pädagogische Psychologie, 1970, 2(4), 241-256.

Kenyon, G. S. The Significance of Physical Activity as a Function of Age, Sex, and Socio-Economic Status of Northern U. S. Adults. International Review of Sport Sociology, 1966, 1, 41-58.

Khan, S. B. Sex Differences in Predictability of Academic Achievement. Measurement and Evaluation in Guidance, 1973, July, 6(2), 88-92.

Kinnane, J. E., and Bannon, M. M. Perceived Parental Influence and Work-Value Orientation. Personnel and Guidance Journal, 1964, 43(3), 273-279.

Klein, R B., and Snyder, F. A. Non-Academic Characteristics and Academic Achievement. Journal of College Student Personnel, 1969, 10, 328-332.

Klemmack, D. L., and Edwards, J. N. Women's Acquisition of Stereotyped Occupational Aspirations. Sociology of Social Research, 1973, July, 57(4), 510-525.

Knudson, E. G. Public Health Nurses' Interest in Occupational Achievement. Nursing Research, 1968, 17(4), 327-335.

Krieger, S. F. Need Achievement and Perceived Parental Child-Rearing Attitudes of Career Women and Homemakers. Unpublished doctoral dissertation, Ohio State University. Dissertation Abstracts International, 1972, May, 32(11-B), 6621.

_____. Nach and Perceived Parental Child-Rearing Attitudes of Career Women and Homemakers. Journal of Vocational Behavior, 1972, 2, 419-432.

Kriesberg, L. Rearing Children for Educational Achievement in Fatherless Families. Journal of Marriage and the Family, 1967, 29(2), 288-301.

Krippner, S. Junior High School Students' Vocational Preferences and Their Parents' Occupational Levels. Personnel and Guidance Journal, 1963, 41, 590-595.

Kundsin, R. B. (ed.). Women and Success: The Anatomy of Achievement. New York: William Morrow, 1974.

Lakshminarayana, H. D. Parental Aspirations for Education and Occupation to Their Children in a South Indian Community. Indian Journal of Social Research, 1972, August, 13(2), 136-143.

Landers, D. A. Sibling-Sex-Status and Ordinal Position of Female Physical Education Majors and Their Sport Participation and Interests. Unpublished doctoral dissertation, University of Illinois, 1968.

_____. Sibling-Sex-Status and Ordinal Position Effects' on Females' Sport Participation and Interests. Journal of Social Psychology, 1970, 80, 247-248.

_____. Sibling-Sex and Ordinal Position as Factors in Sport Participation. Paper presented at the Third International Symposium on Sociology of Sport, Waterloo, Ontario, August 1971.

Lansky, K. K. Reported Parental Behavior and Subsequent Achievement in Males and Females. Unpublished doctoral dissertation, Ohio University. Dissertation Abstracts International, 1975, February, 35(8-B), 4183-4184.

Lansky, L. M., Crandall, V. J., Kagan, J., and Baker, C. T. Sex Differences in Aggression and Its Correlates in Middle-Class Adolescents. Child Development, 1961, 32, 45-58.

Larsen, M. S. Female Achievement Conflict Related to Parental Sex-Typing and Identification. Unpublished doctoral dissertation, Michigan State University. Dissertation Abstracts International, 1970, 30(10-B), 4794-4795.

LaRussa, G. Parental Androgyny and Career Orientation: Mother Didn't Work. Symposium presentation at the American Psychological Association Convention, San Francisco, 1977.

Lee, B. L., and King, P. Vocational Choices of Ninth Grade Girls and Their Parents' Occupational Levels. Vocational Guidance Quarterly, 1964, 12(3), 163-167.

LeMay, M. Birth Order and Scholastic Aptitude and Achievement. Journal of Consulting and Clinical Psychology, 1970, 34(2), 287.

Levine, A. G. Marital and Occupational Plans of Women in Professional Schools: Law, Medicine, Nursing, Teaching. Unpublished doctoral dissertation, Yale University, 1968.

LeVine, R. A. Parental Goals: A Cross-Cultural View. Teachers College Record, 1974, December, 76, 226-239.

Levitt, E. S. A Study of Four Career Patterns and Associated Life History Characteristics Among Female Professional Librarians. Unpublished doctoral dissertation, New York University. Dissertation Abstracts International, 1971, January, 31(7-B), 4381.

_____. Vocational Development of Professional Women: A Review. Journal of Vocational Behavior, 1971, October, 1(4), 375-385.

Lozoff, M. M. Fathers and Autonomy in Women. In R. B. Kundsin (ed.), Women and Success: The Anatomy of Achievement. New York: William Morrow, 1974, 103-109.

Lueptow, L. B. Parental Status and Influence and the Achievement Orientations of High School Seniors. Sociology of Education, 1975, Winter, 48(1), 91-110.

Lynn, D. B. Curvilinear Relation Between Cognitive Functioning and

Distance of Child from Parent of the Same Sex. Psychological Review, 1969, 76(2), 236-240.

McClure, R. F. Birth Order, Income, Sex, and School Related Attitudes. Journal of Experimental Education, 1971, Summer, 39, 73-74.

McDill, E. L., and Coleman, J. Family and Peer Influences in College Plans of High School Students. Sociology of Education, 1965, Winter, 38, 112-126.

MacDonald, A. P., Jr. Internal-External Locus of Control: Parental Antecedents. Journal of Consulting and Clinical Psychology, 1971, 37(1), 141-147.

McLaughlin, G. W., Hunt, W. K., and Montgomery, J. R. Socioeconomic Status and Career Aspirations and Perceptions of Women Seniors in High School. Vocational Guidance Quarterly, 1976, December, 25(2), 155-162.

McPherson, L. I. The Effects of Social Class on Females' Perceptions of Traditional Sex-Role Adherence in Occupations. Unpublished doctoral dissertation, Arizona State University. Dissertation Abstracts International, 1971, March, 31(9-A), 4467.

Maimon, P. D. The Influence of Child Rearing Practices on the Development of Need for Achievement. Unpublished doctoral dissertation, Texas Technical University. Dissertation Abstracts International, 1973, February, 33(8-B), 3952.

Manley, R. O. Parental Warmth as Related to Sex Differences in Children's Achievement Orientation. Paper presented at the American Educational Research Association meeting, Washington, D. C., 1975. Also available from ERIC (ED113633), 1976.

──────. Parental Warmth and Hostility as Related to Sex Differences in Children's Achievement Orientation. Psychology of Women Quarterly, 1977, Spring, 1(3), 229-246.

Marino, C. D., and McCowan, R. J. The Effects of Parent Absence on Children. Child Study Journal, 1976, 6(3), 165-182.

Martin, D. [Self-Image, Performance and Professional Choice Among Female Engineering Students.] Bulletin de Psychologie, 1972-1973, 26(17-18), 954-960.

Martin, S. The Effect of Perceived Parental Influence on Need Achievement of Women in Traditional and Non-traditional Academic Majors. Unpublished doctoral dissertation, University of Oklahoma. Dissertation Abstracts International, 1975, October, 36(4-A), 2106.

Medvene, A. M. Occupational Choice of Graduate Students in Psychology as a Function of Early Parent-Child Interactions. *Journal of Counseling Psychology*, 1969, September, 16, 385-389.

Miller, S. J. Parent Child Relations and Women's Achievement Orientations. Paper presented at the American Sociological Association meeting, New York, 1973. Also available from ERIC (ED084487), 1974.

Miller, S. R. An Investigation of the Relationship between Mothers' General Fearfulness, Their Daughters' Locus of Control and General Fearfulness in the Daughter. Unpublished doctoral dissertation, New York University. *Dissertation Abstracts International*, 1974, November, 35(5-B), 2281.

Mintz, E. The Prejudice of Parents. In F. L. Denmark (ed.), *Who Discriminates Against Women?* (Issue 15). Beverly Hills: Sage, 1974, 9-23. Also in *International Journal of Group Tensions*, 1974, March, 4(1), 6-20.

Monson, R. G. The Relationship Between Nuclear Family Structure and Female Achievement. Unpublished doctoral dissertation, University of Florida, 1972. *Dissertation Abstracts International*, 1974, 34(6-A), 3578. Also available from ERIC (ADG73-29195), 1972.

Morris, L. D. A Socio-Psychological Study of Highly Skilled Women Field Hockey Players. *International Journal of Sport Psychology*, 1975, 6(3), 134-147.

Mowsesian, R., Heath, B. R., and Rothney, J. W. Superior Students' Occupational Preferences and Their Fathers' Occupations. *Personnel and Guidance Journal*, 1966, 45(3), 238-242.

Muhlenkamp, A. F., and Parsons, J. L. Characteristics of Nurses: An Overview of Recent Research Published in a Nursing Research Periodical. *Journal of Vocational Behavior*, 1972, July, 2(3), 261-273.

Munday, D. A. The Relationship of Role Models to the Career Orientation of Female College Students. Unpublished doctoral dissertation, University of Maryland. *Dissertation Abstracts International*, 1975, August, 36(2-A), 712-713.

Munz, D. C., Smouse, A. D., and Letchworth, G. Achievement Motivation and Ordinal Position of Birth. *Psychological Reports*, 1968, 23(1), 175-180.

Murlidharan, R., and Topa, V. Need for Achievement and Independence Training. *Indian Journal of Psychology*, 1970, March, 45(1), 1-21.

Muth, P. New Slant on Achievement: Home Makes a Difference; NAEP and IEA Surveys. *Compact*, 1973, November, 7, 13-14.

Nash, J. M. Prediction of Academic Achievement of Women at a Private Junior College Through Use of Certain Intellective and Family Relationships Measures. Unpublished doctoral dissertation, Boston University. Dissertation Abstracts International, 1970, November, 31(5-A), 2113-2114.

Nichols, R. C Parental Attitudes of Mothers of Intelligent Adolescents and Creativity of Their Children. Child Development, 1964, December, 35, 1041-1049.

Nowicki, S., and Segal, W. Perceived Parental Characteristics, Locus of Control Orientation, and Behavioral Correlates of Locus of Control. Developmental Psychology, 1974, January, 10(1), 33-37.

Nunn, C. Z. Familial Determinants of Achievement Motivation. Unpublished doctoral dissertation, University of North Carolina. Dissertation Abstracts, 1967, 27(11-A), 3937.

Nuttall, E. V., and Nuttall, R. L. Parent-Child Relationships and Effective Academic Motivation. Journal of Psychology, 1976, September, 94(1), 127-133.

_____, _____, Polit, D., and Hunter, J. B. The Effects of Family Size, Birth Order, Sibling Separation and Crowding on the Academic Achievement of Boys and Girls. American Educational Research Journal, 1976, Summer, 13(3), 217-223.

Nuttall, R. L. Do the Factors Affecting Academic Achievement Differ by the Socioeconomic Status or Sex of the Student? JSAS Catalog of Selected Documents in Psychology, 1972, Summer, 2, 122-123.

Nuzum, R E. Inferred Parental Identification and Perceived Parental Relationship as Related to Career and Home-Making-Orientation in Above-Average Ability College Women. Unpublished doctoral dissertation, Washington State University. Dissertation Abstracts International, 1970, December, 31(6-A), 2689-2690.

O'Leary, V. E., and Braun, J. S. Antecedents and Personality Correlates of Academic Careerism in Women. Proceedings of the Annual Convention of the American Psychological Association, 1972, 7(Pt. 1), 277-278.

Oliver, L. W. The Relationship of Parental Attitudes and Parental Identification to Career and Homemaking Orientation in College Women. Journal of Vocational Behavior, 1975, 7(1), 1-12.

Olsen, N. J. Sex Differences in Child Training Antecedents of Achievement Motivation Among Chinese Children. Journal of Social Psychology, 1971, April, 83(2), 303-304.

Osborn, M. E. The Impact of Differing Parental Educational Level on the Educational Achievement, Attitude, Aspiration, and Expectation of the Child. Journal of Educational Research, 1971, December, 65(4), 163-167.

Osofsky, J. D., and O'Connell, E. Parent-Child Interaction: Daughters' Effects Upon Mothers' and Fathers' Behaviors. Developmental Psychology, 1972, 7(2), 157-168.

Otto, L. B., Haller, A. O., and Meier, R. P. High School Students' Levels of Occupational Aspiration: Variations by Sex, Socioeconomic Status, and Grade in School. Paper presented at the Rural Sociological Society meeting, Maryland, August 1973.

Patrick, T A. Personality and Family Background Characteristics of Women Who Enter Male-Dominated Professions. Unpublished doctoral dissertation, Columbia University. Dissertation Abstracts International, 1974, 34(5-A), 2396.

Perrone, P. A. Values and Occupational Preferences of Junior High School Girls. Personnel and Guidance Journal, 1965, 44(3), 253-257.

Peterson, E. H. Parental Identification Factors and Career Commitment In College Subjects. Dissertation Abstracts International, 1972, February, 32(8-B), 4849.

Peterson, R. E. Peer-Conformity and Achievement Motivation as Functions of Sex, Intellectual Ability, and Family Social Status. Unpublished doctoral dissertation, University of California, Berkeley. Dissertation Abstracts, 1963, 24(3), 1272-1273.

Picou, J. S., and Curry, E. W. Structural, Interpersonal, and Behavioral Correlates of Female Adolescents' Occupational Choices. Adolescence, 1973, Fall, 8(31), 521-532.

Pierce, J. V. Sex Differences in Achievement Motivation of Able High School Students. Cooperative Research Project No. 1097, University of Chicago, 1961.

Platt, J. J., Moskalski, D. D., and Eisenman, R. Sex and Birth Order, and Future Expectations of Occupational Status and Salary. Journal of Individual Psychology, 1968, 24(2), 170-173.

Plost, M., and Rosen, M. J. Effect of Career Models on Occupational Preferences of Adolescents. Audio Visual Communication Review, 1974, Spring, 22, 41-50.

Pope, S. K. Effects of Female Career Role Models on Occupational Aspirations, Attitude, and Personalities of High School Seniors. Unpublished doctoral dissertation, University of Missouri. Dissertation Abstracts International, 1972, March, 32(9-A), 4964-4965.

Poppleton, P. K. Puberty, Family Size and the Educational Progress of Girls. British Journal of Educational Psychology, 1968, 38(3), 286-292.

Porter, J. B. The Vocational Choice of Freshmen College Women as Influenced by Psychological Needs and Parent-Child Relationships. Unpublished doctoral dissertation, University of Oklahoma. Dissertation Abstracts, 1967, 27(11-A), 3730.

Portz, E. Influence of Birth Order, Sibling Sex on Sports Participation. In D. Harris (ed.), Women and Sport: A National Research Conference. Penn State HPER Series No. 2, 1973, 225-234.

Pratt, L., and Hasslocher, P. Research on Women In Cultural Affairs. University Woman, 1962, 1(2), 7-8.

Prenter, I. L., and Stewart, R. A. Educational and Vocational Aspirations of New Zealand Adolescent Girls, in Relation to Achievement and Motivation. New Zealand Journal of Educational Studies, 1972, May, 7(1), 38-44.

Quarter, J., Kirsh, S., Dimitri, O., and Postl, B. Values and Role Satisfaction Performance and Commitment Among Early Adolescents. Adolescence, 1976, Summer, 11, 243-259.

Query, J. M., and Kuruvilla, T. C. Male and Female Adolescent Achievement and Maternal Employment. Adolescence, 1975, Fall, 10(39), 353-356.

Regan, C. A. Attitudes Toward Parents and Achievement Motivation of Freshmen Women in a Selective Urban University in Relation to Mothers' Career Patterns. Dissertation Abstracts International, 1973, June, 33(12-A), 6738-6739.

Reimanis, G. A Study of Home Environment and Readiness for Achievement at School. Final Report. Washington, D. C.: Bureau of Research, Office of Education, 1970. Also available from ERIC (ED041637), 1970.

Rhine, W. R. Birth Order Differences in Conformity and Level of Achievement Arousal. Child Development, 1968, 39(3), 987-996.

Ridgeway, C. L., and Seater, B. B. Role Models, Significant Others, and the Importance of Male Influence on College Women. Sociological Symposium, 1976, Spring, 15, 49-64.

Ringness, T. A. Identification Patterns, Achievement Values, and Behavior Orientations as Predictors of Academic Achievement of Eighth-Grade Girls. Final Report. Washington, D. C.: Bureau of Research, Office of Education, 1968. Also available from ERIC (ED031759), 1970.

_____. Identifying Figures, Their Achievement Values, and Children's Values as Related to Actual and Predicted Achievement. Journal of Educational Psychology, 1970, 61(3), 174-185.

Roodin, P. A., Broughton, A., and Vaught, G. M. Effects of Birth Order, Sex, and Family Size on Field Dependence and Locus of Control. Perceptual and Motor Skills, 1974, August, 39(1), 671-676.

Rosenbluh, E. S., and Haarman, G. B. Birth Order, Need for Achievement, College Attendance, and Socio-Cultural Learning. Psychology, 1970, 7(2), 8-12.

Rosenfeld, H. M. Relationships of Ordinal Position to Affiliation and Achievement Motives: Direction and Generality. Journal of Personality, 1966, December, 34, 467-480.

Rosenthal, E. R. Structural Patterns of Women's Occupational Choice. Unpublished doctoral dissertation, Cornell University, 1974. Dissertation Abstracts International, 1974, 35 (6-A), 3901. Also available from ERIC (ADG74-26310), 1974.

Rossi, A. S. Women in Science: Why So Few? Science, 1965, May, 28, 148(3674), 1196-1202.

Rothbart, M. K. Birth Order and Mother-Child Interaction in an Achievement Situation. Journal of Personality and Social Psychology, 1971, February, 17(2), 113-120.

Rubin, D. Mother and Father Schemata of Achievers and Underachievers in Primary School Arithmetic. Psychological Reports, 1968, 23(3, Pt. 2), 1215-1221.

Ruble, D. N., and Nakamura, C. Y. Task Orientation Versus Social Orientation in Young Children and Their Attention to Relevant Social Class. Child Development, 1972, 43, 471-480.

Rushing, W A. Adolescent-Parent Relationship and Mobility Aspirations. Social Forces, 1964, December, 43, 2, 157-166.

Sampson, E. E Birth Order, Need Achievement, and Conformity. Journal of Abnormal and Social Psychology, 1962, February, 64(2), 155-159.

Sandis, E. E. The Transmission of Mothers' Educational Ambitions, as Related to Specific Socialization Techniques. Journal of Marriage and the Family, 1970, 32(2), 204-211.

Sandler, B. E., and Scalia, F. A. The Relationship Between Birth Order, Sex, and Leadership in a Religious Organization. The Journal of Social Psychology, 1975, 95, 279-280.

Schaefer, C. E. A Psychological Study of 10 Exceptionally Creative Adolescent Girls. Exceptional Children, 1970, 36(6), 431-441.

Scheck, D. C., Emerick, R., and El-Assal, M. M. Adolescent's Perceptions of Parent-Child Relations and the Development of Internal-External Control Orientation. Journal of Marriage and the Family, 1973, 35, 634-654.

Schneider, L. R. The Relationship between Identification with Mother and Home or Career Orientation in Women. Unpublished doctoral dissertation, Columbia University. Dissertation Abstracts, 1962, 23(5), 1787.

Schoenfeldt, L. F. Ability, Family Socioeconomic Level, and Advanced Education in Nursing. Measurement and Evaluation in Guidance, 1968, 1, 182-189.

Schwarzweller, H. K. Values and Occupational Choice. Social Forces, 1960, 39, 126-135.

Severance, L. J., and Gottsegen, A. J. Modeling Influences on the Achievement of College Men and Women. Paper presented at the American Psychological Association Convention, San Francisco, 1977.

Sewell, W. H., and Orenstein, A. M. Community of Residence and Occupational Choice. American Journal of Sociology, 1965, 70, 551-563.

———, and Shah, V. P. Socioeconomic Status, Intelligence, and the Attainment of Higher Education. Sociology of Education, 1967, 40(1), 1-23.

———, and ———. Parents' Education and Children's Educational Aspirations and Achievements. American Sociological Review, 1968, 33, 191-209.

———, and ———. Social Class, Parental Encouragement, and Educational Aspirations. American Journal of Sociology, 1968, March, 73(5), 559-572.

Shack, S. Widening Horizons. School Guidance Worker, 1977, January, 32(3), 42-49.

Shaver, P., French, J. R., and Cobb, S. Birth Order of Medical Students and the Occupational Ambitions of Their Parents. International Journal of Psychology, 1970, 5(3), 197-207.

Shaw, M. C., and White, D. L. The Relationship between Child-Parent Identification and Academic Underachievement. Journal of Clinical Psychology, 1965, 21, 10-13.

Shea, P. D. Parental Influence on College Planning by Boys and

Girls of High Ability During the Sixth to the Ninth Grades. Unpublished doctoral dissertation, Harvard University, 1964.

Shelton, P. B. Achievement Motivation in Professional Women. Unpublished doctoral dissertation, University of California, Berkeley. Dissertation Abstracts, 1968, 28(10-A), 4274.

Sherwood, E. B. The Antecedents of Career Choice for Women in Two Professions. Unpublished doctoral dissertation, University of Maryland. Dissertation Abstracts International, 1976, April, 36(10-A), 6995.

Shore, M. F., and Leiman, A. H. Parental Perceptions of the Student as Related to Academic Achievement in Junior College. Journal of Experimental Education, 1965, Summer, 33, 391-394.

Shuval, J. T. Occupational Interests and Sex-Role Congruence. Human Relations, 1963, 16(2), 171-183.

Siegel, A. E., and Curtis, E. A. Familial Correlates of Orientation Toward Future Employment among College Women. Journal of Educational Psychology, 1963, 54(1), 33-37.

Simpson, R. L., and Simpson, I. H. Occupational Choice Among Career-Oriented College Women. Marriage and Family Living, 1961, November, 23(4), 377-383.

Singer, E. Birth Order, Educational Aspirations, and Educational Attainment. Unpublished doctoral dissertation, Columbia University. Dissertation Abstracts, 1967, 27(8-A), 2638.

Smelser, W. T. Adolescent and Adult Occupational Choice as a Function of Family Socioeconomic History. Sociometry, 1963, 4, 393-409.

Snyder, E. E., and Spreitzer, E. Correlates of Sport Participation Among Adolescent Girls. Research Quarterly, 1976, December, 47(4), 804-809.

Solomon, D., Houlihan, K. A., Busse, T. V., and Parelius, R. J. Parent Behavior and Child Academic Achievement, Achievement Striving and Related Personality Characteristics. Genetic Psychology Monographs, 1971, 83, 173-273.

Sorenson, J., and Winters, C. J. Parental Influence on Women's Career Development. In S. Osipow (ed.), Emerging Woman--Career Analysis and Outlooks. Columbus, OH: Charles E. Merrill, 1975, 37-50.

Sostek, A. B. The Relation of Identification and Parent-Child Climate to Occupational Choice. Unpublished doctoral dissertation, Boston University. Dissertation Abstracts, 1963, 24(4), 1690.

Stacey, B. Achievement Motivation, Occupational Choice and Inter-Generation Occupational Mobility. Human Relations, 1969, 22(3), 275-281.

Standley, K., and Soule, B. Women in Male-Dominated Professions: Contrasts in Their Personal and Vocational Histories. Journal of Vocational Behavior, 1974, April, 4(2), 245-258.

Stehbens, J. A., and Carr, D. L. Perceptions of Parental Attitudes by Students Varying in Intellectual Ability and Educational Efficiency. Psychology in the Schools, 1970, 7(1), 67-73.

Steinke, B. K., and Kaczkowski, H. R. Parents Influence the Occupational Choice of Ninth Grade Girls. Vocational Guidance Quarterly, 1961, 9, 101-103.

Straus, J. H., and Straus, M. A. Family Roles and Sex Differences in Creativity of Children in Bombay and Minneapolis. Journal of Marriage and the Family, 1968, 30(1), 46-53.

Tangri, S. S. Role-Innovation in Occupational Choice Among College Women. Unpublished doctoral dissertation, University of Michigan, 1969.

──────. Determinants of Occupational Role Innovation Among College Women. Journal of Social Issues, 1972, 28(2), 177-199. Also in M. T. S. Mednick et al. (eds.), Women and Achievement: Social and Motivational Analyses. New York: Halsted, 1975, 255-273.

Teahan, J. E. Parental Attitudes and College Success. Journal of Educational Psychology, 1963, 54(2), 104-109.

Teevan, R. C., and McGhee, P. E. Childhood Development of Fear of Failure Motivations. Journal of Personality and Social Psychology, 1972, 21, 345-348.

TenElshof, A., and Mehl, D. Academic Achievement in College Women. Journal of the National Association for Women Deans, Administrators, and Counselors, 1976, Fall, 40(1), 7-10.

Thornburg, K. R., and Weeks, M. O. Vocational Role Expectations of Five-Year-Old Children and Their Parents. Sex Roles: A Journal of Research, 1975, 1(4), 395-396.

Tidball, M. E. Women Role Models. In Graduate and Professional Education of Women. Proceedings of a Conference Sponsored by the American Association of University Women. Washington, D. C.: American Association of University Women, 1974, 56-59.

Trent, J. W., and Medsker, L. L. Beyond High School: A Psychosociological Study of 10,000 High School Graduates. San Francisco: Jossey-Bass, 1968.

Tyler, F. B., Rafferty, J. E., and Tyler, B. B. Relationships among Motivations of Parents and Their Children. Journal of Genetic Psychology, 1962, 101, 69-81.

Unkel, E. A Study of the Interaction of Socioeconomic Groups and Sex Factors with the Discrepancy Between Anticipated Achievement and Actual Achievement in Elementary School Mathematics. Arithmetic Teacher, 1966, 13, 662-670.

Venerable, W. R. Parental Influence on College and Vocational Decisions. Journal of the National Association of College Administrators and Counselors, 1974, July, 19, 9-12.

Veres, H. C. Two-Year College Women: Dimensions of Career Choice and Career Commitment. Unpublished doctoral dissertation, Cornell University. Dissertation Abstracts International, 1974, 35(2-A), 831.

Veroff, J., Feld, S., and Gurin, G. Achievement Motivation and Religious Background. American Sociological Review, 1962, 27, 205-217.

Vetter, B. Female 'Role Models' Deemed Important. American Psychological Association Monitor, 1973, August, 4(8), 3.

Viernstein, M. C., and Hogan, R. Parental Personality Factors and Achievement Motivation in Talented Adolescents. Journal of Youth and Adolescence, 1975, June, 4(2), 183-190.

Wallace, J. L., and Leonard, T. H. Factors Affecting Vocational and Educational Decision-Making of High School Girls. Journal of Home Economics, 1971, April, 63, 241-245.

Warriner, C. C., Foster, D. A., and Trites, D. K. Failure to Complete as a Family Characteristic: A College Sample. Journal of Educational Research, 1966, 59, 466-468.

Watley, D. J. Career Progress of Merit Scholars. National Merit Scholarship Corporation Research Reports, 1968, 4(1).

_____. Career Progress: A Longitudinal Study of Gifted Students. Journal of Counseling Psychology, 1969, 16(2, Pt. 1), 100-108.

Weller, L., Shlomi, A., and Zimont, G. Birth Order, Sex, and Occupational Interest. Journal of Vocational Behavior, 1976, February, 8(1), 45-50.

Werts, C. E. Social Class and Career Choice of College Freshmen. National Merit Scholarship Corporation Research Reports, 1965, 1, (8).

_____. Career Choice Patterns: Ability and Social Class. National Merit Scholarship Corporation Research Reports, 1966, 2(3).

_____. Career Choice Patterns. Sociology of Education, 1967, Fall, 40, 348-358.

_____. A Comparison of Male Versus Female College Attendance Probabilities. Sociology of Education, 1968, 41(1), 103-110.

_____, and Watley, D. J. The Relationship of Parental Education on Achievement Test Performance of Girls Versus Boys. Sociology of Education, 1970, Spring, 43(2), 186-194.

White, K. Social Background Variables Related to Career Commitment of Women Teachers. Personnel and Guidance Journal, 1967, March, 45, 648-652.

Wiggins, R. G. Parent-Teenager Perceptions Related to Academic Aspirations. Unpublished doctoral dissertation, University of Georgia. Dissertation Abstracts International, 1971, May, 31(11-A), 5864.

Willerman, L., and Stafford, R. E. Maternal Effects on Intellectual Functioning. Behavior Genetics, 1972, 2(4), 321-325.

Williams, J. H. Growing Up Female. In Psychology of Women: Behavior in a Biosocial Context. New York: W. W. Norton, 1977, 158-195.

Williams, T. H. Educational Aspirations: Longitudinal Evidence on Their Development in Canadian Youth. Sociology of Education, 1972, Spring, 45(2), 107-133.

Williamson, S. Z. Effects of Maternal Employment on the Scholastic Performance of Children. Journal of Home Economics, 1970, October, 62, 609-613.

Withycombe-Brocato, C. J. The Mature Graduate Woman Student: Who is She? Unpublished doctoral dissertation, U. S. International University, 1969.

Witty, P. A. Study of Pupils' Interests, Grades 9, 10, 11, 12. Education, 1961, 82, 169-174.

Wolkon, G. H., and Levinger, G. Birth Order and Need for Achievement. Psychological Reports, 1965, 16, 73-74.

Wolkon, K. A. Prediction of Pioneer Vocational Choice in College Women. Unpublished doctoral dissertation, Boston College, 1970.

Work Values and Background Factors as Predictors of Women's Desires to Work. Ohio Studies in Personnel Research, Monograph No. 108, Ohio State University, Bureau of Business Research, 1962.

Wyer, R. S., Jr. Self-Acceptance, Discrepancy between Parents'

Perceptions of Their Children, and Goal-Seeking Effectiveness. Journal of Personality and Social Psychology, 1965, 2, 311-316.

Wylie, R. C., and Hutchins, E. B. Schoolwork Ability Estimates and Aspirations as a Function of Socioeconomic Level, Race, and Sex. Psychological Reports, 1967, Monographic Supplement 3-V21.

Yarrow, M., Scott, P., DeLeeuw, L., and Heinig, C. Child-Rearing in Families of Working and Non-Working Mothers. Sociometry, 1962, June, 25(2), 122-140.

Yudkin, S., and Holme, A. Working Mothers and Their Children. London: Sphere Books, 1969.

Zanducci, R. The Effect of Mother's Employment on the Achievement, Aspirations, and Expectations of the Child. Personnel and Guidance Journal, 1967, 46, 263-267.

Zissis, C. The Relationship of Selected Variables to Career-Marriage Plans of University Freshman Women. Unpublished doctoral dissertation, University of Michigan. Dissertation Abstracts International, 1962, 23(1), 128.

Zuckerman, D. M. Self-Concept, Family Background, and Personal Traits which Predict the Life Goals and Sex-Role Attitudes of Technical College and University Women. Unpublished doctoral dissertation, Ohio State University, 1977.

III

SOCIAL-PSYCHOLOGICAL FORCES
AND WOMEN'S AMBITION

An-drog-y-ny: n. from the Greek roots andro and gynos, meaning "male" and "female"; a condition under which the characteristics of the sexes--and the human impulses expressed by men and women--are not rigidly assigned.

A. SELF-CONCEPT, SELF-ESTEEM

Aguren, C. T. An Exploration of Self-Actualization, Self-Concept, Locus of Control, and Other Characteristics as Exhibited in Selected Mature Community College Women. Unpublished doctoral dissertation, North Texas State University. Dissertation Abstracts International, 1975, June, 35(12-A, Pt. 1), 7641-7642.

Alberti, J. M. Correlates of Self-Perception-In-School. Paper presented at the American Educational Research Association meeting, New York, 1971. Also available from ERIC (ED048336), 1971.

Alvord, D. J., and Glass, L. W. Relationships Between Academic Achievement and Self-Concept. Science Education, 1974, April, 58, 175-179.

Anderson, T. B., and Olsen, L. C. Congruence of Self and Ideal-Self and Occupational Choices. Personnel and Guidance Journal, 1965, October, 44, 171-176.

Asche, M. The Interrelationships Between Self-Concepts and Occupational Concepts of Post-High School Vocational-Technical Students. Paper presented at the American Educational Research Association meeting, Chicago, 1974. Also available from ERIC (ED094126), 1974.

Bachtold, L. M. Personality Differences Among High Ability Under-Achievers. Journal of Educational Research, 1969, September, 63(1), 16-18.

Bailey, R. C. Self-Concept Differences in Low and High Achieving

Students. *Journal of Clinical Psychology*, 1971, April, 27(2), 188-191.

_____, and Bailey, K. G. Perceived Ability in Male and Female College Students. *Perceptual and Motor Skills*, 1971, February, 32, 1, 293-294.

_____, and _____. Self-Perceptions of Scholastic Ability at Four Grade Levels. *Journal of Genetic Psychology*, 1974, 124, 197-212.

Baird, L. L. The Relation of Vocational Interests to Life Goals, Self-Ratings of Ability and Personality Traits, and Potential for Achievement. *Journal of Educational Measurement*, 1970, Winter, 7(4), 233-239.

Balaza, E. K. Psycho-Social Study of Outstanding Female Athletes. *Research Quarterly*, 1975, 46(3), 267-273.

Baldwin, J. M. An Analysis of the Relationship Between Self-Esteem, Academic Achievement, and Academic Level of Aspiration for a Group of College Students. Unpublished doctoral dissertation, University of Maryland. *Dissertation Abstracts International*, 1970, July, 31(1-A), 209.

Bardwick, J. M. The Ego and Self-Esteem. In *Psychology of Women: A Study of Biocultural Conflicts*. New York: Harper and Row, 1971, 154-166.

Barker, L. W. An Analysis of Achievement, Motivational, and Perceptual Variables Between Students Classified on the Basis of Success and Persistence in College. Unpublished doctoral dissertation, West Virginia University. *Dissertation Abstracts*, 1968, 29(4-A), 1100.

Baruch, G. K. Feminine Self-Esteem, Self-Ratings of Competence, and Maternal Career Commitment. *Journal of Counseling Psychology*, 1973, September, 20(5), 487-488.

_____. Girls Who Perceive Themselves as Competent: Some Antecedents and Correlates. *Psychology of Women Quarterly*, 1976, 1(1), 38-48.

Bellucci, G., and Hoyer, W. J. Feedback Effects on the Performance and Self-Reinforcing Behavior of Elderly and Young Adult Women. *Journal of Gerontology*, 1975, July, 30(4), 456-460.

Bendo, A. A., and Feldman, H. A Comparison of the Self-Concept of Low-Income Women With and Without Husbands Present. *Cornell Journal of Social Relations*, 1974, Spring, 9(1), 53-85.

Berger, C. R. Sex Differences Related to Self-Esteem Factor Structure. *Journal of Consulting and Clinical Psychology*, 1968, 32(4), 442-446.

Birnbaum, J. A. Life Patterns, Personality Style and Self-Esteem in Gifted Family Oriented and Career Committed Women. Unpublished doctoral dissertation, University of Michigan. Dissertation Abstracts International, 1971, 32(3-B), 1834.

_____. Life Patterns and Self-Esteem in Gifted Family Oriented and Career Committed Women. In M. T. S. Mednick et al. (eds.), Women and Achievement: Social and Motivational Analyses. New York: Halsted, 1975, 396-419.

Blaubergs, M. S. Overcoming the Sexist Barriers to Gifted Women's Achievement. In B. Johnson (ed.), Advantage/Disadvantage Gifted. Ventura, CA: Ventura County Superintendent of Schools Office, 1979.

Bledsoe, J. C. Self-Concepts of Children and Their Intelligence, Achievement, Interests, and Anxiety. Childhood Education, 1967, 43, 436-438.

Bobson, S. Self Concept: An Annotated Bibliography of Selected ERIC References. ERIC-IRCD Urban Disadvantaged Series, Number 32, June, 1973. Available from ERIC (ED076729), 1973.

Boddez, M. An Analysis of the Self-Concept and the Impact of Success and Failure Upon the Perception of Performance and Upon the Self-Concept of Junior High School Students: II. St. Louis University Research Journal, 1973, December, 4(4), 485-547.

Bohan, J. S. Age and Sex Differences in Self-Concept. Adolescence, 1973, Fall, 8(31), 379-384.

Borislow, B. Self-Evaluation and Academic Achievement. Journal of Counseling Psychology, 1962, Fall, 9, 246-254.

Brady, P. J., et al. Locus of Evaluation in Children's Learning from Textbook Material. Paper presented at the American Educational Research Association meeting, Washington, D. C., 1975. Also available from ERIC (ED104954), 1975.

Brannigan, G. G., and Duchnowski, A. J. Outerdirectedness in the Decision Making of High and Low Approval Motivated Children. Journal of Genetic Psychology, 1976, March, 128(1st half), 85-90.

Brinkerhoff, R. Exploration of Ego Development in Adolescent Girls. Unpublished doctoral dissertation, University of Chicago, 1972.

Brookover, W. B., Paterson, A., and Shailer, T. Self-Concept of Ability and School Achievement. Final Report. Cooperative Research Project No. 845. East Lansing, MI: Office of Research and Publications, Michigan State University, 1962.

Bryan, W. E. A Comparison of the Career Orientation of College Women in Contrasting Majors. Unpublished doctoral dissertation, Wayne State University, Detroit, MI, 1968.

Butler, I. C. Self-Concept: Race and Social Class in Adolescent Females. Dissertation Abstracts International, 1974, February, 34(8-B), 4034.

Calsyn, R. J., and Kenny, D. A. Self-Concept of Ability and Perceived Evaluation of Others: Cause or Effect of Academic Achievement? Journal of Educational Psychology, 1977, 69(2), 136-145.

Carlson, R. Sex Differences in Ego Functioning: Exploratory Studies of Agency and Communion. Journal of Consulting and Clinical Psychology, 1971, 37, 267-277.

Chang, T. S. The Relationship Between Children's Self-Concepts, Teacher's Rating, and Academic Achievement. Paper presented at the American Educational Research Association meeting, Washington, D. C., 1975. Also available from ERIC (ED 106699), 1975.

_____. Self-Concepts, Academic Achievement, and Teacher's Rating. Psychology in the Schools, 1976, January, 13(1), 111-113.

Clark, E. T. Sex Differences in the Perception of Academic Achievement Among Elementary School Children. Journal of Psychology, 1967, 67(2), 249-256.

Clifton, M. A., and Smith, H. M. Comparison of Expressed Self-Concepts of Highly Skilled Males and Females Concerning Motor Performance. Perceptual and Motor Skills, 1963, 16(1), 199-201.

Connell, D. M., and Johnson, J. E. Relationship Between Sex-Role Identification and Self-Esteem in Early Adolescents. Developmental Psychology, 1970, 3, 268.

Corwin, R. G. Role Conception and Career Aspiration: A Study of Identity in Nursing. Sociological Quarterly, 1961, April, 2(2), 69-86.

Cotler, S., and Palmer, R. J. Relationships Among Sex, Sociometric, Self, and Test Anxiety Factors and the Academic Achievement of Elementary School Children. Psychology in the Schools, 1970, July, 7, 211-216.

Counselman, E. F. A Comparison of the Self-Concepts, Self-Acceptance, Ideal Self-Concepts, and Career Woman Stereotypes of Career- and Non-Career-Oriented College Senior Women. Unpublished doctoral dissertation, Boston University. Dissertation Abstracts International, 1971, October, 32(4-A), 1996-1997.

Cowan, G., and Moore, L. Female Identity and Occupational Commitment. Paper presented at the American Psychological Association Convention, Denver, 1971. Also available from ERIC (ED056335), 1972.

Cox, D. F., and Bauer, R. A. Self-Confidence and Persuasibility in Women. Public Opinion Quarterly, 1964, 28, 453-466.

Cunningham, T., and Berberian, V. Sex Differences in the Relationship of Self Concept to Locus of Control in Children. Personality and Social Psychology Bulletin, 1976, Summer, 2(3), 277-281.

d'Amorim, M. A., and Nuttin, J. R. [The Perception of One's Own Successes and Failures in Function of the Outcomes of a Partner: The Influence of Task Involvement and Level of Aspiration in Male and Female Subjects.] Psychologica Belgica, 1972, 12(1), 9-31.

Davidson, H. H., and Lang, G. Children's Perceptions of Their Teachers' Feelings Toward Them Related to Self-Perception, School Achievement, and Behavior. Journal of Experimental Education, 1960, December, 29(2), 107-118.

Davis, A. J. Self-Concept, Occupational Role Expectations, and Occupational Choice in Nursing and Social Work. Nursing Research, 1969, 18(1), 55-59.

Davis, F., and Olesen, V. L. Initiation into a Women's Profession: Identity Problems in the Status Transition of Coed to Student Nurse. Sociometry, 1963, 26(1), 89-101.

Deaux, K. Self-Evaluations of Women and Men. In The Behavior of Women and Men. Belmont, CA: Wadsworth, 1976, 35-44.

Denmark, F. L., and Guttentag, M. The Effect of College Attendance on Mature Women: Changes in Self-Concept and Evaluation of Student Role. Journal of Social Psychology, 1966, 69(1), 155-158.

_____, and _____. Dissonance in the Self-Concepts and Educational Concepts of College- and Non-College-Oriented Women. Journal of Counseling Psychology, 1967, 14(2), 113-115.

Dias, S. L. A Study of Personal, Perceptual, and Motivational Factors Influential in Predicting the Aspiration Level of Women and Men Toward the Administrative Roles in Education. Unpublished doctoral dissertation, Boston University. Dissertation Abstracts International, 1975, September, 36(3-A), 1202.

DiSabatino, M. Psychological Factors Inhibiting Women's Occupational Aspirations and Vocational Choices: Implications for Counseling. Vocational Guidance Quarterly, 1976, September, 25(1), 43-49.

Douvan, E. Internal Barriers to Achievement in Women--An Introduction. Women on Campus: 1970--A Symposium, Proceedings of the Symposium. Ann Arbor: University of Michigan, 1970, 2-3.

Duquin, M. E. Perceptions of Sport and Psychological Well-Being. Symposium presentation at the American Psychological Association Convention, Washington, D. C., 1976.

Etaugh, C., and Ropp, J. Children's Self-Evaluation of Performance as a Function of Sex, Age, Feedback, and Sex-Typed Task Label. Journal of Psychology, 1976, 94, 115-122.

Fagerburg, J. E. A Comparative Study of Undergraduate Women in Relation to Selected Personal Characteristics and Certain Effects of Educational Interruption. Unpublished doctoral dissertation, Purdue University. Dissertation Abstracts, 1968, 28 (11-A), 4445-4446.

Farmer, H. S. What Inhibits Achievement and Career Motivation in Women? Counseling Psychologist, 1976, 6(2), 12-15.

_____. Why Women Contribute Less to the Arts, Sciences, and Humanities. A paper presented at the American Educational Research Association meeting, San Francisco, 1976.

Feather, N. T. Change in Confidence Following Success or Failure as a Predictor of Subsequent Performance. Journal of Personality and Social Psychology, 1968, 9, 38-46.

Fekart, M. A. A Correlational Study Between Self-Concept and Academic Achievement of College Freshmen and Seniors. Unpublished doctoral dissertation, Indiana University. Dissertation Abstracts International, 1970, June, 30(12-A), 5283-5284.

Fisher, J. K., and Waetjen, W. B. An Investigation of the Relationship Between the Separation by Sex of Eighth-Grade Boys and Girls and English Achievement and Self-Concept. Journal of Educational Research, 1966, 59(9), 409-412.

Fontana, G. L. An Investigation into the Dynamics of Achievement Motivation in Women. Unpublished doctoral dissertation, University of Michigan. Dissertation Abstracts International, 1971, September, 32(3-B), 1821-1822.

Frankel, P. S. The Relationship of Self-Concept, Sex Role Attitudes, and the Development of Achievement Need in Women. Unpublished doctoral dissertation, Northwestern University. Dissertation Abstracts International, 1970, 30(7-B), 3371-3372.

Frerichs, M. Relationship of Self-Esteem and Internal-External Control to Selected Characteristics of Associate Degree Nursing Students. Nursing Research, 1973, July, 22(4) 350-352.

Friedman, R. J. The Relationship of Self-Ideal Self Concept Disparity to Intellectual Ability and Academic Achievement in Ninth Grade Boys and Girls. Unpublished doctoral dissertation, University of Iowa. Dissertation Abstracts International, 1970, 30(9-A), 3783-3784.

Fry, P. S. Success, Failure, and Self-Assessment Ratings. Journal of Consulting and Clinical Psychology, 1976, June, 44(3), 413-419.

Furst, E. J., Raygor, A. W., and Crofoot, A. P. Basic Motivation and Concept of Nursing as Chosen Profession. Journal of Psychology, 1962, 54(1), 85-100.

Gadzella, B. M., and Fournet, G. P. Sex Differences in Self-Perceptions as Students of Excellence and Academic Performance. Perceptual and Motor Skills, 1976, December, 43(3), 1092-1094.

Gillie, A. C. The Differential Effects of Selected Programs on the Performance, Degree of Satisfaction and Retention of Community College Women Students. Final Report. Washington, D. C.: Office of Education. Also available from ERIC (ED068086), 1973.

Gjesme, T. Achievement-Related Motives and School Performance for Girls. Journal of Personality and Social Psychology, 1973, April, 26(1), 131-136.

Gordon, F. E. Where Happiness Lies: Self-Image, Stereotypes, Work Status, and Happiness. Working paper, Department of Administrative Sciences, Yale University, 1971.

_____, and Hall, D. T. Self-Image and Stereotypes of Femininity: Their Relationship to Women's Role Conflicts and Coping. Journal of Applied Psychology, 1974, 59, 241-243.

Grabe, M. D. Peer Priorities and the Impact of Academic Achievement. Contemporary Educational Psychology, 1976, October, 1(14), 314-318.

Graham, J. M. The Relationship of the Developmental Self-Concept to the Academic Achievement of Sixth-Grade Elementary Students. Unpublished doctoral dissertation, University of Oklahoma. Dissertation Abstracts International, 1975, July, 26(1-A), 117.

Gump, J. P. Sex Role Attitudes and Psychological Well-Being. Journal of Social Issues, 1972, 28(2), 79-92.

Gutmann, D. Women and the Conception of Ego Strength. Merrill-Palmer Quarterly, 1965, 11, 229-240.

Hagey, S. J. Risk Taking, Self Complexity, and Role Choice at

Two Stages in the Lives of College Women. Unpublished doctoral dissertation, University of Oregon. Dissertation Abstracts International, 1971, January, 31(7-A), 3638.

Hales, L. W., and Yackee, K. Self-Concepts, Sex and Work Values. Paper presented at the American Educational Research Association meeting, Chicago, 1974. Also available from ERIC (ED090459), 1974.

Hall, M. Study of the Attitudes of Adolescent Girls to Their Own Physical, Intellectual, Emotional and Social Development. Educational Research, 1963, November, 6, 68-70.

Hammes, R. G. The Relationship Between Self-Esteem and Achievement Motivation. Unpublished doctoral dissertation, Northern Illinois University. Dissertation Abstracts International, 1973, February, 33(8-A), 4173-4174.

Hansen, L. S. The Career Development Process for Women: Current Views and Programs. Pupil Personnel Services, (Minnesota Department of Education), 1975, Spring, 4(2), 23-33.

Hennig, M. Family Dynamics and the Successful Woman Executive. In R. B. Kundsin (ed.), Women and Success: The Anatomy of Achievement. New York: William Morrow, 1974, 88-93.

Hesselbart, S. Self-Concept, Personality Correlates, and Need Achievement in Honors College Women. Paper presented at the American Sociological Association Convention, 1972.

Hollender, J. Sex Differences in Sources of Social Self-Esteem. Journal of Consulting and Clinical Psychology, 1972, 38, 343-347.

Homall, G. M., Juhasz, S., and Juhasz, J. Differences in Self-Perception and Vocational Aspirations of College Women. California Journal of Educational Research, 1975, January, 26(1), 6-10.

Ibrahim, H., and Morrison, N. Self-Actualization and Self-Concept Among Athletes. Research Quarterly, 1976, March, 47(1), 68-79.

Janes, G. D. Student Perceptions, Parent Perceptions, and Teacher Perceptions of Student Abilities, Aspirations, Expectations, and Motivations: Their Relationship to Under- and Over-Achievement. Unpublished doctoral dissertation, University of Iowa. Dissertation Abstracts International, 1971, March, 31(9-A), 4548-4549.

Johnson, B. L., and Kilmann, P. R. Locus of Control and Perceived Confidence in Problem-Solving Abilities. Journal of Clinical Psychology, 1975, January, 31(1), 54-55.

Karre, I. Self-Concept and Sex-Role Stereotype: An Empirical Study with Children. Unpublished doctoral dissertation, University of Colorado, Boulder, 1975. Dissertation Abstracts International, 1975, 36(8-A), 4850. Also available from ERIC (ADG76-03914), 1975.

Keefer, K. E. Characteristics of Students Who Make Accurate and Inaccurate Self-Predictions of College Achievement. Journal of Educational Research, 1971, May, 64(9), 401-404.

Kitching, J. C. The Self-Concept of Middle-Aged Women. Unpublished doctoral dissertation, Florida State University, 1972. Dissertation Abstracts International, 1975, 33(6-B), 2682. Also available from ERIC (ADG72-31404), 1972.

Klein, F. L. Conditioning of Favorable and Unfavorable Self-Evaluative Statements Among High, Middle, and Low Anxious Female College Students. Dissertation Abstracts, 1962, 23(5), 1782.

Knott, T. C. Motivational Factors in Selected Women Candidates for the Master of Religious Education Degree. Unpublished doctoral dissertation, Boston University, 1964. Dissertation Abstracts International, 1964, 25(5), 3140. Also available from ERIC (ADG64-11654), 1964.

Kohr, R. L. A Longitudinal Study of Self Concept from Grade 5 to Grade 9. Paper presented at the National Council on Measurement in Education meeting, Chicago, 1974. Also available from ERIC (ED092566), 1974.

Komorita, N. I. Self-Concept Measures as Related to Achievement in Nursing Education. Unpublished doctoral dissertation, Wayne State University. Dissertation Abstracts International, 1972, June, 32(12-A), 6809.

Korman, A. K. Self-Esteem in Vocational Choice. Journal of Applied Psychology, 1966, 50, 479-486.

_____. Self-Esteem as a Moderator of the Relationship Between Self-Perceived Abilities and Vocational Choice. Journal of Applied Psychology, 1967, 51(1), 65-67.

Kramer, M., McDonnell, C., and Reed, J. L. Self-Actualization and Role Adaptation of Baccalaureate Degree Nurses. Nursing Research, 1972, March, 21(2), 111-123.

Kukla, K. J., and Pargman, D. Comparative Perceptions of Psychological Well-Being as Influenced by Sport Experience in Female Athletes. Research Quarterly, 1976, October, 47, 375-380.

Lacher, M., and Lacher, M. R. Sex Differences in Self Evaluation of Academic Achievement and Ability. Paper presented at the

Midwestern Psychological Association meeting, Chicago, 1975. Also available from ERIC (ED117605), 1976.

Lasky, E. (ed.). Sources of Feminine Self-Esteem. In Humanness: An Exploration into the Mythologies about Women and Men. New York: MSS Informational Corporation, 1975, 63-66.

Lefevre, C. The Mature Woman as Graduate Student: A Study of Changing Self-Conception. Unpublished doctoral dissertation, University of Chicago, 1972.

———. The Mature Woman as a Graduate Student. School Review, 1972, February, 80(2), 281-297.

LeMay, M. L. Self-Actualization and College Achievement at Three Ability Levels. Journal of Counseling Psychology, 1969, 16(6), 582-583.

Lenney, E. Low Self-Confidence Among Women: The Influences of Ability Area and of Social Comparison Cues Upon Women's Self-Evaluations. Unpublished manuscript, Stanford University, 1975.

———. Women's Self-Confidence in Achievement Settings. Psychological Bulletin, 1977, January, 84(1), 1-13.

Lenning, O. T. An Exploratory Study of Factors Differentiating Freshmen Educational Growth. Paper presented at the American College Personnel Association meeting, St. Louis, 1970.

Levenberg, L. H. Accuracy of Academic Self Assessment and Its Relation to Age, Sex, Achievement, I. Q., and Self Esteem. Unpublished doctoral dissertation, Indiana University. Dissertation Abstracts International, 1976, May, 36(11-A), 7299.

Leviton, H. The Implications of the Relationship Between Self-Concept and Academic Achievement. Child Study Journal, 1975, 5(1), 25-35.

Lomax, R. M. Self Concepts of Girls in the Context of a Disadvantaging Environment. Educational Review, 1977, February, 29, 107-119.

Love, B. B. Self-Esteem in Women Related to Occupational Status: A Biracial Study. Unpublished doctoral dissertation, Northwestern University. Dissertation Abstracts International, 1974, December, 35(6-A), 3427.

Lum, M. K. M. A Comparison of Under- and Over-achieving Female College Students. Journal of Educational Psychology, 1960, 51, 109-115.

Lundgren, D. C., and Schwab, M. R. Sex Differences in the Social

Bases of Self-Esteem. Paper presented at the American Psychological Association Convention, New Orleans, 1974.

McBee, M. L., Murray, R., and Suddick, D. Self-Esteem Differences of Professional Women. Journal of the National Association for Women Deans, Administrators, and Counselors, 1976, Summer, 39(4), 186-189.

McCallon, E. L. Self-Ideal Discrepancy and the Correlates Sex and Academic Achievement. Journal of Experimental Education, 1967, Summer, 35, 45-49.

McClain, E. W., and Andrews, H. B. Self-Actualization Among Extremely Superior Students. Journal of College Student Personnel, 1972, November, 13, 505-510.

Maccoby, E. E., and Jacklin, C. N. Achievement Motivation and Self Concept. In The Psychology of Sex Differences. Stanford: Stanford University Press, 1974, 134-163.

McCullough, R. V. Condition Yourself to Achieve Success. Rough Notes, 1974, October, 117(10), 80+.

———. Change Your 'Won't' Power into Will Power. Rough Notes, 1976, March, 119(3), 94+.

McHugh, W. T. A Study of the Differences in Self-Concept and Occupational Role Concepts of Young Women and Middle-aged Women in Occupational Training Programs. Unpublished doctoral dissertation, University of Oregon. Dissertation Abstracts International, 1971, January, 31(7-B), 3273.

Mangieri, J. N., and Olsen, H. D. The Effect of Reading Ability on the Self-Concept-of-Academic Ability of College Students. Paper presented at the American Educational Research Association meeting, Washington, D. C., 1975. Also available from ERIC (ED105436), 1975.

Marcia, J. E., and Friedman, M. L. Ego Identity Status in College Women. Journal of Personality, 1970, June, 38, 249-263.

Marecek, J., and Metee, D. R. Avoidance of Continued Success as a Function of Self-Esteem, Level of Esteem Certainty, and Responsibility for Success. Journal of Personality and Social Psychology, 1972, April, 22(1), 98-107.

Mathes, E. W., and Kahn, A. Physical Attractiveness, Happiness, Neuroticism, and Self-Esteem. Journal of Psychology, 1975, May, 90(1), 27-30.

Mehrens, W. A. Self-Concepts of Graduate Students. Journal of Educational Research, 1967, November, 61(3), 112-113.

Merritt, R. Self-Concept and Achievement in Home Economics. Journal of Home Economics, 1971, January, 63, 38-40.

Michaelson, B. L. Vocational Interests, Self-Concepts, and Attitudes Toward Feminine Roles as Related to the Educational and Vocational Choices of College Women. Unpublished doctoral dissertation, Temple University. Dissertation Abstracts International, 1974, December, 35(6-B), 2994.

Milgram, R. M., and Milgram, N. A. Self-Concept Differences in Student Teachers in Primary, Elementary, Secondary, and Special Education. Psychology in the Schools, 1976, October, 13, 439-441.

Miller, S. M. Effects of Maternal Employment on Sex Role Perception, Interests and Self-Esteem in Kindergarten Girls. Developmental Psychology, 1975, 11(3), 405-406.

Monge, R. H. Structure of the Self-Concept from Adolescence Through Old Age. Experimental Aging Research, 1975, November, 1(2), 281-291.

Morgan, D. D. Perception of Role Conflicts and Self Concepts Among Career and Noncareer College Educated Women. Unpublished doctoral dissertation, Columbia University. Dissertation Abstracts, 1962, 23(5), 1816-1817.

Morrison, R. F., and Sebald, M. Personal Characteristics Differentiating Female Executive from Female Nonexecutive Personnel. Journal of Applied Psychology, 1974, October, 59(5), 656-659.

Morse, J. J. Sense of Competence and Individual Managerial Performance. Psychological Reports, 1976, June, 38(3, Pt. 2), 1195-1198.

Nevill, D., and Damico, S. The Development of a Role Conflict Questionnaire for Women: Some Preliminary Findings. Journal of Consulting and Clinical Psychology, 1974, October, 42(5), 743.

Nicholls, J. G. Effort Is Virtuous, but It's Better to Have Ability: Evaluative Responses to Perceptions of Effort and Ability. Journal of Research in Personality, 1976, September, 10(3), 306-315.

Nichols, I. A., and Shauffer, C. B. Self Concept as a Predictor of Performance in College Women. Paper presented at the American Psychological Association Convention, Washington, D. C., 1975. Also available from ERIC (ED124865), 1969.

O'Brien, E. J., and Epstein, S. Naturally Occurring Changes in

Self-Esteem. Personality and Social Psychology Bulletin, 1974, 1(1), 384-386.

Ohlbaum, J. S. Self-Concepts, Value Characteristics and Self-Actualization of Professional and Non-Professional Women. Unpublished doctoral dissertation, United States International University. Dissertation Abstracts International, 1971, August, 32(2-B), 1221-1222.

O'Leary, V. E. Some Attitudinal Barriers to Occupational Aspirations in Women. Psychological Bulletin, 1974, 81(11), 809-826.

Osipow, S. H. (ed.). Perspective and Issues. In Emerging Women: Career Analysis and Outlooks. Columbus, OH: Charles C. Merrill, 1975, 147-158.

Ozehosky, R. J., and Clark, E. T. Children's Self-Concept and Kindergarten Achievement. Journal of Psychology, 1970, July, 75, 185-192.

Pallone, N. J., and Hosinski, M. Reality-Testing a Vocational Choice: Congruence between Self, Ideal, and Occupational Percepts among Student Nurses. Personnel and Guidance Journal, 1967, 45(7), 666-670.

Palmer, A. B., and Wohl, J. Some Personality Characteristics of Honors Students. College Student Journal, 1972, April, 6(2), 106-111.

Patterson, L. E. Girls's Careers--Expression of Identity. In H. J. Peters and J. C. Hansen (eds.), Vocational Guidance and Career Development. New York: Macmillan, 1977.

Picou, J. S., and Curry, E. W. Structural, Interpersonal, and Behavioral Correlates of Female Adolescents' Occupational Choices. Adolescence, 1973, Fall, 8(31), 421-432.

Ponzo, Z. Relations among Sex-Role Identity and Selected Intellectual and Nonintellectual Factors for High School Freshmen and Seniors. Unpublished doctoral dissertation, University of Wisconsin. Dissertation Abstracts, 1967, 28(8-A), 2990.

──────. A Study to Determine Relations in Role Identity, Scholastic Aptitude, Achievement, and Non-Academic Factors among Male and Female Students. Final Report. Washington, D. C.: Office of Education, Bureau of Research, 1967. Also available from ERIC (ED028488), 1969.

Porter, J. Sex-Role Concepts, Their Relationship to Psychological Well-Being and to Future Plans in Female College Seniors. Unpublished doctoral dissertation, University of Rochester. Dissertation Abstracts, 1967, 28(5-A), 1903.

Primavera, L. H., Simon, W. E., and Primavera, A. M. The Relationship between Self-Esteem and Academic Achievement: An Investigation of Sex Differences. Psychology in the Schools, 1974, April, 11(2), 213-216.

Putnam, B. A., and Hansen, J. C. Relationship of Self-Concept and Feminine Role Concept to Vocational Maturity in Young Women. Journal of Counseling Psychology, 1972, September, 19(5), 436-440.

Quimby, V. Differences in the Self-Ideal Relationship of an Achieved Group and an Underachieved Group. California Journal of Educational Research, 1967, 18(1), 23-31.

Rappaport, A. F., Payne, D., and Steinmann, A. Perceptual Differences between Married and Single College Women for the Concepts of Self, Ideal Woman, and Man's Ideal Woman. Journal of Marriage and the Family, 1970, August, 32(3), 441-442.

Resnick, H., Fauble, M. L., and Osipow, S. H. Vocational Crystallization and Self-Esteem in College Students. Journal of Counseling Psychology, 1970, September, 17(5), 465-467.

Richardson, M. S. Self-Concepts and Role Concepts in the Career Orientation of College Women. Unpublished doctoral dissertation, New York University. Dissertation Abstracts International, 1973, 33(B), 5001-5002.

_____. Self-Concepts and Role Concepts in the Career Orientation of College Women. Journal of Counseling Psychology, 1975, March, 22(2), 122-126.

Robitaille, D. F. A Comparison of Boys' and Girls' Feelings of Self-Confidence in Arithmetic Computation. Mathematics, Education Diagnostic and Instructional Center (MEDIC), Report No. 3-76, University of British Columbia, Vancouver, 1976. Also available from ERIC (ED128229), 1977.

Rose, C. Women's Sex-Role Attitudes: A Historical Perspective. New Directions for Higher Education, 1975, Autumn, 11, 1-31.

Rosenberg, F. R., and Simmons, R. G. Sex Differences in Self-Concept in Adolescence. Sex Roles: A Journal of Research, 1975, 1, 147-160.

Rosenkrantz, P., Vogel, S., Bee, H., Broverman, I., and Broverman, D. M. Sex-Role Stereotypes and Self-Concepts in College Students. Journal of Consulting and Clinical Psychology, 1968, 32, 287-295.

Rosenthal, J. C. A Study of the Self-Actualizing Process of Selected University Freshmen Women Students. Unpublished doctoral dissertation, Colorado State College. Dissertation Abstracts, 1968, 28(11-A), 4451.

Ryckman, R. M., and Sherman, M. F. Interactive Effects of Locus of Control and Sex of Subject on Confidence Ratings and Performance in Achievement-Related Situations. Paper presented at the American Psychological Association Convention, Honolulu, 1972.

Sands, B. L. Relationship Between Family Life Teachers' Self-Actualization and Self-Perception of Competency. Journal of Home Economics, 1971, February, 63, 113-115.

Sappenfield, B. R., and Harris, C. L. Self-Reported Masculinity-Femininity as Related to Self-Esteem. Psychological Reports, 1975, 37, 669-670.

Schaefer, C. E. A Psychological Study of 10 Exceptionally Creative Adolescent Girls. Exceptional Children, 1970, 36(6), 431-441.

Schmidt, J. A. Self-Concepts and Career Exploration. Elementary School Guidance and Counselor, 1976, December, 11, 149-153.

Schofield, L. F., and Caple, R. B. Self-Concepts of Mature and Young Women Students. Journal of College Student Personnel, 1971, July, 12(4), 297-302.

Schomburg, T. E. A Correlative Study of Body Concept, Academic Achievement, Level of Aspiration, Race and Sex. Unpublished doctoral dissertation, American University. Dissertation Abstracts International, 1975, June, 35(12-A, Pt. 1), 7662.

Sciortino, R. Factorial Study of Motivational Self-Ratings by Female Subjects. Psychological Reports, 1967, 21(2), 565-570.

Sears, R. R. Relation of Early Socialization Experiences to Self-Concepts and Gender Role in Middle Childhood. Child Development, 1970, 41(2), 267-289.

Seeman, J. Personality Integration in College Women. Journal of Personality and Social Psychology, 1966, July, 4(1), 91-93.

Self, P. A. P. Self-Concepts, Attitudes, and Values of Women Honor Students. Dissertation Abstracts International, 1974, 34(A), 7595.

Shaw, M. C., Edson, K., and Bell, H. M. The Self-Concept of Bright Under-Achieving High School Students as Revealed by an Adjective Check List. Personnel and Guidance Journal, 1960, 39, 193-196.

―――, and Alves, G. J. The Self-Concept of Bright Academic Under-Achievers: Continued. Personnel and Guidance Journal, 1963, 42, 401-403.

Shrauger, J. S., and Terbovic, M. L. Self-Evaluation and Assessments of Performance by Self and Others. Journal of Consulting and Clinical Psychology, 1976, August, 44(4), 564-572.

Simmons, W. D. Superior Women College Students: A Study of Their Self Concepts and Academic Motivation. Final Report. Washington, D. C.: Office of Education, Bureau of Research, 1968. Also available from ERIC (ED022420), 1969.

_____. Superior Women College Students: A Study of Their Self Concepts and Academic Motivation. Unpublished doctoral dissertation, University of Illinois. Dissertation Abstracts, 1969, 29(8-A), 2453.

Simon, W. E., and Simon, M. G. Self-Esteem, Intelligence and Standardized Academic Achievement. Psychology in the Schools, 1975, January, 12, 97-100.

Slaney, F. J. Some Correlates of Achievement Motivation in Women in Student Personnel Work. Unpublished doctoral dissertation, Ohio State University. Dissertation Abstracts International, 1973, April, 33(10-A), 5523-5524.

Small, A., Nakamura, C. Y., and Ruble, D. N. Sex Differences in Children's Outer Directedness and Self Perceptions in a Problem Solving Situation. Unpublished manuscript, University of California, Los Angeles, 1973.

Smalley, D. Are We Lowering the Self-Esteem of Girls? School and Community, 1973, April, 59, 19.

Smith, B. D., and Teevan, R. C. Relationships Among Self-Ideal Congruence, Adjustment, and Fear-of-failure Motivation. Journal of Personality, 1971, March, 39(1), 44-56.

Smith, H. M., and Clifton, M. A. Sex Differences in Expressed Self-Concepts Concerning the Performance of Selected Motor Skills. Perceptual and Motor Skills, 1962, 14, 71-73.

Smokler, C. B. The Development of Self-Esteem and Femininity in Early Adolescence. Unpublished doctoral dissertation, University of Michigan. Dissertation Abstracts International, 1975, January, 35(7-B), 3599-3600.

Snyder, E. E., and Kivlin, J. E. Women Athletes and Aspects of Psychological Well-Being and Body Image. Research Quarterly, 1975, May, 46(2), 191-199.

Soares, A. T., and Soares, L. M. A Comparative Study of the Self-Perceptions of Disadvantaged Children in Elementary and Secondary Schools. Paper presented at the American Psychological Association Convention, Washington, D. C., 1969. Also available from ERIC (ED036578), 1970.

Spaulding, R. Achievement, Creativity, and Self-Concept Correlates of Teacher-Pupil Transactions in Elementary School. Cooperative Research Project No. 1352. Washington, D.C.: Office of Education, 1963.

Spence, J.T., Helmreich, R., and Stapp, J. Ratings of Self and Peers on Sex Role Attributes and Their Relation to Self-Esteem and Conceptions of Masculinity and Femininity. Journal of Personality and Social Psychology, 1975, July, 32(1), 29-39.

Spiegel, J. Sex Role Concepts. How Women and Men See Themselves and Each Other. A Selected Annotated Bibliography. Washington, D.C.: Business and Professional Women's Foundation, 1969.

Stake, J.E., and Stake, M. Performance Self-Esteem and Dominance in Mixed-Sex Dyads. Paper presented at the American Psychological Association Convention, San Francisco, 1977.

Stanwyck, D.J., and Felker, D.W. Intellectual Achievement Responsibility and Anxiety as Functions of Self-Concept of Third to Sixth Grade Boys and Girls. Paper presented at the American Educational Research Association meeting, New York, 1973. Also available from ERIC (ED080903), 1974.

Steinmann, A., and Fox, D.J. Specific Areas of Agreement and Conflict in Women's Self-Perception and Their Perception of Men's Ideal Woman in Two South American Urban Communities and an Urban Community in the United States. Journal of Marriage and the Family, 1969, May, 31(2), 281-289.

———, Levi, J., and Fox, D.J. Self-Concept of College Women Compared with Their Concept of Ideal Woman and Men's Ideal Woman. Journal of Counseling Psychology, 1964, 11(4), 370-374.

Stephan, W.G., Rosenfield, D., and Stephan, C. Egotism in Males and Females. Journal of Personality and Social Psychology, 1976, 34(6), 1161-1167.

Stericker, A.B., and Johnson, J.E. Sex-Role Identification and Self-Esteem in College Students: Do Men and Women Differ? Sex Roles: A Journal of Research, 1977, 3(1), 19-26.

Stewart, A.J., and Winter, D.G. Self-Definition and Social Definition in Women. Journal of Personality, 1974, 42(2), 238-259.

Stillwell, L.J. An Investigation of the Interrelationships Among Global Self Concept, Role Self Concept and Achievement. Unpublished doctoral dissertation, Western Reserve University. Dissertation Abstracts, 1966, 27(3-A), 682.

Sundheim, B.J.M. The Relationship Among "n" Achievement, "n" Affiliation, Sex-Role Concepts, Academic Grades, and Curricular Choice. Dissertation Abstracts, 1963, 23, 3471.

Taylor, P. H. Role and Role Conflicts in a Group of Middleclass Wives and Mothers. Sociological Review, 1964, November, 12(3), 317-327.

Taylor, R. G. Personality Traits and Discrepant Achievement: A Review. Journal of Counseling Psychology, 1964, 11, 76-82.

Tessler, Richard C., and Schwartz, S. H. Help Seeking, Self-Esteem, and Achievement Motivation: An Attributional Analysis. Journal of Personality and Social Psychology, 1972, March, 21(3), 318-326.

Turner, B. F. Self-Concepts of Older Women. Symposium presentation at the American Psychological Association Convention, San Francisco, 1977.

Vacher, C. J. D. The Self Concept of Underachieving Freshmen and Upper-Class Women College Students. Journal of College Student Personnel, 1963, 5, 28-31+.

Vaught, G. M., and Rosenbaum, G. A Note on the Ego-Strength Scale and Sex Differences in College Students. Psychological Record, 1966, 16(1), 87-89.

Veres, H. C. Dimensions of Career Commitment in Two-Year College Women. Unpublished doctoral dissertation, Cornell University. Dissertation Abstracts International, 1974, 35(2-A), 831.

Vincent, M. F. Comparison of Self-Concepts of College Women: Athletes and Physical Education Majors. Research Quarterly, 1976, May, 47(2), 218-225.

Voss, J. H., and Skinner, D. A. Concepts of Self and Ideal Woman Held by College Women: A Replication. Journal of College Student Personnel, 1975, May, 16(3), 210-213.

Wallston, B. S. The Effects of Sex-Role Ideology, Self-Esteem, and Expected Future Interactions with an Audience on Male Help Seeking. Sex Roles: A Journal of Research, 1976, 2(4), 353-365.

Warren, N. T. Self-Esteem and Sources of Cognitive Bias in the Evaluation of Past Performance. Journal of Consulting and Clinical Psychology, 1976, December, 44(6), 966-975.

Weis, S. J. F. Self Esteem and Self Implementation in Role Saliency of Women. Unpublished manuscript, Pennsylvania State University, 1970.

West, C. K., and Fish, J. A. Relationships Between Self-Concept and School Achievement: A Survey of Empirical Investigations. Final Report. Washington, D. C.: National Institute of Education, 1973. Also available from ERIC (ED092239), 1974.

Wetter, R. E. Levels of Self-Esteem Associated with Four Sex Role Categories. Paper presented at the American Psychological Association Convention, Chicago, 1975.

Whiteside, W. Age and Sex Differences in Self-Perception as Related to Ideal Trait Selections: Use of Tennessee Self Concept Scale. Adolescence, 1976, Winter, 11, 585-592.

Wiggins, R. G. Differences in Self-Perceptions of Ninth Grade Boys and Girls. Adolescence, 1973, Winter, 8, 491-496.

Winters, C. J., and Sorenson, J. Individual Factors Related to Career Orientation in Women. In S. H. Osipow (Ed.), Emerging Women: Career Analysis and Outlooks. Columbus, OH: Charles E. Merrill, 1975, 51-68.

Withycombe-Brocato, C. J. The Mature Graduate Woman Student: Who Is She? Unpublished doctoral dissertation, United States International University, 1969.

Wylie, R. C. The Self Concept. Lincoln: University of Nebraska Press, 1961.

Ziegler, S. Self-Perception of Athletes and Coaches. In D. Harris (ed.), Women and Sport: A National Research Conference, Penn State HPER Series No. 2, 1973, 293-305.

Zuckerman, D. M. Self-Concept, Family Background, and Personal Traits Which Predict the Life Goals and Sex-Role Attitudes of Technical College and University Women. Unpublished doctoral dissertation, Ohio State University, 1977.

B. PERSONALITY CHARACTERISTICS

Ahluwalia, S. P., and Sidhu, N. A Study of Personal Problems of Some Adolescent Girls and Their Effect on Academic Achievement. Journal of Psychological Researches, 1969, 13(1), 56-57.

Ali, S. N., and Akhter, M. Motivational Effect of Level of Aspiration on Performance in Adjusted and Maladjusted Individuals. Manas, 1973, 20(1), 1-7.

Alper, T. G. Achievement Motivation in College Women: A Now-You-See-It-Now-You-Don't Phenomenon. American Psychologist, 1974, 29(3), 194-203.

Alutto, J. A., Hrebiniak, L. G., and Alonso, R. C. A Study of Differential Socialization for Members of One Professional Occupation. Journal of Health and Social Behavior, 1971, June, 12(2), 140-147.

Anderson, L. B., and Spencer, P. A. Personal Adjustment and Academic Predictability Among College Freshmen. Journal of Applied Psychology, 1963, 47(2), 97-100.

Angrist, S. S. Personality Maladjustment and Career Aspirations of College Women. Sociological Symposium, 1970, Fall, 5, 1-8.

Apostal, R. A. Personality Type and Preferred College Subculture. Journal of College Student Personnel, 1970, May, 11(3), 206-209.

Astin, A. W. Personal and Environmental Factors Associated with College Dropouts Among High Aptitude Students. Journal of Educational Psychology, 1965, 55, 219-227.

Astin, H. S. Personal and Environmental Factors in Career Decisions of Young Women. Final Report. Washington, D. C.: Bureau of Social Research, 1970.

Avila, D. L. An Inverted Factor Analysis of Personality Differences Between Career- and Homemaking-Oriented Women. Unpublished doctoral dissertation, University of Nebraska. Dissertation Abstracts, 1964, 25(1), 609.

_____. Inverted Factor Analysis of Personality Differences Between Career- and Homemaking-Oriented Women. Journal of Educational Research, 1967, May, 60, 416-418.

Bachtold, L. M. Personality Differences Among High Ability Underachievers. Journal of Educational Research, 1969, September, 63(1), 16-18.

_____. Similarities in Personality Profiles of College and Career Women. Psychological Reports, 1973, October, 33(2), 429-430.

_____. Personality Characteristics of Women of Distinction. Psychology of Women Quarterly, 1976, Fall, 1(1), 70-78.

_____, and Werner, E. E. Personality Profiles of Gifted Women: Psychologists. American Psychologist, 1970, 25(3), 234-243.

_____, and _____. Personality Profiles of Women Psychologists: Three Generations. Developmental Psychology, 1971, September, 5(2), 273-278.

_____, and _____. Personality Characteristics of Women Scientists. Psychological Reports, 1972, October, 31(2), 391-396.

_____, and _____. Personality Characteristics of Creative Women. Perceptual and Motor Skills, 1973, February, 36(1), 311-319.

_____, and _____. Personality Profiles of Gifted Women: Authors and Artists. Unpublished manuscript, University of California, Davis, n. d.

Bailey, J. T., and Claus, K. E. Comparative Analysis of the Personality Structure of Nursing Students. Nursing Research, 1969, July, 18(4), 320-326.

Balazs, E. K. Psycho-Social Study of Outstanding Female Athletes. Research Quarterly, 1975, 46(3), 267-273.

―――, and Nickerson, E. A Personality Needs Profile of Some Outstanding Female Athletes. Journal of Clinical Psychology, 1976, January, 32(1), 45-49.

Barger, B., and Hall, E. Personality Patterns and Achievement in College. Educational and Psychological Measurement, 1964, 24, 339-346.

Barnett, R. C. Vocational Planning of College Women: A Psycho-Social Study. Proceedings of the Annual Convention of the American Psychological Association, 1967, 2, 345-346.

―――. Personality Correlates of Vocational Planning. Genetic Psychology Monographs, 1971, May, 83(2), 309-356.

Benedetti, C. R. Similarities and Differences in the Leadership Styles and Personal Characteristics of Women in Educational Administration and Women in Business Administration. Unpublished doctoral dissertation, Western Michigan University. Dissertation Abstracts International, 1975, September, 36(3-A), 1188-1189.

Benreti-Fuchs, K. M., and Meadows, W. M. Interest, Mental Health, and Attitudinal Correlates of Academic Achievement Among University Students. British Journal of Educational Psychology, 1976, June, 46(2), 212-219.

Berman, G., and Eisenberg, M. Psycho-Social Aspects of Academic Achievement. American Journal of Orthopsychiatry, 1971, April, 41(3), 406-415.

Bezler, A. G. Characteristics of High School Girls Choosing Traditional or Pioneer Vocations. Personnel and Guidance Journal, 1967, 45, 659-664.

Birnbaum, J. A. Life Patterns, Personality Style, and Self-Esteem in Gifted Family-Oriented and Career-Committed Women. Unpublished doctoral dissertation, University of Michigan. Dissertation Abstracts International, 1971, 32(3-B), 1894.

―――. Life Patterns and Self-Esteem in Gifted Family-Oriented and Career-Committed Women. In M. T. S. Mednick, et al.

(eds.), Women and Achievement: Social and Motivational Analyses. New York: Halsted, 1975, 396-419.

Blank, S. An Investigation of Personality Variables of Female Junior College Students Choosing Male and Female Dominated Careers. Unpublished doctoral dissertation, University of Miami, Florida. Dissertation Abstracts International, 1975, June, 35(12-B, Pt. 1), 6065.

Blankstein, K. R., Darte, E., and Donaldson, P. A Further Correlate of Sensation Seeking: Achieving Tendency. Perceptual and Motor Skills, 1976, June, 42(3, Pt. 2), 1251-1255.

Blaubergs, M. S. Personality Characteristics of Eminent Women. A lecture for the Focus on Women Lecture Series, Sponsored by the University of Georgia, Athens, Spring 1977.

———. Overcoming the Sexist Barriers to Gifted Women's Achievement. In B. Johnson (ed.), Advantage/Disadvantage Gifted. Ventura, CA: Ventura County Superintendent of Schools Office, 1979.

Brockway, B. S. Assertive Training for Professional Women. Social Work, 1976, November, 21(6), 498-505.

Bruch, C. B., and Morse, J. A. Initial Study of Creative (Productive) Women Under the Bruch-Morse Model. Gifted Child Quarterly, 1972, Winter, 16(4), 282-289.

Burton, E. C. State and Trait Anxiety, Achievement Motivation and Skill Attainment in College Women. Research Quarterly, 1971, May, 42(2), 139-144.

Carney, R. E., and McKeachie, W. J. Religion, Sex, Social Class, Probability of Success, and Student Personality. Journal for the Scientific Study of Religion, 1963, 3, 32-42.

Cartwright, L. K. Women in Medical School. Unpublished doctoral dissertation, University of California, Berkeley. Dissertation Abstracts International, 1971, April, 31(10-B), 6237.

———. Personality and Family Background of a Sample of Women Medical Students at the University of California. Journal of American Medical Women's Association, 1972, 27, 260-266.

———. Personality Differences in Male and Female Medical Students. Psychiatry in Medicine, 1972, July, 3(3), 213-218.

———. Conscious Factors Entering into Decisions of Women to Study Medicine. Journal of Social Issues, 1972, 28(2), 201-215.

Cashdan, S., and Welsh, G. S. Personality Correlates of Creative

Potential in Talented High School Students. Journal of Personality, 1966, 34(3), 445-455.

Chabassol, D. J., and Thomas, D. C. Anxiety, Aptitude, Achievement and Performance in Female Teachers. Alberta Journal of Educational Research, 1967, 13(4), 291-294.

Chance, J. E. Personality Differences and Level of Aspiration. Journal of Consulting Psychology, 1960, April, 24, 111-115.

Clay, J. T. Personality Traits of Female Intercollegiate Athletes and Female Intercollegiate Athletic Coaches. Unpublished doctoral dissertation, University of Utah. Dissertation Abstracts International, 1975, February, 35(8-A), 5090.

Clements, K. Emotional Characteristics of Mature Women Students in Education. Available from ERIC (ED087980), 1974.

Cleveland, S. Personality Patterns Associated with the Professions of Dietitian and Nurse. Journal of Health and Human Behavior, 1961, 2, 113-124.

Clopton, J. R., and Neuringer, C. An MMPI Scale to Measure Scholastic Personality in Women. Perceptual and Motor Skills, 1973, December, 37(3), 963-966.

Constantini, E., and Craik, K. H. Women as Politicians: The Social Background, Personality, and Political Careers of Female Party Leaders. Journal of Social Issues, 1972, 28(2), 217-236.

Cook, B. I. Role Aspirations as Evidenced in Senior Women. Unpublished doctoral dissertation, Purdue University. Dissertation Abstracts, 1968, 28(A), 2067.

Corbin, C. B. Attitudes Toward Physical Activity of Champion Women Basketball Players. International Journal of Sport Psychology, 1976, 7(1), 14-21.

Cotier, S., and Palmer, R. J. Relationships Among Sex, Sociometric, Self, and Test Anxiety Factors and the Academic Achievement of Elementary School Children. Psychology in the Schools, 1970, July, 7, 211-216.

Crandall, V. C. Personality Characteristics and Social and Achievement Behaviors Associated with Children's Social Desirability Response Tendencies. Journal of Personality and Social Psychology, 1966, 4(5), 477-486.

Crouch, J. G. The Role of Sex, Anxiety, and Independence as Moderator Variables in the Achievement of College Freshmen. Dissertation Abstracts, 1968, 29(11-A), 3827.

Crovitz, E. K. Personality Traits of Female P. A. Program Applicants and Admittees. Paper presented at the American Psychological Association Convention, Chicago, 1975.

Davids, A. Psychological Characteristics of High School Male and Female Potential Scientists in Comparison with Academic Underachievers. Psychology in the Schools, 1966, 3(1), 79-87.

Davis, J. A. Nonintellectual Factors in College Student Achievement. In From High School to College: Reading for Counselors. New York: College Entrance Examination Board, 1965.

Desiderato, O., and Koskinen, P. Anxiety, Study Habits, and Academic Achievement. Journal of Counseling Psychology, 1969, 16(2, Pt. 1), 162-165.

DiMarco, N., and Whitsitt, S. E. A Comparison of Female Supervisors in Business and Government Organizations. Journal of Vocational Behavior, 1975, April, 6(2), 185-196.

DiSabatino, M. Psychological Factors Inhibiting Women's Occupational Aspirations and Vocational Choices: Implications for Counseling. Vocational Guidance Quarterly, 1976, 25(1), 43-49.

Donnan, H. H. An Evaluative Study of Selected Personality Measures in the Prediction of Achievement and Survival of Students at the University of North Carolina. Unpublished doctoral dissertation, University of North Carolina. Dissertation Abstracts, 1967, 27(8-A), 2388-2389.

Doty, C. N., and Hoeflin, R. M. A Descriptive Study of Thirty-Five Unmarried Graduate Women. Journal of Marriage and the Family, 1964, February, 26, 1, 91-94.

Dua, P. S. Personality Characteristics Differentiating Women Leaders from Nonleaders in a University. Journal of the National Association of Women Deans and Counselors, 1964, Spring, 27, 128-132.

Dunteman, G. H. Discriminant Analysis of the MMPI for Female College Students in Health and Education. Journal of Experimental Education, 1967, Spring, 35, 85-90.

Durflinger, G. W. Academic and Personality Differences Between Women Students Who Do Complete the Elementary Teaching Credential Program and Those Who Do Not. Educational and Psychological Measurement, 1963, Winter, 23, 775-783.

Edwards, C. N. The Student Nurse: A Study in Sex Role Transition. Psychological Reports, 1969, 25(3), 975-990.

Elton, C. F., and Rose, H. A. Significance of Personality in the Vocational Choice of College Women. Journal of Counseling Psychology, 1967, July 14(4), 293-298.

Entwistle, N. J. Personality and Academic Attainment. <u>British Journal of Educational Psychology</u>, 1972, June, 42, 137-151.

Erb, E. D. Conformity and Achievement in College. <u>Personnel and Guidance Journal</u>, 1961, January, 39, 361-366.

Fagerburg, J. E. A Comparative Study of Undergraduate Women in Relation to Selected Personal Characteristics and Certain Effects of Educational Interruption. Unpublished doctoral dissertation, Purdue University. <u>Dissertation Abstracts,</u> 1968, 28(11-A), 4445-4446.

Faunce, P. S. Personality Characteristics and Vocational Interests Related to the College Persistence of Academically Gifted Women. Unpublished doctoral dissertation, University of Minnesota. <u>Dissertation Abstracts,</u> 1967, 28(1-B), 338.

_____. Personality Characteristics and Vocational Interests Related to the College Persistence of Academically Gifted Women. <u>Journal of Counseling Psychology,</u> 1968, 15(1), 31-40.

_____. Withdrawal of Academically Gifted Women. <u>Journal of College Student Personnel</u>, 1968, May, 9(3), 171-176.

_____. <u>The Effects of Personality Characteristics of High, Middle, and Low Ability Students on College Persistence.</u> Final Report. Washington, D. C.: Office of Education, Bureau of Research, 1973. Also available from ERIC (ED083503), 1974.

Feld, S. C., and Lewis, J. The Assessment of Achievement Anxieties in Children. In C. P. Smith (ed.), <u>Achievement-Related Motives in Children.</u> New York: Russell Sage Foundation, 1969, 151-199.

Fennema, E., and Sherman, J. A. Selected Cognitive and Affective Factors Related to Mathematics Achievement by Males and Females. Paper presented to the American Association for the Advancement of Science meeting, Boston, February 1976.

Feulner, P. N. Women in the Professions: A Social-Psychological Study. <u>Dissertation Abstracts International</u>, 1974, February, 34(8-A, Pt. 2), 5309.

Field, R. S. Personality Variables and Problem Solving Performance: An Investigation of the Relationship between Field-Dependence-Independence, Sex-Role Identification, Problem Difficulty and Problem Solving Performance. Unpublished doctoral dissertation, 1968.

Frieze, I., Parsons, J., and Ruble, D. N. Some Determinants of Career Aspirations in College Women. Paper read at UCLA Symposium on Sex Roles and Sex Differences, Los Angeles, 1972.

Frost, B. P. Anxiety and Educational Achievement. British Journal of Educational Psychology, 1968, 38(3), 293-301.

Fruen, M. A., Rothman, A. I., and Steiner, J. W. Comparison of Characteristics of Male and Female Medical School Applicants. Journal of Medical Education, 1974, February, 49(2), 137-145.

Gardiner, H. W. Performance of Student Nurses on the Edwards Personal Preference Schedule. Journal of Psychology, 1976, November, 94, 297-300.

Goerss, K. V. W. A Study of Personality Factors of Selected Women Administrators in Higher Education. Unpublished doctoral dissertation, University of Southern Mississippi. Dissertation Abstracts International, 1975, 36(A), 1942.

Goldman, E. K. Need Achievement as a Motivational Basis for the Risky Shift. Journal of Personality, 1975, June, 43(2), 346-356.

Gottsdanker, J. S. Intellectual Interest Patterns of Gifted College Students. Educational and Psychological Measurement, 1968, 28(2), 361-366.

Green, L. H. An Investigation of Factors Which Influence the Vocational Classification of Career Oriented and Home Oriented Women. Unpublished doctoral dissertation, Ohio State University. Dissertation Abstracts International, 1971, October, 32(4-B), 2377-2378.

Gysbers, N. C., Johnston, J. A., and Gust, T. Characteristics of Homemaker- and Career-Oriented Women. Journal of Counseling Psychology, 1968, November, 15(6), 541-546.

Hannah, W. Personality Differentials Between Lower Division Dropouts and Stay-ins. Journal of College Student Personnel, 1971, January, 12(1), 16-19.

Harmatz, M. G. The Effects of Anxiety, Motivating Instructions, Success and Failure Reports, and Sex of Subject Upon Level of Aspiration and Performance. Unpublished Master's thesis, University of Washington, 1962.

Heilbrun, A. B., Jr. Personality Factors in College Dropout. Journal of Applied Psychology, 1965, 49, 1-7.

Helson, R. Narrowness in Creative Women. Psychological Reports, 1966, 19(2), 618.

_____. Personality of Women with Imaginative and Artistic Interests: The Role of Masculinity, Originality, and Other Characteristics in Their Creativity. Journal of Personality, 1966, 34, 1-25.

———. Personality Characteristics and Developmental History of Creative College Women. Genetic Psychology Monographs, 1967, 76(2), 205-256.

———. Women Mathematicians and the Creative Personality. Journal of Consulting and Clinical Psychology, 1971, 36(2), 210-220. Also in J. M. Bardwick (ed.), Readings on the Psychology of Women. New York: Harper and Row, 1972, 93-100.

———. Subtypes of Creative Men and Women in Mathematics. Paper presented at the American Association for the Advancement of Science meeting, Boston, February 1976.

———. Personality, Style, and Product in Creative Women. In K. Paige (ed.), Women: Social and Psychological Perspective. Sunderland, MA: Sinauer Associates, in press.

Henschel, B. J. S. A Comparison of the Personality Variables of Women Administrators and Women Teachers in Education. Unpublished doctoral dissertation, University of Utah. Dissertation Abstracts, 1965, 25(A), 6313.

Herron, E. W. Relationship of Experimentally Aroused Achievement Motivation to Academic Achievement Anxiety. Journal of Abnormal and Social Psychology, 1964, 69, 690-694.

Hesselbart, S. Self-Concept, Personality Correlates, and Need Achievement in Honors College Women. Paper presented at the American Sociological Association Convention, 1972.

Hill, K. T. Social Reinforcement as a Function of Test Anxiety and Success-Failure Experiences. Child Development, 1967, 38, 723-737.

———, and Dusek, J. B. Children's Achievement Expectations as a Function of Social Reinforcement, Sex of S, and Test Anxiety. Child Development, 1969, 40(2), 547-557.

———, and Sarason, S. B. The Relation of Test Anxiety and Defensiveness to Test and School Performance Over the Elementary School Years: A Further Longitudinal Study. Monograph of the Society for Research in Child Development. Chicago: University of Chicago Press, 1966.

Hoban-Hopkins, F. T. A Study of the Relationships Between Freshman Student Nurses' Academic Performance, SAT Scores and Specified Personality Variables. Unpublished doctoral dissertation, University of Toledo. Dissertation Abstracts International, 1976, April, 36(10-A), 6473-6474.

Honigfeld, G., and Spigel, I. M. Achievement Motivation and Field Independence. Journal of Consulting Psychology, 1960, 24, 550-551.

Hoyt, D., and Kennedy, C. Interest and Personality Correlates of Career-Motivated and Homemaking-Motivated College Women. Journal of Consulting Psychology, 1963, 66, 59-66.

Isaacs, A. F. Athletic Prowess and Giftedness: III. A Former World Champion Archer Tells How She Did It. Gifted Child Quarterly, 1970, Fall, 14(3), 154-158.

Isaacson, R. L. Relation Between n Achievement, Test Anxiety, and Curricular Choices. Journal of Abnormal and Social Psychology, 1964, 68(4), 447-452.

Izard, C. E. Personality Characteristics (EPPS), Level of Expectation, and Performance. Journal of Consulting Psychology, 1962, 26(4), 394.

James, R. J. Traits Associated with the Initial and Persistent Interest in the Study of College Science. Journal of Research in Science Teaching, 1972, 9(3), 231-234.

Jantzen, A. C. Some Characteristics of Female Occupational Therapists. Unpublished doctoral dissertation, Boston College, 1971. Dissertation Abstracts International, 1971, 32(4-B), 2244. Also available from ERIC (ADG71-23996), 1971.

Joesting, J., and Whitehead, G. I. Comparison of Women's Studies Students with Female Golf Star Athletes on the 16 PF. Perceptual and Motor Skills, 1976, April, 42(2), 477-478.

Johnson, D. E. Personality Characteristics in Relation to College Persistence. Journal of Counseling Psychology, 1970, 17(2), 162-167.

Johnson, P. A. Comparison of Personality Traits of Superior Skilled Women Athletes in Basketball, Bowling, Field Hockey, and Golf. Research Quarterly, 1972, December, 43, 409-415.

Johnson, R. W., and Leonard, L. C. Psychological Test Characteristics and Performance of Nursing Students. Nursing Research, 1970, March, 19(2), 147-150.

Karman, F. J. Women: Personal and Environmental Factors in Role Identification and Career Choice. Unpublished doctoral dissertation, University of California, Los Angeles. Dissertation Abstracts International, 1972, October, 33(4-A), 1440. Also available from ERIC (ED084383), 1973.

Kass, N. Risk in Decision-Making as a Function of Age, Sex, and Probability Preference. Child Development, 1964, 35, 577-582.

Katz, J. (ed.). Career and Autonomy in College Women. In

Class, Character and Career: Determinants of Occupational Choice in College Students. Stanford: Institute for the Study of Human Problems, Stanford University, 1969, 146-147.

Kestenbaum, J. M., and Weiner, B. Achievement Performance Related to Achievement Motivation and Text Anxiety. Journal of Consulting and Clinical Psychology, 1970, 34(3), 343-344.

Khan, S. B. Affective Correlates of Academic Achievement. Journal of Educational Psychology, 1969, June, 60(3), 216-221.

_____. Dimensions of Manifest Anxiety and Their Relationship to College Achievement. Journal of Consulting and Clinical Psychology, 1970, October, 35(2), 223-228.

Knafle, J. D. Relationship of Behavior Ratings to Grades Earned by Female High School Students. Journal of Educational Research, 1972, November, 66, 106-110.

Kogan, N., and Dorros, K. Sex Differences in Risk Taking and Its Attribution. Paper presented at the American Psychological Association Convention, Chicago, 1975.

Krall, V. Personality Factors in Nursing School Success and Failure. Nursing Research, 1970, May, 19(3), 265-267.

Kundsin, R. B. (ed.). Women and Success: The Anatomy of Achievement. New York: William Morrow, 1974.

Lansky, L. M., Crandall, V. J., Kagan, J., and Baker, C. T. Sex Differences in Aggression and Its Correlates in Middle-Class Adolescents. Child Development, 1961, 32, 45-58.

LaRussa, G. W. Portia's Decision: Women's Motives for Studying Law and Their Later Career Satisfaction as Attorneys. Psychology of Women Quarterly, 1977, Summer, 1(4), 350-364.

_____. Prospective Portia: Her Personality Characteristics and Value Orientation. Paper presented at the American Psychological Association Convention, San Francisco, 1977.

Laws, J. L. Psychological Dimensions of Women's Work-Force Participation. Sloan Management Review, 1974, Spring, 15(3), 49-52.

Lenning, O. T. An Exploratory Study of Factors Differentiating Freshmen Educational Growth. Paper presented at the American College Personnel Association meeting, St. Louis, 1970.

Lerch, H. A. Four Female Collegiate Track Athletes: An Analysis of Personal Constructs. Research Quarterly, 1976, December, 47(4), 687-691.

Liddicoat, J. P. Differences Between Under- and Overachievers at a Small Liberal Arts Women's College. Unpublished doctoral dissertation, Lehigh University. Dissertation Abstracts International, 1972, May, 32(11-A), 6133-6134.

Long, J. M. Sex Differences in Academic Predictions Based on Scholastic, Personality, and Interest Factors. Journal of Experimental Education, 1964, 32, 239-248.

Lovett, S. L. Personality Characteristics and Antecedents of Vocational Choice of Graduate Women Students in Science Research. Unpublished doctoral dissertation, University of California, Berkeley. Dissertation Abstracts, 1969, 29(12-A), 4287-4288.

Loyd, L. L. Personality Characteristics of Selected Women Educators. Dissertation Abstracts International, 1976, 37(A), 743.

McGowan, B., and Liu, P. Y. Creativity and Mental Health of Self-Renewing Women. Measurement and Evaluation in Guidance, 1970, 3(3), 138-146.

McKeachie, W. J. Interaction of Achievement Cues and Facilitating Anxiety in the Achievement of Women. Journal of Applied Psychology, 1969, 53(2, Pt. 1), 147-148.

_____, and Lin, Y. G. Achievement Standards, Debilitating Anxiety, Intelligence and College Women's Achievement. Psychological Record, 1969, 19(3), 457-459.

McKenzie, S. P. A Comparative Study of Feminine Role Perceptions, Selected Personality Characteristics, and Traditional Attitudes of Professional Women and Housewives. Unpublished doctoral dissertation, University of Houston. Dissertation Abstracts International, 1972, 32(10), 5615-5616.

Malumphy, T. M. Personality of Women Athletes in Intercollegiate Competition. Research Quarterly, 1968, October, 39, 610-620.

Manaster, G. J., Friedman, S. T., and Larson, D. Premedical Students' Survivability and Specialization: A Social and Psychological Study. Psychological Reports, 1967, August, 39(1), 35-45.

Mannes, M. The Problems of Creative Women. In Man and Civilization: The Potential of Woman. New York: McGraw-Hill, 1963.

Maquire, U. Effects of Anxiety on Learning, Task Performance and Level of Aspiration in Secondary Modern School Children. British Journal of Educational Psychology, 1966, February, 36, 109-112.

Marlowe, L., and Bessmer, M. If Shakespeare Had a Sister: The

Psychology of Creative Women. Symposium presentation at the American Psychological Association Convention, Washington, D.C., 1976.

Marple, B. L. N. Adult Women Students Compared with Younger Students on Selected Personality Variables. Unpublished doctoral dissertation, Boston College. Dissertation Abstracts International, 1975, March, 35(9-A), 5820.

———. Adult Women Students Compared with Younger Students on Selected Personality Variables. Journal of the National Association for Women Deans, Administrators, and Counselors, 1976, Fall, 40, 11-15.

Martens, R., and Gill, D. L. State Anxiety Among Successful and Unsuccessful Competitors Who Differ in Competitive Trait Anxiety; Sport Competition Anxiety Test. Research Quarterly, 1976, December, 47, 698-708.

Masih, L. K. Career Saliency and Its Relation to Certain Needs, Interests, and Job Values. Personnel and Guidance Journal, 1967, 45(7), 653-658.

Math Mystique; Fear of Figuring. Time, 1977, March 14, 109, 36.

Matis, E. E. An Analysis of Differences in Interests, Personality Needs, and Personality Structures between College Women Majoring in Speech Pathology and College Women Majoring in Other Professional Areas. Unpublished doctoral dissertation, University of Alabama. Dissertation Abstracts, 1969, 29(12-A), 4290-4291.

Matthews, E. Employment Implications of Psychological Characteristics of Men and Women. In W. C. Byham and M. Katzell (eds.), Women in the Work Force: Confrontation with Change. New York: Behavioral Publications, 1972, 27-42.

Mayer, W. K. Vocational Interest Patterns of Teaching and Non-Teaching Female College Graduates. Unpublished doctoral dissertation, University of Florida. Dissertation Abstracts, 1967, 27(9-A), 2831.

Meehan, W. J. A Correlation of Selected Personal Characteristics of Students Identified as High- or Low-Variable on Academic Performance. Unpublished doctoral dissertation, Oklahoma State University. Dissertation Abstracts International, 1975, April, 35(10-A), 6369-6370.

Meir, E. I. Relationship between Intrinsic Needs and Women's Persistence at Work. Journal of Applied Psychology, 1972, August, 56(4), 293-296.

Menoff, B. R. An Investigation of Competitive and Cooperative Behavior in Female Athletes and Nonathletes. Unpublished doctoral dissertation, California School of Professional Psychology, Los Angeles. Dissertation Abstracts International, 1976, May, 36(11-B), 5810.

Meredith, C., and Bradley, J. A Consideration of Art-Science Personality Differences with Particular Reference to the Thing-Person Dimension. Educational Studies, 1976, March, 2(1), 33-44.

Michael, W. B., Haney, R., and Gershon, A. Intellective and Non-Intellective Predictors of Success in Nursing Training. Educational and Psychological Measurement, 1963, 23, 817-821.

Mitchell, B. A. An Investigation into Personality Factors of Administrators of Women's Centers. Dissertation Abstracts International, 1976, 37(A), 1936.

Mogar, R. E. Competition, Achievement, and Personality. Journal of Counseling Psychology, 1962, Summer, 9, 168-172.

Morris, E. The Personality Traits and Psychological Needs of Education Homemakers and Career Women. Unpublished doctoral dissertation, Arizona State University, 1974.

Morris, L. W., Finkelstein, C. S., and Fisher, W. R. Components of School Anxiety: Developmental Trends and Sex Differences. Journal of Genetic Psychology, 1976, March, 128 (1st half), 49-57.

Morrison, R. F., and Sebald, M. L. Personal Characteristics Differentiating Female Executive from Female Nonexecutive Personnel. Journal of Applied Psychology, 1974, October, 59(5), 656-659.

Morse, J. Problems of Gifted Women. Unpublished manuscript, University of Georgia, 1970.

Muhlenkamp, A. F., and Parsons, J. L. Characteristics of Nurses: An Overview of Recent Research Published in a Nursing Research Periodical. Journal of Vocational Behavior, 1972, July, 2(3), 261-273.

Mulvey, M. Psychological and Social Factors in Prediction of Career Patterns in Women. Genetic Psychology Monographs, 1963, 68, 309-386.

Mushier, C. L. A Cross-Sectional Study of the Personality Factors of Girls and Women in Competitive Lacrosse. Unpublished doctoral dissertation, University of Southern California. Dissertation Abstracts International, 1970, August, 31(2-A), 635-636.

_____. Personality and Selected Women Athletes: A Cross Sectional Study. International Journal of Sport Psychology, 1972, 3(1), 25-31.

Myers, A. E. Risk Taking and Academic Success and Their Relation to an Objective Measure of Achievement Motivation. Educational and Psychological Measurement, 1965, 25, 355-363.

Nelson, I. M. Personality Traits and Occupational Values Associated with Choice of Clinical Specialty in Nursing. Unpublished doctoral dissertation, American University. Dissertation Abstracts International, 1974, July, 35(1-A), 175-176.

Nikkari, J. G. Freshman-to-Senior Personality Changes in Basic Collegiate Student Nurses as Compared to Changes in Females in a Liberal Arts College in a Large Midwestern State University. Unpublished doctoral dissertation, University of Michigan. Dissertation Abstracts International, 1970, August, 31(2-B), 774-775.

Norfleet, M. A. Personality Characteristics of Achieving and Under-Achieving High Ability Senior Women. Personnel and Guidance Journal, 1968, 46(10), 976-980.

O'Connor, K. A., and Webb, J. L. Investigation of Personality Traits of College Female Athletes and Nonathletes. Research Quarterly, 1976, May, 47(2), 203-210.

Odell, M. Q. Sex Differences in the Relationship between Anxiety and Need for Achievement and in the Relationship between Anxiety and Need for Affiliation. Unpublished doctoral dissertation, George Washington University. Dissertation Abstracts International, 1969, 30(4-B), 1904.

O'Leary, V. E., and Braun, J. S. Antecedents and Personality Correlates of Academic Careerism in Women. Proceedings of the 80th Annual Convention of the American Psychological Association, 1972, 7, 277-278.

Oliver, L. W. Achievement and Affiliation Motivation in Career-Oriented and Homemaking-Oriented College Women. Journal of Vocational Behavior, 1974, June, 4(3), 275-281.

O'Mahoney, M. T., and Labbie, S. Dimensions of the Image of Nursing in Relation to Academic Success and Factors of Personality. Proceedings of the 81st Annual Convention of the American Psychological Association, Montreal, Canada, 1973, 8, 25-26.

Page, M. J. A Descriptive Analysis of Selected Attitudes, Interests, and Personality Characteristics of Mature College Women. Unpublished doctoral dissertation, North Texas State University. Dissertation Abstracts International, 1972, January, 32(7-A), 3699-3700.

Parsons, J. E., Frieze, I. H., and Ruble, D. N. Intrapsychic Factors Influencing Career Aspirations in College Women. Sex Roles: A Journal of Research, 1978, 4(3), 337-347.

Patrick, T. A. Personality and Family Background Characteristics of Women Who Enter Male-Dominated Professions. Unpublished doctoral dissertation, Columbia University. Dissertation Abstracts International, 1973, 34(5-A), 2396.

Pelechano, V. [Personality, Motivation and Academic Achievement.] Revista de Psicologia General y Aplicada, 1972, January, 27 (114-115), 69-86.

Pfiffner, V. T. Composite Profile of a Top-Level California Community College Woman Administrator. Journal of the National Association for Women Deans, Administrators, and Counselors, 1976, Fall, 40(1), 16-17.

Phillips, B. N. Sex, Social Class, and Anxiety as Sources of Variation in School Achievement. Journal of Educational Psychology, 1962, 53, 316-322.

_____, Hindsman, E., and McGuire, C. Factors Associated with Anxiety and Their Relation to the School Achievement of Adolescents. Psychological Reports, 1960, 7, 365-372.

Phillips, V. K., and Hudgins, A. L. Relationship between Creativity, Sex, and Rule-Orientation Behavior. Perceptual and Motor Skills, 1974, June, 38(3, Pt. 2), 1163-1171.

Pietrofesa, J. J. A Comparison of the Personality Need Structure of College Students Enrolled in Different Academic Majors. National Catholic Guidance Conference Journal, 1970, Summer, 14(4), 218-228.

Porter, J. B. The Vocational Choice of Freshmen College Women as Influenced by Psychological Needs and Parent-Child Relationships. Unpublished doctoral dissertation, University of Oklahoma. Dissertation Abstracts, 1967, 27(11-A), 3730.

Rand, L. M. Characteristics of Career- and Homemaking-Oriented College Freshman Women. Unpublished doctoral dissertation, University of Iowa, 1966.

_____. Masculinity or Femininity? Differentiating Career-Oriented and Homemaking-Oriented College Freshmen Women. Journal of Counseling Psychology, 1968, 15(5), 444-450.

Raynor, J. O. Relationships between Achievement-Related Motives, Future Orientation, and Academic Performance. Journal of Personality and Social Psychology, 1970, 15(1), 28-33.

Reilly, D. E. A Comparative Analysis of Selected Nonintellective

Characteristics of College Graduate and Noncollege Graduate Women Who Entered a Collegiate Nursing Program. Unpublished doctoral dissertation, New York University. Dissertation Abstracts, 1968, 28(10-B), 4180.

Reiter, H. H. Prediction of College Success from Measures of Anxiety, Achievement Motivation, and Scholastic Aptitude. Psychological Reports, 1964, 15, 23-26.

Renner, H. L. A Comparison of the Characteristics and Institutional Perceptions of Mature Married Women Persisters and Non-Persisters at a Small, Urban College. Unpublished doctoral dissertation, University of Maryland. Dissertation Abstracts International, 1975, December, 36(6-A), 3417.

Rettig, J. L. Vocational Choice Patterns and Personality Characteristics of Women in Three Occupational Groups. Unpublished doctoral dissertation, University of California, Los Angeles, 1962. Also available from ERIC (ADG02-59126), 1962.

Rezler, A. G. Characteristics of High School Girls Choosing Traditional or Pioneer Vocations. Personnel and Guidance Journal, 1967, 45(7), 659-665.

Rhude, B. E. A Description of the Vocational and Personal Development of a Few Women B. D. Candidates. Dissertation Abstracts, 1968, 28(7-A), 2565-2566.

Roberts, G. C. Sex and Achievement Motivation Effects on Risk Taking. Research Quarterly, 1975, March, 46(1), 58-70.

Romine, B. H. The Effects of the Interaction between a Personality Characteristic and an Environmental Characteristic on the Achievement of Female College Freshmen When Ability Is Controlled. Unpublished doctoral dissertation, Duke University. Dissertation Abstracts International, 1970, June, 30(12-A), 5301.

Rose, H. A., and Elton, C. F. Sex and Occupational Choice. Journal of Counseling Psychology, 1971, 18(5), 456-461.

Rosen, J. L., and Wallace, D. Personality Antecedents of Career Direction in Middle-Aged Women Educators. Paper presented at the American Psychological Association Convention, Washington, D. C., 1976.

Roskam, A. H. Patterns of Autonomy in High Achieving Adolescent Girls Who Differ in Need for Approval. Dissertation Abstracts International, 1972, September, 33(3-B), 1295-1296.

Roth, R. M., and Puri, P. Direction of Aggression and the Nonachievement Syndrome. Journal of Counseling Psychology, 1967, 14(3), 277-281.

Ruffer, W. A. Two Studies of Personality: Female Graduate Students in Physical Education. Perceptual and Motor Skills, 1976, June, 42(3, Pt. 2), 1268-1270.

Ryan, M. P. Personality Motives, Career Stages, and Work Status Among Nurses. Unpublished doctoral dissertation, Boston University. Dissertation Abstracts International, 1971, October, 32(4-A), 2195.

Ryback, D. The Student Nurse. Journal of Psychiatric Nursing and Mental Health Services, 1968, July, 6(4), 219-223.

Salkind, N. J., and Poggio, J. P. Sex Differences in the Relationship Between Impulsivity and Intellectual Performance. Paper presented at the American Psychological Association Convention, Chicago, 1975.

Sattler, J. M., and Neuringer, C. Personality Characteristics Associated with Over and Underachievers: A Review. Journal of College Student Personnel, 1965, 6, 284-288.

Schmidt, M. R. Personality Change in College Women. Journal of College Student Personnel, 1970, November, 11, 414-418.

Schneier, C. E., and Bartol, K. M. Characteristics of Male Versus Female Emergent Leaders: Exploratory Investigation. Symposium presentation at the American Psychological Association Convention, San Francisco, 1977.

Schwarzer, R. [Test Anxiety, Socioeconomic Status, and Scholastic Achievement.] Psychologie in Erziehung und Unterricht, 1975, 22(1), 16-22.

Sedlacek, C. G. Selected Factors Affecting Certainty and Persistence of Vocational Choice for College Women. Unpublished doctoral dissertation, University of North Dakota. Dissertation Abstracts, 1969, 29(11-A), 3843-3844.

Seeman, J. Personality Integration in College Women. Journal of Personality and Social Psychology, 1966, 4, 91-93.

Shell, L. G. Achievement Motivation in Elementary School Children. Unpublished doctoral dissertation, Colorado State College. Dissertation Abstracts, 1967, 27(8-A), 2409-2410.

Simons, R. H., and Bibb, J. J., Jr. Achievement Motivation, Test Anxiety, and Underachievement in the Elementary School. Journal of Educational Research, 1974, April, 67(8), 366-369.

Sinha, S. Occupational Choice of Extrovert and Introvert Female Students. Indian Psychological Review, 1966, 3(1), 59-62.

Smith, D. G. Personality Differences Between Persisters and Withdrawers in a Small Women's College. Research in Higher Education, 1976, 5(1), 15-25.

Smith, M. A. Compliance and Defiance as It Relates to Role Conflict in Women. Unpublished doctoral dissertation, University of Michigan. Dissertation Abstracts, 1961, 22, 646-647.

Solomon, D., Houlihan, K. A., Busse, T. V., and Parelius, R. J. Parent Behavior and Child Academic Achievement, Achievement Striving, and Related Personality Characteristics. Genetic Psychology Monographs, 1971, 83, 173-273.

Sontag, L. W., and Kibler, M. O. Personality and Other Correlates of I. Q. Change in Women. In J. E. Birren (ed.), Relations of Development and Aging. Springfield, IL: Charles C. Thomas, 1964.

Spiegel, D., and Keith-Spiegel, P. Multiple Predictors of Course Grades for College Men and Women. Journal of College Student Personnel, 1971, January, 12(1), 44-48.

Stanwyck, D. J., and Felker, D. W. Intellectual Achievement Responsibility and Anxiety as Functions of Self-Concept of Third to Sixth Grade Boys and Girls. Paper presented at the American Educational Research Association meeting, New York, 1973.

Stevens, H. A., and Osborn, M. O. Characteristics of Home Economics Graduates. Journal of Home Economics, 1965, December, 57, 773-777.

Stewart, A. J. Longitudinal Prediction from Personality to Life Outcomes among College-Educated Women. Unpublished doctoral dissertation, Harvard University, 1975.

Stewart, D. W., and Louisa, V. Intelligence, Academic Achievement, and Personality: A Canonical Variate Analysis. Psychology in the Schools, 1976, October, 13, 468-470.

Stix, D. L. Discrepant Achievement in College as a Function of Anxiety and Repression. Personnel and Guidance Journal, 1967, April, 45, 804-807.

Stodt, M. M. Autonomy and Complexity in Women Teachers in Leadership Positions. Unpublished doctoral dissertation, Columbia University. Dissertation Abstracts International, 1972, July, 33(1-A), 199.

Stone, L. A., and Foster, J. M. Academic Achievement as a Function of Psychological Needs. Personnel and Guidance Journal, 1964, September, 43, 52-56.

Swaminathan, K. Affiliation and Achievement Motives and Cues in Relation to Conformity and Independence in College Students.

Unpublished doctoral dissertation, University of Michigan. Dissertation Abstracts International, 1971, June, 31(12-B), 7583.

Swisdak, B., and Flaherty, M. R. A Study of Personality Differences between College Graduates and Dropouts. Journal of Psychology, 1964, 57, 25-28.

Szabo, M., and Feldhusen, J. F. Personality and Intellective Predictors and Academic Success in an Independent Study Science Course at the College Level. Psychological Reports, 1970, April, 26(2), 493-494.

Tangri, S. S. Determinants of Occupational Role Innovation Among College Women. Journal of Social Issues, 1972, 28(2), 177-199. Also in M. T. S. Mednick et al. (eds.), Women and Achievement: Social and Motivational Analyses. New York: Halsted, 1975, 255-273.

_____. Effects of Background, Personality, College and Post-College Experience on Women's Post-Graduate Employment. Washington, D. C.: U. S. Commission on Civil Rights, 1974.

Taylor, R. G., and Farquhar, W. Personality, Motivation and Achievement: Theoretical Constructs and Empirical Factors. Journal of Counseling Psychology, 1965, 12(2), 186-191.

Thurston, J. R., Brunclik, H. L., and Feldhusen, J. F. Personality and the Prediction of Success in Nursing Education. Nursing Research, 1969, May, 18(3), 258-262.

Tinsley, D. E. Characteristics of Women with Different Patterns of Career Orientation. Unpublished doctoral dissertation, University of Minnesota. Dissertation Abstracts International, 1972, December, 33(6-B), 2797.

Tobias, S., Kremnitzer, S., and Cohen, A. Accuracy, Anxiety, and Achievement in Mathematics. Paper presented at the American Psychological Association Convention, San Francisco, 1977.

Todd, F. J. Differences between Normal and Under-Achievers of Superior Ability. Journal of Applied Psychology, 1962, June, 46, 183-190.

Trent, J. W., and Medsker, L. L. Beyond High School: A Psychosociological Study of 10,000 High School Graduates. San Francisco: Jossey-Bass, 1968.

Trent, S. J. A Study of the Relationship of Personality Factors to Academic Achievement. Unpublished doctoral dissertation, University of Tennessee. Dissertation Abstracts, 1969, 29(7-A), 2129.

Trigg, L. J., and Perlman, D. Social Influences on Women's Pursuit of a Nontraditional Career. Psychology of Women Quarterly, 1976, Winter, 1(2), 138-150.

Tuel, J. K., and Wursten, R. The Influence of Intra-Personal Variables on Academic Achievement. California Journal of Educational Research, 1965, 16, 58-64.

Tyler, L. E. The Antecedents of Two Varieties of Vocational Interests. Genetic Psychology Monographs, 1964, 70(2), 177-227.

Vaughan, R. P. Personality Characteristics of Exceptional College Students. Proceedings of the 74th Annual Convention of the American Psychological Association, 1966, 281-282.

Veroff, J. Social Comparison and Development of Achievement Motivation. In C. P. Smith (ed.), Achievement-Related Motives in Children. New York: Russell Sage Foundation, 1969, 46-101.

Vetter, L., and Lewis, E. C. Some Correlates of Homemaking Versus Career Preference Among College Home Economics Students. Personnel and Guidance Journal, 1964, February, 42(6), 593-598.

Wagman, M. University Achievement and Daydreaming Behavior. Journal of Counseling Psychology, 1968, 15(2), 196-198.

Watson, D., and Siegel, J. Test Anxiety, Motive to Avoid Failure and Motive to Approach Success. Journal of Experimental Research in Personality, 1966, 1(4), 236-243.

Weiner, B., and Potepan, P. Personality Correlates and Affective Reactions towards Exams of Succeeding and Failing College Students. Journal of Educational Psychology, 1970, 61(2), 144-151.

Welliver, T. J. Risk-taking Judgments and Other Related Variables of College Women Who Are Highly Decided or Highly Undecided About Their Career Goals. Dissertation Abstracts International, 1974, 34(A), 6397.

Wendt, D. T., and Patterson, T. W. Personality Characteristics of Women in Intercollegiate Competition. Perceptual and Motor Skills, 1974, June, 38(3, Pt. 1), 861-862.

Werner, E. E., and Bachtold, L. M. Personality Factors of Gifted Boys and Girls in Middle Childhood and Adolescence. Psychology in the Schools, 1969, 6(2), 177-182.

White, R. F. Female Identity and Career Choice: The Nursing Case. In A. Theodore (ed.), The Professional Woman. Cambridge, MA: Schenkman, 1971, 275-289.

Whitely, M. P., and Poulsen, S. B. Assertiveness and Sexual Satisfaction in Employed Professional Women. Journal of Marriage and the Family, 1975, August, 37(3), 573-581.

Widdop, J. H., and Widdop, V. A. Comparison of the Personality Traits of Female Education and Physical Education Students. Research Quarterly, 1975, October, 46(3), 274-281.

Williams, D. E. A Study of Selected Personality and Occupational Aspiration Variables Associated with Achievement Level. Unpublished doctoral dissertation, Oklahoma State University. Dissertation Abstracts, 1967, 27(12-A), 4143-4144.

Williams, J. M., Hoepner, B. J., Moody, D. L., and Ogilvie, B. C. Personality Traits of Champion Level Female Fencers. Research Quarterly, 1970, October, 41(3), 446-453.

Wills, B. S. Personality Variables Which Discriminate between Groups Differing in Level of Self-Actualization. Journal of Counseling Psychology, 1974, May, 21(3), 222-227.

Winters, C. J., and Sorensen, J. Individual Factors Related to Career Orientation in Women. In S. H. Osipow (ed.), Emerging Woman: Career Analysis and Outlooks. Columbus, OH: Charles E. Merrill, 1975, 51-68.

Wrightsman, L. S., Jr. Effects of Anxiety, Achievement Motivation, and Task Importance upon Performance on an Intelligence Test. Journal of Educational Psychology, 1962, June, 53, 150-156.

Wyer, R. S., Jr. Behavioral Correlates of Academic Achievement: Conformity Underachievement- and Affiliation-Incentive Conditions. Journal of Personality and Social Psychology, 1967, 6, 255-263.

Yoshida, T. A Study of Personality Factors Determining Goal Setting Behavior: Experimental Analysis of Level of Aspiration. Journal of Child Development, 1971, January, 7, 22-34.

Young, F. A., and Brown, M. Effects of Test Anxiety and Testing Conditions on Intelligence Test Scores of Elementary School Boys and Girls. Psychological Reports, 1973, April, 32(2), 643-649.

Zatlin, C. E., Storandt, M., and Botwinick, J. Personality and Values of Women Continuing Their Education after Thirty-five Years of Age. Journal of Gerontology, 1973, April, 28(2), 216-221.

Zissis, C. The Relationship of Selected Variables to Career-Marriage Plans of University Freshman Women. Unpublished doctoral dissertation, University of Michigan, Ann Arbor, 1962.

C. INTERESTS, VALUES

Anderson, R. P., and Lawlis, G. F. Strong Vocational Interest

Blank and Culturally Handicapped Women. Journal of Counseling Psychology, 1972, January, 19(1), 83-84.

Astin, H. S. Career Development of Girls During the High School Years. Journal of Counseling Psychology, 1968, 15(6), 536-540.

―――― . Stability and Change in the Career Plans of Ninth Grade Girls. Personnel and Guidance Journal, 1968, June, 46(10), 961-966.

Bachtold, L. M. Women, Eminence, and Career-Value Relationships. Journal of Social Psychology, 1975, April, 95(2), 187-192.

Bailey, L. J. An Investigation of the Vocational Behavior of Selected Women Vocational Education Students. Unpublished doctoral dissertation, University of Illinois. Dissertation Abstracts, 1969, 29(12-A), 4364.

Banreti-Fuchs, K. M., and Meadows, W. M. Interest, Mental Health, and Attitudinal Correlates of Academic Achievement Among University Students. British Journal of Educational Psychology, 1976, June, 46(2), 212-219.

Bowden, S. S. The Influence of Work Values in the Life Planning of Tenth-Grade Girls. Unpublished doctoral dissertation, Oregon State University, 1975. Dissertation Abstracts International, 1975, 35(7-B), 3428. Also available from ERIC (ADG75-01093), 1975.

Brown, N. W. A Study of the Interests of Baccalaureate Registered Nurses in Relation to Aptitudes, Achievement, and Attitudes, and the Development of an Occupational Scale for the Strong Vocational Interest Blank. Dissertation Abstracts, 1966, 27 (1-B), 290.

Bryan, W. E. A Comparison of the Career Orientation of College Women in Contrasting Majors. Unpublished doctoral dissertation, Wayne State University, Detroit, MI, 1968.

Campbell, D. P. The Vocational Interests of Beautiful Women. Personnel and Guidance Journal, 1967, June, 45, 968-972.

―――― , and Schuell, H. The Vocational Interests of Women in Speech Pathology and Audiology. American Speech and Hearing Association, 1967, 9(3), 67-72.

―――― , and Soliman, A. M. The Vocational Interests of Women in Psychology: 1942-1966. American Psychologist, 1968, 23, 158-163.

Cartwright, L. K. Women in Medical School. Dissertation Abstracts International, 1971, April, 31(10-B), 6237.

Cole, C. W. , and Miller, C. D. Relevance of Expressed Values to Academic Performance. Journal of Counseling Psychology, 1967, 14(3), 272-276.

Cozy, H. M. Post High School Academic Achievement in the Context of Specified Value Indicants in High School Cumulative Records of Scholastically Superior Women. Unpublished doctoral dissertation, University of Wisconsin. Dissertation Abstracts International, 1973, February, 33(8-A), 4084-4085.

Davis, J. A. Undergraduate Career Decisions: Correlates of Occupational Choice. Chicago: Aldine, 1965.

Doherty, W. J. , and Corsini, D. A. Creativity, Intelligence, and Moral Development in College Women. Journal of Creative Behavior, 1976, 10(4), 276-284.

Dunteman, G. H. Discriminant Analyses of the SVIB for Female Students in Five College Curricula. Journal of Applied Psychology, 1966, December, 50, 509-515.

Eyde, L. D. Work Values and Background Factors as Predictors of Women's Desire to Work. Unpublished doctoral dissertation, Ohio State University. Dissertation Abstracts International, 1960, March, 20, 3829.

_____. Work Values and Background Factors as Predictors of Women's Desire to Work. Columbus, OH: Bureau of Business Research, Ohio State University, 1962.

Faunce, P. S. Personality Characteristics and Vocational Interests Related to the College Persistence of Academically Gifted Women. Unpublished doctoral dissertation, University of Minnesota. Dissertation Abstracts International, 1967, 28(1), 338.

_____. Personality Characteristics and Vocational Interests Related to the College Persistence of Academically Gifted Women. Journal of Counseling Psychology, 1968, 15(1), 31-40.

_____. Withdrawal of Academically Gifted Women. Journal of College Student Personnel, 1968, May, 9(3), 171-176.

_____. Vocational Interests of High Ability College Women. Journal of College Student Personnel, 1971, November, 12(6), 430-437.

Fox, L. H. The Values of Gifted Youth. In D. P. Keating (ed.), Intellectual Talent: Research and Development. Baltimore, MD: Johns Hopkins University Press, 1976.

_____, and Denham, S. A. Values and Career Interests of Mathematically and Scientifically Precocious Youth. In J. C. Stanley, D. P. Keating, and L. H. Fox (eds.), Mathematical Talent: Discovery, Description, and Development. Baltimore, MD: Johns Hopkins University Press, 1974, 140-175.

Glogowski, D., and Lanning, W. Relationships Among Age Category, Curriculum Selected, and Work Values for Women in a Community College. Vocational Guidance Quarterly, 1976, December, 25, 119-125.

Gottsdanker, J. S. Intellectual Interest Patterns of Gifted College Students. Educational and Psychological Measurement, 1968, 28(2), 361-366.

Gough, H. G. Strong Vocational Interest Blank Profiles of Women in Law, Mathematics, Medicine, and Psychology. Psychological Reports, 1975, 37, 127-134.

Hall, B. A. Occupational Values and Family Perspectives: A Study of Premedical and Prenursing Women. Unpublished doctoral dissertation, University of Colorado, Boulder, 1974. Dissertation Abstracts International, 1974, 35(4-A), 2407. Also available from ERIC (ADG74-22349), 1974.

Harmon, L. W. Women's Working Patterns Related to Their SVIB Housewife and "Own" Occupational Scores. Journal of Counseling Psychology, 1967, 14(4), 299-301.

_____. Predictive Power Over Ten Years of Measured Social Service and Scientific Interests Among College Women. Journal of Applied Psychology, 1969, 53(3, Pt. 1), 193-198.

_____. The Childhood and Adolescent Career Plans of College Women. Journal of Vocational Behavior, 1971, January, 1(1), 45-56.

Harris, C. M., and Smith, S. W. Man Teacher--Woman Teacher: Does it Matter? Elementary School Journal, 1976, February, 76(5), 285-288.

Haskins, M. J. Characteristics of Professional Women Students in Physical Education as Indicated by the Opinion, Attitude, and Interest Survey. Perceptual and Motor Skills, 1968, 27(3, Pt. 1), 875-879.

Helso, H. Generality of Sex Differences in Creative Style. Journal of Personality, 1968, 36(1), 33-48.

Helson, R. Narrowness in Creative Women. Psychological Reports, 1966, 19(2), 618.

Herrick, J. S. Work Motives of Female Executives. Public Personnel Management, 1973, September, 2(5), 380-387.

Hoyt, D., and Kennedy, C. Interest and Personality Correlates of

Career-Motivated and Homemaking-Motivated College Women. Journal of Consulting Psychology, 1963, 66, 59-66.

Jantzen, A. C. Some Characteristics of Female Occupational Therapists. Unpublished doctoral dissertation, University of Michigan. Dissertation Abstracts International. 1971, 32(4-B), 2244.

Karman, F. J. Women: Personal and Environmental Factors in Role Identification and Career Choice. Unpublished doctoral dissertation, University of California, Los Angeles. Dissertation Abstracts International, 1972, October, 33(4-A), 1440. Also available from ERIC (ED084383), 1973.

Kosa, J., Rachiele, L., and Schommer, D. Marriage, Career, and Religiousness among Catholic College Girls. Marriage and Family Living, 1962, 24, 376-380.

LaRussa, G. W. Prospective Portia: Her Personality Characteristics and Value Orientation. Paper presented at the American Psychological Association Convention, San Francisco, 1977.

Levitt, E. S. Vocational Development of Professional Women: A Review. Journal of Vocational Behavior, 1971, October, 1(4), 375-385.

Long, J. M. Sex Differences in Academic Prediction Based on Scholastic, Personality and Interest Factors. Journal of Experimental Education, 1964, 32, 239-248.

McCloud, T. E. Persistency as a Motivational Factor of Vocational Interest in the Prediction of Academic Success of Twelfth-Grade Superior Students. Psychology, 1968, 5(4), 34-46.

Masih, L. K. Career Saliency and Its Relation to Certain Needs, Interests and Job Values. Personnel and Guidance Journal, 1967, 45(7), 653-658.

Mawardi, B. H., and Tagiuri, R. Value Orientation and Professional Choice in Men and Women. Unpublished manuscript, Harvard University Graduate School of Business Administration, n. d.

Montague, A. C. A Factorial Analysis of the "Basic" Interest Patterns of Two Hundred Women College Students in Various Curricular Groups. Unpublished doctoral dissertation, Temple University. Dissertation Abstracts, 1961, 22(1), 324.

Mooney, R. F. A Multiple Discriminant Analysis of the Interest Patterns of High School Girls. Unpublished doctoral dissertation, Boston College, 1968.

Morrill, W. H., Miller, C. D., and Thomas, L. E. Educational and Vocational Interests of College Women. Vocational Guidance Quarterly, 1970, December, 19(2), 85-88.

Muhlenkamp, A. F., and Parsons, J. L. Characteristics of Nurses: An Overview of Recent Research. Journal of Vocational Behavior, 1972, July, 2(3), 261-273.

Munley, P. H. Interests of Career and Homemaking Oriented Women. Journal of Vocational Behavior, 1974, January, 4(1), 43-48.

Nelson, I. M. Personality Traits and Occupational Values Associated with Choice of Clinical Speciality in Nursing. Unpublished doctoral dissertation, American University. Dissertation Abstracts International, 1974, July, 35(1-A), 175-176.

Ohlbaum, J. S. Self-Concepts, Value Characteristics and Self-Actualization of Professional and Nonprofessional Women. Unpublished doctoral dissertation, United States International University. Dissertation Abstracts International, 1971, 32(B), 1221-1222.

O'Neil, P. M., and Madaus, G. F. Differences in Interest Patterns between Graduates of Diploma and Basic Collegiate Programs in Nursing. Journal of Counseling Psychology, 1966, 13(3), 300-305.

Osipow, S. H. (ed.). Perspective and Issues. In Emerging Woman: Career Analysis and Outlooks. Columbus, OH: Charles E. Merrill, 1975, 147-158.

Page, M. J. A Descriptive Analysis of Selected Attitudes, Interests, and Personality Characteristics of Mature College Women. Unpublished doctoral dissertation, North Texas State University. Dissertation Abstracts International, 1972, January, 32(7-A), 3699-3700.

Perrone, P. A. Values and Occupational Preferences of Junior High School Girls. Personnel and Guidance Journal, 1965, 44(3), 253-257.

Perry, D. K., and Cannon, W. M. Vocational Interests of Female Computer Programmers. Journal of Applied Psychology, 1968, 52(1, Pt. 1), 31-35.

Peterson, R. A. Vocational Interest Patterns of Male and Female Medical Students Over a Four-Year Period. Journal of Counseling Psychology, 1972, January, 19(1), 21-25.

Quarter, J., Kirsh, S., Dimitri, O., and Postl, B. Values and Role Satisfaction Performance and Commitment Among Early Adolescents. Adolescence, 1976, Summer, 11, 243-259.

Reed, H. B. College Students' Motivations Related to Voluntary Dropout and Under-Overachievement. Journal of Educational Research, 1968, 61, 412-416.

Reitz, H. J. Career Orientation and Academic Achievement among

Elementary Education Majors. Journal of Counseling Psychology, 1970, 17(3), 205-209.

Rezier, A. G. Characteristics of High School Girls Choosing Traditional or Pioneer Vocations. Personnel and Guidance Journal, 1967, 45(7), 659-665.

Rose, H. A., and Elton, C. F. Sex and Occupational Choice. Journal of Counseling Psychology, 1971, September, 18(5), 456-461.

Schissel, R. F. Differential Interest Characteristics of Career Women. Unpublished doctoral dissertation, University of Nebraska. Dissertation Abstracts, 1967, 28(6-A), 2103.

_____. Development of a Career-Orientation Scale for Women. Journal of Counseling Psychology, 1968, May, 15(3), 257-262.

Schwarzweller, H. K. Values and Occupational Choice. Social Forces, 1960, 39, 126-135.

Sedlacek, C. G. Selected Factors Affecting Certainty and Persistence of Vocational Choice for College Women. Dissertation Abstracts, 1969, 29(11-A), 3843-3844.

Self, P. A. P. Self-Concepts, Attitudes, and Values of Women Honor Students. Dissertation Abstracts International, 1974, 34(A), 7595.

Smith, M. E. The Values Most Highly Esteemed by Men and Women in Who's Who Suggested as One Reason for the Great Difference in Representation of the Two Sexes in Those Books. Journal of Social Psychology, 1962, 58(2), 339-344.

Tipton, R. M. Vocational Identification and Academic Achievement. Journal of Counseling Psychology, 1966, Winter, 13, 425-430.

Todd, F. J., Terrell, G., and Frank, C. E. Differences between Normal and Underachievers of Superior Ability. In M. Kornrich (ed.), Underachievement. Springfield, IL: Charles C. Thomas, 1965, 399-414.

Vetter, L., and Lewis, E. C. Some Correlates of Homemaking Versus Career Preference Among College Home Economics Students. Personnel and Guidance Journal, 1964, 42(6), 593-598.

Wagman, M. Interests and Values of Career and Homemaking Oriented Women. Personnel and Guidance Journal, 1966, 44(8), 794-801.

Walberg, H. J. Dimensions of Interests in Boys and Girls Studying Physics. Science Education, 1967, 45, 320-326.

Winters, C. J., and Sorensen, J. Individual Factors Related to

Career Orientation in Women. In S. H. Osipow (ed.), Emerging Woman: Career Analysis and Outlooks. Columbus, OH: Charles E. Merrill, 1975, 51-68.

Withycombe-Brocato, C. J. The Mature Graduate Woman Student: Who Is She? Unpublished doctoral dissertation, U.S. International University, 1969.

Zatlin, C. E., Storandt, M., and Botwinick, J. Personality and Values of Women Continuing Their Education after Thirty-Five Years of Age. Journal of Gerontology, 1973, April, 28(2), 216-221.

Zissis, C. The Relationship of Selected Variables to Career-Marriage Plans of University Freshman Women. Unpublished doctoral dissertation, University of Michigan, Ann Arbor, 1962.

D. FEAR OF SUCCESS, FEAR OF FAILURE

Allen, J. L., and Boivin, M. R. Women's Will to Fail in a Disjunctive Reaction Time Competitive Task. Bulletin of the Psychonomic Society, 1976, November, 8(5), 401-402.

Althof, S. E. The Effects of Competitive and Non-Competitive Conditions in High and Low Fear of Success College Women on Verbal Problem Solving Ability. Unpublished Master's thesis, Oklahoma State University, 1973.

_____. A Study of the Personality Variables Related to Fear of Success in College Women. Unpublished doctoral dissertation, Oklahoma State University. Dissertation Abstracts International, 1976, April, 36(10-B), 5242.

Argote, L. M., Fisher, J. E., McDonald, P. J., and O'Neal, E. C. Competitiveness in Males and in Females: Situational Determinants of Fear of Success Behavior. Sex Roles: A Journal of Research, 1976, 2(3), 295-303.

Baruch, G. K. The Motive to Avoid Success and Career Aspirations of 5th and 10th Grade Girls. Paper presented at the American Psychological Association Convention, Montreal, 1973.

_____. Sex-Role Stereotyping, the Motive to Avoid Success, and Parental Identification: A Comparison of Preadolescent and Adolescent Girls. Sex Roles: A Journal of Research, 1975, 1(4), 303-309.

Berkan, J. The Effect of Information about Sex Appropriateness of Tasks on the Fear of Success Motive. Senior essay, Yale University, 1972.

Berman, V. A. The Motive to Avoid Success: A Test of Basic Assumptions. Unpublished doctoral dissertation, Northwestern University, 1973.

Bernstein, A. W. Fear of Failure in College Women. Unpublished doctoral dissertation, Michigan State University, 1975.

Bishop, J. D. The Motive to Avoid Success in Women and Men: An Assessment of Sex-Role Identity and Situational Factors. Unpublished doctoral dissertation, Cornell University. Dissertation Abstracts International, 1974, 34(B), 6256-6257.

Blaubergs, M. S. Overcoming the Sexist Barriers to Gifted Women's Achievement. In B. Johnson (ed.), Advantage/Disadvantage Gifted. Ventura, CA: Ventura County Superintendent of Schools Office, 1979.

Bongort, K. J. Expressions of Fear of Success in the Prisoner's Dilemma Games Played by Male-Female Pairs. Unpublished manuscript, University of Michigan, 1974.

Bonz, M. H. The Effects of Pictorial Modeling Stimuli on the Achievement Behavior of Women. Unpublished doctoral dissertation, University of Maryland. Dissertation Abstracts International, 1975, April, 35(10-A), 6447-6448.

Brandt, D. A., and Kline, K. H. Complete Reanalysis of Horner's Classic Fear-of-Success Study. Paper presented at the American Psychological Association Convention, San Francisco, 1977.

Breedlove, C., and Cicirelli, V. G. Women's Fear of Success in Relation to Personal Characteristics and Type of Occupation. Journal of Psychology, 1974, 86(2), 181-190.

Bremer, T. H., and Wittig, M. A. Deviance and Overload as Determinants of Fear-of-Success Scores. Paper presented at the American Psychological Association Convention, San Francisco, 1977.

Brenton, M. Wanting, Fearing, Avoiding Success. Seventeen, 1976, April, 35, 186-187+.

Bright, M. H. Fear of Success and Traditionality of Occupational Choice. Unpublished Master's thesis, Howard University, 1970.

Brothers, J. How to Be Unafraid of Success. Harper's Bazaar, 1976, January, 109, 97+.

Brown, M., Jennings, J., and Vanik, V. The Motive to Avoid Success: Achievement Conflicts in Men and Women. Humboldt Journal of Social Relations, 1973, Fall, 1(1), 48-52.

_____, _____, and _____. The Motive to Avoid Success: A Further Examination. Journal of Research in Personality, 1974, 8, 172-176.

Buehlmann, B. B. The Relationship between Avoidance of Success and Other Selected Characteristics of College Females. Unpublished doctoral dissertation, Illinois State University. Dissertation Abstracts International, 1974, September, 35(3-B), 1376-1377.

Burghardt, N. R. The Motive to Avoid Success in School-aged Males and Females. Unpublished doctoral dissertation, University of Michigan, 1973.

———. The Motive to Avoid Success in School-aged Males and Females. Paper presented at the American Psychological Association Convention, Montreal, 1973.

Burke, B. W. Fear of Success and Orientation toward the Future in Adolescents. Unpublished manuscript, Wellesley College, 1971.

Burnstein, E. Fear of Failure, Achievement Motivation, and Aspiring to Prestigeful Occupations. Journal of Abnormal and Social Psychology, 1963, 67, 189-193.

Caballero, C. M., Giles, P., and Shaver, P. Sex-Role Traditionalism and Fear of Success. Sex Roles: A Journal of Research, 1975, 1(4), 319-326.

Calef, S. R. The Effect of Sex-Role Identification on the Motive to Avoid Success. Unpublished master's thesis, University of Florida, 1972.

Cherry, F., and Deaux, K. Fear of Success Versus Fear of Gender-Inconsistent Behavior: A Sex Similarity. Paper presented at the Midwestern Psychological Association meeting, Chicago, 1975.

Cohen, N. E. Explorations in the Fear of Success. Unpublished doctoral dissertation, Columbia University, 1974.

Coleman, N. C. The Motive to Avoid Success as a Function of Sex, Intelligence, and Achievement Motivation. Unpublished master's thesis, University of Oregon, 1974.

Coles, B. K., and Mausner, B. Behavioral and Fantasied Measures of Avoidance of Success in Men and Women: A Replication. Unpublished manuscript, Beaver College, 1974.

Condry, J. and Dyer, S. Fear of Success: Attribution of Cause to the Victim. Journal of Social Issues, 1976, Summer, 32(3), 63-84.

Current Trends in Research on 'Fear of Success.' Sex Roles: A Journal of Research, 1976, 2(3), 211-216.

Curtis, R. C., Zanna, M. P., and Campbell, W. W., Jr. Sex, Fear of Success, and the Perceptions and Performance of Law School Students. American Educational Research Journal, 1975, Summer, 12(3), 287-297.

Dalsimer, K. Fear of Academic Success in Adolescent Girls. Journal of Child Psychiatry, 1975, 14, 719-730.

Depner, C. E. Understanding Female Careerism: Fear of Success and New Directions. Sex Roles: A Journal of Research, 1976, 2(3), 259-268.

DiSabatino, M. Psychological Factors Inhibiting Women's Occupational Aspirations and Vocational Choices: Implications for Counseling. Vocational Guidance Quarterly, 1976, September, 25(1), 43-49.

Dorn, R. S. The Effects of Sex Role Awareness Groups on Fear of Success, Verbal Task Performance, and Sex Role Attitudes of Undergraduate Women. Unpublished doctoral dissertation, Boston University. Dissertation Abstracts International, 1975, September, 36(3-A), 1386.

Eme, R., and Lawrence, L. Fear of Success and Academic Under Achievement. Sex Roles: A Journal of Research, 1976, 2(3), 269-271.

English, P. Conditions Leading to the Development and Arousal of a Motive to Avoid Success in Females. Unpublished manuscript, Harvard University, 1973.

_____. A Review of the Literature on the Motive to Avoid Success. Unpublished manuscript, Harvard University, 1973.

Farmer, H. S. What Inhibits Achievement and Career Motivation in Women? The Counseling Psychologist, 1976, 6(2), 12-15.

Feather, N. T. Positive and Negative Reactions to Male and Female Success and Failure in Relation to the Perceived Status and Sex-Typed Appropriateness of Occupations. Unpublished manuscript, Flinders University, Australia, 1974.

_____, and Raphelson, A. C. Fear of Success in Australian and American Student Groups: Motive or Sex-Role Stereotype? Journal of Personality, 1974, June, 42(2), 190-201.

_____, and Simon, J. G. Fear of Success and Causal Attribution for Outcome. Journal of Personality, 1973, December, 41(4), 525-542.

Feij, J. A. Fear of Failure and Reluctance to Participate in Psychological Research: Replication for Female Subjects. Psychological Reports, 1976, June, 38(3, Pt. 2), 1134.

Fitzgerald, L. F. Sex, Occupational Membership, and the Measurement of Psychological Androgyny. Paper presented at the American Psychological Association Convention, Washington, D. C., 1976.

Fleming, J. Comment on 'Do Women Fear Success.' By David Tresemer. SIGNS: Journal of Women in Culture and Society, 1977, 2(3), 706-717.

_____, and Horner, M. S. Sex and Race Differences in Fear of Success Imagery. Unpublished manuscript, Harvard University, 1973.

Freedberg, S. What Are Women Afraid of? Harvard Crimson, 1975, October 25, 3.

Garske, J. P. Motive to Avoid Success, Sensitivity to Rejection, and Male Feedback as Determinants of Female Performance in a Cross-Sexed Competition. Paper presented at the Midwestern Psychological Association meeting, 1975.

Gearty, J. Z., and Milner, J. S. The Motive to Avoid Success in Women. Paper presented at the Southeastern Psychological Association Meeting, Hollywood, FL, 1974.

_____, and _____. Academic Major, Gender of Examiner, and the Motive to Avoid Success in Women. Journal of Clinical Psychology, 1975, January, 31, 13-14.

Gilmore, B. To Achieve or Not to Achieve: The Question of Women. Paper presented at the Gerontological Society meeting, Louisville, KY, October, 1975.

_____. Women's Need Achievement and Need to Avoid Success: Relationships with Other Variables. Unpublished doctoral dissertation, Illinois Institute of Technology. Dissertation Abstracts International, 1975, June, 35(12-B, Pt. 1), 6071.

Glancy, D. J. Women in Law: The Dependable Ones. Harvard Law School Bulletin, 1970, 21, 23-33.

Good, L. R., and Good, K. C. An Objective Measure of the Motive to Avoid Success. Psychological Reports, 1973, 33, 1009-1010.

Goodmonson, C. W. The Motive to Avoid Success in College Students: Effects of Counseling. Dissertation Abstracts International, 1974, 34(B), 6209-6210.

Gornick, V. Why Women Fear Success. MS., 1972, Spring, 50-

54. Also in F. Klagsbrun (ed.), The First Ms. Reader. New York: Warner Paperback Library, 1973, 26-35; and in B. Stanford (ed.), On Being Female. New York: Washington Square Press, 1974, 25-35.

———. Why Radcliffe Women Are Afraid of Success. New York Times Magazine, 1973, February 4, 56-57.

Grainger, B. The Motive to Avoid Success and Its Relationship to Sex-Role Orientation in College Women. Unpublished undergraduate thesis, Wellesley College, 1971.

———, Kostick, B., and Staley, Y. The Role of the Stimulus-Cue in Horner's Motive to Avoid Success. Unpublished undergraduate paper, Wellesley College, 1973.

Green, E., and Olsen, N. J. Reactions to Female Success Among French and American Students. Unpublished manuscript, Stanford University, 1974.

Greenspan, L. J. Sex Role Orientation, Achievement Motivation and the Motive to Avoid Success in College Women. Unpublished doctoral dissertation, Case Western Reserve University. Dissertation Abstracts International, 1975, March, 35(9-A), 5813-5814.

Gross, H. J., and Detterbeck, J. L. Adjustment and Achievement as a Function of the Motive to Avoid Success in College Women. Paper presented at the Western Psychological Association meeting, 1972.

Groszko, M. G. Sex Differences in the Need to Achieve and Fear of Success. Unpublished doctoral dissertation, Adelphi University. Dissertation Abstracts International, 1974, November, 35(5-B), 2429-2430.

———, and Morgenstern, R. Institutional Discrimination: The Case of Achievement-Oriented Women in Higher Education. International Journal of Group Tensions, 1974, 4(1), 82-92.

Gruber, S. New Options and Women's Fear of Success. Symposium presentation at the American Psychological Association Convention, Chicago, 1975.

Haimowitz, M. L., and Haimowitz, N. R. (eds.). The Evil Eye: Fear of Success. In Human Development. New York: Thomas Y. Crowell, 1966, 677-685.

Halprin, R. The Motive to Avoid Success: Personality and Performance Correlates in Alone and Group Testing Situations. Unpublished Honors thesis, Smith College, 1974.

Harvey, A. L. Goal-Setting as Compensation for Fear-of-Success. Adolescence, 1975, 10(37), 137-142.

Hays, J.R. The Dangerous Sex. New York: Pocket Books, 1972.

Heilbrun, A.B., Jr., Kleemeier, C., and Piccola, G. Developmental and Situational Correlates of Achievement Behavior in College Females. Journal of Personality, 1974, 42, 420-436.

Hermans, H.J.M., ter Laak, J.J.F., and Maes, P.C.J.M. Achievement Motivation and Fear of Failure in Family and School. Developmental Psychology, 1972, 6(3), 520-528.

Hertzog, J., and Walker, C.E. Effects of Sex and Need to Avoid Success on Verbal Mediation of Experimenter Bias. Psychological Reports, 1973, 32, 1235-1238.

Hoffman, L.W. Early Childhood Experiences and Women's Achievement Motives. Journal of Social Issues, 1972, Spring, 28(2), 129-156.

———. Fear of Success in Males and Females: 1965 and 1971. Journal of Consulting and Clinical Psychology, 1974, 42(3), 353-358. Also in M.T.S. Mednick et al. (eds.), Women and Achievement: Social and Motivational Analyses. New York: Halsted, 1975, 221-230.

———. A Re-examination of the Fear of Success. In D.G. McGuigan (ed.), New Research on Women at the University of Michigan. Ann Arbor: University of Michigan, Center for Continuing Education of Women, 1974, 105-111.

———. Fear of Success in 1965 and 1974: A Follow-up Study. Journal of Consulting and Clinical Psychology, 1977, 45(2), 310-321.

Holbrook, J.E. Situational Effects on the Measurement of Women's Fear of Success. Unpublished doctoral dissertation, University of Houston. Dissertation Abstracts International, 1975, May, 35(11-B), 5643.

Hopkins, Linda B. Assessment of the Motive to Avoid Success in Men and Women Using Male and Female Cue Characters. Unpublished Master's thesis, Temple University, 1974.

Horner, M.S. Sex Differences in Achievement Motivation and Performance in Competitive and Non-Competitive Situations. Unpublished doctoral dissertation, University of Michigan. Dissertation Abstracts International, 1969, 30(1-B), 407.

———. Fail: Bright Women. Psychology Today, 1969, November, 3(6), 36-38. Also in E. Adams and M.L. Briscoe (eds.), Up Against the Wall, Mother. Beverly Hills, CA: Glencoe, 1971, 379-386; and in A. Theodore (ed.), The Professional Woman. Cambridge, MA: Schenkman, 1971, 252-259.

———. Femininity and Successful Achievement: A Basic Inconsistency. In J.M. Bardwick et al. (eds.), Feminine Personality and Conflict. Monterey, CA: Brooks/Cole, 1970, 45-76. Also in M.H. Garskof (ed.), Roles Women Play: Readings Toward Women's Liberation. Monterey, CA: Brooks/Cole, 1971, 97-122.

_____. Follow-up Studies on the Motive to Avoid Success in Women. Paper presented at the American Psychological Association Convention, Miami, 1970.

_____. The Motive to Avoid Success and Changing Aspirations of College Women. In Women on Campus: 1970, a Symposium. Ann Arbor: University of Michigan, Center for the Continuing Education of Women, 1970, 12-23. Also in J.M. Bardwick (ed.), Readings on the Psychology of Women. New York: Harper and Row, 1972, 62-67.

_____. The Psychological Significance of Success in Competitive Achievement Situations: A Threat as Well as a Promise. In H.I. Day et al. (eds.), Intrinsic Motivation: A New Direction in Education. New York: Holt, Rinehart and Winston, 1971, 46-60.

_____. Human Motivation. In Psychology Today: An Introduction. (2nd ed.). Del Mar, CA: Communications/Research/Machines, 1972, 369-385.

_____. Toward an Understanding of Achievement-Related Conflicts in Women. Journal of Social Issues, 1972, 28(2), 157-176. Also in J. Stacey et al. (eds.), And Jill Came Tumbling After: Sexism in American Education. New York: Dell, 1974, 43-63; and in E. Lasky (ed.), Humanness: An Exploration into the Mythologies about Women and Men. New York: MSS Informational Corporation, 1975, 226-244; and in M.T.S. Mednick et al. (eds.), Women and Achievement: Social and Motivational Analyses. New York: Halsted Press, 1975, 206-220; and in R.K. Unger and F.L. Denmark (eds.), Woman: Dependent or Independent Variable? New York: Psychological Dimensions, 1975, 703-722.

_____. A Psychological Barrier to Achievement in Women: The Motive to Avoid Success. In D.C. McClelland and R.S. Steele (eds.), Human Motivation. Morristown, NJ: General Learning Press, 1973, 222-230.

_____. Success Avoidant Motivation and Behavior; Its Development Correlates and Situational Determinants. Final Report. Washington, D.C.: Office of Education, 1973. Also available from ERIC (ED101221), 1975.

_____. Why Bright Women Fear Success. In C. Tavris (ed.), The Female Experience. From the editors of Psychology Today, Del Mar, CA: Communications/Research/Machines, 1973, 54-57.

228 / Fear of Success/Failure

_____. The Measurement and Behavioral Implications of Fear of Success in Women. In J. W. Atkinson and J. O. Raynor (eds.), Motivation and Achievement. New York: Halsted Press, 1974, 91-117

_____. A Bright Woman Is Caught in a Double Bind. (Originally published as Fail: Bright Woman). In H. H. Frank (ed.), Women in the Organization. Philadelphia: University of Pennsylvania Press, 1977, 216-222.

_____, and Rhoem, W. The Motive to Avoid Success as a Function of Age, Occupation and Progress at School. Unpublished manuscript, University of Michigan, 1968.

_____, Tresemer, D. W., Berens, A. E., and Watson, R. I., Jr. Scoring Manual for an Empirically Derived Scoring System for Motive to Avoid Success. Unpublished Manuscript, Harvard University, 1973. Also paper presented at the American Psychological Association Convention, Montreal, 1973.

_____, and Walsh, M. The Causes and Consequences of the Existence of Psychological Barriers to Self-Actualization. In R. B. Kundsin (ed.), Women and Success: The Anatomy of Achievement. New York: William Morrow, 1974, 138-144.

House, G. F. Orientations to Achievement: Autonomous, Social Comparison, and External. Unpublished doctoral dissertation, University of Michigan, 1973.

Howe, K. G., and Zanna, M. P. Sex-Appropriateness of the Task and Achievement Behavior. Paper presented at the Eastern Psychological Association meeting, New York, 1975.

Hundert, J. Women's 'Motive to Avoid Success' in Tasks Defined as 'Masculine or Feminine.' Unpublished manuscript, McMaster University, Ontario. 1974.

Jackaway, R. Sex Differences in the Development of Fear of Success. Child Study Journal, 1974, 4(2), 71-79.

_____, Steinberg, C., and Teevan, R. An Exploration of Sex Differences in Fear of Success, and the Relationship Between Fear of Success and Fear of Failure. Unpublished manuscript, State University of New York, Albany, 1972.

_____, and Teevan, R. Fear of Failure and Fear of Success: Two Dimensions of the Same Motive. Sex Roles: A Journal of Research, 1976, 2(3), 283-293.

Jacoby, G. Some Remarks Regarding Matina S. Horner's Article, "Toward an Understanding of Achievement-Related Conflicts in Women," and Some Personal Observations. Unpublished manuscript, Smith College, 1974.

Jellison, J. M., Jackson-White, R., and Bruder, R. A. Fear of Success?--A Situational Approach. Paper presented at the Western Psychological Association meeting, San Francisco, April 1974.

_____, _____, _____, and Martyna, W. Achievement Behavior: A Situational Interpretation. Sex Roles: A Journal of Research, 1975, 1(4), 369-384.

Jones, L. J. Beyond the Fear of Success: A Research Design with Implications for Career Development. Unpublished manuscript, University of Minnesota, 1976.

Jordan, J. The Relationship of Sex-Role Orientation to Competitive and Noncompetitive Behaviors. Unpublished doctoral dissertation, Harvard University, 1973.

Juran, S. H. Sex Differences in Negative Achievement Motivation. Unpublished master's thesis, Brooklyn College, 1972.

_____. Measure of Stereotyping in Fear of Success Cues. Paper presented at the American Psychological Association Convention, Washington, D. C., 1976.

Karabenick, S. A. Fear of Success, Achievement and Affiliation Dispositions, and the Performance of Men and Women Under Individual and Competitive Conditions. Journal of Personality, 1977, March, 45, 117-149.

_____, and Marshall, J. M. Performance of Females as a Function of Fear of Success, Fear of Failure, Type of Opponent, and Performance-Contingent Feedback. Journal of Personality, 1974, 42(2), 220-237.

_____, _____, and Karabenick, J. D. Effects of Fear of Success, Fear of Failure, Type of Opponent, and Feedback on Female Achievement Performance. Journal of Research in Personality, 1976, December, 10(4), 369-385.

Katkovsky, W. Motive to Avoid Success, Locus of Control, and Reinforcement Avoidance. Paper presented at the American Psychological Association Convention, Washington, D. C., 1976.

Kenkel, M. B. E. The Influence of Social Response and Sex-Role Stereotypes on the Motive to Avoid Success. Unpublished Master's thesis, Miami University, Oxford, OH, 1974.

Kimball, B., and Leahy, R. L. Fear of Success in Males and Females: Effects of Developmental Level and Sex-Linked Course of Study. Sex Roles: A Journal of Research, 1976, 2(3), 273-281.

Kimball, M. M. Woman and Success--A Basic Conflict? In M.

Stevenson (ed.), Women in Canada. Toronto: New Press, 1973, 119-135.

Knapp, J. J. Fear of Academic Success: A Comparison of Academically Above-Average, Single, Male and Female College Students. Unpublished Master's thesis, University of Florida, 1972.

Korr, W. Fear of Success and Anxiety in Male-, Female-, and Non-competitive Situations. Unpublished manuscript, State University of New York at Buffalo, 1973.

Kresojevich, I. Z. Motivation to Avoid Success in Women as Related to Year in School, Academic Achievement and Success Context. Unpublished doctoral dissertation, Michigan State University. Dissertation Abstracts International, 1972, November, 33(5-B), 2348-2349.

Krishnan, A. The Relationship of Motive to Avoid Success and Selected Socio-Cultural Variables to Resultant Achievement Motivation in Twelfth Graders. Unpublished doctoral dissertation, Kent State University. Dissertation Abstracts International, 1976, May, 36(11-A), 7298.

_____, and Larson, G. L. Achievement Motivation Correlates in Students Showing Fear of Success Imagery. Paper presented at the American Psychological Association Convention, Washington, D.C., 1976.

Krussell, J. L. Attribution of Responsibility for Performance Outcomes of Males and Females. Unpublished doctoral dissertation, University of Rochester, 1973.

Lanzafame, L. J. The Effect of Fear of Success and Significance of the Male Partner on Female Performance on an Intellectual Decision-Making Task. Unpublished doctoral dissertation, University of Connecticut. Dissertation Abstracts International, 1974, August, 35(2-B), 1052-1053.

Lavach, J., and Lanier, H. B. Motive to Avoid Success in 7th, 8th, 9th and 10th Grade High-Achieving Girls. Journal of Educational Research, 1975, Fall, 68, 216-218.

_____, and _____. Motive to Avoid Success in High-Achieving Girls. Paper presented at the American Psychological Association Convention, Washington, D.C., 1976.

Levine, A., and Crumrine, J. Women and the Fear of Success: A Problem in Replication. American Journal of Sociology, 1975, 80(4), 964-974.

Levine, R., Reis, H. T., Sue, E., and Turner, G. Fear of Failure in Males: A More Salient Factor Than Fear of Success in Females? Sex Roles: A Journal of Research, 1976, 2(4), 389-398.

Lockheed-Katz, Jill. Female Motive to Avoid Success: A Psychological Barrier or a Response to Deviancy? Princeton, NJ: Educational Testing Service, 1973. Also in Sex Roles: A Journal of Research, 1975, 1(1), 41-50.

McGuinness, E. The Effects of Success Avoidance, Sex of Competitor, and Level of Task Difficulty on Performance. Paper presented at the Eastern Psychological Association meeting, April 1974.

_____. Success Avoidance and Competitive Performance. Unpublished manuscript, Rutgers University, 1974.

Major, B. N. Effects on Females' Performance of Fear of Success, Physical Attractiveness, and Competitor's Sex. Unpublished Master's thesis, Miami University, 1975.

_____, and Sherman, R. C. The Competitive Women: Fear of Success, Attractiveness, and Competitor Sex. Paper presented at the American Psychological Association Convention, Chicago, 1975.

Makosky, V. P. Fear of Success, Sex Role Orientation of the Task and Competitive Condition as Variables Affecting Woman's Performance in Achievement-Oriented Situations. Paper presented at the Midwestern Psychological Association meeting, Cleveland, 1972.

_____. Sex-Role Compatibility of Task and of Competitor, and Fear of Success as Variables Affecting Women's Performance. Sex Roles: A Journal of Research, 1976, 2(3), 237-248.

Malone, M., and Reynolds, M. K. The Effects of 'Fear of Success' in Women in the Prisoner's Dilemma Game. Unpublished manuscript, University of Michigan, n. d.

Marshall, J., and Karabenick, S. Validity of an Empirically Derived Projective Measure of Fear of Success. Journal of Consulting and Clinical Psychology, 1977, 45(4), 564-574.

Martyna, W. The Motive to Avoid Success and Female Satisfaction with Performance in Achievement-Oriented Situations. Unpublished manuscript, University of Southern California, 1973.

Maxwell, P. G., and Gonzalez, A. E. J. Traditional and Non-Traditional Role Choice and Need for Failure Among College Women. Psychological Reports, 1972, 31, 545-546.

Mednick, M. T. S. Motivational and Personality Factors Related to Career Goals of Black College Women. Washington, D. C.: U. S. Department of Labor, Manpower Administration, 1973.

_____, and Puryear, G. R. Motivational and Personality Factors Related to Career Goals of Black College Women. Journal of Social and Behavioral Sciences, 1975, 21, 1-30.

Midgley, N., and Abrams, M. S. Fear of Success and Locus of Control in Young Women. Journal of Consulting and Clinical Psychology, 1974, October, 42(5), 737.

Miller, B. S. Sex Differences in Attitudes Toward Achievement in Adolescence. Unpublished Honors thesis, University of Michigan, 1972.

Monahan, L., Kuhn, D., and Shaver, P. Intrapsychic Versus Cultural Explanations of the 'Fear of Success' Motive. Journal of Personality and Social Psychology, 1974, 29(1), 60-64.

Moore, K. A. Fear of Success: The Distribution, Correlates, Reliability and Consequences for Fertility of Fear of Success Among Respondents in a Metropolitan Survey Population. Unpublished manuscript, University of Michigan, 1974. Also a paper presented at the American Psychological Association Convention, New Orleans, 1974.

──────. Fear of Success: Four Hypotheses. Paper presented at the Conference for New Research on Women, University of Michigan, March 1975.

Moore, L. L. The Relationship of Academic Group Membership to the Motive to Avoid Success in Women. Unpublished doctoral dissertation, University of Virginia. Dissertation Abstracts International, 1972, 32(8-A), 4355.

Morgan, S. W., and Mausner, B. Behavioral and Fantasied Indicators of Avoidance of Success in Men and Women. Journal of Personality, 1973, 41(3), 457-470.

Most Women Fear Success, Doctor Claims. National Enquirer, 1973, 47(23), 32.

Murphy-Berman, V. Motive to Avoid Success: A Test of Basic Assumptions. Representative Research in Social Psychology, 1975, January, 6(1), 37-44.

──────. Effects of Success and Failure on Perceptions of Gender Identity. Sex Roles: A Journal of Research, 1976, 2(4), 367-374.

O'Connell, A. Effects of Manipulated Status on Performance, Goal Setting, Need Achievement, Anxiety, and Fear of Success. Paper presented at the Eastern Psychological Association meeting, Washington, D. C., May 1973.

O'Leary, V. E. The Motive to Avoid Success: Antecedents, Correlates and Arousal Contexts: Some Speculative Results. Paper presented at the Michigan Psychological Association Convention, April 1974.

_____. Some Attitudinal Barriers to Occupational Aspirations in Women. Psychological Bulletin, 1974, 81(11), 809-826.

_____, and Hammack, B. Sex-Role Orientation and Achievement Context as Determinants of the Motive to Avoid Success. Sex Roles: A Journal of Research, 1975, 1(3), 225-234.

Pappo, M. Fear of Success: A Theoretical Analysis and the Construction and Validation of a Measuring Instrument. Unpublished doctoral dissertation, Columbia University. Dissertation Abstracts International, 1973, 34(B), 421.

Parker, V. J. Fear of Success, Sex-Role Orientation of the Task, and Competition Condition as Variables Affecting Women's Performance in Achievement-Oriented Situations. Unpublished doctoral dissertation, Ohio University. Dissertation Abstracts International, 1972, March, 32(9-B), 5495.

Patty, R. S. A. The Arousal of the Motive to Avoid Success: An Extension and Test of the Theory. Unpublished manuscript, University of Nebraska, 1973. Dissertation Abstracts International, 1973, 34(A), 2768-2769.

_____. Performance as a Function of Motive to Avoid Success and Intellectual, Interpersonal, or Neutral Instructions. Unpublished manuscript, Wake Forest University, 1974.

_____. Motive to Avoid Success: Intellectual, Interpersonal or Neutral Task Instructions. Paper presented at the American Psychological Association Convention, Chicago, 1975.

_____. Motive to Avoid Success and Instructional Set. Sex Roles: A Journal of Research, 1976, 2(1), 81-83.

_____, and Ferrell, M. A Preliminary Note on the Motive to Avoid Success and the Menstrual Cycle. Journal of Psychology, 1974, 36, 173-177.

_____, and Safford, S. F. Motive to Avoid Success, State-Trait Anxiety, and Performance. Paper presented at the NATO Conference on the Dimensions of Stress and Anxiety, Oslo, Norway, 1975.

_____, and Shelley, H. P. Motive to Avoid Success: A Profile. Paper presented at the Southeastern Psychological Association meeting, Hollywood, FL, 1974.

Peplau, L. A. The Impact of Fear of Success, Sex-Role Attitudes and Opposite Sex Relationship on Women's Intellectual Performance: An Experimental Study of Competition in Dating Couples. Unpublished doctoral dissertation, Harvard University, 1973.

_____. When Do Women Fear Successful Achievement? Unpublished manuscript, University of California, Los Angeles, 1974.

_____. Fear of Success in Dating Couples. *Sex Roles: A Journal of Research*, 1976, 2(3), 249-258.

_____. Impact of Fear of Success and Sex-Role Attitudes on Women's Competitive Achievement. *Journal of Personality and Social Psychology*, 1976, 34(4), 561-568.

Pleck, J. H. Male Threat from Female Competence: An Experimental Study in College Dating Couples. Unpublished doctoral dissertation, Harvard University. *Dissertation Abstracts International*, 1974, 34(B), 6221.

Porjesz, Y. R. The Femininity-Achievement Conflict: An Expanded Formulation of the Motive to Avoid Success in Females. *Dissertation Abstracts International*, 1974, November, 35(5-B), 2443-2444.

Prescott, D. Efficacy-Related Imagery, Education, and Politics. Unpublished Honors thesis, Harvard University, 1971.

Pryor, S. Developmental Changes and Sex Differences in the Motive to Avoid Success. Unpublished Honor's thesis, Wellesley College, 1973.

Rider, E. A. The Barrier to Female Achievement: Motive to Avoid Success or Social Proscription? Paper presented at the Washington State Psychological Association meeting, May 1973.

Robbins, L., and Robbins, E. Comment on: Towards an Understanding of Achievement-Related Conflicts in Women. *Journal of Social Issues*, 1973, 29(1), 133-137.

Robbins, R. B. Achievement Performance and Fantasy Arousal in College Women as a Function of the Motive to Avoid Success, Problem Format, and Relationship to Experimenter. Unpublished doctoral dissertation, Temple University. *Dissertation Abstracts International*, 1973, 34(B), 2950.

Robison, K. A. Fear of Success and Future Orientation. Paper presented at the American Psychological Association Convention, New Orleans, 1974.

Romer, N. The Motive to Avoid Success and Its Effect on Performance in School-Age Males and Females. *Developmental Psychology*, 1975, 11, 689-699.

_____. Sex Differences in the Development of the Motive to Avoid Success, Sex Role Identity, and Performance in Competitive and Non-Competitive Situations. *Psychology of Women Quarterly*, 1977, Spring, 1(3), 260-272.

Rossi, A. Case Against Full Time Motherhood. *Redbook*, 1965, March, 124, 51+.

Rudikoff, S. Women and Success. Commentary, 1974, October, 58(4), 49-59.

Schnitzer, P. K. The Motive to Avoid Success: Exploring the Nature of the Fear. Psychology of Women Quarterly, 1977, 1(3), 273-282.

Schwenn, M. Arousal of the Motive to Avoid Success at Radcliffe College. Unpublished manuscript, Radcliffe College, 1970.

_____. A Study of Fear of Success in Eighteen Radcliffe Undergraduates. Unpublished manuscript, Radcliffe College, 1970.

_____. Arousal of the Motive to Avoid Success. Unpublished Honors thesis, Harvard University, 1971.

Sex and Success: Views of M. Horner. Time, 1972, March 20, 99, 46.

Shaver, P. Questions Concerning Fear of Success and Its Conceptual Relatives. Sex Roles: A Journal of Research, 1976, 2(3), 305-320.

Shinn, M. Secondary School Coeducation and the Fears of Success and Failure. Unpublished Honors thesis, Harvard University, 1973.

Short, J. C. The Effect of the Sex-Role Orientation of the Situation on the Arousal of the Motive to Avoid Success. Unpublished Master's thesis, University of Western Ontario, 1973.

Simon, B. D. Women's Fears of Success Increase at Radcliffe, McClelland Study Shows. Harvard Crimson, 1975, October 23, 1+.

Smith, B. D., and Teevan, R. C. Relationships Among Self-Ideal Congruence, Adjustment, and Fear-Of-Failure Motivation. Journal of Personality, 1971, March, 39(1), 44-56.

Smith, C. P. Fear of Success: Qualms and Queries. In F. L. Denmark (ed.), Women--Volume I: A PDI Research Reference Work. New York: Psychological Dimensions, 1976, 141-160.

Solomon, L. Z. Perception of a Successful Person of the Same Sex or the Opposite Sex. Journal of Social Psychology, 1975, February, 95(1), 133-134.

Sorrentino, R. N., and Short, J. A. Performance in Women as a Function of Fear of Success and Sex-Role Orientation. Unpublished manuscript, University of Western Ontario, 1973.

_____, and _____. Effects of Fear of Success on Women's Performance at Masculine Versus Feminine Tasks. Journal of Research in Personality, 1974, 8, 277-290.

Spence, J. T. The Thematic Apperception Test and Attitudes Toward Achievement in Women: A New Look at the Motive to Avoid Success and a New Method of Measurement. Journal of Consulting and Clinical Psychology, 1974, 42, 422-437.

Stake, J. E. Effect of Probability of Forthcoming Success on Sex Differences in Goal Setting: A Test of the Fear of Success Hypothesis. Journal of Consulting and Clinical Psychology, 1976, 44(3), 444-448.

———. Success and Failure: Factors in Female Aspiration Behavior. Unpublished manuscript, University of Missouri-St. Louis, n. d.

Stericker, A. B. Fear-of-Success in Male and Female College Students: Sex-Role Identification and Self-Esteem as Factors. Unpublished doctoral dissertation, Loyola University. Dissertation Abstracts International, 1976, May, 36(11-B), 5819-5820.

Stewart, A. J. Longitudinal Prediction from Personality to Life Outcomes Among College-Educated Women. Unpublished doctoral dissertation, Harvard University, 1975.

Stewart, V. M. Correlational Studies of the "Motive to Avoid Success" in Women. Unpublished manuscript, York University, Ontario, 1974.

Stokowski, B. Motive to Avoid Success. Unpublished manuscript, University of Minnesota, 1976.

Sturm, S. G. An Examination of the Motive to Avoid Success, Performance, Locus of Control, and Role Orientation. Unpublished doctoral dissertation, University of Tennessee. Dissertation Abstracts International, 1975, February, 35(8-B), 4198.

Teevan, R. C., and Smith, B. D. Relationships of Fear-of-Failure and Need Achievement Motivation to a Confirming-Interval Measure of Aspirational Levels. Psychological Reports, 1975, June, 36(3), 967-976.

Thurber, S., and Friedle, R. Internal-External Control, Interpersonal Trust, and the Motive to Avoid Success in College Women. Journal of Psychology, 1976, 92, 141-143.

Tomlinson-Keasey, C. Role Variables: Their Influence on Female Motivational Constructs. Journal of Counseling Psychology, 1974, May, 21(3), 232-237.

Tresemer, D. Fear of Success: Popular, but Unproven. In C. Tavris (ed.), The Female Experience, from the editors of Psychology Today, Del Mar, CA: Communications/Research/Machines, 1973, 58-62. Also in Psychology Today, 1974, March 7(10), 82-85. And in H. H. Frank (ed.), Women in the Organization. Philadelphia: University of Pennsylvania Press, 1977, 223-233.

_____. Success Avoidance and Gender Role. Unpublished doctoral dissertation, Harvard University. Dissertation Abstracts International, 1975, February, 35(8-B), 4263.

_____. The Cumulative Record of Research on "Fear of Success." Sex Roles: A Journal of Research, 1976, 2(3), 217-236.

_____. Do Women Fear Success? SIGNS: Journal of Women in Culture and Society, 1976, 1(4), 863-874.

_____. Research on Fear of Success: Full Annotated Bibliography. JSAS Catalog of Selected Documents in Psychology, 1976, May, 6, 38-39.

_____. A Reply to Fleming. SIGNS: Journal of Women in Culture and Society, 1977, 2(3), 718-720.

_____, and Pleck, J. Sex-Role Boundaries and Resistance to Sex-Role Change. Women's Studies, 1974, 2, 61-78.

Turner, M. E. Sex Role Attitudes and Fear of Success in Relation to Achievement Behavior in Women. Unpublished doctoral dissertation, Fordham University. Dissertation Abstracts International, 1974, November, 35(5-B), 2451-2452.

Unger, R. K., and Krooth, D. M. Female Role Perception and Attitudes Toward Competence as Related to the Activism in Housewives. Paper presented at the American Psychological Association Convention, New Orleans, 1974.

Veroff, J., McClelland, L., and Marquis, K. Measuring Intellectual and Achievement Motivation in Surveys. Final report. Washington, D. C.: Office of Educational Opportunity, 1971 (3 volumes).

Walton, J. Adolescent Thinking and the Fear of Success. Unpublished doctoral dissertation, Boston University. Dissertation Abstracts International, 1975, September, 36(3-B), 1422.

Watson, R. I., Jr. Female and Male Response to the Succeeding Female Cue. Unpublished manuscript, Harvard University, 1971.

Wellens, G. J. The Motive to Avoid Success in High School Seniors: N-Achievement Shifts and Psychosocial Correlates. Unpublished doctoral dissertation, Illinois Institute of Technology. Dissertation Abstracts International, 1973, May, 33(11-B), 5529.

Williams, D., and King, M. Sex Role Attitudes and Fear of Success as Correlates of Sex Role Behavior. Journal of College Student Personnel, 1976, November, 17(6), 480-484.

Winchel, R., Fenner, D., and Shaver, P. Impact of Coeducation on "Fear of Success" Imagery Expressed by Male and Female High School Students. Journal of Educational Psychology, 1974, October, 66(5), 726-730.

Wood, M. M., and Greenfeld, S. T. Women Managers and Fear of Success: A Study in the Field. Sex Roles: A Journal of Research, 1976, 2(4), 375-387.

Zalman, R. Expression of Fear of Success in a Mixed-Sex Triad Game. Unpublished honors thesis, University of Michigan, 1973.

Zanna, M. P. Intellectual Competition and the Female Student. Final report. Washington, D. C.: Office of Education, 1973. Also available from ERIC (ED072389), 1973.

Zaro, J. S. An Experimental Study of Role Conflict in Women. Unpublished doctoral dissertation, University of Connecticut. Dissertation Abstracts International, 1972, 33(B), 2828.

_____. The Effects of Motive to Avoid Success on Women's Competitive Behavior. Unpublished manuscript, University of Washington, 1975.

Zuckerman, M., and Allison, S. N. An Objective Measure of Fear of Success: Construction and Validation. Journal of Personality Assessment, 1976, 40(4), 422-430.

_____, _____, and Marion, S. P. The Effects of the Motive to Avoid Success on Performance and Attribution of Success and Failure. Unpublished manuscript, University of Rochester, New York, 1974.

_____, and Wheeler, L. To Dispel Fantasies About the Fantasy-Based Measure of Fear of Success. Psychological Bulletin, 1975, 82, 932-946.

E. EXPECTATIONS, CONTROL, AND ATTRIBUTED CAUSES OF SUCCESS/FAILURE

1. EXPECTATIONS OF SUCCESS/FAILURE

Altshuler, R. J. The Effects of Skill Versus Chance Instructional Sets, Schedule of Reinforcement, and Sex on Expectancies of Success and Temporal Persistence. Unpublished doctoral dissertation, Hofstra University. Dissertation Abstracts International, 1974, December, 35(6-B), 3048.

_____, and Kassinove, H. The Effects of Skill and Chance Instructional Sets, Schedule of Reinforcement, and Sex on Children's Temporal Persistence. Child Development, 1975, March, 46, 258-262.

Batlis, N. C., and Waters, L. K. Locus of Control and Achievement Motivation as Moderators of the Expectancy-Academic Performance Relationship. Educational and Psychological Measurement, 1973, 33, 895-902.

Battle, E. S. Motivational Determinants of Academic Task Persistence. Journal of Personality and Social Psychology, 1965, 2, 209-218.

Brickman, P., and Hendricks, M. Expectancy for Gradual or Sudden Improvement Reaction to Success and Failure. Journal of Personality and Social Psychology, 1975, 32(5), 893-900.

_____, Linsenmeier, J. A. W., and McCareins, A. G. Performance Enhancement by Relevant Success and Irrelevant Failure. Journal of Personality and Social Psychology, 1976, 33(2), 149-160.

Cole, D., King, K., and Newcomb, A. Grade Expectations as a Function of Sex, Academic Discipline, and Sex of Instructor. Psychology of Women Quarterly, 1977, Summer, 1(4), 380-385.

Cousins, R. B. The Effects of Task and Sex of Co-Actor on Female Expectancy Level and Performance. Unpublished doctoral dissertation, Indiana University, 1973. Dissertation Abstracts International, 1973, 34(3-A), 937. Also available from ERIC (ADG73-21035), 1973.

Crandall, V. C. Sex Differences in Achievement Expectancies. Paper presented at the conference on The Development of Achievement Related Motives and Self-Esteem, City University of New York, 1967.

_____. Expectancy of Reinforcement and Academic Competence. Journal of Personality, 1968, 36(4), 635-648.

_____. Sex Differences in the Expectancy of Intellectual and Academic Reinforcement. In C. P. Smith (ed.), Achievement Related Motives in Children. New York: Russell Sage Foundation, 1969, 11-45. Also in R. K. Unger, and F. L. Denmark (eds.), Woman: Dependent or Independent Variable? New York: Psychological Dimensions, 1975, 659-686.

Crandall, V. J., Katkovsky, W., and Preston, A. Motivational and Ability Determinants of Young Children's Intellectual Achievement Behaviors. Child Development, 1962, 33, 643-661.

Croke, J. A. Sex Differences in Causal Attributions and Expectancies for Success as a Function of the Sex-Role Appropriateness of the Task. Unpublished manuscript, University of California, Los Angeles, 1973.

Deever, S. G. Ratings of Task Oriented Expectancy for Success as a Function of Internal Control and Field Independence. Unpublished doctoral dissertation, University of Florida. Dissertation Abstracts, 1968, 29(1-B), 365.

Dweck, C. S. The Role of Expectations and Attributions on the Alleviation of Learned Helplessness. Journal of Personality and Social Psychology, 1975, 31, 674-685.

―――, and Gilliard, D. Expectancy Statements as Determinants of Reactions to Failure: Sex Differences in Persistence and Expectancy Change. Journal of Personality and Social Psychology, 1975, 32(6), 1077-1084.

Feather, N. T. The Effect of Differential Failure on Expectation of Success, Reported Anxiety, and Response Uncertainty. Journal of Personality, 1963, 31(3), 289-312.

―――. Valence of Outcome and Expectation of Success in Relation to Task Difficulty and Perceived Locus of Control. Journal of Personality and Social Psychology, 1967, 7, 372-386.

―――, and Simon, J. G. Causal Attributions for Success and Failure in Relation to Expectations of Success Based Upon Selective or Manipulative Control. Journal of Personality, 1971, 39, 527-541.

Frieze, I. H. Women's Expectations for and Causal Attributions of Success and Failure. In M. T. S. Mednick et al. (eds.), Women and Achievement: Social and Motivational Analyses. New York: Halsted Press, 1975, 158-171.

Glasser, K. J. Sex-Role Orientation of the Task and Expectancy of Success as Variables Affecting the Achievement Behavior of Male and Female College Students. Unpublished doctoral dissertation, Princeton University. Dissertation Abstracts International, 1975, March, 34(9-B), 4707.

Hill, K. T., and Dusek, J. B. Children's Achievement Expectations as a Function of Social Reinforcement, Sex of Subject, and Test Anxiety. Child Development, 1969, 40, 547-557.

Hodges, K. Sex Differences in Achievement: The Role of Expectancies for Success. Unpublished senior thesis, Princeton University, 1974.

House, W. C. Actual and Perceived Differences in Male and Female Expectancies and Minimum Goal Levels as a Function of Competition. Journal of Personality and Social Psychology, 1974, 29, 454-563.

―――. Actual and Perceived Differences in Male and Female Expectations and Goal Levels as a Function of Competition. Journal of Personality, 1974, 42, 493-509.

_____, and Perney, V. Valence of Expected and Unexpected Outcomes as a Function of Locus of Control and Type of Expectancy. Journal of Personality and Social Psychology, 1974, 29, 454-463.

Izard, C. E. Personality Characteristics (EPPS), Level of Expectation and Performance. Journal of Consulting Psychology, 1962, 26(4), 394.

Jackaway, R. Achievement Attributions and the Low Expectation Cycle in Females. Paper presented at the American Psychological Association Convention, Chicago, 1975.

Kahn, A., Nelson, R. E., and Gaedert, W. P. Sex Differences in Achievement Expectations, Achievement Behavior, and Success Attributions. Symposium presentation at the American Psychological Association Convention, San Francisco, 1977.

McMahan, I. D. Relationships Between Causal Attributions and Expectancy of Success. Journal of Personality and Social Psychology, 1973, 28, 108-114.

_____. Sex Differences in Expectancy of Success as a Function of the Task. Paper presented at the Eastern Psychological Association meeting, New York, 1975.

Montanelli, D. S., and Hill, K. T. Children's Achievement Expectations and Performance as a Function of Two Consecutive Reinforcement Experiences, Sex of Subject, and Sex of Experimenter. Journal of Personality and Social Psychology, 1969, 13, 115-128.

Nowicki, S., and Walker, C. The Role of Generalized and Specific Expectancies in Determining Academic Achievement. Journal of Social Psychology, 1974, December, 94(2), 275-280.

Olson, L. A. Academic Attitudes, Expectations, and Achievement. Improving College and University Teaching, 1965, 13, 39-41.

Parsons, J. The Development of Achievement Expectancies in Girls and Boys. Paper presented at the Eastern Psychological Association meeting, Philadelphia, April, 1974.

Parsons, J. E. Sex Differences in Attributional Patterns and Expectancy for Success. Paper presented at the Eastern Psychological Association meeting, New York, 1975.

_____, and Ruble, D. N. Attributional and Cognitive Processes Underlying the Development of Achievement-Related Expectancies. Unpublished manuscript, 1975.

_____, _____, Hodges, K. L., and Small, A. W. Cognitive-Developmental Factors in Emerging Sex Differences in Achievement Related Expectancies. Journal of Social Issues, 1976, 32(3), 47-61.

Raban, R. Need Achievement in College Women: The Effects of Success or Failure. Connecticut College Psychology Journal, 1965, 2, 24-48.

Stein, A. H., Pohly, S. R., and Mueller, E. The Influence of Masculine, Feminine, and Neutral Tasks on Children's Achievement Behavior, Expectancies of Success and Attainment Values. Child Development, 1971, 42, 195-207.

Szilagyi, A. D., and Sims, H. P., Jr. Locus of Control and Expectancies Across Multiple Occupational Levels. Journal of Applied Psychology, 1975, October, 60, 638-640.

Valle, V. A. The Effect of the Stability of Attributions on Future Expectations. Personality and Social Psychology Bulletin, 1974, 1(1), 97-99.

_____, and Frieze, I. H. The Stability of Causal Attributions as a Mediator in Changing Expectations for Success. Journal of Personality and Social Psychology, 1976, 33, 579-587.

Vollmer, F. Determinants of Expectancy of Examination Results. Scandinavian Journal of Psychology, 1976, 17(3), 238-245.

E. EXPECTATIONS, CONTROL, CAUSES (continued)

2. INTERNAL-EXTERNAL
CONTROL OF SUCCESS/FAILURE

Aguren, C. T. An Exploration of Self-Actualization, Self-Concept, Locus of Control, and Other Characteristics as Exhibited in Selected Mature Community College Women. Unpublished doctoral dissertation, North Texas State University. Dissertation Abstracts International, 1975, June, 35(12-A, Pt. 1), 7641-7642.

Allen, G. J., Giat, L., and Cherney, R. J. Locus of Control, Test Anxiety, and Student Performance in a Personalized Instruction Course. Journal of Educational Psychology, 1974, December, 66, 968-973.

Bass, B. A., and Stek, R. J. Perceived Locus of Control and Self-Actualization: Failure to Replicate. Perceptual and Motor Skills, 1972, 35, 646.

Batlis, N. C., and Waters, L. K. Locus of Control and Achievement Motivation as Moderators of the Expectancy-Academic Performance Relationship. Educational and Psychological Measurement, 1973, 33, 895-902.

Battle, E. S., and Rotter, J. B. Children's Feelings of Personal

Control as Related to Social Class and Ethnic Group. Journal of Personality, 1963, 31, 482-490.

Becker, W. M. Internal-External Scale Correlated with Edwards Personal Preference Schedule. Psychological Reports, 1974, December, 35(3), 1182.

Biondo, J., and MacDonald, A. P. Internal-External Locus of Control and Response to Influence Attempts. Journal of Personality, 1971, 39, 407-419.

Bolen, L. M., and Torrance, E. P. Influence on Creative Thinking of Locus of Control, Cooperation, and Sex. Paper presented at the American Psychological Association Convention, Washington, D. C., 1976.

Boor, M. Dimensions of Internal-External Control and Academic Achievement. Journal of Social Psychology, 1973, June, 90(1), 163-164.

_____. Dimensions of Internal-External Control and Marital Status, Sex, Age, and College Class. Journal of Social Psychology, 1974, October, 94(1), 145-146.

Bradley, R. H. Sex, Race, Socioeconomic Status, Locus of Control, and Classroom Behavior Among Junior High School Students. Unpublished doctoral dissertation, University of North Carolina. Dissertation Abstracts International, 1974, December, 35(6-A), 3505-3506.

Brandt, J. D. Internal Versus External Locus of Control and Performance in Controlled and Motivated Reading-Rate Improvement and Instruction. Journal of Counseling Psychology, 1975, September, 22, 377-383.

Brannigan, G. G., and Tolor, A. Sex Differences in Adaptive Styles. Journal of Genetic Psychology, 1971, September, 119(1), 143-149.

Brissett, M., and Nowicki, S. Internal Versus External Control of Reinforcement and Reaction to Frustration. Journal of Personality and Social Psychology, 1973, 25, 35-44.

Brooks, M., and Hounshell, P. B. Study of Locus of Control and Science Achievement. Journal of Research in Science Teaching, 1975, April, 12, 175-181.

Bryant, B. K., and Trockel, J. F. Personal History of Psychological Stress Related to Locus of Control Orientation Among College Women. Journal of Consulting and Clinical Psychology, 1976, 44(2), 266-271.

Burlin, F. D. An Investigation of the Relationship of Ideal and Real

Occupational Aspiration to Locus of Control and to Other Social and Psychological Variables in Adolescent Females. Unpublished doctoral dissertation, Syracuse University. Dissertation Abstracts International, 1975, July, 36(1-A), 181-182.

_____. Locus of Control and Female Occupational Aspirations. Journal of Counseling Psychology, 1976, 23(2), 126-129.

Butterfield, E. C. Locus of Control, Test Anxiety, Reactions to Frustration, and Achievement Attitudes. Journal of Personality, 1964, September, 32, 355-370.

Cash, T. F., and Begley, P. J. Internal-External Control, Achievement Orientation and Physical Attractiveness of College Students. Psychological Reports, 1976, 38, 1205-1206.

Chance, J. E. Internal Control of Reinforcements and the School Learning Process. Paper presented at the Society for Research in Child Development meeting, Minneapolis, 1965.

_____, and Goldstein, A. G. Locus of Control and Performance on Embedded Figures. Perception and Psychophysics, 1971, 9, 33-34.

Chandler, T. A. Locus of Control: A Proposal for Change. Psychology in the Schools, 1975, July, 12(3), 334-339.

Clark, M. A., and Ford, E. G. Measurement Internal-External Locus of Control of Reinforcement as it Relates to Sex, Social Class, Achievement and Parent's Education in Sixth and Seventh Grade Children. Unpublished Master's thesis, University of North Carolina, 1970.

Clifford, M. M., and Cleary, T. A. The Relationship Between Children's Academic Performance and Achievement Accountability. Child Development, 1972, 43(2), 647-655.

Cohen, S., and Oden, S. An Examination of Creativity and Locus of Control in Children. Journal of Genetic Psychology, 1974, June, 124(2), 179-185.

Crandall, V. C., Katkovsky, W., and Crandall, V. J. Children's Belief in Their Own Control of Reinforcements in Intellectual-Academic Achievement Situations. Child Development, 1965, 36(1), 91-109.

_____, and Lacey B. W. Children's Perceptions of Internal-External Control in Intellectual-Academic Situations and Their Embedded Figures Test Performance. Child Development, 1972, 43, 1123-1134.

Cunningham, T., and Berberian, V. Sex Differences in the Relationship of Self Concept to Locus of Control in Children. Personality and Social Psychology Bulletin, 1976, Summer, 2(3), 277-281.

Davis, W. L., and Davis, D. E. Internal-External Control and Attribution of Responsibility for Success and Failure. Journal of Personality, 1972, March, 40(1), 123-136.

_____, and Phares, E. J. Parental Antecedents of Internal-External Control of Reinforcement. Psychological Reports, 1969, 24, 427-436.

deCharms, R. in collaboration with D. J. Shea. Enhancing Motivation: Change in the Classroom. New York: Irvington, 1976.

Dissinger, J. K. Locus of Control in Achievement: Measurement and Empirical Assessment. Unpublished doctoral dissertation, Purdue University. Dissertation Abstracts, 1968, 29(11-A), 3868-3869.

Doctor, R. Locus of Control of Reinforcement and Responsiveness to Social Influence. Journal of Personality, 1971, 39, 542-551.

DuCette, J., and Wolk, S. Locus of Control and Extreme Behavior. Journal of Consulting and Clinical Psychology, 1972, October, 39(2), 253-258.

Duke, M. P., and Nowicki, S. Locus of Control and Achievement: The Confirmation of a Theoretical Expectation. Journal of Psychology, 1974, July, 87(2), 263-267.

Durand, D., and Shea, D. Enterpreneurial Activity as a Function of Achievement Motivation and Reinforcement Control. Journal of Psychology, 1974, September, 88(1), 57-63.

Durka, D. W. Self Actualization and Internal Control in Nursing Students. Unpublished doctoral dissertation, University of Michigan. Dissertation Abstracts International, 1974, July, 35(1-A), 254.

Eisemann, R., and Platt, J. J. Birth Order and Sex Differences in Academic Achievement and Internal-External Control. Journal of General Psychology, 1968, 78, 279-285.

Fanelli, G. C. The Effect of Locus of Control and Need Achievement on Performance, Self Rating and Attribution of Responsibility. Proceedings of the 81st Annual Convention of the American Psychological Association, Montreal, Canada, 1973, 8, 609-610.

Feather, N. T. Some Personality Correlates of External Control. Australian Journal of Psychology, 1967, 19(3), 253-260.

_____. Valence of Outcome and Expectation of Success in Relation to Task Difficulty and Perceived Locus of Control. Journal of Personality and Social Psychology, 1967, 7, 372-386.

———. Change in Confidence Following Success or Failure as a Predictor of Subsequent Performance. Journal of Personality and Social Psychology, 1968, 9(1), 38-46.

Finn, J. A., and Straub, W. F. Locus of Control Among Dutch and American Women Softball Players. Research Quarterly, 1977, March, 48, 56-60.

Flavin, J. R. Race and Sex of Experimenter and Subject as Possible Covariables Affecting Responses to Julian B. Rotter's Locus of Control Questionnaire. Unpublished doctoral dissertation, University of Houston. Dissertation Abstracts International, 1975, May, 35(11-B), 5662.

Foster, N. J. Women: Locus of Control and Attitudes Toward Femininity and Masculinity. Dissertation Abstracts International, 1975, April, 35(10-B), 5109.

Gable, R. K., Thompson, D. L., and Glanstein, P. J. Perceptions of Personal Control and Conformity of Vocational Choice as Correlates of Vocational Development. Journal of Vocational Behavior, 1976, June, 8(3), 259-267.

Garrett, A. M., and Willoughby, R. H. The Effects of External and Internal Orientation on Success and Failure Experience in the Classroom. Paper presented at the Society for Research in Child Development meeting, Minneapolis, 1971.

Gilliland, L. L. Internal Versus External Locus of Control and the High-Level Athletic Competitor. Perceptual and Motor Skills, 1974, August, 39(1), 38.

Goldston, J., Zimmermann, M., Seni, C., and Gadzella, B. M. Study Habits and Attitudes Characteristic of Sex and Locus-of-Control Groups. Psychological Reports, 1977, February, 40(1), 271-274.

Gozali, H., Cleary, T. A., Walster, G. W., and Gozali, J. Relationship Between the Internal-External Control Construct and Achievement. Journal of Educational Psychology, 1973, February, 64(1), 9-14.

Green, L. H. An Investigation of Factors Which Influence the Vocational Classification of Career Oriented and Home Oriented Women. Unpublished doctoral dissertation, Ohio State University. Dissertation Abstracts International, 1971, October, 32 (4-B), 2377-2378.

Green, R. G. Locus of Control. In Personality: The Skein of Behavior. St. Louis, MO: C. V. Mosby, 1976, 230-253.

Harvey, J. H., Barnes, R. D., Sperry, D. L., and Harris, B. Perceived Choice as a Function of Internal-External Locus of Control. Journal of Personality, 1974, September, 42(3), 437-452.

Hasak, P. Relationships between Locus of Control, Parental Antecedents, and Personality Dimensions. Unpublished Master's thesis, University of Kentucky, 1974.

Hiroto, D. S. Validation of the Learned Helplessness Hypothesis with Humans. Paper presented at the American Psychological Association Convention, Honolulu, 1972.

_____. Locus of Control and Learned Helplessness. Journal of Experimental Psychology, 1974, February, 102(2), 187-193.

Hjelle, L. A. Internal-External Control as a Determinant of Academic Achievement. Psychological Reports, 1970, February, 26(1), 326.

_____. Social Desirability as a Variable in the Locus of Control Scale. Psychological Reports, 1971, 28, 807-816.

Hochreich, D. J. Sex-Role Stereotypes for Internal-External Control and Interpersonal Trust. Journal of Consulting and Clinical Psychology, 1975, April, 43(2), 273.

Hollis, R. E., and Woods, E. M. Sex Differences in Predictability of Academic Achievement from Internal-External Control. Paper presented at the American Psychological Association Convention, Washington, D. C., 1976.

House, W. C., and Perney, V. Valence of Expected and Unexpected Outcomes as a Function of Locus of Control and Type of Expectancy. Journal of Personality and Social Psychology, 1974, 29, 454-463.

Hrycenko, I., and Minton, H. L. Internal-External Control, Power Position, and Satisfaction in Task-Oriented Groups. Journal of Personality and Social Psychology, 1974, December, 30(6), 871-878.

Hsieh, T. T., Shybut, J., and Lotsof, E. J. Internal Versus External Control and Ethnic Group Membership: A Cross-Cultural Comparison. Journal of Consulting and Clinical Psychology, 1969, February, 33(1), 122-124.

Jacobs, K. W. Sixteen PF Correlates of Locus of Control. Psychological Reports, 1976, June, 38(3, Pt. 2), 1170.

Janzen, H. L., and Beeken, D. An Analysis of the Applicability of the Locus of Control Construct. Alberta Journal of Educational Research, 1973, December, 19(4), 295-302.

Joe, V. C. A Review of the Internal-External Control Construct as a Personality Variable. Psychological Reports, 1971, 28, 619-640.

_____. Social Desirability and the I-E Scale. Psychological Reports, 1972, 30, 44-46.

Johnson, B. L., and Kilmann, P. R. Locus of Control and Perceived Confidence in Problem-Solving Abilities. The Journal of Clinical Psychology, 1975, January, 31(1), 54-55.

_____, and _____. The Relationship Between Recalled Parental Attitudes and Internal-External Control. Journal of Clinical Psychology, 1975, January, 31(1), 40-42.

Johnson, H. N. The Relevancy of the Internal-External Locus of Control Construct as a Dimension of Vocational Choice and Vocational Choice Satisfaction. Unpublished doctoral dissertation, University of Iowa. Dissertation Abstracts International, 1975, January, 35(7-A), 4158-4159.

Katkovsky, W., Crandall, V., and Good, S. Parental Antecedents of Children's Beliefs in Internal-External Control of Reinforcements in Intellectual Achievement Situations. Child Development, 1967, September, 38(3), 765-776.

Kearney, M., and Kearney, J. F. Multi-Dimensionality of Locus of Control in Females. Paper presented at the American Psychological Association Convention, San Francisco, 1977.

Keller, J. M. Sex Similarities and Differences in the Relationship Between Locus of Control and OPI. Paper presented at the American Educational Research Association meeting, 1974. Also available from ERIC (ED089154), 1974.

_____, and Pugh, R. C. Sex Similarities and Differences in Locus of Control in Relation to Academic Adjustment Measures. Measurement and Evaluation in Guidance, 1976, October, 9(3), 110-118.

Kipnis, D. M. Inner Direction, Other Direction, and Achievement Motivation. Human Development, 1974, 17(5), 321-343.

Krovetz, M. L. Explaining Success or Failure as a Function of One's Locus of Control. Journal of Personality, 1974, 42, 175-189.

Lancaster, S. L. The Nature of the Relationship between Locus of Control and Academic Achievement. Unpublished doctoral dissertation, University of Virginia. Dissertation Abstracts International, 1975, February, 35(8-A), 4865-4866.

Lavoie, J. C., and Adams, G. R. A Comparative Test of Locus of Control Measures and IQ as Predictors of Children's Task Performance. Paper presented at the Society for Research in Child Development meeting, Denver, 1975. Also available from ERIC (ED118248), 1976.

Lefcourt, H. M. The Effects of Cue Explication upon Persons Maintaining External Control Expectancies. Journal of Personality and Social Psychology, 1967, 5, 372-378.

_____. Changes in the Locus of Control. In Locus of Control: Current Trends in Theory and Research. New York: Halsted Press, 1976, 111-126.

_____. Current Status of Theory and Research. In Locus of Control: Current Trends in Theory and Research. New York: Halsted Press, 1976, 140-155.

_____. Locus of Control and Achievement-Related Behavior. In Locus of Control: Current Trends in Theory and Research. New York: Halsted Press, 1976, 66-78.

_____. Locus of Control: Current Trends in Theory and Research. New York: Halsted Press, 1976.

_____. The Social Antecedents of Locus of Control. In Locus of Control: Current Trends in Theory and Research. New York: Halsted Press, 1976, 96-110.

Levenson, H. Perceived Parental Antecedents of Internal, Powerful Others, and Chance Locus of Control Orientations. Developmental Psychology, 1973, 9(2), 260-265.

_____, and Mahler, I. Attitudes Toward Others and Components of Internal-External Locus of Control. Psychological Reports, 1975, February, 36(1), 209-210.

Levine, R. V. Attributions to Self and Others as a Function of Perceived Locus of Control, Self-Esteem and Task Outcome. Unpublished doctoral dissertation, New York University. Dissertation Abstracts International, 1974, August, 35(2-B), 1106-1107.

Lewis, P., Dawes, A. S., and Cheney, T. Effects of Sensitivity Training on Belief in Internal Control of Interpersonal Relationships. Psychotherapy: Theory, Research and Practice, 1974, Fall, 11(3), 282-284.

Lichtenstein, K. A New Locus of Control Scale Sensitive to Women. Symposium presentation at the American Psychological Association Convention, San Francisco, 1977.

Lintner, A. C., and DuCette, J. Effects of Locus of Control, Academic Failure and Task Dimensions on a Student's Responsiveness to Praise; Aptitude-Treatment Interaction. American Educational Research Journal, 1974, Summer, 11, 231-239.

McCarthy, P. A. The Effects of Pupil Performance Pattern and Locus of Control of the Perceiver on Teacher Attribution of Pupil Ability. Unpublished doctoral dissertation, Indiana University. Dissertation Abstracts International, 1975, June, 35 (12-A), 7758.

MacDonald, A. P., Jr. Internal-External Locus of Control: Parental Antecedents. Journal of Consulting and Clinical Psychology, 1971, 37(1), 141-147.

McGhee, P. E., and Crandall, V. C. Beliefs in Internal-External Control of Reinforcements and Academic Performance. Child Development, 1968, 39(1), 91-102.

Marecek, J., and Frasch, C. Locus of Control and College Women's Role Expectations. Journal of Counseling Psychology, 1977, 24(2), 132-136.

Massari, D. J., and Rosenblum, D. C. Locus of Control, Interpersonal Trust and Academic Achievement. Psychological Reports, 1972, October, 31(2), 355-360.

Messer, S. B. The Relation of Internal-External Control to Academic Performance. Child Development, 1972, December, 43(4), 1456-1462.

Miller, S. R. An Investigation of the Relationship between Mothers' General Fearfulness, Their Daughters' Locus of Control and General Fearfulness in the Daughter. Unpublished doctoral dissertation, New York University. Dissertation Abstracts International, 1974, November, 35(5-B), 2281.

Minnigerode, F. A. Attitudes Toward Women, Sex-Role Stereotyping and Locus of Control. Psychological Reports, 1976, June, 38(3, Pt. 2), 1301-1302.

Mirels, H. L. Dimensions of Internal Versus External Control. Journal of Consulting and Clinical Psychology, 1970, April, 34(2), 226-228.

Murray, H. B., and Staebler, B. K. The Effects of Teacher-Student Locus of Control on Intellectual Achievement. Proceedings of the 81st Convention of the American Psychological Association, Montreal, Canada, 1973, 8, 699-700.

_____, and _____. Teacher's Locus of Control and Student Achievement Gains. Journal of School Psychology, 1974, Winter, 12(3), 305-309.

Nicholls, J. G. Effort is Virtuous, but It's Better to Have Ability: Evaluative Responses to Perceptions of Effort and Ability. Journal of Research in Personality, 1976, September, 10(3), 306-315.

Nowicki, S. Factor Structure of Locus of Control in Children.

Paper presented at the American Psychological Association Convention, Montreal, 1973.

_____. Predicting Academic Achievement of Females from a Locus of Control Orientation: Some Problems and Some Solutions. Paper presented at the American Psychological Association Convention, Montreal, 1973. Also available from ERIC (ED087542), 1973.

_____, and Duke, M. P. A Preschool and Primary Internal-External Control Scale. Developmental Psychology, 1974, 10, 874-880.

_____, and Roundtree, J. Correlates of Locus of Control in a Secondary School Population. Developmental Psychology, 1971, 4, 477-478.

_____, and Segal, W. Perceived Parental Characteristics, Locus of Control Orientation, and Behavioral Correlates of Locus of Control. Developmental Psychology, 1974, January, 10(1), 33-37.

_____, and Walker, C. Achievement in Relation to Locus of Control: Identification of a New Source of Variance. Journal of Genetic Psychology, 1973, September, 123(1), 63-67.

Organ, D. W., and Greene, C. N. Role Ambiguity, Locus of Control, and Work Satisfaction. Journal of Applied Psychology, 1974, February, 59, 101-102.

Parsons, O. A., Schneider, J. M., and Hansen, A. S. Internal-External Locus of Control and National Stereotypes in Denmark and the United States. Journal of Consulting and Clinical Psychology, 1970, 35, 30-37.

Pawlicki, R. E. Locus of Control and the Effectiveness of Social Reinforcers. Journal of Genetic Psychology, 1974, September, 125(1), 153-159.

_____, and Almquist, C. Authoritarianism, Locus of Control and Tolerance of Ambiguity as Reflected in Membership and Nonmembership in a Women's Liberation Group. Psychological Reports, 1973, 32(3, Pt. 2), 1331-1337.

Penk, W. E. Age Changes and Correlates of Internal-External Locus of Control Scale. Psychological Reports, 1969, 25, 856.

Phares, E. J. Antecedents of Locus of Control Beliefs. In Locus of Control in Personality. Morristown, NJ: General Learning Press, 1976, 144-156.

_____. Locus of Control and Achievement in Children. In Locus of Control in Personality. Morristown, NJ: General Learning Press, 1976, 106-118.

_____. Locus of Control as a Determinant Over the Environment. In Locus of Control in Personality. Morristown, NJ: General Learning Press, 1976, 60-79.

_____. Locus of Control in Personality. Morristown, NJ: General Learning Press, 1976.

_____. Locus of Control in the Social Context. In Locus of Control in Personality. Morristown, NJ: General Learning Press, 1976, 80-105.

Phipps-Sanger, S., and Alker, H. Dimensions of Internal-External Locus of Control and the Women's Liberation Movement. Journal of Social Issues, 1972, 28(4), 115-129.

Platt, J. J., Pomeranz, D., Eisenman, R., and DeLisser, O. Importance of Considering Sex Differences in Relationships Between Locus of Control and Other Personality Variables. Proceedings of the 78th Annual Convention of the American Psychological Association, 1970, 5, 463-464.

Powell, A., and Centa, D. Adult Locus of Control and Mental Ability. Psychological Reports, 1972, 30, 829-830.

_____, and Vega, M. Correlates of Adult Locus of Control. Psychological Reports, 1972, April, 30(2), 455-460.

Prociuk, T. J., and Breen, L. J. Defensive Externality and Its Relation to Academic Performance. Journal of Personality and Social Psychology, 1975, March, 31(3), 549-556.

_____, _____, and Lussier, R. J. Hopelessness, Internal-External Locus of Control, and Depression. Journal of Clinical Psychology, 1976, 32, 299-300.

_____, and Lussier, R. J. Internal-External Locus of Control: An Analysis and Bibliography of Two Years of Research (1973-1974). Psychological Reports, 1975, December, 37(3, Pt. 2), 1323-1337.

Ramanaiah, N. V., Ribich, F. D., and Schmeck, R. R. Internal-External Control of Reinforcement as Determinant of Study Habits and Academic Attitudes. Journal of Research in Personality, 1975, 9, 375-384.

Reid, I., and Cohen, L. Achievement Orientation, Intellectual Achievement Responsibility and Choice Between Degree and Certificate Courses in College of Education. British Journal of Educational Psychology, 1973, February, 43(1), 63-66.

Reimanis, G. School Performance, Intelligence, and Locus of Reinforcement Control Scales. Psychology in the Schools, 1973, April, 10, 207-211.

_____. Effects of Locus of Reinforcement Control Modification Procedures in Early Graders and College Students. Journal of Educational Research, 1974, November, 68(3), 124-127.

Roodin, P. A., Broghton, A., and Vaught, G. M. Effects of Birth Order, Sex, and Family Size on Field Dependence and Locus of Control. Perceptual and Motor Skills, 1974, August, 39(1), 671-676.

Rotter, J. B. Generalized Expectancies for Internal Versus External Control of Reinforcement. Psychological Monographs, 1966, 80(1), 1-28.

_____. Some Problems and Misconceptions Related to the Construct of Internal Versus External Control of Reinforcement. Journal of Consulting and Clinical Psychology, 1975, February, 43(1), 56-67.

Ryckman, R. M., Martens, J. L., Rodda, W. C., and Sherman, M. F. Locus of Control and Attitudes Toward Women's Liberation in a College Population. Journal of Social Psychology, 1972, 87, 157-158.

_____, Rodda, W. C., and Stone, W. F. Performance Time as a Function of Sex, Locus of Control, and Task Requirements. Journal of Social Psychology, 1971, 85, 299-305.

_____, and Sherman, M. F. Interaction Effects of Locus of Control and Sex of Subject on Confidence Ratings and Performance in Achievement-Related Situations. Paper presented at the American Psychological Association Convention, Honolulu, 1972.

_____, and _____. Locus of Control and Perceived Ability Level as Determinants of Partner and Opponent Choice. Journal of Social Psychology, 1974, October, 94(1), 103-110.

Samson, D. F. An Investigation of the Effects of External and Internal Evaluation Upon Motivation. Unpublished doctoral dissertation, University of Illinois. Dissertation Abstracts International, 1971, 31(9-A), 4561.

Scheck, D. C., Emerick, R., and El-Assal, M. M. Adolescent's Perceptions of Parent-Child Relations and the Development of Internal-External Control Orientation. Journal of Marriage and the Family, 1973, 35, 634-654.

Schneider, J. M. Skill Versus Chance Activity Preferences and Locus of Control. Journal of Consulting and Clinical Psychology, 1968, June, 32(3), 333-337.

_____. College Students' Belief in Personal Control, 1966-1970. Journal of Individual Psychology, 1971, 27, 188.

_____. Relationship Between Locus of Control and Activity Preferences: Effects of Masculinity, Activity and Skill. Journal of Consulting and Clinical Psychology, 1972, April, 38(2), 225-230.

———, and Parsons, O. A. Categories on the Locus of Control Scale and Cross-Cultural Comparisons in Denmark and the United States. Journal of Cross-Cultural Psychology, 1970, 1, 131-138.

Seeman, J. Personality Integration in College Women. Journal of Personality and Social Psychology, 1966, 4(1), 91-93.

Seidner, C. J., Horne, M. D., and Harasymiw, S. J. Locus of Control and Achievement: Mediating Effects of Peer Status. Paper presented at the American Psychological Association Convention, Washington, D. C., 1976.

Shea, J. B. A Preliminary Investigation of Expectancy Changes in Locus of Control Among Aged White Women as Related to Skill and Chance Tasks. Unpublished doctoral dissertation, University of North Carolina, Greensboro, 1973. Dissertation Abstracts International, 1974, 34 (5-B), 2136. Also available from ERIC (ADG73-26407), 1973.

Shelton, P. B. Achievement Motivation in Professional Women. Unpublished doctoral dissertation, University of California, Berkeley. Dissertation Abstracts, 1968, 28(10-A), 4274.

Srull, T. K., and Karabenick, S. A. Effects of Personality-Situation Locus of Control Congruence. Journal of Personality and Social Psychology, 1975, 32(4), 617-628.

Staats, S. et al. Internal Versus External Locus of Control for Three Age Groups. International Journal of Aging and Human Development, 1974, Winter, 5(1), 7-10.

Stein, A. H. The Influence of Social Reinforcement on the Achievement Behavior of Fourth-Grade Boys and Girls. Child Development, 1969, 40(3), 727-736.

Stephens, M. W. Dimensions of Locus of Control: Impact of Early Educational Experiences. Proceedings of the 80th Annual Convention of the American Psychological Association, 1972, 7(Pt. 1), 317-318.

Stone, G. L., and Jackson, T. Internal-External Control as a Determinant of the Effectiveness of Modeling and Instructions. Journal of Counseling Psychology, 1975, July, 22(4), 294-298.

Szilagyi, A. D., and Sims, H. P., Jr. Locus of Control and Expectancies Across Multiple Occupational Levels. Journal of Applied Psychology, 1975, October, 60, 638-640.

Thomas, H. Underlying Constructs of Locus of Control of Reinforcement. Paper presented at the American Educational Research Association meeting, Washington, D. C., April 1975.

Thornhill, M. A., Thornhill, G. J., and Youngman, M. B. A Computerized Bibliography and Locus of Control. Psychological Reports, 1975, April, 36(2), 505-506.

Thurber, S. Defensive Externality and Academic Achievement by Women. Psychological Reports, 1972, 30, 454.

Warehime, R. G. Generalized Expectancy for Locus of Control and Academic Performance. Psychological Reports, 1972, February, 30(1), 314.

Watson, D., and Baumal, E. Effects of Locus of Control and Expectation of Future Control Upon Present Performance. Journal of Personality and Social Psychology, 1967, 6(2), 212-215.

Weiner, M. J., and Daughtry, T. Locus of Control as a Determinant of Information Seeking. Personality and Social Psychology Bulletin, 1975, Summer, 1(3), 505-508.

Wolfgang, A., and Potvin, R. Internality as a Determinant of Classroom Participation and Academic Performance Among Elementary Students. Paper presented at the American Psychological Association Convention, Montreal, 1973.

Wolk, S., and DuCette, J. Locus of Control and Achievement Motivation: Theoretical Overlap and Methodological Divergence. Psychological Reports, 1971, December, 29(3, Pt. 1), 755-758.

_____, and _____. The Moderating Effect of Locus of Control in Relation to Achievement-Motivation Variables. Journal of Personality, 1973, March, 41(1), 59-70.

Zikmund, W. G., and Miller, S. J. Internal/External Control of Reinforcement and Women's Participation in Direct Social Action. Psychological Reports, 1974, June, 34(3, Pt. 2), 1163-1166.

E. EXPECTATIONS, CONTROL, CAUSES (continued)

3. ATTRIBUTED CAUSES
OF SUCCESS/FAILURE

Adler, S. Determinants of Causal Attributions for Academic Performance. Unpublished doctoral dissertation, New York University. Dissertation Abstracts International, 1976, May, 36(11-B), 5846.

Ames, C., Ames, R., and Felker, D. W. Informational and Dispositional Determinants of Children's Achievement Attributions. Journal of Educational Psychology, 1976, 68(1), 63-69.

Bar-Tal, D., and Frieze, I. H. Achievement Motivation and Gender as Determinants of Attributions for Success and Failure. Washington, D. C.: National Institute of Education, 1975. Also Available from ERIC (ED118518), 1976.

_____, and _____. Attributions of Success and Failure for Actors and Observers. Journal of Research in Personality, 1976, September, 10(3), 256-265.

_____, and _____. Achievement Motivation for Males and Females as a Determinant of Attributions for Success and Failure. Sex Roles: A Journal of Research, 1977, June, 3(3), 301-313.

Beckman, L. J. Effects of Students' Performance on Teachers' and Observers' Attributions of Causality. Journal of Educational Psychology, 1970, 61, 76-82.

_____. Causal Attributions of Teachers and Parents Regarding Children's Performance. Psychology in the Schools, 1976, April, 13(2), 212-218.

Berg, P. A., and Hyde, J. S. Gender and Race Differences in Causal Attributions in Achievement Situations. Paper presented at the American Psychological Association Convention, Washington, D. C., 1976.

Crandall, V. C. Children's Achievement Responsibility and Their Achievement Behaviors. NIMH Progress Report, 1965, December, Grant No. MH-02238, 110-117.

Croke, J. A. Sex Differences in Causal Attributions and Expectancies for Success as a Function of the Sex-Role Appropriateness of the Task. Unpublished manuscript, University of California, Los Angeles, 1973.

Davis, W. L., and Davis, D. E. Internal-External Control and Attribution of Responsibility for Success and Failure. Journal of Personality, 1972, March, 40(1), 123-136.

Deaux, K. Sex and Helping: Expectations and Attributions. Symposium presentation at the American Psychological Association Convention, Honolulu, 1972.

_____. Ahhh, She Was Just Lucky. Psychology Today, 1976, December, 10, 70+.

_____. Sex: A Perspective on the Attribution Process. In J. H. Harvey, W. J. Ickes and R. F. Kidd (eds.), New Directions in Attribution Research: I. New York: Halsted Press, 1976, 335-352.

_____. Stereotypes of Women and Men: Performance Evaluation. In The Behavior of Women and Men. Monterey, CA: Brooks/Cole, 1976, 23-34.

_____, and Emswiller, T. Explanations of Successful Performance on Sex-Linked Tasks: What Is Skill for the Male Is Luck for the Female. Journal of Personality and Social Psychology, 1974, January, 29(1), 80-85.

_____, and Farris, E. Attributing Causes for One's Own Performance: The Effects of Sex, Norms, and Outcome. Journal of Research in Personality, 1977, March, 11(1), 59-72.

_____, White, L., and Farris, E. Skill Versus Luck: Field and Laboratory Studies of Male and Female Preferences. Journal of Personality and Social Psychology, 1975, October, 32(4), 629-636.

Dipboye, R. L. Effects of Initial Performance as Moderated by Causal Attributions and Sex. Perceptual and Motor Skills, 1976, June, 42(3, Pt. 1), 791-794.

Dweck, C. S., and Reppucci, N. D. Learned Helplessness and Reinforcement Responsibility in Children. Journal of Personality and Social Psychology, 1973, 25, 109-116.

Erkut, S. Sex Differences in Attribution of Achievement and Actual Achievement. Paper presented at the American Psychological Association Convention, San Francisco, 1977.

Etaugh, C., and Brown, B. Perceiving the Causes of Success and Failure of Male and Female Performers. Developmental Psychology, 1975, 11, 103.

_____, and Hadley, T. Causal Attributions of Male and Female Performance by Young Children. Psychology of Women Quarterly, 1977, Fall, 2(1), 16-23.

_____, and Ropp, J. Children's Self-Evaluation of Performance as a Function of Sex, Age, Feedback, and Sex-Typed Task Label. Journal of Psychology, 1976, September, 94(1), 115-122.

Feather, N. T. Attribution of Responsibility and Valence of Success and Failure in Relation to Initial Confidence and Task Performance. Journal of Personality and Social Psychology, 1969, 13(2), 129-144.

_____, and Simon, J. G. Attribution of Responsibility and Valence of Outcome in Relation to Initial Confidence and Success and Failure of Self and Other. Journal of Personality and Social Psychology, 1971, 18(2), 173-188.

_____, and _____. Causal Attributions for Success and Failure in Relation to Expectations of Success Based Upon Selective or Manipulative Control. Journal of Personality, 1971, 39, 527-541.

_____, and _____. Luck and the Unexpected Outcome: A Field Replication of Laboratory Findings. Australian Journal of Psychology, 1972, 24(1), 113-117.

_____, and _____. Reactions to Male and Female Success and Failure in Sex-Linked Occupations: Impressions of Personality, Causal Attributions, and Perceived Likelihood of Different Consequences. Journal of Personality and Social Psychology, 1975, 31(1), 20-31.

Feldman-Summers, S., and Kiesler, S. B. Those Who Are Number Two Try Harder: The Effect of Sex on Attributions of Causalty. Journal of Personality and Social Psychology, 1974, December, 30(6), 846-855.

Friend, R. M., and Wood, L. E. Adults' Attribution of Responsibility for Success and Failure of Children from Different Social Backgrounds. Psychology in the Schools, 1973, July, 10, 339-344.

Frieze, I. H. Sex Differences in Perceiving the Causes of Success and Failure. Unpublished manuscript, University of Pittsburgh, 1973.

_____. Women's Expectations for and Causal Attributions of Success and Failure. In M. T. S. Mednick et al. (eds.), Women and Achievement: Social and Motivational Analyses. New York: Halsted Press, 1975, 158-171.

_____. Causal Attributions and Information Seeking to Explain Success and Failure. Journal of Research in Personality, 1976, September, 10(3), 293-305.

_____. Internal and External Psychological Barriers for Women in Science. Chapter to appear in J. A. Ramaley (ed.), Covert Discrimination and Women in the Sciences. Boulder, CO: Westview Press, 1978.

_____, Fisher, J., Hanusa, B., McHugh, M., and Valle, V. A. Attributions of Success and Failure as Internal and External Barriers to Achievement in Women. Chapter to appear in J. Sherman and F. Denmark (eds.), Psychology of Women: Future Directions of Research. New York: Psychological Dimensions, 1978.

_____, McHugh, M., Fisher, J., and Valle, V. Attributing the Causes of Success and Failure: Internal and External Barriers to Achievement in Women. Paper presented at New Directions for Research on Women Conference, Madison, WI, 1975.

_____, McHugh, M., and Duquin, M. E. Causal Attributions for

Women and Men and Sports Participation. Symposium presentation at the American Psychological Association Convention, Washington, D. C., 1976.

_____, and Weiner, B. Cue Utilization and Attributional Judgments for Success and Failure. Journal of Personality, 1971, 39, 591-605.

Garland, H. Sometimes Nothing Succeeds Like Success: Reactions to Success and Failure in Sex-Linked Occupations. Psychology of Women Quarterly, 1977, Fall, 2(1), 50-61.

_____, and Price, K. H. Attitudes Toward Women in Management and Attributions for Their Success and Failure in a Managerial Position. Journal of Applied Psychology, 1977, 62(1), 29-33.

Goldberg, C., and Evenbeck, S. Causal Attribution of Success and Failure as a Function of Authoritarianism and Sex. Perceptual and Motor Skills, 1976, April, 42(2), 499-510.

Hansen, R. D., and O'Leary, V. E. Sex-Determined Attributions: Women's Dispositions Vs. Men's Environment. Symposium presentation at the American Psychological Association Convention, San Francisco, 1977.

Ilgen, D. R., and Terborg, J. R. Sex Discrimination and Sex-Role Stereotypes: Are they Synonymous? No! Organizational Behavior and Human Performance, 1975, 14, 154-157.

Jackaway, R. F. Achievement Attributions and the Low Expectation Cycle in Females. Paper presented at the American Psychological Association Convention, Chicago, 1975.

_____. Sex Differences in Achievement Motivation Behavior, and Attributions About Success and Failure. Unpublished doctoral dissertation, State University of New York, Albany. Dissertation Abstracts International, 1975, 35(10-B), 5158.

Jellison, J. M., Jackson-White, R., Bruder, R. A., and Martyna, W. Achievement Behavior: A Situational Interpretation. Sex Roles: A Journal of Research, 1975, 1(4), 369-384.

Johnston, S., Cunningham, J. D., Passer, M. W., and Kanouse, D. E. Effects of Social Influence on Attributions for Success and Failure. Personality and Social Psychology Bulletin, 1974, 1(1), 100-102.

Kahn, A., Nelson, R. E., and Gaedert, W. P. Sex Differences in Achievement Expectations, Achievement Behavior, and Success Attributions. Symposium presentation at the American Psychological Association Convention, San Francisco, 1977.

Krusell, J. L. Attribution of Responsibility for Performance Outcomes of Males and Females. Unpublished doctoral dissertation, University of Rochester. Dissertation Abstracts International, 1974, July, 35(1-B), 481-482.

Kukla, A. Attributional Determinants of Achievement-Related Behavior. Journal of Personality and Social Psychology, 1972, 21, 166-174.

Layden, M. A., and Ickes, W. Self-Esteem and Sex Differences in Attributional Style: Effect on Performance. Paper presented at the American Psychological Association Convention, San Francisco, 1977.

Lee, S. Sex and Sex Role Identity Differences in Attributions for Success and Failure in Subjectively Recalled Life Experiences. Symposium presentation at the American Psychological Association Convention, San Francisco, 1977.

Levine, R. V. Attributions to Self and Others as a Function of Perceived Locus of Control, Self-Esteem and Task Outcome. Unpublished doctoral dissertation, New York University. Dissertation Abstracts International, 1974, August, 35(2-B), 1106-1107.

Libow, J. A., and Mogy, R. B. Task Sex-Appropriateness and Sex Differences in Self-Attribution for Performance. Paper presented at the American Psychological Association Convention, Washington, D. C., 1976.

Luginbuhl, J. E. R., Crowe, D. H., and Kahan, J. P. Causal Attributions for Success and Failure. Journal of Personality and Social Psychology, 1975, 31(1), 86-93.

McArthur, L. Z. Note on Sex Differences in Causal Attribution. Psychological Reports, 1976, 38(1), 29-30.

McHugh, M. C. Sex Differences in Causal Attributions: A Critical Review. Paper presented at the Eastern Psychological Association meeting, New York, 1975.

_____, Fisher, J. E., and Frieze, I. H. The Effects of Competitiveness, Type of Task, Sex, and Outcome on Attributions for One's Own Performance. Unpublished manuscript, University of Pittsburgh, 1975.

McMahan, I. D. Sex Differences in Causal Attribution Following Success and Failure. Paper presented at the Eastern Psychological Association meeting, New York, 1971.

_____. Relationships Between Causal Attributions and Expectancy of Success. Journal of Personality and Social Psychology, 1973, 28, 108-114.

Murray, S. R. Achievement Evaluation: Variations Related to Causal Attribution, Sex, Sex Role, and Outcome. Unpublished manuscript, Howard University, 1976.

_____, and Mednick, M. T. S. Perceiving the Causes of Success and Failure in Achievement: Sex, Race, and Motivational Comparisons. Journal of Consulting and Clinical Psychology, 1975, December, 43(6), 881-884.

Nicholls, J. G. Causal Attributions and Other Achievement-Related Cognitions: Effects of Task Outcome, Attainment Value, and Sex. Journal of Personality and Social Psychology, 1975, March, 31(3), 379-389.

O'Leary, V. E., and Ridley, R. Causal Attributions for Performance: Sex Differences in Sensitivity to Incongruity Between Expectancy and Outcome. Unpublished manuscript, Oakland University, 1975.

Parsons, J. E. Sex Differences in Attributional Patterns and Expectancy for Success. Paper presented at the Eastern Psychological Association meeting, New York, 1975.

_____. Women's Attributional Patterns for Sex-Stereotyped Occupations. Paper presented at the American Psychological Association Convention, San Francisco, 1977.

_____, and Ruble, D. N. Attributional and Cognitive Processes Underlying the Development of Achievement-Related Expectancies. Unpublished manuscript, 1975.

Pasquella, M., Mednick, M. T. S., and Murray, S. R. Causal Attributions for Achievement Outcomes: Sex Role, Sex, and Outcome Comparisons. Paper presented at the American Psychological Association Convention, San Francisco, 1977.

Pines, H. A. An Attributional Analysis of Locus of Control Orientation and Source of Informational Dependence. Journal of Personality and Social Psychology, 1973, 26(2), 262-272.

Rosenfield, D., and Stephan, W. G. Sex Differences in Attributions for Sex-Typed Tasks. Paper presented at the American Psychological Association Convention, San Francisco, 1977.

Ruble, D. N., Parsons, J. E., and Ross, J. Self-Evaluative Responses of Children in an Achievement Setting. Child Development, 1976, December, 47(4), 990-997.

Sasfy, J. H. Some Relationships Between Causality for Task Participation and the Causal Attribution of Task Outcomes. Unpublished doctoral dissertation, Pennsylvania State University. Dissertation Abstracts International, 1975, May, 35(11-A), 7134-7135.

Seligman, C., Paschall, N., and Takata, G. Effects of Physical

Attractiveness on Attribution of Responsibility. Canadian Journal of Behavioural Science, 1974, July, 6(3), 290-296.

Simon, J. G., and Feather, N. T. Causal Attributions for Success and Failure at University Examinations. Journal of Educational Psychology, 1973, February, 64(1), 46-56.

Snyder, H. N., and Frieze, I. H. The Biasing Effect of Causal Belief Structures on Achievement-Related Attributions. Unpublished manuscript, 1977.

Sobel, R. S. The Effects of Success, Failure, and Locus of Control on Postperformance Attribution of Causality. Journal of General Psychology, 1974, July, 91(1), 29-34.

Stabler, J., and Johnson, E. E. Instrumental Performance as a Function of Reinforcement Schedule, Luck Versus Skill Instructions and Sex of Child. Journal of Experimental Child Psychology, 1970, 9, 330-335.

Taynor, J., and Deaux, K. When Women Are More Deserving Than Men: Equity, Attribution, and Perceived Sex Differences. Journal of Personality and Social Psychology, 1973, 28(3), 360-367. Also in F. L. Denmark (ed.), Women--Volume I: A PDI Research Reference Work. New York: Psychological Dimensions, 1976, 423-430.

Terborg, J. R., and Ilgen, D. R. A Theoretical Approach to Sex Discrimination in Traditionally Masculine Occupations. Organizational Behavior and Human Performance, 1975, 13, 352-376.

Valle, V. A. The Effect of the Stability of Attributions on Future Expectations. Personality and Social Psychology Bulletin, 1974, 1(1), 97-99.

_____, and Frieze, I. H. The Stability of Causal Attributions as a Mediator in Changing Expectations for Success. Journal of Personality and Social Psychology, 1976, 33, 579-587.

Weiner, B. Thoughts and Actions Associated with Achievement Motivation. Irish Journal of Education, 1969, Winter, 3(2), 105-116.

_____. Attribution Theory, Achievement Motivation, and the Educational Process. Review of Educational Research, 1972, Spring, 42, 203-215.

_____ (ed.). Achievement Motivation and Attribution Theory. Morristown, NJ: General Learning Press, 1974.

_____ (ed.). Achievement Motivation as Conceptualized by an Attribution Theorist. In Achievement Motivation and Attribution Theory. Morristown, NJ: General Learning Press, 1974.

_____, Frieze, I. H., Kukla, A., Reed, L., Rest, S., and Rosenbaum, R. M. (eds.). Perceiving the Causes of Success and Failure. Morristown, NJ: General Learning Press, 1971.

_____, Heckhausen, H., Meyer, W., and Cook, R. E. Causal Ascriptions and Achievement Behavior: Conceptual Analysis of Effort and Reanalysis of Locus of Control. Journal of Personality and Social Psychology, 1972, 21, 239-248.

_____, and Kukla, A. An Attributional Analysis of Achievement Motivation. Journal of Personality and Social Psychology, 1970, 15(1), 1-20.

_____, and Potepan, P. A. Personality Correlates and Affective Reactions Towards Exams of Succeeding and Failing College Students. Journal of Educational Psychology, 1970, 61(2), 144-151.

Weiner, L. Students' Success and Failure Attributions. Symposium presentation at the American Psychological Association Convention, San Francisco, 1977.

Wyer, R. S., Jr., Henninger, M., and Wolfson, M. Informational Determinants of Females' Self-Attributions and Observers' Judgments of Them in an Achievement Situation. Journal of Personality and Social Psychology, 1975, 32(3), 556-570.

IV

COUNSELING FORCES AND WOMEN'S AMBITION

> Like all sciences and all valuations, the psychology of women has hitherto been considered only from the point of view of men. It is inevitable that the man's position of advantage should cause objective validity to be attributed to his subjective, affective relations to the woman, and ... the psychology of women hitherto actually represents a deposit of the desires and disappointments of men. An additional and very important factor in the situation is that women have adapted themselves to the wishes of men and felt as if their adaptation were their true nature. That is, they see or saw themselves in the way that their men's wishes demanded of them; unconsciously they yielded to the suggestion of masculine thought. --Karen Horney, 1926.

Abramowitz, S. I., and Abramowitz, C. V. Should Prospective Women Clients Seek Out Women Practitioners?: Intimations of a "Ding-Bat" Effect in Clinical Evaluation. Proceedings of the 81st Annual Convention of the American Psychological Association, Montreal, Canada, 1973, 8, 505-506.

———, ———, Jackson, C., and Gomes, B. The Politics of Clinical Judgment: What Nonliberal Examiners Infer About Women Who Do Not Stifle Themselves. Journal of Consulting and Clinical Psychology, 1973, 41, 385-391.

———, Weitz, L. J., Schwartz, J. M., Amira, S., Gomes, B., and Abramowitz, C. V. Comparative Counselor Inferences Toward Women with Medical School Aspirations. Journal of College Student Personnel, 1975, March, 16(2), 128-130.

Adams, J. F., and Rogers, P. A. Counseling the Adolescent Girl on Personal Problems. Personnel and Guidance Journal, 1961, April, 39(8), 672.

Ahrons, C. Counselors' Perceptions of Career Images of Women. Journal of Vocational Behavior, 1976, 8, 197-207.

Alberti, R. E., and Emmons, M. L. Your Perfect Right: A Guide to Assertive Behavior. San Luis Obispo, CA: Impact, 1975.

Almquist, E. M. Career Counseling for Women in 1884: The More Total View. Vocational Guidance Quarterly, 1975, June, 23(4), 298-300.

Amatea, E. S. A Study of the Effects of a Career Planning Program for College Women. Unpublished doctoral dissertation. Dissertation Abstracts International, 1973, 33(A), 5485.

AMEG Commission Report on Sex Bias in Measurement. Measurement and Evaluation in Guidance, 1973, 6, 171-177.

American Association of University Women Educational Foundation. Counseling Techniques for Mature Women. Washington, D. C.: AAUW Educational Foundation, 1966.

American Psychological Association Task Force. Report on Sex Bias and Sex-Role Stereotyping in Psychotherapeutic Practice. American Psychologist, 1975, 30(12), 1169-1175.

Anderson, M., and the Feminist Psychology Group. Sex Role Stereotypes and Clinical Psychologists: An Australian Study. Australian Psychologist, 1975, December, 10(3), 325-331.

Angrist, S. S. Counseling College Women About Careers. Journal of College Student Personnel, 1972, November, 13(6), 494-498.

Arkava, M. L. Alterations in Achievement Motivation Through Counseling Intervention. Journal of Secondary Education, 1969, February, 44, 74-80.

Ashbaugh, J.-A., Levin, C., and Zaccaria, L. Persistence and the Disadvantaged College Student. Journal of Educational Research, 1973, October, 67(2), 64-66.

Asher, J. Psychology Tries to Buy into Psychiatric Standard-Setting Body. APA Monitor, March 1975, 6(3), 1+.

Aslin, A. L. Feminist and Community Mental Health Center Psychotherapists' Mental Health Expectations for Women. Unpublished doctoral dissertation, University of Maryland. Dissertation Abstracts International, 1975, May, 35(11-B), 5630-5631.

Assertion Training. Special Issue. The Counseling Psychologist, 1975, 5(4).

Association for Measurement and Evaluation in Guidance Commission on Sex Bias in Measurement. Report on Sex Bias in Interest Measurement. Measurement and Evaluation in Guidance, 1973, 6, 171-177.

Babcock, R. J., and Kaufman, M. A. Effectiveness of a Career Course. Vocational Guidance Quarterly, 1976, 24(3), 261-266.

Barbier, M. N. Counseling the Mature Woman. Adult Leadership, 1971, November, 20, 187-189+.

Barrett, C. J., Berg, P. I., Eaton, E. M., and Pomeroy, E. L. Implications of Women's Liberation for the Future of Psychotherapy. Psychotherapy: Theory, Research, and Practice, 1974, 11(1), 11-15.

Baum, O. E., and Herring, C. The Pregnant Psychotherapist in Training: Some Preliminary Findings and Impressions. American Journal of Psychiatry, 1975, April, 132(4), 419-422.

Beach, D. R. Attitudes of Counselor Trainees Toward Women. Unpublished doctoral dissertation, Nova University, 1975.

_____, and Kimmel, E. Attitudes Toward Women: A Comparison Study of Counselor Trainees. The Humanist Educator, 1976, June, 14(4), 209-220.

Beesly, M. G. Critical Evaluations: Modern Woman--Implications for Psychotherapy. I. Psychotherapy and Evolving Social-Sexual Roles. Canadian Psychiatric Association Journal, 1973, 18(1), 83-93.

Belin, S. B. Better Work with Women Clients. Social Work, 1976, November, 21(6), 492-497.

Belson, B. A. Supplemental References Re: The Counseling of Women. The Counseling Psychologist, 1973, 4(1), 96-101.

Berg, P., Vega, S., and Corby, N. Sex-Role Stereotypes and Their Influence on the Psychotherapy Process. Symposium presentation at the American Psychological Association Convention, Washington, D. C., 1976.

Berman, M. R., Gelso, C., Greenfeig, B., and Hirsch, R. Treatment Effectiveness: Meeting Needs of Women Exploring New Goals. Paper presented at the American Psychological Association Convention, Washington, D. C., 1976.

Bernard, M. Working Class Women's Anger: Implication for Therapy. Symposium presentation at the American Psychological Association Convention, San Francisco, 1977.

Berry, J. B. The New Womanhood: Counselor Alert. Personnel and Guidance Journal, 1972, October, 51(2), 105-108.

_____. Counseling Older Women: A Perspective. Personnel and Guidance Journal, 1976, November, 55, 130-131.

_____, et al. Counseling Girls and Women: Awareness Analysis Action, Kansas City: University of Missouri, 1966.

Bickel, H. E. An Analysis of the Work Values of Women: Implications for Counseling. Unpublished doctoral dissertation, State University of New York, Albany. Dissertation Abstracts, 1969, 29 (11-A), 3761.

Biggerstaff, M. A. A Framework for Analyzing Women's Roles Within the Social Work Treatment Situation. Unpublished manuscript, University of Southern California, 1975.

_____. Social Work Practitioners' Conceptions of Sex and Social Roles. Unpublished doctoral dissertation, University of Southern California, 1976.

Billingsley, D. Sex-Role Stereotypes and Clinical Judgment: Negative Bias in Psychotherapy. Paper presented at the American Psychological Association Convention, Washington, D. C., 1976.

_____. Sex Bias in Psychotherapy: An Examination of the Effects of Client Sex, Client Pathology, and Therapist Sex on Treatment Planning. Journal of Consulting and Clinical Psychology, 1977, 45(2), 250-256.

Bingham, W. C., and House, E. W. Counselors' Attitudes Toward Women and Work. Vocational Guidance Quarterly, 1973, 22(1), 16-23.

_____, and _____. Counselors View Women and Work: Accuracy of Information. Vocational Guidance Quarterly, 1973, June, 21(4), 262-268.

_____, and _____. ACES' Members Attitudes Toward Women and Work. Counselor Education and Supervision, 1975, March, 14(3), 204-214.

Birk, J. M. Interest Inventories: A Mixed Blessing. Vocational Guidance Quarterly, 1974, June, 22(4), 280-286.

_____. Reducing Sex-Bias--Factors Affecting the Client's View of the Use of Career Interest Inventories. In E. E. Diamond (ed.), Issues of Sex Bias and Sex Fairness in Career Interest Measurement. Washington, D. C.: National Institute of Education, 1975, 101-121.

_____. Providing Life/Career Planning for Women and Girls. Palo Alto: National Consortium on Competency Based Staff Development in Cooperation with American Institutes for Research, 1976.

_____, Cooper, J., and Tanney, M. F. Racial and Sex Role Stereotyping in Career Information Illustration. In D. Wark and E. G. Joselyn (eds.), Student Counseling Bureau Review: Women in Transition. Minneapolis: Student Counseling Bureau, University of Minnesota, 1975, September, 26(1), 42-46.

_____, _____, and _____. Stereotyping in Occupational Outlook Handbook Illustrations: A Follow-Up Study. Paper presented at the American Psychological Association Convention, Chicago, 1975.

_____, and Tanney, M. F. Career Exploration for High School Women: A Model. Paper presented at the American Personnel and Guidance Association Regional Convention, Atlanta, 1973.

Blimline, C. A. The Effect of a Vocational Unit on the Exploration of Nontraditional Career Options. Journal of Vocational Behavior, 1976, October, 9(2), 209-217.

Bloom, L. Z., Coburn, K., and Pearlman, J. The New Assertive Woman. New York: Dell, 1975.

Bobowski, R. C. Project Women: Career Education Program: Maine. American Education, 1975, December, 11, 27-28.

Bogie, D. W., and Bogie, C. E. Counselor-Client Contact Variable and Occupational Aspiration-Expectation Discrepancies. Vocational Guidance Quarterly, 1976, September, 25, 50-58.

Borgers, S. B., Hendrix, J. C., and Price, G. E. Does Counselor Response to Occupational Choice Indicate Sex Stereotyping? Journal of the National Association for Women Deans, Administrators, and Counselors, 1977, Fall, 41(1), 17-20.

Boring, P. Z. Sex Stereotyping in Educational Guidance. Sex Role Stereotyping in the Schools. Washington, D.C.: National Education Association, 1973, 14-22.

Borow, H., (ed.). Career Guidance for a New Age. Boston: Houghton Mifflin Co., 1973.

Borup, J. H. Validity of American College Test for Discerning Potential Academic Achievement Levels; Ethnic and Sex Groups. Journal of Educational Research, 1971, September, 65, 3-6.

Boyd, B., and Griffith, M. E. Critical Professional Need: The Counselor for Women. Adult Leadership, 1973, November, 22, 161-162.

Brandenburg, J. B. Needs of Women Returning to School. Personnel and Guidance Journal, 1974, September, 53, 11-18.

Brashear, D. B., and Willis, K. Claiming Our Own: A Model for Women's Growth. Journal of Marriage and Family Counseling, 1976, July, 2(3), 251-258.

Brebner, R. A. Career Planning and Placement Strategies for Women. Journal of College Placement, 1976, Winter, 36, 19-20.

Brew, A. P. Effects of a Counseling Workshop on Adult Women. Unpublished doctoral dissertation, University of Maryland. Dissertation Abstracts International, 1976, April, 36(10-A), 6467.

Brockway, B. S. Assertive Training for Professional Women. Social Work, 1976, November, 21(6), 498-505.

Brodsky, A. M. The Consciousness-Raising Group as a Model for Therapy with Women. Psychotherapy: Theory, Research, and Practice, 1973, 10, 24-29.

_____. Seeking the Holy Grail: Or, The Status of Women in Counseling. The Counseling Psychologist, 1976, 6(2), 56-58.

Brooks, B. Women's Powerlessness as It Affects Anger in the Therapeutic Relationship. Symposium presentation at the American Psychological Association Convention, San Francisco, 1977.

Brooks, L. Do Androgynous Models Generate Androgynous Counselors? Symposium presentation at the American Psychological Association Convention, Chicago, 1975.

_____. Supermoms Shift Gears: Re-entry Women. The Counseling Psychologist, 1976, 6(2), 33-37.

Broverman, I. K., Broverman, D., Clarkson, F., Rosenkrantz, P., and Vogel, S. Sex-Role Stereotypes and Clinical Judgments of Mental Health. Journal of Consulting and Clinical Psychology, 1970, 34(1), 1-7.

Brown, C. R., and Hellinger, M. L. Therapists' Attitudes toward Women. Journal of Social Work, 1975, July, 20(4), 266-270.

Bullard, D. G. An Investigation of Sex Bias in the Evaluation of Psychotherapists: An Analogue Study. Unpublished doctoral dissertation, Arizona State University. Dissertation Abstracts International, 1975, January, 35(7-B), 3571.

Bundy, D. A., and Hebert, D. J. Relationship of Clients' Sex to Effective Vocational Counseling by Male Counselors. Perceptual and Motor Skills, 1974, August, 39(1, Pt. 2), 653-654.

Bureau of Guidance. Career Guidance for Girls. Sacramento: California Department of Education, 1960.

Business and Professional Women's Foundation. Career Counseling: New Perspectives for Girls and Women: A Selected Annotated Bibliography. Washington, D. C., 1972.

Calia, V. P. Vocational Guidance: After the Fall. Personnel and Guidance Journal, 1966, 45, 320-327.

California State Advisory Commission on the Status of Women. Information for Counselors on Counseling California Girls, Sacramento, 1973. Also available from ERIC (ED094172), 1974.

Campbell, D. P. Women Deserve Better. Personnel and Guidance Journal, 1973, 51(8), 545-549.

Campbell, R. E., and Parsons, J. L. Readiness for Vocational

Planning in Junior High School: A Socio-economic and Geographic Comparison. Journal of Vocational Behavior, 1972, 2, 401-417.

Carey, E. A. (ed.). Issues in the Psychology and Counseling of Women. Additional Resources. Boston: Womanspace, Feminist Therapy Collective, 1976.

_____, Murphy, B. M., and Wasserman, C. Counseling Women: A Bibliography. Boston: Womanspace, Feminist Therapy Collective, 1975.

Carter, D., and Rawlings, E. (eds.). Psychotherapy for Women: Treatment Toward Equality. Springfield, IL: Charles C. Thomas, 1977.

Casey, T. J. The Development of a Leadership Orientation Scale on the SVIB for Women. Measurement and Evaluation in Guidance, 1975, July, 8(2), 96-100.

Chasen, B. Diagnostic Sex-Role Bias and Its Relation to Authoritarianism, Sex-Role Attitudes and Sex of the School Psychologist. Unpublished doctoral dissertation, New York University. Dissertation Abstracts International, 1974, November, 35(5-B), 2400.

_____. Diagnostic Sex-Role Bias and Its Relation to Authoritarianism, Sex-Role Attitudes, and Sex of the School Psychologist. Sex Roles: A Journal of Research, 1975, 1(4), 355-368.

_____, and Weinberg, S. Diagnostic Sex-Role Bias: How Can We Measure It? Journal of Personality Assessment, 1975, 39(6), 620-629.

Cherniss, C. Personality and Ideology: A Personological Study of Women's Liberation. Psychiatry, 1972, 35, 109-125.

Cherry, R., and Cherry, K. The Horney Heresy. Nursing Digest 1975 Review of Psychiatry and Mental Health. Wakefield, MA: Contemporary, 1975, 56-61.

Chesler, P. Men Drive Women Crazy. Psychology Today, 1971, July, 5(2), 18+.

_____. Women as Psychiatrists and Psychotherapeutic Patients. Journal of Marriage and the Family, 1971, 33(4), 446-459.

_____. Patient and Patriarch: Women in the Psychotherapeutic Relationship. In V. Gornick and B. K. Moran (eds.), Woman in Sexist Society: Studies in Power and Powerlessness. New York: Basic Books, 1971, 362-392. Also in S. Cox (ed.), Female Psychology: The Emerging Self. Chicago: Science Research Associates, 1976, 318-334.

_____. Women and Madness. New York: Doubleday, 1972.

_____. A Word about Mental Health and Women. Mental Hygiene, 1973, 57(3), 5-7.

Clarke, E. Sex in Education or a Fair Chance for the Girls. New York: Arno Press, 1972.

Cline-Naffziger, C. A Survey of Counselors' and Other Selected Professionals' Attitudes Toward Women's Roles. Dissertation Abstracts International, 1971, 32(A), 3021.

Coakley, J. Attitudes of Guidance Counselors. In Report of the Massachusetts Governor's Commission on the Status of Women. Boston, 1972.

Cochran, D. J., and Warren, P. M. Career Counseling for Women: A Workshop Format. School Counselor, 1976, November, 24, 123-127.

Cole, N. A. Bias in Selection. Journal of Educational Measurement, 1973, 10, 237-255.

Cole, N. S. On Measuring the Vocational Interests of Women. American College Testing Research Report, 1972, March, (49). Also in Journal of Counseling Psychology, 1973, March, 20(2), 105-112.

_____, and Hanson, G. R. Impact of Interest Inventories on Career Choice. In E. E. Diamond (ed.), Issues of Sex Bias and Sex Fairness in Career Interest Measurement. Washington, D. C.: National Institute of Education, 1975, 1-19. Also available from ERIC (ED095370), 1975.

Collins, A. M., and Sedlacek, W. E. Counselor Ratings of Male and Female Clients. Journal of the National Association for Women Deans, Administrators, and Counselors, 1974, 37, 128-132.

Cook, B. I. Woman's Search for a Way of Becoming. Journal of the National Association of Women Deans and Counselors, 1970, Fall, 34, 23-27.

_____. Roles, Labels, Stereotypes: A Counselor's Challenge. Journal of the National Association of Women Deans and Counselors, 1971, 34(3), 99-105. Also in Sex Role Stereotyping in the Schools. Washington, D. C.: National Education Association, 1973, 40-49.

_____, and Stone, B. Counseling Women. Boston: Houghton Mifflin, 1973.

Cooper, G. Legal Implications of the Use of Standardized Ability

Tests in Employment and Education. Columbia Law Review, 1968, 68, 691-744.

Cooper, J. F. Comparative Impact of the SCII and the Vocational Card Sort on Career Salience and Career Exploration of Women. Journal of Counseling Psychology, 1976, July, 23(4), 348-352.

Counseling Girls and Women, A Guide for Jewish and Other Minority Women. Washington, D.C.: B'nai B'rith Career and Counseling Service, 1973.

Counseling Women. Special issue. Journal of the National Association for Women Deans, Administrators, and Counselors, 1974, Fall, 38(1).

Creaser, J., and Carsello, C. Comparability of Cross-Sex Scores on the Strong-Campbell Interest Inventory. Journal of Counseling Psychology, 1976, July, 23(4), 360-364.

Cross, S. L. The Second Time Around: A Survey of the Counseling Needs of Mature Women Returning to School. Unpublished master's thesis, University of California, Los Angeles, 1975.

Cummings, L. What Psychiatrists Say About Women's Liberation. Family Weekly, 1972, 4.

Daly, E. M. A Theory for the Vocational Counseling of Women. Unpublished doctoral dissertation, Ohio University, 1970.

Dansker, M. M. Counselor Evaluation of Identical Articles Attributed to Male and Female Authors. Unpublished doctoral dissertation, Stanford University. Dissertation Abstracts International, 1973, 34(A), 5621.

Datrin, S., and Galliano, G. For Counselors: A Course for Counseling Women. Counseling Educators and Supervisors, 1976, March, 15, 221-224.

Davis, S. O. Counseling Techniques for Dealing with Mathematics Anxiety. Symposium presentation at the American Psychological Association Convention, San Francisco, 1977.

_____. Encouraging the Career Development of Women in Nontraditional Fields. Symposium presentation at the American Psychological Association Convention, San Francisco, 1977.

Delk, J. L., and Ryan, T. T. Sex Role Stereotyping and A-B Therapist Status: Who is More Chauvinistic? Journal of Consulting and Clinical Psychology, 1975, August, 43(4), 589.

Denebrink, J. Counseling for Careers. Contact, 1972, Fall, 3(6), 30-33.

Dewey, C. R. Exploring Interests: A Non-Sexist Method. Personnel and Guidance Journal, 1974, 52, 311-315.

Diamond, E. E. (ed.). Guidelines for Assessment of Sex Bias and Sex Fairness in Career Interest Inventories. Issues of Sex Bias and Sex Fairness in Career Interest Measurement. Washington, D. C.: National Institute of Education, 1975, XIII-XXIX.

_____ (ed.). Issues of Sex Bias and Sex Fairness in Career Interest Measurement. Washington, D. C.: National Institute of Education, 1975.

DiSabatino, M. Psychological Factors Inhibiting Women's Occupational Aspirations and Vocational Choices: Implications for Counseling. Vocational Guidance Quarterly, 1976, September, 25(1), 43-49.

Donahue, T. J., and Costar, J. W. Counselor Discrimination Against Young Women in Career Selection. Journal of Counseling Psychology, 1977, 24(6), 481-486.

Drews, E. M. Counseling for Self-Actualization in Gifted Girls and Young Women. Journal of Counseling Psychology, 1965, 12(2), 167-175.

Dunteman, G. H. Validities of the Female Form of the Strong Vocational Interest Blank Occupational Therapy, Laboratory Technology, and Nursing Keys. Journal of Experimental Education, 1967, Summer, 35, 53-57.

Dyrud, J. Feminism and Psychotherapy. Symposium presentation at the American Psychological Association Convention, Chicago, 1975.

Eason, J. Life Style Counseling for a Reluctant Leisure Class. Personnel and Guidance Journal, 1972, October, 51(2), 127-132.

Elias, M. Sisterhood Therapy. Human Behavior, 1975, April, 4, 56-61.

Elton, C. F., and Rose, H. A. Significance of Personality in the Vocational Choice of College Women. Journal of Counseling Psychology, 1967, 14(4), 293-298.

_____, and _____. A Vocational Interest Test Minus Sex Bias. Journal of Vocational Behavior, 1975, October, 7(2), 207-214.

Engelhard, P. A. A Survey of Counselors' Attitudes Towards Women. Minnesota Counselor, 1969, 9(1), 14-28.

_____, Jones, K. O., and Stiggins, R. J. Trends in Counselor Attitude About Women's Roles. Journal of Counseling Psychology, 1976, July, 23(4), 365-372.

Entine, A. D. The Mid-Career Counseling Process. Industrial Gerontology, 1976, Spring, 3(2), 105-111.

Erickson, V. L. Psychological Growth for Women: A Cognitive-Developmental Curriculum Intervention. Counseling and Values, 1974, 18(2), 102-116.

──────. Deliberate Psychological Education for Women: From Iphigenia to Antigone. Counselor Education and Supervision, 1975, June, 297-309.

Eyde, L. D. Eliminating Barriers to Career Development of Women. Personnel and Guidance Journal, 1970, September, 49(1), 24-29.

Fabrikant, B. The Psychotherapist and the Female Patient: Perceptions, Misperceptions and Change. In V. Franks and V. Burtle (eds.), Women in Therapy: New Psychotherapies for a Changing Society. New York: Brunner/Mazel, 1974, 83-109.

──────, Landau, D., and Rollenhagen, J. Perceived Female Sex Role Attributes and Psychotherapists' Sex Role Expectations for Female Patients. New Jersey Psychologist, 1973, 23, 13-16.

Facilitating Career Development for Girls and Women. Monograph. Washington, D. C.: National Vocational Guidance Association, 1975.

Faggen-Steckler, J., McCarthy, K. A., and Tittle, C. K. Quantitative Method for Measuring Sex Bias in Standardized Tests. Journal of Educational Measurement, 1974, Fall, 11, 151-161.

Farmer, H. S. Helping Women to Resolve the Home-Career Conflict. Personnel and Guidance Journal, 1971, June, 49(10), 795-801.

──────. Career Counseling. New Directions for Higher Education, 1975, Autumn, 3(3), 61-78.

──────, and Backer, T. E. New Career Options for Women: A Counselor's Sourcebook. New York: Human Sciences Press, 1977.

Fedor, I. Sex Role Conflict and Symptom Formation in Women: Can Behavior Therapy Help? Psychotherapy: Theory, Research and Practice, 1974, 11, 22-29.

Feminists Call Psychiatry Sick. Bergen Record, 1972, June 9, 5.

Fensterhaim, H., and Baer, J. Don't Say Yes When You Want to Say No. New York: David McKay, 1975.

Fiedler, L. Psychological Development Curriculum for Adult Women--Design, Implementation, Assessment. Symposium presentation at the American Psychological Association Convention, San Francisco, 1977.

Fields, R. M. Psychotherapy: The Sexist Machine--Case Histories of Sexism. Symposium presentation at the American Psychological Association Convention, Honolulu, 1972.

_____. Psychotherapy: The Sexist Machine. Reprint from KNOW, Inc., P. O. Box 86031, Pittsburgh, PA 15221.

Fincher, C. Testing and Title VII. Atlanta Economic Review, 1965, 15(6), 15-19.

_____. Differential Validity and Test Bias. Personnel Psychology, 1975, 28, 481-500.

Fischer, J., Dulaney, D. D., Fazio, R. T., Hudark, M. T., and Zivotofsky, E. Are Social Workers Sexists? Social Work, 1976, November, 21(6), 428-433.

Fitzgerald, L. E. Counseling and Guidance for Women: A Selected Annotated Bibliography, 1962-1964. Journal of the National Association of Women Deans and Counselors, 1965, Summer, 28, 183-186.

_____. Women's Changing Expectations ... New Insights, New Demands. The Counseling Psychologist, 1973, 4(1), 90-95.

_____, and Harmon, L. W. (eds.). Counseling Women. Special Issue. The Counseling Psychologist, 1973, 4(1).

Flaugher, R. L. Bias in Testing: A Review and Discussion, (TM Report 36). Princeton, NJ: ERIC Clearinghouse on Tests, Measurement, and Evaluation, 1974.

_____. The New Definitions of Test Fairness in Selection: Developments and Implications. Educational Researcher, 1974, 3(9), 13-16.

Follingstad, D. R., Robinson, E. A., and Pugh, M. Effects of Consciousness-Raising Groups on Measures of Feminism, Self-Esteem, and Social Desirability. Journal of Counseling Psychology, 1977, May, 24, 223-230.

Fox, L. H. Changing Attitudes and Behaviors of Gifted Girls. Symposium presentation at the American Psychological Association Convention, Washington, D. C., 1976.

Frank, A. C., and Kirk, B. A. Factors Within the 1969 SVIB for Women and Relationships to Holland's Theory. Journal of Vocational Behavior, 1974, August, 5(1), 79-94.

Frank, H. H. (ed.). Assertiveness Training. In Women in the Organization. Philadelphia: University of Pennsylvania Press, 1977, 241-245.

Franks, V., and Burtle, V. (eds.). Women in Therapy: New Psychotherapies for a Changing Society. New York: Bunner/Mazel, 1974.

Friedersdorf, N. W. A Comparative Study of Counselor Attitudes Toward the Further Educational and Vocational Plans of High School Girls. Unpublished doctoral dissertation, Purdue University. Dissertation Abstracts International, 1970, 30(A), 4220-4221.

Fuller, F. F. Preferences for Male and Female Counselors. Personnel and Guidance Journal, 1964, 42, 463-467.

Gardner, J. Sexist Counseling Must Stop. Personnel and Guidance Journal, 1971, May, 49(9), 705-714.

Gelb, L. Masculinity-Femininity: A Study in Imposed Inequality. In J. B. Miller (ed.), Psychoanalysis and Women. New York: Penguin Books, 1973, 363-406.

Goerss, K. V. Sexism: A Challenge for School Counselors. Journal of the National Association for Women Deans, Administrators, and Counselors, 1977, Spring, 40(3), 104-107.

Goldberg, B. J. Mental Health Practice as Social Control: Practitioners' Choices of Therapy Goals as a Function of Sex of Client, Situations, and Other Practitioners' Opinions. Unpublished doctoral dissertation, State University of New York, Stony Brook. Dissertation Abstracts International, 1976, April, 36(10-B), 5256.

Goldberg, L. H. Attitudes of Clinical Psychologists Toward Women. Dissertation Abstracts International, 1974, 35(B), 1017-1018.

Gottfredson, G. D. A Note on Sexist Wording in Interest Measurement. Measurement and Evaluation in Guidance, 1976, January, 8(4), 221-223.

_____, and Holland, J. L. Vocational Choices of Men and Women: A Comparison of Predictors from the Self-Directed Search. Journal of Counseling Psychology, 1975, 22(1), 28-34.

_____, and _____. Toward Beneficial Resolution of the Interest Inventory Controversy. Unpublished manuscript, Johns Hopkins University, 1977.

_____, _____, and Gottfredson, L. S. The Relation of Vocational Aspirations and Assessments to Employment Reality. Center for Social Organization of Schools Report, Johns Hopkins University, 1974, September, (181).

Gould, L. J. Toward a More Androgynous Psychotherapy Research. Symposium presentation at the American Psychological Association Convention, San Francisco, 1977.

Gove, W. R. The Relationship between Sex Roles, Marital Status and Mental Illness. Social Forces, 1972, September, 51, 34-44.

_____, and Tudor, J. Adult Sex Roles and Mental Illness. American Journal of Sociology, 1973, January, 78(4), 50-73. Also in Huber, J. (ed.), Changing Women in a Changing Society. Chicago: University of Chicago Press, 1973, 50-93.

Greif, A. C. Developing an Androgynous Perspective Within the Client-Therapist Relationship. Symposium presentation at the American Psychological Association Convention, Washington, D. C., 1976.

Gribbons, W. D., and Lohnes, P. R. Career Development. Available from ERIC (ED010282), 1967.

Grumbine, C. Career Roles for Females in Psychology. In R. E. Hardy and J. G. Cull (eds.), Career Guidance for Young Women: Considerations in Planning Professional Careers. Springfield, IL: Charles C. Thomas, 1974, 112-131.

Grundy, B. L. Career Roles in Medicine. In R. E. Hardy and J. G. Cull (eds.), Career Guidance for Young Women: Considerations in Planning Professional Careers. Springfield, IL: Charles C. Thomas, 1974, 17-26.

Guidance Tests Get A in Sex Bias. Detroit Free Press, 1972, April 5.

Gurin, M. G., Nachmann, B., and Segal, S. J. The Effect of the Social Context in the Vocational Counseling of College Women. Journal of Counseling Psychology, 1963, 10(1), 28-33.

Guttentag, M., and Salastin, S. Women, Men and Mental Health. In L. A. Cater et al. (eds.), Women and Men--Changing Roles, Relationships, and Perceptions. New York: Praeger, 1977.

Guttman, M. A. J. (ed.). Female Perspectives on Sexist Issues in Counselor Education. In Women and ACES: Perspective and Issues. Washington, D. C.: Commission for Women, Association for Counselor Education and Supervision, 1974, 13-20.

_____ (ed.). Women and ACES: Perspective and Issues. Washington, D. C.: Commission for Women, Association for Counselor Education and Supervision, 1974.

Haener, D. The Working Woman: Can Counselors Take the Heat? Personnel and Guidance Journal, 1972, October, 51(2), 109-113.

Hahn, M. C. Equal Rights for Women in Career Development. Personnel, 1970, July/August, 55-59.

Hammond, E. H. Sex Discrimination in Student Personnel Functions. NAASP Journal, 1974, Winter, 11, 27-32.

Hansen, L. S. We Are Furious (Female) but We Can Shape Our Own Development. Personnel and Guidance Journal, 1972, October, 51(2), 87-93.

_____. Practical Approaches to Facilitate the Career Development of Women. School Psychology Digest, 1974, Summer, 3(3), 40-46. Also in Pupil Personnel Services Journal, 1976, 5(1), 1-12.

_____. The Career Development Process for Women: Current Views and Programs. Pupil Personnel Services Journal, 1975, 4(2), 23-33.

_____. Counseling and Career (Self) Development of Women. In H. J. Peters and J. C. Hansen (eds.), Vocational Guidance and Career Development. New York: Macmillan, 1977, 453-454.

_____, and Rapoza, R. S. (eds.). Career Development and Counseling of Women. Springfield, IL: Charles C. Thomas, 1977.

_____, and Tennyson, W. W. Career Development as Self Development: Humanizing the Focus for Career Education. Social Education, 1975, May, 39, 304-309.

Hanson, G. R., and Noeth, R. J. The Psychological Rewards of Work: Implications for the Career Development of Women. Iowa City: American College Testing Program.

_____, and Prediger, D. J. Toward Sex-Fair Vocational Interest Scales: The Uni-Sex ACT Interest Inventory. Unpublished manuscript, American College Testing Program, Iowa City.

_____, _____, and Schussel, R. H. Development and Validation of Sex-Balanced Interest Inventory Scales. ACT Research Report 73, Iowa City: American College Testing Program, 1977.

_____, and Rayman, J. Validity of Sex-Balanced Interest Inventory Scales. Journal of Vocational Behavior, 1976, December, 9(3), 279-291.

Hardee, M. D. Counseling Women Students. Junior College Journal, 1963, December, 34, 16-20.

Harmon, L. W. The Measurement of Women's Interest: The Effect of Using Married Women as Occupational Criterion Groups on the Women's Strong Vocational Interest Blank. Unpublished doctoral dissertation, University of Minnesota. Dissertation Abstracts, 1966, 26(9), 5541.

_____. Women's Interest: Fact or Fiction? Personnel and Guidance Journal, 1967, 45(9), 895-900.

_____. Women's Working Patterns Related to Their SVIB Housewife and Own Occupational Scores. Journal of Counseling Psychology, 1967, July, 14(4), 299-301.

_____. Predictive Power Over Ten Years of Measured Social Service and Scientific Interests Among College Women. Journal of Applied Psychology, 1969, 53(3, Pt. 1), 193-198.

_____. Strong Vocational Interest Blank Profiles of Disadvantaged Women. Journal of Counseling Psychology, 1970, November, 17(6), 519-521.

_____. Tables for Sexual Bias in Interest Testing. Paper presented at the American Personnel and Guidance Association Convention, Chicago, March, 1972.

_____. Sexual Bias in Interest Measurement. Measurement and Evaluation in Guidance, 1973, January, 5(4), 496-501.

_____. Sex Stereotyping in Interest Items: Occupational Titles Versus Activities. Measurement and Evaluation in Guidance, 1976, January, 8(4), 215-220.

_____. Career Counseling for Women. In D. Carter and E. Rawlings (eds.), Psychotherapy for Women: Treatment Toward Equality. Springfield, IL: Charles C. Thomas, 1977, 197-206.

_____, and Campbell, D.P. Use of Interest Inventories with Nonprofessional Women: Stewardesses Versus Dental Assistants. Journal of Counseling Psychology, 1968, 15(1), 17-22.

Harris, S.R. Sex Typing in Girls' Career Choices: A Challenge to Counselors. Vocational Guidance Quarterly, 1974, December, 23(2), 128-133.

Hartsook, J.E., Olch, D.R., and DeWolf, V.A. Personality Characteristics of Women's Assertiveness Training Group Participants. Journal of Counseling Psychology, 1976, 23(4), 322-326.

Harvey, D.W. The Validity of Holland's Vocational Preference Inventory for Adult Women. Unpublished doctoral dissertation, University of Connecticut. Dissertation Abstracts International, 1972, May, 32(11-A), 6129.

_____, and Whinfield, R.W. Extending Holland's Theory to Adult Women. Journal of Vocational Behavior, 1973, April, 3(2), 115-127.

Harway, M. Sex Bias in Counseling Materials. Journal of College Student Personnel, 1977, 18(1), 57-64.

_____. Studying Sex Discrimination in Counseling. Symposium presentation at the American Psychological Association Convention, San Francisco, 1977.

_____, and Astin, H. S. Sex Discrimination in Career Counseling and Education. New York: Praeger, 1977.

_____, _____, and Suhr, J. M. Selected Annotated Bibliography on Counseling Women. JSAS Catalog of Selected Documents in Psychology, 1977, 7(2), 55.

_____, _____, _____, and Whitely, J. M. Guidance and Counseling. Division 35 Newsletter-Psychology of Women, 1976, 3, 13-14.

Havighurst, R. J. Counseling Adolescent Girls in the 1960's. Vocational Guidance Quarterly, 1965, 13(3), 154-157.

Hawley, P. J. Perceptions of Male Models of Femininity Related to Career Choice. Journal of Counseling Psychology, 1972, 19(4), 308-313.

_____. Empirically-Based Counseling Practices for Women. Focus on Guidance, 1976, February, 8(6), 1-12.

Haÿrynen, Y. P. The Flow of New Students to Different University Fields: Career Motivation, Educational Choice and Discriminating Effects of University Admission: A Study of Finnish Female Students. Annales Academiae Scientiarum Fennicae, 1970, B-168.

Heilbrun, A. B., Jr. Counseling Readiness and the Problem-Solving Behavior of Clients. Journal of Consulting and Clinical Psychology, 1968, 32(4), 396-399.

Helwig, A. A. Counselor Bias and Women. Journal of Employment Counseling, 1976, June, 13(2), 58-67.

Hendel, D. D. Evaluation of Mathematics Anxiety Programs. Symposium Presentation at the American Psychological Association Convention, San Francisco, 1977.

Hill, C. E. Sex of Client and Sex and Experience Level of Counselor. Journal of Counseling Psychology, 1975, January, 22, 6-11.

_____. Counselor Reactions to Female Clients. Symposium presentation at the American Psychological Association Convention, Washington, D. C., 1976.

_____. A Research Perspective on Counseling Women. The Counseling Psychologist, 1976, 6(2), 53-55.

_____, Tanney, M. F., Leonard, M. M., and Reiss, J. A. Counselor Reactions to Female Clients: Type of Problem, Age of Client, and Sex of Counselor. Journal of Counseling Psychology, 1977, January, 24(1), 60-65.

Hill, J. W. Selling Women Short: A Psychiatrist's View. In Christian Association for Psychological Studies, Proceedings of the Twenty-first Annual Convention. Grand Rapids, MI: Christian Association for Psychological Studies, 1974.

Hilton, M. E. Special Message to Counselors of Women: Review of the Feminine Mystique, by B. Friedan. Journal of the National Association of Women Deans and Counselors, 1964, Winter, 27, 59-62.

Hiltunen, W. A. Counseling Course for the Mature Woman. Journal of the National Association of Women Deans and Counselors, 1968, Winter, 31, 93-96.

Hipple, J. L. Perceptual Differences in Concepts of the Ideal Woman. School Counselor, 1975, January, 22(3), 180-186.

Hohenshil, T. H. Perspectives on Career Counseling for Women: 1884 and 1974. Vocational Guidance Quarterly, 1974, December, 23, 100-103. Reply: Almquist, E. M., 1975, June, 23, 298-300. Rejoinder: 1975, December, 24, 102-103.

_____. Salmagundi: Career Counseling for Women in 1884: Revisited. Vocational Guidance Quarterly, 1975, December, 25(2), 102-103.

Holland, J. L., and Gottfredson, G. D. Sex Differences, Item Revisions, Validity, and the Self-Directed Search. Measurement and Evaluation in Guidance, 1976, 8, 224-228.

_____, _____, and Gottfredson, L. S. Read Our Reports and Examine the Data--A Response to Prediger and Cole. Journal of Vocational Behavior, 1975, 7, 253-259.

Holroyd, J. Psychotherapy and Women's Liberation. Counseling Psychologist, 1976, 6(2), 22-28.

Hornaday, J. A., and Kuder, G. F. Study of Male Occupational Interest Scales Applied to Women. Educational and Psychological Measurement, 1961, Winter, 21(4), 859-864.

Hosford, R. E. Cognitive Complexity and Counselor Bias in Educational and Vocational Guidance. Symposium presentation at the American Psychological Association Convention, San Francisco, 1977.

Humphrey, F. G. Changing Roles for Women: Implications for Marriage Counselors. Journal of Marriage and Family Counseling, 1975, July, 1(3), 219-227.

Hunter, K. Illuminate the Whole Road: Career Planning for a Young Woman. National Education Association Journal, 1964, November, 53, 62-63.

Huth, C. M. Measuring Women's Interests: How Useful? Personnel and Guidance Journal, 1973, April, 51(8), 539-545.

———. Limits of Vocational Testing for Women. Journal of College Placement, 1973, December, 34, 32-33.

An Imperative for the Seventies: Releasing Creative Womanpower: A Guide for Counselors of Mature Women. St. Louis: University of Missouri, Extension Division, 1969.

Jaghelian, A. Surviving Sexism: Strategies and Consequences. Personnel and Guidance Journal, 1976, February, 54, 307-311.

Jakubowski, P. A. Helping Women Develop Responsible Assertive Behavior. Symposium presentation at the American Psychological Association Convention, Washington, D. C., 1976.

———. Assertive Behavior and Clinical Problems of Women. In D. Carter and E. Rawlings (eds.), Psychotherapy for Women: Treatment Towards Equality. Springfield, IL: Charles C. Thomas, 1977, 147-167.

———, and Lacks, P. B. Assessment Procedures in Assertion Training. The Counseling Psychologist, 1975, 5(4), 84-90.

Jakubowski-Spector, P. Facilitating the Growth of Women Through Assertive Training. The Counseling Psychologist, 1973, 4(1), 75-86.

Johnson, D. H. Subjects' Sex Preferences and Sex-Role Expectancies for Counselors. Paper presented at the American Psychological Association Convention, Washington, D. C., 1976.

Johnson, M. A. Influence of Counselor Gender on Reactivity to Clients. Paper presented at the American Psychological Association Convention, San Francisco, 1977.

Johnson, R. W. Content Analysis of the Strong Vocational Interest Blank for Women. Journal of Vocational Behavior, 1974, August, 5(1), 125-131.

Kalunian, P., Lopatich, G., and Cymerman, S. Changing Sex Role Stereotypes Through Career Development. Psychology in the Schools, 1975, April, 12, 230-233.

Kane, R. D., et al. A Study of Factors Influencing the Participation of Women in Non-traditional Occupations in Postsecondary Area Vocational Training Schools. Final Report. Washington, D. C.: Bureau of Occupational and Adult Education, 1977.

Kaplan, A. G. Androgyny as a Model of Mental Health for Women: From Theory to Therapy. In A. G. Kaplan and J. P. Bean (eds.), Beyond Sex-Role Stereotypes: Readings Toward a Psychology of Androgyny. Boston: Little, Brown, 1976, 320-362.

_____. Clarifying the Concept of Androgyny: Implications for Therapy. Paper presented at the American Psychological Association Convention, Washington, D.C., 1976.

Karelius-Schumacher, K. L. Designing a Counseling Program for the Mature Woman Student. Journal of the National Association for Women Deans, Administrators, and Counselors, 1977, Fall, 41(1), 28-31.

Kaye, B. I., and Scheele, A. M. Leadership Training. New Directions for Higher Education, 1975, Autumn, 11, 79-93.

Kazickas, J. Women Are Asking: Is Therapy Couched in Chauvinism? The Sunday Record, 1973, May 13(3).

Kenworthy, J. A. Androgyny in Psychotherapy: But Will It Sell In Peoria? Symposium presentation at the American Psychological Association Convention, Washington, D.C., 1976.

Kilby, J. E., and Whited, C. Toward a Non-Sexist Approach to Career Counseling. TPGA Journal, 1975, September, 4(2), 76-85.

Kirkbride, V. R. Project Lifeline Introduces College Women to Their Futures. Journal of the National Association of Women Deans and Counselors, 1966, Summer, 29, 174-176.

Klarreich, S. F. Career Counseling for College Women: A New Approach. Dissertation Abstracts International, 1974, 34(A), 6979.

Klein, M. H. Feminists Concepts of Therapy Outcomes. Psychotherapy: Theory, Research and Practice, 1976, Spring, 13(1), 89-95.

Klein, R. R. Sex-Role Stereotype Bias as Reflected in Counselors-Attitudes Toward Their Clients. Unpublished doctoral dissertation, Indiana University. Dissertation Abstracts International, 1975, August, 36(2-A), 706.

Kloedt, A. The Myth of the Vaginal Orgasm. Reprint from KNOW, Inc., P.O. Box 86031, Pittsburgh, PA 15221, 1970.

Knefelkamp, L. L., Widick, C. C., and Stroad, B. Cognitive-Developmental Theory: A Guide to Counseling Women. The Counseling Psychologist, 1976, 6(2), 15-19.

Knox, B. S. Trends in the Counseling of Women in Higher Education, 1957-1973. Ruth Strand Research Award Monograph Series, No. 1, 1975, July. Washington, D.C.: National Association for Women Deans, Administrators, and Counselors.

Konanc, J. T. An Introduction to Women's Issues in Treatment.

Paper presented at the American Psychological Association Convention, Washington, D. C., 1976.

Koontz, E. D. Counseling Women for Responsibilities. Journal of the National Association of Women Deans and Counselors, 1970, 34(1), 13-17.

Krakauer, A. A Good Therapist Is Hard to Find. Ms., 1972, October, 1(4), 33+.

Kravetz, D. F. Consciousness-Raising Groups and Group Therapy: Alternative Mental Health Resources for Women. Psychotherapy: Theory, Research and Practice, 1976, Spring, 13(1), 66-71.

Krohn, M. J. Planning for Career Options. New York: Catalyst, 1975.

Kronsky, B. J. Feminism and Psychotherapy. Journal of Contemporary Psychotherapy, 1971, Spring, 3(2), 89-98.

Lange, J. Women. Menninger Perspective, 1971, June, 2(4), 5-9.

Larson, R. The Influence of Sex-Roles and Symptoms on Clergymen's Perceptions of Mental Illness. Pacific Sociological Review, 1970, 13, 53-61.

Larwood, L., O'Neal, E., and Brennan, P. Increasing the Physical Aggressiveness of Women: The Liberating Effect of Angry Role Play. Paper presented at the Southeastern Psychological Association meeting, New Orleans, 1973.

Leonard, M., Hansen, L. S., and Knefelkamp, L. A Process Model for Changing Counselor Education Departments. In M. A. J. Guttman (ed.), Women and ACES: Perspective and Issues. Washington, D. C.: Commission for Women, Association for Counselor Education and Supervision, 1974, 69-80.

Letchworth, G. E. Women Who Return to College: An Identity-Integrity Approach. Journal of College Student Personnel, 1970, 11(2), 103-106.

Lewis, E. C. Counselors and Girls. Journal of Counseling Psychology, 1965, 12(2), 159-166.

_____. Developing Woman's Potential. Ames: Iowa State University Press, 1968.

Lewis, J. A. (ed.). Women and Counselors. Personnel and Guidance Journal, 1972, October, 51(2), 84-156.

_____. Counselors and Women: Finding Each Other. Personnel and Guidance Journal, 1972, October, 51(2), 147-150.

_____. The Working Woman: Can Counselors Take the Heat? A

Conversation with Dorothy Haener. Personnel and Guidance Journal, 1972, October, 51(2), 109-112.

———, and Lewis, G. J. Attacking Institutional Sexism: Raising Counselor Consciousness. In M. A. J. Guttman (ed.), Women and ACES: Perspective and Issues. Washington, D. C.: Commission for Women, Association for Counselor Education and Supervision, 1974, 63-68.

Lindbloom, C. G. Factors Influencing Activity Changes Following Career Counseling with Mature Women. Unpublished doctoral dissertation, University of Oregon. Dissertation Abstracts International, 1975, February, 35(8-A), 5029.

Linn, R. L., and Werts, C. E. Considerations for Studies of Test Bias. Journal of Educational Measurement, 1971, 8, 1-4.

Little, D. M. The Effects of Modeling of Career Counseling and Sex of Counselor on Interest in Nontraditional Occupations for Women. Unpublished doctoral dissertation. Dissertation Abstracts International, 1974, 34(A), 3994.

———, and Roach, A. J. Videotape Modeling of Interest in Nontraditional Occupations for Women. Journal of Vocational Behavior, 1974, August, 5(1), 133-138.

Livingston, J., and Wirtenberg, T. J. The Impact of a Consciousness-Raising Group on Maximization of Occupational Potential in Fifth Grade Girls. Undergraduate Honors thesis, University of California, Los Angeles, 1975.

Lloyd, M. A. The Effects of Active Versus Passive Participation on Ego-involved Attitudes: Changes in Knowledge and Attitudes Following a Life-Planning Workshop for College Women. Dissertation Abstracts International, 1973, 34(B), 858.

Loyd, D. F. Women Counseling Women: An Art and a Philosophy. Unpublished doctoral dissertation, University of Massachusetts. Dissertation Abstracts International, 1974, July, 35(1-A), 192.

Lunneborg, P. W. Neutralized Interest Inventory: Better Vocational Counseling for Women? Paper presented at the American Psychological Association Convention, Chicago, 1975.

McAllister, A. B. A General Model and Proposed Implementation Plan for Career Education at Mississippi State College for Women. Unpublished doctoral dissertation. Dissertation Abstracts International, 1974, 34(A), 6315.

McClain, E. W. Is the Counselor a Woman? Personnel and Guidance Journal, 1968, 46(5), 444-448.

McComb, A. Exploring the Nurturance Needs of Independent Women in Psychotherapy. Symposium presentation at the American Psychological Association Convention, Washington, D. C., 1976.

McCoy, V., and Cassell, P. Career Exploration Workshop for Women. Lawrence: University of Kansas, 1974.

McEwen, M. K. Counseling Women. A Review of the Research. Journal of College Student Personnel, 1975, September, 16(5), 382-388.

Malik, H. M. A Study of Racism and Sexism in Career Counseling, Job Selection and Placement by Vocational Rehabilitation Counselors in Alaska, Idaho, and Oregon. Unpublished doctoral dissertation, University of Oregon, 1973. Dissertation Abstracts International, 1974, 34(9-A), 6146. Also available from ERIC (ADG74-06860), 1973.

Mander, A. V., and Rush, A. K. Feminism as Therapy. New York: Random House, 1974.

Manis, L. G., and Mochizuki, J. Search for Fulfillment: A Program for Adult Women. Personnel and Guidance Journal, 1972, March, 50(7), 594-599.

Marecek, J. The Special Case of Psychotherapy. Symposium presentation at the American Psychological Association Convention, Chicago, 1975.

_____. Power and Women's Psychological Disorders: Preliminary Observation. Unpublished manuscript, Swarthmore College, n. d.

Maslin, A., and Davis, J. L. Sex-Role Stereotyping as a Factor in Mental Health Standards Among Counselors-in-training. Journal of Counseling Psychology, 1975, March, 22(2), 87-91.

Matthews, E. E. Career Development of Girls. Vocational Guidance Quarterly, 1963, Summer, 11, 273-277.

_____. Counselor and the Adult Woman: Women of Suburbia. Journal of the National Association of Women Deans and Counselors, 1969, Spring, 32(3), 115-122.

_____. Adolescence and Young Adulthood. In E. E. Matthews et al. (eds.), Counseling Girls and Women over the Life Span. Washington, D. C.: The National Vocational Guidance Association, 1972, 23-34.

_____. Infancy, Childhood and Pre-Adolescence. In E. E. Matthews et al. (eds.), Counseling Girls and Women over the Life Span. Washington, D. C.: National Vocational Guidance Association, 1972, 17-22.

_____. Life Stages and the Development of Sex Differences in

Girls and Women. In E. E. Matthews et al. (eds.), Counseling Girls and Women Over the Life Span. Washington, D. C.: National Vocational Guidance Association, 1972, 9-16.

―――. Mature Adulthood and Old Age. In E. E. Matthews et al. (eds.), Counseling Girls and Women over the Life Span. Washington, D. C.: National Vocational Guidance Association, 1972, 35-44.

―――. Girls, Counselors, and Careers: An Action Plan for Vocational Development. School Guidance Worker, 1976, May, 31(5), 15-20.

―――, Feingold, S. N., Weary, B., Berry, J., and Tyler, L. E. Counseling Girls and Women Over the Life Span. Washington, D. C.: National Vocational Guidance Association, 1972.

Medvene, A. M., and Blimline, C. Sources of Differential Perceptions of the Counselor's Role. Journal of the National Association for Women Deans, Administrators, and Counselors, 1977, Fall, 41(1), 25-27.

―――, and Collins, A. M. Occupational Prestige and Appropriateness: The Views of Mental Health Specialists. Journal of Vocational Behavior, 1976, August, 9(1), 63-71.

Mehnert, I. B. The Effects of an Abbreviated Training Paradigm of Female Learning Assertive Behavior. Unpublished doctoral dissertation, University of South Dakota. Dissertation Abstracts International, 1974, December, 35(6-A), 3430.

Menaker, E. The Therapy of Women in Light of Psychoanalytic Theory and the Emergence of a New View. In V. Franks and V. Burtle (eds.), Women in Therapy: New Psychotherapies for a Changing Society. New York: Brunner/Mazel, 1974, 230-246.

Mezzano, J. Concerns of Students and Preferences for Male and Female Counselors. Vocational Guidance Quarterly, 1971, 20, 42-47.

―――. Counselor Response to Male and Female Clients with Conforming and Nonconforming Career Goals in Professional and Technical Areas. Guidelines for Pupil Services, 1973, 11(3), 86-94.

Midlarsky, E. Women and Psychotherapy. Paper presented at the Social Welfare Conference, Metropolitan State College, Denver, May 1976.

―――. Women, Psychopathology, and Psychotherapy: A Partially Annotated Bibliography. JSAS Catalog of Selected Documents in Psychology, 1977, 7(2), 41.

Miller, J. B. (ed.). Psychoanalysis and Women: Contributions to New Theory and Therapy. New York: Penguin Books, 1973.

———. Toward a New Psychology of Women. Boston: Beacon Press, 1976.

Mishler, S. A. Barriers to the Career Development of Women. In S. H. Osipow (ed.), Emerging Woman: Career Analysis and Outlooks. Columbus, OH: Charles E. Merrill, 1975, 117-146.

Mitchell, E. What About Career Education for Girls? Educational Leadership, 1972, December, 30, 233-236.

Moore, S. L. Career Information: A Critical Review. Journal of Employment Counseling, 1976, June, 13(2), 78-84.

Mott, F. L., and Moore, S. F. The Determinants and Consequences of Occupational Information for Young Women. Washington, D. C.: Employment and Training Administration, 1976, Also available from ERIC (ED128597), 1977.

Mulvey, R. B. The Achievement Motive in Women: Implications for Career Development. Journal of Personality and Social Psychology, 1967, May, 260-267.

Munley, P. H., et al. Female College Students' Scores on the Men's and Women's Strong Vocational Interest Blanks. Journal of Counseling Psychology, 1973, May, 20, 285-289.

Murphy, G. New Approaches to Counseling Girls in the 1960's. A Report of the Midwest Regional Pilot Conference. Washington, D. C.: Women's Bureau, U. S. Department of Labor, 1966. Also available from ERIC (ED014576), 1968.

Naffziger, K. G. A Survey of Counselor-Educators' and Other Selected Professionals' Attitudes Towards Women's Roles. Unpublished doctoral dissertation, University of Oregon. Dissertation Abstracts International, 1971, 32(A), 3035-3036.

Nagely, D. L. A Comparison of College Educated Working Mothers in Traditional and Nontraditional Occupations. Journal of Vocational Behavior, 1971, 1, 331-341.

National Institute of Education, Career Education Program. Guidelines for the Assessment of Sex Bias and Sex Fairness in Career Interest Inventories. Measurement and Evaluation in Guidance, 1975, April, 8(1), 7-11. Also in E. E. Diamond (ed.), Issues of Sex Bias and Sex Fairness in Career Interest Measurement. Washington, D. C.: National Institute of Education, 1975, 23-39.

Navin, S. Future Planning of College Women: Counseling Implications. Vocational Guidance Quarterly, 1972, 21(4), 12-17.

Neulinger, J. Perceptions of the Optimally Integrated Person: A Redefinition of Mental Health. Proceedings of the 76th Annual Convention of the American Psychological Association, 1968, 553-554.

Neuman, R. R. When Will the Educational Needs of Women Be Met? Some Questions for the Counselor. Journal of Counseling Psychology, 1963, 10(4), 378-383.

Nichols, C. A Seminar in Personality Development for Mature Women. Journal of the National Association for Women Deans, Administrators, and Counselors, 1974, 37(3), 123-127.

Norman, R. Counselor Response to Female Clients with Deviate and Conforming Career Goals. Journal of Counseling Psychology, 1971, 18, 352-357.

Ohlsen, M. M. Vocational Counseling for Girls and Women. Vocational Guidance Quarterly, 1968, 17(2), 124-127.

Oliver, L. W. Counseling Implications of Recent Research on Women. Personnel and Guidance Journal, 1975, February, 53(6), 430-437.

Oliver, T. C. What About Test Bias and Discrimination? Activity, 1975, December, 13(5), 6.

Osborn, J. Creativity Applied to Career Development. In Facilitating Career Development for Girls and Women. Washington, D. C.: National Vocational Guidance Association, 1975, 71-82.

Osborn, S. M., and Harris, G. G. Assertive Training for Women. Springfield, IL: Charles C. Thomas, 1975.

O'Shea, A. J., and Harrington, T. F. Measuring the Interests of Male and Female Students with the SVIB for Men. Measurement and Evaluation in Guidance, 1974, July, 7(2), 112-117.

Osmond, H., Franks, V., and Burtle, V. Changing Views of Women and Therapeutic Approaches: Some Historical Considerations. In V. Frank and V. Burtle (eds.), Women in Therapy: New Psychotherapies for a Changing Society. New York: Bruner/Mazel, 1974, 3-24.

Otto, K. M. Attitudes of Selected High School Counselors Toward Women. Unpublished master's thesis, Mankato State College, 1973.

Parrish, J. B. Women, Careers and Counseling: The New Era. Journal of the National Association for Women Deans, Administrators, and Counselors, 1974, Fall, 38(1), 11-19.

Pearlman, J., and Mayo, M. Assertive Training for Women: A

Follow-Up. Journal of the National Association for Women Deans, Administrators, and Counselors, 1977, Winter, 40, 49-52.

Pendergrass, V., Kimmel, E., Joesting, J., Petersen, J., and Bush, E. Sex Discrimination Counseling. American Psychologist, 1976, January, 31(1), 36-46.

Peters, H. J., and Hansen, J. C. (eds.). Vocational Guidance and Career Development. New York: Macmillan, 1977.

Phelps, S., and Astin, N. The Assertive Woman. San Luis Obispo, CA: Impact, 1975.

Phillips, P. B., et al. How High School Counselors Can Assist Students to Successfully Enter Government and Industry. Workshop on Vocational and Occupational Guidance in the Sixties and Seventies, 1964. Available from ERIC (ED015250), 1968.

Piel, E. R. The Career Development of Young Women: Theory, Research and Directions for Future Investigation. Paper presented at the American Personnel and Guidance Association Convention, Dallas, 1976.

Pietrofesa, J. J., and Schlossberg, N. K. Counselor Bias and the Female Occupational Role. In N. Glazer-Malbin and H. Y. Waehrer (eds.), Woman in a Man-Made World. Chicago: Rand McNally, 1972, 219-221. Available from ERIC (ED044749), n.d.

Pincus, C., Radding, N., and Lawrence, R. A Professional Counseling Service for Women. Social Work, 1974, March, 19(2), 187-195.

Pinsker, S. Advantages of Handling Women's Anger Within Reciprocal Counseling. Symposium presentation at the American Psychological Association Convention, San Francisco, 1977.

Pinto, L. R., and Feigenbaum, L. Effects of Clinical Counseling on College Achievement. Journal of Counseling Psychology, 1974, September, 21, 409-414.

Plotsky, F. A., and Goad, R. Encouraging Women Through a Career Conference. Personnel and Guidance Journal, 1974, 52(7), 486-488.

Pogrebin, L. C. Working Woman, Career Counseling for the Older Woman. Ladies Home Journal, 1973, August, 90, 68+.

Polster, M. Women in Therapy: A Gestalt Therapist's View. In V. Franks and V. Burtle (eds.), Women in Therapy: New Psychotherapies for a Changing Society. New York: Brunner/Mazel, 1974, 247-262.

Potter, B. A. Increasing Decision-Making Behavior in Women: What the Counselor Can Do. Journal of Instructional Psychology, 1976, Summer, 3(3), 33-39.

Poulous, R., and Sang, B. The 'Presenting Issues' Patients Bring to Feminist and Traditional Psychotherapists. Symposium presentation at the American Psychological Association Convention, Chicago, 1975.

Powell, B. The Empty Nest, Employment, and Psychiatric Symptoms in College-Educated Women. Psychology of Women Quarterly, 1977, Fall, 2(1), 35-43.

Pratt, A. B. Exploring Stereotypes of Popular and Unpopular Occupations Among Women-In-General. Journal of Vocational Behavior, 1975, April, 6(2), 145-164.

Prediger, D. J., and Cole, N. S. Sex-Role Socialization and Employment Realities: Implications for Vocational Interest Measures. American College Testing Research Report, No. 68, 1975, January. Also in Journal of Vocational Behavior, 1975, 7, 239-251.

_____, and _____. It Is Time to Face Some Issues--A Response to Holland, Gottfredson, and Gottfredson. Journal of Vocational Behavior, 1975, 7, 261-263.

_____, and Hanson, G. R. The Distinction Between Sex Restrictiveness and Sex Bias in Interest Inventories. Measurement and Evaluation in Guidance, 1974, July, 7(2), 96-104.

_____, and _____. Holland's Theory of Careers Applied to Women and Men: Analysis of Implicit Assumptions. Journal of Vocational Behavior, 1976, 8, 167-184.

_____, and _____. A Theory of Careers Encounters Sex: Reply to Holland (1976). Journal of Vocational Behavior, 1976, 8, 359-366.

_____, and _____. Evidence Related to Issues of Sex Bias in Interest Inventories. Paper presented at the American Psychological Association Convention, Washington, D. C., 1976.

_____, and _____. Overview of Research on the Viability of Sex-Restrictive Reports of Career Interests. American College Testing Program, Iowa City, n. d.

_____, Roth, J. D., and Noeth, R. J. Career Development of Youth: A Nationwide Study. Personnel and Guidance Journal, 1974, 53, 97-104.

Price, G. E., and Borgers, S. B. An Evaluation of the Sex Stereotyping Effect as Related to Counselor Perceptions of Courses Appropriate for High School Students. Journal of Counseling Psychology, 1977, 24(3), 240-243.

Pringle, M. B. Counseling Women. Counseling and Personnel Services Information Center (CAPS) Capsule, 1971, 4, 11-15.

_____. The Responses of Counselors to Behaviors Associated with Independence and Achievement in Male and Female Clients. Unpublished doctoral dissertation. Dissertation Abstracts International, 1973, 34(A), 1627.

Psathas, G. Toward a Theory of Occupational Choice for Women. Sociology and Social Research, 1968, 52(2), 253-268.

Pyke, S. W. This Column Is About Women: Feminist Counseling: The New Frontier. Ontario Psychologist, 1975, April, 7(1), 43-47.

_____, and Ricks, F. A. The Counselor and the Female Client. School Counselor, 1973, March, 20(4), 280-284.

Ramsey, S. E. Career Exploration for Women. Journal of College Placement, 1973, February, 33, 36-40.

Randolph, C., and Zimmerman, J. A Counselor's Role in Helping Women. In M. A. J. Guttman (ed.), Women and Aces: Perspective and Issues. Washington, D. C.: Commission for Women, Association for Counselor Education and Supervision, 1974, 83-89.

Raskin, B. L. The Relative Effect of Occupational and Socio-Occupational Information of High School Girls' Expressed Opinions of Women Scientists and Science as a Career. Unpublished doctoral dissertation, Johns Hopkins University. Dissertation Abstracts, 1968, 29(5-A), 1455.

Ray, E. M. An Experimental Attempt to Maximize the Professional Potential of Home Economics Teachers Through a Program of Group Counseling in College. Final Report. Washington, D. C.: Office of Education, 1968. Also available from ERIC (ED021782), 1969.

Rayman, J. R. Sex and the Single Interest Inventory: The Empirical Validation of Sex Balanced Vocational Interest Inventory Items. Unpublished doctoral dissertation, University of Iowa. Dissertation Abstracts International, 1975, June, 35(12-A, Pt. 1), 7659-7660.

_____. Sex and the Single Interest Inventory: The Empirical Validation of Sex-Balanced Interest Inventory Items. Journal of Counseling Psychology, 1976, 23, 239-246.

Rehberg, R., and Hotchkiss, L. Educational Decision Maker: Antecedents and Consequences of Career Advice from the Guidance Counselor as a Significant Other in the Process of Social Mobility. Paper presented at the American Sociological Association meeting, Denver, 1971.

Rice, J. K. Vocational Problem Focus and Client and Counselor Gender. Vocational Guidance Quarterly, 1977, September, 26(1), 69-74.

_____, and Goering, M. L. Women in Transition: A Life-Planning Workshop Model. Journal of the National Association for Women Deans, Administrators, and Counselors, 1977, Winter, 40, 57-61.

_____, and Rice, D. G. Implications of Women's Liberation Movement for Psychotherapy. American Journal of Psychiatry, 1973, February, 130(2), 191-196.

Riordan, R. J. Feminine Sex-Role Concepts Among High School Counselors and Students. Unpublished doctoral dissertation, Michigan State University. Dissertation Abstracts, 1966, 27(3-A), 680.

Risch, C., and Beymer, L. A Framework for Investigating Career Choice of Women. Vocational Guidance Quarterly, 1967, December, 16(2), 87-92.

Rohfeld, R. W. High School Women's Assessment of Career Planning Resources. Vocational Guidance Quarterly, 1977, September, 26(1), 79-84.

Roiphe, A. What Women Psychoanalysts Say About Women's Liberation. New York Times Magazine, 1972, February 13, 63.

Rose, H. A., and Elton, C. F. Sex and Occupational Choice. Journal of Counseling Psychology, 1971, September, 18(5), 456-461.

Salwen, L. H. New Conflicts for the New Woman. Psychotherapy: Theory, Research and Practice, 1975, 12, 429-432.

Sandler, B. Legislation and Sex Bias Considerations for the Counseling Psychologist. Symposium presentation at the American Psychological Association Convention, Washington, D. C., 1976.

Saretsky, L. Sex-Related Countertransference Issues of a Female Therapist. Symposium presentation at the American Psychological Association Convention, Washington, D. C., 1976.

Scher, M. Verbal Activity, Sex, Counselor Experience, and Success in Counseling. Journal of Counseling Psychology, 1975, March, 22, 97-101.

Schleman, H. B. Span Plan. Purdue Alumnus, 1969, February, 7-11

Schlossberg, N. K. A Framework for Counseling Women. Personnel and Guidance Journal, 1972, October, 51(2), 137-143.

_____. Liberated Counseling: A Question Mark. Journal of the

National Association for Women Deans, Administrators, and Counselors, 1974, 38(1), 3-10.

_____. Liberated Counseling. In Facilitating Career Development for Girls and Women. Washington, D. C. : National Vocational Guidance Association, 1975, 83-90.

_____, and Goodman, J. Imperative for Change: Counselor Use of the Strong Vocational Interest Blanks. Impact, 1972, 2(1), 26-29.

_____, and Pietrofesa, J. J. Perspectives on Counseling Bias: Implications for Counselor Education. The Counseling Psychologist, 1973, 4(1), 44-54.

Schmaljohn, P. J. Sex-Role Stereotyping in a Selected Group of Materials for Elementary School Career Education. Unpublished doctoral dissertation, University of Northern Colorado. Dissertation Abstracts International, 1975, June, 35(12-A, Pt. 1), 7640.

Scholz, N. T., Prince, J. S., and Miller, G. P. How to Decide: A Guide for Women. New York: College Entrance Examination Board, 1975.

Schwartz, J. L. A Study of Guidance Counselor Sex Biases in the Occupational Recommendations Made for Female Students of Superior Intelligence. Unpublished doctoral dissertation, New York University. Dissertation Abstracts International, 1975, May, 35(11-A), 7069.

Scott, P. A Selected Bibliography on Career Counseling: New Perspectives for Women and Girls. Washington, D. C. : Business and Professional Women's Foundation, 1972.

Sedgwick, B. R. The Contribution of Sex and Traditional Versus Non-Traditional Role Occupation on the Perception of Adjustment by Others. Unpublished doctoral dissertation, University of Kansas. Dissertation Abstracts International, 1973, May, 33(11-B), 5499.

Sedney, M. A. Complexities in Conceptualizing Clients' Problems in Androgynous Terms. Symposium presentation at the American Psychological Association Convention, Washington, D. C., 1976.

Seeman, M. V. Critical Evaluations: Modern Woman--Implications for Psychotherapy. II. Woman's Adjustment to Being Modern. Canadian Psychiatric Association Journal, 1973, 18(1), 84-85.

Seiden, A. M. Overview: Research on the Psychology of Women: II. Women in Families, Work, and Psychotherapy. American Journal of Psychiatry, 1976, October, 133(10), 1111-1123.

Seidenberg, R. Marriage in Life and Literature. New York: Philosophical Library, 1970.

_____. For the Future--Equity? In J.B. Miller (ed.), Psychoanalysis and Women. New York: Penguin Books, 1973, 330-349.

_____. Is Anatomy Destiny? In J.B. Miller (ed.), Psychoanalysis and Women. New York: Penguin Books, 1973, 306-329.

Sell, J.M. Effects of Subjects Self-Esteem, Test Performance of Feedback, and Counselor Attractiveness on Influence in Counseling. Journal of Counseling Psychology, 1974, July, 21, 342-344.

Setne, V.L. Educational-Vocational Development Program for Adult Women. Vocational Guidance Quarterly, 1977, March, 25, 232-237.

Seward, G.H. Sex Roles and Therapy: Sex Roles in Changing Society. New York: Random House, 1970.

_____. Psychotherapy and Culture Conflict. In Community Mental Health. New York: Ronald Press, 1972.

Shainess, N. A Psychiatrist's View: Images of Woman: Past, Present, Overt and Obscured. In R. Morgan (ed.), Sisterhood Is Powerful. New York: Random House, 1970, 230-244.

_____. Is Anatomy Destiny? Panel: The Changing Role of Women Psychiatrists. Journal of American Medical Women's Association, 1973, 28, 293-295.

_____, Tobach, E., and Headley, D. The Mental Health Movement Meets Women's Liberation. Mental Hygiene, 1971, 55, 1-9.

Shapiro, E. One Person's Therapist Is Another Person's Client. Symposium presentation at the American Psychological Association Convention, Washington, D.C., 1976.

_____. Anger Between Women in the Therapeutic Process. Symposium presentation at the American Psychological Association Convention, San Francisco, 1977.

Shapiro, J. Socialization of Sex Roles in the Counseling Setting. In M.E. Lockheed (ed.), Research in Women's Acquisition of Professional and Leadership Roles. Princeton, NJ: Educational Testing Service, 1975, 44-74.

Shaw, D. Assertive Training for Women: Effects on Cognitive Sets. Symposium presentation at the American Psychological Association Convention, San Francisco, 1977.

Sherman, J.A. Freud's 'Theory' and Feminism: A Reply to Juliet

Mitchell. Symposium presentation at the American Psychological Association Convention, Chicago, 1975.

_____. Girls' Attitudes Toward Mathematics: Implications for Counseling. Symposium presentation at the American Psychological Association Convention, Washington, D.C., 1976.

Shishkoff, M. M. Counseling Mature Women for Careers. Journal of the National Association for Women Deans, Administrators, and Counselors, 1973, Summer, 36, 173-177.

Simons, J. A., and Helms, J. E. Influence of Counselors' Marital Status, Sex, and Age on College and Non-College Women's Counselor Preferences. Journal of Counseling Psychology, 1976, July, 23(4), 380-386.

Simpson, E. J. Career Education--Feminine Version. Paper presented at the Regional Seminar/Workshop on Women in the World of Work. Technical Education Research Centers, Chicago, October, 1972.

Smith, J. A. For God's Sake, What Do Those Women Want? Personnel and Guidance Journal, 1972, October, 51(2), 133-136.

Starker, L. Androgynous Perspective on Mental Health Consultation. Symposium presentation at the American Psychological Association Convention, Washington, D.C., 1976.

Staten, B. J. The Effect of Counselor Gender and Sex-Role Attitudes on Change of Female Clients' Sex-Role Attitudes. Unpublished doctoral dissertation, University of Southern California. Dissertation Abstracts International, 1975, April, 35(10-A), 6470.

Steinmann, A. Guidance Personnel and the College Woman. Personnel Journal, 1966, 45(5), 294-299.

_____. Female-Role Perception as a Factor in Counseling. Journal of the National Association of Women Deans and Counselors, 1970, Fall, 34, 27-33.

_____. Perceptions of the Feminine Role Among Male Psychologists. International Mental Health Research Newsletter, 1972, 14(1), 6.

_____. Sex Role Bias in Psychotherapy. International Mental Health Research Newsletter, 1973, 16(2), 8-12.

_____. Cultural Values, Female Role Expectancies, and Therapeutic Goals: Research and Interpretation. In V. Franks and V. Burtle (eds.), Women in Therapy: New Psychotherapies for a Changing Society. New York: Brunner/Mazel, 1974, 51-82.

Stephenson, P. S. Modern Woman: Implications for Psychotherapy. Canadian Psychiatric Association Journal, 1973, 18(1), 79-82.

Stevens, B. The Psychotherapist and Women's Liberation. Social Work, 1971, July, 16(3), 12-18.

Stevenson, G. Career Planning for High School Girls. Outlook Quarterly, 1973, Summer, 17, 22-25.

Strouse, J. (ed.). Women and Analysis: Dialogues on Psychoanalytic Views of Femininity. New York: Grossman, 1974.

Surette, R. F. Career Versus Homemaking: Perspectives and Proposals. Vocational Guidance Quarterly, 1967, December, 16, 82-86.

Tanney, M. F. Face Validity of Interest Measures: Sex-Role Stereotyping. In E. E. Diamond (ed.), Issues of Sex Bias and Sex Fairness in Career Interest Measurement. Washington, D. C.: National Institute of Education, 1975, 89-100.

_____. Unobtrusive Measures of Sexism in Counseling. Symposium presentation at the American Psychological Association Convention, Washington, D. C., 1976.

_____, and Birk, J. M. Women Counselors for Women Clients? A Review of the Research. Counseling Psychologist, 1976, 6(2), 28-32.

Tautfest, P. B. Continuing Education Programs and Their Implications for Counselors. Journal of the National Association of Women Deans and Counselors, 1964, Summer, 27, 194-197.

Tennov, D. Feminism, Psychotherapy and Professionalism. Journal of Contemporary Psychotherapy, 1973, 5, 2-11.

_____. Psychotherapy, Women, and the Women's Movement. Paper presented at the Society for Psychotherapy Research meeting, Philadelphia, June 1973.

_____. Women Evaluate and Describe Their Psychotherapy Outside the Clinical Setting. Paper presented at the Society for Psychotherapy Research meeting, Denver, June 1974.

_____. Psychotherapy: The Hazardous Cure. New York: Abelard-Schuman, 1975.

_____. Women and the Psychotherapy Profession. In Psychotherapy: The Hazardous Cure. New York: Abelard-Schuman, 1975, 196-230.

Teri, L. Sex-Role Development Through Psychotherapy: Confronting Adult Conflicts. Symposium presentation at the American Psychological Association Convention, San Francisco, 1977.

Thomas, A. H. Counselor Response to Divergent Vocational Goals of a Female Client in Terms of Acceptance Appropriateness and Need for Further Counseling. Unpublished doctoral dissertation, Michigan State University. Dissertation Abstracts, 1968, 28(12-A), 4882-4883.

_____, and Stewart, N. R. Counselor Response to Female Clients with Deviate and Conforming Career Goals. Journal of Counseling Psychology, 1971, July, 18(4), 352-357.

Thompson, J. K. Fighting Discrimination: Up Against the Ivied Wall. Social Work, 1976, November, 21(6), 506-511.

Thoresen, C. E., Krumboltz, J. D., and Varenhorst, B. Sex of Counselors and Models: Effect on Client Career Exploration. Journal of Counseling Psychology, 1967, November, 14(6), 503-508.

Tiedt, I. M. Realistic Counseling for High School Girls. The School Counselor, 1972, 19(5), 354-356. Also in J. Stacey et al. (eds.), And Jill Came Tumbling After: Sexism in American Education. New York: Dell, 1974, 236-240; and in D. Gersoni-Stavn (ed.), Sexism and Youth. New York: R. R. Bowker, 1974, 123-126.

Tittle, C. K. Minimizing Sex Bias in Interest Measurement Through the Context of Testing and Interpretive Materials. Paper presented at the American Personnel and Guidance Association Convention, New Orleans, 1973.

_____. Women and Educational Testing. Phi Delta Kappan, 1973, October, 55(2), 118-119.

_____. Women and Educational Testing: A Selective Review of the Research Literature and Testing Practices. New York: Office of Teacher Education, City University of New York, 1973.

_____. Sex Bias in Educational Measurement: Fact or Fiction? Measurement and Evaluation in Guidance, 1974, 6, 219-226.

_____. The Use and Abuse of Vocational Tests. In J. Stacey et al. (eds.), And Jill Came Tumbling After: Sexism in American Education. New York: Dell, 1974, 241-248.

_____, McCarthy, K., and Steckler, J. F. Women and Educational Testing. Princeton, NJ: Educational Testing Service, 1974. Also in J. Pottker and A. Fishel (eds.), Sex Bias in the Schools --Research Evidence. Madison, NJ: Fairleigh Dickinson University Press, 1977, 256-272.

Tobias, S., and Donady, B. Counseling the Math Anxious. Journal of the National Association for Women Deans, Administrators and Counselors, 1977, Fall, 41(1), 13-16.

Torrance, P. Helping the Creatively Gifted Girl Achieve Her Potentiality. Journal of the National Association of Women Deans and Counselors, 1965, 29(1), 28-33.

Torrey, J. Psychoanalysis: A Feminist Review. Women and Psychology Symposium. University of Bridgeport, March 1971.

Trent, I. M. Realistic Counseling for High School Girls. School Counselor, 1972, May, 19, 354-356.

Turkat, D., and Glad, D. Traditional Therapy Fits Traditional Womanhood. Psychological Reports, 1976, December, 39(3, Pt. 1), 834.

Tyler, L. E. Counseling Girls and Women in the Year 2000. In E. E. Matthews et al. (eds.), Counseling Girls and Women Over the Life Span. Washington, D. C.: National Vocational Guidance Association, 1972, 89-96.

Vail, A. F. Dropout from Psychotherapy as Related to Patient-Therapist Discrepancies, Therapist Characteristics, and Interaction in Race and Sex. Unpublished doctoral dissertation, Fordham University. Dissertation Abstracts International, 1974, November, 35(5-B), 2452.

Valley, J. A. The Influence of Race and Sex Upon a Counseling Interview Designed to Increase Need for Achievement in Upward Bound Students. Unpublished doctoral dissertation, Ohio State University. Dissertation Abstracts International, 1976, May, 36(11-B), 5774-5775.

VanderWilt, R. B., and Klocke, R. A. Self-Actualization of Females in an Experimental Orientation Program; Experimental Studies Program at Mankato State College in Conjunction with the Minnesota Outward Bound School. Journal of the National Association of Women Deans and Counselors, 1971, Spring, 34(3), 125-129.

Verheyden-Hilliard, M. E. The Use of Interest Inventories with the Re-Entering Woman. Washington, D. C.: National Institute of Education, 1974. Also available from ERIC (ED095369), 1975.

_____. Counseling: Potential Superbomb Against Sexism. American Education, 1977, April, 13, 12-15.

Verma, M. R. Some Thoughts on the Choice of a Career by Girls. Guidance Review, 1964, 2(1), 13-16.

Veroff, J. Woman Psychotherapist as Support System for Women. Symposium presentation at the American Psychological Association Convention, San Francisco, 1977.

Vetter, L. Career Counseling for Women. The Counseling Psychologist, 1973, 4(1), 54-67.

———. Sex Stereotyping in Illustrations in Career Materials. Paper presented at the American Psychological Association Convention, Chicago, 1975.

———, and Sethney, B. J. Women in the Workforce: Development and Field Testing of Curriculum Materials. Available from ERIC (ED072175), 1971.

———, Stockburger, D. W., and Brose, C. Career Guidance Materials: Implications for Women's Career Development. Columbus, OH: Center for Vocational Education, Ohio State University, 1974.

Vocational Development Special Issue. Journal of the National Association for Women Deans, Administrators, and Counselors, 1974, Summer, 37, 151-178.

Walker, E. F., and Stake, J. E. Changes in Preference for Male and Female Counselors. Unpublished manuscript, University of Missouri, St. Louis, n. d.

Wallace, J. L., and Leonard, T. H. Factors Affecting Vocational and Educational Decision-Making of High School Girls. Journal of Home Economics, 1971, April, 63(4), 241-245.

Walstedt, J. J. The Anatomy of Oppression: A Feminist Analysis of Psychotherapy. Reprint from KNOW, Inc., P. O. Box 86031, Pittsburgh, PA 15221.

Weary, B. A Job Choice of One's Own. In E. E. Matthews et al. (eds.), Counseling Girls and Women over the Life Span. Washington, D. C.: National Vocational Guidance Association, 1972, 65-74.

Webb, A. P. Sex-Role Preferences and Adjustment in Early Adolescents. Child Development, 1963, 34, 609-618.

Webb, S. C. Transferability of a Role-Oriented Interest Inventory from Men to Women in Church-Related Occupations. Journal of Vocational Behavior, 1974, December, 5(3), 347-356.

Webbink, P. Therapist Turned Woman. In J. Agel (ed.), Rough Times. New York: Ballantine Books, 1973, 101-106.

Wells, J., and Magruder, H. Education Programs for Mature Women. Education Digest, 1972, January, 37(5), 42-45.

Werner, J. E. Vocational Choices of Selected Working Women and Holland's Theory. Available from ERIC (ED132455), 1977.

Werner, P. D., and Block, J. Sex Differences in the Eyes of Expert Personality Assessors: Unwarranted Conclusions. Journal of Personality Assessment, 1975, April, 39(2), 110-113.

West, S. D., Jr. Attitudes of High School Teachers, Principals, Guidance Counselors, Librarians, and Teacher Educators Toward the Social, Educational, and Economic Roles of Women. Unpublished doctoral dissertation, University of Florida, 1975.

Westervelt, E. M. Counseling Today's Girls for Tomorrow's Womanhood. In G. Murphy (ed.), New Approaches to Counseling Girls in the 1960's: Report of the Midwest Regional Pilot Conference. Washington, D. C.: Women's Bureau, U. S. Department of Labor, 1966, 19.

White, W. Career Interest Inventories: NIE Issues Test Guidelines for Detecting Sex Bias. APA Monitor, 1975, March, 6(3), 14.

Whitely, R. M. Cognitive Restructuring of Assertive Behavior for Women. Symposium presentation at the American Psychological Association Convention, San Francisco, 1977.

Whitton, M. C. Same-Sex, Cross-Sex, Reliability and Concurrent Validity of the Strong-Campbell Interest Inventory. Journal of Counseling Psychology, 1975, 22(3), 204-210.

Wilk, C. A., and Coplan, V. Assertive Training as a Confidence-Building Technique. Personnel and Guidance Journal, 1977, April, 55, 460-464.

Willis, M. P. Sex Role Stereotypic Responses of Counselors to Personal and Educational Vocational Problems Presented Via Videotape. Unpublished doctoral dissertation, Temple University. Dissertation Abstracts International, 1975, December, 36(6-A), 3421-3422.

Wilson, M. Promoting Growth in College Females through Peer Counseling. Symposium presentation at the American Psychological Association Convention, San Francisco, 1977.

Winfield, A. D. Expanding Career Options for Females. In Facilitating Career Development for Girls and Women. Washington, D. C.: National Vocational Guidance Association, 1975, 7-14.

Wingett, T. J. Career Attitude Maturity and Self-Concept of Eighth Grade Girls after a Career Education Experience. Unpublished doctoral dissertation, University of Wyoming. Dissertation Abstracts International, 1975, January, 35(7-A), 4175.

Wolfe, H. B. Analysis of the Work Values of Women: Implications for Counseling. Journal of the National Association of Women Deans and Counselors, 1969, Fall, 33(1), 13-18.

Wolfe, J. L. What to Do Until the Revolution Comes: An Argument for Women's Therapy Groups. Paper presented at the Women's Conference, Madison, November 1973.

____, and Fodor, I. G. Cognitive/Behavioral Approach to Modifying Assertive Behavior in Women. Paper presented at the American Psychological Association Convention, Chicago, 1975.

Woll, S., and Tiffany, D. W. Housework Versus Employment Preferences for Female Ex-Psychiatric Patients. Vocational Guidance Quarterly, 1969, September, 18, 21-28.

Wolpe, J. The Instigation of Assertive Behavior: Transcripts from Two Cases. Journal of Behavior Therapy and Experimental Psychiatry, 1970, 1, 145-151.

Women and Counselors. Special Issue. Personnel and Guidance Journal, 1972, 51, 84-156.

Women's Bureau. Counseling Girls Toward New Perspectives: A Report of the Middle Atlantic Regional Pilot Conference. Washington, D. C. : U. S. Department of Labor, 1966.

Women's Bureau. Continuing Education Programs and Services for Women. Washington, D. C. : U. S. Department of Labor, 1971.

Women's Bureau. Expanding Opportunities for Girls: Their Special Counseling Needs. Washington, D. C. : U. S. Department of Labor, 1971.

Wysocki, S. R. Differential Effects of Three Group Treatments on Self-Actualization and Attitudes Toward the Sex Roles of Women. Unpublished doctoral dissertation, University of Southern California. Dissertation Abstracts International, 1976, May, 36(11-A), 7316.

Yorburg, B. Psychoanalysis and Women's Liberation. Psychoanalytic Review, 1974, Spring, 61(1), 71-77.

Zapoleon, M. W. Occupational Planning for Women. New York: Harper & Row, 1961.

Zemon-Gass, G., and Gass, S. Women's Use of Language: Implications for Psychotherapy. Symposium presentation at the American Psychological Association Convention, Washington, D. C., 1976.

Zweig, M. Is Women's Liberation a Therapy Group? In J. Agel (ed.), The Radical Therapist. New York: Ballantine Books, 1971.

Zytowski, D. C. Toward a Theory of Career Development for Women. Personnel and Guidance Journal, 1969, March, 47(7), 660-664.

V

EDUCATIONAL FORCES AND WOMEN'S AMBITION

The President of Yale College gives everlasting greeting to all:

Let it be known unto you, that I have tested Miss Lucinda Foote, aged 12, by way of examination, proving that she has made laudable progress in the languages of the learned, viz., the Latin and the Greek; to such an extent that I found her translating and expounding with [perfect] ease, both words and sentences in the whole of Vergil's Aeneid, in selected orations of Cicero, and in the Greek Testament. I testify that were it not for her sex, she would be considered fit to be admitted as a student in the junior [i.e., freshman] class of Yale University. --Given in the Yale College Library December 22, the year of Salvation 1783. --Ezra Stiles, President.

A. GENERAL

Abramson, J. The Invisible Woman: Discrimination in the Academic Profession. San Francisco: Jossey-Bass, 1975.

———. Measuring Success or, Whatever Happened to Affirmative Action. Civil Rights Digest, 1977, Winter, 9(2), 14-27.

Ahlum, C., and Fralley, J. Feminist Studies: The Schools and Sex-Role Stereotyping. In D. Gersoni-Stavn (ed.), Sexism and Youth. New York: R. R. Bowker Co., 1974, 120-122.

Alexander, S. State-by-State Guide to Women's Legal Rights. Los Angeles: Wollstonecraft, 1975.

Allen, D. B., and Hansen, L. S. Sexism in Vocational Education: More than a Ha-Ha. Unpublished manuscript, University of Minnesota, 1974.

Alpert, J. L. The School Psychologist's Impact on Sexism in the Schools. International Encyclopedia of Neurology, Psychiatry, Psychoanalysis and Psychology, in press.

American Federation of Teachers. Changing Sexist Practices in the Classroom. Unpublished manuscript, 1973.

American Women: Their Status and Education. United States. Presidents Commission on the Status of Women. Practical Forecasts in Home Economics, 1963, November, 9, 26-27+.

Anderson, P. R. Woman's Place and the Educational Labeling Process. Humboldt Journal of Social Relations, 1974, Spring/Summer, 1(2), 93-101.

Andreas, C. Educating a New Generation for Whatever It's Worth. In Sex and Caste in America. Englewood Cliffs, NJ: Prentice-Hall, 1971, 27-47.

_____. Keeping People in Their Places: St. Paul, Freud, and Madison Avenue. In Sex and Caste in America. Englewood Cliffs, NJ: Prentice-Hall, 1971, 67-91.

Askins, J. Women and the PDKs. In J. Stacey, S. Bereaud, and J. Daniels (eds.), And Jill Came Tumbling After: Sexism in American Education. New York: Dell, 1974, 348-350.

Astin, H. S. Achieving Educational Equity for Women. NASPA Journal, 1976, Summer, 14, 15-24.

_____ (ed.). Some Action of Her Own: The Adult Woman and Higher Education. Lexington, MA: D. C. Heath, 1976.

_____, Suniewick, N., and Dweck, S. Women: A Bibliography on Their Education and Careers. Washington, D. C.: Human Service Press, 1972.

_____, et al. Sex Discrimination in Education: Access to Postsecondary Education. Washington, D. C.: National Center for Education Statistics, 1976. Also available from ERIC (ED132-967), 1977.

Babcock, R. J., and Kaufman, M. A. Effectiveness of a Career Course. Vocational Guidance Quarterly, 1976, 24(3), 261-266.

Baker, T., and Fitzgerald, W. Women and Education. School Review, 1972, February, 80(2), 155-159.

Bard, J. F. Do Women Have Second Class Status in Education? Pennsylvania Education, 1971, 14-15.

Barrett, C. The Hidden Curriculum in the Schools. Paper presented at the Central New York School Study Council Conference on Women in Education. Syracuse University, Syracuse, NY: 1974.

Bernard, J. S. Academic Women. University Park: Pennsylvania State University Press, 1964.

_____. Second Sex and the Cichlid Effect. Journal of the National Association of Women Deans and Counselors, 1967, Fall, 31, 8-17.

_____. Where Are We Now? Some Thoughts on the Current Scene. Psychology of Women Quarterly, 1976, 1(1), 21-38.

_____. Women's Continuing Education: Wither Bound? In H. S. Astin (ed.), Some Action of Her Own: The Adult Woman and Higher Education. Lexington, MA: D. C. Heath, 1976, 109-124.

Berry, J. Continuing Education for Women for a Pluralistic Society. Washington Newsletter for Women, 1970, 1, 2, 5.

_____. Educational Innovation and an Era. In E. E. Matthews et al. (eds.), Counseling Girls and Women Over the Life Span. Washington, D.C.: National Vocational Guidance Association, 1972, 75-88.

_____, and Kushner, R. A Critical Look at the Queen Bee Syndrome. Journal of the National Association for Women Deans, Administrators and Counselors, 1975, Summer, 38(4, Pt. 2), 173-176.

_____, and Loring, R. Special Programs for Women. In R. Smith (ed.), Handbook of Adult Education in the U.S.A. New York: Macmillan, 1970.

Billings, V. Getting It Together. In The Womansbook. Los Angeles: Wollstonecraft, 1974, 113-143.

Bird, C. Women's Colleges and Women's Lib. Change, 1972, April, 4(3), 60-65.

_____. The Case Against College. New York: David McKay, 1975.

Blackledge, E. H. Welcome the Older Woman to College. Journal of Business Education, 1960, October, 36, 23-24.

Blackwell, G. W. College and the Continuing Education of Women. Educational Record, 1963, January, 44, 33-39.

Blaubergs, M. S. Overcoming the Sexist Barriers to Gifted Women's Achievement. In B. Johnson (ed.), Advantage/Disadvantage Gifted. Ventura, CA: Ventura County Superintendent of Schools Office, 1979.

Bobowski, R. C. Project Women: Career Education Program; Maine. American Education, 1975, December, 11, 27-28.

Boodish, H. M. Trends: Women and Careers. The Social Studies, 1963, January, 54(1), 24-27.

Borgers, S. B. Need for a Consultative, Educational Model to Sensitize Women. Symposium presentation at the American Psychological Association Convention, San Francisco, 1977.

Brandon, G. L. (ed.). Educating Women for the World of Work. American Vocational Journal, 1970, December, 45, 33-48.

Bray, D. W. The Assessment Center: Opportunities for Women. Personnel, 1971, September/October, 48, 30-34.

Breeding, B. Funding Intercollegiate Sports Programs in the Intermountain Area; Sports Competition for Women in Six States Bordering the Rocky Mountains. Physical Educator, 1971, October, 28, 133-134.

Brody, C. M. Do Instructional Materials Reinforce Sex Stereotyping? Educational Leadership, 1973, 31(2), 119-122.

Bromhead, E. Education of Women: Symposium. International Review of Education, 1973, 19(1), 3-180.

Bronfenbrenner, U. The Psychological Costs of Quality and Equality in Education. Child Development, 1967, 38, 909-925.

Brophy, J. and Good, T. L. Feminization of American Elementary Schools. Phi Delta Kappan, 1973, April, 54(8), 564-566. Reply: D. F. Smith, 1973, June, 54, 703-704. Rejoinder: 1973, September, 55, 73-75.

Bross, D. R. Night College Courses for the Older Woman. Adult Leadership, 1967, January, 15, 233-234.

Buccieri, C. Continuing Education: If At First You Don't Succeed. College University Business, 1970, February, 48(2), 84-86.

Buckey, A., Freeark, K., and O'Barr, J. Support for Returning Students. Adult Leadership, 1976, September, 25, 21-23.

Buek, A. P., and Orleans, J. H. Sex Discrimination--A Bar to a Democratic Education: Overview of Title IX of the Education Amendments of 1972. Connecticut Law Review, 1973, 6(1), 1-27.

Bunting, J. W. Relation of Business to Women's Higher Education. Educational Record, 1961, October, 42, 287-295.

Bunting, M. I. Education: A Nurturant if Not a Determinant of Professional Success. In R. B. Kundsin (ed.), Women and Success: The Anatomy of Achievement. New York: William Morrow, 1974, 208-213.

Bureau of the Census. A Statistical Portrait of Women in the U.S. Washington, D.C.: U.S. Department of Commerce, 1976.

Burzynski, H. G. Promised Land of Paraprofessional Careers; Technical Education for Women. American Vocational Journal, 1970, December, 45, 21-23.

Campbell, J. Change for Women--Glacial or Otherwise? Women on Campus: 1970. Ann Arbor: Center for Continuing Education of Women, University of Michigan, 1970, 56-62.

Carnegie Commission on Higher Education. Affirmative Action. In Opportunities for Women in Higher Education. New York: McGraw-Hill, 1973, 127-152.

_____. The Many Roles of College-Educated Women. In Opportunities for Women in Higher Education. New York: McGraw-Hill, 1973, 15-34.

_____. Opportunities for Women in Higher Education. New York: McGraw-Hill, 1973.

Cary, E., and Peratis, K. W. Woman and the Law. Skokie, IL: National Textbook, 1977.

Cater, L. A., Scott, A. F., and Martyna, W. (eds.). Discussions: Institutional Ferment. In Women and Men: Changing Roles, Relationships, and Perceptions. New York: Praeger, 1977, 55-69.

Cegelka, P. T. Sex Role Stereotyping in Special Education: A Look at Secondary Work Study Programs. Exceptional Children, 1976, March, 42(6), 323-328.

Center for Law and Education. Sex Discrimination. Inequality in Education, 18. Cambridge, MA: Harvard University, 1974.

Chafetz, J. S. The Bringing Down of Jane. Masculine/Feminine or Human? An Overview of the Sociology of Sex Roles. Itasca, IL: F. E. Peacock, 1974, 108-156.

Chalmers, E. L. Achieving Equity for Women in Higher Education, Graduate Enrollment and Faculty Status. Journal of Higher Education, 1972, October, 43, 517-524.

Chasen, B. Diagnostic Sex-Role Bias and Its Relation to Authoritarianism, Sex-Role Attitudes and Sex of the School Psychologist. Unpublished doctoral dissertation, New York University. Dissertation Abstracts International, 1974, November, 35(5-B), 2400.

_____. Diagnostic Sex-Role Bias and Its Relation to Authoritarianism, Sex-Role Attitudes, and Sex of the School Psychologist. Sex Roles: Journal of Research, 1975, 1(4), 355-368.

Chisholm, S. Sexism and Racism: One Battle to Fight. Personnel and Guidance Journal, 1972, October, 51(2), 123-125.

Chmaj, B. E. Image, Myth and Beyond: American Women and American Studies. Pittsburgh: KNOW, Inc., 1972.

Chu, D. Review of Research Concerning the Hypothesis That Strenuous Physical Activity Develops Masculine Traits in Women, and Therefore It Should Not Be Encouraged by Physical Educators. Physical Educator, 1972, December, 29, 195-197.

Clarenbach, K. F. Can Continuing Education Adapt? American Association of University Women Journal, 1970, January, 62-65.

_____. School Athletics and Sex Discrimination. Sex Role Stereotyping in the Schools. Washington, D. C.: National Education Association, 1973, 36-39.

Cless, E. L. A Modest Proposal for the Educating of Women. The American Scholar, 1969, 38(4), 618-627.

_____. A Modern Proposal for the Educating of Women. In N. Reeves (ed.), Womankind: Beyond the Stereotypes. Chicago: Aldine, 1971, 310-317.

Cohen, A. Women and Higher Education: Recommendations for Change. Phi Delta Kappan, 1972, November, 53(3), 166.

_____, and Mesrop, A. Women and Higher Education--Creating the Solutions. Washington, D. C.: Task Force on the Status of Women, American Psychological Association, 1972.

Coleman, J. S., Campbell, E. Q., McPartland, J., Mood, A. M., Weinfeld, F. D., and York, R. L. Equality of Education Opportunity. Washington, D. C.: Office of Education, 1966.

Commission on Civil Rights. Subject: Elimination of Sex Discrimination in Athletic Programs. Washington, D. C.: Department of Health, Education and Welfare, 1975.

Committee on the Education and Employment of Women. The Stanford Women in 1972. Stanford: Stanford University, 1972. Also available from ERIC (ED077337), n. d.

Committee to Eliminate Sexual Discrimination in the Public Schools. Let Them Aspire!: A Plea and Proposal for Equality of Opportunity for Males and Females in the Ann Arbor Public Schools--Excerpts. In D. Gersoni-Stavn (ed.), Sexism and Youth. New York: R. R. Bowker, 1974, 127-160.

_____, and the Discrimination in Education Committee of NOW, Ann Arbor Chapter. An Action Proposal to Eliminate Sex Discrimination in the Ann Arbor Public Schools. Reprint from KNOW, Inc., P. O. Box 86031, Pittsburgh, PA 15221, 1972.

Cook, A. H. Sex Discrimination at Universities: An Ombudsman's View. AAUP Bulletin, 1972, September, 58, 280. Also in E. Wasserman et al. (eds.), Women in Academia: Evolving Policies Toward Equal Opportunities. New York: Praeger, 1975, 120-127.

Cooper, G. Legal Implications of the Use of Standardized Ability Tests in Employment and Education. Columbia Law Review, 1968, 68, 691-744.

Corrallo, S. B. The Economic Relevance of Women's Higher Education. Journal of the National Association of Women Deans and Counselors, 1968, Winter, 31(2), 74-78.

Cottle, T. J. College-Reward and Betrayal. Chicago: University of Chicago Press, 1977.

Council for University Women's Progress at the University of Minnesota. Proportion of Doctorates Earned by Women, by Area and Field, 1960-1969. Wash., D.C.: Assc. of American Colleges, 1971.

Craiglow, J. H. A Two-Man Look at Women's Sports. Independent School Bulletin, 1974, December, 34(2), 17-22.

Crase, D. New Dimension in Education: Girl's and Women's Sports. NASSP Bulletin, 1975, November, 59, 104-109.

Cristo, M. G. Factors Influencing Career Mobility and Career Attainment of Women in the Field of Education. Unpublished doctoral dissertation, University of Virginia. Dissertation Abstracts International, 1975, 36(6), 4034.

Crockford, R. E. The Forgotten Sex in Education. Junior College Journal, 1971, October, 42(2), 17-19.

Cronkhite, B. B. New Patterns in Women's Education. Improving College and University Teaching, 1972, Winter, 20(1), 37-42.

Cross, K. P. Beyond the Open Door. San Francisco: Jossey-Bass, 1971.

_____. Women in Higher Education. Washington, D. C.: American Council on Education, 1973.

_____. The Education of Woman Today and Tomorrow. In M. L. McBee and K. A. Blake (eds.), The American Woman: Who Will She Be? Riverside, NJ: Glencoe Press, 1974, 121-135.

Crowe, K. P. A Comparative Analysis of Selected Vocational and Educational Programs, In Terms of Educational Cognitive Style, to Determine if Sex Bias Exists. Unpublished doctoral dissertation, Wayne State University. Dissertation Abstracts International, 1975, June, 35(12-A, Pt. 1), 7645-7646.

Cutler, M. H. Ridding the Schools of Sexism: A Mixed Bag. American School Board Journal, 1973, October, 160, 41+.

Daniels, A. K. A Survey of Research Concerns on Women's Issues. Washington, D. C.: Project on the Status and Education of Women, Association of American Colleges, 1975.

Darden, E. Especially for Women. Roanoke, VA: Leisure Press, 1977.

Davis, A. E. Women as a Minority Group in Higher Academics. In A. Theodore (ed.), The Professional Woman. Cambridge, MA: Schenkman, 1971, 587-598.

Davis, S. A. Encouraging the Career Development of Women in Non-traditional Fields. Symposium presentation at the American Psychological Association Convention, San Francisco, 1977.

Deckard, B. S. The Women's Movement: Political, Socioeconomic, and Psychological Issues. New York: Harper & Row, 1975.

DeCrow, K. Sexism in Education: To Bow Down No Longer. Sexist Justice: How Legal Sexism Affects You. New York: Random House, 1974, 290-302.

Delworth, U. Raising Consciousness About Sexism. Personnel and Guidance Journal, 1973, 51(9), 672-674.

Dennis, L. E. Education and a Woman's Life. Ithaca Conference on the Continuing Education of Women. Washington, D. C.: American Council on Education, 1963.

Dinerman, B. Sex Discrimination in Academia. Journal of Higher Education, 1971, 42(4), 253-264.

Discrimination Against Women. Hearings Before the Special Subcommittee on Education of the Committee on Education and Labor, Washington, D. C.: House of Representatives, Section 805 of H. R. 16098, June/July, 1970.

Dolan, E. F. Higher Education for Women: Time for Reappraisal. Higher Education, 1963, September, 20, 5-13.

_____. Women's Continuing Education: Some National Resources. Journal of the National Association of Women Deans and Counselors, 1965, Fall, 29, 34-38.

Doubrovsky, C. P. (ed.). Report on Sex Bias in the Public Schools. New York: Education Committee, National Organization for Women, New York City Chapter, 1971.

Dunkle, M. C., and Sandler, B. Sex Discrimination Against Students: Implications of Title IX of the Education Amendments of 1972. Inequality in Education, 1974, October, 18, 12-35.

Dunn, N. E., and Hedges, E. You Still Have a Long Way to Go, Baby: Neglected Women Writers; Women's Studies and the High School English Curriculum. Available from ERIC (ED 083617), 1973.

The Educated Woman. Special Issue. Student World, 1966, 59(3).

Education and the Role of Women: Symposium. Today's Education. 1960, December, 49, 48-53.

Education Committee. New York City Chapter, National Organization for Women, Report on Sex Bias in the Public Schools-- Excerpts. In D. Gersoni-Stavn (ed.), Sexism and Youth. New York: R.R. Bowker, 1974, 90-100.

Education, Credit, Sports--Barriers to Women Keep Falling. U.S. News, 1975, July 21, 79, 21-22.

Education for Survival. Final Report, Sex Role Stereotypes Project. Washington, D.C.: National Education Association, 1973.

Education of Women: Adaptation of Report. School Life, 1963, November, 46, 17-19.

Education of Women: Symposium. Saturday Review, 1963, May 18, 46, 64-70+.

Einstein, H., and Sacks, S.R. Women in Search of Autonomy: An Action Design. Social Change, 1975, 5(2), 4-6.

Ekstrom, R.B. Barriers to Women's Participation in Post-Secondary Education: A Review of the Literature. Research Bulletin, Princeton: Educational Testing Service, October, 1972.

_____, and Lockheed, M. Volunteer Experiences to College Credit. Women's Work, 1976, July/August, 20-21.

Elbert, S. Changing Education of American Women. Current History, 1976, May, 70, 220-223+.

Elder, P. Women in Higher Education; Qualified, Except for Sex. NASPA Journal, 1975, Fall, 13(2), 9-17.

Ellis, D.L., Graves, K., Grimstad, K., Marks, D., Pollack, F., Thompson, J., and Wexford, N.E. Women's Work and Women's Studies 1972. Reprint from KNOW Inc., P.O. Box 86031, Pittsburgh, Pa 15221, 1973.

Emma Willard Task Force on Education. Sexism in Education. Emma Willard Task Force on Education, Box No. 14229, Minneapolis, MN, 55414.

_____. Consciousness-Raising in the Classroom: Some Games, Projects, Discussion-Openers, Etc. In D. Gersoni-Stavn (ed.), Sexism and Youth. New York: R.R. Bowker, 1974, 103-106.

Entine, A.D. (ed.). Americans in Middle Years: Career Options and Educational Opportunities. Available from ERIC (ED099608), 1974.

Epstein, C.F. Bringing Women In: Rewards, Publishments, and

the Structure of Achievement. Annals of the New York Academy of Sciences, 1973, 208, 62-70.

──────. Structuring Success for Women: Guidelines for Gatekeepers. Journal of the National Association for Women Deans, Administrators, and Counselors, 1973, Fall, 37(1), 34-42.

Erickson, V. L. Psychological Growth for Women: A Cognitive-Developmental Curriculum Intervention. Unpublished doctoral dissertation, University of Minnesota, 1973.

──────. Psychological Growth for Women: A Cognitive-Developmental Curriculum Intervention. Counseling and Values, 1974, Winter, 18(2), 102-116.

──────. Deliberate Psychological Education for Women: From Iphigenia to Antigone. Counselor Education and Supervision, 1975, 14(4), 297-309.

──────. Deliberate Psychological Education for Women: A Curriculum Follow-Up Study. The Counseling Psychologist, 1977, 6(4), 25-29.

Farber, S. M., and Wilson, R. H. L. (eds.). The Potential of Woman. New York: McGraw-Hill, 1963.

Farley, J. Coeducation and College Women. Cornell Journal of Social Relations, 1974, 9, 87-97.

Farquar, N., and Mohlmar, C. Life Competence: A Non-Sexist Introduction to Practical Arts. Social Education, 1973, October, 37(6), 516-519.

Federbush, M. Let Them Aspire! A Plea and Proposal for Equality of Opportunity for Males and Females in the Ann Arbor Public Schools. Available from ERIC (ED092416), 1973.

──────. Let Them Aspire--Report on Sexism and Ann Arbor Public Schools. Reprint from KNOW Inc., P.O. Box 86031, Pittsburgh, PA 15221, 1973.

Feingold, S. N. Looking to the Future: Careers for Women in the 1970's and 80's. Women's Education, 1966, June, 5(2), 1+.

Feldman, K. A., and Newcomb, T. M. The Impact of College on Students. San Francisco: Jossey-Bass, 1969.

Female Athletics. American Medical Association Committee on the Medical Aspects of Sports. Journal of Physical Education and Recreation, 1976, January, 46, 45-46.

Feshback, N. D. A Primer for Non-Sexism in Schools. Educational Horizons, 1975, Spring, 53(3), 129-137.

General / 313

Fields, C. M. Affirmative Action 4 Years After. The Chronicle of Higher Education, 1974, August 5, 8(39), 1. Also reprint from KNOW Inc., P. O. Box 86031, Pittsburgh, PA 15221, 1974.

Fields, R. M. Public Education: Training for Sexism. KNOW, Inc., P. O. Box 86031, Pittsburgh, PA 15221, 1971.

Fishel, A., and Pottker, J. (eds.). School Boards and Sex Bias in American Education. In Sex Bias in the Schools--Research Evidence. Madison, NJ: Farleigh Dickinson University Press, 1977, 311-319.

Fitzpatrick, B. Women's Inferior Education: An Economic Analysis. New York: Praeger, 1976.

Folger, J. K., Astin, H. S., and Bayer, A. E. (eds.). Human Resources and Higher Education: Staff Report of the Commission on Human Resources and Advanced Education. New York: Russell Sage Foundation, 1970.

Forrest, K. S., and Chang, W. Affirmative Action and Equal Employment: A Bibliography. Available from Affirmative Action Office, San Jose State University, San Jose, CA, n. d.

Franklin, B. M. Career Education and Self Concept: A Median Perspective. Teachers College Record, 1977, February, 78, 285-297.

Frazier, N., and Sadker, M. The Anatomy of Change: A Positive Approach for Educators. In Sexism in School and Society. New York: Harper & Row, 1973, 177-207.

_____, and _____. The Male University. In Sexism in School and Society. New York: Harper & Row, 1973, 144-176.

_____, and _____. Sexism in School and Society. Harper & Row, 1973.

Freeman, J. Dissent. School Review, 1970, 79(1), 115-118.

_____. Women's Liberation and Its Impact on the Campus. Liberal Education, 1971, December, 57(4), 468-478.

_____ (ed.). How to Discriminate Against Women Without Really Trying. In Women: A Feminist Perspective. Palo Alto, CA: Mayfield, 1975, 194-208.

_____. Opportunities for Women in Higher Education. Review. Ms., 1975, September, 4, 47-48.

Friedan, B. What? No Degree for Women's Lib? College Management, 1970, December, 5(12), 14-17.

Friedrich, N. M. Access to Education at All Levels. Annals of the American Academy of Political and Social Science, 1968, January, 375, 133-144.

Froomkin, J. Aspirations, Enrollments, and Resources. Washington, D. C. : U. S. Government Printing Office, 1970.

Froschl, M., Odarenko, D. J., and Weinbaum, S. Women's Lives, Women's Work: A Feminist Approach to the High School Curriculum. Journal of Research and Development in Education, 1977, 10(4), 12-19.

Fry, B. J. Women, the Law, and Higher Education: 1960 to the Present. Unpublished manuscript, Michigan State University, East Lansing, n. d.

Furness, W. T., and Graham, P. A. (eds.). Women in Higher Education. Washington, D. C. : American Council on Education, 1974.

Gaffga, R. H. Employment of Women and Their Education. Adult Leadership, 1976, September, 25, 13-14.

Gager, N. (ed.). Women's Rights Almanac. New York: Harper & Row, 1975.

Galloway, J. M. The Impact of the Admission of Women to the Service Academies on the Role of the Woman Line Officer. American Behavioral Scientist, 1976, May/June, 19(5), 647-664.

Gander, M. J. Sex-Typing in the High School. In J. Pottker, and A. Fishel (eds.), Sex Bias in the Schools--The Research Evidence. Madison, NJ: Fairleigh Dickinson University Press, 1977, 78-91.

Gardner, J. A. E. What Effect Should the Feminist Movement Have on Higher Education? Women Speaking, Hutton Mount, Brentwood, Essex, England, n. d.

Gibbons, A. R., and Eaton, D. Exploring the Nature and Extent of Sex Bias. American Education, 1974, April, 10, 34-35.

Ginzberg, E. Educated American Women. New York: Columbia University Press, 1966.

Girard, K. L. How Schools Fail Women: A Study of Feminists' Perceptions of Their Schooling Experiences and Women's Schooling Needs. Unpublished doctoral dissertation, University of Massachusetts. Dissertation Abstracts International, 1974, November, 35(5-A), 2529-2530.

Gittell, M. The Illusion of Affirmative Action. Change Magazine, 1975, October, 7(8), 39-43.

Glazer-Malbin, N., and Waehrer, H. Y. Woman in a Man-Made World. Chicago: Rand McNally, 1972.

Glenn, H. M., and Walters, J. Feminine Stress in the Twentieth Century. Journal of Home Economics, 1966, November, 58(9), 703-707.

Goldman, F. H. A Turning to Take Next: Alternative Goals in the Education of Women. Brookline, MA: Center for the Study of Liberal Education for Adults, Boston University, 1965.

Gould, J. S., and Pagano, A. Sex Discrimination and Achievement. Journal of the National Association of Women Deans and Counselors, 1972, 35(2), 74-82.

Graham, P. Status Transitions of Women Students, Faculty, and Administrators. In A. Rossi and A. Calderwood (eds.), Academic Women on the Move. New York: Russell Sage Foundation, 1973, 163-172.

Green, E. Road Is Paved with Good Intentions; Title IX and Sex Discrimination; Address, January 25, 1977. Vital Speeches of the Day, 1977, March 1, 43, 300-303.

Greene, M. Honorable Work and Delayed Awakenings: Education and American Women. Phi Delta Kappan, 1976, September, 58, 25-30.

Groseclose, E. Sexism and Schools. In E. Graham (ed.), What Do Women Really Want. Princeton, NJ: Dow Jones Books, 1974, 164-169.

Gross, N. Implementing Organizational Innovations: A Sociological Analysis of Planned Educational Change. New York: Basic Books, 1971.

Groszko, M., and Morgenstern, R. Institutional Discrimination: The Case of Achievement-Oriented Women in Higher Education. International Journal of Group Tensions, 1974, 4, 82-92.

Group for the Advancement of Psychiatry. The Educated Woman. New York: Charles Scribner's, 1975.

Gruchow, N. Discrimination: Women Charge Universities, Colleges with Bias. Science, 1970, May, 168, 559-561.

Guttentag, M. Undoing Sex Stereotypes: Research and Resources for Educators. New York: McGraw-Hill, 1977.

Guttman, M. A. J. (ed.). Female Perspectives on Sexist Issues in Counselor Education. In Women and ACES: Perspective and Issues. Washington, D. C.: Commission for Women, Association for Counselor Education and Supervision, 1974, 13-20.

_____ (ed.). Women and ACES: Perspective and Issues. Washington, D.C.: Commission for Women, Association for Counselor Education and Supervision, 1974.

Hall, E.B. Education and Women's Aims. Ladies Home Journal, 1961, April, 78, 43+.

Handley, A., and Sedlacek, W. Characteristics and Work Attitudes of Women Working on Campus. Journal of the National Association for Women Deans, Administrators and Counselors, 1977, Summer, 40(4), 128-134.

Hansan, J.F., and Green, M.L. Coming of the Second Plague. Physical Educator, 1975, May, 32(2), 64-66.

Hansen, L.S. We Are Furious (Females) But We Can Shape Our Own Development. Personnel and Guidance Journal, 1972, October, 51(2), 87-93.

_____. A Career Development Curriculum Framework to Promote Female Growth. In M.A.J. Guttman (ed.), Women and ACES-- Perspective and Issues. Washington, D.C.: Commission for Women, Association for Counselor Education and Supervision, 1974, 43-62.

_____. Practical Approaches to Facilitate the Career Development of Women. School Psychology Digest, 1974, Summer, 3(3), 40-46. Also in Pupil Personnel Services Journal, 1976, 5(1), 1-12.

_____. The Career Development Process for Women: Current Views and Programs. Pupil Personnel Services Journal, 1975, 4(2), 23-33.

_____. Applied Developmental Intervention for Elementary, Secondary, and College Settings. Symposium presentation at the American Psychological Association Convention, San Francisco, 1977.

Harmon, L.A. Status of Women in Higher Education: 1963-1972; A Selective Bibliography. Ames: Iowa State University, 1972.

Harris, C.M., and Smith, S.W. Man Teacher--Woman Teacher: Does It Matter? Elementary School Journal, 1976, February, 75(5), 285-288.

Harris, P.R. Problems and Solutions in Achieving Equality for Women. In W.T. Furniss and P.A. Graham (eds.), Women in Higher Education. Washington, D.C.: American Council on Education, 1974, 11-26.

Harrison, B.G. Feminist Experiment in Education. In J. Stacey et al. (eds.), And Jill Came Tumbling After: Sexism in American Education. New York: Dell, 1974, 377-389.

General / 317

_____. Unlearning the Lie: Sexism in School. New York: William Morrow, 1974.

Harrison, P., and Jones, B. J. Research and Women in Sports: Closing the Gap. Physical Educator, 1975, May, 32, 84-88.

Hawkins, R. R. The Odds Against Women. Change in Higher Education, 1969, November/December, 34-36. Also in Women on Campus: The Unfinished Liberation. New York: Change Magazine, 1975, 28-33.

Hefner, R., Meda, R., Oleshansky, B., and Nordin, V. D. Sex Role Transcendence as a Guide to Intervention in Educational Systems to End Sex Discrimination in Education. Final Report. Washington, D. C.: National Institute of Education, 1976.

Hembrough, B. L. Two-Fold Educational Challenge: The Student Wife and the Mature Woman Student. Journal of the National Association of Women Deans and Counselors, 1966, Summer, 29, 163-167.

Hendel, D. D. Evaluation of Mathematics Anxiety Programs. Symposium presentation at the American Psychological Association Convention, San Francisco, 1977.

Henley, N. Facing Down the Man. In J. Agel (ed.), Rough Times. New York: Ballantine Books, 1973.

Hicks, N. Women's Groups in 4 Cities Monitor Complaints About Sex Bias in Schools. The New York Times, 1976, August 31, 30.

The Higher Education of Women. Special Issue. Improving College and University Teaching, 1972, Winter, 20(1).

Hipple, J. L., and Hill, A. J. Meeting the Special Needs of Women in Educational Settings. Journal of the National Association of Women Deans and Counselors, 1973, Summer, 36, 170-172.

Hole, J., and Levine, E. Education. In Rebirth of Feminism. New York: Quandrangle Books, 1971, 319-337.

Hollander, H. E., Penney, S., and Haines, J. R. (eds.). Women: Their Future in the University and the Community. Conference Proceedings. New York State Citizens Council; Skidmore College, Saratoga Springs, NY: Office of Higher Education Management Services, New York State Education Department, 1974.

How Should Vocational Education Respond? American Vocational Journal, 1970, December, 45(9), 20+.

Howard, T. M. Is There a Feminine Mystique in Catholic Education. Momentum, 1972, December, 3(4), 49-51.

Howe, F. Sexism, Racism, and the Education of Women. Today's Education, 1973, May, 62, 47-48.

_____. The Education of Women. In J. Stacey et al. (eds.), And Jill Came Tumbling After: Sexism in American Education. New York: Dell, 1974, 64-75.

_____. Equal Opportunity for Women: How Possible and How Quickly. In J. Stacey et al. (eds.), And Jill Came Tumbling After: Sexism in American Education. New York: Dell, 1974, 423-434.

_____. Sexism in Education and the Aspirations of Women. Changing Education, 1974, Winter/Spring, 5, 31-35.

_____ (ed.). Women and the Power to Change. New York: Mc-Graw-Hill, 1975.

_____. Feminism and the Education of Women. In J. Stiehm (ed.), The Frontiers of Knowledge. University Park: University of Southern California Press, 1976, September, 79-93.

Hult, J. Girls and Women's Sports. Journal of Health, Physical Education, Recreation, 1974, June, 45(6), 45-46.

Husbands, S. A. Women's Place in Higher Education? School Review, 1972, 80(2), 261-274.

Jacobs, C., and Eaton, C. Sexism in the Elementary School. Today's Education, 1972, December, 61(9), 20-22.

Jacobs, J. E. Woman and Work: A Selected, Annotated Bibliography. Educational Horizons, 1975, Spring, 53(3), 142-144.

_____, and Alberti, J. M. (eds.). Realizing Human Potential: Alternatives for Women; Symposium. Educational Horizons, 1975, Spring, 53(3), 94-141.

Jacoby, S. Altering Sexism in the Classroom. Learning, 1973, April, 1, 62-67.

Jaffe, L. Women's Place in Academe. The Midwest Quarterly, 1973, October, 15(1), 16-30.

Janeway, E. Women on Campus: The Unfinished Liberation. In Women on Campus: The Unfinished Liberation. New Rochelle, NY: Change Magazine, 1975, 10-27.

Jay, W. T. Sex Stereotyping in Selected Mathematics Textbooks, for Grades Two, Four and Six. Unpublished doctoral dissertation, University of Oregon, 1973.

_____, and Schminke, C. W. Sex Bias in Elementary School Mathematics Texts. The Arithmetic Teacher, 1975, 242-246.

Jencks, C., and Reisman, D. The Academic Revolution. New York: Doubleday, 1968.

Joffe, C. As the Twig Is Bent. In J. Stacey et al. (eds.), And Jill Came Tumbling After: Sexism in American Education. New York: Dell, 1974, 91-109.

Kalunian, P., Lopatich, G., and Cymerman, S. Changing Sex Role Stereotypes Through Career Development. Psychology in the Schools, 1975, April, 12, 230-233.

Kane, R. D. A Study of Factors Influencing the Participation of Women in Non-Traditional Occupations in Postsecondary Area Vocational Training Schools. Final Report. Washington, D. C.: Bureau of Occupational and Adult Education, 1977.

Katz, I. Academic Motivation and Equal Educational Opportunity. Harvard Educational Review, 1968, Winter, 38(1), 57-65.

Kayden, X. Report on Women and Continuing Education. Washington, D. C., Office of Education, 1970.

Keiffer, M. G., and Cullen, D. M. Women Who Discriminate Against Other Women: The Process of Denial. International Journal of Group Tensions, 1974, March, 4(1), 21-33. Also in F. Denmark (ed.), Who Discriminates Against Women (Issue 15). Beverly Hills: Sage, 1974, 24-36; and reprint from KNOW, Inc., P. O. Box 86031, Pittsburgh, PA 15221, n. d.

Kent, M. Higher Education and Gender Role Socialization. Paper presented at the American Association of University Women Symposium on Graduate and Professional Education of Women, Washington, D. C., 1974.

Kerr, W. D., and Johnston, R. L. Self-Actualization for Women Through Continuing Education. Adult Leadership, 1964, December, 13, 177-178.

Kirkpatrick, W. J. The Emerging Role of Women in Institutions of Higher Education in the United States. Unpublished doctoral dissertation, University of Arkansas. Dissertation Abstracts, 1965, 26(2), 797.

Knudsen, D. The Declining Status of Women: Popular Myths and the Failure of Functionalist Thought. Social Forces, 1969, 48(2), 183-193.

Komisar, L. Barriers in Higher Education. In The New Feminism. New York: Warner Books, 1972, 41-45.

_____. Sexism in High School. In The New Feminism. New York: Warner Books, 1972, 32-40.

Kreps, J. Sex in the Market Place: American Women at Work. Baltimore: Johns Hopkins Press, 1971.

Kreuter, G. But Can She Cook? An Historical View of Women in Higher Education in Minnesota. Pupil Personnel Services Journal, 1975, 4(2), 3-10.

Kundsin, R. B. (ed.). Women and Success: The Anatomy of Achievement. New York: William Morrow, 1974.

Kutner, N. G., and Brogan, D. Sources of Sex Discrimination in Educational Systems: A Conceptual Model. Psychology of Women Quarterly, 1976, Fall, 1(1), 50-69.

Lamel, L. Career Expressions of Women. Career Education Monograph Series, 1974, 1(5). Also available from ERIC (ED105-235), 1975.

Lee, P. C., and Gropper, N. B. Sex-Role Culture and Educational Practice. Harvard Educational Review, 1974, 44(3), 369-410.

Lehmann, P. Cutting Sex Bias Out of Vocational Education. Education Digest, 1977, March, 42, 33-35.

Leonard, M., Hansen, L. S., and Knefelkamp, L. A Process Model for Changing Counselor Education Departments. In M. A. J. Guttman (ed.), Women and ACES: Perspective and Issues. Washington, D. C.: Commission for Women, Association for Counselor Education and Supervision, 1974, 69-80.

Letchworth, G. E. Women Who Return to College: An Identity-Integrity Approach. Journal of College Student Personnel, 1970, 11(2), 103-106.

Levine, S. E. OCR and Sex Discrimination. In Graduate and Professional Education of Women. Washington, D. C.: American Association of University Women, 1974, 20-22.

Levy, B. Sex Role Socialization in Schools. In Sex Role Stereotyping in the Schools. Washington, D. C.: National Education Association, 1973, 1-7.

_____, and Stacey, J. Sexism in Elementary School: A Backward and Forward Look. Phi Delta Kappan, 1973, 9(2), 105-109+.

Levy, L. (ed.). Inequality in Education: Sex Discrimination. Cambridge, MA: Center for Law and Education, Harvard University, No. 18, 1974, October.

Lewis, E. C. Developing Woman's Potential. Ames: Iowa State University Press, 1968.

Ley, K. Women in Sports: Where Do We Go from Here Boys?

Title IX Regulations. Phi Delta Kappan, 1974, October, 56, 129-131.

Lightfoot, S. L. Sociology of Education: Perspectives on Women. In M. Millman and R. M. Kanter (eds.), Another Voice: Feminist Perspectives on Social Life and Social Science. New York: Doubleday, 1975, 106-143.

Lipman-Blumen, J. Toward a Homosocial Theory of Sex Roles: An Explanation of the Sex Segregation of Social Institutions. In B. B. Reagan and M. Blaxall (eds.), Women and the Workplace: The Implications of Occupational Segregation. Chicago: University of Chicago Press, 1976, 15-31.

Lloyd, M. A. The Effects of Active Versus Passive Participation on Ego-Involved Attitudes: Changes in Knowledge and Attitudes Following a Life-Planning Workshop for College Women. Dissertation Abstracts International, 1973, 34(2-B), 858.

Lockheed, M. E., and Ekstrom, R. B. Sex Discrimination in Education. A Literature Review and Bibliography. Research Bulletin. Princeton, NJ: Educational Testing Service, 1977.

―――, and Harris, A. Producing Equal Status Contact Between School-Age Boys and Girls. Paper presented at the American Educational Research Association meeting, San Francisco, 1977.

Loeffler, M. The Feminists and Their Impact on the College Community. College Student Journal, 1975, February-March, 9(1), 5-8.

London, J. Continuing Education of Women: A Challenge for Our Society. Adult Leadership, 1966, April, 14, 326-328+.

Long-Laws, J. On Campus with Women. Journal of the National Association for Women Deans, Administrators, and Counselors, 1976, April, 13, 5.

Lopata, H. Z. The Effect of Schooling on Social Contracts of Urban Women. American Journal of Sociology, 1973, November, 79(3), 604-619.

Luchins, E. H. Women and Mathematics: A Contemporary Appraisal. Paper presented at the American Association for the Advancement of Science meeting, Boston, 1976.

Ludovici, L. J. The Final Inequality. New York: Tower Publication, 1971.

Lyon, R. Married Women and the Academic Tradition. Journal of Higher Education, 1964, May, 35, 251-255.

McAllister, A. B. A General Model and Proposed Implementation Plan for Career Education at Mississippi State College for Women. Unpublished doctoral dissertation. Dissertation Abstracts International, 1974, 34, 6315.

Macaulay, J. R. Failure of Affirmative Action for Women at a Major University. Symposium presentation at the American Psychological Association Convention, Chicago, 1975.

Maccia, E. S., Coleman, M. A., Estep, M., and Shiel, T. M., (eds.). Women and Education. Springfield, IL: Charles C. Thomas, 1975.

Maccoby, E. E. Woman's Intellect. In S. M. Farber and R. H. L. Wilson (eds.), Potential of Women. New York: McGraw-Hill, 1963, 24-39.

_____. Feminine Intellect and the Demands of Society. Impact of Science on Society, 1970, 20(1), 13-20.

McCune, S. D. Barriers to Change. In Graduate and Professional Education of Women. Washington, D. C.: American Association of University Women, 1974, 59-62.

_____. Eliminating Sexism: Teacher Education and Change. Journal of Teacher Education, 1975, 26(4), 294-300.

_____. Title IX--Sexism in Education. The Humanist Educator, 1976, June, 14(4), 195-208.

McGrath, P. L. The Unfinished Assignment: Equal Education for Women. Worldwatch Paper 7. Washington, D. C.: Worldwatch, 1976. Also available from ERIC (ED129650), 1977.

Macháček, L. Prispevok k Problému Riešenia Feminizácie Vysokoškolského Štúdia [Feminization of University Studies]. Jednotná Skola, 1967, 19(5), 429-440.

McKnight, D., and Huit, J. Competitive Athletics for Girls: We Must Act. Journal of Health, Physical Education, and Recreation, 1974, June, 45, 45-46.

McLure, G. T. Eliminate Sex Bias in the Curriculum. Educational Leadership, 1973, November, 31(2), 111-113.

_____. Attitudes of School Superintendents Toward Affirmative Action Guidelines for Eliminating Sex Stereotyping in Schools: A Q Analysis. Unpublished doctoral dissertation, University of Iowa. Dissertation Abstracts International, 1974, July, 35(1-A), 135.

_____, Friedman, M., Ries, K., Brunner, T., Hender, J., and Witwer, B. Sex Discriminations in Schools. Today's Education, 1971, November, 60(8), 33-35.

_____, _____, _____, _____, _____, and _____. Outmoded Stereotypes in the School Environment. In Sex Role Stereotyping in the Schools. Washington, D.C.: National Education Association, 1973, 8-13.

McLure, J.W., and McLure, G.T. Cinderella Grows Up: Sex Stereotyping in the Schools. Educational Leadership, 1972, October, 30, 31-33.

McNamara, W.A. Quitting the Doll's House. A Special Report on Women in Higher Education. College and University Journal, 1972, September, 11, 11-14.

Marecek, J. Psychology of Women and Higher Education in the '70's. Paper presented at the American Psychological Association Convention, Chicago, 1975.

Martin, A.M., and Martin, A.G. Educating Women for Identity in Work. American Vocational Journal, 1971, May, 46, 38+.

Mathies, L. Citings on the Educational Horizon. Educational Horizon, 1975, Spring, 53(3), 145-147.

Mathison, M.A. Curricular Interventions and Programming Innovations for Reducing Mathematics Anxiety. Symposium presentation at the American Psychological Association Convention, San Francisco, 1977.

Mednick, M.T.S., Tangri, S.S., and Hoffman, L.W. Women and Achievement: Social and Motivational Analyses. New York: Halsted Press, 1975.

Mendenhall, T.C. Women's Education and the Educated Woman. School and Society, 1960, November 19, 88, 436-439.

Meredith, E., and Meredith, R. Adult Women's Education: A Radical Critique. Journal of the National Association of Women Deans and Counselors, 1971, Spring, 34(3), 111-120.

Merrirr, K. Women in Higher Education: Voices from the Sexual Siberia. In J.I. Roberts (ed.), Women Scholars on Woman: Changing Perceptions of Reality. New York: David McKay, 1975.

Michaels, J.W., and McCulloch, D.H. Rationale and Design for Reducing Sex Differences in Occupational and Educational Attainment by Strengthening Across-Sex Peer Influences. Center for Social Organization of Schools Report, Johns Hopkins University, 1975, May, (196).

Miller, K., and Mendelsohn, M. Education and the Participation of Women in World Development: A Brief Survey. Washington, D.C.: Women's Equity Action League, Education and Legal Defense Fund, n.d.

Millett, K., et al. Token Learning: A Study of Women's Higher Education in America. New York: National Organization for Women, 1968.

Millman, M., and Kanter, R. M. (eds.). Another Voice: Feminist Perspectives on Social Life and Social Science. New York: Doubleday, 1975.

Minuchin, P. The Schooling of Tomorrow's Women. School Review, 1972, 80(2), 199-208. Also in D. Gersoni-Stavn (ed.), Sexism and Youth. New York: R. R. Bowker, 1974, 70-77; and in E. S. Maccia et al. (eds.), Women and Education. Springfield, IL: Charles C. Thomas, 1975, 347-356.

Mitchell, E. What About Career Education for Girls? Educational Leadership, 1972, December, 30, 233-236.

Mitchell, J. I Can Be Anything: Careers and Colleges for Women. New York: College Entrance Examination Board, 1975.

Monsour, K. J. Education and a Woman's Life. In L. E. Dennis (ed.), Education and a Woman's Life: Proceedings of the Itasca Conference on the Continuing Education of Women. Washington, D. C.: American Council on Education, 1963, 9-10.

Mueller, K. H. What It's All About. In L. C. Muller and O. G. Muller (eds.), New Horizons for College Women. Washington, D. C.: Public Affairs Press, 1960, 14.

Muller, L. C., and Muller, O. G. (eds.). New Horizons for College Women. Washington, D. C.: Public Affairs Press, 1960.

Mulligan, K. A Question of Opportunity: Women and Continuing Education. Washington, D. C.: National Advisory Council on Extensions and Continuing Education, 1973.

Mullis, I. V. S. Educational Achievement and Sex Discrimination. Available from ERIC (ED115701), 1976.

Naiman, A. What To Do About Sex Bias in the Curriculum. American Education, 1977, April, 13, 10-11.

Naylor, H. H. Continuing Education for Women. Adult Leadership, 1967, October, 16, 150.

Nell, O. How Do We Know When Opportunities Are Equal? In C. C. Gould and M. W. Wartofsky (eds.), Women and Philosophy: Toward a Theory of Liberation. New York: G. P. Putnam's, 1976, 334-346.

Neugarten, B. Women in the University of Chicago: Report of the Committee on University Women. Prepared for the Committee of the Council of the University Senate, University of

Chicago, 1970. Reprinted in Discrimination Against Women. Hearings Before the Special Subcommittee on Education of the Committee on Education and Labor, Washington, D. C. : House of Representatives, Section 805 of H. R. 16098, June/July, 1970, 754-884.

_____. Education and the Life-Cycle. School Review, 1972, 80(2), 209-216.

New Women and the Campus. College Management, 1971, November, 6, 4.

New York Board of Regents. Equal Opportunity for Women, Position Paper No. 14 of the Regents. Albany, NY: New York State Education Department, 1972.

Newcomer, M. Women's Education: Facts, Findings, and Apparent Trends. Journal of the National Association of Women Deans and Counselors, 1960, October, 24, 35-40.

_____. A Century of Higher Education for American Women. Washington, D. C. : Zenger, 1976.

Nolte, M. C. Women in Education: A Long, Long Way to Go. The American School Board Journal, 1973, October, 160, 38-40.

Nordlie, P. G. The Use of Quantitative Measures to Assess Changes in Institutional Discrimination. Paper presented at the American Psychological Association Convention, Washington, D. C. , 1976.

OCR Statement on Sex Discrimination. College and University Bulletin, 1972, March 1, 24(10).

Oleshansky, B. A Model of Sex-Role Transcendence: Role Polarity and Sex Discrimination in Education. Washington, D. C. : National Institute of Education, 1974.

Oltman, R. M. Campus 1970--Where Do Women Stand? American Association of University Women Journal, 1970, November, 64, 14-15.

_____. The Evolving Role of the Women's Liberation Movement in Higher Education. Available from ERIC (ED049489), 1971.

On Campus with Women. Newsletter of the Project on the Status and Education of Women. Washington, D. C. : Association of American Colleges.

On Women in Educational Research and Development. Educational Researcher, 1975, October, 4(9), 3-4.

Opportunities for Women in Higher Education. A Digest of Reports of the Carnegie Commission on Higher Education. New York: McGraw-Hill, 1974. Also in Intellect, 1974, January, 102, 208-209.

Ornstein, A. C. What Does Affirmative Action Affirm? A Viewpoint. Phi Delta Kappan, 1975, December, 45, 242-250.

Osborn, J. Creativity Applied to Career Development. In Facilitating Career Development for Girls and Women. Washington, D. C.: National Vocational Guidance Association, 1975, 71-82.

Osborn, R. H. Developing New Horizons for Women. Adult Leadership, 1971, April, 19, 326-328.

Overman, S. J. Women and Students in the Medieval Universities. Journal of the National Association for Women Deans, Administrators and Counselors, 1974, Winter, 37(2), 88-93.

Painter, E. Women: The Last of the Discriminated. Journal of the National Association of Women Deans and Counselors, 1971, 34(1), 50-62.

Parsons, T. The School Class as a Social System: Some of Its Functions in American Society. In Socialization and Schools. Cambridge, MA: President and Fellows of Harvard College, 1968, 69-90.

Paxton, K. They Care: New Occupational Program for Women. American Vocational Journal, 1967, April, 42, 38-40.

Pender, A. Attention Men: The Women Are Coming. Contemporary Education, 1972, February, 43(4), 219-223.

Pennsylvania Department of Education. Sexism in Education. Joint Task Force Report, Harrisburg, PA: Pennsylvania Human Relations Commission, 1972.

Pietrofesa, J. J. Education and Guidance of Women. Catholic Education Review, 1967, November, 65, 517-523.

Pifer, A. Women in Higher Education. Paper presented at the Southern Association of Colleges and Schools, Miami, FL, 1971.

Pirsig, N., Eaton, G., and Jacobs, C. Action on Sexism in Education. American Education, 1973, June, 9, 24-28.

Plost, M., and Rosen, M. J. Report on Sex Bias in the Public Schools. Available from ERIC (ED090131), 1973.

Plotsky, F. A., and Goad, R. Encouraging Women Through a Career Conference. Personnel and Guidance Journal, 1974, March, 52, 486-488.

Polowy, C. I. Federal Remedies for Discrimination in University

Employment. In Graduate and Professional Education of Women. Washington, D. C.: American Association of University Women, 1974, 16-20.

Pottker, J., and Fishel, A. (eds.). Sex Bias in the Schools-- The Research Evidence. Madison, NJ: Fairleigh Dickinson University Press, 1977.

Pratt, L. V. The Educating of Modern Woman, University Woman, 1962, 1(1), 5-8.

Project on the Status and Education of Women. Minority Women. On Campus with Women. Washington, D. C.: Association of American Colleges, 1977, June 17, 7-8.

Pullen, D. L. The Educational Establishment: Wasted Women. In M. L. Thompson (ed.), Voices of the New Feminism. Boston: Beacon Press, 1970, 115-135.

Punke, H. H. Sex and Equal Opportunity in Higher Education. NASSP Bulletin, 1961, November, 45, 121-128.

Quinn, R. P., Tabor, J. M., and Gordon, L. K. The Decision to Discriminate. Ann Arbor: Institute for Social Research, University of Michigan, 1968.

Raffel, N. K. Women's Movement and Its Impact on Higher Education. Liberal Education, 1973, May, 59, 246-254.

Resource Center on Sex Roles in Education. Research Action Notes. Washington, D. C.: National Foundation for the Improvement of Education, 1975, April.

Revolution II: Thinking Female. College and University Business, 1970, 48(2), 70.

Rich, A. Toward a Woman-Centered University. The Chronicle of Higher Education, 1975, July 21, 32. Also in F. Howe (ed.), Women and the Power to Change. New York: McGraw-Hill, 1975, 15-46.

Richardson, B. Sexism in Higher Education. New York: Seabury Press, 1974.

Rieder, C. H. Work, Women and Vocational Education. American Education, 1977, June, 13, 27-30.

Riesman, D. Some Dilemmas of Women's Education. Educational Record, 1965, 46, 424-434. Also in E. S. Maccia et al. (eds.), Women and Education. Springfield, IL: Charles C. Thomas, 1975, 146-160.

_____. Dilemmas for Women in Higher Education. Harvard Today, 1974, Summer, 17(4), 8-9.

Roberts, J. I. (ed.). Beyond Intellectual Sexism: A New Woman, A New Morality. New York: David McKay, 1976.

_____. Women's Right to Choose, or Men's Right to Dominate. In W. T. Furniss and P. A. Graham (eds.), Women in Higher Education. Washington, D. C.: American Council on Education, 1974, 50-55.

Robinson, L. H. The Status of Academic Women, Review 5. Available from ERIC (ED048523), 1971.

_____. Institutional Analysis of Sex Discrimination: A Review and Annotated Bibliography. Available from ERIC (ED076176), 1973.

Roby, P. Structural and Internalized Barriers to Women in Higher Education. In J. Bernard (ed.), Women and the Public Interest. Chicago: Aldine, 1971. Also in C. Safilios-Rothschild (ed.), Sociology of Women. Lexington, MA: Xerox College Publishing, 1971, 121-140; and in J. Freeman (ed.), Women: A Feminist Perspective. Palo Alto: Mayfield, 1975, 171-193.

_____. Women and American Higher Education. Annals of the American Academy of Political and Social Science, 1972, 404, 118-139. Also reprint from KNOW, Inc., P. O. Box 86031, Pittsburg, PA 15221.

Rose, C. (ed.). Meeting Women's New Educational Needs. New Directions for Higher Education, 1975, Autumn, 3(3). Also in Meeting Women's New Educational Needs. San Francisco: Jossey-Bass, 1975.

Rosen, R. Sexism in History. In J. Stacey et al. (eds.), And Jill Came Tumbling After: Sexism in American Education. New York: Dell, 1977, 326-334.

Ross, S. C. Education. In The Rights of Women: The Basic American Civil Liberties Union Guide to a Woman's Rights. New York: Avon Books, 1973, 116-147.

Rossi, A. S. Discrimination and Demography Restrict Opportunities for Academic Women. College and University Business, February, 1970. Also in J. Stacey et al. (eds.), And Jill Came Tumbling After: Sexism in American Education. New York: Dell, 1974, 366-374.

_____, and Calderwood, A. (eds.). Academic Women on the Move. New York: Russell Sage Foundation, 1973.

Rothchild, N. Sexism in the Schools: A Handbook for Action. Available from ERIC (ED090108), 1973.

Rothwell, C. E. The Milieu of the Educated Woman. In L. E. Dennis (ed.), Education and a Woman's Life: Proceedings of the Itasca Conference on the Continuing Education of Women. Washington, D. C.: American Council on Education, 1963, 42.

Rubin-Rabson, G. How High Are the Odds Against Women? American Psychologist, 1974, 29, 916-917.

Rumbarger, M. L. Internal Remedies for Sex Discrimination in Colleges and Universities. In A. S. Rossi and A. Calderwood (eds.), Academic Women on the Move. New York: Russell Sage Foundation, 1973, 425-438.

Rutherford, M. Reinforced Concrete; Sexism in Secondary Education. English Journal, 1974, March, 63, 25-33.

Ryten, E. Our Best Educated Women (Canada). Canadian Business Review, 1975, Summer, 2, 12-16.

Saario, T. N. School Policies and Sex Bias. Available from ERIC (ED090661), 1974.

_____, Jacklin, C., and Tittle, C. Sex Role Stereotyping in the Public Schools. Harvard Educational Review, 1973, 43, 386-416.

Sadker, M., and Frazier, N. Sex Bias: The Hidden Curriculum in the Elementary School. In Sexism in School and Society. New York: Harper & Row, 1973, 76-113.

_____, and Sadker, D. Sexual Discrimination in the Elementary School. National Elementary Principal, 1972, 52, 41-45.

_____, and _____. Sexism in Schools: An Issue for the 70's. Education Digest, 1974, April, 39(8), 58-61. Also in Journal of the National Association for Women Deans, Administrators, and Counselors, 1974, Winter, 37(2), 69-74.

Safilios-Rothschild, C. Social Policy to Liberate Women. In Women and Social Policy. Englewood Cliffs, NJ: Prentice-Hall, 1974, 17-71.

Salter, A. Politics in the Preschool. Sex Role Stereotypes Teacher's Guide. Reprint from KNOW, Inc., P. O. Box 86031, Pittsburgh, PA 15221, 1975.

Sandler, B. What Women Really Want on the Campus. The Chronicle of Higher Education, 1972, April 24, 8.

_____. Women in Higher Education (address). Vital Speeches of the Day, 1972, June 15, 38, 532-537.

_____. Sex Discrimination, Educational Institutions, and the Law: A New Issue on Campus. In E. Wasserman et al. (eds.), Women in Academia: Evolving Policies Toward Equal Opportunities. New York: Praeger, 1975, 20-36.

Sassower, D. L. Women's Rights in Higher Education. Current, 1972, November, 145, 29-34.

Schetlin, E. M. Sexism, Racism and the Crucial K-12 Years. Journal of the National Association for Women Deans, Administrators, and Counselors, 1977, Spring, 40(3), 102-103.

Schleman, H. G. Span Plan. Purdue Alumnus, 1969, February, 7-11.

Schletzer, V. M., Cless, E. L., McCune, C. W., Mantini, B. K., and Loeffler, D. L. Continuing Education for Women: A Five-Year Report of the Minnesota Plan. Minneapolis: University of Minnesota, 1967.

Schlossberg, N. K. The Right to Be Wrong Is Gone: Women in Academe. Educational Record, 1974, Fall, 55(4), 257-262.

Schneider, J., and Hacker, S. Sex Role Imagery and Use of the Generic 'Man' in Introductory Texts: A Case in the Sociology of Sociology. American Sociologist, 1973, 8, 12-18.

Schreiber, K. J. Sexist Issues in Child Advocacy. Clinical Psychologist, 1976, Winter, 29(2), 22-23.

Schuck, V. Sexism and Scholarship: A Brief Overview of Women, Academia, and the Disciplines. Social Science Quarterly, 1974, December, 55(3), 563-585.

Schumacher, D. Changing the School Environment. In D. Gersoni-Stavn (ed.), Sexism and Youth. New York: R. R. Bowker, 1974, 113-119.

Schwartz, P., and Lever, J. Women in the Male World of Higher Education. In A. S. Rossi and A. Calderwood (eds.), Academic Women on the Move. New York: Russell Sage Foundation, 1973, 57-77.

Scott, A. The Half-Eaten Apple: A Look at Sex Discrimination in the University. Available from ERIC (ED041566), 1970.

_____. It's Time for Equal Education. In J. Stacey et al. (eds.), And Jill Came Tumbling After: Sexism in American Education. New York: Dell, 1974, 399-409.

Scott, P., and Horhn, M. Sexism in Education. Social Studies Journal, 1973, Winter, 2(4).

_____, and _____. Self-Study Guide to Sexism in Schools. Available from ERIC (ED097289), 1974.

Scott, R., and Holt, L. The New Wave: A College Responds to Women Returnees. Phi Delta Kappan, 1976, December, 58(4), 338-339.

Scully, M. Women in Higher Education: Challenging the Status Quo. The Chronicle of Higher Education, 1972, February 9, 4, 2-5.

Sewell, W. H. Inequality of Opportunity for Higher Education. American Sociological Review, 1971, October, 36, 793-809.

Sex Discrimination in Education: An Overview. In R. E. Hardy and J. G. Cull (eds.), Career Guidance for Young Women: Considerations in Planning Professional Careers. Springfield, IL: Charles C. Thomas, 1974, 147-169.

Sex Role Stereotyping in the Schools. Washington, D. C.: National Education Association, 1973.

Sexism and Bias. A Special Issue. Journal of the National Association for Women Deans, Administrators, and Counselors, 1974, Winter, 37(2).

Sexism in the Elementary School; Schools and Sex-Role Stereotyping; Symposium. Today's Education, 1972, December, 61, 20-29.

Sexton, P. Higher Education. In Women in Education. Bloomington, IN: Phi Delta Kappa Educational Foundation, 1976, 75-88.

———. Women In Education. Bloomington, IN: Phi Delta Kappa Educational Foundation, 1976.

Shack, S. The Two-Thirds Minority: Women in Canadian Education. Toronto: University of Toronto, 1973.

Shaffer, H. G., and Shaffer, J. P. Job Discrimination Against Faculty Wives. Journal of Higher Education, 1966, January, 36, 10-15.

Shapley, D. University Women's Rights; Whose Feet Are Dragging? Science, 1972, January 14, 175, 151-154.

Shinn, M. Secondary School Co-Education and Fears of Success and Failure. Unpublished undergraduate thesis, Harvard University, 1973.

Silver, P. F. Attitudes Toward Sex Role Differentiation in Education. Implications for Title IX Implementation. Journal of Research and Development in Education, 1977, 10(2), 26-35.

Smith, M. P. He Only Does It to Annoy. In S. Anderson (ed.), Sex Differences and Discrimination in Education. Worthington, OH: Charles A. Jones, 1972, 28-43.

Spaulding, J. What Does Education Do to Women? Sounds of Change: A Report in Counseling and Programming for Women's Career Opportunities. Los Angeles: University of California, 1974, 85-86.

Spiegel, J. Continuing Education for Women. A Selected Annotated Bibliography. Washington, D. C.: Business and Professional Women's Foundation, 1967.

Sports. On Campus with Women. 1977, June, 17, 8. Washington, D. C.: Project on the Status and Education of Women, Association of American Colleges.

Stacey, J., Béreaud, S., and Daniels, J. (eds.). And Jill Came Tumbling After: Sexism in American Education. New York: Dell, 1974.

Starer, R., and Denmark, F. Discrimination Against Aspiring Women. In F. Denmark (ed.), Who Discriminates Against Women. Issue 15. Beverly Hills: Sage, 1974, 67-72. Also in International Journal of Group Tensions, 1974, March, 4(1), 65-70.

Steele, M. H. On Women Becoming in Education. Delta Kappa Gamma Bulletin, 1972, Spring, 38, 48-52.

_____. Women in Vocational Education. Project Baseline Supplemental Report. Flagstaff: Northern Arizona University, 1974.

Steiger, J. M. Vocational Preparation for Women: A Critical Analysis. State of Illinois, Board of Vocational and Technical Education, Research and Development Unit, 1974, December, 1-15.

_____, and Cooper, S. Vocational Preparation of Women. A report to the Secretary's Advisory Committee on the Rights and Responsibilities of Women. Washington, D. C.: U. S. Department of Health, Education and Welfare, 1975.

Stiles, L. J., and Nystrand, P. M. The Politics of Sex in Education. Educational Forum, 1974, 38(4), 431-440.

Stimpson, C. (Edited in conjunction with the Congressional Information Service) Discrimination Against Women: Congressional Hearing on Equal Rights in Education and Employment. New York: R. R. Bowker, 1973.

Strommer, D. W. Feminism and the Education of Women. Education Digest, 1976, May, 41, 39-42.

_____. Whither Thou Goest: Feminism and the Education of Women. Journal of the National Association for Women Deans, Administrators, and Counselors, 1976, Winter, 39(2), 81-89.

Sugnet, C. J. The Uncertain Progress of Affirmative Action. In Women on Campus: The Unfinished Liberation. New York: Change Magazine, 1975, 53-68.

Taylor, H. The Demands of Modern Society. In L. C. Muller and O. G. Muller (eds.), New Horizons for College Women. Washington, D. C.: Public Affairs Press, 1960, 88-100.

Thetford, M. The Case for the Career Book in Grades Five to Eight: A Feminist View. Elementary English, 1973, 50(7), 1059-1060+

Thompson, J. K. Fighting Discrimination: Up Against the Ivied Wall. Social Work, 1976, November, 21(6), 506-511.

Tibbetts, S. L. Sex Role Stereotyping in the Lower Grades: Part of the Solution. Journal of Vocational Behavior, 1975, 6, 255-261.

_____. Elementary Schools: Do They Stereotype or Feminize? Journal of the National Association for Women Deans, Administrators, and Counselors, 1976, Fall, 40(1), 27-33.

Tidball, M. E. Perspective on Academic Women and Affirmative Action. Educational Record, 1973, 54, 130-135.

Tilly, C. H. Reflections on the Future of Universities and of University Women. In Women on Campus: 1970: Proceedings of the Symposium. Ann Arbor: University of Michigan, Center for the Continuing Education of Women, 1970, 50-55.

Tinsley, A., Reuben, E., and Crothers, D. Academic Women, Sex Discrimination and the Law. MLA Commission on the Status of Women, 1975.

Title IX, Public Law 92-318. Education Amendments of 1972. 1972, June 23.

Title IX Rules. Guideposts, 1974, September, 28, 17(2), 6.

Tittle, C. K., Saario, T. N., and Denker, E. R. Women in Educational Research: Their Status from Student to Employee. Educational Researcher, 1975, October, 4(9), 15-24.

Tobias, S. Female Studies: Its Origins, Its Organization and Prospect. Paper distributed at the Modern Language Association meeting, New York City, 1970.

_____. The Case for Women's Studies. Connecticut Conference on the Status of Women. 51% Minority. Washington, D.C.: National Education Association, 1972, 17-21.

_____. Sexual Politics in the Classroom. In Sex Role Stereotyping in the Schools. Washington, D.C.: National Education Association, 1973, 31-35.

Tompkins, P. Change and Challenge for the Educated Woman. Saturday Review, 1963, May 18, 46, 69-70+.

Toward a Nonsexist School. American Education, 1977, April, 13, 7-9.

Trecker, J. L. Woman's Place Is in the Curriculum. Saturday Review, 1971, October 16, 54, 83-86+.

Trippot, L. Elementary Education--A Man's World. Instructor, 1968, November, 78(3), 50-52.

Trow, J. J. Higher Education for Women. Improving College and University Teaching, 1972, Winter, 20(1), 19-20.

Truex, D. Focus on Feminine Ferment. Journal of College Student Personnel, 1970, 11(5), 323-331.

_____. Education of Women, the Student Personnel Profession, and the New Feminism. Journal of the National Association of Women Deans and Counselors, 1971, Fall, 35(1), 13-20.

Tuck, M.G. The Effect of Different Factors on the Level of Academic Achievement in England and Wales. Social Science Research, 1974, June, 3(2), 141-149.

Ulrich, C. But I Am My Body: Schools and Physical Survival. Education for Survival. Final Report. Sex Role Stereotypes Project. Washington, D.C.: National Education Association, 1973.

Useem, R.H. What Does Society Expect Higher Education to Do for Women: Who Knows and Who Cares? Washington, D.C.: National Education Association, 1966.

Van Alstyne, C., and Withers, J.S. Women and Minorities in Administration of Higher Education Institutions: Employment Patterns and Salary Comparisons. Washington, D.C.: College and University Personnel Association, 1977.

Verheyden-Hilliard, M.E. Cinderella Doesn't Live Here Anymore. Womanpower, 1975, November, 34-37. Also reprint from KNOW, Inc., P.O. Box 86031, Pittsburgh, PA 15221.

_____. Getting Ready to Go: Not Propriety but Right. Educational Horizons, 1975, Spring, 53(3), 138-141.

_____. A Handbook for Workshops on Sex Equality in Education. Washington, D. C.: American Personnel and Guidance Association, 1975.

_____. The Sexist Humanist and the Oppression of Girls. The Humanist Educator, 1976, June, 14(4), 142-148.

Vetter, L., and Sethney, B. J. Women in the Workforce: Development and Field Testing of Curriculum Materials. Available from ERIC (ED072175), 1971.

Vriend, T. J. The Community College in the Career Development of Women. In Facilitating Career Development for Girls and Women. Washington, D. C.: National Vocational Guidance Association, 1975, 67-70.

Wanted, More Women in Higher Education. Science News, 1973, September 22, 104, 182.

Watkins, B. More Women Coming Back to Campus. The Chronicle of Higher Education, 1974, 9(14), 6.

Watts, J. Married Women Among Pupils; Effects of Higher Leaving Age. The Times (London) Educational Supplement, 1967, October 6, 2733, 705.

Weitzman, L. J. Legal Requirements, Structures, and Strategies for Eliminating Sex Discrimination in Academe. In E. Wasserman, A. Y. Lewin, and L. H. Bleiweis (eds.), Women in Academia: Evolving Policies Toward Equal Opportunities. New York: Praeger, 1975, 45-81.

Wells, J., and Magruder, H. Education Programs for Mature Women. Education Digest, 1972, January, 37(5), 42-45.

Wernick, W., Tiedeman, D., Eddy, J., and Bosdell, B. A Career Education Primer for Educators: With a Bibliography of ERIC Career Education Literature. Available from ERIC (ED-078216), 1975.

Wertheimer, B. Into the Mainstream: Equal Educational Opportunity for Working Women. Journal of Research and Development in Education, 1977, 10(4), 61-76.

West, A. G. (ed.). Report on Sex Bias in the Public Schools. New York: National Organization for Women, Education Committee, 1971.

Westervelt, E. WOW: A Model for Encouraging Women's Potential. American Association of University Women Journal, 1970, January, 63(2), 69-76.

_____. Femininity in American Women: The Influence of Education. Journal of the National Association of Women Deans and Counselors, 1971, Fall, 35, 2-12.

──────. A Tide in the Affairs of Women: The Psychological Impact of Feminism on Educated Women. The Counseling Psychologist, 1973, 4(1), 3-26.

──────. Barriers to Women's Participation in Postsecondary Education: A Review of Research and Commentary as of 1973-74. Washington, D.C.: U.S. Office of Education, 1975. Also available from ERIC (ED111256), 1975.

──────, and Fixter, D. Women's Higher and Continuing Education: An Annotated Bibliography with Selected References on Related Aspects of Women's Lives. New York: College Entrance Examination Board, 1971.

White, B.C. The Inter-American Specialized Conference on the Integral Education of Women. Journal of the National Association for Women Deans, Administrators, and Counselors, 1974, Winter, 37(2), 94-96.

Wigney, T. The Education of Women and Girls in a Changing Society--A Selected Bibliography with Annotations. Educational Research Series No. 36. Toronto: University of Toronto, Ontario College of Education, Department of Educational Research, 1965.

Wild, C.L. Statistical Issues Raised by Title IX Requirements on Admission Procedures. Journal of the National Association for Women Deans, Administrators, and Counselors, 1977, Winter, 40, 53-56.

Wilkerson, M.B. Information, Research, and Counseling: The Women's Center at Berkeley. Public Affairs Report, 1975, June, 16, 1-6.

Williams, K.L., Parks, B.J., and Finley, C.J. Measures of Educational Equity for Women: A Research Monograph. Palo Alto, CA: American Institutes for Research, 1977.

Willson, N. Until Now. English Journal, 1976, May, 65(5), 8-10.

Winch, R.F., and Thrash, P.A. Aspects of College Experience and Their Relevance to the Activities of Later Life: A Story of 740 Northwestern Alumnae. Journal of the National Association of Women Deans and Counselors, 1963, June, 26, 30-37.

Wirtenberg, T.J., and Nakamura, C.Y. Education: Barrier or Boon to Changing Occupational Roles of Women? Journal of Social Issues, 1976, 32(3), 165-179.

Women and Education. Special Issue. School Review, 1972, February, 80(2).

Women Around the World. The Annals of the American Academy of Political and Social Science, 1968, January.

Women in Education. Special Issue. Edcentric, 1971, December, 3.

Women on Campus: 1970--A Symposium. Ann Arbor: University of Michigan, Center for Continuing Education of Women, 1970.

Women on Campus: The Unfinished Liberation. New York: Change Magazine, 1975.

Women's Bureau. Plans for Widening Women's Educational Opportunities. Washington, D. C.: Employment Standards Administration, n. d.

_____. Expanding Opportunities for Girls. Washington, D. C.: U. S. Department of Labor, 1970.

_____. Continuing Education Programs and Services for Women. Washington, D. C.: U. S. Department of Labor, 1971.

_____. Continuing Education for Women: Current Developments. Washington, D. C.: U. S. Department of Labor, 1974.

_____. Trends in Educational Attainment of Women. Washington, D. C.: U. S. Department of Labor. Yearly reports.

Women's Centers, Where Are They? Washington, D. C.: Project on the Status and Education of Women, Association of American Colleges, 1975.

Women's Equity Action League. Facts About Women in Education. Available from WEAL, 1821 National Press Bldg., Washington, D. C. 20045, 1975.

Women's Sports. San Mateo, CA: Women's Sports Publishing Co., Vol. 1 published 1974. Continuing monthly publication covering women in sports.

Woodring, P. Sexism on the Campus. Saturday Review, 1970, May 16, 53, 80+.

Yates, B., Werner, S., Rosen, D. (eds.). We'll Do It Ourselves: Combatting Sexism in Education. Lincoln: Nebraska Curriculum Development Center, University of Nebraska, 1974.

Yee, A. H. Are the Schools a "Feminized Society?" Educational Leadership, 1973, 31(2), 128-133.

Zimmer, T. A. Sexism in Higher Education: A Cross-national Analysis. Pacific Sociological Review, 1975, January, 18, 55-67.

Zimmerman, B. B. Jack and Jill: This Is the World That Jack

Built: And Jill Came Tumbling After. Livermore, CA: Status of Women Committee, California State Division of the American Association of University Women, 1972.

Zinberg, D. College: When the Future Becomes the Present. In R. B. Kundsin (ed.), Women and Success: The Anatomy of Achievement. New York: William Morrow, 1974, 129-137.

Zwerdling, D. Womanpower Problem: Sex Discrimination on Campus. New Republic, 1971, March 20, 164, 11-13.

B. STUDENTS

Abramowitz, S. I., and Abramowitz, C. V. Sex Role Psychodynamics in Psychotherapy Supervision. American Journal of Psychotherapy, 1976, October, 30(4), 583-592.

Adams, G. R., and LaVoie, J. C. Effect of Student's Sex, Conduct, and Facial Attractiveness on Teacher Expectancy. Education, 1974, Fall, 93, 76-83.

Adams, P. W. The Effect of the Life Career Simulation Game Upon Decision Making Processes of Sophomore High School Students. Unpublished doctoral dissertation, University of South Dakota, 1971.

Albjerg, M. H. Why Do Bright Girls Not Take Stiff Courses? Educational Forum, 1961, January, 25, 141-144.

Alexander, K. L., and Eckland, B. K. Sex Differences in the Educational Attainment Process. American Sociological Review, 1974, 39(5), 668-682.

_____, and _____. High School Context, College Quality, and Educational Attainment: Institutional Constraints in Educational Stratification. Center for Social Organization of Schools Report, Johns Hopkins University, 1976, July, 214.

Alpert, J. L., and Hummel-Rossi, B. Differences in Teacher Behavior Toward Boys and Girls in Third Grade Classrooms. Educational Research Quarterly, 1976, Fall, 1(3), 29-39.

Angrist, S. S. The Impact of Higher Education on Women. Paper prepared for the School of Urban and Public Affairs, Carnegie-Mellon University, 1970.

Arlow, P., and Froschl, M. Women in the High School Curriculum. Women's Studies Newsletter, 1975, 3(3,4,), 12-22.

Arnold, R. D. The Achievement of Boys and Girls Taught by Men and Women Teachers. Elementary School Journal, 1968, 68(7), 367-372.

Asher, S. R., and Gottman, J. M. Sex of Teacher and Student Reading Achievement. Paper presented at the American Educational Research Association meeting, April 1972.

_____, and _____. Sex of Teacher and Student Reading Achievement. Journal of Educational Psychology, 1973, October, 65, 168-171.

Astin, A. W. Differential College Effects on the Motivation of Talented Students to Obtain the PhD. Journal of Educational Psychology, 1963, 54(1), 63-71.

_____. Identification, Motivation, and Training of Talented Students. School and Society, 1964, April 18, 92(2243), 186-189.

Astin, H. S. Preparing Women for Careers in Science and Technology. Paper presented at the Massachusetts Institute of Technology Conference on Women in Science and Technology, May 1973.

Attwood, C. L. Women in Fellowship and Training Programs. Washington, D. C.: Project on the Status and Education of Women, Association of American Colleges, 1972.

Badner, G., Jr. Hey, Coach! Can Betty Sue and I Get in the Game Now? Pennsylvania State Board Ruling. Pennsylvania School Journal, 1974, December, 123, 68-70+.

Baggett, L. R. A Science Career for You? National Business Woman, 1960, May, 39(5), 6-7+.

Bagley, M. T. The Effects of Teacher Expectations and Verbal Interaction on Academic Achievement of First Grade Children. Unpublished doctoral dissertation, University of Texas, Austin. Dissertation Abstracts International, 1975, February, 35(8-A), 5162.

Baird, L. L. Entrance of Women to Graduate and Professional Education. Paper presented at the American Psychological Association Convention, Washington, D. C., 1976.

Baum, O. E., and Herring, C. The Pregnant Psychotherapist in Training: Some Preliminary Findings and Impressions. American Journal of Psychiatry, 1975, April, 132(4), 419-422.

Becker, M., Katasaky, M., and Seidel, H. A Follow-Up Study of Unsuccessful Applicants to Medical Schools. Journal of Medical Education, 1973, 48, 991-1001.

Benedek, E. P. Training the Woman Resident to Be a Psychiatrist.

American Journal of Psychiatry, 1973, October, 130(10), 1131-1135.

Bengelsdorf, W. Women's Stake in Low Tuition. Washington, D. C.: American Association of State Colleges and Universities, 1974. Also available from ERIC (ED096933), 1974.

Bernard, J., and Holmstrom, E. Women Entering College, 1970: Pioneers and Traditionalists. Unpublished manuscript, 1973.

Bernstein, J. The Elementary School: Training Ground for Sex Role Stereotypes. Personnel and Guidance Journal, 1972, October, 51(2), 97-104.

Biber, H., Miller, L. B., and Dyer, J. L. Feminization in Preschool. Developmental Psychology, 1972, 7, 86.

Bickel, P. J., Hammel, E. A., and O'Connell, J. W. Sex Bias in Graduate Admissions: Data from Berkeley. Science, 1975, 187, 398-404.

Bikman, M. Where Do All the Women PhD's Go? In S. Stambler (ed.), Women's Liberation: Blueprint for the Future. New York: Charter Communications, 105-109.

Birk, J., and Tanney, M. Career Exploration for High School Women: A Model. Paper presented at the American Personnel and Guidance Association Regional Convention, Atlanta, 1973.

Bisconti, A. S., and Astin, H. S. Undergraduate and Graduate Study in Scientific Fields. ACE Research Reports, Washington, D. C.: American Council on Education, 1973, 8(3).

Bishop, J. F. Profile: The Woman in Liberal Arts. Journal of College Placement, 1965, April, 25, 37+.

Bjorkquist, D. C. Women and Industrial Education. School Shop, 1973, March, 32, 58-62.

Blaska, B. Women in Academe--The Need for Support Groups. Journal of the National Association for Women Deans, Administrators, and Counselors. 1976, Summer, 39(4), 173-178.

Blaufarb, M. Equal Opportunity for Girls in Athletics. Today's Education, 1974, November, 63(4), 52-55.

Blum, L. The New "Women in Science" Program Is Booming with Students. Mills Quarterly, 1975, Summer, 14-16.

Bod and Man at Yale; Charge of Sex Discrimination for Tolerating Sexual Coercion of Female Students by Male Teachers. Time, 1977, August 8, 110, 52-53.

Boutwell, W. D. What's Happening in Education? Sex Differences in Children's Learning Behavior. PTA Magazine, 1963, June, 57, 25.

Brager, G., and Michael, J. A. The Sex Distribution in Social Work: Causes and Consequences. Social Casework, 1969, 50(10), 595-601.

Brandenburg, J. B. The Needs of Women Returning to School. Personnel and Guidance Journal, 1974, September, 53(1), 11-18.

Brandt, L. J., and Hayden, M. E. Male and Female Teacher Attitudes as a Function of Students' Ascribed Motivation and Performance Levels. Journal of Educational Psychology, 1974, 66(3), 309-314.

Brodsky, A. M. Graduate Women in Psychology in the Southeast. Report to the Committee on the Status of Women of the Southeastern Psychological Association, Southeastern Psychological Association Convention, New Orleans, 1973.

_____. Women as Graduate Students. American Psychologist, 1974, 29, 523-526.

Brody, C. Do Instructional Materials Reinforce Sex Stereotyping? Educational Leadership, 1973, November, 3, 120.

Brookhart, R. A. An Analysis of the Changing Problems of a Business Education Program in the Liberal Arts College, with Special Emphasis on the Problems of the Preparation of Women for Teaching and Business Employment. Dissertation Abstracts, 1967, 28(1-A), 29. Unpublished doctoral dissertation, University of Iowa, 1967. Also available from ERIC (ADG67-09045), 1967.

Brookshire, M. L., and Lumsden, H. H. Women, Jobs and Mobility; Attitudes of College Seniors, Graduate Students and Recruiters. Journal of College Placement, 1975, Spring, 35, 75-79.

Bull, J. High School Women: Oppression and Liberation. In S. Stambler (ed.), Women's Liberation: Blueprint for the Future. New York: Charter Communications, 95-105.

Bunker, J. P., and Pool, J. G. The Case for More Women in Medicine: The Stanford Program. New England Journal of Medicine, 1971, 53, 285.

Burstyn, J. Educational Experiences for Women at Carnegie-Mellon University: A Brief History. Western Pennsylvania Historical Magazine, 1973, 56, 141-153.

Bushnell, J. H. Student Culture at Vassar. In N. Sanford (ed.),

The American College. New York: John Wiley, 1962, 489-514.

Cahill, N. J. Women Researchers Analyze Education, Job Barriers. Science, 1977, December 2, 198, 917-918.

Campbell, M. A. Why Would a Girl Go into Medicine? Old Westbury, New York: The Feminist Press, 1973.

Cancian, F. The Stanford Woman in 1972. (Committee on Education and Employment of Women in the University.) Unpublished manuscript, Stanford University, 1972.

Canty, E. M. Effects of Women's Studies Courses on Women's Attitudes and Goals. Paper presented at the American Psychological Association Convention, San Francisco, 1977.

Carlsen, M. L. A Four-Year Retrospective View of the Educational Experience of a Group of Mature Women Undergraduate Students. Unpublished doctoral dissertation, University of Washington. Dissertation Abstracts International, 1974, July, 35(1-A), 153.

Carnegie Commission on Higher Education. Women as Undergraduates. In Opportunities for Women in Higher Education: Their Current Participation, Prospects for the Future, and Recommendations for Action. New York: McGraw-Hill, 1973, 61-80.

_____. Women Entering Higher Education. In Opportunities for Women in Higher Education: Their Current Participation, Prospects for the Future, and Recommendations for Action. New York: McGraw-Hill, 1973, 35-60.

_____. Women in Graduate and Professional Schools. In Opportunities for Women in Higher Education: Their Current Participation, Prospects for the Future, and Recommendations for Action. New York: McGraw-Hill, 1973, 81-108.

Cascario, E. F. The Male Teacher and Reading Achievement of First-Grade Boys and Girls. Unpublished doctoral dissertation, Lehigh University, 1971.

Casserly, P. L. An Assessment of Factors Affecting Female Participation in Advanced Placement Programs in Mathematics, Chemistry and Physics. Report. Washington, D. C. : National Science Foundation, 1975.

Centra, J. A. Women, Men, and the Doctorate. Princeton, NJ: Educational Testing Service, 1974.

Chalmers, E. L., Jr. Achieving Equity for Women in Higher Education Graduate Enrollment and Faculty Status. Journal of Higher Education, 1972, 43, 517-524.

Chandler, T. M. Factors Which Have Influenced Careers at Texas Woman's University. Unpublished doctoral dissertation, Texas Woman's University. American Doctoral Dissertation, 1971, 11(97), 218. Also available from ERIC (ADG02-366600), 1971.

Chang, T. S. Self-Concepts, Academic Achievement, and Teacher's Rating. Psychology in the Schools, 1976, January, 13(1), 111-113.

Chasen, B. Sex-Role Stereotyping and Prekindergarten Teachers. Elementary School Journal, 1974, 4, 220-235.

Cherry, L. Teacher-Child Verbal Interaction: An Approach to the Study of Sex Differences. In B. Thorne and N. Henley (eds.), Language and Sex: Differences and Dominance. Boston: Newbury House, 1975, 172-183.

Christensen, K. C., and Sedlacek, W. E. Differential Faculty Attitudes Toward Blacks, Females and Students in General. Counseling Center Research Report #13-72, College Park: University of Maryland, 1972.

Christensen, S., Melder, J., and Weisbrod, B. A. Factors Affecting College Attendance. Madison: University of Wisconsin, Institute for Research on Poverty, 1972.

Chu, D. Review of Research Concerning the Hypothesis that Strenuous Physical Activity Develops Masculine Traits in Women, and Therefore It Should Not Be Encouraged by Physical Educators. Physical Educator, 1972, December, 29, 195-197.

Clarke, G. F. Case Study: From Coed to M. D. Contact, 1972, Fall, 3(6), 19-22.

Clifford, M. M., and Walster, E. The Effect of Sex on College Admission, Work Evaluation, and Job Interviews. Journal of Experimental Education, 1972, Winter, 41(2), 1-5. Also in J. Pottker and A. Fishel (eds.), Sex Bias in the Schools--Research Evidence. Madison, NJ: Fairleigh Dickinson University Press, 1977, 335-343.

_____, and _____. The Effect of Physical Attractiveness on Teacher Expectations. Sociology of Education, 1973, Spring 46(2), 248-258.

Cole, D., Kraig, K., and Newcomb, A. Grade Expectations as a Function of Sex, Academic Discipline, and Sex of Instructor. Psychology of Women Quarterly, 1977, Summer, 1(4), 380-385.

Cooley, F. R. Women Doctoral Students: Differential Perceptions of Their Role Behavior in the Academic Environment. Unpublished doctoral dissertation, University of Wisconsin. Dissertation Abstracts International, 1970, June, 30(12-A), 5228-5229.

Cottle, T. J. (ed.). College Woman. In College: Reward and Betrayal. Chicago: University of Chicago Press, 1977, 128-135.

Crase, D. Question of Athletic Competition for Elementary School Age Girls. Journal of Physical Education, 1976, September, 73, 13+.

Crosman, A. M., and Gustav, A. Academic Success of Older People. Psychology in the Schools, 1966, July, 3(3), 256-258.

Cross, K. P. College Women: A Research Description. Journal of the National Association of Women Deans and Counselors, 1968, 31, 12-21.

_____. The Undergraduate Woman. Research Report Number 5. Washington, D. C.: American Association for Higher Education, 1971, March.

_____. The Woman Student. In W. T. Furniss and P. A. Graham, (eds.), Women in Higher Education. Washington, D. C.: American Council on Education, 1972, 29-49.

_____. Women Want Equality in Higher Education. The Research Reporter, 1972, 7(4), 5-8.

_____. Women as New Students. In Beyond the Open Door: New Students to Higher Education. San Francisco: Jossey-Bass, 1974, 133-154. Also in M. T. S. Mednick et al. (eds.), Women and Achievement: Social and Motivational Analyses: New York: Halsted Press, 1975, 339-354.

Crovitz, E. Comparisons of Male and Female Physicians Associate Program Applicants. Journal of Medical Education, 1975, 50(7), 672-676.

Dale, R. R., and Miller, P. M. Academic Progress of University Students from Co-Educational and Single-Sex Schools. The British Journal of Educational Psychology, 1972, November, 42, 317-319.

Dalton, S., Anastasiow, M., and Brigman, S. L. The Relationship of Underachievement and College Attrition. Journal of College Student Personnel, 1977, November, 18(6), 501-505.

Darley, J. G. Promise and Performance: A Study of Ability and Achievement in Higher Education. Berkeley: University of California, Center for the Study of Higher Education, 1962.

Darling, R. W. College Women: Do They Fit the Research Description? Journal of the National Association of Women Deans and Counselors, 1968, Fall, 32, 22-25.

Davidson, H. H., and Lang, G. Children's Perceptions of Their

Teachers' Feelings Toward Them Related to Self-Perception, School Achievement, and Behavior. Journal of Experimental Education, 1960, December, 29(2), 107-118.

Davis, J. Great Aspirations: The Graduate School Plans of America's College Seniors. Chicago: Aldine, 1964.

Davis, L. Your Future Is Now; College Education. Vogue, 1977, August, 167, 94.

Davis, O., and Slobodian, J. Teacher Behavior Toward Boys and Girls in First Grade Reading Instruction. American Educational Research Journal, 1967, 4, 261-269.

Davis, S. O. Factors Related to the Persistence of Women in a Four-Year Institute of Technology. Unpublished doctoral dissertation, University of Minnesota, 1973.

_____. A Researcher's-Eye View: Women Students, Technical Majors, and Retention. IEEE Transactions on Education, 1975, February, E-18(1), 25-29.

_____. Women in Technology: Myths, Realities, and Action. In D. Wark and E. G. Joselyn (eds.), Student Counseling Bureau Review: Women in Transition. Minneapolis: University of Minnesota, Student Counseling Bureau, 1975, September, 26(1), 67-72.

DeCrow, K. What You Are Taught in School About Being a Woman. In The Young Woman's Guide to Liberation: Alternatives to the Half-Life While the Choice Is Still Yours. New York: Bobbs-Merrill, 1971, 40-61.

Dement, A. L. The College Woman as a Science Major. Journal of Higher Education, 1962, December, 33(9), 487-490.

_____. What Brings and Holds Women Science Majors? College and University, 1963, Fall, 39, 44-50.

Denise, Sister Mary. Role of the Intellectual Girl. America, 1961, April, 105(4), 191-192.

Denmark, F., and Guttentag, M. The Effect of College Attendance on Mature Women: Changes in Self-Concept and Evaluation of Student Role. Journal of Social Psychology, 1966, 69(1), 155-158.

Dickerson, K. G. Are Female College Students Influenced by the Expectations They Perceive Their Faculty and Administration Have for Them? Journal of the National Association for Women Deans, Administrators, and Counselors, 1974, 37(4), 167-172.

Dobbert, M. L. Sexual Complementarity in the Social Structure of

Schools. Council on Anthropology and Education Quarterly, 1975, August, 6(3), 9-13.

Donnalley, M. J. A Study of the Factors Which Influence Women College Students to Withdraw Before Completing Their Degree Requirements. Unpublished doctoral dissertation, University of Virginia. Dissertation Abstracts, 1967, 27(8-A), 2388.

Doty, B. A. Some Academic Characteristics of the Mature Coed. Journal of Educational Research, 1967, December, 61, 163-165.

Douvan, E. The Role of Models in Women's Professional Development. Psychology of Women Quarterly, 1976, 1, 5-20.

Dresselhaus, M. S. Some Personal Views on Engineering Education for Women. IEEE Transactions on Education, 1975, February, E-18(1), 30-34.

Dube, W. F. Woman Students in U. S. Medical Schools: Past and Present Trends. Journal of Medical Education, 1973, 48, 186-189.

Dunkle, M. C., and Sandler, B. Sex Discrimination Against Students: Implications of Title IX of the Education Amendments of 1972. Inequality in Education, 1974, October, 18, 12-35.

Dusek, J. B., and O'Connell, E. J. Teacher Expectancy Effects on the Achievement Test Performance of Elementary School Children. Journal of Educational Psychology, 1973, December, 65, 371-377.

Dyer, S. E. The Flow Through the System: Differential Levels of Educational Attainment for Women and Minorities. Symposium presentation at the American Psychological Association Convention, San Francisco, 1977.

Egin, A. W., Leppaluoto, J., and Fodor, I. Male and Female-- The Mutually Disadvantaged: The School Psychologist's Role in Expanding Options for Both Sexes. School Psychology Digest, 1973, 2(3), 2-10.

Eiden, L. J. Trends in Female Degree Recipients. American Education, 1976, November, 12, back cover.

Ellis, J. R. The Effects of Same Sex Class Organization on Junior High School Students' Academic Achievement, Self-Discipline, Self-Concept, Sex Role Identification and Attitudes Toward School. Final Report. Washington, D. C.: Office of Education, 1968. Also available from ERIC (ED035939), 1970.

_____, and Peterson, J. L. Effects of Same Sex Class Organization on Junior High School Students' Academic Achievement, Self-Discipline, Self-Concept, Sex Role Identification, and Attitude Toward School. Journal of Educational Research, 1971, July, 64, 455-464.

Elmore, P. B., and LaPointe, K. A. Effects of Teacher Sex and Student Sex on the Evaluation of College Instructors. Journal of Educational Psychology, 1974, 66, 386-389.

Elovson, A. C. The Reported Impact of Women's Studies Courses on Students' Lives. Symposium presentation at the American Psychological Association Convention, San Francisco, 1977.

Engineering Add Lib. Urbana-Champaign: University of Illinois, College of Engineering, 1973.

Falbo, T. The Attributional Explanation of Academic Performance by Kindergarteners and Their Teachers. Proceedings of the 81st Annual Convention of the American Psychological Association, 1973, 8(1), 123-124.

_____. Achievement Attributions of Kindergarteners. Developmental Psychology, 1975, 11, 529-530.

Farley, J. Graduate Women: Career Aspirations and Desired Family Size. American Psychologist, 1970, 25, 1099-1100.

_____. Coeducation and College Women. Cornell Journal of Social Relations, 1973, Spring, 9(1), 87-97.

Faunce, P. S. Academic Careers of Gifted Women. Personnel and Guidance Journal, 1967, 46(3), 252-257.

_____. Withdrawal of Academically Gifted Women. Journal of College Student Personnel, 1968, May, 9(3), 171-176.

Feldman, K. A., and Newcomb, T. M. The Impact of College on Students. San Francisco: Jossey-Bass, 1969.

Feldman, S. D. Escape from the Doll's House: Women in Graduate and Professional School Education. Unpublished doctoral dissertation, University of Washington, 1972. Dissertation Abstracts International, 1972, 33(5-A), 2509. Also available from ERIC (ADG72-28596), 1972.

_____. Impediment or Stimulant? Marital Status and Graduate Education. American Journal of Sociology, 1973, 78(4), 982-994.

_____. Escape from the Doll's House: Women in Graduate and Professional School Education. New York: McGraw-Hill, 1974.

Female College Students Risking Unemployment. Intellect, 1977, January, 105, 211.

Fennema, E. Mathematics Learning and the Sexes: A Review. Journal for Research in Mathematics Education, 1974, 5, 126-139.

_____. Sex Differences in Mathematics Learning: Why? The Elementary School Journal, 1974, 75, 183-190.

_____. What Difference Does It Make? (If Boys Learn Math Better Than Girls). Wisconsin Teacher of Mathematics, 1974, 25, 6-7.

_____. Women and Girls in the Public Schools: Defeat or Liberation? In J. I. Roberts (ed.), Beyond Intellectual Sexism: A New Woman, A New Morality. New York: David McKay, 1976, 343-352.

_____, and Sherman, J. A. Selected Cognitive and Affective Factors Related to Mathematics Achievement by Males and Females. Paper presented at the American Association for the Advancement of Science meeting, Boston, February 1976.

Ferber, M. A., and Huber, J. A. Sex of Student and Instructor: A Study of Student Bias. American Journal of Sociology, 1975, 80, 949-963.

Fields, C. M. Women Seeking Greater Shares of Fellowships. The Chronicle of Higher Education, 1972, December 11, 7, 1+.

Flanagan, J. C. Project Talent: The American High School Student. Pittsburgh: University of Pittsburgh Press, 1964.

Fley, J. The Time to Be Properly Vicious. Journal of the National Association for Women Deans, Administrators, and Counselors, 1974, 37(2), 53-58.

Follett, C. F., Hendel, D. D., and Klohs, W. L. A. Men and Women in the College of Veterinary Medicine: Their Comment About Student Services. Minneapolis: University of Minnesota, Measurement Services Center, 1975.

Forslund, M. A., and Hull, R. E. Sex-Role Identification and Achievement at Preadolescence. Rocky Mountain Social Science Journal, 1972, January, 9(1), 105-110.

_____, and _____. Teacher Sex and Achievement Among Elementary School Pupils. Education, 1974, Fall, 95(1), 87-89.

Fox, G. L. The Woman Graduate Student in Sociology. Women on Campus: 1970--A Symposium. Ann Arbor: University of Michigan, Center for Continuing Education of Women, 1970, 32-35.

_____. Student Careers of Graduate Student Women in Sociology at an Elite Department. Available from ERIC (ED074900), 1973.

Fox, L. H. Career Interests and Mathematical Acceleration for

Girls. Paper presented at the American Psychological Association Convention, Chicago, 1975.

_____. Facilitating the Development of Mathematical Talent in Young Women. Unpublished doctoral dissertation, Johns Hopkins University. Dissertation Abstracts International, 1975, January, 35(7-B), 3553.

_____. Changing Behaviors and Attitudes of Gifted Girls. Paper presented at the American Psychological Association Convention, Washington, D.C., 1976.

_____. Mathematics Education for Women: Implications for Change. Paper presented to the American Association for the Advancement of Science meeting, Boston, February 1976.

_____. Women and the Career Relevance of Mathematics and Science. School Science and Mathematics, 1976, April, 76, 347-353.

Frank, H.H., and Katcher, A.H. Perceptions of Freshwomen Dental and Medical Students by Their Freshman Peers. In M.E. Lockheed (ed.), Research in Woman's Acquisition of Professional and Leadership Roles. Princeton, NJ: Educational Testing Service, 1975, 75-96.

_____, and _____. The Socialization of Freshwomen Medical Students. Paper presented at the American Educational Research Association meeting, Washington, D.C., 1975. Also available from ERIC (ED106728), 1975.

Frazier, N., and Sadker, M. Living Down to Expectations: The High School Years. In Sexism in School and Society. New York: Harper & Row, 1973, 114-143.

_____, and _____. School Against Boys! School Against Girls! The Instructor, 1973, 83(7), 92-97.

Freedman, M.B. The Role of the Educated Woman: An Empirical Study of the Attitudes of a Group of College Women. Journal of College Student Personnel, 1965, 6, 145-155.

Fried, F.E. Women in Medicine: The Training Years. Journal of Operational Psychiatry, 1974, Spring/Summer, 5(2), 101-102.

Friskey, E.A. College Women and Careers. AAUP Bulletin, 1974, September, 60, 317-319.

Frohreich, D.S. Programs for Women in Engineering--Directory. West Lafayette, IN: Purdue University, Department of Freshman Engineering, 1974.

_____. How Colleges Try to Attract More Women Students. IEEE Transactions on Education, 1975, February, E-18(1), 41-46.

Furst, E. J., Raygor, A. W., and Crofoot, A. P. Basic Motivation and Concept of Nursing as Chosen Profession. Journal of Psychology, 1962, 54(1), 85-100.

Gilliland, L. L. Internal Versus External Locus of Control and the High-Level Athletic Competitor. Perceptual and Motor Skills, 1974, August, 39(1), 38.

Goad, R., and Plotsky, F. A. Through The Maze: A Graduate Women's Workshop to Explore Professional and Personal Issues. Journal of the National Association for Women Deans, Administrators, and Counselors, 1976, Spring, 39(3), 116-119.

Goebes, D. D., and Shore, M. F. Behavioral Expectations of Students as Related to the Sex of the Teacher. Psychology in the Schools, 1975, April, 12, 222-224.

Goldberg, P. Misogyny and the College Girl. Paper presented at the Eastern Psychological Association meeting, Boston, 1967.

Goldstein, M. Z. Preventive Mental Health Efforts for Women Medical Students. Journal of Medical Education, 1975, March, 50(3), 289-291.

Good, T. L., Sikes, J. N., and Brophy, J. E. Effects of Teacher Sex and Student Sex on Classroom Interaction. Journal of Educational Psychology, 1973, August, 65(1), 74-87.

Goodwin, G. C. The Woman Doctoral Recipient: A Study of the Difficulties Encountered in Pursuing Graduate Degrees. Unpublished doctoral dissertation, Oklahoma State University. Dissertation Abstracts International, 1967, 27(A), 4038.

_____. The Woman Doctoral Recipient: Difficulties in Pursuing Graduate Degrees. Symposium presentation at the American Psychological Association Convention, San Francisco, 1977.

Graduate and Professional Education of Women. Washington, D. C.: American Association of University Women, 1974.

Grebner, F. Sex as a Parameter of Athletic Eligibility. Physical Educator, 1974, December, 31, 205-207.

Groszko, M., and Morgenstern, R. Institutional Discrimination: The Case of Achievement-Oriented Women in Higher Education. International Journal of Group Tensions, 1974, 4(1), 82-92. Also in F. Denmark (ed.), Who Discriminates Against Women? Issue 15. Beverly Hills: Sage Publications, 1974, 84-94.

Group for the Advancement of Psychiatry. College and After. In The Educated Woman: Prospects and Problems. New York: Scribner's, 1975, 82-112.

_____. Expectations of Women in College. In The Educated Women: Prospects and Problems. New York: Scribner's, 1975, 35-51.

Groves, R., and Daly, J. T. Girls on Boys Teams. Journal of Health, Physical Education, and Recreation, 1974, October, 45, 25-26.

Grumbine, C. Career Roles for Females in Psychology. In R. E. Hardy and J. G. Cull (eds.), Career Guidance for Young Women: Considerations in Planning Professional Careers. Springfield, IL: Charles C. Thomas, 1974, 112-131.

Grundy, B. L. Career Roles in Medicine. In R. E. Hardy and J. G. Cull (eds.), Career Guidance for Young Women: Considerations in Planning Professional Careers. Springfield, IL: Charles C. Thomas, 1974, 17-26.

Guttentag, M., and Bray, H. Teachers as Mediators of Sex-Role Standards. In A. G. Sargent (ed.), Beyond Sex Roles. St. Paul, MN: West, 1977, 395-411.

Guttman, M. A. J. Is the Gray Mare Only a Workhorse? Personnel and Guidance Journal, 1972, October, 51(2), 115-121.

Hands, S. L. An Evaluation of a Course for Women Directed Toward the Development of Self-Actualizing Life-Styles. Unpublished doctoral dissertation, University of Texas, Dallas. Dissertation Abstracts International, 1975, February, 35(8-A), 5117-5118.

Hanson, G. R., Cole, N. S., and Lamb, R. R. Sex Bias in Selective College Admissions. In J. Pottker and A. Fishel (eds.), Sex Bias in the Schools--Research Evidence. Madison, NJ: Fairleigh Dickinson University Press, 1977, 335-343.

Harkleroad, M. A. Selective Effect of Higher Education on Catholic Women's Career Orientations. Unpublished doctoral dissertation, Catholic University of America, 1973. Dissertation Abstracts International, 1973, 33(12-A), 7073. Also available from ERIC (ADG73-13061), 1973.

Harmon, L. W. Variables Related to Women's Persistence in Educational Plans. Journal of Vocational Behavior, 1972, 2, 143-153.

Harvard University. Preliminary Report on the Status of Women at Harvard. Cambridge, MA: Harvard University, 1970.

Hatch, D. D. Differential Impact of College on Males and Females. Women on Campus: 1970--A Symposium. Ann Arbor: University of Michigan, Center for Continuing Education of Women, 1970, 24-31.

Hayrynen, Y. P. The Flow of New Students to Different University Fields: Career Motivation, Educational Choice and Discriminating Effects of University Admission: A Study of Finnish Female Students. Annales Academiae Scientiarum Fennicae, 1970, B-168, 142.

Heist, P. A. A Commentary on the Motivation and Education of College Women. Journal of the National Association of Women Deans and Counselors, 1962, January, 25(2), 51-59.

Herman, M. H. Student Perceptions of the Need for a Women's Studies Program. College Student Journal, 1973, 7(3), 3-6.

Hilberman, E., Konanc, J., Perez-Reyes, M., Hunter, R., Scagnelli, J., and Sanders, S. Support Groups for Women in Medical School: A First-Year Program. Journal of Medical Education, 1975, September, 50, 867-875.

Hill, A. J., and Hipple, J. Recruitment and Retention of Undergraduate College Women. Journal of the National Association of Women Deans and Counselors, 1972, Winter, 35(2), 70-73.

Hitchman, G. S. The Professional Socialization of Women and Men in Two Canadian Graduate Schools. Unpublished doctoral dissertation, York University, Canada, 1976. Dissertation Abstracts International, 1976, 3(12-A), 7979. Also available from ERIC (ADG03-10605), 1976.

Hochman, L. M., and Nietfeld, C. R. Differences in Sources of Financing of Female and Male Michigan State University Graduate Students. Journal of College Student Personnel, 1977, 17(1), 55-60.

Hofer, B. Blueprint for Career Development; College Influences on the Role Development of Female Undergraduates. American Education, 1969, October, 5, back cover.

Hoffman, B. H. Co-eds in Rebellion. Ladies Home Journal, 1965, October, 82, 82-84+.

Hoffman, D. S., and Hoeflin, R. Freshman and Sophomore Women: What Do They Want Most in the Future? Journal of College Student Personnel, 1972, November, 13, 490-493.

Holliday, F. G. T. Failing the Girls? The Times (London) Educational Supplement, 1977, March 11, 3223, 40.

Holmstrom, E. I. Barriers to Women in Graduate School. In Graduate and Professional Education of Women. Washington, D. C.: American Association of University Women, 1974, 53-56.

_____. The New Pioneers: Women Engineering Students. Paper presented at the Cornell University College of Engineering Conference, Ithaca, NY, 1975.

_____, and Holmstrom, R. W. The Plight of the Woman Doctoral Student. American Educational Research Journal, 1974, Winter, 11(1), 1-17.

Horst, L. Women Students in Engineering: Current View. Paper presented at the American Psychological Association Convention, San Francisco, 1977.

Howe, F. (ed.). Women and the Power to Change. New York: McGraw-Hill, 1975.

Howell, M. C. What Medical Schools Teach About Women. New England Journal of Medicine, 1974, 291, 304-307.

Increase in Women Law Students. Intellect, 1974, Summer, 102, 489-490.

Istiphan, I. Role Expectations of American Undergraduate College Women in a Western Coeducational Institution. Unpublished doctoral dissertation, University of Southern California, 1962. Dissertation Abstracts International, 1963, 23(7), 2613. Also available from ERIC (ADG62-06068), 1962.

Jackson, P., and Lahaderne, H. Inequalities of Teacher-Pupil Contacts. Psychology in Schools, 1967, 4, 204-211.

Jacobs, A. D. Women in Law School: Structural Constraint and Personal Choice in the Formation of Professional Identity. Journal of Legal Education, 1972, 24, 462-472.

Jaeger, R. M., and Feijo, T. D. Race and Sex as Concomitants of Composite Halo in Teachers' Evaluative Rating of Pupils. Journal of Educational Psychology, 1975, April, 67, 226-237.

Janes, G. D. Student Perceptions, Parent Perceptions, and Teacher Perceptions of Student Abilities, Aspirations, Expectations, and Motivations: Their Relationship to Under- and Over-Achievement. Dissertation Abstracts International, 1971, March, 31(9-A), 4548-4549.

Jansen, D. G., Bonk, E. C., and Robb, G. P. Graduate Students in Education: A Comparison of Counselor, Supervisor, and Teacher Candidates. Counselor Education and Supervision, 1973, September, 13(1), 53-61.

Jenkins, E. K. The Perceived Institutional Barriers of Undergraduate Women Who Discontinued Their Education at a Southern Urban University. Unpublished doctoral dissertation, Georgia State University. Dissertation Abstracts International, 1975, October, 36(4-A), 2025-2026.

Johns Hopkins University. Career Patterns of Unaccepted Applicants to Medical School: A Case Study in Reactions to a

Blocked Career Pathway. Baltimore, MD: Office of Health Manpower Studies, 1975. Also available from ERIC (ED106448), 1975.

Johnson, D. G., and Hutchins, E. B. Doctor or Dropout? A Study of Medical Student Attrition. Journal of Medical Education, 1966, 41(1099), 1269.

_____, and Sedlacek, W. E. Retention by Sex and Race of the 1968-1972 U.S. Medical School Entrants. Journal of Medical Education, 1975, 50(10), 925-933.

Johnson, T. P. Girls on the Boys' Team: Equal Protection in School Athletics. NASSP Bulletin, 1974, October, 58, 55-65.

Kemer, B. J. A Study of the Relationship Between the Sex of the Student and the Assignment of Marks by Secondary School Teachers. Unpublished doctoral dissertation, Michigan State University, 1965.

Kenworthy, J., Koufacos, C., and Sherman, J. Women and Therapy: A Survey of Internship Programs. Psychology of Women Quarterly, 1976, 1(2), 125-137.

Kenyon, G. S. Explaining Sport Involvement. Paper presented at the Fall Conference of Eastern Association of Physical Education for College Women, Lake Placid, NY, October 1969.

Kidd, T. R., and Woodman, W. F. Sex and Orientations Toward Winning in Sport. Research Quarterly, 1975, December, 46, 476-483.

Kiehle, T. J., Bramble, J., and Mason, E. J. Teachers' Expectations: Ratings of Student Performance as Biased by Student Characteristics. Journal of Experimental Education, 1974, Fall, 43(1), 54-60.

Kirkbride, V. R. Project Lifeline Introduces College Women to Their Futures. Journal of the National Association of Women Deans and Counselors, 1966, Summer, 29, 174-176.

Knowles, L. W. Brenden Versus Independent District 742: Girl Athletes Get a Sporting Chance. Nation's Schools, 1973, March, 91(3), 38-39.

Koniorita, N. I. Self-Concept Measures as Related to Achievement in Nursing Education. Unpublished doctoral dissertation. Dissertation Abstracts International, 1972, June, 32(12-A), 6809.

Kramer, N. A. Discrimination and the Woman Law Student. Women on Campus: 1970--A Symposium. Ann Arbor: University of Michigan, Center for Continuing Education of Women, 1970, 39-41.

Lafevre, C. The Mature Woman as Graduate Student. School Review, 1972, February, 80(2), 281-297.

Lavine, T. Z. The Motive to Achieve Limited Success: The New Woman Law School Applicant. In W. T. Furniss and P. A. Graham (eds.), Women in Higher Education. Washington, D. C.: American Council on Education, 1974.

Lavoie, J. C., and Adams, G. R. Pygmalion in the Classroom: An Experimental Investigation of the Characteristics of Children on Teacher Expectancy. Paper presented at the Midwest Psychological Association Annual meeting, Chicago, May, 1973. Also available from ERIC (ED088973), 1974.

Lee, D. E., Wilson, B. D., and Quisenberry, D. J. Stereotypes of Academic Minorities. Perceptual and Motor Skills, 1975, June, 40(3), 947-952.

Leifer, A., and Lesser, G. The Development of Career Education in Young Children. Washington, D. C.: National Institute of Education, 1977.

Leland, C., and Lozoff, M. College Influences on the Role Development of Female Undergraduates. Stanford: Stanford University, Institute for the Study of Human Problems, 1969. Also available from ERIC (ED026975), 1969.

Levine, A. Forging a "Feminine Identity": Women in Four Professional Schools. American Journal of Psychoanalysis, 1975, 35, 63-67.

Levitin, T. E., and Chananie, J. D. Responses of Female Primary School Teachers to Sex-Typed Behaviors in Male and Female Children. Child Development, 1972, December, 43(4), 1309-1316.

Levy, B. B. Do Teachers Sell Girls Short? Today's Education, 1972, 61(9), 27-29.

_____. Do Schools Sell Girls Short? In J. Stacey et al. (eds.), And Jill Came Tumbling After: Sexism in American Education. New York: Dell, 1974, 142-146.

_____. Teachers' Judgments of Achievement-Related and Pupil Role Behaviors of Elementary School Girls and Boys. Unpublished doctoral dissertation, Columbia University. Dissertation Abstracts International, 1975, April, 35(10-B), 5085.

Lewis, E. C. Choice and Conflict for the College Woman. Journal of the National Association of Women Deans and Counselors, 1969, Summer, 32, 176-182.

_____. Choice and Conflict for the College Woman. Education Digest, 1969, November, 35, 52-54.

_____. Women in Graduate School. Graduate Comment, 1969, 12, 29-34.

_____, Wolins, L., and Yelsma, J.J. The Academic Interests of College Women. A Factorial Study. Personnel and Guidance Journal, 1967, 46(3), 258-262.

Liebman, J. S. Women in Engineering at the University of Illinois in Urbana-Champaign. IEEE Transactions on Education, 1975, February, E-18(1), 47-49.

Lockheed, M. E., and Ekstrom, R. B. Sex Discrimination in Education: A Literature Review and Bibliography. Princeton, NJ: Educational Testing Service, 1977.

Lowrey, B. Those 'Emerging Women' as Undergraduates. The Washington Post, 1976, September 15, Section A, 21.

Ludeman, W. W. Declining Female College Attendance: Causes and Implications. Educational Forum, 1961, May, 25, 505-507.

Lunneborg, P. W., and Lillie, C. Sexism in Graduate Admissions. American Psychologist, 1973, February, 187-189.

McBee, M. L., and Suddick, D. E. Differential Freshman Admission by Sex. Journal of the National Association for Women Deans, Administrators, and Counselors, 1974, 37(2), 75-77.

McCanne, L., Green, F., Keating, L. A., and McCanne, T. Women Students: Their Attitudes and Frustrations. Symposium presentation at the American Psychological Association Convention, San Francisco, 1977.

MacDonald, C. Increasing Women's Participation in the Sciences: An Experiment in Mathematics Education. Paper presented at the American Association for the Advancement of Science meeting, Boston, February 1976.

McGrath, E. M. Female Medical Students and Specialty Interest. Unpublished doctoral dissertation, George Washington University. Dissertation Abstracts International, 1976, May, 36 (11-B), 5806-5808.

Malumphy, T. M. Athletics and Competition for Girls. Women in Sports. Washington, D. C.: National Education Association, 1971.

Marsalis, L. W. A Study of the Impact of Attitudes on Academic Performance of Students at the Mississippi State College for Women. Unpublished doctoral dissertation, University of Southern Mississippi. Dissertation Abstracts International, 1971, February, 31(8-A), 3962-3963.

Marshak, W. P., Gillman, D. C., and Nelson, L. D. Cadet Attitudes

During the Admission of Women to the U.S. Air Force Academy. Paper presented at the American Psychological Association Convention, San Francisco, 1977.

Mason, E. J. Teachers' Observations and Expectations of Boys and Girls as Influenced by Biased Psychological Reports and Knowledge of the Effects of Bias. Journal of Educational Psychology, 1973, October, 65, 238-243.

Mathews, M. R. The Training and Practice of Women Physicians: A Case Study. Journal of Medical Education, 1970, 45(12), 1016-1024.

Mathis, L. R. Where Women Study Engineering. Vocational Guidance Quarterly, 1967, June, 15, 281-282.

Meade, C. Strategies for Defining and Eliminating Sexism in Graduate Training. Symposium presentation at the American Psychological Association Convention, San Francisco, 1977.

Merenda, P. F., and Reilly, R. Validity of Selection Criteria in Determining Success of Graduate Students in Psychology. Psychological Reports, 1971, February, 28(1), 259-266.

Merry, P. E. A Descriptive Study of Mature and Younger Women in an Associate Degree Nursing Program. Unpublished doctoral dissertation, University of Southern California. Dissertation Abstracts International, 1974, August, 35(2-A), 823.

Meyer, W. J. and Thompson, G. G. Teacher Interactions with Boys, as Contrasted with Girls. In R. Kuhlems and G. G. Thompson (eds.), Psychological Studies of Human Development. New York: Appleton-Century-Crofts, 1963, 510-518.

Miles, B. Harmful Lessons Little Girls Learn in School. Redbook, 1971, March, 136(86), 168-169.

Miles, M. B., and Charters, W. W. (eds.). Inequalities of Teacher Pupil Contacts. In Learning in Social Settings: New Readings in the Sociology of Education. Boston: Allyn and Bacon, 1970, 94-103.

Milgram, R. M., and Milgram, N. A. Self-Concept Differences in Student Teachers in Primary, Elementary, Secondary, and Special Education. Psychology in the Schools, 1976, October, 13, 439-441.

Miner, J. B. The School of Business Study: Change in Female Students. In Studies in Management Education. New York: Springer, 1965.

Mitchell, S. B. Women and the Doctorate: A Study of Enabling or Impeding Factors Among Oklahoma's Doctoral Recipients in the

Attainment and Use of the Degree. Unpublished doctoral dissertation, 1969.

_____, and Alciatore, R. T. Women Doctoral Recipients Evaluate Their Training. Educational Forum, 1970, 34, 533-539.

Mooney, J. D. Attrition Among Ph. D. Candidates: An Analysis of a Cohort of Recent Woodrow Wilson Fellows. Journal of Human Resources, 1968, 3(1), 47-62.

Moore, K. M. The Cooling Out of Two-Year College Women. Personnel and Guidance Journal, 1975, April, 53(8), 578-583.

Moose, M. E. Different Kind of Shopping: On Being a Woman in IA. School Shop, 1974, November, 34, 41.

More Access of Women to Graduate Study. Intellect, 1974, December, 103, 149-150.

Motta, R. W., and Vane, J. R. An Investigation of Teacher Perceptions of Sex-Typed Behaviors. Journal of Educational Research, 1976, July-August, 69(10), 363-368.

Mullaney, T. R. The Womanschool. Change, 1975, October, 7(8), 15-18.

Myers, C. H. Special Problems Encountered by Mature Women Undergraduates. Journal of the National Association of Women Deans and Counselors, 1964, Spring, 27, 137-139.

Nadelson, C., and Notman, M. Success or Failure: Women as Medical School Applicants. Paper presented at the American Psychological Association Convention, Montreal, 1973.

National Organization for Women. Report on Sex Bias in the Public Schools. New York: National Organization for Women, New York Chapter, 1972.

Newman, J. E. Sex Differences in the Organizational Assimilation of Beginning Graduate Students in Psychology. Journal of Educational Psychology, 1974, February, 66(1), 129-138.

Newton, H. Women at West Point! Ladies Home Journal, 1976, May, 93, 59.

Nichols, C. A Seminar in Personality Development for Mature Women. Journal of the National Association for Women Deans, Administrators, and Counselors, 1974, 37(3), 123-127.

No Girls (or Lady Teachers) Please. Nation's Schools, 1969, April, 83(4), 68-69.

Notman, M., and Nadelson, C. C. Medicine: A Career Conflict

for Women. American Journal of Psychiatry, 1973, 130(10), 1123-1127.

Oglesby, C. A. Jocks and Jockarinas: Will You Really Need a Program to Tell the Difference? Symposium presentation at the American Psychological Association Convention, Washington, D. C. , 1976.

Olesen, V. L. , and Whittaker, E. W. Instant Life: College Women Report on Immersion in the Adult World. Journal of the National Association of Women Deans and Counselors, 1966, Spring, 29, 131-135.

Oltman, R. M. Graduate and Professional Education of Women. Improving College and University Teaching. 1975, 23, 5-6.

O'Rourke, M. C. The Impact of the Educational Environment Upon the Development of a Professional Self-Image. Unpublished doctoral dissertation, University of Notre Dame. Dissertation Abstracts, 1963, 23(8), 3008-3009.

Palfrey, C. F. Headteachers' Expectations and Their Pupils' Self-Concepts. Educational Research, 1973, February, 15(2), 123-127.

Pascarella, E. T. Interaction of Sex and Year of Enrollment in Student Perceptions of the University Climate. Research in Higher Education, 1976, 4, 149-163.

Pascoe, E. J. A+ for Older College Women. McCalls, 1977, March, 104, 45.

Patterson, M. , and Sells, L. Women Dropouts from Higher Education. In A. S. Rossi and A. Calderwood (eds.), Academic Women on the Move. New York: Russell Sage Foundation, 1973, 79-91.

Payne, D. A. , Wells, R. A. , and Clarke, R. R. Another Contribution to Estimating Success in Graduate School: A Search for Sex Differences and Comparison Between Three Degree Types. Educational and Psychological Measurement, 1971, Summer, 31, 497-503.

Peltier, G. L. Sex Differences in the School: Problem and Proposed Solution. Phi Delta Kappan, 1968, 50(3), 182-185.

Pleck, J. H. Sex Role Issues in Clinical Training. In Psychotherapy: Theory, Research and Practice. 1976, Spring, 13(1), 17-19.

Plotsky, F. A. Some Characteristics that Influence Learning for the Returning Woman Student. Educational Horizons, 1974, Spring, 52, 135-137.

_____. Women to Women: A Program for Older Women Students and Younger Women Undergraduates. Journal of College Student Personnel, 1975, May, 16, 248.

Potter, E. F. Correlates of Oral Participation in Classrooms. Paper presented at the American Educational Research Association meeting, San Francisco, 1976. Also available from ERIC (ED121744), 1976.

Radcliffe Institute. Wasted Women. Senior Scholastic, 1960, December, 77, 1+.

Radcliffe Institute Conference on Women, Spring, 1972. Cambridge, MA: Radcliffe Institute, 1972.

Raderman, R., and Allen, D. V. Registered Nurse Students in a Baccalaureate Program: Factors Associated with Completion. Nursing Research, 1974, January, 23(1), 71-73.

Randolph, K. S. The Mature Woman in Doctoral Programs. Unpublished doctoral dissertation, Indiana University, 1965.

Reed, H. B. College Students' Motivations Related to Voluntary Dropout and Under-Overachievement. Journal of Educational Research, 1968, 61, 412-416.

Reeling, P. A. Undergraduate Female Students as Potential Recruits to the Library Profession. Unpublished doctoral dissertation, Columbia University, 1969. Dissertation Abstracts International, 1969, 30(10-A), 4470. Also available from ERIC (ADG70-7053), 1969.

Rees, M. The Graduate Education of Women. In W. T. Furniss and P. A. Graham (eds.), Women in Higher Education. Washington, D. C.: American Council on Education, 1974.

Reisman, D. Observations on Contemporary College Students--Especially Women. In P. K. Manning (ed.), Youth: Divergent Perspectives. New York: John C. Wiley, 1973, 136-154.

Report of the Task Force on the Status of Women in Psychology. American Psychologist, 1973, July, 28(7), 611-616.

Resources Analysis Branch. Special Report on Women and Graduate Study. Resources for Medical Research Report No. 13. Washington, D. C.: National Institutes of Health, Office of Program Planning and Evaluation, 1968.

Rice, J. K. Perceptions of Males and Females Concerning Their Graduate Education Experience in Counseling. Journal of the National Association for Women Deans, Administrators, and Counselors, 1977, Fall, 41(1), 32-37.

Ricks, F. A., and Pyke, S. W. Teacher Perceptions and Attitudes that Foster or Maintain Sex Role Differences. Interchange, 1973, 4(1), 26-33.

Riverside California NOW Education Task Force. Just Like a Girl She Gives Up. Redlands, CA: National Organization for Women, Education Task Force, n. d.

Roby, P. Structural and Internalized Barriers to Women in Higher Education. In C. Safilios-Rothschild (ed.), Toward a Sociology of Women. Lexington, MA: Xerox College Publishing, 1972, 121-140.

─────. Institutional Barriers to Women Students in Higher Education. In A. S. Rossi and A. Calderwood (eds.), Academic Women on the Move. New York: Russell Sage Foundation, 1973, 37-56.

Roe, A. Women in Science. Personnel and Guidance Journal, 1966, 44(8), 784-787.

Rose, C. A. The Impact of College on Women's Attitudes Toward Their Role in Society. Unpublished doctoral dissertation, University of California, Los Angeles. Dissertation Abstracts International, 1975, February, 35(8-A), 5065-5066.

Rosenthal, R., and Jacobson, L. Self-Fulfilling Prophecies in the Classroom: Teachers' Expectations as Unintended Determinants of Pupils' Intellectual Competence. In M. Deutsch, I. Katz, and A. R. Jensen (eds.), Social Class, Race, and Psychological Development. New York: Holt, Rinehart and Winston, 1968, 219-253.

Ross, M. B., and Salvia, J. Attractiveness as a Biasing Factor in Teacher Judgments. American Journal of Mental Deficiency, 1975, July, 80(1), 96-98.

Rossi, A. S. The Status of Women in Graduate Departments of Sociology: 1968-1969. American Sociologist, 1970, Fall, 5, 1-12.

Rubin, R. A. Sex Discrimination in Interscholastic High School Athletes. Syracuse Law Review, 1974, April, 25, 535-574.

Rudd, M. H. That Burgeoning Law School Enrollment is Portia. American Bar Association Journal, 1974, 60, 182-184.

Russin, J. M. (ed.). What Educated Women Want: Report: Views of Vassar Seniors. Newsweek, 1966, June 13, 67, 68-72+.

Saario, T. N., Jacklin, C. N., and Tittle, C. K. Sex Role Stereotyping in the Public Schools. In P. M. Insel and L. F. Jacobson (eds.), What Do You Expect? An Inquiry into Self-Fulfilling Prophecies. Menlo Park, CA: Cummings, 1975, 137-163.

Sachdeva, D. Women Students at a Southern California State University. Journal of the National Association for Women Deans, Administrators, and Counselors, 1977, Fall, 41(1), 38-41.

Samara, B. M. Teachers Conceptions of Children's Sex Roles as Related to Attitudes about the Women's Liberation Movement and Personal Background Data. Unpublished doctoral dissertation, Temple University. Dissertation Abstracts International, 1974, December, 35(6-A), 3532-3533.

Schab, F. Southern College Women. American Association of University Women Journal, 1967, 60, 142-148.

Schaeffer, R. G. The Campus Recruiting Scene. The Conference Board Record, 1974, March, 11(3), 41-45.

Schmidt-Relenberg, N. Die Berufstätigkeit der Frau in den Leitbildern von Abiturientinnen [The Images of Female High School Graduates Regarding Professional Work for Women.] Soz. Welt, 1965, 16(2), 133-150.

Schneider, L. Our Failures Only Marry: Bryn Mawr and the Failure of Feminism. In J. Stacey et al. (eds.), And Jill Came Tumbling After: Sexism in American Education. New York: Dell, 1974, 279-292.

Scholz, N. T., Prince, J. S., and Miller, G. P. How to Decide: A Guide for Women. New York: College Entrance Examination Board, 1975.

Schumacher, E. E. The Roles of the Elementary School Teacher as Perceived by Freshmen Women Students. Unpublished doctoral dissertation. Dissertation Abstracts, 1965, 27(3-A), 693.

Schwartz, P., and Lever, J. Women in the Male World of Higher Education. In A. S. Rossi and A. Calderwood (eds.), Academic Women on the Move. New York: Russell Sage Foundation, 1973, 57-77.

Scott, A. Preliminary Report on the Status of Graduate Women: University of California, Berkeley. Prepared for the Graduate Assembly's Committee on the Status of Women, Berkeley, 1973.

Sears, P. S. The Effect of Classroom Conditions on the Strength of Achievement Motive and Work Output on Elementary School Children. Final report. Washington, D. C.: U. S. Office of Education, 1963.

_____, and Feldman, D. H. Teacher Interactions with Boys and with Girls. National Elementary Principal, 1966, 46(2), 30-35. Also in J. Stacey et al. (eds.), And Jill Came Tumbling After: Sexism in American Education. New York: Dell, 1974, 147-158.

Selby, R., and Lewko, J. H. Children's Attitudes Toward Females in Sports: Their Relationship with Sex, Grade, and Sports Participation. Research Quarterly, 1976, October, 47, 453-463.

Sells, L. W. Sex and Discipline Differences in Doctoral Attrition. Unpublished doctoral dissertation, University of California, Berkeley, 1975.

_____. Sex and Discipline Differences in Professional Socialization. In M. E. Lockheed (ed.), Research on Women's Acquisition of Professional and Leadership Roles. Princeton, NJ: Educational Testing Service, 1975, 18-35.

Serbin, L. A., and O'Leary, K. D. How Nursery Schools Teach Girls to Shut Up. Psychology Today, 1975, December, 9, 56-58+.

_____, _____, Kent, R. N., and Tonick, I. J. A Comparison of Teacher Response to the Pre-Academic and Problem Behavior of Boys and Girls. Child Development, 1973, 44, 796-804.

Shaman, J. M. College Admissions Policies on Sex and the Equal Protection Clause. Buffalo Law Review, 1971, April, 20, 609-623.

Shapley, D. Medical Education: Those Sexist Putdowns May Be Illegal. Science, 1974, April, 184(4135), 449-451.

Sharp, L. M. Education and Employment: The Early Careers of College Graduates. Baltimore: Johns Hopkins Press, 1970.

Siegel, A. E., and Carr, R. G. The Education of Women at Stanford. In H. L. Packer (ed.), The Study of Education at Stanford: Report to the University. (Vol. 7.). Stanford: Stanford University, 1969.

Simon, R. J., Clark, S. M., and Galway, K. The Woman Ph. D. A Recent Profile. Social Problems, 1967, 15, 221-236.

Singleton, D. Sex as a Determinant of Responses to Patient Management Problems by Physicians and Medical Students. Symposium presentation at the American Psychological Association Convention, San Francisco, 1977.

Slee, F. W. The Feminine Image Factor in Girls' Attitudes to School Subjects. The British Journal of Educational Psychology, 1968, June, 38(2), 212-214.

Smart, M., Hechinger, G., and Hechinger, F. M. How Not to Waste College on Girls; with Study-Discussion Program. Parents' Magazine, 1964, February, 39, 40, 70-71+.

Smith, W. S. Science Education in the Affective Domain: The Effect of a Self-Awareness Treatment on Career Choice of Talented High School Women. Paper presented at the National Association of Research in Science Teaching meeting, April 1976.

Snyder, E. E., and Spreitzer, E. Correlates of Sport Participation Among Adolescent Girls. Research Quarterly, 1976, December, 47, 804-809.

_____, and _____. Participation in Sports as Related to Educational Expectations Among High School Girls. Sociology of Education, 1977, January, 50, 47-55.

Society of Woman Engineers. Report on Women Undergraduate Engineering Students: Biennial Survey. New York, 1974.

Solano, C. H. Teacher and Pupil Stereotypes of Gifted Girls and Boys. Symposium presentation at the American Psychological Association Convention, Washington, D. C., 1976.

Solmon, L. C. Women in Doctoral Education: Clues and Puzzles Regarding Institutional Discrimination. Research in Higher Education, 1973, 1(4), 299-332.

_____. Male and Female Graduate Students: The Question of Equal Opportunity. New York: Praeger, 1976.

Solomons, H. H. Sex-Role Mediated Achievement Behaviors in Coeducational Physical Education. Paper presented at the American Psychological Association Convention, Washington, D. C., 1976.

Sorotzkin, F., Fleming, E. S., and Anttonen, R. G. Teacher Knowledge of Standardized Test Information and Its Effect on Pupil IQ and Achievement. Journal of Experimental Education, 1974, Fall, 43(1), 79-85.

Spaulding, R. Achievement, Creativity and Self-Concept Correlates of Teacher Pupil Transactions in Elementary Schools. Washington, D. C.: U. S. Office of Education, 1963.

Stafford, M. P. Freshman Expectations and Assimilation Into the College Environment. Unpublished doctoral dissertation, Syracuse University. Dissertation Abstracts International, 1972, 32(A), 4434.

Stafford, R. L. Are the Schools Failing Our Daughters? New York State Education, 1969, April, 56, 14-16.

Stanford Committee on the Education and Employment of Women in the University. The Stanford Woman in 1972: A Study of Undergraduate Choice of Academic Fields and Future Occupations. Stanford: Stanford University, 1972.

Still, E. Tribulations and Advantages of Being a Mature Student.

The Times (London) Educational Supplement, 1968, August 9, 2777, 258.

Stivers, J. Student Loans and the Education of Women. Washington, D. C.: Center for Women Policy Studies, 1974.

Stoessel, J. Student Development for College Women: The Need for Role Models. Orient, 1976/1977, Fall, Winter, 12, 1-9.

Stokes, S. Graduate Women in Political Science--A Recent Research Study. Women on Campus: 1970--A Symposium. Ann Arbor: University of Michigan, Center for the Continuing Education of Women, 1970, 36-38.

Sturtz, S. A. Age Differences in College Student Satisfaction. Journal of College Student Personnel, 1971, March, 12(3), 220-222.

Suchner, R. W., and More, D. M. Stereotypes of Males and Females in Two Occupations. Journal of Vocational Behavior, 1975, February, 6(1), 1-8.

Taines, B. Older Women, Newer Students. Community and Junior College Journal, 1973, August, 44, 17.

Tamir, P. The Relationship Between Achievement in Biology and Cognitive Preference Styles in High School Students. The British Journal of Educational Psychology, 1976, February, 46(1), 57-67.

Thistlethwaite, D. L. Fields of Study and Development of Motivation Advanced Training. Journal of Educational Psychology, 1962, April, 53, 53-64. Discussion. 1962, December, 53, 303-315. Discussion. 1963, February, 54, 63-71.

_____., and Wheeler, N. Effects of Teacher and Peer Subcultures Upon Student Aspirations. Journal of Educational Psychology, 1966, 57(1), 35-47.

Trickett, P., and Trickett, E. The Experience and Effects of Attending Independent Secondary Schools on Female Students. Symposium presentation at the American Psychological Association Convention, San Francisco, 1977.

20 Women to Study Law at Notre Dame. New York Times. 1969, September 14.

Vander Wilt, R. B., and Klocke, R. A. Self Actualization of Females in an Experimental Orientation Program. Journal of the National Association of Women Deans and Counselors, 1971, Spring, 34(3), 125-129.

Vaughter, R. M., and Sullivan, W. J. Influence of Sex of Instructor upon Achievement-Related Behaviors. Paper presented at the

American Psychological Association Convention, Washington, D.C., 1976.

Verheyden-Hilliard, M.E. Cinderella Doesn't Live Here Anymore. Womanpower, 1975, November, 34-37.

Vestin, M. A Freer Choice: A Program for Equality Between the Sexes in Education and School. Journal of Research and Development in Education, 1977, November, 10(4), 53-60.

Vetter, B.M. More Women for Higher Education. Science, 1972, November 24, 178, 815.

Virginia Woman Wins In-State Tuition Rights. The Chronicle of Higher Education, 1973, February 26, 4.

Vroegh, K. Sex of Teacher and Academic Achievement: A Review of Research. Elementary School Journal, 1976, April, 76(7), 389-405.

Wallace, W.L. The Perspective of College Women. In A. Theodore (ed.), The Professional Woman. Cambridge, MA: Schenkman, 1970, 381-396.

Wallach, A. A View from the Law School. In F. Howe (ed.), Women and the Power to Change. New York: McGraw-Hill, 1975, 81-126.

Walster, E., Cleary, T.A., and Clifford, M.M. The Effects of Race and Sex on College Admissions. Sociology of Education, 1971, 44, 237-244.

Waters, E.B. Exercising New Options: Adult Women Compared with Men and Younger Women at a Community College. Dissertation Abstracts International, 1974, 34(A), 3896-3897.

Weisman, C.S., Morlock, L.L., Sack, D.G., and Levine, D.M. Sex Differences in Response to a Blocked Career Pathway Among Unaccepted Medical School Applicants. Sociology of Work and Occupations, 1976, May, 3(2), 187-208.

Werts, C.E. Sex Differences in College Attendance. National Merit Scholarship Corporation Research Reports, 1966, 2(6). Evanston, IL: National Merit Scholarship Corporation.

———. A Comparison of Male Versus Female College Attendance Probabilities. Sociology of Education, 1968, Winter, 41, 103-110.

West, S.D., Jr. Attitudes of High School Teachers, Principals, Guidance Counselors, Librarians, and Teacher Educators Toward the Social, Educational, and Economic Roles of Women. Unpublished doctoral dissertation, University of Florida, 1975.

White, M. S. Psychological and Social Barriers to Women in Science. Science, 1970, October 23, 170(3956), 413-416. Also in C. Safilios-Rothschild (ed.), Toward a Sociology of Women. Lexington, MA: Xerox College Publishing, 1972, 300-308; and in J. Freeman (ed.), Women: A Feminist Perspective. Palo Alto: Mayfield, 1975, 227-237.

Wiggins, N., Blackburn, M., and Hackman, J. R. Prediction of First-Year Success in Psychology. Proceedings of the 76th Annual Convention of the American Psychological Association, 1968, 4, 237-238.

Wilson, B., Lee, D., and Quisenberry, D. Measures of Stereotype Toward College Women Physical Education Majors. Physical Educator, 1974, October, 31(3), 140-142.

Wilson, K. M. Today's Women Students: New Outlooks, Options. Findings, 1974, 1, 5-8.

Wirtenberg, T. J. The Impact of a Sex-Desegregated Practical Arts Course on Maximization of Occupational Potential in Seventh Grade Girls. Unpublished doctoral dissertation, University of California, Los Angeles, 1975.

Withey, S., et al. Women Students in U. S. Medical Schools: Past and Present Trends. Journal of Medical Education, 1973, February, 48, 186-189.

Withycombe-Brocato, C. J. The Mature Graduate Woman Student: Who Is She? Unpublished doctoral dissertation, U. S. International University, San Diego. Dissertation Abstracts International, 1970, November, 31(5-B), 2973-2974.

Women and the Doctorate: Educational Testing Service Survey. Intellect, 1976, January, 104, 284.

Women in Engineering. Atlanta: Georgia Institute of Technology, Engineering College, 1974.

_____. Cambridge, MA: Massachusetts Institute of Technology, Office of the Dean of Engineering, n. d.

_____. West Lafayette, IN: Purdue University, Purdue Student Section of the Society of Women Engineers, n. d.

Women Spark Gain in Science, Math Degrees. Science News Letter, 1961, December 30, 80, 432.

Women Students Urged: Set a Higher Career Goal. Journal of College Placement, 1963, February, 23, 65.

Work, C. E. Measuring and Improving Awareness and Attitudes of Girls Toward Engineering. Houghton, MI: Michigan Technological University, n. d.

368 / Educational Forces

Wright, C. R. Success or Failure in Earning Graduate Degrees. Sociology of Education, 1964, Fall, 38, 73-97.

Yount, D. Women Undergraduates Discover Physics Is Still a Man's World. Physics Teacher, 1970, April, 8, 193-194.

Yudin, L. W., Ring, S. I., Nowakiwska, M., and Heinemann, S. H. School Dropout or College Bound: Study in Contrast. Journal of Educational Research, 1973, October, 67(2), 87-93.

Zinberg, D. College: When the Future Becomes the Present. In R. B. Kundsin (ed.), Women and Success: The Anatomy of Achievement. New York: William Morrow, 1974, 129-137.

C. FACULTY

Abramson, J. The Invisible Woman: Discrimination in the Academic Profession. San Francisco: Jossey-Bass, 1975.

Affirmative Action--How Far Must It Go? Detroit Free Press, 1972, March 27.

American Association of University Professors. Nearly Keeping Up. Report on the Economic Status of the Profession, 1975-1976. American Association of University Professors Bulletin, 1976, Summer.

Association of American Medical Colleges. Faculty Rank by Sex and Age for 78 of the United States Medical Schools in Operation in 1968-1969 Academic Year. Faculty Roster, 1970.

Astin, H. S., and Bayer, A. E. Sex Discrimination in Academe. Educational Record, 1972, Spring, 53(2), 101-118. Also in A. S. Rossi and A. Calderwood (eds.), Academic Women on the Move. New York: Russell Sage Foundation, 1973, 333-358; and in M. T. S. Mednick et al. (eds.), Women and Achievement: Social and Motivational Analyses. New York: Halsted Press, 1975, 372-395.

Baker, M. Women as a Minority Group in the Academic Profession. Unpublished doctoral dissertation, University of Alberta, Canada, 1975. American Doctoral Dissertations, 11(97), 1975. Also available from ERIC (ADG029-3388), 1975.

Baron, A. S., and Reeves, E. T. How Effective Has Affirmative Action Legislation Been. Personnel Administrator, 1977, January, 22(1), 47-49.

Basualdo, E. A. The Status and Role of Female Vocational Faculty in Comprehensive High Schools. Vocational-Technical Education Research Report, 1975, August, 13(5).

Bayer, A. E., and Astin, H. S. Sex Differences in Academic Rank and Salary Among Science Doctorates in Teaching. Journal of Human Resources, 1968, Spring, 111(2), 191-200.

_____, and _____. Sex Differentials in the Academic Reward System. Science, 1975, May 23, 188, 796-802. Reply, 1975, December 19, 190, 1154+.

Bernard, J. S. Academic Women. University Park, PA: Pennsylvania State University Press, 1964.

_____. My Four Revolutions: An Autobiographical History of the American Sociological Association. American Journal of Sociology, 1973, 78, 773-791.

_____. The Present Situation in the Academic World of Women Trained in Engineering. In J. A. Mattfeld and C. G. Van Aken (eds.), Women and the Scientific Professions. Cambridge: Massachusetts Institute of Technology Press, 1975, 163-182.

Berry, J., and Kushner, R. A Critical Look at the Queen Bee Syndrome. Journal of the National Association for Women Deans, Administrators, and Counselors, 1975, Summer, 38(4), 173-176.

Berry, M., and Fitzgerald, L. The Profile and Status of National Association of Women Deans and Counselors Members. Journal of the National Association of Women Deans and Counselors, 1971, Winter, 34(2), 50-59.

Berwald, H. Attitudes Toward Women College Teachers in Institutions of Higher Education Accredited by the North Central Association. Dissertation Abstracts International, 1963, 23, 4161.

Bikman, M. Where Do All the Women PhD's Go? In S. Stambler (ed.), Women's Liberation: Blueprint for the Future. New York: Charter Communications, 1970, 105-109.

Blaska, B. Women in Academe--The Need for Support Groups. Journal of the National Association for Women Deans, Administrators, and Counselors, 1976, Summer, 39(4), 173-178.

Brandt, L. J., and Hayden, M. E. Male and Female Teacher Attitudes as a Function of Students' Ascribed Motivation and Performance Levels. Journal of Educational Psychology, 1974, 66(3), 309-314.

Bruce, J. D. The Search for Women Faculty Members. IEEE Transactions on Education, 1975, February, E-18(1), 53-57.

Budner, S., and Meyer, J. Women Professors. Unpublished manuscript, n. d.

Bunting, M. I., Graham, P. A., and Wasserman, E. R. Academic

Freedom and Incentive for Women. Educational Record, 1970, Fall, 51(4), 386-391.

Cancian, F. The Stanford Woman in 1972. Unpublished manuscript, 1972.

Carnegie Commission on Higher Education: Women as Faculty Members and Academic Administrators. In Opportunities for Women in Higher Education. New York: McGraw-Hill, 1973, 109-126.

Chalmers, E. L., Jr. Achieving Equity for Women in Higher Education Graduate Enrollment and Faculty Status. Journal of Higher Education, 1972, 43, 517-524.

Chinas, B. L. Women on College Faculties: Letter. Science, 1970, May 23, 168, 917.

Clark, L. Fact and Fantasy: A Recent Profile of Women in Academia. Peabody Journal of Education, 1977, January, 54, 103-109.

Colson, E., and Scott, E. Report of the Subcommittee on the Status of Academic Women on the Berkeley Campus. Berkeley: University of California, 1970.

Daniels, A. K. Feminist Perspectives in Sociological Research. In M. Millman and R. M. Kanter (eds.), Another Voice: Feminist Perspectives on Social Life and Social Science. New York: Doubleday, 1976, 340-380.

Davis, A. E. Women as a Minority Group in Higher Academics. American Sociologist, 1969, 4, 95-99.

Davis, F., and Olesen, V. L. The Career Outlook of Professionally Educated Women. Psychiatry, 1965, 28, 334-345.

Egelston, J. C. Sex Bias in Publications and Grant Awards. Journal of the National Association for Women Deans, Administrators and Counselors, 1976, Winter, 39(2), 66-69.

Ehrlich, C. The Male Sociologist's Burden: The Place of Women in Marriage and Family Texts. Journal of Marriage and the Family. 1971, 33(3), 421-430.

Elbe, K. E. Strengthening the Position of Women Faculty Members. Journal of the National Association of Women Deans and Counselors, 1972, 35(4), 165.

Ellman, M. Academic Women. In J. Stacey et al. (eds.), And Jill Came Tumbling After: Sexism in American Education. New York: Dell, 1974, 358-365.

Emig, J. Another Prejudice, One Woman in Academe Fights Back. Mount Holyoke Alumnae Quarterly, 1970, Fall.

Epstein, C. F. Encountering the Male Establishment: Sex-Status Limits on Women's Careers in the Professions. American Journal of Sociology, 1970, May, 75(6), 965-982.

_____. A Different Angle of Vision: Notes on the Selective Eye of Sociology. Social Science Quarterly, 1974, December, 55(3), 645-656.

_____. Mind, Matter and Mentors: The Making of a Sociologist. In J. Stiehm (ed.), The Frontiers of Knowledge. University Park, CA: University of Southern California Press, 1976, 23-37.

Ezorsky, G. The Fight over University Women. New York Review of Books, 1976, May 16, 21, 32-39.

Faculty Women Are Paid 17% Less Than Men. The Chronicle of Higher Education, 1973, March 12, 7(23), 6.

Fava, S. F. The Status of Women in Professional Sociology. American Sociological Review, 1960, 25(2), 271-272.

Ferber, M. A., and Huber, J. A. Sex of Student and Instructor: A Study of Student Bias. American Journal of Sociology, 1975, January, 80(4), 949-963.

_____, and Loeb, J. W. Performance, Rewards, and Perceptions of Sex Discrimination Among Male and Female Faculty. American Journal of Sociology, 1973, 78, 995-1002. Also in J. Huber (ed.), Changing Women in a Changing Society. Chicago: University of Chicago Press, 1973, 233-240.

Feulner, P. N. Women in the Professions: A Social-Psychological Study. Unpublished doctoral dissertation. Dissertation Abstracts International, 1974, February, 34(8-A, Pt. 2), 5309.

Fidell, L. Empirical Verification of Sex Discrimination in Hiring Practices in Psychology. American Psychologist, 1970, 25, 1094-1098. Also in R. K. Unger and F. L. Denmark (eds.), Woman: Dependent or Independent Variable? New York: Psychological Dimensions, 1975, 773-785.

Fley, J. The Time to Be Properly Vicious. Journal of the National Association for Women Deans, Administrators, and Counselors, 1974, 37(2), 53-58.

Forest, C. A., Sr. The Religious Academic Woman: A Study of Adjustment to Multiple Roles. Unpublished doctoral dissertation, Fordam University. Dissertation Abstracts, 1966, 27(6-A), 1939.

Freeman, J. Women on the Social Science Faculties Since 1892, University of Chicago. Speech presented at the Minority Groups Workshop of the Political Science Association Conference and the University Panel of the Status of Women, Chicago, 1969. Reprinted in Discrimination Against Women. Hearings Before the Special Subcommittee on Education of the Committee on Education and Labor, Washington, D. C. : House of Representatives, Section 805 of H. R. 16098, 1970, June/July, 994+.

Gardner, J. E. Autobiographical Notes Relevant to Sex Discrimination in Academic Psychology. Physiology and Behavior, 1968, 3, 709-712.

Giventer, L. L. A Systems Approach to the Problem of Sex Discrimination in Higher Education Faculty Employment. Unpublished doctoral dissertation, University of Pittsburgh, 1977. Dissertation Abstracts International, 1977, 38(1-A), 468. Also available from ERIC (ADG77-15163), 1977.

Gordon, N. M., Morton, T. E., and Braden, I. C. Faculty Salaries: Is There Discrimination by Sex, Race and Discipline? American Economic Review, 1974, June, 64(3), 419-427.

Gottsegen, G. B., and Gottsegen, M. G. Women and School Psychology. School Psychology Digest, 1973, Summer, 2(3), 24-27.

Gould, S. H., and van den Berghe, P. L. Particularism in Sociology Departments' Hiring Practices. Race, 1973, July, 15(1), 106-111.

Graham, P. A. Women in Academe. Science, 1970, September 25, 169, 1284-1290. Also in C. Safilios-Rothschild (ed.), Toward a Sociology of Women. Lexington, MA: Xerox College Publishing, 1972, 261-276.

Grandjean, B. D., Aiken, L. H., and Bonjean, C. M. Professional Autonomy and the Work Satisfaction of Nursing Educators. Nursing Research, 1976, May-June, 25(3), 216-221.

Greenwald, C. Who Says a Woman Can't Raise a Family and Teach, Too? The Chronicle of Higher Education, 1974, September 10, 7(42), 16.

A Grievance Handbook for Women Educators. Washington, D. C. : National Association for Women Deans, Administrators, and Counselors, 1977.

Groth, N. J. Success and Creativity in Male and Female Professors. Gifted Child Quarterly, 1975, Winter, 19(4), 328-335.

Guttman, M. A. J. Is the Gray Mare Only a Workhorse? Personnel and Guidance Journal, 1972, October, 51(2), 115-122.

_____, and Hicks, L. Characteristics of Female Members of ACES. Counselor Education and Supervision, 1974, March, 13(3), 165-171.

Hall, K. P. Sex Status in Teacher Groups. In M. E. Lockheed (ed.), Research on Women's Acquisition of Professional and Leadership Roles. Princeton, NJ: Educational Testing Service, 1975, 97-118.

Harlan, A., Bernstein, V., and Kerr, S. Sex, Productivity and Reward in Academe. Paper presented at the American Psychological Association Convention, New Orleans, 1974.

Harmon, L. The Female Psychologist--Strategies for Successful Publication. Symposium presentation at the American Psychological Association Convention, San Francisco, 1977.

Harris, A. S. The Second Sex in Academe. American Association of University Professors Bulletin, 1970, 56, 283-295. Also in Art in America, 1972, May, 60, 18-19; and in J. Stacey, et al. (eds.), And Jill Came Tumbling After: Sexism in American Education. New York: Dell, 1974, 293-316; and in E. S. Maccia et al. (eds.), Women and Education. Springfield, IL: Charles C. Thomas, 1975, 161-194.

Harris, B. F., and Lightner, J. Woman's Image in Abnormal Psychology: Professionalism Versus Pathology. Paper presented at the American Psychological Association Convention, San Francisco, 1977.

Harris, M. B. Sex Role Stereotypes and Teacher Evaluations. Journal of Educational Psychology, 1975, 67(6), 751-756.

_____. The Effects of Sex, Sex-Stereotyped Descriptions, and Institutions on Evaluations of Teachers. Sex Roles: A Journal of Research, 1976, 2(1), 15-22.

Harris, R. D. Coping with Role Conflict: My Story. Illinois Teacher of Home Economics, 1975, May-June, 18(5), 280-284.

Haslett, B. J. Influence of Student Ability and Sex on Students' Attitudes Towards Teachers. Education, 1976, Spring, 96, 268-275.

Heilman, M. E. Miss, Mrs., or Ms., or None of the Above. American Psychologist, 1975, April, 30(4), 516-518.

Henschel, B. J. S. A Comparison of the Personality Variables of Women Administrators and Women Teachers in Education. Unpublished doctoral dissertation, University of Utah. Dissertation Abstracts, 1964, 25(A), 6313.

Holden, C. Women in Michigan; Academic Sexism Under Siege. Science, 1972, November 24, 178, 841-844.

Hole, J., and Levine, E. Professions. In Rebirth of Feminism. New York: Quadrangle Books, 1971, 338-371.

Hopkins, E. B. Unemployed! An Academic Woman's Saga? In Women on Campus: The Unfinished Liberation. New York: Change Magazine, 1975, 140-151.

Horing, L. S. Affirmative Action Through Affirmative Attitudes. In E. Wasserman et al. (eds.), Women in Academia: Evolving Policies Toward Equal Opportunities. New York: Praeger Publishers, 1975, 8-19.

How Harvard Rules Women. Boston: New England Free Press, 1970.

Howe, F. (ed.). Women and the Power to Change. New York: McGraw-Hill, 1975.

Hughes, H. M. (ed.). The Status of Women in Sociology: 1968-1972. Washington, D. C.: American Sociological Association, 1973.

———. Women in Academic Sociology, 1925-1975. Sociological Focus, 1975, August, 8(3), 215-222.

Iacobacci, R. F. Women of Mathematics. The Arithmetic Teacher, 1970, April, 17, 316-324.

Jacobs, K. F., and Woman, C. S. Strategies of Women Academics. In H. H. Frank (ed.), Women in the Organization. Philadelphia: University of Pennsylvania Press, 1977, 256-262.

Jaffe, L. Women's Place in Academe. The Midwest Quarterly, 1973, October, 15(1), 16-30.

Johnson, G. E., and Stafford, F. P. Earnings and Promotion of Women Faculty. American Economic Review, 1974, December, 64, 888-903.

———, and ———. Women and the Academic Labor Market. In C. B. Lloyd (ed.), Sex, Discrimination, and the Division of Labor. New York: Columbia University Press, 1975, 201-222.

Jones, R. H. Sex Prejudice: Effects on the Inferential Process of Judging Hireability. Dissertation Abstracts International, 1970, 31(3-A), 1013.

Katz, J. Career and Autonomy in College Women. In J. Katz, (ed.). Class, Character, and Career. Stanford, CA: Stanford University Press, 1969.

Keiffer, M. G., and Cullen, D. M. Discrimination Experienced by Academic Female Psychologists. Paper presented at the American Psychological Association Convention, Washington, D. C., 1969.

_____, and _____. Women Who Discriminate Against Other Women: The Process of Denial. In F. Denmark (ed.), Who Discriminates Against Women? Issue 15. Beverly Hills: Sage Publications, 1974, 24-36. Also in International Journal of Group Tensions, 1974, March, 4(1), 21-33.

Kirshstein, R. J. Sex Differences in the Academic Work Structure. Unpublished doctoral dissertation, University of Massachusetts, 1976. Dissertation Abstracts International, 1976, 37(9-A), 6089. Also available from ERIC (ADG77-06486), 1976.

Kitchener, K. S., Corazzini, J. G., and Huebner, L. A. A Study of Counseling Center Hiring Practices: What Does It Take for a Woman to Be Hired? Journal of Counseling Psychology, 1975, September, 22(5), 440-445.

Kreps, J. M. Sex and the Scholarly Girl; Review of Academic Women, by J. Bernard. AAUP Bulletin, 1965, March, 51(1), 30-33.

Krosky, B. J. Sex Role Stereotyping in Home Economics Curricula in Selected Senior High Schools in Colorado. Unpublished doctoral dissertation, University of Northern Colorado. Dissertation Abstracts International, 1975, March, 35(9-A), 5781-5782.

Kuhlen, R. G. Needs, Perceived Need Satisfaction Opportunities and Satisfaction with Occupation. Journal of Applied Psychology, 1963, 47(1), 56-64.

Ladd, E. C., Jr., and Lipset, S. M. Faculty Women: Little Gain in Status. 1975, Ladd-Lipset Survey of U. S. Professoriate. The Chronicle of Higher Education, 1975, September 29, 11, 2.

Landon, G. L. Perceptions of Sex Role Stereotyping and Women Teachers' Administrative Career Aspirations. Unpublished doctoral dissertation, University of Wisconsin. Dissertation Abstracts International, 1975, September, 36(3-A), 1214-1215.

LaSorte, M. A. Academic Women's Salaries: Equal Pay for Equal Work? Journal of Higher Education, 1971, April, 42(4), 265-278.

_____. Sex Differences in Salary Among Academic Sociology Teachers. American Sociologist, 1971, November, 6(4), 304-307.

Laws, J. L. A Feminist Analysis of Relative Deprivation in Academic Women. Review of Radical Political Economics, 1972, 4(2), 107-119.

_____. The Psychology of Tokenism: An Analysis. Sex Roles: A Journal of Research, 1975, 1(1), 51-67.

Leffler, A., Gillespie, D. L., and Ratner, E. L. Academic Feminists and the Women's Movement. The Insurgent Sociologist, 1973, Fall, 4(1), 44-55.

Leon, G. R. The Mother-Professional Model in Academia. American Psychologist, 1970, 25(9), 874-875.

Lester, R. A. Antibias Regulation of Universities: Faculty Problems and Their Solutions. New York: McGraw-Hill, 1974.

Levy, B. Do Teachers Sell Girls Short? Today's Education, 1972, 61, 27-29.

Lewin, A. Y., and Duchan, L. Women in Academia: A Study of the Hiring Decision in Departments of Physical Science. Science, 1971, September 3, 173, 892-895.

Liberating Academe. Saturday Review, 1971, March 20, 54, 48.

Lipman-Blumen, J., Stivers, P. E., Tickamyer, A. R., and Brainard, S. Participation of Women in the Educational Research Community. Educational Researcher, 1975, October, 4(9), 5-13.

Loeb, J. W., and Ferber, M. A. Rank, Pay, and Representation of Women Faculty: The Report of the Committee on the Status of Women. Urbana: University of Illinois, Urbana AAUP Chapter, 1970.

_____, and _____. Sex as Predictive of Salary and Status on a University Faculty. Paper presented at the National Council on Measurement in Education meeting, New York, February 1971.

_____, and _____. Representation, Performance, and Status of Women on the Faculty at the Urbana-Champaign Campus of the University of Illinois. In A. Rossi (ed.), Academic Women on the Move. New York: Russell Sage Foundation, 1973, 239-254.

Long, T. E., et al. Role Perceptions of Female Faculty and Their Administrators in Post-Secondary Proprietary Schools. Vocational-Technical Education Research Report, 1975, July, 13(4).

Lopata, H. Z. Review Essay: Sociology. SIGNS: Journal of Women in Culture and Society, 1976, 2(1), 165-176.

Lovano-Kerr, J., Semler, V., and Zimmerman, E. Profile of Art Educators in Higher Education: Male/Female Comparative Data. Studies in Art Education, 1977, 18(2), 21-37.

Lyon, C., and Saario, T. Women in Public Education: Sexual Discrimination in Promotions. Phi Delta Kappan, 1973, 55, 120-123.

McCune, S. D. Eliminating Sexism: Teacher Education and Change. Journal of Teacher Education, 1975, 26(4), 294-300.

McEwen, M., and Shertzer, B. Analysis of Differences in Professional Attitudes and Beliefs Between Male and Female Members of the College Student Personnel Profession. Journal of the National Association for Women Deans, Administrators, and Counselors, 1975, Spring, 36, 136-143.

McIntosh, G. R. A Personal Journal of a Woman in Academia, Or, The Making of a Feminist. Reprint from KNOW, Inc., P. O. Box 86031, Pittsburgh, PA 15221, 1974.

McIntosh, J. C. Differences Between Women Teachers Who Do and Do Not Seek Promotion. Journal of Educational Administration, 1974, 12(2), 28-41.

Mackie, M. Students' Perceptions of Female Professors. Journal of Vocational Behavior, 1976, June, 8(3), 337-348.

McNeel, S. P., et al. Social Psychology Job Applicants: Normative Information and the Question of Sexism. Personality and Social Psychology Bulletin, 1975, Fall, 1(4), 570-574.

Manpower Resources for Scientific Activities at Universities and Colleges. Washington, D. C.: National Science Foundation, 1975.

Marcus, L. R. Has Advertising Produced Results in Faculty Hiring? Educational Record, 1976, Fall, 57(4), 247-250.

Marsalis, L. W. A Study of the Impact of Attitudes on Academic Performance of Students at the Mississippi State College for Women. Dissertation Abstracts International, 1971, February, 31 (8-A), 3962-3963.

Martin, M. Pedagogical Arguments for Preferential Hiring and Tenuring of Women Teachers in the University. In C. C. Gould and M. W. Wartofsky (eds.), Women and Philosophy: Toward a Theory of Liberation. New York: G. P. Putnam's, 1976, 325-333.

Masterman, M. Falling Through the Grid or What Has Happened to the Scarce Women Academics? (An Analysis Constructed by Playing the Panoramix Game.) Journal for the Theory of Social Behaviour, 1974, April, 4(1), 97-107.

Mears, J. Women in Australian Psychology: Identity. Australian Psychologist, 1975, December, 10(3), 293-297.

Miller, M. M. Women in University Teaching. American Association of University Women Journal, 1961, March, 54, 152-154.

Miller, S. B. Bias in Academia. In E. Graham (ed.), What Do

Women Really Want? Princeton, NJ: Dow Jones Books, 1974, 143-147.

Mischel, H. N. Sex Bias in the Evaluation of Professional Achievements. Journal of Educational Psychology, 1974, 66(2), 157-166.

Mitchell, J. M., and Starr, R. R. A Regional Approach for Analyzing the Recruitment of Academic Women. American Behavioral Scientist, 1971, November/December, 15(2), 183-205.

Morlock, L. Discipline Variation in the Status of Academic Women. In A. S. Rossi and A. Calderwood (eds.), Academic Women on the Move. New York: Russell Sage Foundation, 1973, 255-312.

NEA Du Shane Emergency Fund Division. Discriminating Against the Pregnant Teacher. Today's Education, 1971, 60(9), 33-35.

Neugarten, B. L. Women in a University; With Reply by J. Freedman. School Review, 1970, November, 79, 109-118.

Nixon, M. Women Administrators and Women Teachers: A Comparative Study. Unpublished doctoral dissertation, University of Alberta, 1975.

_____, and Gue, L. R. Women Administrators and Women Teachers: A Comparative Study. Alberta Journal of Educational Research, 1975, September, 21(3), 196-206.

_____, and _____. Professional Role Orientation of Women Administrators and Women Teachers. Canadian Administrator, 1975, November, 15(2), 1-5.

No Girls (or Lady Teachers) Please. Nation's Schools, 1969, April, 83(4), 68-69.

Oltman, R. M. The Evolving Role of the Women's Liberation Movement in Higher Education. Available from ERIC (ED049489), 1971.

_____. Focus on Women in Academe, 1980. Improving College and University Teaching, 1972, Winter, 20, 73-75.

Osipow, S. The Female Psychologist--Strategies for Successful Publication. Symposium presentation at the American Psychological Association Convention, Washington, D. C., 1976.

Packard, S. Analysis of Current Statistics and Trends as They Influence the Status and Future for Women in the Art Academe. Studies in Art Education, 1977, 19(2), 38-48.

Painter, E. G. Women: The Last of the Discriminated. Journal of the National Association of Women Deans and Counselors. 1971, Winter, 35(2), 59-61.

Parrish, J. B. Women in Top Level Teaching and Research. American Association of University Women Journal, 1962, 55(2), 99-103+.

Patten, F. G. Portrait of a Teacher. In J. Stacey et al. (eds.), And Jill Came Tumbling After: Sexism in American Education. New York: Dell, 1974, 353-357.

Patterson, M. Alice in Wonderland: A Study of Women Faculty in Graduate Departments of Sociology. American Sociologist, 1971, 6, 226-231.

Peden, I. C. Recruiting, Retention and Promotion of Women Faculty: Tactical Considerations for Affirmative Action. Paper presented to the ASEE meeting, Troy, NY, June 1974.

_____, and Sloan, M. E. Faculty Women: Strategies for the Future. IEEE Transactions on Education, 1975, February, E-18(1), 57-65.

Perun, P. J. Academic Women Social Scientists in Retirement: Factors Affecting Productivity. Symposium presentation at the American Psychological Association Convention, Washington, D. C., 1976.

Peterson, I. College Hiring of Women Said to Slip. New York Times, 1972, November 30, 44.

Petit, Sister R. M. Attitudinal Study of Faculty Women in Higher Education in Northwest United States. Unpublished doctoral dissertation. Dissertation Abstracts International, 1972, 33(A), 1572.

Pottker, J. Overt and Covert Forms of Discrimination Against Academic Women. In J. Pottker and A. Fishel (eds.), Sex Bias in the Schools--Research Evidence. Madison, NJ: Fairleigh Dickinson University Press, 1977, 380-410.

Randour, M. L. Research and Funding Issues for Women in Counseling Psychology. Symposium presentation at the American Psychological Association Convention, San Francisco, 1977.

Reich, A. Teaching Is a Good Profession ... for a Woman. In J. Stacey et al. (eds.), And Jill Came Tumbling After: Sexism in American Education. New York: Dell, 1974, 337-343.

Report of the Task Force on the Status of Women in Psychology. American Psychologist, 1973, July, 28(7), 611-615.

Reuben, E., and Hoffmann, L. (eds.). Unladylike and Unprofessional: Academic Women and Academic Unions. Modern Language Association Commission on the Status of Women in the Profession, 1975.

Revolution II: Thinking Female. Special Issue. College and University Business, 1970, February, 48(2).

Riley, S. B. New Sources of College Teachers. American Association of University Women Journal, 1961, March, 54, 131-134.

Ritchie, J. W. Profile of the Local Teacher Organization Leader: Male Domination in a Predominantly Female Occupation. Unpublished doctoral dissertation, University of Cincinnati. Dissertation Abstracts International, 1974, November, 35(5-A), 2549-2550.

Roberts, J. Creating a Facade of Change: Informal Mechanisms Used to Impede the Changing Status of Women in Academe. Reprint from KNOW, Inc., P.O. Box 86031, Pittsburgh, PA 15221, 1975.

Robinson, L. H. The Status of Academic Women. Available from ERIC (ED048523), 1971.

──────. Institutional Variation in the Status of Academic Women. In A. S. Rossi and A. Calderwood (eds.), Academic Women on the Move. New York: Russell Sage Foundation, 1973, 199-238.

Roby, P. Structural and Internalized Barriers to Women in Higher Education. In C. Safilios-Rothschild (ed.), Toward a Sociology of Women. Lexington, MA: Xerox College Publishing, 1972, 121-140.

Rosen, R. A. Occupational Role Innovators and Sex Role Attitudes. Journal of Medical Education, 1974, June, 49(6), 554-561.

Ross, D. R. The Story of the Top 1% of the Women at Michigan State University. East Lansing: Michigan State University, Counseling Center, 1963.

Rossi, A. S. Discrimination and Demography Restrict Opportunities for Academic Women. College and University Business, 1970, February, 48, 74-78. Also in J. Stacey et al. (eds.), And Jill Came Tumbling After: Sexism in American Education. New York: Dell, 1974, 366-374.

──────. Status of Women in Graduate Departments of Sociology, 1968-1969. American Sociologist, 1970, 5(1), 1-12.

──────. American Association of University Professors, Committee on the Status of Women in the Profession. Annual Report. Towson, MD: Goucher College, 1971.

_____, and Calderwood, A. (eds.). Academic Women on the Move. New York: Russell Sage Foundation, 1973.

Sandler, B. Sex Discrimination at the University of Maryland. College Park, MD: Women's Equity Action League, 1969.

_____. A New Weapon in the Fight for Equal Pay. The Chronicle of Higher Education, 1973, February 26, 6.

Sarvas, A. F. An Analysis of the Relationship Between Perceptions of Vocational Female Faculty and Administrators Toward Female Faculty in Four Institutional Types. Available from ERIC (ED118993), 1976.

Schuck, V. Women in Political Science: Some Preliminary Observations. Newsletter of the American Political Science Association, 1969, Fall, 2(4), 642-653.

Schumacher, E. E. The Roles of the Elementary School Teacher as Perceived by Freshmen Women Students. Dissertation Abstracts, 1965, 27(3-A), 693.

Schwendinger, J., and Schwendinger, H. Sociology's Founding Fathers: Sexists to a Man. Journal of Marriage and the Family, 1971, November, 33(4), 783-799.

Scott, E. L. Developing Criteria and Measures of Equal Opportunities for Women. In E. Wasserman et al. (eds.), Women in Academia: Evolving Policies Toward Equal Opportunities. New York: Praeger, 1975, 82-114.

Seltz, J. Woman Teacher Means Second-Class Professional. Teacher, 1972, 90, 44-45.

Sexton, P. Academic Women. In Women in Education. Bloomington, IN: Phi Delta Kappa Educational Foundation, 1976, 121-134.

Shortridge, K. Women as University Nigger. The Daily Magazine, 1970, April 12.

Showalter, E. Women and the Literary Curriculum. College English, 1971, May, 32(8), 855-862. Also in A Case for Equity: Women in English Departments. Washington, D.C.: National Council of Teachers of English, 9-17; and in J. Stacey et al. (eds.), And Jill Came Tumbling After: Sexism in American Education. New York: Dell, 1974, 317-325.

Simon, R. J., Clark, S. M., and Galway, K. The Woman PhD: A Recent Profile. Social Problems, 1967, 15, 221-236. Also in M. T. S. Mednick et al (eds.), Women and Achievement: Social and Motivational Analyses. NY: Halsted, 1975, 355-371.

_____, _____, and Tifft, L. L. Of Nepotism, Marriage, and the

Pursuit of an Academic Career. Sociology of Education, 1966, Fall, 39, 344-358.

Simpson, L. A. A Study of Employing Agents' Attitudes Toward Academic Women in Higher Education. Unpublished doctoral dissertation, Pennsylvania State University. Dissertation Abstracts, 1969, 29(12-A), 4203-4204.

_____. Attitudes of Higher Education Employing Agents Toward Academic Women. Comment, 1969, 12.

_____. Myth Is Better than a Miss: Men Get the Edge in Academic Employment. College and University Business, 1970, February, 48, 72-73.

Sinowitz, B. E. College Faculty Women Fight Sex Bias. Today's Education, 1974, September, 63, 58-59+.

Smith, G. M. Faculty Women at the Bargaining Table. AAUP Bulletin, 1973, December, 59, 403.

Soldwedel, B. The Profile and Status of N. A. W. D. A. C. Members. Journal of the National Association for Women Deans, Administrators, and Counselors, 1977, Summer, 40(4), 123.

Solomon, L. D. The Mobility of Academic Scientists: A Comparison of Male and Female Faculty Members. Cornell Journal of Social Relations, 1970, Fall, 5(2), 120-132.

Sprik, J. Historical Perspectives of Female Student Personnel Work. Unpublished manuscript, Michigan State University, East Lansing, n. d.

Standards for Women in Higher Education: Affirmative Policy in Achieving Sex Equality in the Academic Community. Washington, D. C.: American Association of University Women, n. d.

Starting Salaries: Teaching Vs. Private Industry (Women). Summary of Economic Status of the Teaching Profession, 1968; Research Report. NEA Research Bulletin, 1968, March, 46, 12.

Stasz, C., Weinberg, S., and McDonald, F. J. The Influence of Sex of Student and Sex of Teacher on Student's Achievement and Evaluation of the Teacher. JSAS Catalog of Selected Documents in Psychology, 1974, 4, 54.

Status of Women Faculty and Administrators in Higher Education Institutions, 1971-1972. Available from ERIC (ED080034), 1973.

Stoll, C. S. Sexism in Social Science. In Female and Male: Socialization, Social Roles, and Social Structures. Dubuque, IA: William C. Brown, 1974, 57-75.

Story, M. W. Some Attitudes that Indicate Job Satisfaction in Vocational Home Economics Teachers Graduated from Two Different Curriculums at Michigan State University. Unpublished doctoral dissertation, Michigan State University. Dissertation Abstracts, 1968, 28(10-A), 4033-4034.

Strong, C. R. A Study of Attitudes Toward the Selection of Women Faculty in Collegiate Schools of Business in the Southeastern USA. Unpublished doctoral dissertation, University of Alabama, 1972. Dissertation Abstracts International, 1972, 33(6-A), 2573. Also available from ERIC (ADG72-33136), 1972.

Theodore, A. Academic Women in Protest. Available from ERIC (ED091989), 1974.

Thetford, M. L. Today's Changing Roles: An Approach to Nonsexist Teaching. Teaching Resources with Curriculum Related Activities: 1. Elementary 2. Intermediate and Secondary. Available from ERIC (ED098086), 1974.

Tidball, M. E. Perspective on Academic Women and Affirmative Action. Educational Record, 1973, 54, 130-135.

Torrance, P. Helping the Creatively Gifted Girl Achieve Her Potentiality. Journal of the National Association of Women Deans and Counselors, 1965, 29(1), 28-33.

Truax, A. Research on the Status of Faculty Women, University of Minnesota. Minneapolis: University of Minnesota, Minnesota Planning and Counseling Center for Women, 1970.

Voss, V. With a Telling Tongue. Mademoiselle, 1967, March, 64, 152-153+.

Wasserman, E., Lewin, A. Y., and Bleiweis, L. H. (eds.). Women in Academia: Evolving Policies Toward Equal Opportunities. New York: Praeger, 1975.

West, S. D., Jr. Attitudes of High School Teachers, Principals, Guidance Counselors, Librarians, and Teacher Educators Toward the Social, Educational, and Economic Roles of Women. Unpublished doctoral dissertation, University of Florida, 1975.

White, M. S. Psychological and Social Barriers to Women in Science. Science, 1970, October 23, 170(3956), 413-416. Also in C. Safilios-Rothschild (ed.), Toward a Sociology of Women. Lexington, MA: Xerox College Publishing, 1972, 300-308; and in J. Freeman (ed.), Women: A Feminist Perspective. Palo Alto: Mayfield, 1975, 227-237.

Why Women Need Less Pay (And Other Myths). The Chronicle of Higher Education, 1973, March 12, 7(23), 9.

Wilson, D., and Doyle, K. O., Jr. Student Ratings of Instruction;

Student and Instructor Sex Interactions. Journal of Higher Education, 1976, July, 47, 465-470.

Withey, S. Women PhD's Hurt More Than Men by Job Shortage, Survey Shows. The Chronicle of Higher Education, 1971, January 11, 5(14), 4.

_____, et al. Women Physicists Are Bucking the Tide at Harvard. Boston Globe, 1972, November 24.

Women and the Doctorate. Intellect, 1976, January, 104, 284.

Women in Colleges: Status, Teaching, and Feminist Criticism. Special Issue. College English, 1971, May, 32(8).

Women Writing and Teaching. Special Issue. College English, 1972, October, 34(1).

Women's Caucus, Political Science Department, University of Chicago. The Halls of Academe. In R. Morgan (ed.), Sisterhood Is Powerful. New York: Random House, 1970, 101.

Woodring, P. Sexism on the Campus: Women's Rights in Teaching and Administrative Positions. Saturday Review, 1970, May 16, 53, 80+.

D. ADMINISTRATORS

Abramson, P. Women Excel as Elementary Principals. Senior Scholastic, 1976, May 4, 108, TE5.

Arter, M. H. Role of Women in Administration in State Universities and Land Grant Colleges. Unpublished doctoral dissertation, Arizona State University, 1972. Dissertation Abstracts International, 1972, 32(A), 5559. Also available from ERIC (ED086085), 1972.

Asper, L. B. Factors Affecting the Entry of Women into Administrative Positions of the Manitoba School System. Unpublished Masters thesis, University of Manitoba, 1974.

Astin, A. W. A Study of Administrative Positions with Regard to Women. UCLA Educator, 1977, Spring. Los Angeles: UCLA Graduate School of Education.

Bach, L. Of Women, School Administration, and Discipline. Phi Delta Kappan, 1976, March, 463-466.

Bacon, P. A. PA's--Most Are Middle-Aged and Male. College and University Business, 1974, February, 56, 22-24.

Baine, E. V. Women Holders of Leadership Positions on the Coeducational Campus. Journal of the National Association of Women Deans and Counselors, 1968, Fall, 32, 39.

Bernard, J. S. Academic Women. University Park: Pennsylvania State University Press, 1964.

Bruker, R., Jass, R., and Schefelbein, B. The Role of Women in Management in Our Profession--Three Points of View. College and University, 1974, Fall, 50, 46-59.

Burns, D. M. Women in Educational Administration: A Study of Leadership in California Public Schools. Unpublished doctoral dissertation, University of Oregon. Dissertation Abstracts, 1964, 25(A), 2821-2822.

Carroll, M. A. Women in Administration in Higher Education. Contemporary Education, 1972, February, 43(4), 214-218.

Clarke, E. A. Women in Administrative Positions in Public Education. Philadelphia: Temple University, Recruitment Leadership and Training Institute, 1974.

Cobbley, L. O. Study of Attitudes and Opportunities for Women in Six Western States to Become Elementary School Principals. Unpublished doctoral dissertation, Brigham Young University. Dissertation Abstracts International, 1970, 31(A), 4409.

College and University Personnel Association. Women and Minorities in Administration of Higher Education Institutions: Employment Patterns and Salary Comparisons. Washington, D. C. : CUPA, n. d.

Collins, L. About Those Few Females Who Scale the Heights of School Management. American School Board Journal, 1976, June, 163(6), 24-27.

Coursen, D. Women and Minorities in Administration. Arlington, VA: National Association of Elementary School Principals, 1975.

Crosby, J. W. An Exploratory Study of Women Superintendents. Unpublished doctoral dissertation, University of Massachusetts. Dissertation Abstracts International, 1974, 34(A), 3742.

Dale, C. T. Women Are Still Missing Persons in Administrative and Supervisory Jobs. Educational Leadership, 1973, 31(2), 123-127.

Dias, S. L. A Study of Personal, Perceptual, and Motivational Factors Influential in Predicting the Aspiration Level of Women and Men Toward the Administrative Roles in Education. Unpublished doctoral dissertation. Dissertation Abstracts International, 1975, September, 36(3-A), 1202.

_____. The Aspiration Levels of Women for Administrative Careers in Education: Predictive Factors and Implications for Effecting Change. Paper presented at the American Educational Research Association meeting, San Francisco, 1976. Also available from ERIC (ED119376), 1976.

Dunn, C. J. College Deans of Women: A Synthesis of the Literature. Personnel and Guidance Journal, 1968, February, 46(6), 550-554.

Eaton, L. L. A Survey of Women Graduates in the Field of Educational Administration. Unpublished doctoral dissertation, Eastern Michigan University, 1970.

Estler, S. E. Women as Leaders in Public Education. SIGNS: Journal of Women in Culture and Society, 1975, Winter, 1(2), 363-386.

Fecher, A. A. R. Career Patterns of Women in College and University Administration. Unpublished doctoral dissertation, Indiana University. Dissertation Abstracts International, 1973, 33(A), 6115.

Fishel, A., and Pottker, J. Women Lose Out: Is There Sex Discrimination in School Administration? Clearing House, 1973, 47, 387-391.

_____, and _____. Women in Educational Governance: A Statistical Portrait. Educational Researcher, 1974, 3, 4-7. Also in Sex Bias in the Schools--Research Evidence. Madison, NJ: Fairleigh Dickinson University Press, 1977, 505-513.

_____, and _____. Performance of Women Principals: A Review of Behavioral and Attitudinal Studies. Journal of the National Association for Women Deans, Administrators, and Counselors, 1975, Spring, 38, 110-117. Also in Sex Bias in the Schools--Research Evidence. Madison, NJ: Fairleigh Dickenson University Press, 1977, 289-299.

Fleming, J. T. Assessment of Employment Practices Toward Women Administrators in Institutions of Higher Education. Unpublished doctoral dissertation, Arizona State University. Dissertation Abstracts International, 1974, 35(A), 4184.

Gardner, H. R. Women Administrators in Higher Education in Illinois: A Study of Current Career Patterns. Unpublished doctoral dissertation, Indiana University. Dissertation Abstracts, 1966, 27(A), 1686.

Gasser, M. H. Career Patterns of Women Administrators in Higher Education: Barriers and Constraints. Unpublished doctoral dissertation, Southern Illinois University. Dissertation Abstracts International, 1976, 36(A), 7893.

Gateways and Barriers for Women in the University Community. Proceedings of Cornell University's Mary Donlou Alger Conference for Trustees and Administrators. Washington, D. C.: Association of Governing Boards, 1976.

Gillies, J. In Defense of the Dean of Women: A New Role for a New World. Journal of the National Association for Women Deans, Administrators, and Counselors, 1975, Summer, 38, 156-162.

Goerss, K. V. W. A Study of Personality Factors of Selected Women Administrators in Higher Education. Dissertation Abstracts International, 1975, 36, 1942.

_____. Women Administrators in Education: A Review of Research 1960-1976. Ruth Strang Research Award Monograph Series, No. 3. Washington, D. C.: National Association for Women Deans, Administrators, and Counselors, 1977, July.

Gordon, R. S., and Ball, P. G. Survival Dynamics for Women in Educational Administration. Journal of the National Association for Women Deans, Administrators, and Counselors, 1977, Winter, 40(2), 46-48.

Grambs, J. D. Women and Administration: Confrontation or Accommodation? Theory Into Practice, 1976, October, 15, 293-300.

Gross, N., and Trask, A. Men and Women as Elementary Principals. Cambridge, MA: Harvard University, Graduate School of Education, 1965.

Guttman, M. A. J. Is the Gray Mare Only a Workhorse? Personnel and Guidance Journal, 1972, October, 51(2), 115-121.

_____, and Hicks, L. Characteristics of Female Members of ACES. Counselor Education and Supervision, 1974, March, 13(3), 165-171.

Haller, L. M. The Future Role of the Highest Ranking Woman Student Personnel Administrator in the College or University and a Suggested Training Program. Unpublished doctoral dissertation, Michigan State University. Dissertation Abstracts, 1968, 28(10-A), 3933.

Hare, N. The Vanishing Woman Principal. National Elementary Principal, 1966, April, 45(5), 12-13.

Haun, H. T. A Study of Work Satisfaction and Dissatisfaction Among Selected Women Leaders in Higher Education. Unpublished doctoral dissertation, University of Tennessee. Dissertation Abstracts International, 1975, September, 36(3-A), 1330.

Henschel, B. J. S. A Comparison of the Personality Variables of

Women Administrators and Women Teachers in Education. Unpublished doctoral dissertation, University of Utah. Dissertation Abstracts, 1964, 25(A), 6313.

Holland, J. L. Relations Between the Chief School Administrator's Selection of Principal Candidates and the Candidates' Qualifications, Attitudes on Educational Issues and Sex. Unpublished doctoral dissertation, Fordham University. Dissertation Abstracts International, 1973, 34(A), 2213-2214.

Howard, S. Why Aren't Women Administering Our Schools? Arlington, VA: National Council of Administrative Women in Education, 1975.

Hoyle, J. Who Shall Be Principal--A Man or a Woman? National Elementary Principal, 1969, January, 48(3), 23-24.

Hulett, S. A. Women Administrators in Missouri. School and Community, 1977, January, 63, 16+.

Ingraham, M. Mirror of Brass: Compensation and Working Conditions of College and University Administrators. Madison: University of Wisconsin Press, 1968.

Jenkins, W. J. A Study of the Attitudes of Elementary School Teachers in Selected Schools in Montgomery County, Pennsylvania, Toward the Woman Elementary School Principal. Unpublished doctoral dissertation, Temple University. Dissertation Abstracts, 1966, 27(5-A), 1223-1224.

Johnson, D. What Is the Future of Women in School Administration? In Women: A Significant National Resource. Washington, D. C.: National Council of Administrative Women in Education, 1971, 35.

Johnson, J. L. Women Leaders in National Guidance and Counseling Associations: Some Implications of Their Backgrounds and Leadership Roles. Dissertation Abstracts International, 1973, 33, 2713.

Kaufmann, S. Few Women Get Positions of Power in Academe, Survey Discloses. The Chronicle of Higher Education, 1970, November 30, 5, 1+.

Kaye, B. W. Moving Women into Educational Administration. Available from ERIC (ED105549), 1975.

Kobayashi, K. A Comparison of Organizational Climate of Schools Administered by Female and Male Elementary School Principals. Unpublished doctoral dissertation, University of the Pacific. Dissertation Abstracts International, 1974, 35(A), 129-130.

Koontz, E. D. The Double Standard in Education. In The Best Kept

Administrators / 389

Secret of the Past 5,000 Years: Women Are Ready for Leadership in Education. Bloomington, IN: Phi Delta Kappa Educational Foundation, 1972, 39-41.

――――. The Best Kept Secret of the Past 5,000 Years: Women Are Ready for Leadership in Education. Bloomington, IN: Phi Delta Kappa Educational Foundation, 1972.

Krause, J. L. A Study of Teacher Attitudes Toward Their Women Secondary School Principals in New Jersey. Unpublished doctoral dissertation, Temple University. Dissertation Abstracts, 1964, 25(A), 967-968.

Krohn, B. The Puzzling Case of the Missing Ms. Nation's Schools and Colleges, 1974, November, 1, 32-38.

LaBarthe, E. R. A Study of the Motivation of Women in Administrative and Supervisory Positions in Selected Unified School Districts in Southern California. Unpublished doctoral dissertation, University of California. Dissertation Abstracts International, 1974, 34(A), 3695-3696.

Landon, G. L. Perceptions of Sex Role Stereotyping and Women Teachers' Administrative Career Aspirations. Unpublished doctoral dissertation, University of Wisconsin. Dissertation Abstracts International, 1975, September, 36(3-A), 1214-1215.

Lemon, D. K. A Study of the Attitude of Selected Groups Toward the Employment of Women for Administrative Positions in Public Schools. Unpublished doctoral dissertation, University of Kansas. Dissertation Abstracts, 1968, 29(6-A), 1718-1719.

Linton, D. L. Teachers' Perceptions of Women as Principals in an Elementary School District. Unpublished doctoral dissertation, U.S. International University. Dissertation Abstracts International, 1974, 35(A), 1354.

Long, T. E., et al. Role Perceptions of Female Faculty and Their Administrators in Post-Secondary Proprietary Schools. Vocational-Technical Education Research Report, 1975, July, 13(4).

Longstreth, C. A. An Analysis of the Perceptions of the Leadership Behavior of Male and Female Secondary School Principals in Florida. Unpublished doctoral dissertation, University of Miami. Dissertation Abstracts International, 1973, 34(A), 2224-2225.

Lupini, D. Women in Administration--Where Are They? Education Canada, 1975, Winter, 15, 17-22.

McCorkle, E. M. Top-Level Women Administrators in Higher Education: A Study of Women Presidents, Chief Academic Officers, and Academic Deans in Federal Regions I, VI, and X. Dissertation Abstracts International, 1975, 36(A), 7238.

McIntosh, J. C. Differences Between Women Teachers Who Do and Do Not Seek Promotion. Journal of Educational Administration, 1974, 12(2), 28-41.

McLure, G. T., and McLure, J. W. Women and Educational Administration. The Humanist Educator, 1976, June, 14(4), 188-193.

McLure, J. W., and McLure, G. T. The Case of the Vanishing Woman: Implications for the Preparation of Women in Educational Administration. In D. F. Musella et al. (eds.), Leadership Development for Women in Education. Toronto: The Ontario Council for Leadership in Education, 1975, 6-9.

Matheny, P. H. P. A Study of the Attitudes of Selected Male and Female Teachers, Administrators and Board of Education Presidents Toward Women in Educational Administrative Positions. Unpublished doctoral dissertation, Northwestern University. Dissertation Abstracts International, 1973, 34(A), 2976.

Mattes, L., and Watkins, J. F. Women in Administration in Schools of Education. Intellect, 1973, November, 102, 132-133.

Michael, J. A. Women/Men in Leadership Roles in Art Education. Studies in Art Education, 1977, 18(2), 7-20.

Mickish, G. Can Women Function as Successfully as Men in the Role of Elementary Principal? Boulder, CO: University of Colorado, Bureau of Educational Research, 1971.

_____. Can Women Function as Successfully as Men in the Role of Elementary Principal? Research Reports on Educational Administration, 1971, 2(4).

Milanovich, A. Gentlemen Before Ladies? Women Teachers Aspiring to Elementary Principalships Are Being Discriminated Against. New York State Educator, 1966, December, 54, 18-19.

Miner, J. B. Motivation to Manage Among Women: Studies of Business Managers and Educational Administrators. Journal of Vocational Behavior, 1974, 5, 197-208.

Morsink, H. A. A Comparative Study of the Leader Behavior of Men and Women Secondary School Principals. Unpublished doctoral dissertation. Dissertation Abstracts, 1966, 27(A), 2793.

_____. Leader Behavior of Men and Women Secondary School Principals. Educational Horizons, 1968-69, 69-94.

_____. Leader Behavior of Men and Women Principals. National Association of Secondary School Principals Bulletin, 1970, September, 54, 80-87.

Administrators / 391

National Council of Administrative Women in Education. Wanted: More Women in Educational Leadership. Washington, D. C. : National Education Association, 1965.

Neidig, M. B. Women Applicants for Administrative Positions: Attitudes Held by Administrators and School Boards. Unpublished doctoral dissertation, University of Iowa. Dissertation Abstracts International, 1973, 34(A), 2982.

_____. Rise and Decline of Women Administrators. National Elementary Principals, 1976, November, 56, 53-54.

Nieboer, N. A. There Is a Certain Kind of Woman. Journal of the National Association for Women Deans, Administrators, and Counselors, 1975, 38(3), 99-103. Also in The Education Digest, 1975, 41, 60-62.

Nixon, M. Women Administrators and Women Teachers: A Comparative Study. Unpublished doctoral dissertation, University of Alberta, 1975.

_____, and Gue, L. R. Women Administrators and Women Teachers: A Comparative Study. Alberta Journal of Educational Research, 1975, September, 21(3), 196-206.

_____, and _____. The Professional Role Orientation of Women Administrators and Women Teachers. Canadian Administrator, 1975, November, 15(2), 1-5.

_____, and Hrynyk, N. P. Women in School Administration: A Study of the Deployment of Women in Positions of Administrative Responsibility in Alberta Schools. Occasional Papers, 1973, March. Edmonton: Alberta Teachers Association.

Norman, B. A Study of Women in Leadership Positions in North Carolina. Delta Kappa Gamma Bulletin, 1970, 36, 10-14.

O'Brien, G. M. The Trials of Women's-College Presidents. The Chronicle of Higher Education, 1977, August 1, 14(21), 8-9.

Oltman, R. M. The Evolving Role of the Women's Liberation Movement in Higher Education. Available from ERIC (ED049489), 1971.

Painter, E. G. Women: The Last of the Discriminated. Journal of the National Association of Women Deans and Counselors, 1971, Winter, 34, 59-61.

Palmieri, P., and Shakeshaft, C. S. Up the Front Staircase: A Proposal for Women to Achieve Parity with Men in the Field of Educational Administration. Journal of the National Association for Women Deans, Administrators, and Counselors, 1976, 39(2), 58-65.

Peterson, M. A Woman Administrator Speaks: Openness and Secrecy in Educational Administration. Journal of the National Association for Women Deans, Administrators, and Counselors, 1975, Spring, 38(3), 124-131.

Pfiffner, V. T. Factors Associated with Women in Major Administrative Positions in California Community Colleges. Unpublished doctoral dissertation, University of Southern California. Dissertation Abstracts International, 1973, 33(A), 4888.

_____. Women as Leaders in Higher Education in These Changing Times. Delta Kappa Gamma Bulletin, 1975, 41(3), 5-10.

_____. Composite Profile of a Top-Level California Community College Woman Administrator. Journal of the National Association for Women Deans, Administrators, and Counselors, 1976, 40(1), 16-17.

Preparing Women for College Posts. Intellect, 1974, March, 102, 345-346.

Pruitt, G. S. Women in Leadership of Alternative Schools. Dissertation Abstracts International, 1976, 37(A), 80.

Rader, H. B. Women in Higher Education Administration: Annotated Bibliography. Washington, D. C.: National Association for Women Deans, Administrators and Counselors, 1976.

Ralston, Y. L. An Analysis of Attitudes as Barriers to the Selection of Women as College Presidents in Florida. Unpublished doctoral dissertation, University of Mississippi. Dissertation Abstracts International, 1975, May, 35(11-A), 6992.

Recruitment, Leadership and Training Institute. Women in Administrative Positions in Public Education. Philadelphia: Temple University, 1974.

Reeves, M. E. An Analysis of Job Satisfaction of Women Administrators in Higher Education. Journal of the National Association for Women Deans, Administrators, and Counselors, 1975, Spring, 38(3), 132-135.

Reilly, T. M. Women in Key Positions. Delta Kappa Gamma Bulletin, 1976, Fall, 43, 55-58.

Rideout, A. H. The Upward Mobility of Women in Higher Education: A Profile of Women Home Economics Administrators. Dissertation Abstracts International, 1974, 35(A), 2604.

Rossi, A. S., and Calderwood, A. Academic Women on the Move. New York: Russell Sage Foundation, 1973.

Roussell, C. Relationship of Sex of Department Head to Department Climate. Administrative Science Quarterly, 1974, June, 19(2), 211-220.

Sarvas, A. F. An Analysis of the Relationship Between Perceptions of Vocational Female Faculty and Administrators Toward Female Faculty in Four Institutional Types. Available from ERIC (ED118993), 1976.

Schetlin, E. M. Wonderland and Looking-Glass: Women in Administration. Journal of the National Association for Women Deans, Administrators, and Counselors, 1975, 38(3), 104-109.

_____. Remembering the Ladies: Abigail Adams and the Women Deans, Administrators, and Counselors. Journal of the National Association for Women Deans, Administrators, and Counselors, 1976, Summer, 39(4), 163-167.

Schlack, M. J. A Comparison of Personal Characteristics and Leadership Styles of University Upper Management and Middle Management Women Student Personnel Administrators. Unpublished doctoral dissertation. Dissertation Abstracts International, 1974, 35(A), 852.

Schmuck, P. A. Deterrents to Women's Careers in School Management. Sex Roles: A Journal of Research, 1975, 1(4), 339-353.

Scriven, A. L. A Study of Women Occupying Administrative Positions in the Central Office of Large School Districts. Unpublished doctoral dissertation, University of Florida. Dissertation Abstracts International, 1973, 33(A), 6920.

Seawell, W., and Canady, R. L. Where Have All the Women Gone? National Elementary Principal, 1974, 53, 46-48.

Sexton, P. Male Dominance and School Leadership. In Women in Education. Bloomington, IN: Phi Delta Kappa Educational Foundation, 1976, 55-60.

Sizemore, B. A. Will the Woman Administrator Make a Difference? Paper presented at the American Association of School Administrators meeting, Atlantic City, February 1973. Also available from ERIC (ED078497), 1973.

Soldwedel, B. The Profile and Status of N. A. W. D. A. C. Members. Journal of the National Association for Women Deans, Administrators, and Counselors, 1977, Summer, 40(4), 123.

Spence, B. A. Sex of Teachers as a Factor in Their Perception of Selected Leadership Characteristics of Male and Female Elementary School Principals. Unpublished doctoral dissertation, Purdue University. Dissertation Abstracts International, 1971, 32(A), 2985.

Status of Women Faculty and Administrators in Higher Education Institutions 1971-1972. Available from ERIC (ED080034), 1973.

Stevenson, F. B. Women Administrators in Big Ten Universities. Unpublished doctoral dissertation. Dissertation Abstracts International, 1973, 34(A), 5533.

Strache, L. K. Personality Characteristics of Men and Women Administrators: Actual Versus Perceived. Paper presented at the American Psychological Association Convention, Washington, D. C., 1976.

Taylor, S. S. The Attitudes of Superintendents and Board of Education Members in Connecticut Toward the Employment and Effectiveness of Women as Public School Administrators. Unpublished doctoral dissertation, University of Connecticut. Dissertation Abstracts International, 1971, July, 32(1-A), 145.

_____. Educational Leadership: A Male Domain? Phi Delta Kappan, 1973, 55, 124-128.

_____. The Attitudes of Superintendents and Board of Education Members Toward the Employment and Effectiveness of Women as Public-School Administrators. In J. Pottker and A. Fishel (eds.), Sex Bias in the Schools--Research Evidence. Madison, NJ: Fairleigh Dickinson University Press, 1977, 300-310.

Tessler, S. E. Profiles of Selected Women College Presidents Reflecting the Emerging Role of Women in Higher Education. Unpublished doctoral dissertation. Dissertation Abstracts International, 1976, 37(A), 840.

Thurston, A. J. A Woman President?!--A Study of Two-Year College Presidents. Journal of the National Association for Women Deans, Administrators, and Counselors, 1975, Spring, 38(3), 118-123.

Timmons, J. E. A Study of Attitudes Toward Women School Administrators and the Aspirations of Women Teachers for Administrative Positions in the State of Indiana. Unpublished doctoral dissertation, Indiana University. Dissertation Abstracts International, 1974, 34(8-A), 4660.

Timpano, D. M., and Knight, L. W. Sex Discrimination in the Selection of School District Administrators: What Can Be Done? Washington, D. C.: National Institute of Education, 1977.

Tuttle, H. I. Actual and Ideal Perceptions of the Role of the Dean of Women by Students, Administrators, Faculty, and Staff at Upper Iowa College. Unpublished doctoral dissertation. Dissertation Abstracts, 1968, 29(4-A), 1113.

Tyler, L. E. Must University Administration Remain A Man's

World? Wayne State University Graduate Comment, 1969, 12, 6-11.

Valentine, C. Women in University Administration. Innovator, 1975, January 20, 6, 3.

VanMeir, E. J. Sexual Discrimination in School Administration Opportunities. Journal of the National Association for Women Deans, Administrators, and Counselors, 1975, 38(4), 163-167.

Verheyden-Hilliard, M. E. Training Ground for Women in Administration. Education Digest, 1975, November, 41, 33-35.

Vos, C. Problems and Solutions for Women Student Personnel Administrators. Unpublished manuscript, Michigan State University, East Lansing, n. d.

Walsh, P. A. Career Patterns of Women Administrators in Higher Education Institutions in California. Unpublished doctoral dissertation. Dissertation Abstracts International, 1975, 36(A), 3323.

Warwick, E. B. Attitudes Toward Women in Administrative Positions as Related to Curricular Implementation and Change. Unpublished doctoral dissertation, University of Wisconsin. Dissertation Abstracts, 1967, 28(A), 1256-1257.

West, S. D., Jr. Attitudes of High School Teachers, Principals, Guidance Counselors, Librarians, and Teacher Educators Toward the Social, Educational, and Economic Roles of Women. Unpublished doctoral dissertation, University of Florida, 1975.

White, B. Current Status of Professional and Administrative Women in Higher Education. Unpublished manuscript, Michigan State University, East Lansing, n. d.

Whitney, M. E. Women Student Personnel Administrators: The Past and the Future. Journal of College Student Personnel, 1971, January, 12, 7-10.

Whitten, J. E. Women Teachers' Perceptions Concerning Career Aspirations of the Elementary Principalship in Selected Schools in Texas. Unpublished doctoral dissertation, University of Houston. Dissertation Abstracts International, 1975, November, 36(5-A), 2566-2567.

Winkler, K. J. Women Administrators Seek Way Out of Isolation. The Chronicle of Higher Education, 1973, November 5, 8, 5.

Woman's View from the Top. Community and Junior College Journal, 1976, 46(4), 16-20.

Women in Administration: Symposium. Journal of the National Association for Women Deans, Administrators, and Counselors, 1975, Spring/Summer, 38, 99-143+.

Woodring, P. Sexism on the Campus: Women's Rights in Teaching and Administrative Positions. Saturday Review, 1970, May, 53, 80+.

Zimmerman, J. N. The Status of Women in Educational Administrative Positions Within the Central Offices of Public Schools. Unpublished doctoral dissertation, Temple University. Dissertation Abstracts International, 1971, 32(A), 1826.

VI

OCCUPATIONAL FORCES AND WOMEN'S AMBITION

I'm squeezed, I'm frustrated, because I conduct five concerts a year, sometimes six, and I'd like to conduct five concerts a month. I cannot play my instrument, which is the orchestra.... I want to conduct professional orchestras. And I want to conduct in New York. I want to conduct in California, in San Francisco. I want to conduct in Russia. Every single time I hear the name, Evgenie Svetlana, I die inside, because she is a woman, in Russia, conducting all the time.... It's a perpetual heartbreak. --Antonia Brico.

A. GENERAL

Abzug, B. S. Last Hired, First Fired. Saturday Review, 1976, August 7, 3, 16-17.

Affirmative Action--How Far Must It Go? Detroit Free Press, 1972, March.

Alexander, S. State-by-State Guide to Women's Legal Rights. Los Angeles: Wolstonecraft, 1975.

Almquist, E. M. Women in the Labor Force. SIGNS: Journal of Women in Culture and Society, 1977, Summer, 2(4), 843-855.

American Women: Their Status and Education. United States Presents Commission on the Status of Women. Practical Forecast for Home Economics, 1963, November, 9, 26-27+.

America's New Working Woman: Interviews. Harper's Bazaar, 1977, August, 110, 72-83.

Amundsen, K. Institutional Sexism. In The Silenced Majority: Women and American Democracy. Englewood Cliffs, NJ: Prentice-Hall, 1971, 42-61.

_____. On Her Own: Down and Under. In The Silenced Majority: Women and American Democracy. Englewood Cliffs, NJ: Prentice-Hall, 1971, 19-41.

Anastasi, A. Sources of Bias in the Prediction of Job Performance: Technical Critique. In L. A. Crooks (ed.), An Investigation of Sources of Bias in the Prediction of Job Performance: A Six-Year Study. Princeton, NJ: Educational Testing Service, 1972.

Anderson, R. E., and Terstine, R. J. Our Working Women, an Under-Utilized Resource. Business Horizons, 1973, February, 16(1), 55-62.

Andreas, C. Keeping People in Their Places: St. Paul, Freud, and Madison Avenue. In Sex and Caste in America. Englewood Cliffs, NJ: Prentice-Hall, 1971, 67-91.

_____. The World of Work: Supply and Demand in a Male-Dominated Society. In Sex and Caste in America. Englewood Cliffs, NJ: Prentice-Hall, 1971, 48-66.

Are We Wasting Women? Life, 1961, July 28, 51, 36B.

Ashburn, E. A. Motivation, Personality, and Work-Related Characteristics of Women in Male-Dominated Professions. Ruth Strang Research Award Monograph Series No. 2. National Association for Women Deans, Administrators, and Counselors, Washington, D. C. : 1977.

Astin, H. S. Factors Associated with the Participation of Women Doctorates in the Labor Force. Personnel and Guidance Journal, 1967, November, 46, 240-246.

_____. The Woman Doctorate in America. New York: Russell Sage Foundation, 1969.

_____. Women and Work. In J. Sherman and F. Denmark (eds.), Psychology of Women: Future Directions of Research. New York: Psychological Dimensions, 1978.

_____, Suniewick, N., and Dweck, S. Women: A Bibliography on Their Education and Careers. New York: Behavioral Publications, 1974.

Athanassiades, J. C. An Investigation of Some Communication Patterns of Female Subordinates in Hierarchial Organizations. Human Relations, 1974, March, 27(3), 195-209.

Atlanta, Georgia, NOW Chapter. Sex Discrimination in Employment. Reprint from KNOW Inc., P. O. Box 86031, Pittsburgh, PA 15221.

Ayella, M. E., and Williamson, J. B. The Social Mobility of Women: A Causal Model of Socioeconomic Success. Sociological Quarterly, 1976, Autumn, 17(4), 534-554.

Baer, M. F. Work Life Expectancy of Women. Personnel and Guidance Journal, 1968, March, 46, 720.

Baetjer, A. M. Health Problems Among Employed Women. Journal of the National Association of Women Deans and Counselors, 1966, Summer, 29, 156-159.

Barbash, J. Industrialism and Woman's Status. Vocational Guidance Quarterly, 1964, Autumn, 13, 21-27.

Barnal, L. Status of Women at HEW. LD, Federal Women's Program. Washington, D. C. : Department of Health, Education and Welfare.

Barnard, T. M. The Conflict Between State Protective Legislation and Federal Laws Prohibiting Sex Discrimination: Is It Resolved? Wayne Law Review, 1971, 17, 25-65.

Barron, P. S. E. A Comparison of the Individual Characteristics, Extrinsic Rewards and Occupational Mobility of Women in Male and Female Occupations. Unpublished doctoral dissertation, University of Chicago, 1975. Dissertation Abstracts International, 1976, 36(12-A), 8304. Also available from ERIC (ADG 029-0725), 1975.

Bars Against Women. Time, 1971, January 11, 97, 31.

Bartnoff, J. Title VII and Employment Discrimination in Upper Level Jobs. Columbia Law Review, 1973, 73, 1614-1640.

Bartol, K. M. Relationship of Sex and Professional Training Area to Job Orientation. Journal of Applied Psychology, 1976, 61, 368-370.

Bass, B. M., Krusell, J., and Alexander, R. A. Male Manager's Attitude Toward Working Women. American Behavioral Scientist, 1971, 15, 63-78.

Bazaar's Guide to Success on the Job; Symposium. Harper's Bazaar, 1977, August, 110, 84-89+.

Becker, G. S. The Economics of Discrimination. Chicago: The University of Chicago Press, 1971.

Beckham, B., and Aronson, H. Selection of Jury Foremen as a Measure of Social Status of Women. Symposium presentation at the American Psychological Association Convention, San Francisco, 1977.

Bedeian, A. G., Armenakis, A. A., and Kemp, B. W. Relation of Sex to Perceived Legitimacy of Organizational Influence. Journal of Psychology, 1976, 94, 93-99.

Bell, C. S. Economics, Sex, and Gender. Social Science Quarterly, 1974, December, 55(3), 615-631.

Bell, D. On Meritocracy and Equality. Public Interest, 1972, 29, 29-68.

Bem, S. L., and Bem, D. J. Sex-Segregated Want Ads: Do They Discourage Female Job Applicants? Reprint from KNOW, Inc., P.O. Box 86031, Pittsburgh, PA 15221, 1970.

———, and ———. Does Sex-Biased Job Advertising Aid and Abet Sex Discrimination? Journal of Applied Social Psychology, 1973, 3(1), 6-18.

Benston, M. The Political Economy of Women's Liberation. In M. H. Garskof (ed.), Roles Women Play: Readings Toward Women's Liberation. Monterey, CA: Brooks/Cole, 1971, 194-205.

Bergmann, B. The Economics of Women's Liberation. Challenge, 1973, May-June, 16(2), 11-17.

———, and Gray, M. Equality in Retirement Benefits. In S. Crowell (ed.), Civil Rights Digest, 1975, Fall, 8(1), 25-27.

Bernard, J. Female Workers: The Myth and the Reality. Washington, D.C.: Women's Bureau, Department of Labor, 1967.

———. Sexism and Discrimination. American Sociologist, 1970, November, 5, 374-375.

———. The Jobs of Women. In Women and the Public Interest. Chicago: Aldine-Atherton, 1971, 105-135.

———. Women and the Public Interest. Chicago: Aldine-Atherton, 1971.

———. Women and New Social Structures. In M. L. McBee and K. A. Blake (eds.), The American Woman: Who Will She Be? Riverside, NJ: Glencoe Press, 1974, 81-93.

———. The Impact of Sexism and Racism on Employment Status and Earnings. In Women, Wives, Mothers: Values and Options. Chicago: Aldine, 1975, 200-212.

———. Historical and Structural Barriers to Occupational Desegregation. In M. Blaxall and B. Reagan (eds.), Women and the Workplace: The Implications of Occupational Segregation. Chicago: University of Chicago Press, 1976.

Bernard, S. Women's Economic Status: Some Cliches and Some Facts. In J. Freeman (ed.), Women: A Feminist Perspective. Palo Alto, CA: Mayfield, 1975, 238-241.

Bernstein, M. C., and Williams, L. G. Professor Higgins' Complaint; or, The Pension Treatment of Women Who Refuse to

Act Like Men. Educational Record, 1974, Fall, 55(4), 248-256.

Berry, J., et al. Development of Permanent Part-Time Employment Opportunities for Girls and Women. Kansas City: University of Missouri, 1968.

Bettelheim, B. Growing Up Female. Harper's, 1962, October, 225(1349), 120-128.

Bickner, M. L. Women at Work: An Annotated Bibliography. Los Angeles: Institute of Industrial Relations, 1974.

Bigoness, W. J. Effect of Applicant's Sex, Race, and Performance on Employers' Performance Ratings: Some Additional Findings. Journal of Applied Psychology, 1976, 61(1), 80-84.

Billings, V. Getting It Together. In The Womansbook. Los Angeles: Wollstonecraft, 1974, 113-143.

Bing, E. The Effect of Child Rearing Practices on Development of Differential Cognitive Abilities. Child Development, 1963, 34, 631-648.

Bird, C. Everything a Woman Needs to Know to Get Paid What She's Worth. New York: David McKay, 1974.

Bishop, J. F. College Women as Part-Time Workers. Journal of College Placement, 1968, December, 29, 113-114+.

Blau, F. D. Women in the Labor Force: An Overview. In J. Freeman (ed.), Women: A Feminist Perspective. Palo Alto, CA: Mayfield, 1975, 211-226.

Blaubergs, M. S. Overcoming the Sexist Barriers to Gifted Women's Achievement. In B. Johnson (ed.), Advantage/Disadvantage Gifted. Ventura, CA: Ventura County Superintendent of Schools Office, 1979.

Blaxall, M., and Reagan, B. (eds.). Occupational Segregation in International Women's Year. SIGNS: Journal of Women In Culture and Society, 1976, Spring Supplement, 1(3, Pt. 2), 1-5.

_____, and _____ (eds.). Women and the Workplace: The Implications of Occupational Segregation. Chicago: University of Chicago Press, 1976.

Blitz, R. C. Women in the Professions, 1870-1970. Monthly Labor Review, 1974, May, 97, 34-39.

_____. An International Comparison of Women's Participation in the Professions. Journal of Developing Areas, 1975, July, 9, 499-510.

Bloustein, E. J. Man's Work Goes from Sun to Sun, but Woman's Work Is Never Done. Psychology Today, 1968, March, 1, 38-41+.

Bogan, F. A. Work Experience of the Population: Spotlight on Women and Youths. Monthly Labor Review, 1969, June, 92, 44-50.

Boodish, H. M. Trends: Women and Careers. Social Studies, 1963, January, 54(1), 24-27.

Bose, C. E. Jobs and Gender: Sex and Occupational Prestige. Baltimore: Johns Hopkins University, Center for Metropolitan Planning and Research, 1973.

_____. Women and Jobs: Sexual Influences on Occupational Prestige. Unpublished doctoral dissertation. Johns Hopkins University, 1973.

Boulding, K., Leavitt, H. J., Mason, K. O., and Tangri, S. S. The Social Institutions of Occupational Change. SIGNS: A Journal of Women in Culture and Society, 1976, Spring, 1(3,2), 75-86.

Bowman, G. What Helps or Harms Promotability. Harvard Business Review, 1964, January-February, 42(1), 6-27.

Boyer, E. Women--Are the Technical Occupational Programs Attracting Them? Available from ERIC (ED085065), 1973.

Boyle, B. M. Equal Opportunity for Women Is Smart Business. Harvard Business Review, 1973, 51(3), 85-96. Also in H. H. Frank (ed.), Women in the Organization. Philadelphia: University of Pennsylvania Press, 1977, 173-190.

Bray, D. W. The Assessment Center--Opportunities for Women. Personnel, 1971, September/October, 48(5), 30-34.

Breaking In: Women in Non-Traditional Jobs. Women's Work, 1975, July/August, 1(4), 4.

Bridges, W. P., and Berk, R. A. Determinants of White Collar Income: An Evaluation of Equal Pay for Equal Work. Social Science Research, 1974, September, 3(3), 211-233.

Brief, A. P., and Wallace, M. J., Jr. The Impact of Employee Sex and Performance on the Allocation of Organizational Rewards. Journal of Psychology, 1976, 92, 25-34.

Broad, M. Developing Women's Resources: Challenges for the HRD Consultant. Training and Development Journal, 1975, September, 6-9.

Bronson, G. F. More Well-Educated Women Find Firms Willing to

Hire Them for Less Than Full-Time Employment. The Wall Street Journal, 1972, September 8, 8.

Brooks, T. R. Working Women. Dun's Review, 1963, August, 82, 62-63.

Brothers, J. How to Be Unafraid of Success. Harper's Bazaar, 1976, January, 109, 96-97+.

Brown, G. D. How Type of Employment Affects Earnings Differences by Sex. Monthly Labor Review, 1976, July, 25-30.

Brown, H. G. Sex and the Office. New York: Pocket Books, 1965.

Brown, R. H., III. Sex Discrimination: It Isn't Funny, It's Illegal, and the Battle Has Just Begun. Good Government, 1971, Winter, 88(4).

Bryant, B. E. American Women Today and Tomorrow. Washington, D. C.: National Commission on the Observance of International Women's Year, 1977.

Buckley, J. E. Pay Difference Between Men and Women in the Same Job. Monthly Labor Review, 1971, 94, 36-39.

Bunker, B. B., and Seashore, E. W. Power, Collusion, Intimacy-Sexuality, Support-Breaking the Sex Role Stereotypes in Social and Organizational Settings. In A. G. Sargent (ed.), Beyond Sex Roles. St. Paul, MN.: West, 1977, 356-370.

Bunting, M. I. Our Greatest Waste of Talent Is Women; With Introductory Comments. Life, 1961, January 13, 50, 63-64.

_____. Huge Waste: Educated Womanpower. New York Times Magazine, 1961, May 7, 23+.

Bureau of Labor Statistics. U. S. Working Women: A Chartbook. Bulletin 1880. Washington, D. C.: U. S. Department of Labor, 1975.

Bureau of the Census. 1970 Census of Population: Employment Status and Work Experience. Washington, D. C.: U. S. Department of Commerce, n. d.

_____. 1970 Census of Population: Occupational Characteristics. Washington, D. C.: U. S. Department of Commerce, n. d.

_____. A Statistical Portrait of Women in the U. S. Washington, D. C.: U. S. Department of Commerce, 1976.

Burk, D. Liberty, Justice and Equality for All? Business Education World, 1967, April, 47(8), 14-15.

Cain, G. G. Married Women in the Labor Force; An Economic Analysis. Chicago: University of Chicago Press, 1966.

Calder, B., and Ross, M. Sexual Discrimination and Work Performance. Personality and Social Psychology Bulletin, 1977, 3, 429-433.

Caldwell, O. J. American Women and International Affairs. Journal of the National Association of Women Deans and Counselors, 1968, Spring, 31, 122-126.

Campbell, D. P. The Clash Between Beautiful Women and Science. Paper presented at the American Psychological Association Convention, San Francisco, 1968.

Campbell, J. T., Crooks, L. A., Mahoney, M. H., and Rock, D. A. An Investigation of Sources of Bias in the Prediction of Job Performance. Princeton, NJ: Educational Testing Service, 1973.

Cantwell, M. Success, That Dirty Little Word. Mademoiselle, 1974, February, 78, 108-109.

Careers and Women. Senior Scholastic, 1964, November 11, 85(9), 22.

Careers of Ph. D's: Academic Versus Nonacademic, A Second Report on Follow-Ups of Doctorate Cohorts, 1935-1960. Washington, D. C.: National Academy of Sciences, 1968.

Carpenter, R. L., and Shearer, K. D. Sex and Salary Update. Library Journal, 1974, January 15, 101-107.

Cary, E., and Peratis, K. W. Woman and the Law. Skokie, IL: National Textbook, 1977.

The Case for Non-Traditional Work. Women's Work, 1975, July/August, 1(4), 4.

Cash, T. F., Gillen, B. and Burns, D. S. Sexism and 'Beautyism' in Personnel Consultant Decision Making. Journal of Applied Psychology, 1977, June, 62(3), 301-310.

Cater, L. A., Scott, A. F., and Martyna, W., (eds.). Discussions: Women, Power and Politics. In Women and Men: Changing Roles, Relationships, and Perceptions. New York: Praeger, 1977, 17-28.

Cavanagh, B. K. Legal Stereotypes and the Feminine Personality. Civil Liberties Law Review, 1971, 6, 261-285.

Cecil, E. A., Paul, R. J., and Olins, R. A. Perceived Importance of Selected Variables Used to Evaluate Male and Female Job Applicants. Personnel Psychology, 1973, 26, 397-404.

Chafe, W. H. The American Woman: Her Changing Social, Economic, and Political Role, 1920-1970. New York: Oxford University Press, 1972.

Chafetz, J. S. The Bringing Down of Jane. Masculine/Feminine or Human? An Overview of the Sociology of Sex Roles. Itasca, IL: F. E. Peacock, 1974, 108-156.

Changes in the Labor Force Status of Women. Monthly Labor Review, 1973, August, 96, 76.

Chapman, J. B., and Luthans, F. The Female Leadership Dilemma. Public Personnel Management, 1975, 4, 173-179.

Chapman, J. R. (ed.). Economic Independence for Women: The Foundation for Equal Rights. Beverly Hills, CA: Sage, 1976.

Chisholm, S. The 51% Minority. An address delivered at the Conference on Women's Employment sponsored by the Chicago Area Chapter of the National Organization for Women. Chicago, January 1970.

Christen, S. R., and Syptak, F. M. Helping Women to Move Up--A Successful First Step. Training and Development Journal, 1976, October, 30(10), 42-45.

Churchill, N. C., and Shank, J. K. Affirmative-Action and Guilt-Edged Goals. Harvard Business Review, 1976, March/April, 54(2), 111-116.

Cimons, M. Occupational Health V. Civil Rights for Women. New Republic, 1977, May 21, 176, 24.

Citizens' Advisory Council on the Status of Women. Women in 1975. Washington, D. C.: U. S. Gov. Printing Office, 1976.

Clarke, P., and Esposito, V. A Study of Occupational Advice for Women in Magazines. Journalism Quarterly, 1966, Autumn, 43(3), 477-485. Also in A. Theodore (ed.), The Professional Woman. Cambridge, MA: Schenkman, 1971.

Clawson, A. H. Liberation from Low Pay and Limited Opportunity. American Vocational Journal, 1970, December, 45, 31-32.

Cohen, M. S. Married Women in the Labor Force: An Analysis of Participation Rates. Monthly Labor Review, 1969, October, 92, 31-35.

_____. Sex Differences in Compensation. Journal of Human Resources, 1971, Fall, 6(4), 434-447.

Cohen, S. L., and Bunker, K. A. Subtle Effects of Sex Role Stereotypes on Recruiters' Hiring Decisions. Journal of Applied Psychology, 1975, 60(5), 566-572.

Commission on the Status of Women. Participation of Women in the Economic and Social Development of Their Countries. New York: United Nations, 1970.

Commission on Civil Rights. 8 Fact Sheets: Statistics on Effects of Racism and Sexism in the United States. U.S. Civil Rights Commission, 1973. Also reprint from KNOW, Inc., P.O. Box 86031, Pittsburgh, PA 15221.

_____. Last Hired, First Fired: Layoffs and Civil Rights. Washington, D.C.: U.S. Commission on Civil Rights, 1977.

Condran, G. A. Income Differentials Between Men and Women: United States, 1960. Paper presented at the Population Association meeting, Washington, D. C., April 1971.

Conyers, J. E. An Exploratory Study of Employers' Attitudes Toward Working Mothers. Sociology and Social Research, 1961, January, 45(2), 145-156.

Cooney, R.S. Female Professional Work Opportunities: A Cross-National Study. Demography, 1975, February, 12, 107-120.

Cooper, G. Legal Implications of the Use of Standardized Ability Tests in Employment and Education. Columbia Law Review, 1968, 68, 691-744.

The Corporate Woman: How Men Adjust to a Female Boss. Business Week, 1977, September 5, 90-94.

Coser, R. L., and Rokoff, G. Women in the Occupational World: Social Disruption and Conflict. Social Problems, 1971, Spring, 18, 535-554.

Costello, T. Where Do We Go from Here? In M. E. Katzell and W. C. Byham (eds.), Women in the Work Force: Confrontation with Change. New York: Behavioral Publications, 1972, 71-76.

Cousins, M. Why Women Don't Succeed. This Week Magazine, 1964, February 9, 10-11+.

Cowan, J. Demilitarizing the Corporation. Management Review, 1974, September, 63(9), 34-39.

Cowley, S.C., Lord, M., and Whitman, L. Women at Work. Newsweek, 1976, December 6, 88(23), 68-81.

Coyle, J.M. Job Involvement, Work Satisfaction, and Attitudes Toward Retirement of Business and Professional Women. Unpublished doctoral dissertation, Texas Woman's University, 1976. Dissertation Abstracts International, 1976, 87(7-A), 4630. Also available from ERIC (ADG77-0735), 1976.

Crooks, L. A. (ed.). An Investigation of Sources of Bias in the Prediction of Job Performance: A Six-Year Study. Princeton, NJ: Educational Testing Service, 1972.

Crouch, D. R. Going Up! New Rules for Women on the Job. Redbook, 1977, August, 149, 102-103+.

Crowley, J. E., Levitin, T. E., and Quinn, R. P. Facts and Fictions About American Working Women. Ann Arbor: University of Michigan, Institute for Social Research, Survey Research Center, 1973. Also available from ERIC (ED074235), 1973.

_____, _____, and _____. Seven Deadly Half-Truths About Women. Psychology Today, 1973, March, 6, 94-96. Also in C. Tavris (ed.), The Female Experience. From the editors of Psychology Today. Del Mar, CA: Communications Research Machines, 1973, 76-78.

Cunningham, R. M. Women Who Made It Offer Insights (Some Unintended) Into Their Problems. College and University Business, 1970, February, 48, 56-61.

Dana, C. M. Stumpin' and Hand-Pumpin': A Do It Yourself Guide to Entering Politics. Women's Work, 1976, March/April, 2(2), 7-8.

_____. Negotiating a Salary. Women's Work, 1976, July/August, 2(4), 15-16.

Daniels, A. K. The World of Work. In A Survey of Research Concerns of Women's Issues. Washington, D. C.: Association of American Colleges, 1975, 17-23.

Darian, J. C. Labor Force Participation of Married Women in the United States: An Investigation of the Role of Occupation. Unpublished doctoral dissertation, University of Pennsylvania, 1972. Dissertation Abstracts International, 1972, 33(4-A), 1860. Also available from ERIC (ADG72-25561), 1972.

Dauterive, J. W. Human Capital and Labor Market Structure: A Study of Interpersonal Differences in Wages Among Mature Career Women. Unpublished doctoral dissertation, Texas Technical University, 1976. Dissertation Abstracts International, 1977, 37(10-A), 6617. Also available from ERIC (ADG77-08743), 1976.

Davidson, S. Social Security and Women. Women's Work, 1976, May/June, 2(3), 24-25.

Davis, F., and Olesen, V. Initiation Into a Woman's Profession. Sociometry, 1963, 26, 89-101.

_____, and _____. The Career Outlook of Professionally Educated Women. Psychiatry, 1965, 28, 334-345.

Davis, W. Need Sex Desegregation. Science News Letter, 1964, July 11, 86, 22.

Deckard, B. S. The Women's Movement: Political, Socioeconomic, and Psychological Issues. New York: Harper & Row, 1975.

DeCrow, K. The Outer World Is Where the Fun Is. In The Young Woman's Guide to Liberation: Alternatives to the Half-Life While the Choice Is Still Yours. New York: Bobbs-Merrill, 1971, 181-197.

_____. Money and Employment (1): A Breach of the Duty of Fair Representation. In Sexist Justice: How Legal Sexism Affects You. New York: Random House, 1974, 64-86.

_____. Money and Employment (2): Sex and the Job Market. In Sexist Justice: How Legal Sexism Affects You. New York: Random House, 1974, 87-110.

_____. Sexist Justice: How Legal Sexism Affects You. New York: Random House, 1974.

De Fazio, M. Women's Role in Contemporary Society; The Report of the New York City Commission on Human Rights. New York: New York City Commission on Human Rights, 1970.

DeJong, P. Y. Factors Instrumental in Female Occupational Status: A Comparison to Factors Instrumental in Male Occupational Status. Unpublished doctoral dissertation, Western Michigan University, 1972. Dissertation Abstracts International, 1972, 33(7-A), 3788. Also available from ERIC (ADG73-01333), 1972.

_____, Brawer, M. J., and Robin, S. S. Patterns of Female Intergenerational Occupational Mobility: A Comparison with Male Patterns of Intergenerational Occupational Mobility. American Sociological Review, 1971, December, 36(6), 1033-1042.

Delgado, J. A Study of Women's Attitudes Toward Achieving Higher Level Jobs. M. B. A. thesis. Los Angeles: Pepperdine University, 1975.

Denmark, F. L. (ed.). Who Discriminates Against Women? An Overview with Editorial License. In Who Discriminates Against Women: Issue 15. Beverly Hills: Sage Publications, 1974, 5-7.

_____. Who Discriminates Against Women? Issue 15. Beverly Hills: Sage Publications, 1974.

_____. Styles of Leadership. Presidential address, Division 35. Presented at the American Psychological Association Convention, Washington, D. C., 1976.

Department of Labor. Women--Their Social and Economic Status. Selected references. Washington, D. C.: U. S. Gov. Printing Office, 1970.

Deutsch, R. Sex-linked Role Behavior in Three Employment Groups. Symposium presentation at the American Psychological Association Convention, San Francisco, 1977.

Developing New Horizons for Women: Bibliography. Washington, D. C.: George Washington University Press, 1970.

Diamond, E. Clues to Being More Successful: Achievement Motivation Tests. Readers Digest, 1975, May, 106, 88-91.

Diesler, S. B. Acturial Prejudice Toward Women and Its Implications. Journal of Applied Social Psychology, 1975, 5, 201-216.

Dipboye, R. L., Arvey, R., and Terpstra, D. Equal Employment and the Interview. Personnel Journal, 1976, 55, 520-523.

_____, _____, and _____. Sex and Physical Attractiveness of Raters and Applicants as Determinants of Resumé Evaluations. Journal of Applied Psychology, 1977, 62(3), 288-294.

_____, Fromkin, H. L., and Wiback, K. Relative Importance of Applicant Sex, Attractiveness, and Scholastic Standing in Evaluation of Job Applicant Resumes. Journal of Applied Psychology, 1975, 60(1), 39-43.

_____, and Wiley, J. W. Reactions of College Recruiters and Students to Male and Female Job Applicants Described with Stereotypic Male and Female Traits. Unpublished manuscript, 1976.

_____, and _____. Reactions of College Recruiters to Interviewee Sex and Self-Presentation Style. Journal of Vocational Behavior, 1977, 10, 1-12.

_____, and _____. The Effects of Interviewee Self-Presentation Style and Sex: Replication and Extension of Previous Research. Unpublished manuscript, University of Tennessee, n. d.

Dipietro, A. E. Competition or Monopsonistic Discrimination: An Analysis of the Position of Women in American Labor Markets. Unpublished doctoral dissertation, University of Pittsburgh, 1974. Dissertation Abstracts International, 1975, 36(1-A), 0413. Also available from ERIC (ADG75-06355), 1974.

Discrimination Against Women. Hearings Before the Special Subcommittee on Education of the Committee on Education and Labor, Washington, D. C.: House of Representatives, Section 805 of H. R. 16098, June/July, 1970.

Dobbins, M. P. The Earnings Gap Between Women and Men. Washington, D. C.: Women's Bureau, U. S. Department of Labor, 1976.

———. Economic Status of Women in International Women's Year. American Economic Review, 1976, May, 66, 205-228.

———. Capital Shifts to Sectors of Female Labor. Unpublished manuscript. University of Alabama, Tuscaloosa, n. d.

Donlon, M. H. Politics, Power and Your Granddaughter. Association of University Women Journal, 1960, January, 53, 77-79.

Dorsen, N. Equal Rights for Women: A Symposium on the Proposed Constitutional Amendment. Civil Liberties Law Review, 1972, March, 6(2), 216-224.

Dresselhaus, M. S. Investigating the Solid State. In J. Stiehm (ed.), The Frontiers of Knowledge. University Park: University of Southern California Press, 1976, 39-50.

Drews, E. M. Big Waste of Brain Power: Our Gifted Girls. Parents Magazine, 1960, April, 35, 44-45+.

Duff, F., and Parrish, J. Sex Differences in Employment of College Graduates. Journal of the National Association for Women Deans, Administrators, and Counselors, 1977, Summer, 40(4), 155-160.

Duncan, B., and Evers, M. Measuring Change in Attitudes Toward Women's Work. In K. C. Land and S. Spilerman (eds.), Social Indicator Models. New York: Russell Sage Foundation, 1975.

DuPont, H. Playing the Part-Time Game. Women's Work, 1976, November/December, 2(6), 17-20.

Dutton, R. E. Sex as a Factor in Occupational Choice. Personnel Journal, 1967, 46(8), 510-513.

East, C. The Current Status of the Employment of Women. In M. E. Katzell and W. C. Byham (eds.), Women in the Work Force: Confrontation with Change. New York: Behavioral Publications, 1972, 7-14+.

Ebert, P. C. Advising Congress Informally on Issues Affecting Women. Paper presented at the American Psychological Association Convention, San Francisco, 1977.

Edwards, R. C., and Gordon, M. (eds.). Equality of Opportunity and Treatment of Women Workers. Report VIII. Geneva, Switzerland: International Labor Office, 1974.

_____, and _____ (eds.). Exploitation from 9 to 5, Report of the Twentieth Century Fund Task Force on Women and Employment. Lexington, MA: Lexington Books, 1975.

Einstein, H., and Sacks, S. R. Women in Search of Autonomy: An Action Design. Social Change, 1975, 5(2), 4-6.

Ellis, D. L., Graves, K., Grinstad, K., Marks, D., Pollack, F., Thompson, J., and Wexford, M. E. Women's Work and Women's Studies 1972. Available from KNOW, Inc., P. O. Box 86031, Pittsburgh, PA 15221, 1973.

Ellmann, M. In America, the Great Brain Divide. Vogue, 1969, May, 153(9), 152+.

_____. Thinking About Women. New York: Harcourt Brace Jovanovich, 1970.

Emerson, T. I. In Support of the Equal Rights Amendment. Civil Liberties Law Review, 1972, March, 6(2), 226-233.

Employment Discrimination: Statistics and Preferences Under Title VII. Virginia Law Review, 1973, 59, 463-491.

Employment Trends. Women's Work. 1975, January/February, 1(1), 4.

Entine, A. D. (ed.). Americans in Middle Years; Career Options and Educational Opportunities. Available from ERIC (ED099608), 1974.

Epstein, C. F. Encountering the Male Establishment: Sex-Status Limits on Women's Careers in the Professions. American Journal of Sociology, 1970, 75(6), 965-982. Also in A. Theodore (ed.), The Professional Woman. Cambridge, MA: Schenkman, 1970, 52-73; and in R. K. Unger and F. L. Denmark (eds.), Woman: Dependent or Independent Variable? New York: Psychological Dimensions, 1975, 751-772.

_____ (ed.). Inside Professional Life: Interaction, Performance, and Impediments. In Woman's Place: Options and Limits in Professional Careers. Berkeley: University of California Press, 1970, 167-197.

_____ (ed.). Professions in a Changing World: New Contexts. In Woman's Place: Options and Limits in Professional Careers. Berkeley: University of California Press, 1970, 198-204.

_____ (ed.). The Structure of Professions: How They Affect

Women's Participation. In Woman's Place: Options and Limits in Professional Careers. Berkeley: University of California Press, 1970, 151-166.

―――― (ed). Woman's Place: Options and Limits in Professional Careers. Berkeley: University of California Press, 1970.

――――. Review of the Woman Doctorate in America by H. S. Astin. American Journal of Sociology, 1971, September, 77(2), 359-361.

――――. Bringing Women In: Rewards, Punishments, and the Structure of Achievement. Annals of the New York Academy of Sciences, 1973, March, 62-70. Also in R. B. Kundsin (ed.), Women and Success: Anatomy of Achievement. New York: William Morrow, 1974, 12-13; and in F. L. Denmark (ed.), Women--Volume I: A PDI Research Reference Work. New York: Psychological Dimensions, 1976, 123-132.

――――. Structuring Success for Women: Guidelines for Gatekeepers. Journal of the National Association for Women Deans, Administrators, and Counselors, 1973, Fall, 37(1), 34-42. Also in The Education Digest, 1974, February, 39, 56-59.

――――. Women Versus Success. Educational Horizons, 1974, Spring, 52, 107-109.

――――. Ambiguity as Social Control: Consequences for the Integration of Women in Professional Elites. In P. L. Stewart and M. G. Cantor (eds.), Varieties of Work Experience. New York: Halsted Press, 1974, 26-38.

――――. I. Institutional Barriers: What Keeps Women Out of the Executive Suite? In G. E. Gordon and M. H. Strober (eds.), Bringing Women Into Management. New York: McGraw-Hill, 1975, 7-21.

Equal but Different. The Times (London) Educational Supplement, 1961, March 3, 2389, 426.

Equal Employment Opportunity Commission. Guidelines on Employment Selection Procedures. Federal Register, 1970, 35(149), 12333-12336.

Equal Rights for Men and Women, 1971. Hearings Before Subcommittee No. 4 on H. J. 35, 208 and Related Bills and H. R. 916 and Related Bills. Washington, D. C.: U. S. Government Printing Office, 1971.

Equality for Uglies. Time, 1972, February 21, 99, 8.

Equality of Rights Shall Not Be Abridged ... on Account of Sex. Washington, D. C.: Common Cause, 1972.

Etaugh, C. F. Attitudes of Professionals Toward the Married Professional Woman. Psychological Reports, 1973, 32, 775-780.

Etzkowitz, M. The Male Sister: Sexual Separation of Labor in Society. Journal of Marriage and the Family, 1971, 33(3), 431-434.

Evans, V. M. Unisex Jobs and Non-Traditional Employment. Personnel, 1975, November/December, 52, 31-37.

Fader, S. S. Brave New Jobs for Women. McCalls, 1972, May, 99, 65.

Falk, W. W., and Cosby, A. G. Women and the Occupational Choice Process, 1974. Unpublished manuscript, Texas A & M University, n. d.

Farley, J. Women Going Back to Work: Preliminary Problems. Journal of Employment Counseling, 1970, December, 7(4), 130-136.

_____, and Kelly, J. A Woman's Job Roster: Is It Helping? Journal of the National Association for Women Deans, Administrators, and Counselors, 1976, Summer, 39(4), 190-195.

Farmer, H. S. What Inhibits Achievement and Career Motivation in Women. Counseling Psychologist, 1976, 6(2), 12-14.

_____. Why Women Contribute Less to the Arts, Sciences, and Humanities. Paper presented at the American Educational Research Association meeting, San Francisco, 1976.

_____, and Backer, T. E. New Career Options for Women: A Selected Annotated Bibliography. New York: Human Sciences Press, 1977.

Farrell, W. Women's and Men's Liberation Groups: Political Power Within the System and Outside the System. In J. Jaquette (ed.), Women in Politics. New York: John Wiley, 1974.

Faunce, P. S. Psychological Barriers to Occupational Success for Women. Contact, Journal of the Minnesota College Personnel Association, 1977, Spring, 8(2), 8-15. Also in the Journal of the National Association for Women Deans, Administrators, and Counselors, 1977, Summer, 40(4), 140-144.

Featherman, D. L., and Hauser, R. M. Sexual Inequalities and Socioeconomic Achievements in the U. S., 1962-1973. Paper presented at the Population Association of America meeting, Seattle, 1975.

Feingold, S. N. Looking to the Future: Careers for Women in the 1970's and 80's. Women's Education, 1966, June, 5(2), 1-7.

_____. Career Barriers: Are They Falling Down? In Facilitating Career Development for Girls and Women. Washington, D. C.: National Vocational Guidance Association, 1975, 15-28.

Ferber, M. A., and Lowry, H. M. The Sex Differential in Earnings: A Reappraisal. Industrial and Labor Relations Review, 1976, April, 29(3), 377-387.

Ferree, M. M. A Woman for President? Changing Responses, 1958-72. Public Opinion Quarterly, 1974, Fall, 38(3), 390-399.

Ferriss, A. L. Indicators of Trends in the Status of American Women. New York: Russell Sage Foundation, 1971.

Feshbach, N. D. How Not to Succeed in the Professions Without Really Trying, or The Seven Stages of Women. Educational Horizons, 1973-1974, Winter, 52, 67-71.

Fidell, L. S., and DeLamater, J. (eds.). Women in the Professions: What's All the Fuss About? Beverly Hills, CA: Sage Publications, 1971.

Fitzgerald, L. E. Women's Changing Expectations: New Insights, New Demands. The Counseling Psychologist, 1973, 4(1), 90-95.

Flanders, D. P., and Anderson, P. E. Sex Discrimination in Employment: Theory and Practice. Industrial and Labor Relations Review, 1973, 26, 938-955.

Fley, J. A. The Time to Be Properly Vicious. Journal of the National Association for Women Deans, Administrators, and Counselors, 1974, Winter, 37(2), 53-58.

For Women a Difficult Climb to the Top. Business Week, 1969, August 2, 42-44.

Forrest, K. S., and Chang, W. Affirmative Action and Equal Employment: A Bibliography. San Jose, CA: San Jose State University, Affirmative Action Office, 1977.

Fox B. Create Your Own Job. Women's Work, 1976, May/June, 2(3), 22-23.

Fox, H. W., and Renas, S. R. Stereotypes of Women in the Media and Their Impact on Women's Careers. Human Resource Management, 1977, Spring, 16(1), 28-31.

Fox, J. H. Women, Work, and Retirement. Unpublished doctoral dissertation, Duke University, 1976. Dissertation Abstracts International, 1976, 37(2-A), 1235. Also available from ERIC, (ADG76-18951), 1976.

Francis, A. Let's Stop Wasting Women's Potential. Canadian Counsellor, 1973, October, 7(4), 218-231.

Frank, F. D., and Drucker, J. The Influence of Evaluatee's Sex on Evaluations of a Response on a Managerial Selection Instrument. Sex Roles: A Journal of Research, 1977, 3(1), 59-64.

Frank, H. H. Women in the Organization. Philadelphia: University of Pennsylvania Press, 1977.

_____, and Hooks, K. The Workplace Woman. In H. H. Frank (ed.), Women in the Organization. Philadelphia: University of Pennsylvania Press, 1977, 163-172.

Franzwa, H. Working Women in Fact and Fiction. Journal of Communications, 1974, 24, 104-109.

Freeman, J. How to Discriminate Against Women Without Really Trying. In J. Freeman (ed.), Women: A Feminist Perspective. Palo Alto, CA: Mayfield, 1975, 194-208.

Fretz, C. F., and Hayman, J. Progress for Women--Men Are Still More Equal. Harvard Business Review, 1973, September/October, 51(5), 133-142.

Fried, M. G. In Defense of Preferential Hiring. In C. C. Gould and M. W. Wartofsky (eds.), Women and Philosophy: Toward a Theory of Liberation. New York: G. P. Putnam's, 1976, 309-319.

Friedman, B., et al. Women's Work and Women's Studies, 1973-1974, a Bibliography. New York: Barnard College Women's Center, 1975.

Fuchs, V. R. Differences in Hourly Earnings Between Men and Women. Monthly Labor Review. 1971, May, 94, 9-16. Also in N. Glazer-Malbin and H. Y. Waehrer (eds.), Woman in a Man-Made World: A Socioeconomic Handbook. Chicago: Rand McNally, 1972, 222-227.

_____. Recent Trends and Long-Run Prospects for Female Earnings. American Economic Review, 1974, May, 64, 236-242.

_____. Women's Earnings: Recent Trends and Long-Run Prospects. Monthly Labor Review, 1974, 97, 23-25.

_____. A Note on Sex Segregation in Professional Occupations. Explorations in Economic Research, 1975, 2, 105-111.

Furugori, T. A Micro Labor Supply Model of Women Under the Existence of Discrimination. Unpublished doctoral dissertation, State University of New York, Buffalo. Dissertation Abstracts International, 1975, April, 35(10-A), 6316.

Gager, N. (ed.). Women's Rights Almanac. New York: Harper & Row, 1975.

Galenson, M. Women and Work: An International Comparison. Ithaca, NY: Cornell University, School of Industrial and Labor Relations, 1973.

Gallese, L. R. Up-the-Ladder Blues. In E. Graham (ed.), What Do Women Really Want. Chicopee, MA: Dow Jones Books, 1974, 48-53.

Galvin, R. Sex and Success. Time, 1972, March 20, 46-47.

Garfinkle, S. H. Occupations of Women and Black Workers, 1962-1974. Monthly Labor Review, 1975, November, 98, 25-34.

Gaudreau, P. A. Investigation of Sex Differences Across Job Levels. Paper presented at the American Psychological Association Convention, Chicago, 1975.

Gaylin, J. Executives Versus the Career Woman. Psychology Today, 1976, January, 9, 22.

Geis, F. L. Women and Power: A Social Comparison Theory Analysis. Symposium presentation at the American Psychological Association Convention, Chicago, 1975.

George, E. L. The Women Appointees of the Roosevelt and Truman Administrations: A Study of Their Impact and Effectiveness. Unpublished doctoral dissertation, American University, 1972. Dissertation Abstracts International, 1972, 33(5-A), 2284. Also available from ERIC (ADG72-30092), 1972.

Gerard, G. B. Financial Independence for Professional Women. Journal of Home Economics, 1960, February, 52, 91-94.

Gery, G. J. Hiring Minorities and Women--The Selection Process. Personnel Journal, 1974, December, 53(12), 906-909.

_____. Equal Opportunity--Planning and Managing the Process of Change. Personnel Journal, 1977, April, 56(4), 184-191+.

Ginzberg, E. The Development of Human Resources. New York: McGraw-Hill, 1966.

_____. Paycheck and Apron--Revolution in Womanpower. Industrial Relations, 1968, 7(3), 193-203.

Giving Them Confidence: Back to Work. The Times (London) Educational Supplement, 1964, October 2, 2576, 536.

Glazer-Malbin, N., and Waehrer, H. Y. Woman in a Man-Made World: A Socioeconomic Handbook. Chicago: Rand McNally, 1972.

General / 417

Glenn, H. M., and Walters, J. Feminine Stress in the Twentieth Century. Journal of Home Economics, 1966, November, 58(9), 703-707.

Goetz, T. E., and Herman, J. B. Effects of Supervisor's Sex and Subordinate Sex on Job Satisfaction and Productivity. Paper presented at the American Psychological Association Convention, Washington, D. C., 1976.

Gold, S. S. Alternative National Goals and Women's Employment. Science, 1973, 179, 656-660.

Gordon, M. S. Introduction: Women in the Labor Forces. Industrial Relations, 1968, 7(3), 187-192.

_____ (ed.). Higher Education and the Labor Market. New York: McGraw-Hill, 1974.

Gordon, N. M., and Morton, T. E. A Low Mobility Model of Wage Discrimination--With Special Reference to Sex Differentials. Journal of Economic Theory, 1974, March, 7, 241-253.

Gottfredson, G. D., Holland, J. L., and Gottfredson, L. S. The Relation of Vocational Aspirations and Assessments to Employment Reality. Journal of Vocational Behavior, 1975, 7, 135-148.

Gould, J., and Pagano, A. Sex Discrimination and Achievement. Journal of the National Association of Women Deans and Counselors, 1972, Winter, 35, 74-82.

Gould, K. Goals and Timetables Versus Quotas: Nondiscrimination or Reverse Discrimination? Journal of the National Association for Women Deans, Administrators, and Counselors, 1976, Fall, 40(1), 3-6.

Graham, L. Who's in Charge Here? Not Women! New York Times Magazine, 1962, September 2, 8+.

Graham, S. Sex Discrimination Against the American Working Woman. American Behavioral Scientist, 1971, November/December, 15, 79-96.

Gray, B. M. Sex Bias and Cyclical Unemployment. In N. Glazer-Malbin and H. Y. Waehrer (eds.), Woman in a Man-Made Society: A Socioeconomic Handbook. Chicago: Rand McNally, 1972, 235-237.

Green, E. Unreasoning Prejudice Hinders Attainment of Women's Dreams. Delta Kappa Gamma Bulletin, 1970, Fall, 37, 8-17.

Greenwald, C. S. Part-Time Work and Flexible Hours Employment. Paper presented at the Workshop on Research Needed to Improve the Employment and Employability of Women. Washington, D.C.: U.S. Department of Labor, 1974.

Griffiths, M.W. Can We Still Afford Occupational Segregation? Some Remarks. In B.B. Reagan and M. Blaxall (eds.), Women in the Workplace: The Implications of Occupational Segregation. Chicago: University of Chicago Press, 1976, 7-14.

Grimm, J.W., and Stern, R.N. Sex Roles and Internal Labor Market Structures: The Female Semi-Professions. Social Problems, 1974, June, 21(5), 690-705.

Gronau, R. Wage Comparison--A Selectivity Bias. Journal of Political Economy, 1974, November/December, 82, 1119-1143.

Grosgebauer, C.H. Volunteer to Career. Women's Work, 1976, July/August, 2(4), 17-19.

Gross, A. Success: How Much Is Enough? Mademoiselle, 1975, March, 81, 136-137+.

Gross, E. Plus Ca Change ... ? The Sexual Structure of Occupations over Time. Social Problems, 1968, Fall, 16(2), 198-208. Also in A. Theodore (ed.), The Professional Woman. Cambridge, MA: Schenkman, 1968, 39-51.

Grossman, A.S. Women in the Labor Force: The Early Years. Monthly Labor Review, 1975, November, 98, 3-9.

Gubbels, R. The Supply and Demand for Women Workers. In N. Glazer-Malbin and H.Y. Waehrer (eds.), Woman in a Man-Made World: A Socioeconomic Handbook. Chicago: Rand McNally, 1972, 208-218.

Guidance Associates Incorporated. Jobs and Gender. New York: Harcourt Brace Jovanovich, 1971.

Gullahorn, J.E. Equality and Social Structure. In E. Donelson and J.E. Gullahorn (eds.). Women: A Psychological Perspective. New York: Wiley, 1977, 266-281.

Gumperz, E. Women: The Last Minority? Columbia University Forum, 1967, 11, 30-34.

Gurin, P. Psychological Issues in the Study of Employment Discrimination. Unpublished manuscript, University of Michigan, Ann Arbor, 1974.

Gwartney, J. Discrimination and Income Differentials. American Economic Review, 1970, June, 60, 396-408.

Haener, D. What Is Labor Doing About Women in the Work Force. In M.E. Katzell and W.C. Byham (eds.), Women in the Work

Force: Confrontation with Change. New York: Behavioral Publications, 1972, 43-52.

Hagen, R. L., and Kahn, A. Discrimination Against Competent Women. Journal of Applied Social Psychology, 1975, 5, 362-376.

Hall, G. Changing Sex Roles in the Labor Force. Phi Delta Kappan, 1973, October, 55(2), 135-137.

Hall, O. Gender and the Division of Labor. In Implications of Traditional Divisions Between Men's Work and Women's Work in Our Society. Ottawa: Department of Labour of Canada, Women's Bureau, 1964.

Hamilton, M. G. College Woman: Qualities for Success in the Business World. Balance Sheet, 1968, December, 50, 152-153+.

Hamilton, M. T. A Study of Wage Discrimination by Sex: A Sample Survey in the Chicago Area. Unpublished doctoral dissertation, University of Pennsylvania, 1969.

──────. Sex and Income Inequality Among the Employed. Annals of the American Academy of Political and Social Science, 1973, September, 409, 42-52.

Hanau, D. O. Another First for Women; Bell System and University of Vermont. Journal of College Placement, 1966, April, 26, 47-48+.

Hancock, W. L. B. An Analysis of the Impact of Federal Laws and Regulations on Opportunities for Women in Management. Unpublished doctoral dissertation, Mississippi State University, 1973. Dissertation Abstracts International, 1973, 34(5-A), 2095. Also available from ERIC (ADG73-25709), 1973.

Hansen, D. Sex Differences and Supervisors. Paper presented at the American Psychological Association Convention, New Orleans, 1974.

Hansen, L. S. The Career Development Process for Women: Current Views and Programs. Pupil Personnel Services, (Minnesota Department of Education), 1975, Spring, 4(2), 23-33.

Harragan, B. L. Why Corporations Are Teaching Men to Think Like Women ... and Other Game Plans They May Not Have Been Briefed On. Ms., 1977, June, 5(12), 62-63+.

Harrison, E. The Working Women: Barriers in Employment. Public Administration Review, 1964, June, 24, 78-85.

Hart, L. B. Training Women to Become Effective Leaders: A

Case Study. Unpublished doctoral dissertation, University of Massachusetts. Dissertation Abstracts International, 1975, May, 35(11-A), 6977.

Hartmann, H. I. The Historical Roots of Occupational Segregation. Capitalism, Patriarch, and Job Segregation by Sex. SIGNS: Journal of Women in Culture and Society, 1976, Spring, 1(3, Part 2), 137-169.

──── . Women's Work in the United States. Current History, 1976, May, 70, 215-219+.

Heath, K. G. Legislation and Its Implications for Elimination of Sex Bias. Journal of the National Association for Women Deans, Administrators, and Counselors, 1974, Winter, 37(2), 58-69.

Hedges, J. N. Women Workers and Manpower Demands in the 1970's. Monthly Labor Review, 1970, 93, 19-29.

────, and Barnett, J. Working Women and the Division of Household Tasks. Monthly Labor Review, 1972, 97, 4-22.

Heide, W. S. Women's Liberation Means Putting Sex in Its Place. In M. E. Katzell and W. C. Byham (eds.), Women in the Work Force: Confrontation with Change. New York: Behavioral Publications, 1972, 15-26.

Heilman, M. Sex of Co-Worker as a Moderator of Self-Deprecating Attitudes in Women. Symposium presentation at the American Psychological Association Convention, San Francisco, 1977.

Helping Women to Come Back: Training and Retraining. The Times (London) Educational Supplement, 1965, May 14, 2608, 1510.

Helson, R. The Changing Image of the Career Woman. Journal of Social Issues, 1972, 28(2), 33-46. Also in M. T. S. Mednick et al. (eds.), Women and Achievement: Social and Motivational Analyses. New York: Halsted Press, 1975, 420-431.

Hendrick, H. W. The White Male Club: Experiential Explorations of Racism and Sexism. Symposium presentation at the American Psychological Association Convention, Chicago, 1975.

Henley, N. Facing Down the Man. Reprint from KNOW, Inc., P.O. Box 86031, Pittsburgh, PA 15221, 1970.

Herman, D. D. More Career Opportunities for Women--Whose Responsibility. Personnel Journal, 1974, June, 53(6), 414-417.

Herzfeld, N. K. Status of Women. Commonweal, 1960, February 5, 71, 515-518.

Higginson, M. How Women Can Get Ahead in a Man's World; Interview. U.S. News & World Report, 1976, March 29, 80, 46-48.

Highlights of Report of the President's Commission on the Status of Women. Journal of the National Association of Women Deans, and Counselors, 1963, October, 27, 47-48.

Hilton, I. Jobs for the Girls. The Times (London) Educational Supplement, 1970, March 13, 2860, 44-45.

Hochschild, A. R. Inside the Clockwork of Male Careers. In F. Howe (ed.), Women and the Power to Change. New York: McGraw-Hill, 1975, 47-80.

Hoffer, W. Career Conditioning for the New Woman. School Management, 1973, March, 17, 34-36.

Hogan, P. A Woman Is Not a Girl and Other Lessons in Corporate Speech. Business and Society Review, 1975, Summer, 14, 34-38.

Hollander, H. E., Penney, S., and Haines, J. R. (eds.). Women: Their Future in the University and The Community; Conference Proceedings. New York State Citizens Council; Skidmore College, Saratoga Springs, NY; Office of Higher Education Management Services, New York State Education Department, October, 1974.

Holm, J. M. Employment and Women: Cinderella Is Dead! Journal of the National Association of Women Deans and Counselors, 1970, Fall, 34, 6-13.

Holmberg, J. J. Changing Occupational Status, 1960-1970: The Impact of Increased Female Labor Force Participation. Unpublished doctoral dissertation, Fordham University, 1977. Dissertation Abstracts International, 1977, 38(1-A), 500. Also available from ERIC (ADG77-14895), 1977.

Holstein, R. Status of Women. NEA Journal, 1963, November, 52, 68.

Hood, K. E. Sex and Status: Influence on the Evaluation of Professionals. Paper presented at the American Psychological Association Convention. Washington, D. C., 1976.

Horn, M. T. The Road to Financial Independence. Women's Work, 1976, March/April, 2(2), 12-13+.

How Bosses Feel About Women's Lib: Job Policies Unaffected. Business Week, 1970, September 5, 2140, 18-19.

How Can These Situations Be Remedied? Job Discrimination Against Women: Excerpt from HEW report. Harvard Business Review, 1974, September, 52, 89.

How to Get Along--And Ahead--In the Office. Business Week, 1976, March 22, 2424, 107-110.

How to Invade a Man's World; Ideas of Successful Men. Harper's Bazaar, 1977, January, 110, 54+.

Howe, F., (ed.). Impact ERA; Limitations and Possibilities. Edited by the Equal Rights Amendment Project of the California Commission on the Status of Women. Millbrae, CA: Les Femmes Publishing, 1976.

Howell, M.C. Professional Women and the Feminist Movement. Journal of the National Association for Women Deans, Administrators, and Counselors, 1974, 37(2), 84-87.

Hoyte, S.K. The Women's Job Corps--Patterns of Behavior Relating to Success or Failure. Unpublished doctoral dissertation, Catholic University of America, 1969. Dissertation Abstracts International, 1969, 30(6-A), 2630. Also available from ERIC (ADG69-19922), 1969.

Huber, J. (ed.). Demographic Influence on Female Employment for the Status of Women. In Changing Women in a Changing Society. Chicago: University of Chicago Press, 1973, 184-199.

Hughes, M.M. The Sexual Barrier. Legal and Economic Aspects of Employment. Women and American Law, No. 1, 1970, November. Order from M.M. Hughes, 2422 Fox Plaza, San Francisco, CA 94102.

_____. Supplement No. 1. The Sexual Barrier. Legal and Economic Aspects of Employment. Order from M.M. Hughes, 2422 Fox Plaza, San Francisco, CA 94102.

Hulin, C.L., and Smith, P.C. Sex Differences in Job Satisfaction. Journal of Applied Psychology, 1964, April, 48, 88-92.

Hummer, P.M. The Decade of Elusive Promise: Professional Women in the United States, 1920-1930. Unpublished doctoral dissertation, Duke University, 1976. Dissertation Abstracts International, 1976, 37(6-A), 3852. Also available from ERIC (ADG76-27977), 1976.

Hunt, C.L. Female Occupational Roles and Urban Sex Ratios in the United States, Japan and the Philippines. Social Forces, 1965, May, 43(3), 407-417.

Introduction of Women's Education Act of 1972. Congressional Record House, 1972, April 18.

Jackson, J., and Huber, J. So You Really Want to Hire Blacks and Women? Sociological Abstracts, 1973, December, 21(7), (Supplement 37), 227-228.

Jacobs, J. E. Woman and Work: A Selected, Annotated Bibliography. Educational Horizons, 1975, Spring, 53(3), 142-144.

_____, and Alberti, J. M. (eds.). Realizing Human Potential: Alternatives for Women; Symposium. Educational Horizons, 1975, Spring, 53(3), 94-148.

Jacobson, C. J. Women Workers: Profile of a Growing Force. American Federationist, 1974, July, 81, 9-15.

Jacobson, M. B., and Effertz, J. Sex Roles and Leadership: Perceptions of the Leaders and the Led. Organizational Behavior and Human Performance, 1974, 12, 383-396.

Johnson, B. L., and Hayghe, H. Labor Force Participation of Married Women. Monthly Labor Review, 1977, June, 100, 32-36.

Johnson, P. B. Social Power and Sex Role Stereotyping. Dissertation Abstracts International, 1974, November, 35(5-B), 2406.

_____. Women and Power: Toward a Theory of Effectiveness. Journal of Social Issues, 1976, 32(3), 99-110.

Johnstone, E. Women in Economic Life: Rights and Opportunities. Annals of the American Academy of Political and Social Science. 1968, January, 375, 102-114.

Jong, E. Succeed at Your Own Risk. Vogue, 1975, October, 165, 216-217.

Jongeward, D., and Scott, D. The Organization Women: Then and Now. In Affirmative Action for Women: A Practical Guide. Reading, MA: Addison-Wesley, 1973, 1-14.

Kahn, S. E. Effects of a Program in Awareness of Sex-Role Stereotypes for Helping Professionals. Unpublished doctoral dissertation, Arizona State University. Dissertation Abstracts International, 1975, October, 36(4-A), 2027.

Kahne, H. Women in the Professions--Career Considerations and Job Placement Techniques. Journal of Economic Issues, 1971, September, 5(3), 28.

_____. Women in Professional Occupations: New Complexities for Chosen Roles. Journal of the National Association for Women Deans, Administrators, and Counselors, 1976, Summer, 39(4), 179-185.

_____, and Kohen, A. I. Economic Perspectives on the Roles of Women in the American Economy. Journal of Economic Literature, 1975, December, 13(4), 1249-1292.

Kaley, M. M. Attitudes Toward the Dual Role of the Married Professional Woman. American Psychologist, 1971, March, 26(3), 301-306.

Kanter, R. M. The Impact of Hierarchical Structures on the Work Behavior of Women and Men. Social Problems, 1974, April, 23(4), 415-430.

_____. Women and the Structure of Organizations: Explorations in Theory and Behavior. In M. Millman and R. M. Kanter (eds.), Another Voice: Feminist Perspectives on Social Life and Social Science. New York: Doubleday, 1975, 34-74.

_____. Why Bosses Turn Bitchy. Psychology Today, 1976, May, 9(12), 56-59.

_____. Men and Women of the Corporation. New York: Basic Books, 1977.

_____. Power Games in the Corporation. Psychology Today, 1977, July, 11(2), 48-53+.

_____. Women in Organizations: Sex Roles, Group Dynamics, and Change Strategies. In A. G. Sargent (ed.), Beyond Sex Roles. St. Paul, MN: West, 1977, 371-386.

Kaser, J. How to Get Along with Career Women: Guidelines for Career Men. Phi Delta Kappan, 1976, March, 56(7), 468.

Katzell, M. E., and Byham, W. C. (eds.). Women in the Work Force. New York: Behavioral Publications, 1972.

Kay, M. J. A Positive Approach to Promoting Women. Personnel Administrator, 1975, June, 36-39.

Kellen, K. The Coming Age of Woman Power. New York: Peter H. Wyden, 1972.

Keller, S. The Future Status of Women in America. In C. F. Westoff and R. Parke, Jr. (eds.), Demographic and Social Aspects of Population Growth, vol. 1. Washington, D. C.: Commission on Population Growth and the American Future 1972.

Keniston, E., and Keniston, K. An American Anachronism: The Image of Women and Work. The American Scholar, 1964, 33(3), 355-375.

Keyserling, M. D. Facing the Facts about Women's Lives Today. In New Approaches to Counseling Girls in the 1960's: Report of the Midwest Regional Pilot Conference. Washington, D. C.: U. S. Government Printing Office, 1966, 9.

_____. Goals--Ways of Fuller Utilization. In Exploding the Myths: Report of a Conference on Expanding Employment Opportunities for Career Women. Washington, D. C. : Women's Bureau, U. S. Department of Labor, 1967.

Kieffer, M. G. , and Cullen, D. M. Women Who Discriminate Against Other Women: The Process of Denial. International Journal of Group Tensions, 1974, March, 4(1), 21-33. Also in F. Denmark (ed.), Who Discriminates Against Women? Issue 15. Beverly Hills, CA: Sage Publications, 1974, 24-36. And a reprint from KNOW, Inc. P. O. Box 86031, Pittsburgh, PA 15221.

Kievit, M. B. Women in Gainful and Useful Employment. Journal of Home Economics, 1968, November, 60, 697-702.

_____. Review and Synthesis of Research on Women in the World of Work. Columbus: Ohio State University, Center for Vocational and Technical Education, 1972.

Kimball, M. M. Women and Success: A Basic Conflict. In M. Stephenson (ed.), Women in Canada. Toronto: New Press, 1973, 119-135.

King, A. G. Futures for College Women in New York. New York: Alumnae Advisory Center, 1960.

King, P. A Strategy for Change. In D. Jongeward and D. Scott (eds.), Affirmative Action for Women: A Practical Guide. Reading, MA: Addison-Wesley, 1973, 139-152.

Kirkpatrick, J. J. , and Lasswell, H. D. Political Woman. New York: Basic Books, 1974.

Kirschstein, R. L. A Woman Has to Be a Bit Better than a Man; Interview. U. S. News & World Report, 1975, April 26, 80(17), 50-51.

Klein, D. P. Women in the Labor Force: The Middle Years. Monthly Labor Review, 1975, November, 98, 10-16.

Klein, V. The Demand for Professional Woman-Power. British Journal of Sociology, 1966, June, 17(2), 183-197.

Knotts, R. E. L. Manifest Needs of Professional Female Workers in Business Oriented Occupations. Unpublished doctoral dissertation, Texas A & M University, 1972. Dissertation Abstracts International, 1973, 33(8-A), 3865. Also available from ERIC (ADG73-03547), 1972.

Knudsen, D. D. The Declining Status of Women: Popular Myths and the Failure of Functionalist Thought. Social Forces, 1969, 48(2), 183-193.

Koenig, R. The Persons in the Office. Harper's, 1976, February, 252(1509), 87-88+.

Kohen, A. I., Breinich, S. C., and Shields, P. Women and the Economy: A Bibliography and a Review of the Literature on Sex Differentiation in the Labor Market. Columbus: Ohio State University, Center for Human Resource Research, 1975.

_____, and Roderick, R. D. Causes of Differentials in Early Labor Market Success Among Young Women. Proceedings of the American Statistical Association, Social Statistics Section, 1972, 329-334.

_____, and _____. The Effects of Race and Sex Discrimination on Early-Career Earnings. Columbus: Ohio State University, Center for Human Resource Research, 1975.

Koontz, E. D. Women as a Minority Group. In M. L. Thompson (ed.), Voices of the New Feminism. Boston: Beacon Press, 1970, 77-86.

_____. Women and Jobs in a Changing World. American Vocational Journal, 1970, December, 45, 13-15.

_____. The Progress of the Woman Worker: An Unfinished Story. Issues in Industrial Society, 1971, 2, 29-31.

_____. The Double Standard in the Professions. In The Best Kept Secret of the Past 5,000 Years: Women Are Ready for Leadership in Education. Bloomington, IN: Phi Delta Kappa Educational Foundation, 1972, 41-44.

_____. Plans for Widening Women's Educational Opportunities. Washington, D. C.: U. S. Government Printing Office, 1972.

_____. Fighting Stereotypes: Women Want Up the Career Ladder. American Vocational Journal, 1973, May, 48, 35-36.

Korda, M. Woman and Power. In Power: How to Get It, How to Use It. New York: Random House, 1975, 213-249.

_____. Getting Women off the Boat and into the Power Swim. Harper's Bazaar, 1976, February, 109, 119+.

Kranz, H. Are Merit and Equity Compatible? Public Administration Review, 1974, September/October, 34(5), 434-439.

Kreps, J. M. Status of Women; Address, July 19, 1962. Vital Speeches of the Day, 1962, September 1, 28, 698-701.

_____. Sex in the Marketplace: American Women at Work. Baltimore: Johns Hopkins Press, 1971.

_____. The Sources of Inequality. In E. Ginzberg and A. M. Yohalem (eds.), Corporate Lib: Women's Challenge to Management. Baltimore: Johns Hopkins Press, 1973, 85-96.

General / 427

Also in H. H. Frank (ed.), Women in the Organization. Philadelphia: University of Pennsylvania Press, 1977, 154-162.

_____. The Occupations: Wider Economic Opportunity. In M. L. McBee and K. A. Blake (eds.), The American Woman: Who Will She Be? Riverside, NJ: Glencoe Press, 1974, 67-80.

_____. Women and the American Economy: A Look to the 1980's. Englewood Cliffs, NJ: Prentice-Hall, 1976.

Landau, E. A., and Dunahoo, K. L. Sex Discrimination in Employment: A Survey of State and Federal Remedies. Drake Law Review, 1971, 20, 417-527.

Lantier, F. Nouvelles Perspectives sur le Travail Feminin. [New Outlook on the Employment of Women.] International Review and Applied Psychology, 1969, 18(1), 41-52.

Laws, J. L. Psychological Dimensions of Women's Work-Force Participation. Sloan Management Review, 1974, Spring, 15(3), 49-52.

_____. Psychological Dimensions of Work Force Participation of Women. In P. A. Wallace (ed), Equal Employment Opportunity and the AT&T Case. Boston: MIT Press, 1975.

Lear, F. EEO Compliance--Behind the Corporate Mask. Harvard Business Review, 1975, July/August, 53(4), 138-146.

Lecht, L. A. Women at Work. Conference Board Record, 1976, September, 13(9), 16-21.

Lederer, M. New Job Opportunities for Women. Skokie, IL: Publications International, 1975.

Lee, M. D. Personal and Organizational Factors Associated with the Success of Women in Traditionally Male-Oriented Jobs. Symposium presentation at the American Psychological Association Convention, San Francisco, 1977.

Length of Working Life for Men and Women, 1970. Monthly Labor Review, 1976, February, 31-35.

Levinson, R. M. Sex Discrimination and Employment Practices: An Experiment with Unconventional Job Inquiries. Social Problems, 1975, April, 22(4), 533-543.

Levitin, T. , Quinn, R. P. , and Staines, G. L. Sex Discrimination Against the American Working Woman. American Behavioral Scientist, 1971, November, 15(2), 237-254. Also in M. T. S. Mednick et al. (eds.), Women and Achievement: Social and Motivational Analyses. New York: Halsted Press, 1975, 326-338.

428 / Occupational Forces

____, ____, and ____. A Woman Is 58% of a Man. Psychology Today, 1973, March, 6, 89-92. Also in C. Tavris, (ed.), The Female Experience. From the editors of Psychology Today. Del Mar, CA: Communications/Research/Machines, 1973, 71-74; and in D. G. McGuigan (ed.), New Research on Women: At the University of Michigan. Ann Arbor: University of Michigan, Center for Continuing Education of Women, 1974, 152-158.

Levitt, M. J. Political Attitudes of American Women: A Study of the Effects of Work and Education on Their Political Role. Unpublished doctoral dissertation, University of Maryland, 1965. Dissertation Abstracts International, 1966, 27(6-A), 1880. Also available from ERIC (ADG66-00933), 1965.

Levy, R. Woman Who Wasn't There. Dun's Review, 1972, June, 99, 63-65.

Lewis, A. Things That College Never Taught Me. Journal of College Placement, 1975, 35(2), 52-55.

Lifton, R. J. (ed.). The Woman in America. Boston: Houghton Mifflin, 1965.

Lindsey, K. Sexual Harassment on the Job: How to Spot It and How to Stop It. Ms., 1977, November, 6(5), 47-51.

Lipman-Blumen, J. Role De-Differentiation as a System Response to Crisis: Occupational and Political Roles of Women. Sociological Inquiry, 1973, 43(2), 105-129.

____. Toward a Homosocial Theory of Sex Roles: An Explanation of the Sex Segregation of Social Institutions. In B. B. Reagan and M. Blaxall (eds.), Women and the Workplace: The Implications of Occupational Segregation. Chicago: University of Chicago Press, 1976, 15-31. Also in SIGNS: Journal of Women in Culture and Society, 1976, Spring, 1(3, Pt. 2), 15-32.

Little, D. M., and Roach, A. J. Occupations for Women. Journal of Vocational Behavior, 1974, August, 5(1), 133-138.

Lloyd, B. J. Womanpower, the Future Manpower. Journal of Business Education, 1963, January, 38, 150-152.

Lloyd, C. B. (ed.). Sex, Discrimination, and the Division of Labor. New York: Columbia University Press, 1975.

Lockheed, M. E., and Hall, K. P. Conceptualizing Sex as a Status Characteristic: Applications to Leadership Training Strategies. Journal of Social Issues, 1976, 32(3), 111-124.

Lofft, V. M. Train Women to Manage. Sales Meeting Magazine, 1974, March, 23(3), 56-57+.

Long Road for Women; Report of Council of Economic Advisors. Time, 1973, February 12, 101, 69.

Lopata, H. Z. Occupation Housewife. New York: Oxford University Press, 1971.

_____, and Steinhart, F. Work Histories of American Urban Women. Gerontologist, 1971, 11(4:2), 27-36.

Luce, C. B. Without Portfolio; Status of Women Today. McCall's, 1965, March, 92, 26+.

_____. Woman. A Technological Castaway. Britannica Yearbook, 1973, Special Report. Chicago: Encyclopaedia Britannica, 1973, 28.

Lyle, J. R., and Ross, J. L. Occupational Discrimination in Industrial and Non-Industrial Firms. In Women in Industry. Lexington, MA: D. C. Heath, 1973, 51-78.

_____, and _____. Women in Industry. Lexington, MA: D. C. Heath, 1973.

McBee, M. L., Murray, R., and Suddick, D. E. Self-Esteem Differences of Professional Women. Journal of the National Association for Women Deans, Administrators, and Counselors, 1976, Summer, 39(4), 186-189.

McBee, S. Report on the Status of Women. McCalls, 1970, September, 97, 128.

McClendon, M. J. The Occupational Status Attainment Processes of Males and Females. American Sociological Review, 1976, February, 41(1), 52-64.

McEaddy, B. J. Women in the Labor Force, the Later Years. Monthly Labor Review, 1975, November, 98(11), 17-24.

McKim, J. Women and Employment: Bibliography. Santa Anna, CA: Santa Anna College, 1973.

McLaughlin, S. D. Occupational Characteristics and the Male-Female Income Differential. Unpublished doctoral dissertation, Washington State University, 1975. Dissertation Abstracts International, 1975, 36(8-A), 5560. Also available from ERIC, (ADG76-04367), 1975.

Macleod, J. Rate Your Employer. In F. Klagsbrun (ed.), The First Ms Reader. New York: Warner Books, 1973, 87-90.

McNally, G. B. Patterns of Female Labor Force Activity. Industrial Relations, 1968, 7(3), 204-218.

Macy, J. W., Jr. Unless We Begin Now: Womanpower Address, July 25, 1966. Vital Speeches of the Day, 1966, 32(22), 678-682.

Madden, J. F. The Economics of Sex Discrimination. Lexington, MA: D. C. Heath, 1973.

———. Discrimination--A Manifestation of Male Market Power? In C. B. Lloyd (ed.), Sex, Discrimination, and the Division of Labor. New York: Columbia University Press, 1975, 146-174.

Mahood, W. No Woman Need Apply. Social Science Record, 1975, Spring, 12(3), 13-17.

Malkiel, B. G., and Malkiel, J. A. Male-Female Pay Differentials in Professional Employment. American Economic Review, 1973, September, 693-705.

Mandel, W. M. Soviet Women in the Work Force and Professions. American Behavioral Scientist, 1971, November, 15(2), 255-280.

Mandle, J. D. Women's Liberation: Humanizing Rather than Polarizing. The Annals of the American Academy of Political and Social Science, 1971, September, 397, 119-128. Also reprint from MSS Information Corp., 655 Madison Ave., New York, NY 10021.

Manpower Administration. Dual Careers: A Longitudinal Study of the Labor Experience of Women. Manpower Research and Development Monograph, no. 21. Washington, D. C.: U. S. Department of Labor, 1972.

Marconi, K. M. Predicting the Occupational Behavior of American Women. Unpublished doctoral dissertation, George Washington University, 1976. Dissertation Abstracts International, 1977, 37(12-A), 7982. Also available from ERIC (ADG77-10115), 1976.

Marrett, C. B. Centralization in Female Organizations: Reassessing the Evidence. Social Problems, 1972, Winter, 19(3), 348-357.

Marshall, K. K. Power of Women. Saturday Review, 1962, August 4, 45, 13. Reply, Baker, K. 1962, September 22, 45, 21.

Martin, W. T., and Poston, D. L., Jr. The Occupational Composition of White Females: Sexism, Racism and Occupational Differentiation. Social Forces, 1972, March, 50(3), 349-355.

Mathews, J. J., Collins, W. E., and Cobb, B. B. A Sex Comparison of Reasons for Attrition in a Male-Dominated Occupation. Personnel Psychology, 1974, Winter, 27(4), 535-541.

Matthews, E. E. Personalizing Occupational Freedom for Girls and Women. Proceedings of the Rutgers Guidance Conference. October, 1970. Also available from ERIC (ED075734), 1973.

Matthies, M. T. The Developing Law on Equal Employment Opportunity. Journal of Contemporary Business, 1976, Winter, 5(1), 29-46.

Maymi, C. R. Women Workers and the Women's Movement. Human Ecology Forum, 1973, 4(2), 19-20.

Mead, M., and Kaplan, F. B. (eds.). American Women: The Report of the President's Commission on the Status of Women and Other Publications of the Commission. New York: Scribner's, 1965.

Medsger, B. Women at Work. Women's Work, 1976, May/June, 2(3), 15-19.

Medvene, A. M., and Collins, A. Occupational Prestige and Its Relationship to Traditional and Nontraditional Views of Women's Roles. Journal of Counseling Psychology, 1974, March, 21(2), 139-143.

Megargee, E. I. Influence of Sex Roles on the Manifestation of Leadership. Journal of Applied Psychology, 1969, 53(5), 377-382.

Mepham, G. J. Equal Opportunity and Equal Pay: A Review of Objectives, Problems and Progress. London: Institute of Personnel Management, 1974.

Merriam, E. Ogress in the Office. Nation, 1962, June 23, 194, 556-557.

Messe, L. A., and Callahan, C. M. Sex Differences in the Allocation of Pay. Unpublished manuscript, Michigan State University, 1974.

Miles, C. Sex Stereotyping in the Job Market/Getting Your Head Straight for Work. Women's Work, 1975, September/October, 1(5), 11-12.

Miller, F. L. Womanpower; Rediscovering a Prime Resource. Journal of Home Economics, 1968, November, 60, 693-696.

Miller, J., Labovitz, S., and Fry, L. Differences in the Organizational Experiences of Women and Men: Resources, Vested Interests, and Discrimination. Paper presented at the American Sociological Association meeting, Montreal, 1974.

Millett, K. Sexual Politics. New York: Doubleday, 1970.

Millman, M., and Kanter, R. M. (eds.). Another Voice: Feminist Perspectives on Social Life and Social Science. New York: Doubleday, 1975.

Mincer, J. The Labor Participation of Married Women: A Study of Labor Supply. In N. Glazer-Malbin and H. Y. Waehrer (eds.), Woman in a Man-Made World: A Socioeconomic Handbook. Chicago: Rand McNally, 1972, 198-202.

_____, and Polacheck, S. Family Investments in Human Capital: Earnings of Women. Journal of Political Economy, 1974, March/April, 82, 76-110.

Mischel, H. N. Sex Bias in the Evaluation of Professional Achievements. Journal of Educational Psychology, 1974, April, 66(2), 157-166.

Mitchell, J. Non-traditional Occupations for Women: The U. S. Experience. Washington, D. C. : Conference for Women of the Hemisphere on Non-traditional Occupations and Career Opportunities--the U. S. Experience, 1974.

Mitchell, S. B. Women and the Doctorate: A Study of Enabling or Impeding Factors Among Oklahoma's Doctoral Recipients in the Attainment and Use of the Degree. Unpublished doctoral dissertation, 1969.

_____, and Alciatore, R. T. Women Doctoral Recipients Evaluate Their Training. Educational Forum, 1970, 34, 533-539.

Moran, R. D. Reducing Discrimination: Role of the Equal Pay Act. Monthly Labor Review, 1970, 93, 30-34. Also in N. Glazer-Malbin and H. Y. Waehrer (eds.), Woman in a Man-Made World: A Socioeconomic Handbook. Chicago: Rand McNally, 1972, 238-244.

Morgenthaler, E. Corporate Liberation. In E. Graham (ed.), What Do Women Really Want? Princeton: Dow Jones Books, 1974, 17-23.

Morris, J. Exposing Nonconventional Careers for Women. School and Community, 1975, November, 23, 127-131.

Morris, R. Women at the Top. Training and Development Journal, 1977, May, 31(5), 39-42.

Moser, C. H. Mature Women--The New Labor Force. Industrial Gerontology, 1974, Spring, 1, 14-25.

Moses, J. L. , and Boehm, V. R. Relationship of Assessment Center Performance to Management Progress of Women. Journal of Applied Psychology, 1975, August, 60(4), 527-529.

Move Over, Men. Nation's Business, 1974, August, 62(8), 28-34.

Moving Up. Women's Work, 1975, May/June, 5.

Munnell, B. Sexual Harrassment on the Job. Do It Now, 1976, December, 9(11), 2.

Murphy, L. K. Ambiguity, Sex, Cognitive Complexity: Effects on Treatment of Subordinate Personnel. Paper presented at the American Psychological Association Convention, San Francisco, 1977.

Myerson, B. What Insurance Companies Do to Women; A New Look. Redbook, 1977, June, 149, 74+.

Nell, O. How Do We Know When Opportunities Are Equal? In C. C. Gould and M. W. Wartofsky (eds.), Women and Philosophy: Toward a Theory of Liberation. New York: G. P. Putnam's, 1976, 334-346.

Nelson, M. C. W. The Information Channels Used by Certain Professional Women to Gain Employment: Arlington County, Virginia. Unpublished doctoral dissertation, American University, 1973. Dissertation Abstracts International, 1973, 34(6-A), 3568. Also available from ERIC (ADG73-29645), 1973.

Nelson, S. (ed.). The Challenge Before Us: Full Employment and the Economy. Do It Now, 1976, December, Special Insert, 1-4.

Newland, J. E. Women at Work. Journal of Business Education, 1961, October, 37, 17-18.

Newman, D., and Benton, R. Now Is the Time for All Good Parties to Come to the Aid of the Girls. Mademoiselle, 1966, September, 63, 88+.

Nezzer, M. Woman's Position in the Labor Force. Unpublished manuscript, University of Minnesota, Minneapolis, 1969.

Niemi, B. The Female-Male Differential in Unemployment Rates. Industrial and Labor Relations Review, 1974, April, 27(3), 331-350.

Nieva, V. F., and Gutek, B. A. Women and Work: A Bibliography of Psychological Research. JSAS Catalog of Selected Documents in Psychology, 1976, May, 6, 50.

Notestine, E. B., and Kerlin, L. Salary Comparisons of Men and Women: A Look at Recent College Graduates. Vocational Guidance Quarterly, 1975, 24(1), 56-60.

Now, At Last, Better Jobs for Women. Changing Times, 1972, November, 26, 37-39.

Oaxaca, R. Male-Female Wage Differentials in Urban Labor Markets. International Economic Review, 1973, October, 14, 693-709.

———. Sex Discrimination in Wages. In O. Ashenfelter and A. Rees (eds.), Discrimination in Labor Markets. Princeton, NJ: Princeton University Press, 1973, 124-151.

Odiorne, G. S. The Corporation and the Women's Revolution. Training and Development Journal, 1975, May, 29(5), 3-11.

O'Leary, V. E. Opening Job Doors for Mature Women. Manpower, 1973, August, 8-12.

———. Some Attitudinal Barriers to Occupational Aspirations in Women. Psychological Bulletin, 1974, November, 81(11), 809-826.

Olesen, V. L., and Whittaker, E. W. Instant Life: College Women Report on Immersion in the Adult World. Journal of the National Association of Women Deans and Counselors, 1966, Spring, 29, 131-135.

Oltman, R. M. Women in the Professional Caucuses. American Behavioral Scientist, 1971, November, 15(2), 281-302.

One Company's Freewheeling Approach to Worktimes. Women's Work, 1976, July/August, 2(4), 11-12.

O'Neill, P. Variables Affecting Assignment of Occupations to Men and Women. Paper presented at the American Psychological Association Convention, Chicago, 1975.

O'Neill, W. L. (ed.), Women at Work. New York: Quadrangle/The New York Times, 1972.

Oppenheimer, V. K. The Female Labor Force in the U.S.: Factors Governing Its Growth and Changing Composition. Unpublished doctoral dissertation, University of California, Berkeley. Dissertation Abstracts International, 1966, 27(8-A), 2632.

———. The Sex-Labeling of Jobs. Industrial Relations, 1968, 7(3), 219-234.

———. The Female Labor Force in the United States: Demographic and Economic Factors Concerning Its Growth and Changing Composition. Population Monograph Series No. 5, Berkeley: University of California Press, 1970.

———. Demographic Influence on Female Employment and the Status of Women. American Journal of Sociology, 1973, January, 78(4), 946-961.

———. The Sex-Labeling of Jobs. In M. T. S. Mednick et al.

(eds.), Women and Achievement: Social and Motivational Analyses. New York: Halsted Press, 1975, 307-325.

Osipow, S. H. (ed.). Emerging Woman: Career Analysis and Outlook. Columbus, OH: Charles E. Merrill, 1975.

Otten, A. L. Two-Career Couples. The Wall Street Journal, 1976, July 29, 188(20), 10.

Parnes, H. S., Spitz, R. S., Miljus, R., and Associates. Career Thresholds, Vol. I. Manpower Research Monograph No. 16. Washington, D. C.: Manpower Administration, U. S. Department of Labor, 1970.

Parrish, J. B. Professional Womanpower as a National Resource. Quarterly Review of Economics and Business, 1961, February, 1(1), 54-63.

_____. Top Level Training of Women in the United States, 1900-1960. Journal of the National Association of Women Deans, and Counselors, 1962, January, 25, 67-73.

_____. Revolution in Employment for Women. Education Digest, 1964, October, 30, 50-52.

_____. College Women and Jobs: Another Look at the 1970's. Journal of College Placement, 1971, April, 31, 34-38.

_____. Women in Professional Training. Monthly Labor Review, 1974, May, 97, 41-43.

Paul, R. J. Some Correlates of Role Ambiguity; Men and Women in the Same Work Environment. Educational Administration Quarterly, 1975, Autumn, 11, 85-98.

Pender, A. Attention Men: The Women Are Coming. Contemporary Education, 1972, February, 43(4), 219-223.

Perrella, V. C. Women and the Labor Force. Monthly Labor Review, 1968, February, 91(2), 1-12.

Peterson, E. Needs and Opportunities for Educated Women. In L. E. Dennis (ed.), Education and a Woman's Life: Proceedings of the Itasca Conference on the Continuing Education of Women. Washington, D. C.: American Council on Education, 1963, 64+.

_____. Working Women. Daedalus, 1964, 92(2), 671-699.

Petty, M. M., and Lee, G. K. Moderating Effects of Sex of Supervisor and Subordinate on Relationships Between Supervisor Behavior and Subordinate Satisfaction. Journal of Applied Psychology, 1975, 60, 624-628.

Pietrofesa, J. J. Women and the World of Work. Catholic Educational Review, 1968, 66(4), 256-259.

Pifer, A. Women Working: Toward a New Society. 1976 Annual Report, Carnegie Corporation of New York, 1976, 3-18.

Pogrebin, L. C. How to Make It In a Man's World. New York: Bantam Books, 1971.

——. Working Woman: The Success Syndrome. Ladies Home Journal, 1974, July, 91, 42+.

Polachek, S. W. Discontinuous Labor Force Participation and Its Effects on Women's Market Earnings. In C. Lloyd (ed.), Sex, Discrimination and the Division of Labor. New York: Columbia University Press, 1975, 90-122.

——. Work Experience and the Difference Between Male and Female Wages. Unpublished doctoral dissertation, Columbia University, 1975. Dissertation Abstracts International, 1975, 36(3-A), 1673. Also available from ERIC (ADG75-18429), 1975.

——. Occupational Segregation: An Alternative Hypothesis. Journal of Contemporary Business, 1976, Winter, 5(1), 1-12.

Polk, B. B. Male Power and the Women's Movement. Journal of Applied Behavioral Science, 1974, 10(3), 415-431.

Poloma, M. M. The Married Professional Woman: An Empirical Examination of Three Myths. Unpublished doctoral dissertation, Case Western Reserve University, 1970.

Pottinger, J. S. Race, Sex, and Jobs: The Drive Toward Equality. In E. Wasserman, A. Y. Lewin, and L. H. Bleiweis (eds.), Women in Academia: Evolving Policies Toward Equal Opportunities. New York: Praeger, 1975, 37-44.

Powell, G. N. Sex and Sex-Role Identification: Implications for Organizational Research. Symposium presentation at the American Psychological Association Convention, San Francisco, 1977.

Prather, J. Why Can't Women Be More Like Men: A Summary of the Sociopsychological Factors Hindering Women's Advancement in the Professions. American Behavioral Scientist, 1971, November, 15(2), 172-182.

President's Commission on the Status of Women. American Women. Washington, D. C.: U. S. Government Printing Office, 1963.

Pressman, S. Sex Discrimination in Employment and What You Can Do About It. Women Lawyers Journal, 1968, Fall.

Problems on Job Rights of Women. U. S. News & World Report, 1965, August 30, 59, 77.

Professional Women's Caucus, Report of Founding Conference. Sixteen Reports on the Status of Women in the Professions, 1970.

Puddefoot, S., Weston, M., Watson, S., and Shaw, S. (eds.). Women Who Made It in a Man's World; Interviews. The Times (London) Educational Supplement, 1974, March 9, 2067, 42.

Quinn, F. X. Women at Work--(1)--The Facts. Social Order, 1962, February, 12(2), 65-71.

Ramey, E. Well, Fellows, What Did Happen at the Bay of Pigs? And Who Was in Control? McCall's, 1971, January, 28, 81-82.

Reagan, B. B., and Blaxall, M. (eds.). Introduction: Occupational Segregation in International Women's Year. In Women and the Workplace: The Implications of Occupational Segregation. Chicago: University of Chicago Press, 1976, 1-5.

Reeves, N. Curious Guest for Womanpower. Nation, 1963, August 24, 197, 89-91.

Reilly, M. E., and Bouvier, L. F. Population Profiles Number 15, Women in American Society. Washington, CT: Center for Information on America, n. d.

Revised Order No. 4: Putting New Rules into Effect. Detroit Free Press, 1972, March 27.

Rice, P. What Drives Professional Women. St. Louis Post-Dispatch, 1974, April 21, 3+.

Riley, M., Johnson, M., and Boocock, S. Women's Changing Occupational Role: A Research Report. American Behavioral Scientist, 1963, 6, 33-37.

Ripley, T. M. Discrimination Against Women Professionals in a Male-Dominated Profession by Women Consumers. Unpublished doctoral dissertation, University of Oregon. Dissertation Abstracts International, 1972, May, 32(11-A), 6219.

Ritter, K. V., and Hargens, L. L. Occupational Positions and Class Identification of Married Working Women: A Test of the Asymmetry Hypothesis. American Journal of Sociology, 1975, 80(4), 934-948.

Robbins, P. F. People in Glass Houses: Sex Discrimination at the U. N. Ms., 1975, January, 3, 46-49.

Roby, P. A. Toward Full Equality: More Job Education for Women. Scholarly Review, 1976, February, 84, 181-211.

Roebling, M. G. Power and Influence of Women; Address, May 27, 1965. Vital Speeches of the Day, 1965, September 1, 31, 689-691.

Roesch, R. Women in Action: Their Questions and Their Answers. New York: John Day, 1967.

Rohrlich, L. T., and Vatter, E. L. Women in the World of Work: Past, Present, and Future. Women's Studies, 1973, 1, 263-277.

Rosen, B., and Jerdee, T. H. Influence of Sex Role Stereotypes on Personnel Decisions. Journal of Applied Psychology, 1974, 59(1), 9-14.

_____, and _____. Effects of Employee's Sex and Threatening Versus Pleading Appeals on Managerial Evaluations of Grievances. Journal of Applied Psychology, 1975, 60(4), 442-445.

Rosenberg, D. Clearing the Way for the Growth of Women Subordinates. Supervisory Management, 1976, January, 21(1), 9-12.

Rosow, J. M. (ed.). The Worker and the Job: Coping with Change. Englewood Cliffs, NJ: Prentice-Hall, 1974.

Ross, S. C. Employment Discrimination. In The Rights of Women: The Basic American Civil Liberties Union Guide to a Woman's Rights. New York: Avon Books, 1973, 31-115.

Rossi, A. S. Women and Professional Advancement: Excerpts from Address, September 2, 1969. Science, 1969, October 17, 166, 356.

_____. Discrimination and Demography Restrict Women. College and University Business, 1970, February, 48(2), 74-78.

_____. Job Discrimination and What Women Can Do About It. The Atlantic Monthly, 1970, March, 225(3), 90-102.

Rotter, N. G. Effects of Worker Sex upon Perceived Commitment and Merited Salary. Paper presented at the American Psychological Association Convention, Washington, D. C., 1976.

Royal Commission. Report on the Status of Women. Ottawa: Information Canada, 1970.

Rubin-Rabson, G. How High Are the Odds Against Women? American Psychologist, 1974, 29, 916-917.

Rudikoff, S. Women and Success. Commentary, 1974, October, 58(4), 49-59.

_____. Women and Success. Commentary, 1975, February, 59, 7+.

Rytina, N. F. Female Labor Force Participation and Occupational Status: 1965-1970. Unpublished doctoral dissertation, Duke University, 1976. Dissertation Abstracts International, 1977, 37(12-A), 7991. Also available from ERIC (ADG77-11858), 1976.

Safilios-Rothschild, C. Social Policy to Liberate Women. In Women and Social Policy. Englewood Cliffs, NJ: Prentice-Hall, 1974, 17-71.

Safran, C. On the Job: What It Takes for a Woman to Get Ahead. Redbook, 1977, January, 148, 52+.

Sandler, B. Women: The Last Minority. Journal of College Placement, 1971-1972, December-January, 32(2), 50.

Sangerman, H. A Look at the Equal Pay Act in Practice. Labor Law Journal, 1971, May, 22(5), 259-265.

Sawhill, I. V. The Economics of Discrimination Against Women: Some New Findings. Journal of Human Resources, 1973, Summer, 8, 383-396.

Scates, A. Y. Women Moving Ahead. American Education, 1966, March, 2, 1-4.

Schaeffer, R. G. The Campus Recruiting Scene. Conference Board Record, 1974, March, 11(3), 41-45.

Schien, V. Implications and Obstacles to Full Participation of the Woman Worker. Bests Review L/H, 1972, April, 72(12), 22+.

Schnepper, J. A. Women and Occupational Segregation. Intellect, 1977, June, 105, 415-417.

Schonberger, R. J. Inflexible Working Conditions Keep Women 'Unliberated.' Personnel Journal, 1971, 50, 834-845.

Schuler, R. S. Sex, Organizational Level, and Outcome Importance: Where the Differences Are. Personnel Psychology, 1975, Autumn, 28(3), 365-375.

Schwartz, F. N. Converging Work Roles of Men and Women. Innovation Business and Society Review, 1973, Fall, (7), 71-75.

_____. New Work Patterns for the Better Use of Womanpower. Management Review, 1974, May, 63(5), 4-12.

Scott, A. Feminism Versus the Feds. Issues in Industrial Society, 1971, 2(1), 32-46. Ithaca, NY: Cornell University, State School of Industrial and Labor Relations.

_____ (ed.). What Is Happening to American Women? Atlanta: Southern Newspaper Publishers Association, 1970.

Sedaka, J. B. Why Not a Woman? Women in New Careers Program for Training for Non-Traditional Jobs. American Education, 1975, December, 11(10), 11-15. Also in Education Digest, 1976, March, 41(7), 22-25.

Seed, S. Saturday's Child: Thirty-Six Women Talk About Their Jobs. New York: Bantam Books, 1973.

Seidenberg, F. A. The Submissive Majority: Modern Trends in the Law Concerning Women's Rights. Cornell Law Review, 1970, January, 55(2), 262-283.

_____. No Room at the Top: Case Histories of Disturbed (or Disturbing) Females. Psychiatric Opinion, 1972, June, 9(3), 24-28.

Seifer, N. Absent from the Majority: Working Class Women in America. New York: Institute for Human Relations, 1973.

Self, G. Women on the Move: Some Common Psychological Problems. Paper presented to the Governor's Commission on the Status of Women, Las Vegas, June 1969.

Self-Evaluation Is Key to Career Planning, Hyde Says. Marketing News, 1977, February 25, 10(16), 5.

Sells, L. W. High School Mathematics as the Critical Filter in the Job Market. In Developing Opportunities for Minorities in Graduate Education. Proceedings of the Conference on Minority Graduate Education at the University of California, Berkeley, 1973.

_____. Sex and Discipline Differences in Professional Socialization. Unpublished manuscript, University of California, Berkeley, n. d.

A Senator's Reaction to Report on Working Women and Children. Monthly Labor Review, 1975, October, 36-38.

Sex and Equal Employment Rights. Monthly Labor Review, 1967, August, 90, 3-4.

Sex and Nonsense. New Republic, 1965, September 4, 153, 10.

Shanahan, E. Women and Money: All the Pigs Are More Equal. The New York Times (The Week in Review), 1973, July 29, 5.

Shapiro, H. J. Job Motivations of Males and Females: An Empirical Study. Psychological Reports, 1975, April, 36(2), 647-654.

Shapiro, R. Should You Work for a Woman? Stereotyped Female Boss. Harper's Bazaar, 1977, August, 110, 85+.

Sharma, P. C. Status of Women Bibliography: A Selective Bibliography of Government Publications. Bowling Green, OH: Bowling Green State University Library, Government Documents Service, 1973.

_____. Female Working Role (Underdeveloped States) and Economic Development: A Selected Research Bibliography. Monticello, IL: Council of Planning Librarians, 1974.

_____. A Special Bicentennial Focus on Women: Their Progress, Problems, Concerns in 1976. American Association of University Women Journal, 1976, April, 69, 1-27.

Sharp, L. M. Education and Employment: The Early Careers of College Graduates. Baltimore: Johns Hopkins Press, 1970.

Shea, J. R., Spitz, R. S., and Zeller, F. A. Dual Careers: A Longitudinal Study of Labor Market Experience of Women, Volume I. Columbus, OH: Ohio State University, Center for Human Resource Research, 1970.

Sheldon, E. B. Social Indicators on the Status of Women. Paper presented at the American Psychological Association Convention, Chicago, 1975.

Shepherd, J. Is Someone Kidding the College Girl? Creativity in College, Then Typing in a New York Office. Look, 1966, January 11, 30, 36-38.

Simon, R. J., Clark, S. M., and Galway, K. The Woman Ph. D.: A Recent Profile. Social Problems, 1967, Fall, 51(2), 221-236. Also in J. M. Bardwick (ed.), Readings on the Psychology of Women. New York: Harper & Row, 1972, 83-93; and in M. T. S. Mednick et al. (eds.), Women and Achievement: Social and Motivational Analyses. New York: Halsted Press, 1975, 355-371.

Simpson, R. L., and Simpson, I. H. Women and Bureaucracy in the Semi-Professions. In A. Etzioni, (ed.), The Semi-Professions and Their Organization. New York: Free Press, 1969, 196-265.

Six Reasons College Women Miss Good Jobs. Changing Times. 1974, March, 28, 45-47.

Slocum, W. L. Occupational Careers in Organizations: A Sociological Perspective. Personnel and Guidance Journal, 1965, May, 43, 858-866.

Smith, G. Help Wanted: Female. New Brunswick, NJ: Rutgers State University Press, 1964.

Smuts, R.W. Women and Work in America. New York: Schocken Books, 1971.

Sokeitous, J. F., and McFadden, K. Myths About Working Women. Reprint from KNOW, Inc., P.O. Box 86031, Pittsburgh, PA 15221, 1974.

Sokoloff, N. J. A Description and Analysis of the Economic Position of Women in American Society. Unpublished manuscript, Columbia University, n. d.

Solomon, L. Labor Force Participation of Women: A Study of Arkansas. Unpublished doctoral dissertation, University of Arkansas. Dissertation Abstracts International, 1970, 31(6-A), 2572.

Some Good Employment Prospects. Women's Work, 1975, March/April, 1(2), 2.

Somerville, R. The Urban Working Woman in the USSR: An Historical Overview. In A. Michel (ed.), Family Issues of Employed Women in Europe and America. Leiden: Brill Press, 1971, 91-103.

Sommers, D. Occupational Rankings for Men and Women by Earnings. Monthly Labor Review, 1974, August, 97(8), 34-51.

Sorkin, A. L. On the Occupational Status of Women, 1870-1970. The American Journal of Economics and Sociology, 1973, July 32(3), 235-243.

Space May Be a Man's World. Science Digest, 1965, March, 57, 23-24.

Staines, G., et al. Alternative Methods for Measuring Sex Discrimination in Occupational Incomes. In R. P. Quinn and T. W. Mangiore et al. (eds.), 1969-1970 Survey of Working Conditions: Chronicles of an Unfinished Enterprise. Ann Arbor: University of Michigan Survey Research Center, 1973. Also in F. L. Denmark (ed.), Women--Volume I: A PDI Research Reference Work. New York: Psychological Dimensions, 1976, 275-300.

_____, Tavris, C., and Jayaratne, T. E. The Queen Bee Syndrome. In C. Tavris (ed.), The Female Experience. From the Editors of Psychology Today. Del Mar, CA: Communications/Research/Machines, 1973, 63-66. Also in Psychology Today, 1974, January, 7(8), 55-60.

Starer, R., and Denmark, F. Discrimination Against Aspiring Women. In F. Denmark (ed.), Who Discriminates Against Women? Issue 15. Beverly Hills: Sage Publications, 1974, 67-72. Also in International Journal of Group Tensions, 1974, March, 4(1), 65-70.

Status of Women. United States. President's Commission on the Status of Women. Higher Education, 1963, October, 20, 18-20.

Steigenga-Kouwe, S. E. De Vrouwelijke Bevolking en de Werkgelegenheid voor Vrouwen [The Female Population and the Work Opportunity for Women.] Mens en Onderneming, 1972, May, 26(3), 167-180.

Stein, R. L. Economic Status of Families Headed by Women. In N. Glazer-Malbin and H. Y. Waehrer (eds.), Woman in a Man-Made World: A Socioeconomic Handbook. Chicago: Rand McNally, 1972, 254-264.

Steinem, G. Women Voters Can't Be Trusted. Ms., 1972, July, 1, 47+.

Stevenson, M. Women's Wages and Job Segregation. Politics and Society, 1973, 83-96.

_____. Relative Wages and Sex Segregation by Occupation. In C. B. Lloyd (ed.), Sex, Discrimination, and the Division of Labor. New York: Columbia University Press, 1975, 175-200.

Stewart, P. L., and Cantor, M. G. Varieties of Work Experience. New York: Halsted Press, 1974.

Stimpson, C. (edited in conjunction with the Congressional Information-Service). Discrimination Against Women: Congressional Hearing on Equal Rights in Education and Employment. New York: R. R. Bowker, 1973.

Strober, M. H. Women and Men in the World of Work: Present and Future. In L. A. Cater et al. (eds.), Women and Men: Changing Roles, Relationships, and Perceptions. New York: Praeger Publishers, 1977, 119-152.

_____, and Gordon, F. E. (eds.). Conclusion: Problems and Opportunities. In Bringing Women into Management. New York: McGraw-Hill, 1975, 157-168.

Stroink, P. L. Jonge Werkneemsters Alleen Maar "Bruidjesvan-Morgen?" [Are Young Female Employees Only "Brides-of-Tomorrow?"] Mens en Onderneming, 1972, July, 26(4), 258-266.

Suelzle, M. Women in Labor. Transaction, 1970, 8, 50-59.

Sumner, H. L. The Historical Development of Women's Work in the United States. Proceedings of the Academy of Political Science, 1971, 30, 101-113.

Suter, L. E., and Miller, H. P. Income Differences Between Men and Career Women. American Journal of Sociology, 1973, 78, 962-974. Also in J. Huber (ed.), Changing Women in a Changing Society. Chicago: University of Chicago Press, 1973, 200-212.

Sweet, J. A. Women in the Labor Force. New York: Harcourt Brace Jovanovich, 1973.

Swerdloff, S. Job Opportunities for Women College Graduates. Monthly Labor Review, 1964, April, 37, 396-400.

Szymanski, A. Racism and Sexism as Functional Substitutes in the Labor Market. Sociological Quarterly, 1976, Winter, 17(1), 65-73.

Tangri, S. S. Can Research on Women Be More Effective in Shaping Policy? Paper presented at the American Psychological Association Convention, San Francisco, 1977.

Tavris, C., and Offir, C. Earning the Bread Versus Baking It: The Sociological Perspective. In The Longest War: Sex Differences in Perspective. New York: Harcourt Brace Jovanovich, 1977, 201-234.

Terborg, J. R., and Ilgen, D. R. A Theoretical Approach to Sex Discrimination in Traditionally Masculine Occupations. Organizational Behavior and Human Performance, 1975, June, 13(3), 352-376.

Thalberg, I. Reverse Discrimination and the Future. In C. C. Gould and M. W. Wartofsky (eds.), Women and Philosophy: Toward a Theory of Liberation. New York: G. P. Putnam's, 1976, 294-308.

Theodore, A. The Professional Woman. Cambridge, MA: Schenkman, 1971.

Thomas, J. L. Why Women Work--(2)--The Significance. Social Order, 1962, February, 12(2), 72-76.

Tidball, M. E. The Search for Talented Women. Change Magazine, 1974, May, 6(4), 51-52+. Also in Women on Campus: The Unfinished Liberation. New York: Change Magazine, 1975, 152-159.

Toporoff, R. Generating Role Types Concerning the Occupational Participation of Women in the Twentieth Century. Unpublished doctoral dissertation, Washington State University, 1972. Dissertation Abstracts International, 1973, 32(12-A), 7107. Also available from ERIC (ADG72-18494), 1972.

Tornabene, L. L. (ed.). Boss Ladies; Symposium. Esquire, 1965, January, 63(1), 102-108+.

Torrey, J. W. The Consequences of Equal Opportunity for Women. Journal of Contemporary Business, 1976, Winter, 5(1), 13-27.

Treiman, D. J., and Terrell, K. Women, Work and Wages: Trends in the Female Occupation Structure. In K. C. Land and S. Spilerman (eds.), Social Indicator Models. New York: Russell Sage Foundation, 1975, 157-199.

_____, and _____. Sex and the Process of Status Attainment: A Comparison of Working Women and Men. American Sociological Review, 1975, April, 40(2), 174-200.

Trewick, O. No Place for Women, or Several? Catholic World, 1970, February, 210, 215-219.

Tsuchigane, R., and Dodge, N. Economic Discrimination Against Women in the United States: Measures and Changes. Lexington, MA: Lexington Books, 1974.

Tyree, A., and Treas, J. The Occupational and Marital Mobility of Women. American Sociological Review, 1974, June, 39(3), 293-302.

Ulbrich, H. H. Women and Wages. Atlanta Economic Review, 1976, March-April, 26(2), 44-46.

Ullrich, M. F., and Holden, J. D. Attitudes Toward Equal Employment. Symposium presentation at the American Psychological Association Convention, Washington, D. C., 1976.

Up the Ladder, Finally. Business Week, 1975, November 24, 58-68.

Van Dusen, R. A., and Sheldon, E. B. The Changing Status of American Women: A Life Cycle Perspective. American Psychologist, 1976, February, 31(2), 106-116. Also in H. J. Peters and J. C. Hansen (eds.), Vocational Guidance and Career Development. New York: Macmillan, 1977.

Vanek, J. Variations in a Sixty Hour Week: Trends in Women's Time in Work in the USA. Ekistics, 1975, 39, 37-39.

Vaughter, R. M., Ginorio, A. B., and Trilling, B. A. The Failure of Trait Theories to Predict Success. SIGNS: Journal of Women in Culture and Society, 1977, 2(3), 664-674.

Verheyden-Hilliard, M. E. Cinderella Doesn't Live Here Anymore. Womanpower, 1975, November, 34-37.

Vetterling, M. Some Common Sense Notes on Preferential Hiring. In C. C. Gould and M. W. Wartofsky (eds.), Women and Philosophy: Toward a Theory of Liberation. New York: G. P. Putnam's, 1976, 320-325.

Vogel, E. Some Suggestions for the Advancement of Working Women. International Labour Review, 1975, July, 112, 29-43.

_____. Womenpower. Manpower, 1975, November, 7, 2-44.

Waldman, E. Changes in the Labor Force Activity of Women. Monthly Labor Review, 1970, June, 93, 10-18. Also in N. Glazer-Malbin and H. Y. Waehrer (eds.), Woman in a Man-Made World: A Socioeconomic Handbook. Chicago: Rand McNally, 1972, 30-38.

_____, and McEaddy, B. J. Where Women Work--An Analysis by Industry and Occupation. Monthly Labor Review, 1974, May, 97(5), 3-13.

Waler, Y. K., et al. Evaluation of the Availability and Effectiveness of MDTA Institutional Training and Employment Services for Women: Reanalysis of the MDTA Outcomes Study. Available from ERIC (ED095279), 1974.

Wall, J. A., Jr., and Organ, D. W. Representative's Bargaining: Effects of Negotiating with a Constituent or Opposing Representative of the Opposite Sex. Paper presented at the American Psychological Association Convention, San Francisco, 1977.

Wallace, M. R. Reflections on Women at Work. Across the Board, 1976, November, 13(11), 39-42.

Walt, D. E. The Motivation for Women to Work in High-Level Professional Positions. Unpublished doctoral dissertation, American University. Dissertation Abstracts, 1962, 23(5), 1817-1818.

Wang, L. The Female Status Attainment Process and Occupational Mobility. Unpublished Master's thesis, University of Wisconsin, 1973.

Wardle, M. G. Women's Physiological Reactions to Physically Demanding Work. Psychology of Women Quarterly, 1976, Winter, 1(2), 151-159.

Ware, C. Woman Power, The Movement for Women's Liberation. New York: Tower Publications, 1970.

WEAL Joins in Suit Against University of Denver. Detroit Free Press, 1972, April 30.

Weiss, J. A., Ramirez, F. O., and Tracy, T. Female Participation in the Occupational System: A Comparative Institutional Analysis. Social Problems, 1976, June, 23(5), 593-608.

Wells, T. Equalizing Advancement Between Women and Men. Training and Development Journal, 1973, August, 27(8), 20-24.

Westervelt, E. Releasing Women's Potentialities. Albany: State University of New York Press, 1969.

White, W. S. Public Women. Harper's, 1960, January, 220, 86-88.

Wigny, L. Role of Woman in the World of Today; address, October 3, 1960. Vital Speeches of the Day, 1960, December 15, 27, 143-146.

Wilensky, H. L. Women's Work: Economic Growth, Ideology, Structure. Industrial Relations, 1968, May, 7, 235-248.

Wilkerson, M. B. Women and the Economy. Journal of Political Economy, 1976, Spring, 8, 1-122.

_____. Women and Work. Research and Development Monograph 46. Washington, D. C. : U. S. Department of Labor, Employment and Training Administration, 1977.

Wilks, J. What Government Is Doing About Women in the Work Force. In M. E. Katzell and W. C. Byham (eds.), Women in the Work Force: Confrontation with Change. New York: Behavioral Publications, 1972, 63-69.

Williams, D. L., and Lewis, S. A. Effects of Sex-Role Attitudes on Integrative Bargaining. Paper presented at the American Psychological Association Convention, Washington, D. C., 1976.

Williams, K. L., Parks, B. J., and Finley, C. J. Measures of Educational Equity for Women: A Research Monograph. Palo Alto, CA: American Institutes for Research, 1977.

Wolfe, H. B. Women in the World of Work. Albany, University of the State of New York, State Education Department, Division of Research, 1969.

Wolfgang, M. What Price Women's 'Equality'? Dissent, 1971, June, 18(3), 265-266.

Wolman, C. S., and Frank, H. H. The Solo Woman in a Professional Peer Group. American Journal of Orthopsychiatry, 1975, January, 45(1), 164-171. Also in H. H. Frank (ed.), Women in the Organization. Philadelphia: University of Pennsylvania Press, 1977, 246-255.

Womanpower. Senior Scholastic. 1962, November 7, 81(9), 17-19.

Woman's Place. The Atlantic, 1970, March, 225(3), 81-126.

Women as Key to Development. Science News, 1976, June 26, 109, 407.

Women at Work: Anything He Can Do. Senior Scholastic, 1970, November 9, 97, 15.

Women at Work: Symposium. Monthly Labor Review, 1970, June, 93, 3-44.

Women Can Make It to the Top; Symposium. U.S. News & World Report, 1976, April 26, 80, 49-54.

Women Entering Job Force at "Extraordinary" Pace. New York Times, 1976, September 12, 1.

Women in Organizations: Sex Roles, Group Dynamics, and Change Strategies. In A. Sargent (ed.), Beyond Sex Roles. St. Paul, MN: West, 1976, 371-387.

Women in the Work Force. Management Review, 1970, 59, 20-23.

Women: Their Impact Grows in the Job Market. U.S. News & World Report, 1977, June 6, 82, 58-59.

Women to the Forefront. Behavior Today, 1973, 4(8), 1.

Women Who Head Families: A Socioeconomic Analysis. Monthly Labor Review, 1976, June, 99(6), 3-9.

Women Work Longer, Harder on the Job than Men Do, Institute for Social Research Use Study Finds. ISR Newsletter. Ann Arbor: University of Michigan, Institute for Social Research, 1977, Summer, 8.

Women's Bureau, Canada. Women in the Labour Force: Facts and Figures, 1973. Ottawa, 1974.

Women's Bureau, U.S. Dept. of Labor. Facts About Women's Absenteeism and Labor Turnover. Washington, D.C.: U.S. Gov. Printing Office, 1969. Also in N. Glazer-Malbin and H.Y. Waehrer (eds.), Woman in a Man-Made Society: A Socioeconomic Handbook. Chicago: Rand McNally, 1972, 265-271.

———. 1965 Handbook on Women Workers. (Bulletin no. 290). Washington, D.C.: U.S. Gov. Printing Office, 1965.

———. Bibliography on American Women Workers. Washington, D.C.: U.S. Gov. Printing Office, 1966.

———. Exploding the Myths: A Report of a Conference on Expanding Employment Opportunities for Career Women. Washington, D.C.: U.S. Gov. Printing Office, 1967.

———. Job Horizons for College Women. Washington, D.C.: U.S. Gov. Printing Office, 1967.

———. Underutilization of Women Workers. Washington, D.C.: U.S. Gov. Printing Office, 1967.

General / 449

_____. 1969 Handbook on Women Workers. (Bulletin no. 294), Washington, D. C. : U. S. Gov. Printing Office, 1969.

_____. Trends in the Educational Attainment of Women. Washington, D. C. : U. S. Gov. Printing Office, 1969.

_____. Fact Sheet on the Earnings Gap. Washington, D. C. : U. S. Gov. Printing Office, 1970.

_____. Jobfinding Techniques for Mature Women. Washington, D. C. : U. S. Gov. Printing Office, 1970.

_____. Bibliography. In American Women at the Crossroads: Directions for the Future; Report of the Fiftieth Anniversary Conference of the Women's Bureau of the Department of Labor, June 1970. Washington, D. C. : U. S. Gov. Printing Office, 1971, 81-126.

_____. Fact Sheet on the Earnings Gap. Washington, D. C. : U. S. Gov. Printing Office, 1971.

_____. Underutilization of Women Workers. Washington, D. C. : U. S. Gov. Printing Office, 1971.

_____. A Guide to Sources of Data on Women and Women Workers for the United States and for Regions, States, and Local Areas. Washington, D. C. : U. S. Gov. Printing Office, 1972.

_____. Handbook on Women Workers. Washington, D. C. : U. S. Gov. Printing Office, 1972.

_____. Why Women Work. Washington, D. C. : U. S. Gov. Printing Office, 1972.

_____. Women Workers in Regional Areas and in Large States and Metropolitan Areas, 1971. Washington, D. C. : U. S. Gov. Printing Office, 1972.

_____. Careers for Women in the Seventies. Washington, D. C. : U. S. Gov. Printing Office, 1973.

_____. Highlights of Women's Employment and Education. Washington, D. C. : U. S. Gov. Printing Office, 1973.

_____. Twenty Facts on Women Workers. Washington, D. C. : U. S. Gov. Printing Office, 1973.

_____. Women Workers Today. Washington, D. C. : U. S. Gov. Printing Office, 1973.

_____. The Comprehensive Employment and Training Act of 1973,

How Women and Women's Groups Can Help. Washington, D.C.: U.S. Gov. Printing Office, 1974.

_____. The Myth and the Reality. Washington, D.C.: U.S. Gov. Printing Office, 1974.

_____. Fact Sheet on the Earnings Gap. Washington, D.C.: U.S. Gov. Printing Office, 1975.

_____. 1975 Handbook on Women Workers. Washington, D.C.: U.S. Gov. Printing Office, 1975.

_____. Women Workers Today. Washington, D.C.: U.S. Gov. Printing Office, 1975.

_____. The Earnings Gap Between Women and Men. Washington, D.C.: U.S. Gov. Printing Office, 1976.

_____. Mature Women Workers, A Profile. Washington, D.C.: U.S. Gov. Printing Office, 1976.

_____. Why Women Work. Washington, D.C.: U.S. Gov. Printing Office, 1976.

_____. Women Workers Today. Washington, D.C.: U.S. Gov. Printing Office, 1976.

_____. Brief Highlights of Major Federal Laws and Order on Sex Discrimination in Employment. Washington, D.C.: U.S. Gov. Printing Office, 1977.

Women's Sports. San Mateo, CA: Women's Sports Publishing, Vol. 1 published 1974. Continuing monthly publication covering women in sports.

Women's Work: Economic Growth, Ideology, Structure. Industrial Relations, 1968, May, 7, 235-248.

"Women's Year" Sparks Nation's Effort Toward Employment Equality. Commerce Today, 1975, December 8, 6(5), 4-6.

Wyman, C. Striking Back: How to File a Complaint with the EEOC. Women's Work, 1975, September/October, 1(5), 14-15.

Zapoleon, M.W. Occupational Planning for Women. New York: Harper & Row, 1961.

Zellman, G.L. Politics and Power. In I.H. Frieze et al. (eds.), Women and Sex Roles: A Social Psychological Perspective. New York: W.W. Norton, 1977.

Zellner, H. Discrimination Against Women, Occupational Segregation and the Relative Wage. American Economic Review, 1972, 62, 157-176.

_____. The Determinants of Occupational Segregation. In C. B. Lloyd (ed.), Sex, Discrimination, and the Division of Labor. New York: Columbia University Press, 1975, 125-145.

B. SPECIFIC

BUSINESS, MANAGEMENT, INDUSTRY

ABA's New Spokeswoman Gets Set to Tell Banking's Story on TV. Banking, 1975, June, 67(6), 32.

Acker, J., and Van Houten, D. R. Differential Recruitment and Control: The Sex Structuring of Organizations. Administrative Science Quarterly, 1974, June, 19(2), 152-163.

Adams, K. A. Assertive-Management Training for Professional Women. Symposium presentation at the American Psychological Association Convention, San Francisco, 1977.

_____, and Wukasch-Williamson, L. C. Assertiveness Training, Androgyny, and Professional Women. Paper presented at the American Psychological Association Convention, Washington, D. C., 1976.

Ahern, D. D. The Economics of Being a Woman. New York: Macmillan, 1976.

Alpander, G. G., and Gutmann, J. E. Contents and Techniques of Management-Development Programs for Women. Personnel Journal, 1976, February, 55(2), 76-79.

Arvis, P. F. Factors Affecting the Recruitment and Advancement of Women to Managerial Positions in Federal Agencies. Unpublished doctoral dissertation, American University, 1973. Dissertation Abstracts International, 1973, 34(6-A), 3511. Also available from ERIC (ADG73-29637), 1973.

Ashburn, E. A. Motivation, Personality, and Work-Related Characteristics of Women in Male-Dominated Professions. Ruth Strang Research Award Monograph Series No. 2. Washington, D. C.: National Association for Women Deans, Administrators, and Counselors, 1977.

Athanassiades, J. C. Myths of Women in Management--What Every Businessman Ought to Know About Women but May Be Afraid to Ask. Atlanta Economic Review, 1975, May/June, 25(3), 4-9.

Back from the Home to Business. Business Week, 1967, October 7, 92-93+.

Bailyn, L. Notes on the Role of Choice in the Psychology of Professional Women. Daedalus, 1964, 93(2), 700-710. Also in R. J. Lifton (ed.), The Woman in America. Boston: Houghton Mifflin, 1965, 236-246.

Barcelona, C. T., and Lelievre, C. C. Women in Accounting--Eddies and Mainstream Currents. The Woman CPA, 1975, January, 37(1), 3-6+.

_____, _____, and Lelievre, T. W. The Profession's Underutilized Resource--The Women CPA. Journal of Accountancy, 1975, November, 140(5), 58-64.

Barnes, M., and Rothenberg, S. The Search for Women Managers: Fiction or Reality. Employee Relations Law Journal, 1975, Autumn, 1(2), 280-292.

Bartol, K. Male Versus Female Leaders: The Effect of Leader Need for Dominance on Follower Satisfaction. Academy of Management Journal, 1974, 17, 225-233.

_____, and Bartol, R. A. Women in Managerial and Professional Positions: The United States and the Soviet Union. Industrial and Labor Relations Review. 1975, July, 28(4), 524-534.

Bass, B. M., Krusell, J., and Alexander, R. A. Male Managers' Attitudes Toward Working Women. American Behavioral Scientist, 1971, November, 15(2), 221-236.

Bates, M. Home Economist as a Leader in Business. Forecast for Home Economics, 1968, March, 13, 42-43.

Batt, R. Creating a Professional Identity. American Journal of Psychoanalysis, 1972, 32(2), 156-162.

Beck, E. L. An Analysis of Selected Factors Relevant to the Employment Status in Business Offices of Married Women College Graduates. Unpublished doctoral dissertation, Indiana University, 1963.

_____. Prospect for Advancement in Business of the Married Woman College Graduate. Journal of the National Association of Women Deans and Counselors, 1964, Spring, 27, 114-119. Also in the Journal of Business Education, 1964, March 32, 17-21.

Bedeian, A. G., and Armenakis, A. A. Male-Female Differences in Perceived Organizational Legitimacy. Human Resource Management, 1975, Winter, 14(4), 5-9.

_____, and _____. Male Vs. Female Managers. Intellect, 1976, July, 105, 8.

_____, _____, and Kemp, B. W. Relation of Sex to Perceived Legitimacy of Organizational Influence. Journal of Psychology, 1976, September, 94(1), 93-99.

Bell, C. S. Report of the Committee on the Status of Women in the Economics Profession. American Economic Review, 1973, May, 63, 508-511.

Bender, M. A Profile of the Woman Boss. New York Times, 1971, February 23, 120, 49-50.

Bennett, W. W. Institutional Barriers to the Utilization of Women in Top Management. Unpublished doctoral dissertation, University of Florida, 1964. Dissertation Abstracts International, 1965, 25(10), 5605. Also available from ERIC (ADG65-02413), 1964.

Berlew, D. C., and Hall, D. T. The Socialization of Managers: Effects of Expectations on Performance. Administrative Science Quarterly, 1966, 11, 207-223.

Bernard, J. (ed.). Cases in Point. In Women and the Public Interest. Chicago: Aldine-Atherton, 1971, 136-146.

Betancourt, J. Women in Focus. Dayton, OH: Pflaum, 1974.

Bird, C. Women in Business: The Invisible Bar. Personnel, 1968, May/June, 29-35.

Boehm, V. R. The Competent Woman Manager: Will Success Spoil Women's Lib? Paper presented at the American Psychological Association Convention, Chicago, 1975.

Bolton, E. B., and Humphreys, L. W. A Training Model for Women--An Androgynous Approach. Personnel Journal, 1977, May, 56(5), 230-234.

Bon, R. J. Why Not Give Today's Credit Women Credit? Credit and Financial Management, 1969, September, 71(9), 22-23.

Booth, A. N. Future of Women in Business and Professions; Address, July 18, 1960. Vital Speeches of the Day, 1960, October 1, 26, 761-763.

Bowman, G. W. Why No Women in Management Development? Training in Business and Management, 1969, August, 6(8), 38-43+.

_____, Worthy, N. B., and Greyser, S. A. Are Women Executives People? Harvard Business Review, 1965, July, 43(4), 14-16+.

Bradford, D.L., Sargent, A.G., and Sprague, M.S. Executive Man and Woman: The Issue of Sexuality. In F.E. Gordon and M.H. Strober (eds.), Bringing Women into Management. New York: McGraw-Hill, 1975, 39-58.

Brenner, M.H. Management Development Activities for Women. Paper presented at the American Psychological Association Convention, Miami, 1970.

Brief, A.P., and Oliver, R.L. Male-Female Differences in Work Attitudes Among Retail Sales Managers. Journal of Applied Psychology, 1976, August, 61(4), 526-528.

Bruker, R., Jass, R., and Schefelbein, B. The Role of Women in Management in Our Profession--Three Points of View. College and University, 1974, Fall, 50, 46-59.

Bryce, R.A. Characteristics of Women Holding Executive, Managerial and Other High Level Positions in Four Areas of Business. Unpublished doctoral dissertation, Colorado State College, 1969.

Burke, R.J., and Weir, T. Readying the Sexes for Women in Management. Business Horizons, 1977, June, 20(3), 30-35.

Business and Professional Women's Foundation. Woman Executives. A Selected Annotated Bibliography. Washington, D.C.: 1970.

Buzenberg, M.E. Training and Development of WOMEN Executives: A Model. Collegiate News and Views, 1975, Fall, 19-22.

Carlson, E. Woman's Place. Newsweek, 1975, April 21, 85(16), 82.

Carruth, E. Some Executives' Wives Are Executives Too. Fortune, 1973, December, 88, 114-119.

Chapman, J.B. A Comparative Analysis of Male and Female Leadership Styles in Similar Work Environments. Unpublished doctoral dissertation, University of Nebraska, 1974. Dissertation Abstracts International, 1974, 35(5-A), 2456. Also available from ERIC (ADG74-23882), 1974.

Chernik, D.A., and Phelan, J.G. Attitudes of Women in Management: I. Job Satisfaction: A Study of Perceived Need Satisfaction as a Function of Job Level. International Journal of Social Psychiatry, 1974, Spring/Summer, 20(1-2), 94-98.

Chung, K.H. Manager's Perceptional Responses in Employee Evaluation. Academy of Management Proceedings, 1973, August, 354-359.

Cliche Thinking Still Bars Gains by Women--Schein. Marketing News, 1977, February 25, 10(16), 3-4.

Clutterbuck, D. Dow Makes the Most of Womanpower. International Management, 1976, November, 31(11), 27-28.

Commissioner Greenwald's Address to the MBA. U. S. Investor/ Eastern Banker, 1975, June 16, 86(12), 33-45.

Cook, S. M. H. Personal Value Profile of Selected Women Executives. Unpublished doctoral dissertation, Texas Technical University, 1973. Dissertation Abstracts International, 1974, 35 (1-A), 26. Also available from ERIC (ADG74-15287), 1973.

Cooley, R. P. The Woman Executive--An Enlightened Investment in the Future of Banks. Bank Administration, 1974, February, 50(2), 6-7.

Coonrod, C. Careers in Real Estate. Women's Work, 1975, September/October, 1(5), 16-18.

Corporate Lib. Wall Street Journal, 1972, March 20, 179(55), 1, 17.

Corporate Woman: Up the Ladder Finally. Business Week, 1975, November 24, 58-68. Also in H. H. Frank (ed.), Women in the Organization. Philadelphia: University of Pennsylvania Press, 1977, 271-290.

The Corporate Woman: Stress Has No Gender. Business Week, 1976, November 15, 73-74.

Daddio, S. Oh! The Obstacle to Women in Management. In D. Jongeward and D. Scott (eds.), Affirmative Action for Women: A Practical Guide. Reading, MA: Addison-Wesley, 1973, 153-172.

Dainton, P. M. Women Executives: Is There Room at the Top? Personnel Management, 1967, 49(379), 15-19.

Dale, C. Women Are Still Missing Persons in Administrative and Supervisory Jobs. Educational Leadership, 1973, 31, 123-127.

Dawkins, L. B. Women Executives in Business, Industry, and the Professions. Unpublished doctoral dissertation, University of Texas, Austin, 1962. Dissertation Abstracts International, 1962, 23(5), 1542. Also available from ERIC (ADG62-04832), 1962.

Day, D., and Stogdill, R. Leader Behavior of Male and Female Supervisors: A Comparative Study. Personnel Psychology, 1972, 25(2), 353-360.

Deaux, K. Women in Management: Causal Explanations of Performance. Paper presented at the American Psychological Association Convention, New Orleans, 1974.

Diamond, H. Wanted: More Women in Management. Educational Horizons, 1975, Spring, 53(3), 125-128.

Diesler, S. B. Actuarial Prejudice Toward Women and Its Implications. Journal of Applied Social Psychology, 1975, 5, 201-216.

DiMarco, N., and Whitsitt, S. E. A Comparison of Female Supervisors in Business and Government Organizations. Journal of Vocational Behavior, 1975, April, 6(2), 185-196.

Do Women Managers Really Like Themselves. Training, 1977, May, 14(5), 16.

Doll, P. A. A Comparative Study of Top Level Male and Female Executives in Harris County. Unpublished doctoral dissertation, University of Houston. Dissertation Abstracts, 1966, 26(11), 6883-6884.

Donnelly, C. Keys to the Executive Powder Room. Money, 1976, August, 5(8), 28-32.

A Double Standard for Women Manager's Pay. Business Week, 1977, November 28, 61-62.

Draznin, J. N. Women Communicators in the Business Community. Supervision, 1976, August, 38(8), 2-3.

DuPont, H. The MBA: Ticket to Where the Jobs Are? Women's Work, 1976, May/June, 2(3), 9-11.

Eberly, M. Executive Woman. American Association of University Women Journal, 1961, May, 54, 215-218.

Ekberg-Jordan, S. Women in Management--Some Today, Many More Tomorrow. Atlanta Economic Review, 1976, March/April, 26(2), 6-8.

Eklund, C. G. Women in Business: Address April 24, 1976. Vital Speeches of the Day, 1976, June 15, 42, 539-542.

Feilke, J. F. Women, Women Everywhere, But Not a Manager in Sight. Iron Age, 1970, August 27, 206(1), 63-65.

Female Executives Become a Target for Ads. Business Week, 1977, August 22, 6.

Feminist Business Association. Dealing with the Real World: 13 Papers by Feminist Entrepreneurs. Kerhonkson meeting, October 1973. Also available from KNOW, Inc., P.O. Box 86031, Pittsburgh, PA 15221.

Fogarty, M. P., Allen, A. J., Allen, I., and Walters, P. A. Women in Top Jobs: Four Studies in Achievement. London: Allen and Unwin, 1971.

_____, Rapoport, R., and Rapoport, R. N. Women in Top Jobs: Four Studies in Achievement and Sex, Career and Family. Prepared jointly by Political and Economic Planning and the Tavistock Institute. London: Allen, 1968.

_____, _____, and _____. Sex, Career and Family. Beverly Hills, CA: Sage Publications, 1974.

Foster, G. H. Banking as a Career Area for Women. In R. E. Hardy and J. G. Cull (eds.), Career Guidance for Young Women: Considerations in Planning Professional Careers. Springfield, IL: Charles C. Thomas, 1974, 64-73.

Francke, C. A. Perceived Performance Differences Between Women and Men Supervisors and Implications for Training. Unpublished doctoral dissertation, Michigan State University. Dissertation Abstracts International, 1975, September, 36(3-A), 1349-1350.

French, P. Women in Management--Success at the First Level. Supervisory Management, 1975, March, 20(3), 14-17.

Gackenbach, J. I., Burke, M., et al. A 'Women in Business' Seminar--Exploring an Approach to Change in Sex-Role Awareness. Atlanta Economic Review, 1976, March/April, 26(2), 32-37.

The Game's Played that Way, Lady! Forbes, 1977, July 15, 120(2), 56+.

Garland, H., and Price, K. H. Attitudes Toward Women in Management and Attributions for Their Success and Failure in a Managerial Position. Journal of Applied Psychology, 1977, February, 62(1), 29-33.

Ginzberg, E., and Yohalem, A. M. (eds.). Corporate Lib: Women's Challenge to Management. Baltimore: Johns Hopkins University Press, 1973.

Goldfield, R. J. Choosing a Word-Processing Supervisor. The Office, 1974, February, 79(2), 36-38.

Goodman, N. C. Women and Management. Radcliffe Institute Working Paper, Cambridge, MA, 1975.

Gordon, F. E. Bringing Women into Management: The Role of the Senior Executive. In F. E. Gordon and M. H. Strober (eds.), Bringing Women into Management. New York: McGraw-Hill, 1975, 113-130.

_____, and Strober, M. H. (eds.). Bringing Women into Management. New York: McGraw-Hill, 1975.

Hackamack, L. C., and Solid, A. B. The Woman Executive: There Is Still Ample Room for Progress. Business Horizons, 1972, April, 15(2), 89-93.

Hackett, C. W. Doing Business with the SBA. Women's Work, 1975, November/December, 1(6), 23-24.

Hansen, P. Sex Differences and Supervision. Paper presented at the American Psychological Association Convention, New Orleans, 1974.

Harris, C., Johnson, A. C., and Westling, J. H. How Affirmative Has Business Been in Dealing with Women BBA's? Unpublished manuscript, University of Wisconsin, Madison, 1974.

Have You Considered Accounting? New York: Catalyst, 1975.

Helmich, D. L. Male and Female Presidents: Some Implications of Leadership Style. Human Resources Management, 1974, 13, 25-26.

Hennig, M. M. Career Development for Women Executives. Unpublished doctoral dissertation, Harvard Business School, 1970. American Doctoral Dissertations, 1971, 11(97), 42. Also available from ERIC (ADG02-49697), 1971.

_____, and Jardim, A. Behavioral Differences Stressed in Women's Management Training. New York Times, 1974, February 11, 123, 53.

_____, and _____. The Managerial Woman. New York: Doubleday, 1977.

_____, and _____. Women Executives in the Old-Boy Network; Excerpt from the Managerial Woman. Psychology Today, 1977, January, 10, 76-78+.

Herrick, J. S. Work Motives of Female Executives. Public Personnel Management, 1973, September/October, 380-387.

Hieronymus, B. Feminist Entrepreneurs. In E. Graham (ed.), What Do Women Really Want?, Princeton: Dow Jones Books, 1974, 88-94.

Hilton, M. J. The Employment Status of Men and Women Baccalaureate Graduates from the College of Business Administration at the University of Tennessee from 1969-1973. Unpublished doctoral dissertation, University of Tennessee, 1974. Dissertation Abstracts International, 1974, 35(8-A), 4787. Also available from ERIC (ADG75-03603), 1974.

Hogadone, E. B. Careers for Women with Business Degrees. Journal of Business Education, 1969, January, 44, 163.

Honomichl, J. J. Market Research Good Field for Women, Panel Says. Advertising Age, 1975, October 13, 46(41), 60.

Hunt, P. J. Women Supervisors: A Study of Their Performance

and the Group Interaction in a Simulated Organization. Dissertation Abstracts International, 1974, September, 35(3-B), 1437.

Insights, Learning, Achievement in the 'Spirit of 1976.' Life Association News, 1976, December, 71(12), 101-105.

It's Slow, But Women Are Moving into the Executive Suite. U.S. News & World Report, 1974, September, 77(14), 43-45.

Jacklin, C. N., and Maccoby, E. E. Sex Differences and Their Implications for Management. In F. E. Gordon and M. H. Strober (eds.), Bringing Women into Management. New York: McGraw-Hill, 1975, 23-28.

Jacob, N. L. (ed.). Women in Business: A New Look. Special Issue. Journal of Contemporary Business, 1976, Winter, 5(1).

Jancura, E. G. Women in Accounting--A 1977 Profile. Woman CPA, 1977, April, 39(2), 8-12.

Janeway, E. Women in Business. In Between Myth and Morning: Women Awakening. New York: William Morrow, 1974, 47-54.

Jongeward, D., and Scott, D. Affirmative Action for Women: A Practical Guide for Women and Management. Reading, MA: Addison-Wesley, 1975.

Kanter, R. M. Men and Women of the Corporation. New York: Basic Books, 1977.

Kay, M. J. What Do Women in Personnel Do? Personnel Journal, 1969, 48(10), 810-812.

_____. A Positive Approach to Women in Management. Personnel Journal, 1972, January, 51(1), 38-41.

Kelley, J. Women in Management: An Examination of Role Conflict. Unpublished manuscript, University of Minnesota, Department of Sociology, 1976.

Klarke, L. S. Women and Insurance. Managers Magazine, 1976, 51(4), 24-30.

Knotts, R. E. Manifest Needs of Professional Female Workers in Business-Related Occupations. Journal of Business Research, 1975, July, 3(3), 267-276.

Knudsen, K., and Gould, K. The Rise of Womanagement. Innovation, 1971, September, 24, 14.

Koehn, H. E. Attitude--The Success Element for Women in Business. Journal of Systems Management, 1976, March, 27(3), 12-15.

Koff, L. A. Age, Experience, and Success Among Women Managers. Management Review, 1973, November, 62(11), 65-66.

_____, and Handlon, J. H. Women in Management--Key to Success or Failure. Personnel Administrator, 1975, April, 20(2), 24-28.

Kriebel, C. Mothers in Business. Harper's Bazaar, 1972, July, 105, 90.

Kuhlmann, H. G. A Study of the Attitudes Toward Women in Business. Unpublished doctoral dissertation, Ohio State University, 1973. Dissertation Abstracts International, 1973, 34(5-A), 2098. Also available from ERIC (ADG73-26856), 1973.

Landon, D. D. Adam's Rib--Can Do. Life Association News, 1974, August, 69(8), 59-63.

Larwood, L., and Blackmore, J. Sex Discrimination in Managerial Selection: Testing Predictions of the Vertical Dyad Linkage Model. Paper presented at the Academy of Management meeting, Kansas City, 1976. Also in Sex Roles, 1978, June, 4(3) 359-367.

_____, Zalkind, D., and Legault, J. The Bank Job: A Field Study of Sexually Discriminatory Performance on a Neutral-Role Task. Journal of Applied Social Psychology, 1975, 5(1), 68-74.

Ledbetter, R. B. Current Attitudes Held by Selected Top Corporate Management Regarding the Role of Women as Executives. Unpublished doctoral dissertation, United States International University, San Diego. Dissertation Abstracts International, 1970, November, 31(5-B), 2961-2962.

Loring, R., and Wells, T. Breakthrough: Women into Management. New York: Van Nostrand Reinhold, 1972.

Lublin, J. S. The Managers: Mrs. Lowe Has to Deal with Stress and Sexism as Bank-Branch Head. Wall Street Journal, 1977, April 26, 189(81), 1+.

Lyle, J. R., and Ross, J. L. Women in the Managerial Elite. In Women in Industry. Lexington, MA: D. C. Heath, 1973, 79-92.

_____, and _____. Women in Industry. Lexington, MA: D. C. Heath, 1973.

Lynch, E. M. The Executive Suite: Feminine Style. New York: AMACOM, 1973.

McCord, B. Identifying and Developing Women for Management Positions. Training and Development Journal, 1971, November, 25(11), 2.

McCullough, R. V. Agency 'Specialists' May Achieve Rapid Success. Rough Notes, 1975, February, 118(2), 68-70.

McKemie-Belt, V. L. The Women in the Business of Economics. In R. E. Hardy and J. G. Cull (eds.), Career Guidance for Young Women: Considerations in Planning Professional Careers. Springfield, IL: Charles C. Thomas, 1974, 50-63.

Maclennan, L. The Case for Women Internal Auditors. Internal Auditor, 1974, September/October, 31(5), 36-42.

Madam Executive; Views of M. Hennig and A. Jardim. Time, 1974, February 18, 163, 76-77.

Madame Corporation President? Senior Scholastic, 1973, September 27, 103, 24-25.

Malan, M. Job-Sharing Couple Finds It's a Corporate Ideal. Nashville Tennessean, 1975.

Manhardt, P. J. Job Orientation of Male and Female College Graduates in Business. Personnel Psychology, 1972, Summer, 25(2), 361-368.

Martin, C. R., Jr. Support for Women's Lib: Management Performance. Southern Journal of Business, 1972, 7, 19-28.

Masters, R. J. Management Training for Women. Training and Development Journal, 1974, June, 28(6), 29.

Mathys, N., and Staszak, J. Women in Management--No Room in the Middle. Supervisory Management, 1975, March, 20(3), 10-13.

Matson, P. L. Bank's Criteria Could Be Met Only by a Tailor Made Affirmative Action Program. Banking, 1976, November, 68(11), 46+.

Matteson, M. T. Attitudes Toward Women as Managers: Sex or Role-Differences? Psychological Reports, 1976, August, 39(1), 166.

Meet Ms Calling Officer. Banking, 1975, November, 67(11), 74-78.

Merritt, D. H. Discrimination and the Woman Executive: Convention Blocks Use of a Resource. Business Horizons, 1969, December, 12(6), 15-22.

Meyer, P. Women Executives Are Different. Dun's Review, 1975, January, 105, 46-48.

Miner, J. B. Motivational Potential for Upgrading Among Minority and Female Managers. Journal of Applied Psychology, 1977, 62(6), 691-697.

Mitzner, P. L. Impact of EEO Rulings on the Insurance Industry. Spectator, 1975, March, 183(3), 23-28.

Montgomery, J. Including Women in Formerly All-Male Sales Teams. Training and Development Journal, 1975, November, 29(11), 22-27.

More Companies Turning to Women for Senior Marketing Posts. Here's a Report on Two of Them. Mark II, 1976, May/June, 17(4), 18+.

Morse, J. L. Sense of Competence and Individual Managerial Performance. Psychological Reports, 1976, June, 38(3), 1195-1198.

NAIW. The Career Woman in Insurance. Journal of American Insurance, 1975, Fall, 51(3), 29-32.

National Organization for Women. Women and Minorities in Corporate Positions: The Shape of the Future. Unpublished manuscript, n. d.

Nemeth, S. E. Women at General Motors Institute. IEEE Transactions on Education, 1975, February, E-18(1), 36-37.

Norton, S. D. Bibliography on Criteria of Managerial Success and on the Assessment Center and Other Predictors of Managerial Success. JSAS Catalog of Selected Documents in Psychology, 1976, Spring, 6, 53.

O'Brien, M. How Major-Company Marketing Ranks Are Opening to Women. National Petroleum News, 1976, October, 68(10), 50-52.

Orth, C. D., III, and Jacobs, F. Women in Management: Pattern for Change. Harvard Business Review, 1971, July/August, 49, 139-147.

Paisios, J., and Ringo, M. A New Dimension in Executive Recruiting. California Management Review, 1972, Spring, 14(3), 20-23.

Pearson, K. G. Business Opportunities for Women in Real Estate. Intellect, 1975, January, 103, 217-218.

Perham, J. Women, Industry's Newest Challenge: With Editorial Comment. Dun's Review, 1966, August, 88(23), 36-37+.

Peters, L. H., Terborg, J. R., and Taynor, J. Women as Managers Scale: A Measure of Attitudes Toward Women in Management Positions. JSAS Catalog of Selected Documents in Psychology, 1974, Winter, 4, 27.

Prather, J. E. When the Girls Move In: A Sociological Analysis of the Feminization of the Bank Teller's Job. Journal of Marriage and the Family, 1971, November, 33(4), 777-782.

Putnam, L., and Heinen, J. S. Women in Management--The Fallacy of the Trait Approach. MSU Business Topics, 1976, Summer, 24(3), 47-53.

Quadango, J. Occupational Sex-Typing and Internal Labor Market Distributions: An Assessment of Medical Specialities. Social Problems, 1976, April, 23(4), 415-430.

Quinn, R. P., Kahn, R. L., Tabor, J. M., and Gordon, L. K. The Chosen Few: A Study of Discrimination in Executive Selection. Ann Arbor: University of Michigan, Institute for Social Research, Survey Research Center, 1968.

_____, Tabor, J. M., and Gordon, L. M. The Decision to Discriminate: A Study of Executive Selection. Ann Arbor: University of Michigan, Institute for Social Research, Survey Research Center, 1968.

Ramey, E. R. Sex Hormones and Executive Ability. In R. B. Kundsin (ed.), Women and Success: The Anatomy of Achievement. New York: William Morrow, 1974, 248-256. Also in S. Cox (ed.), Female Psychology: The Emerging Self. Chicago: Science Research Associates, 1976, 20-30.

Reeves, N. The Relation of Woman and World as Milieu: In the Marketplace. In Womankind: Beyond the Stereotypes. Chicago: Aldine, 1973, 52-62.

Roark, A. C. Business Graduates Find It Helps to Be Female or Black--or Both. The Chronicle of Higher Education, 1977, August 1, 14(21), 5-6.

Roberts, M. L., and Ekstrom, R. B. Goal Orientation and Commitment to Working of MBA Women. Paper presented at the American Psychological Association Convention, San Francisco, 1977.

Robertson, W. The Ten Highest-Ranking Women in Big Business. Fortune, 1973, April, 87(4), 81-89.

Robinson, J. A. Women Managers: Aids and Barriers in Their Career Paths, Performance and Advancement. Unpublished doctoral dissertation, University of California, Berkeley, 1974. Dissertation Abstracts International, 1975, April, 35(10-A), 6310-6311. Also available from ERIC (ADG75-08241), 1974.

Rosen, B., and Jerdee, T. H. Effects of Applicant's Sex and Difficulty of Job on Evaluations of Candidates for Managerial Positions. Journal of Applied Psychology, 1974, 59, 511-512.

_____, and _____. Sex Stereotyping in the Executive Suite. Harvard Business Review, 1974, March/April, 52(2), 45-58.

_____, and _____. Effects of Employee's Sex and Threatening Versus Pleading Appeals on Managerial Evaluations of Grievances. Journal of Applied Psychology, 1975, August, 60(4), 442-445.

_____, _____, and Prestwich, T. Dual-Career Marital Adjustment: Potential Effects of Discriminatory Managerial Attitudes. Journal of Marriage and the Family, 1975, 37(3).

Ross-Skinner, J. European Women: Heading for the Executive Suite. Dun's Review, 1976, October, 108, 80-82+.

Schein, V. E. Fair Employment of Women Through Personnel Research. Personnel Journal, 1972, May, 51(5), 330-335.

_____. The Relationship Between Sex Role Stereotypes and Requisite Management Characteristics. Journal of Applied Psychology, 1973, 57(2), 95-100. Also in F. L. Denmark (ed.), Women--Volume I: A PDI Research Reference Work. New York: Psychological Dimensions, 1976, 393-398.

_____. Relationships Between Sex Role Stereotypes and Requisite Management Characteristics Among Female Managers. Journal of Applied Psychology, 1975, June, 60, 340-344.

Schoonover, J. W. Why Men Fear Women in Business. Saturday Evening Post, 1974, October, 246, 48-49.

Schreiber, C. Changing Places: Women and Men in Non-Traditional Clerical, Craft and Technical Jobs. Symposium presentation at the American Psychological Association Convention, San Francisco, 1977.

Schwartz, E. B. An Evaluation of the Application and Implementation of Title VII as It Applies to Women in Management. Unpublished doctoral dissertation, Georgia State University, 1969. Dissertation Abstracts International, 1970, 30(10-A), 4080. Also in American Doctoral Dissertations, 1970, 11(97), 39. Also available from ERIC (ADG70-6690), 1969.

_____. Entrepreneurship: A New Female Frontier. Journal of Contemporary Business, 1976, Winter, 5(1), 47-76.

_____, and Rago, J. J., Jr. Beyond Tokenism: Women as True Corporate Peers: Can Organization Cope with Male Executives Who Resist Working with Women as Peers? Business Horizons, 1973, December, 16(2), 69-76.

Sedaka, J. B. Why Not a Woman? Women in New Careers Program, for Training for Non-Traditional Jobs. American Education, 1975, December, 11, 11-15.

Shafer, S. M. Factors Affecting the Utilization of Women in Professional and Managerial Roles: England, East and West Germany. Comparative Education, 1974, March, 10, 1-11.

Shapiro, R. Will an MBA Make You a VIP? Careers of Women. Harper's Bazaar, 1977, June, 110, 49+.

Shaughnessy, S. The National Association of Insurance Women--A Commitment to Education. Bests Review P/L, 1974, September, 75(5), 26-28+.

Smith, J. Business and the Radicals: The Women: They Want Action. Dun's Review, 1970, June, 95, 46+.

Smith, L. What's It Like for Women Executives? Dun's Review, 1975, December, 106(6), 58-61.

Spain, J. Leading Businesswoman's Perspective on Management; Interview. Nation's Business, 1977, March, 65, 70-72+.

Stanley, B. M. A Comparative Analysis of the Work of the Male and Female First-Line Office Supervisor. Unpublished doctoral dissertation, Arizona State University, 1972. Dissertation Abstracts International, 1972, 33(5-A), 1915. Also available from ERIC (ADG72-30137), 1972.

Starting a Business: Women Show It's Not Just a Man's World. U. S. News & World Report, 1977, August 29, 83, 55-56.

Stead, B. A. Real Equal Opportunity for Women Executives. Business Horizons, 1974, August, 17(4), 87-92.

_____. Educating Women for Administration. Business Horizons, 1975, April, 18(2), 51-56.

_____. Women in Management: Address. Vital Speeches of the Day, 1975, July 15, 41(19), 589-591.

Steers, R. M. Task-Goal Attributes, in Achievement, and Supervisory Performance. Organizational Behavior and Human Performance, 1975, June, 13(3), 392-403.

Steichen, E. Of Women and Banking. Burroughs Clearing House, 1973, December, 58(3), 20-21+.

Strober, M. H. Bringing Women into Management: Basic Strategies. In F. E. Gordon and M. H. Strober (eds.), Bringing Women into Management. New York: McGraw-Hill, 1975, 77-96.

Templeton, J. F. Women as Managers, Still a Long Way to Go. Personnel, 1972, September/October, 49(5), 30-37.

Terborg, J. R. Integration of Women into Management Positions:

A Research Review. Symposium presentation at the American Psychological Association Convention, Washington, D.C., 1976.

_____. Women in Management: A Research Review. Journal of Applied Psychology, 1977, 62(6), 647-664.

_____, Peters, L.H., Ilgen, D.R., and Smith, F. Organizational and Personal Correlates of Attitudes Toward Women as Managers. Academy of Management Journal, 1977, March, 20(1), 89-100.

Thompson, M.H. Today's Business Woman: Her Characteristics, Her Need for Further Education, Her Future in Management. Unpublished manuscript, University of California, Los Angeles, 1963.

To Succeed in Business, Women Need to Work Well with Others. Marketing News, 1977, February 25, 10(16), 4.

Top Women Executives Don't Match Stereotype. Seattle Times, 1972, July 10, D2.

Tritsch, C. Anatomy of a Seminar Part 3--'Shyness Didn't Count,' Say Two Participants. Sales Meeting Magazine, 1974, October, 23(10), 87-92+.

Twilight Comes to the All-Male Business Club. Business Week, 1976, December 20, 2463, 65.

Upward Bound (The Professions and Business). Women's Work, 1975, January/February, 1(1), 5.

Walker, Y.K., et al. Women in Health Careers. Washington, D.C.: U.S. Department of Health, Education, and Welfare, 1976.

Warman, J.P. Women Agents Can Find Their Own Markets. Life Association News, 1976, February, 71(2), 41-43.

Warren, V.L. 6 Female Sellers and How They Do It. Marketing Times, 1975, March/April, 22(2), 10-13.

The Way to a Government Job. Women's Work, 1975, May/June, 1(3), 2.

Wexley, K.N., and Nemeroff, W.F. Effectiveness of Positive Reinforcement and Goal Setting as Methods of Management Development. Journal of Applied Psychology, 1975, August, 60(4), 446-450.

Why Women Need Their Own MBA Programs. Business Week, 1974, February 23, 102.

Willett, R.S. Working in 'A Man's World': The Woman Executive.

In V. Gornick, and B. K. Moran, (eds.), Woman in Sexist Society: Studies in Power and Powerlessness. New York: Basic Books, 1971.

WLRT Programs Stress Transferable Ideas. Life Association News, 1975, November, 70(11), 141-148.

Women Are Losing Out; The Race for Executive Jobs. Michigan Education Journal, 1965, April, 42, 23.

Women in Banking: Making the Transition to Management. Carnegie Quarterly, 1973, Spring, 24(2), 5-7.

Women's Progress in Management to Take Time and Self Study. Marketing News, 1977, February 25, 10(16), 1+.

Women's Role in Banking Improving Rapidly. U. S. Investor/Eastern Banker, 1975, June 2, 86(11), 35-36.

Woods, M. M. What Does It Take for a Woman to Make It in Management? Personnel Journal, 1975, January, 54(1), 38-41+.

_____. Women in Management: How Is It Working Out? Advanced Management Journal, 1976, 41(1), 22-30.

Worthington, B. Women Ad Managers Propel Daily's Ad Linage Upwards. Editor and Publisher, 1975, March 29, 108(13), 18-20.

Yorks, L. What Mother Never Told You About Life in the Corporation. Management Review, 1976, April, 65(4), 13-19.

You Still Have a Long Way to Go Baby. Business Week, 1971, September 25, 74-76.

Young, Successful, and First; Eight Young Women--From Rabbi to Sportscaster. Saturday Evening Post, 1974, October, 246, 50-53+.

B. SPECIFIC (continued)

2. SCIENCES, ENGINEERING, MATHEMATICS

Abelson, P. H. Special Opportunity. Science, 1964, July 10, 145, 115. Discussion. 1964, September 11, 145, 1123.

Ancker-Johnson, B. Physicist. Educational Horizons, 1975, Spring 53(3), 116-121.

Association for Women in Mathematics (Philadelphia Chapter). Remarks on Women in Mathematics. American Mathematical Monthly, 1972, 79, 903-904.

Astin, H. S. Preparing Women for Careers in Science and Technology. Paper presented at the Massachusetts Institute of Technology Workshop on Women in Science and Technology, Boston, May 1973.

―――. Women Scientists and Scholarly Productivity. Symposium presentation at the American Psychological Association Convention, San Francisco, 1977.

Baggett, L. R. A Science Career for You? National Business Woman, 1960, May, 39(5), 6-7+.

Bernard, J. (ed.). Cases in Point. In Women and the Public Interest. Chicago: Aldine-Atherton, 1971, 136-146.

―――. The Present Situation in the Academic World of Women Trained in Engineering. In J. A. Mattfeld and C. G. Van Aken (eds.), Women and the Scientific Professions. Cambridge, MA: MIT Press, 1965, 163-182.

Berreman, G. D. On the Role of Women. Bulletin of the Atomic Scientists, 1966, November, 22, 26-28.

Block, J. S., and Parrish, J. B. (eds.). Future for Women in Science and Engineering: Excerpts from address, July 1967. Bulletin of Atomic Scientists, 1968, May, 24, 46-49.

Bolt, R. H. The Present Situation of Women Scientists and Engineers in Industry and Government. In J. A. Mattfeld and C. G. Van Aken (eds.), Women and the Scientific Professions. Cambridge, MA: MIT Press, 1965.

Brief Descriptions of 28 Studies and Experimental Projects Related to Careers in Science for Women Funded by the National Science Foundation in Fiscal Years 1974 and 1975. Washington, D. C.: National Science Foundation, n. d.

Brown, J. M. A Woman in the World of Engineering. IEEE Transactions on Education, 1975, February, E-18(1), 3-10.

Bryn, K. New Era for Women in Science. Science Digest, 1972, November, 72, 54-59.

―――. Sexism in Science: Women Fight Back. Science Digest, 1975, December, 78, 26-33.

Bunting, M. I. Creating Opportunities for Women in Science. In E. Wasserman et al. (eds.), Women in Academia: Evolving Policies Toward Equal Opportunities. New York: Praeger, 1975, 115-119.

Cahill, N. J. Women Researchers Analyze Education, Job Barriers. Science, 1977, December, 198, 917-918.

Campbell, D. P. The Clash Between Beautiful Women and Science. In A. Theodore (ed.), The Professional Woman. Cambridge, MA: Schenkman, 1971, 135-141.

Carr, B. C. What Barriers Impede Women's Science Careers? Physics Today, 1976, August, 29, 63.

Chan, J. Coming Soon: Women in Space. McCalls, 1977, April, 104, 56-57.

David, D. Career Patterns and Values: A Study of Men and Women in Science and Engineering. New York: Columbia University, Bureau of Applied Social Research, 1973.

De Bellefonds, J. Women and Engineering. Impact of Science on Society, 1964, 14(4), 249-267.

Durrant, S. A. On the Role of Women: G. D. Berreman: Reply with Rejoinder. Bulletin of Atomic Scientists, 1967, March, 23, 28-29.

Edgerton, H. A. Women in Science Careers. Journal of the National Association for Women Deans, Administrators, and Counselors, 1962, June, 25(4), 166-169.

Ellsberg, H. New Old Worlds to Conquer; Women in Marine Science. Mademoiselle, 1964, June, 59, 106-108+.

Engineering Manpower Commission of the Engineers' Joint Council. Women and Minority Engineering Students. New York, 1974.

Epstein, C. F. Success Among Women. Chemical Technology, 1973, January, 3, 8-13.

Estrin, T. Ms. Biomedical Engineer: A New Professional Opportunity for Women. IEEE Transactions on Education, 1975, February, E-18(1), 11-14.

Few Women Choose Science as Career. Science News Letter, 1961, November 4, 80, 305.

Franson, M. H. The New Woman and the New Engineering. Engineering: Cornell Quarterly, 1972, Summer, 2, 13-33.

Frieze, I. H. Internal and External Psychological Barriers for Women in Science. In J. A. Ramaley (ed.), Covert Discrimination and Women in the Sciences. American Association for the Advancement of Science Symposium Series, 1977.

Gardner, G. H. F. The Status of Women in the Field of Computing.

Computers and Automation, 1970, January. Also Reprint from KNOW, Inc., P.O. Box 86031, Pittsburgh, PA 15221.

Goldsmith, N. F. Women in Science: Symposium and Job Mart. Science, 1970, May 29, 168, 1124-1127+.

Gray, M. Women in Mathematics. American Mathematical Monthly, 1972, 79(5), 475-479.

Hansen, R. A., and Neujahr, J. L. A Comparison of Career Development Between Males and Females Gifted in Science. Proceedings of the 81st Annual Convention of the American Psychological Association, Montreal, Canada, 1973, 8, 669-670.

———, and ———. Career Development of Males and Females Gifted in Science. Journal of Educational Research, 1974, September, 68, 43-45.

Helson, R. Subtypes of Creative Men and Women in Mathematics. Paper presented at the American Association for the Advancement of Science meeting, Boston, 1976.

———. Women as Mathematicians. Symposium presentation at the American Psychological Association Convention, San Francisco, 1977.

Honigman, R. Women in Engineering. A report to the Conference of Professional and Academic Women, Professional Women's Caucus, Washington, D. C., June 1970.

Kashket, E. R., Robbins, M. L., Leive, L., and Huang, A. S. Status of Women Microbiologists. Science, 1974, February 8, 183, 488-494.

Killian, J. R., Jr. Enhancing the Role of Women in Science, Engineering, and the Social Sciences. In J. A. Mattfeld and C. G. Van Aken (eds.), Women and the Scientific Professions. Cambridge, MA: MIT Press, 1965.

Kotel, J. The Ms. Factor in ASME. Mechanical Engineering, 1973, July, 95(7), 9-21.

Kundsin, R. B. Why Nobody Wants Women in Science. Science Digest, 1965, October, 58, 60-65.

——— (ed.). Women and Success: The Anatomy of Achievement. New York: William Morrow, 1974.

Larney, V. H. Female Mathematicians, Where Are You? American Mathematical Monthly, 1973, 80(3), 310-313.

Levine, R., and Rolwing, R. H. Reasons Why Qualified Women Do Not Pursue Mathematical Careers. Delta Kappa Gamma Bulletin, 1977, Winter, 43, 40-48.

Lubkin, G. B. Women in Physics. Physics Today, 1971, April, 24, 23-27.

———. Discrimination Against Women in Physics. Physics Today, 1972, July, 25, 61-62.

Luchins, E. H. Women in Mathematics: A Contemporary Appraisal. Paper presented to the American Association for the Advancement of Science meeting, Boston, February 1976.

McAffee, N. Women in Engineering. New Engineer, 1973, March, 2, 6-7.

Maccoby, E. E. Feminine Intellect and the Demands of Science. Impact of Science on Society, 1970, 20(1), 13-28.

Marcus, G. H. Status of Women in the Nuclear Industry. Bulletin of the Atomic Scientists, 1976, April, 32, 34-39.

Mattfeld, J. A., and Van Aken, C. G. (eds.), Women and the Scientific Professions. Cambridge, MA: MIT Press, 1965.

Medalen, J. I. Women in Engineering--1 Percent to 10 Percent in Four Years. IEEE Transactions on Education, 1975, February, E-18(1), 38-40.

Motz, A. B. The Roles of the Married Woman in Science. Journal of Marriage and Family, 1961, 23, 374-376.

National Research Council. Employment Status of Ph. D. Scientists and Engineers, 1973 and 1975. Washington, D. C.: National Academy of Sciences, n. d.

———. Doctoral Scientists and Engineers in the United States, 1975 Profile. Washington, D. C.: National Academy of Sciences, n. d.

O'Brien, J. E. Opportunities and Challenges for Women Engineers. Available from ERIC (ED101117), 1974.

Office of Experimental Projects and Programs. Summary of Studies and Experimental Programs to Discover Barriers in the Participation of Women in Science. Unpublished report. Washington, D. C.: National Science Foundation, 1974.

Osen, L. M. Women in Mathematics. Cambridge, MA: MIT Press, 1974.

Parrish, J. B. Are There Women in Engineering's Future? American Association of University Women Journal, 1965, 59(1), 29-31.

———. Employment of Women Chemists in Industrial Laboratories. Science, 1965, April 30, 148, 657-658.

_____. Women BS Graduates in Chemistry: A Survey of Career Experience. Journal of Chemical Education, 1965, April, 42, 216-217.

_____. Women in Engineering: Some Perspectives on the Past, Present, and Future. Paper presented at the Engineering Foundation Research Conference, New England College, Henniker, NH, July 1971.

Peden, I. C., and Bee, H. L. Characteristics of Women Currently Employed as Engineers, Technicians, Programmers, and Draftsmen. In The Access of Technical Careers to Women in the West Coast States of the United States of America. New York: United Nations Educational, Scientific, and Cultural Organization, 1968.

Pendleton, C. Women in Science: Reshaping the Stereotypes. Science News, 1975, March 15, 107, 171+.

Perrucci, C. C. The Female Engineer and Scientist: Factors Associated with the Pursuit of a Professional Career. Unpublished manuscript, 1968.

_____. Minority Status and the Pursuit of Professional Careers: Women in Science and Engineering. Social Forces, 1970, December, 49(2), 245-259. Also in D. B. Targ (ed.), Marriage and the Family: A Critical Analysis and Proposals for Change. New York: David McKay, 1974, 376-397.

A Place for Women. Cambridge, MA: MIT, 1973.

Ray, C. D. Biomedical Engineering--The Beauty and the Beast. Naturwissenschaften, 1973, August, 60(8), 375-381.

Register of Women and Minority Males with Doctorates in Civil Engineering, Mechanics, and Allied Fields. Urbana, IL: University of Illinois-Urbana, n. d.

Reskin, B. F. Sex Differences in the Professional Life Chances of Chemists. Unpublished doctoral dissertation, University of Washington, 1973. Dissertation Abstracts International, 1974, 34(8-A), 5341. Also available from ERIC (ADG74-02229), 1973.

_____. Sex Differences in Status Attainment in Science: The Case of the Postdoctoral Fellowship. American Sociological Review, 1976, August, 41(4), 597-612.

Robin, S. S. The Female in Engineering. In R. Perrucci and J. E. Gerstl (eds.), The Engineers and the Social System. New York: John Wiley, 1969, 203-218.

Rossi, A. S. Who Wants Women Scientists? In J. A. Mattfeld and C. G. Van Aken (eds.), Women and the Scientific Professions. Cambridge, MA: MIT Press, 1965.

_____. Barriers to the Career Choice of Engineering, Medicine, or Science Among American Women. In J. A. Mattfeld and C. G. Van Aken (eds.), Women and the Scientific Professions. Cambridge, MA: MIT Press, 1965, 51-127. Also in J. M. Bardwick (ed.), Readings on the Psychology of Women. New York: Harper and Row, 1972, 72-83.

_____. Women in Science: Why So Few? In C. Safilios-Rothschild (ed.), Toward a Sociology of Women. Lexington, MA: Xerox College Publishing, 1972, 141-153.

Rossiter, M. W. Women Scientists in America Before 1920. American Scientist, 1974, May/June, 62(3), 312-323.

Ruina, E. Women in Science and Technology. Cambridge, MA: MIT Press, 1973.

Sandell, S. Male-Female Salary Differences Among Scientists with Ph.D.'s. Unpublished doctoral dissertation, University of Minnesota, 1973.

Schilling, G. F., and Hunt, K. Women in Science and Technology: U.S./U.S.S.R. Comparisons. Santa Monica, CA: Rand, 1974.

Science's Sex Desegregation. Science News Letter, 1962, March 3, 81, 138-139.

Scientific Manpower Commission. The Impact of Federal Programs and Policies on Manpower Planning for Scientists and Engineers. Washington, D.C., 1977.

Sidlofsky, S., and Goodings, G. J. The Canadian Female Engineer: Role Confusion--Oh, No! Sociological Focus, 1973, Winter, 6(1), 14-29.

Simmons, J. E. Women in Science: AAAS Symposium. Science, 1970, October 9, 170, 201.

Sloan, M. E. Opportunities for Women in Engineering. IEEE Transactions on Education, 1975, February, E-18(1), 1-3.

_____. Women Engineers in the United States. Educational Horizons, 1975, Spring, 53(3), 102-105.

_____, and Peden, I. C. Some Comparisons Between Women and Ethnic Minority Engineers. IEEE Transactions on Education, 1974, February, E-17(1), 7-9.

Statistics Committee. A Profile of the Woman Engineer. Unpublished manuscript. New York: Society of Women Engineers, 1972.

Tittle, C. K., McCarthy, K., and Steckler, J. F. Women and Educational Testing. Princeton, NJ: Educational Testing Service,

474 / Occupational Forces

1974. Also in J. Pottker and A. Fishel (eds.), Sex Bias in the Schools--Research Evidence. Madison, NJ: Fairleigh Dickinson University Press, 1977, 256-272.

Very Favorable Outlook for Women in Research. Science News Letter, 1965, June 19, 87, 392.

Vetter, B. M. Women and Minority Scientists. Science, 1975, September 5, 189, 751.

──────. Supply and Demand for Scientists and Engineers--A Review of Selected Studies. Washington, D. C.: Scientific Manpower Commission, n. d.

White, M. S. Psychological and Social Barriers to Women in Science. Science, 1970, October 23, 170, 413-416. Also in C. Safilios-Rothschild (ed.), Toward a Sociology of Women. Lexington, MA: Xerox College Publishing, 1972, 300-308; and in J. Freeman (ed.), Women: A Feminist Perspective. Palo Alto: Mayfield, 1975, 227-237.

Wilson, M. Unliberated Labs of American Science. Harper's Bazaar, 1972, September, 105, 18.

Wolfle, D. Women in Science and Engineering. Science, 1964, September 25, 145, 1389.

──────. Women in Science and Engineering. Science, 1965, April 2, 148, 21. Discussion, 1965, May 14, 893-894.

Women and Aviation; Symposium, with Editorial Comment. Flying, 1965, August, 77(28), 30-45+.

Women in Engineering. Special issue. Engineering Manpower Bulletin, 1972, May, (21).

Women in Engineering. Special issue. IEEE Transactions on Education, 1975, February, E-18(1).

Women in Science and Technology: Careers for Today and Tomorrow. Iowa City: American College Testing Program, 1975.

Zimmerman, J. Some Salaries Are More Equal than Others. Chemistry, 1971, February, 44, 4.

B. SPECIFIC (continued)

3. HEALTH SCIENCES

Bernard, J. (ed.). Cases in Point. In Women and the Public Interest. Chicago: Aldine-Atherton, 1971, 136-146.

Bowers, J. J. Women in Medicine: An International Study. New England Journal of Medicine, 1966, August, 275, 362-365.

Bullough, B., and Bullough, V. L. The Causes and Consequences of the Differentiation of the Nursing Role. In P. L. Stewart and M. G. Cantor (eds.), Varieties of Work Experience. New York: John Wiley, 1974, 292-300.

_____, and _____. Sex Discrimination in Health Care. Nursing Outlook, 1975, January, 23, 40-45.

Campbell, M. A. Why Would a Girl Go into Medicine? Medical Education in the United States: A Guide for Women. Old Westbury, NY: The Feminist Press, n.d.

Cartwright, L. K. Career Satisfaction and Role Harmony in Young Women Physicians. Symposium presentation at the American Psychological Association Convention, San Francisco, 1977.

Center for Women in Medicine. Women in Medicine: Action Planning for the 1970's. Philadelphia: Medical College of Pennsylvania, 1974.

Comisarow, R. W. Work Motivation of Female Health Field Workers. Unpublished doctoral dissertation, Case Western Reserve University. Dissertation Abstracts International, 1971, January, 31(7-B), 4378.

Doan, B., Levy, J., and Levy, D. R. Les Femmes dans la Médecine et les Professions Liberales [Women in Medicine and Other Liberal Professions.] C. Sociol. Demog. Med., 1964, October-December, 4(4), 123-136.

Ducker, D. G. The Effects of Two Sources of Role Strain on Women Physicians. Unpublished doctoral dissertation. Dissertation Abstracts International, 1975, January, 35(7-B), 3552.

Ehrenreich, B., and English, D. Witches, Midwives, and Nurses: A History of Women Healers. Old Westbury, NY: The Feminist Press, 1977.

Fay, M. Why So Few Women Doctors? Today's Health, 1963, June, 41, 46-49+.

Feulner, P. N. Women in the Professions: A Social-Psychological Study. Unpublished doctoral dissertation. Dissertation Abstracts International, 1974, February, 34(8-A, Pt. 2), 5309.

Gibbons, K. M., and Grosgebauer, C. The New Health Practitioners. Women's Work, 1976, November/December, 2(6), 8-13.

Gilbert, M. Women in Medicine. In R. Morgan (ed.), Sisterhood Is Powerful. New York: Random House, 1970, 62-65.

Giuliani, B., and Centra, J. A. The Woman Veterinarian. Personnel and Guidance Journal, 1968, 46(10), 971-975.

Gloeckner, M. L. The Challenge of Medicine for Women Today. Journal of the American Medical Women's Association, 1960, March, 15, 271-274.

Grandjean, B. D., Aiken, L. H., and Bonjean, C. M. Professional Autonomy and the Work Satisfaction of Nursing Educators. Nursing Research, 1976, May-June, 25(3), 216-221.

Haavio-Mannila, E., and Jaakkola, R. Sex Roles and the Medical Profession, Research Report No. 150. Helsinki: University of Helsinki, Institute of Sociology, 1970.

The Health Professions. Women's Work, 1976, November/December, 2(6), 7.

Health Resources Administration. Minorities and Women in Health Fields. Washington, D. C.: Department of Health, Education, and Welfare, n. d.

Hill, R. E. The Leadership Role as a Factor in Commitment and Satisfaction Among Registered Nurses. Unpublished doctoral dissertation, Purdue University. Dissertation Abstracts International, 1971, April, 31(10-B), 6314.

Hoffman, R. Can Women Take Medicine? Mademoiselle, 1963, September, 57, 127-129+.

Hole, J., and Levine, E. Professions. In Rebirth of Feminism. New York: Quadrangle/The New York Times, 1971, 338-371.

Jantzen, A. C. Some Characteristics of Female Occupational Therapists, 1970: I. Descriptive Study. American Journal of Occupational Therapy. 1972, January, 26(1), 19-26.

_____. Some Characteristics of Female Occupational Therapists, 1970: III. A Comparison: Faculty and Clinical Practitioners. American Journal of Occupational Therapy, 1972, April, 26(3), 150-154.

Kaplan, H. I. Women Physicians: The More Effective Recruitment and Utilization of Their Talents and the Resistance to It--The Final Conclusions of a Seven Year Study. Women Physicians, 1970, 25, 561-570.

_____. Women Physicians. New Physician, 1971, 20, 11-19.

Kirk, K. W. A National Survey of Women Pharmacists: Their Attitudes, Career Practice Patterns, and Vocational Interests. Unpublished doctoral dissertation, University of Wisconsin, Madison, 1972. Dissertation Abstracts International, 1972, 33(6-B), 2675. Also available from ERIC (ADG72-233191), 1972.

Kosa, J., and Coker, R. E., Jr. The Female Physician in Public Health: Conflict and Reconciliation of the Sex and Professional Roles. Sociology and Social Research, 1965, April, 49(3), 294-305. Also in A. Theodore (ed.), The Professional Woman. Cambridge, MA: Schenkman, 1971, 195-206.

Kramer, M., McDonnell, C., and Reed, J. L. Self-Actualization and Role Adaptation of Baccalaureate Degree Nurses. Nursing Research, 1972, March, 21(2), 111-123.

Lopate, C. Women in Medicine. Baltimore: Johns Hopkins University Press, 1968.

Lower, D., and Krain, M. Minorities and Women in the Health Fields. Washington, D. C.: U. S. Gov. Printing Office, 1976.

Lynn, N. B., Vaden, A. G., and Vaden, R. E. The Challenges of Men in a Woman's World. Public Personnel Management, 1975, January-February, 4(1), 4-17.

Mathews, M. R. The Training and Practice of Women Physicians: A Case Study. Journal of Medical Education, 1970, 45(12), 1016-1024.

Menninger, K. The Psychological Advantages of the Woman Physician. Bulletin of the Menninger Clinic, 1973, 37(4), 333-340.

Midlarsky, E. The Female Mental Health Professional: A Wasted Resource. Paper presented at the Colorado Mental Health Association meeting, Colorado Springs, September 1976.

Miller, M. H. Work Roles for the Associate Degree Graduate. American Journal of Nursing, 1974, March, 74(3), 468-470.

Nadelson, C., and Notman, M. The Woman Physician. Journal of Medical Education, 1972, March, 47, 176-183.

Navarro, V. Women in Health Care. New England Journal of Medicine, 1975, February, 292(8), 398-402.

Orbach, N. R. F. The Evolution of a Professional: The Case of Women in Dentistry. Unpublished doctoral dissertation, University of Illinois, Chicago Circle, 1977. Dissertation Abstracts International, 1977, 38(1-A), 492. Also available from ERIC (ADG77-15332), 1977.

Pennell, M., and Renshaw, J. E. Distribution of Women Physicians. Journal of the American Medical Women's Association, 1972, April, 27, 197-203.

_____, and Showell, S. Women in Health Careers: Status of Women in Health Careers in the United States and Other Selected Countries. Available from ERIC (ED113553), 1975.

Phelps, C. E. Women in American Medicine. Journal of Medical Education, 1968, 43, 916-924.

Powers, L., Wiesenfelder, H., and Parmelee, R. Practice Patterns of Women and Men Physicians. Preliminary report to the American Association of Medical Colleges, October 1966.

Pullum, C. A. Women, Medicine and Misconceptions. Journal of the American Medical Women's Association, 1963, July, 18, 563-565.

Quadagno, J. Occupational Sex-Typing and Internal Labor Market Distributions: An Assessment of Medical Specialties. Social Problems, 1976, 23(4), 442-453.

Ray, C. D. Biomedical Engineering. The Beauty and the Beast. Naturwissenschaften, 1973, August, 60(8), 375-381.

Renshaw, J. E., and Pennell, M. Distribution of Women Physicians. The Women Physician, 1971, 26(4), 187-195.

Roeske, N. A. Women in Psychiatry: Past and Present Areas of Concern. American Journal of Psychiatry, 1973, October, 130(10), 1127-1131.

_____. Women in Psychiatry: A Review. American Journal of Psychiatry, 1976, April, 133(4), 365-372.

Ryan, M. P. Personality Motives, Career Stages, and Work Status Among Nurses. Dissertation Abstracts International, 1971, October, 32(4-A), 2195.

Saleh, S. E., Lee, R. J., and Prien, E. P. Why Nurses Leave Their Jobs: An Analysis of Female Turnover. Personnel Administration, 1965, January-February, 28(1), 25-28.

Seaver, J. Women Doctors, In Spite of Everything. New York Times Magazine, 1961, March 26, 27+.

Shapiro, C. S. A Woman in a Non-Traditional Role: A Surgeon. Educational Horizons, 1975, Spring, 53(3), 106-109.

Shuval, J. T. Sex Role Differentiation in the Professions: The Case of Israeli Dentists. Journal of Health and Social Behavior, 1970, September, 11(3), 236-244.

Silver, G. A. Women in Medicine. Nation, 1975, June 21, 220, 741.

Singleton, D. Sex as a Determinant of Responses to Patient Management Problems by Physicians and Medical Students. Symposium presentation at the American Psychological Association Convention, San Francisco, 1977.

Stein, L. Male and Female: The Doctor-Nurse Game. In J. P. Spradley and D. W. McCurdy (eds.), Conformity and Conflict: Readings in Cultural Anthropology. Boston: Little, Brown, 1971.

Sullivan, M. A New Era: Challenges for the Woman Physician. Journal of the American Medical Woman's Association, 1974, January, 29, 9-11.

Technical Education Research Center. Pathways to a Career in Dentistry. Cambridge, MA: Tufts University School of Dental Medicine, n. d.

Walsh, M. R. Sexual Barriers in the Medical Profession: A Case Study of Boston Women Physicians, 1835-1973. Unpublished doctoral dissertation, Boston University, 1974. American Doctoral Dissertations, 1974, 11(97). Also available from ERIC (ADG02-85521), 1974.

_____. "Doctors Wanted: No Women Need Apply." Sexual Barriers in the Medical Profession. New Haven, CT: Yale University Press, 1976.

_____. Successful Femininity: The Superwoman Mystique Among Female Physicians. Symposium presentation at the American Psychological Association Convention, San Francisco, 1977.

Why There Aren't More Woman Doctors. Science Digest, 1963, May, 53(5), 29.

Williams, J. J. Patients and Prejudice: Lay Attitudes Toward Women Physicians. American Journal of Sociology, 1964, January, 51, 282-287.

Williams, P. A. Women in Medicine: Some Themes and Variations. Journal of Medical Education, 1971, 46(7, Pt. 1), 584-591.

Wilson, M. F. Women in Medicine: Improving Prospects? Journal of Medical Education, 1972, 47(4), 303-304.

Wilson, V. An Analysis of Femininity in Nursing. American Behavioral Scientist, 1971, November, 15(2), 213-220.

Women in Medicine: Action Planning for the 1970's. Philadelphia: Center for Women in Medicine, Medical College of Pennsylvania, 1974.

Women in Medicine. Palo Alto, CA: Stanford University School of Medicine, n. d.

Women M. D.'s Join the Fight. Medical World News, 1970, 11(43), 22-28.

Women Physicians: A Selected List of Books. Philadelphia: The Medical College of Pennsylvania, 1972.

Women's Action Programs, Office of Special Concerns. Exploratory Study of Females in Health Professions Schools. Washington, D. C. : Department of Health, Education, and Welfare, 1976.

B. SPECIFIC (continued)

4. SOCIAL AND BEHAVIORAL SCIENCES

American Historical Association. Committee on the Status of Women. Final Report. Washington, D. C. : American Historical Association, 1971.

American Political Science Association. Women in Political Science. Studies and Reports of the American Political Science Association Committee on the Status of Women in the Profession, 1969-1971, Washington, D. C. , 1971.

Astin, H. S. Employment and Career Status of Women Psychologists. American Psychologist, 1972, May, 27(5), 371-381.

_____. Legislation and Sex Bias Considerations for the Counseling Psychologist. Symposium presentation at the American Psychological Association Convention, San Francisco, 1977.

Babchuk, N. , Massey, R. , and Gordon, C. W. Men and Women in Community Agencies: A Note on Power and Prestige. In N. Glazer-Malbin and H. Y. Waehrer (eds.), Woman in a Man-Made World: A Socioeconomic Handbook. Chicago: Rand McNally, 1972, 248-253.

Bates, M. Home Economist as a Leader in Business. Practical Forecast for Home Economics, 1968, March, 13, F42-43.

Benetar, J. Admissions: Notes from a Woman Psychiatrist. New York: Bantam Books, 1974.

Berman, E. The Woman Psychiatrist as Therapist and Academician. Journal of Medical Education, 1972, November, 47(11), 890-893.

Bernstein, M. D. , and Russo, N. F. The History of Psychology Revisited: Or, Up with Our Foremothers. American Psychologist, 1974, February, 29(2), 130-134.

Boneau, C. A. , and Cuca, J. M. An Overview of Psychology's Human Resources: Characteristics and Salaries from the 1972

APA Survey. American Psychologist, 1974, November, 29(11), 821-839.

Bryson, R. B., Bryson, J. B., Licht, M. H., and Licht, B. G. The Professional Pair: Husband and Wife Psychologists. American Psychologist, 1976, 31, 10-16.

Butler, M., and Paisley, W. Status of Professional Couples in Psychology. Psychology of Women Quarterly, 1977, Summer, 1(4), 307-318.

Carter, C. A. Advantages of Being a Woman Therapist. Psychotherapy: Theory, Research and Practice, 1971, Winter, 8(4), 297-300.

Cates, J. N. Sex and Salary. American Psychologist, 1973, October, 28(10), 929.

Chesler, P. Women as Psychiatric and Psychotherapeutic Patients. Journal of Marriage and the Family, 1971, 33(4), 746-759.

Cohn, E., and Kidder, L. The Merit of Sex: A Look at the Differences in Salaries Given to Men and Women. Symposium presentation at the American Psychological Association Convention, San Francisco, 1977.

Cole, J. Women in Science. Paper presented at the American Sociological Society meeting, Denver, 1971.

Cosper, W. B. Consider the Higher Educational Limbo of Married Home Economists. Journal of Home Economics, 1968, November, 60, 721-723.

Dalgleish, L. Women and Psychology Hearing Group Report. Australian Psychologist, 1975, December, 10(3), 339-344.

Fabian, J. J. The Hazards of Being a Professional Woman. Professional Psychology, 1972, Fall, 3(4), 324-326.

Fanshel, D. Status Differentials: Men and Women in Social Work. Social Work, 1976, November, 21(6), 448-454.

Farmer, H. S. Why Women Contribute Less to the Arts and Sciences. Paper presented at the American Psychological Association Convention, Washington, D. C., 1976.

Fein, L. G. Women in International Psychology. International Understanding, 1974, Spring, 9/10, 97-107.

Fidell, L. S. Empirical Verification of Sex Discrimination in Hiring Practices in Psychology. American Psychologist, 1970, 25, 1094-1098. Also in R. K. Unger and F. L. Denmark (eds.), Woman: Dependent or Independent Variable? New York: Psychological Dimensions, 1975, 773-786.

Fields, R. M. The Status of Women in Psychology: How Many and How Come? In F. L. Denmark (ed.), Who Discriminates Against Women? Issue 15. Beverly Hills, CA: Sage Publications, 1974, 95-103. Also in International Journal of Group Tensions, 1974, March, 4(1), 93-121.

Gilligan, M. B. Developmental Stages of Occupational Therapy and the Feminist Movement. American Journal of Occupational Therapy. 1976, October, 30(9), 560-567.

Gottsegen, G. B., and Gottsegen, M. G. Women and School Psychology. School Psychology Digest, 1973, Summer, 2(3), 24-27.

Grieve, N. Women in Psychology: As Practitioners. Australian Psychologist, 1975, December, 10(3), 299-301.

Groot, H., Preston, T., Powell, A., and McCormick, N. Women's Place in Clinical Psychology: On the Quality of Women's Power in the Administration of Psychological Services in Mental Health and Medical Settings. Paper presented at the WAWP Convention, 1976.

Guttman, M. A. J. Is the Gray Mare Only a Workhorse? Personnel and Guidance Journal, 1972, October, 51(2), 115-122.

_____, and Hicks, L. Characteristics of Female Members of ACES. Counselor Education and Supervision, 1974, March, 13(3), 165-171.

Guyer, L., and Fidell, L. Publications of Men and Women Psychologists: Do Women Publish Less? American Psychologist, 1973, February, 28(2), 157-160.

Harrower, M. Women in Independent or Free-Lance Practice. International Understanding, 1974, Spring, 9(10), 88-96.

Herberg, D. M. The Career Patterns of Female Social Workers. Unpublished manuscript, University of Michigan, Ann Arbor, n. d.

Hilberman, E., Gispert, M., and Harper, J. Impact of a District Branch Task Force on Women. American Journal of Psychiatry, 1976, October, 133(10), 1159-1164.

Hoffman, D. T., Scally, B., Deering, A., and Kott, E. Women in Psychology. Paper presented at the American Psychological Association Convention, Miami, FL, 1970.

Holroyd, J. C. Problems of Women Therapists in Relation to Their Profession. Symposium presentation at the American Psychological Association Convention, Chicago, 1975.

Jackson, A. Problems Experienced by Female Therapists in Establishing an Alliance. Paper presented at the American Psychological Association Convention, Honolulu, 1972.

Keith-Spiegel, P., and Farell, J. Client Discrimination Against Female Psychotherapists. Paper presented at the WAWP Convention, Anaheim, CA, April 1973.

Kenworthy, J. A. Problems of Women Therapists in Relation to Training. Symposium presentation at the American Psychological Association Convention, Chicago, 1975.

Killian, J. R., Jr. Enhancing the Role of Women in Science, Engineering, and the Social Sciences. In J. A. Mattfeld and C. G. Van Aken (eds.), Women and the Scientific Professions. Cambridge, MA: MIT Press, 1965.

Kimmel, E. Status of Women in the Psychological Community in the Southeast: A Case Study. American Psychologist, 1974, 29, 519-540.

_____. Contributions to the History of Psychology: XXIV Role of Women Psychologists in the South. Psychological Reports, 1976, April, 38(2), 611-618.

Kitchener, K. S., Corazzini, J. G., and Huebner, L. A. A Study of Counseling Center Hiring Practices: What Does It Take for a Woman to Be Hired? Journal of Counseling Psychology, 1975, September, 22(5), 440-445.

Lewin, T. F. The Employment Experience of Married Women Social Caseworkers: A Study of One Hundred Graduates of the New York School of Social Work, Columbia University. Unpublished doctoral dissertation, University of Chicago, 1962. American Doctoral Dissertations, 1962, 11(96), 203. Also available from ERIC (ADG02-61494), 1962.

Lopata, H. Z. Review Essay: Sociology. SIGNS: Journal of Women in Culture and Society, 1976, 2(1), 165-176.

Lord, E. Discussion: Women in National and International Psychology. International Understanding, 1974, Spring, 9(10), 108-114.

McMurray, G. L. Social Work. Report to the Professional and Academic Women's meeting, Professional Women's Caucus, Washington, D. C., 1970.

Magoon, T. M., and Golann, S. E. Nontraditionally Trained Women as Mental Health Counselors/Psychotherapists. Personnel and Guidance Journal, 1966, April, 44, 788-793.

Mausner, J. S., and Steppacher, R. C. Suicide in Professionals: A Study of Male and Female Psychologists. American Journal of Epidemiology, 1973, 98(6), 436-445.

Monts, E. A., and Burger, L. J. The Status of Home Economics and the Status of Women. In J. I. Roberts (ed.), Beyond Intellectual Sexism: A New Woman. A New Reality. New York: David McKay, 1976, 381-386.

Nader, L. Anthropological Charting of the Frontier. In J. Stiehm (ed.), The Frontiers of Knowledge. University Park, Los Angeles: University of Southern California Press, 1976, 63-78.

Nelson, C. Women in Clinical Psychology. International Understanding, 1974, Spring, 9(10), 78-87.

O'Leary, V. E. Some Attitudinal Barriers to Occupational Aspirations in Women. Psychological Bulletin, 1974, 81(11), 809-826.

Pendergrass, V. E. Women as Clinicians in Private Practice. American Psychologist, 1974, 29, 533-535.

Randour, M. L. Research and Funding Issues for Women in Counseling Psychology. Symposium presentation at the American Psychological Association Convention, San Francisco, 1977.

Report of Ad Hoc Committee on the Role of Women in Anthropology. Presented at the American Anthropological Association meeting, San Diego, November 1970.

Report of the Task Force on the Status of Women in Psychology. American Psychologist, 1973, July, 28(7), 611-616.

Rosen, R. Sexism in History or, Writing Women's History Is a Tricky Business. Journal of Marriage and the Family, 1971, August, 33(3), 541-543.

Rosenblatt, A., Turner, E. M., Patterson, A. R., and Rollesson, C. K. Predominance of Male Authors in Social Work Publications. Social Casework, 1970, 51(7), 421-430. Also in A. Theodore (ed.), The Professional Woman. Cambridge, MA: Schenkman, 1971.

Rubin-Rabson, G. How High Are the Odds Against Women? American Psychologist, 1974, December, 29(12), 916-917.

Schein, V. E. The Woman Industrial Psychologist: Illusion or Reality? American Psychologist, 1971, 26(8), 708-712.

Scher, M. Women Psychiatrists in the United States. American Journal of Psychiatry, 1973, October, 130(10), 1118-1122.

Sexton, V. S. Women's Accomplishments in American Psychology: A Brief Survey. Pakistan Journal of Psychology, 1969, 2(1), 29-35.

―――. Women in American Psychology: An Overview. International Understanding, 1974, Spring, 9(10), 66-77.

Shelton, B. Feminism: Implications for Employment Counselors. Journal of Employment Counseling, 1976, September, 13(3), 116-121.

Smith, D. Women's Perspective as a Radical Critique of Sociology. Sociological Inquiry, 1974, 44, 1+.

Stedman, L. A., and Anderson, P. S. Employer Acceptance of the Mature Home Economist. Journal of Home Economics, 1965, December, 57, 767-772.

Stoll, C. S. Sexism in Social Science. In Female and Male: Socialization, Social Roles, and Social Structures. Dubuque, IA: William C. Brown, 1974, 57-75.

Teghtsoonian, M. Sexual Bias in the Selection of Editors of Psychological Journals. Paper presented at the Eastern Psychological Association meeting, April, 1972.

_____. Distribution by Sex of Authors and Editors of Psychological Journals, 1970-1972: Are There Enough Women Editors? American Psychologist, 1974, April, 29(4), 262-269.

Tyler, L. Introductory Statement: Women in National and International Psychology. International Understanding, 1974, Spring, 9(10), 64-65.

Valentich, M. E. Sex Differences in Career Management Among Social Workers. Unpublished doctoral dissertation, University of Denver, 1975. Dissertation Abstracts International, 1975, 36 (7-A), 4765. Also available from ERIC (ADG75-01232), 1975.

Vetter, B. M. Survey Paints Picture of Psychology Manpower. APA Monitor, 1973, 4, 3.

Walton, R. G. Women in Social Work. Boston: Routledge and Kegan Paul, Ltd., 1975.

Wilkie, J. R., and Allen, I. L. Women Sociologists and Co-Authorship with Men. American Sociologist, 1975, 10, 19-24.

Wittig, M. A., and Nolfi, S. L. Sex Differences in the Training, Recruitment, and Employment of Psychologists. Status of Women Committee of the Western Psychological Association, n. d.

Women Who Work in Historical Settings. Women's Work, 1976, January/February, 2(1), 21-22.

B. SPECIFIC (continued)

5. LAW AND LAW ENFORCEMENT

Boalt Hall Women's Association of the School of Law at the University of California. Wanted by the Law: Women. Berkeley: University of California, School of Law, n. d.

Brownlee, J. Where Is the Professional Woman. Women Lawyers Journal, 1967, Winter, 53(1), 14-16.

Coles, F. S. Women in Litigation Practice: Success and the Woman Lawyer. Unpublished doctoral dissertation, University of California, Berkeley, 1974. Dissertation Abstracts International, 1975, 36(1-A). Also available from ERIC (ADG75-15137), 1974.

Epstein, C. F. Women and Professional Careers: The Case of the Woman Lawyer. Unpublished doctoral dissertation, Columbia University, 1968. Dissertation Abstracts International, 1969, 30(2-A), 824. Also available from ERIC (ADG69-09188), 1968.

————. Women Lawyers and Their Profession: Inconsistency of Social Controls and Their Consequences for Professional Performance. In A. Theodore (ed.), The Professional Woman. Cambridge, MA: Schenkman, 1971, 669-684.

Feulner, P. N. Women in the Professions: A Social-Psychological Study. Dissertation Abstracts International, 1974, February, 34(8-A, Pt. 2), 5309.

Glancy, D. J. HLS Survey Women in Law. Harvard Law School Bulletin, 1970, 21(5), 22-33.

Golden Gate Law School Women's Association. Women and the Law. San Francisco: Golden Gate Law School, n. d.

Grossblat, M., and Sikes, B. H. (eds.). Women Lawyers: Supplementary Data to the 1971 Lawyer Statistical Report. Chicago: American Bar Foundation, 1973.

Hole, J., and Levine, E. Professions. In Rebirth of Feminism. New York: Quadrangle/The New York Times, 1971, 338-371.

Kanowitz, L. Women and the Law: The Unfinished Revolution. Albuquerque: University of New Mexico Press, 1971.

LaRussa, G. W. Portia's Decision: Women's Motives for Studying Law and Their Later Career Satisfaction as Attorneys. Psychology of Women Quarterly, 1977, Summer, 1(4), 350-364.

Melchionne, T. M. Current Status and Problems of Women Police.

Journal of Criminal Law, Criminology and Police Science, 1967, June, 58(2), 257-260.

Morneau, R. H., Jr. Women in Law Enforcement: A Social-Psychological Study. Unpublished doctoral dissertation, University of Southern California, 1975. *Dissertation Abstracts International*, 1976, 36(11-A), 7635. Also available from ERIC (ADG 02-84382), 1975.

Price, B. R. A Study of Leadership Strength of Female Police Executives. *Journal of Police Science and Administration*, 1974, June, 2(2), 219-226.

Sciacco, A., Jr. Some Observations About Women and Their Role in the Field of Corrections. *American Journal of Corrections*, 1972, 34(2), 10-12.

Sherman, L. J. A Psychological View of Women in Policing. *Journal of Police Science and Administration*, 1973, December, 1(4), 383-394.

Smith, D. *Justice Is a Woman*. Philadelphia: Dorrance, 1966.

Stout, E. Women in Probation and Parole: Should Female Officers Supervise Male Offenders? *Crime and Delinquency*, 1973, January, 19(1), 61-71.

Tolchin, S. The Exclusion of Women from the Judicial Process. *SIGNS: Journal of Women in Culture and Society*, 1977, Summer, 2(4), 877-887.

White, J. J. Women in the Law. *Michigan Law Review*, 1967, 65, 1051-1122. Abridged form in C. Safilios-Rothschild (ed.), *Toward a Sociology of Women*. Lexington, MA: Xerox College Publishing, 1972, 277-299. Also in A. Theodore (ed.), *The Professional Woman*. Cambridge, MA: Schenkman, 1971.

Women and Law. Stanford, CA: Stanford University Law School, n. d.

B. SPECIFIC (continued)

6. GOVERNMENT AND POLITICS

Baer, M. F. Women in Federal Government. *Personnel and Guidance Journal*, 1962, January, 40, 416-417.

Carper, J. Four Women Who Can Improve Your Life; Government's New Consumer Advocates. *American Home*, 1977, August, 80, 42-43.

Constantini, E., and Craik, K. H. Women as Politicians: The Social Background, Personality, and Political Careers of Female Party Leaders. Journal of Social Issues, 1972, 28(2), 217-236.

Diamond, I. Sex Roles in the State House. New Haven: Yale University Press, 1971.

DiMarco, N., and Whitsitt, S. E. A Comparison of Female Supervisors in Business and Government Organizations. Journal of Vocational Behavior, 1975, 6, 185-196.

Dubeck, P. J. Women and Access to Political Office: A Comparison of Female and Male State Legislators. Sociological Quarterly, 1976, Winter, 17(1), 42-52.

Erskine, H. The Polls: Women's Role. Public Opinion Quarterly, 1971, Summer, 35(2), 275-290.

Eyde, L. D. The Status of Women in State and Local Government. Public Personnel Management, 1973, 2, 205-211.

Fleming, G. J. Why Women in Politics; Address, November 15, 1959. Vital Speeches of the Day, 1960, January 1, 26, 172-173.

Foote, F. L. Role Stress and Cultural Resources: A Study of the Role of the Woman Member of Congress. Unpublished doctoral dissertation. Dissertation Abstracts, 1968, 28(10-A), 4284-4285.

Gehlen, F. L. Legislative Role Performance of Female Legislators. Sex Roles: A Journal of Research, 1977, 3(1), 1-18.

Gibbons, K. M. Women in Politics. Women's Work, 1976, March/April, 2(2), 3-6.

Grafton, S. Women in Politics: The Coming Breakthrough. McCall's, 1962, September, 89, 102-103+.

Gruberg, M. Woman in American Politics: An Assessment and Sourcebook. Oshkosh, WI: Academia Press, 1968.

Haavio-Mannila, E. Sex Roles in Politics. In C. Safilios-Rothschild (ed.), Toward a Sociology of Women. Lexington, MA: Xerox College Publishing, 1972, 154-172.

Hole, J., and Levine, E. Professions. In Rebirth of Feminism. New York: Quadrangle/New York Times, 1971, 338-371.

Jaquette, J. S. (ed.). Women in Politics. New York: John Wiley, 1974.

Johnson, M., and Stanwick, K. Profile of Women Holding Office.

In Women in Public Office: A Biographical Directory and Statistical Analysis. New York: R.R. Bowker, 1976.

_____, and _____. Women in Public Office: A Biographical Directory and Statistical Analysis. New York: R.R. Bowker, 1976.

Kirkpatrick, J.J. Political Woman. New York: Basic Books, 1974.

Ludovici, L.J. The Final Inequality. New York: Tower Publications, 1971.

McDonnell, J.J. The Employment of Women in Selected Positions in Local New Jersey Governmental and Educational Subdivisions: An Analysis of Women as Public Sector Employees in Terms of Salary Trends, Job Occupancy and Membership in Collective Bargaining Units. Unpublished doctoral dissertation, Rutgers University, 1975. Dissertation Abstracts International, 1975, 36(7-A), 4798. Also available from ERIC (ADG76-01120), 1975.

Maslow, A.P. Job Factors, Attitudes, and Preferences Affecting the Relative Advancement and Turnover of Men and Women in Federal Careers. Paper presented at the American Psychological Association Convention, Miami, FL, 1970.

Merritt, S.A. Political Women and Political Men: Sex Differences in Motivations and Adaptations of Elected Local Political Officials. Unpublished doctoral dissertation, Case Western Reserve University, 1975. Dissertation Abstracts International, 1975, 36(9-A), 6283. Also available from ERIC (ADG75-27941), 1975.

Oltman, R.M. Women in the Professional Caucuses. American Behavioral Scientist, 1971, 15(2), 281-302.

Poland, N. FCC Commissioner Margita E. White. Matrix, 1976, Fall, 62(1), 14-16+.

Rizzo, A.M. Patterns of Person-Group Relationships for Female and Male Mid-Level Managers in Three Governmental Agencies. Unpublished doctoral dissertation, Syracuse University, 1974. Dissertation Abstracts International, 1975, 36(10-A), 6950. Also available from ERIC (ADG76-07932), 1974.

Samuels, C. The Forgotten Five Million: Women in Public Employment. New York: Women's Action Alliance, n.d.

Schneider, F., and Rall, M. Attitudes Towards Male and Female Political Candidates. Paper presented at the American Psychological Association Convention, Washington, D.C., 1976.

Schwindt, H.D. Mr. President: These Women Belong in Your Cabinet. Ms., 1977, January, 5(7), 91-94.

Shanahan, E. Women Score Significant Gains at All Levels of Government. New York Times, 1974, November 7, 1, 32.

Smith, K. S. The Characteristics and Motivation of American Women Who Seek Positions of Political Leadership. Unpublished doctoral dissertation, New School for Social Research, 1976. Dissertation Abstracts International, 1976, 37(2-A), 1203. Also available from ERIC (ADG76-18116), 1976.

Spain, J. B. Women in Government and Affirmative Action. In D. Jongeward and D. Scott (eds.), Affirmative Action for Women: A Practical Guide. Reading, MA: Addison-Wesley, 1973, 71-90.

Stucker, J. J. Women's Political Role. Current History, 1976, May, 70, 211-214+.

Thomas, J. L. Why Women Work--The Significance. Social Order, 1962, February, 12(2), 72-76.

Women in Government. Women's Work, 1975, May/June, 1(3), 22.

B. SPECIFIC (continued)

7. ARTS, MUSIC, MEDIA

Affirmative Action for Women in 1971: A Report of the Modern Language Association Commission on the Status of Women in the Profession. Publication of the Modern Language Association, 1972, May, 87, 531+.

Batterberry, M., and Batterberry, A. Women Artists? Harper's Bazaar, 1971, July, 104, 73.

Braunagel, J. S. Job Mobility as Related to Career Progression of Female Academic Librarians in the South. Unpublished doctoral dissertation, Florida State University, 1975. Dissertation Abstracts International, 1976, 37(1-A), 10. Also available from ERIC (ADG76-16515), 1975.

Brico, A. One Undeflected Step at a Time. In J. Stiehm (ed.), The Frontiers of Knowledge. University Park, Los Angeles: University of Southern California Press, 1976, 9-21.

Cantor, M. G. Women and Public Broadcasting. Journal of Communication, 1977, Winter, 27(1), 14-19.

Carpenter, R., and Shearer, K. Sex and Salary Survey. Library Journal, 1972, November, 15, 36-83.

Cochrane, D. G. Women in Art: A Progress Report; with Directory of Organizations, Publications, and Slide Registries. American Artist, 1972, December, 36, 52-56.

Davis, D. Designing Women: Brooklyn Museum Exhibition. Women in American Architecture. Newsweek, 1977, March 7, 89, 79-80.

Dinneiman, B. Women in Architecture. Architectural Forum, 1969, December, 131(5), 50.

Fenner, M. Women in Educational Journalism. Contemporary Education, 1972, February, 43(4), 209-213.

Furman, L. A House Is Not a Home: Women in Publishing. In R. Morgan (ed.), Sisterhood Is Powerful. New York: Random House, 1970, 66-69. Also in H. H. Frank (ed.), Women in the Organization. Philadelphia: University of Pennsylvania Press, 1977, 263-265.

Garrison, D. The Tender Technicians: The Feminization of Public Librarianship, 1876-1905. Journal of Social History, 1972-1973, Winter, 6(2), 131-159. Also in M. Hartman and L. W. Banner (eds.), Clio's Consciousness Raised. New York: Harper & Row, 1974, 158-178; and in F. L. Denmark (ed.), Women--Volume I: A PDI Research Reference Work. New York: Psychological Dimensions, 1976, 221-250.

Guyer, L., and Fidell, L. Publications of Women Psychologists. Do Women Publish Less? American Psychologist, 1973, February, 28(2), 157-160.

Haskell, M. From Reverence to Rape: The Treatment of Women in the Movies. New York: Holt, Rinehart and Winston, 1974.

Hess, T. B., and Baker, E. C. (eds.), Art and Sexual Politics: Why Have There Been No Great Women Artists? New York: P. F. Collier, 1973.

Hixon, D. L., and Hennessee, D. Women in Music: A Biobibliography. Metuchen, NJ: Scarecrow Press, 1975.

Hole, J., and Levine, E. Professions. In Rebirth of Feminism. New York: Quadrangle/New York Times, 1971, 338-371.

The Invisible Woman Is Visible. Newsweek, 1971, November 15, 78(20), 130-131.

Josephine, H. B., and Leita, C. Beyond Awareness: Women in Libraries Organize for Change: Women Library Workers. School Library Journal, 1977, January, 23, 32-33.

Kay, J. H. Architecture: Women in American Architecture: A History and Contemporary Perspective, Exhibition. Nation, 1977, April 16, 224, 474-476.

Lowenthal, H. Healthy Anger: Discrimination Against Women Librarians. Library Journal, 1971, September 1, 96, 2597-2599.

McBee, S. Open Sesame! Women Journalists in National Press Club. McCall's, 1971, July, 98, 45.

Modern Language Association, Commission on Status of Women. The Status of Women: A Summary. Towson, MD: Goucher College, n. d.

Murtagh, R. Women in the Arts. Music Journal, 1963, October, 21(7), 54+.

Nettl, P. Women in Music. Music Journal, 1960, February, 18, 8-9+.

Nochlin, L. Why Have There Been No Great Women Artists? Art News, 1971, January, 69, 22-39.

———. Why Are There No Great Women Artists? In V. Gornick and B. K. Moran (eds.), Woman in Sexist Society. New York: Basic Books, 1971, 480-510.

Peterson, K., and Wilson, J. J. Women Artists. Harper & Row, 1976.

Piomelli, R. Pains and Pleasures of a Woman Architect. Educational Horizons, 1975, Spring, 53(3), 110-115.

Podis, E. Musical Careers for Women. Music Journal, 1960, October, 18(7), 22+.

Reuter, B. A. The Career Development of the Professional Female Artist Compared to that of the Male. Unpublished doctoral dissertation, Columbia University, 1974. Dissertation Abstracts International, 1974, 35(6-A), 3597. Also available from ERIC (ADG74-26615), 1974.

Reuter, M. Does the Woman Writer Exist? Report of Symposium Sponsored by Doubleday. Publishers Weekly, 1976, April 5, 209, 24+.

Rodger, W. Art Isn't a Man's World. Hobbies, 1977, 82, 148-149.

Rosen, M. Popcorn Venus. New York: Avon Books, 1973.

Sex Differentials in Art Exhibition Reviews: A Statistical Study. Los Angeles: Tamarind Lithography Workshop, 1973.

Showalter, E. Women Writers and the Double Standard. In V. Gornick and B. K. Moran (eds.), Woman in Sexist Society. New York: Basic Books, 1971, 452-479.

Smith, D. C., and Harwood, K. Women in Broadcasting. Journal of Broadcasting, 1966, Fall, 10(4), 339-356.

Smith, S. (ed.). Women Who Make Movies. New York: Hopkinson and Blake, 1975.

Sorel, C. Equal Opportunity for Women Pianists. Music Journal, 1968, March, 26, 40-41+.

Strainchamps, E. (ed.). Rooms with No View. New York: Harper & Row, 1974.

Tabak, M. N. Notes on Pesky Problems: The Right to Be Creative. Craft Horizons, 1973, October, 33(5), 41+.

Ten-Point Plan Developed to Advance Women in Media. Editor and Publisher, 1975, September 27, 108(39), 11.

Van Gelder, L. The Trials of Lois Lane: Women in Journalism. In R. Morgan (ed.), Sisterhood Is Powerful. New York: Random House, 1970, 81-85.

Women Design Space; Brooklyn Museum Exhibition, Women in American Architecture. Ms., 1977, March, 5, 62-67.

Women's Liberation, Women Artists and Art Throughout History. Special Issue. Art News 69, 1971, January 9.

B. SPECIFIC (continued)

8. RELIGION

ALC Commission on Women in Church and Society. Women: A Questioning of the Past and Present. Minneapolis: Augsburg, 1975.

Andover-Newton Quarterly XII. Special Issue on Women's Liberation and Theology. 1972, March.

Balasuriya, T. Women in the Church. Commonweal, 1976, January 16, 103, 39-42.

Beeson, T. Anglican Women Priests: Has Their Time Come? Christian Century, 1975, May 28, 92, 542-543.

Bock, E. W. The Female Clergy: A Case of Professional Marginality. American Journal of Sociology, 1967, March, 72(5), 531-539.

The Chicago Theological Seminary Register. Woman, 1970, March, LX(3).

Controversy Over Women as Ministers. Intellect, 1975, March, 103, 353-354.

Cowley, S.C., and Lisle, L. Women in the Pulpit. Newsweek, 1975, October 13, 86, 70-71.

Daly, M. The Church and the Second Sex. New York: Harper & Row, 1968.

———. Toward Partnership in the Church. In M. L. Thompson (ed.), Voices of the New Feminism. Boston: Beacon Press, 1970, 136-151.

———. After the Death of God the Father. Commonweal, 1971, March 12, 94(1), 7-11.

———. The Courage to See; Religious Implications of the New Sisterhood. The Christian Century, 1971, September 22, 88(38), 1108-1111.

Doely, S. B. Women's Liberation and the Church. New York: Association Press, 1970.

First at the Cradle, Last at the Cross. Christianity Today, 1973, March 16, 17, 26-27.

Forest, C. A., Sr. The Religious Academic Woman: A Study of Adjustment to Multiple Roles. Unpublished doctoral dissertation, Fordham University. Dissertation Abstracts, 1966, 27(6-A), 1939.

Gilfeather, K. Women and Ministry. America, 1976, October 2, 135, 191-194.

Grelsch, J. R. Mother Church's Daughters: Distaff Dissent. Christianity Today, 1970, June 5, 14, 37-38.

Grindle, E. S. Career Roles in the Ministry. In R. E. Hardy and J. G. Cull (eds.), Career Guidance for Young Women: Considerations in Planning Professional Careers. Springfield, IL: Charles C. Thomas, 1974, 65-100.

Harper, M. A. Woman's Role in the Church. America, 1966, July 23, 115, 91-93.

Heinzelmann, G. Priesthood and Women. Commonweal, 1965, January 15, 81, 504-508, and 1965, February 12, 81, 626. Discussion, 1965, March 5, 682 and 1965, March 26, 746-747.

Henning, C. M. Women in the Priesthood. Commonweal, 1977, February 15, 99, 475.

Hole, J., and Levine, E. The Church. In Rebirth of Feminism. New York: Quadrangle/New York Times, 1971, 372-396.

Horwitz, S. Women in the Pulpit. Seventeen, 1975, December, 34, 92-93.

Jones, A. R., and Taylor, L. Differential Recruitment of Female Professionals: A Case Study of Clergywomen. Paper presented at the Southern Sociological Society meeting, Atlanta, April 1964.

Kelly, S. Putting Sisters in Their Place. America, 1966, March 5, 114, 329-330.

Kumlien, C. D. Suffragette Nuns. Commonweal, 1964, October 16, 81, 95-97.

Mead, M. Women as Priests: A New Challenge. Redbook, 1975, June, 145, 31-32+.

Northcott, C. Women in Anglican Pulpits? Christian Century, 1963, November 6, 80, 1360.

_____. Women Priests in England? Christian Century, 1968, January 24, 85, 101-102.

Novak, M. Feminine-Masculine Theology. Commonweal, 1972, June 2, 96(13), 302+.

On Ordaining Women Priests. America, 1974, August 24, 131, 65.

Raming, I. The Exclusion of Women from the Priesthood: Divine Law or Sex Discrimination? Metuchen, NJ: Scarecrow Press, 1976.

Ruether, R. R. (ed.). Misogynism and Virginal Feminism in the Fathers of the Church. In Religion and Sexism. New York: Simon and Schuster, 1974, 164-166.

Schmidt, R. A. Second-Class Citizenship in the Kingdom of God. Christianity Today, 1971, January 1, 15, 13-14.

Sex and the Sacraments. Christian Century, 1968, November 13, 85, 1425.

Smith, S. D., and Carlson, H. Sex-Role Attitudes and Androgyny in Religious Women. Symposium presentation at the American Psychological Association Convention, San Francisco, 1977.

Swidler, A. Male Church. Commonweal, 1966, June 24, 83, 387-389.

Tygart, C. E. The Clergy. In P. L. Stewart and M. G. Cantor (eds.), Varieties of Work Experience. New York: John Wiley, 1974, 80-96.

Verdesi, E. H. The Professionally-Trained Woman in the Presbyterian Church: The Role of Power in the Achievement of Status and Equality. Unpublished doctoral dissertation, Columbia

University. Dissertation Abstracts International, 1975, 36(3-A), 1408-1409.

Wedel, C. C. Women in Organized Religion. In D. Jongeward and D. Scott (eds.), Affirmative Action for Women: A Practical Guide. Reading, MA: Addison-Wesley, 1973, 91-120.

Weldman, J. Methodist Women Clergy Map Strategies; First National Consultation of Ordained Women in the United Methodist Church. Christian Century, 1975, February 26, 92, 188-189.

Woman. Special Issue. Chicago Theological Seminary Register, 1970, March, 60(3).

Woman Intellectual and the Church: Symposium. Commonweal, 1967, January 27, 85, 446-456.

Woman's Place in the Church. America, 1970, February 28, 122, 204.

Women and Religion: 1972. Proceedings of the Working Group on Women and Religion. Missoula, MT: American Academy of Religion, 1973.

Women in the Limelight. Christianity Today, 1976, June 18, 20, 36.

Women in Theological Education: Past, Present and Future. Special Issue. Theological Education, 1972, Summer, 8.

B. SPECIFIC (continued)

9. ATHLETICS

Brown, J. M. Women in Physical Education: The Dribble Index of Liberation. In J. E. Roberts (ed.), Beyond Intellectual Sexism: A New Woman, A New Reality. New York: David McKay, 1976, 365-380.

Felshin, J. A View of Imperatives for Women in Sport. AAHPER Update, 1974, February. Also reprint from KNOW, Inc., P.O. Box 86031, Pittsburgh, PA 15221, 1974.

Gilbert, B., and Williamson, N. Sport Is Unfair to Women. Sports Illustrated, 1973, May 28, 38(21), 88-92+.

Hart, M. Women Sit in the Back of the Bus. Psychology Today, 1971, October, 5(5), 64-66.

Heide, W. Feminism for the Health of It. In C. Oglesby (ed.),

Women and Sport: From Myth to Reality. Philadelphia: Lea and Febiger, 1978.

Kane, J. E. Motivation and Performance. In D. V. Harris (ed.), Women and Sport. College Park: Pennsylvania State University Press, 1973, 141-156.

Kaplan, J. Everyone Can Do It! Marathon Runners. Seventeen, 1977, March, 36, 66+.

Morgan, W. P. (ed.). Research Studies on the Female Athletes: Symposium. Journal of Physical Education and Recreation, 1975, January, 47, 37.

Ogilvie, B. The Unanswered Question: Competition, Its Effects on Femininity. Santa Barbara, CA: Olympic Development Committee, 1967.

Oglesby, C. The Forest Must Be Planted All at Once. In C. Oglesby (ed.), Women and Sport: From Myth to Reality. Philadelphia: Lea and Febiger, 1978.

Project on the Status and Education of Women. What Constitutes Equality for Women in Sports? Washington, D. C.: Association of American Colleges, 1974.

Two Pros. Time, March 20, 1972, 99(12), 103. Also in B. Stanford (ed.), On Being Female. New York: Washington Square Press, 1974, 169-171.

Women's Sports. San Mateo, CA: Women's Sports Publishing, Vol. 1 published 1974. Continuing monthly publication covering women in sports.

B. SPECIFIC (continued)

10. MILITARY

Bird, C. Let's Draft Women Too! In C. Safilios-Rothschild (ed.), Toward a Sociology of Women. Lexington, MA: Xerox College Publishing, 1972, 173-176.

Horn, E. L. The Problems Associated with the Retention of Young Enlisted Women in the U. S. Navy. Monterey, CA: Naval Postgraduate School, 1965.

Military Service: An Open Door to Learning for America's Young Women. Adult Leadership, 1966, January, 14, 229+.

Ogilvie, B., Johnsgard, K. W., and Merritt, E. Female Parachutists as Contrasted with Other High Level Competitors (Pt. 3). Fort Rucker, AL: U.S. Army AeroMedical Research Laboratory, 1973.

Plog, S. C., and Kahn, O. L. Reenlistment and Retention of Effective Women in the Women's Army Corps: An Exploratory Research Investigation. Washington, D. C. : U. S. Army Research Institute for the Behavioral and Social Sciences, 1974.

Schnall, S. Women in the Military. In R. Morgan (ed.), Sisterhood Is Powerful. New York: Random House, 1970, 76-80.

Thomas, P. J. Why Women Enlist: The Navy as an Occupational Choice. San Diego: Navy Personnel Research and Development Center, 1976.

_____, and Durning, K. P. The Military Woman. Symposium presentation at the American Psychological Association Convention, Washington, D. C., 1976.

_____, and _____. The Military Woman and the Navy Wife. Paper presented at the American Psychological Association Convention, Washington, D. C., 1976.

Vitola, B. M., Mullins, C. J., and Weeks, J. L. Characteristics of Women in the Air Force: 1970 through 1973. U. S. AFHRL Technical Report, 1974, July, 59.

_____, and Wilbourn, J. M. Comparative Performance of Male and Female Enlistees on Air Force Selection Measures. U.S. AFHRL Technical Report, 1971, February, 9.

B. SPECIFIC (continued)

11. PROFESSIONAL

Alpenfels, E. J. Women in the Professional World. In B. Cassara (ed.), American Women: The Changing Image. Boston: Beacon Press, 1962, 73-89.

Astin, H. The Woman Doctorate in America. New York: Russell Sage Foundation, 1969.

Bailyn, L. Notes on the Role of Choice in the Psychology of Professional Women. In R. T. Lifton (ed.), The Woman in America. Boston: Houghton Mifflin, 1965, 236-246.

Bernard, J. (ed.). Women at the Professional Level. In Women and the Public Interest. Chicago: Aldine-Atherton, 1971, 179-196.

Blitz, R. C. Women in the Professions, 1870-1970. Monthly Labor Review, 1974, May, 97, 34-39.

Brooke, M. H. Status Incongruence and Support for Change in Sex-Role Ideology: A Study of Women in Various Professions. Unpublished doctoral dissertation. Dissertation Abstracts International, 1976, May, 36(11-B), 5858-5859.

DeLamater, J., and Fidell, L. S. On the Status of Women. In L. S. Fidell and J. DeLamater (eds.), Women in the Professions: What's All the Fuss About? Beverly Hills: Sage Publications, 1971.

Epstein, C. F. Encountering the Male Establishment: Sex-Status Limits on Women's Careers in the Professions. American Journal of Sociology, 1970, May, 75(6), 965-982.

Fabian, J. J. The Hazards of Being a Professional Woman. Professional Psychology, 1972, Fall, 3(4), 324-326.

Gullahorn, J. E. The Woman Professional. In E. Donelson and J. E. Gullahorn (eds.), Women: A Psychological Perspective. New York: John Wiley, 1977, 247-265.

Kahne, H. The Women in Professional Occupations: New Complexities for Chosen Roles. Journal of the National Association for Women Deans, Administrators, and Counselors, 1976, Summer, 39(4), 179-185.

Kaley, M. M. Attitudes Toward the Dual Role of the Married Professional Woman. American Psychologist, 1971, March, 26(3), 301-306.

Mandel, W. M. Soviet Women in the Work Force and Professions. American Behavioral Scientist, 1971, November, 15(2), 255-280.

Prather, J. Why Can't Women Be More Like Men: A Summary of the Sociopsychological Factors Hindering Women's Advancement in the Professions. American Behavioral Scientist, 1971, November/December, 15(2), 172-182.

Spiegel, J. A Selected Annotated Bibliography: Women Executives. Washington, D. C.: Business and Professional Women's Foundation, 1970.

Theodore, A. The Professional Woman: Trends and Prospects. In A. Theodore (ed.), The Professional Woman. Cambridge, MA: Schenkman, 1971, 1-35.

Upward Bound (The Professions and Business). Women's Work, 1975, January/February, 1(1), 5.

Walt, D. E. The Motivation for Women to Work in High-Level Professional Positions. Unpublished doctoral dissertation, American University, 1962.

VII

CAREER DEVELOPMENT, ORIENTATION, AND CONTINGENCIES

Do Everything. -- Frances Willard motto.

A. CAREER DEVELOPMENT AND ORIENTATION

Almquist, E. M. Occupational Choice and Career Salience Among College Women. Unpublished doctoral dissertation, University of Kansas, 1969. Dissertation Abstracts International, 1969, 30(6-A), 2634. Also available from ERIC (ADG69-21484), 1969.

⸺. Sex Stereotypes in Occupational Choice: The Case for College Women. Journal of Vocational Behavior, 1974, August, 5(1), 13-21.

⸺, and Angrist, S. S. Career Salience and Atypicality of Occupational Choice Among College Women. Journal of Marriage and the Family, 1970, 32(2), 242-249.

⸺, and ⸺. Role Model Influences on College Women's Career Aspirations. Paper presented at the American Sociological Association meeting, 1970.

Altman, S. L., and Grossman, F. K. Women's Career Plans and Maternal Employment. Psychology of Women Quarterly, 1977, Summer, 1(4), 365-376.

Angrist, S. S. Sources of Influence on Women's Career Aspirations: Family, College, and Self. Paper prepared for the School of Urban and Public Affairs, Carnegie-Mellon University, Pittsburgh, 1970.

⸺. Measuring Women's Career Commitment. Sociological Focus, 1971-72, Winter, 5(2), 29-39.

⸺. Changes in Women's Work Aspirations During College (or Work Does Not Equal Career). International Journal of Sociology of the Family, 1972, 2(1), 87-97.

⸺. Variations in Women's Adult Aspirations During College. Journal of Marriage and the Family, 1972, 34(3), 465-468.

_____, and Almquist, E. M. Career Commitment Is Hard to Learn. In Careers and Contingencies. New York: Dunellen, 1975, 27-44.

_____, and _____. Career Women Are Different, Not Deviant. In Careers and Contingencies. New York: Dunellen, 1975, 169-186.

_____, and _____. Careers and Contingencies. New York: Dunellen, 1975.

_____, and _____. College Fosters Career Interests, But.... In Careers and Contingencies. New York: Dunellen, 1975, 45-65.

_____, and _____. Education, Work and Women's Lives. In Careers and Contingencies. New York: Dunellen, 1975, 7-25.

_____, and _____. False Explanations of Women's Career Choices. In Careers and Contingencies. New York: Dunellen, 1975, 105-123.

_____, and _____. How Women Choose an Occupation. In Careers and Contingencies. New York: Dunellen, 1975, 125-145.

_____, and _____. Women Use Role Models for Adult Life. In Careers and Contingencies. New York: Dunellen, 1975, 147-168.

Astin, A. W., and Nichols, R. C. Life Goals and Vocational Choice. Journal of Applied Psychology, 1964, 48, 50-58.

Astin, H. S. Factors Associated with the Participation of Women Doctorates in the Labor Force. Personnel and Guidance Journal, 1967, 46, 240-246.

_____. Patterns of Career Choice Over Time. Personnel and Guidance Journal, 1967, 45, 541-546.

_____. Career Development of Girls During the High School Years. Journal of Counseling Psychology, 1968, 15, 536-540.

_____. Stability and Change in the Career Plans of Ninth Grade Girls. Personnel and Guidance Journal, 1968, 46(10), 961-966.

_____. Career Profiles of Women Doctorates. In A. S. Rossi and A. Calderwood (eds.), Academic Women on the Move. New York: Russell Sage Foundation, 1973, 139-162.

_____. The Role of Continuing Education in the Development of Adult Women. Paper presented at the American Psychological Association Convention, Chicago, 1975.

_____ (ed.). A Profile of the Women in Continuing Education.

502 / Career Development

In Some Action of Her Own: The Adult Woman and Higher Education. Lexington, MA: D.C. Heath, 1976, 57-88.

_____. Continuing Education and the Development of Adult Women. The Counseling Psychologist, 1976, 6(1), 55-60.

_____, and Myint, T. Career Development of Young Women During the Post-High School Years. Journal of Counseling Psychology, 1971, July, 18(4), 369-393.

_____, Suniewick, N., and Dweck, S. Women, A Bibliography on Their Education and Careers. New York: Behavioral Publishers, 1974.

Bachtold, L.M. Women, Eminence, and Career-Value Relationships. Journal of Social Psychology, 1975, April, 95(2), 187-192.

Bailey, P. I'm Going to Start All Over Again--and Be a Doctor. Redbook, 1974, December, 144, 80+.

Bardwick, J.M. Changes in Motive and Roles During Different Stages in Life. In Psychology of Women: A Study of Biocultural Conflicts. New York: Harper & Row, 1971, 188-205.

Baruch, R.W. The Interruption and Resumption of Women's Careers. Harvard Studies and Career Development, 1966, 50, 353-360.

_____. The Achievement Motive in Women: A Study of the Implications for Career Development. Unpublished doctoral dissertation, Harvard University. Dissertation Abstracts, 1967, 28(1-A), 102.

_____. The Achievement Motive in Women: Implications for Career Development. Journal of Personality and Social Psychology, 1967, 5(3), 260-267.

Benetar, J. Admissions: Notes from a Woman Psychiatrist. New York: Bantam Books, 1974.

Berry, J. Aspirations of Alumnae for Continuing Education. Journal of the National Association of Women Deans and Counselors, 1964, Summer, 27, 197-198.

Birnbaum, J.A. Life Patterns and Self Esteem in Gifted Family Oriented and Career Committed Women. In M.T.S. Mednick et al. (eds.), Women and Achievement: Social and Motivational Analyses. New York: Halsted Press, 1975, 396-419.

Blackwell, G.W. The College and the Continuing Education of Women. In L.E. Dennis (ed.), Education and a Woman's Life: Proceedings of the Itasca Conference on the Continuing Education of

Women. Washington, D.C.: American Council on Education, 1963, 74-85.

Blai, B., Jr. Job Satisfaction and Work Values for Women. Journal of the National Association for Women Deans, Administrators, and Counselors, 1974, 37(4), 151-157.

Blake, C. H., Jr. Women's Mobility and Their Motivations for Working in the Madison, Wisconsin, Labor Market. Unpublished doctoral dissertation, University of Wisconsin. Dissertation Abstracts, 1967, 28(2-A), 332.

Bowers, T. A. Student Attitudes Toward Journalism as a Major and a Career. Journalism Quarterly, 1974, Summer, 51(2), 265-270.

Boyd, B. J. A Study of the Relationship Between the Job Satisfactions of Women and Selected Demographic Characteristics. Dissertation Abstracts International, 1975, February, 35(8-A), 5226.

Brooks, B. Mother Is a Freshperson: Study of Women in Transition. Symposium presentation at the American Psychological Association Convention, San Francisco, 1977.

Brooks, L. Supermoms Shift Gears: Re-Entry Women. The Counseling Psychologist, 1976, 6(2), 33-37.

Conaway, C. Y., and Niple, M. L. Working Patterns of Mothers and Grandmothers of Freshman Women at the Ohio State University, 1955 and 1965. Journal of the National Association of Women Deans and Counselors, 1966, Summer, 29, 167-170.

Cooperman, I. G. Second Careers: War Wives and Widows. Vocational Guidance Quarterly, 1971, 20, 103-111.

Counselman, E. F. A Comparison of the Self-Concepts, Self-Acceptance, Ideal Self-Concepts, and Career Woman Stereotypes of Career and Non-Career Oriented College Senior Women. Unpublished doctoral dissertation. Dissertation Abstracts International, 1971, 32(A), 1996-1997.

David, D. S. Career Patterns and Values: A Study of Men and Women in Science and Engineering. Unpublished doctoral dissertation, Columbia University, 1972. American Doctoral Dissertations, 1972, 11(97). Also available from ERIC (ADG02-63001), 1972.

Davis, F., and Olesen, V. L. The Career Outlook of Professionally Educated Women. Psychiatry, 1965, 28(4), 334-345.

Davis, N. J., and Bumpass, L. L. The Continuation of Education after Marriage Among Women in the United States: 1970. Demography, 1976, May, 13, 161-174.

Denmark, F. L., Baxter, B. K., and Shirk, E. J. The Future Goals of College Women. Unpublished manuscript, City University of New York, 1973.

deWolf, V. A. Factors Related to Postgraduate Educational Aspirations of Women College Graduates. Paper presented at the American Psychological Association Convention, Washington, D. C., 1976.

Dexter, E. W. Career Women of America. Clifton, NJ: Augustus M. Kelley, 1972.

Dias, S. L. A Study of Personal, Perceptual, and Motivational Factors Influential in Predicting the Aspiration Level of Women and Men Toward the Administrative Roles in Education. Dissertation Abstracts International, 1975, September, 36(3-A), 1202.

Doty, B. A. Why Do Mature Women Return to College? Journal of the National Association of Women Deans and Counselors, 1966, Summer, 29, 171-174.

Durchholz, P., and O'Connor, J. Why Women Go Back to College. In Women on Campus: The Unfinished Liberation. New York: Change Magazine, 1975, 236-241.

Edgerton, H. A. Women in Science Careers. Journal of the National Association of Women Deans and Counselors, 1962, June, 25(4), 166-169.

Entine, A. D. At Mid-Life They Return to College and Change Careers. Journal of College Placement, 1967, April/May, 27(4), 50-57.

Eyde, L. D. Work Motivation of Women College Graduates: Five-Year Follow-Up. Journal of Counseling Psychology, 1968, 15(2), 199-202.

Farmer, H. S., and Backer, T. E. New Career Options for Women. New York: Human Science Press, 1977.

Faunce, P. S. Academic Careers of Gifted Women. Personnel and Guidance Journal, 1967, November, 46(3), 252-257.

Fogarty, M. P., Allen, A. J., Allen, I., and Walters, P. A. Women in Top Jobs: Four Studies in Achievement. London: Allen and Unwin, 1971.

_____, Rapoport, R., and Rapoport, R. N. Women in Top Jobs. London: Political and Economic Planning, 1968.

_____, _____, and _____. Sex, Career and Family. Beverly Hills: Sage Publications, 1974.

Friend, J. G. Personal and Vocational Interplay in Identity Building: A Longitudinal Study. Boston: Branden Press, 1973.

Friskey, E. A. College Women and Careers. AAUP Bulletin, 1974, 60, 317-319.

Fuchs, R. Different Meanings of Employment for Women. Human Relations, 1971, December, 24(6), 495-499.

Gannon, M. J., and Hendrickson, D. H. Career Orientation and Job Satisfaction Among Working Wives. Journal of Applied Psychology, 1973, June, 57(3), 339-340.

Gifted Girls 50 Years Later; Ongoing Psychological Study Conducted by Stanford University Researchers. Intellect, 1976, May, 104, 553-554.

Gifted Women Are Queried on Life Satisfaction for Ninth Time in 50 Years. Aging, 1976, January, 255, 6.

Ginzberg, E., and Yohalem, A. M. Longer View of the Educated Woman; Excerpts from Educated American Women: Self-Portraits. Sociology and Society, 1966, November 12, 94, 391-392+.

_____, and _____. Educated American Women: Life Styles and Self-Portraits. New York: Columbia University Press, 1966.

Giuliani, B., and Centra, J. A. The Woman Veterinarian. Personnel and Guidance Journal, 1968, 46(10), 971-975.

Glenn, N. D., Taylor, P. A., and Weaver, C. N. Age and Job Satisfaction Among Males and Females: A Multivariate, Multisurvey Study. Journal of Applied Psychology, 1977, April, 62, 189-193.

Glick, R. Practitioners and Non-Practitioners in a Group of Women Physicians. Unpublished doctoral dissertation, Western Reserve University. Dissertation Abstracts, 1966, 26(11), 6845.

Gold, S. S. The Power of Values III: The Professional Commitment of Educated Women. In K. Baier and N. Rescher (eds.), Technology and American Values. Glencoe, IL: Free Press, 1968, 266-293.

Gottlieb, D., and Bell, M. L. Work Expectations and Work Realities: A Study of Graduating College Seniors. Youth and Society, 1975, September, 7(1), 69-83.

Gross, A. (ed.). Great Women; Great Careers; Great Mothers? Their Daughters Talk: Interviews. Mademoiselle, 1975, June, 81, 120-123+.

Gross, R. Mother Goes to School. Parents Magazine, 1977, April, 52, 18+.

Haber, S. Career/Family Orientations in Female College Seniors. Paper presented at the American Psychological Association Convention, San Francisco, 1977.

Hacker, S. L. S. Patterns of Work and Leisure: An Investigation of the Relationships Between Childhood and Current Styles of Leisure and Current Career Behavior Among Young Women Graduates in the Field of Public School Education. Unpublished doctoral dissertation, University of Chicago, 1969. American Doctoral Dissertations, 1969, 11(96), 286. Also available from ERIC (ADG02-21579), 1969.

Hall, B. A. Occupational Values and Family Perspectives: A Study of Premedical and Prenursing Women. Unpublished doctoral dissertation, University of Colorado, Boulder, 1974. Dissertation Abstracts International, 1974, 35(4-A), 2407. Also available from ERIC (ADG74-22349), 1974.

Hansen, G. R., and Noeth, R. J. Career Status and Occupational Patterns of Women: Five Years After Beginning Post Secondary Vocational-Technical Transfer Programs. Paper presented at the American Personnel and Guidance Association Convention, 1976.

Hansen, L. S. The Career Development Process for Women: Current Views and Programs. Pupil Personnel Services, (Minnesota Department of Education) 1975, Spring, 4(2), 23-33.

Harlow, D. N., and Sedlacek, W. E. Career Orientation of High School and University Women. Journal of the National Association for Women Deans, Administrators, and Counselors, 1974, 37(4), 161-166.

Harmon, L. W. Anatomy of Career Commitment in Women. Journal of Counseling Psychology, 1970, 17(1), 77-80.

_____. Toward Understanding the Changing Phenomena of Women's Career Development. Invited address presented at the American Psychological Association Convention, San Francisco, 1977.

Heist, P. Motivation of College Women Today: A Closer Look. American Association of University Women Journal, 1962, 56(1), 17-19.

Helson, R. Personality Characteristics and Developmental History of Creative College Women. Genetic Psychology Monographs, 1967, 76, 205-256.

_____. The Changing Image of the Career Woman. Journal of Social Issues, 1972, 28, 33-46.

Herberg, D. M. C. Career Patterns and Work Participation of Graduate Female Social Workers. Unpublished doctoral dissertation, University of Michigan, 1970. Dissertation Abstracts International, 1970, 32(2-A), 1097. Also available from ERIC (ADG 71-15177), 1970.

_____. Social Research of Women's Professional Careers. In D. G. McGuigan (ed.), New Research on Women: At the University of Michigan. Ann Arbor: University of Michigan, Center for Continuing Education of Women, 1974, 159-162.

Herman, M. H. Career Orientation of High School and University Women. Journal of the National Association for Women Deans, Administrators, and Counselors, 1974, 37(4), 161-166.

Hiestand, D. L. Changing Careers After Thirty-Five: New Horizons Through Professional and Graduate Study. New York: Columbia University Press, 1971.

Highlights in Career of PhD's: Academic Versus Nonacademic; A Second Report on Follow-Ups of Doctorate Cohorts, 1935-1960. Washington, D. C.: National Academy of Sciences, 1968.

Hohenshil, T. H. (ed.). New Dimensions in the Career Development of Women. Available from ERIC (ED098437), 1974.

Holmstrom, L. L. Women's Career Patterns: Appearance and Reality. Journal of the National Association of Women Deans and Counselors, 1973, 36(2), 76-81.

James, E. T., James, J. W., and Boyer, P. S. (eds.). Notable American Women 1607-1950: A Biographical Dictionary. Cambridge, MA: Harvard University Press, 1974.

Jantzen, A. C. Some Characteristics of Female Occupational Therapists, 1970: I. Descriptive Study. American Journal of Occupational Therapy, 1972, January, 26(1), 19-26.

_____. Some Characteristics of Female Occupational Therapists, 1970: III. A Comparison: Faculty and Clinical Practitioners. American Journal of Occupational Therapy, 1972, April, 26(3), 150-154.

Jerdee, T. H., and Rosen, B. Factors Influencing the Career Commitment of Women. Symposium presentation at the American Psychological Association Convention, Washington, D. C., 1976.

Jones, J. G. Career Patterns of Women Physicians. Unpublished doctoral dissertation, Brandeis University, 1971. Dissertation Abstracts International, 1971, 32(7-A), 4125. Also available from ERIC (ADG72-01581), 1971.

Joseph, J. A Research Note on Attitudes to Work and Marriage of Six Hundred Adolescent Girls. British Journal of Sociology, 1961, June, 12(2), 176-183.

Katz, J., Comstock, P., and Lozoff, M.M. Educational and Occupational Aspirations of Adult Women: Report to the College Entrance Examination Board. Stanford: Stanford University, Institute for the Study of Human Problems, 1970.

Kundsin, R.B. (ed.). Women and Success: The Anatomy of Achievement. New York: William Morrow, 1974.

LaBarthe, E.R. A Study of the Motivation of Women in Administrative and Supervisory Positions in Selected Unified School Districts in Southern California. Unpublished doctoral dissertation. Dissertation Abstracts International, 1973, 34(A), 3695.

Ladan, C.J., and Crooks, M.M. Some Factors Influencing the Decision of Mature Women to Enroll for Continuing Education. Canadian Counsellor, 1975, October, 10(1), 29-36.

LaRussa, G.W. Portia's Decision: Women's Motives for Studying Law and Their Later Career Satisfaction as Attorneys. Psychology of Women Quarterly, 1977, Summer, 1(4), 350-364.

Laws, J.L. Work Aspiration of Women: False Leads and New Starts. In B.B. Reagan and M. Blaxall (eds.), Women and the Workplace: The Implications of Occupational Segregation. Chicago: University of Chicago Press, 1976, 33-49.

Lee, S.L., Ray, E.M., Vetter, L., Murphy, L., and Sethney, B.J. High School Senior Girls and the World of Work: Occupational Knowledge Attitudes and Plans. Columbus: Ohio State University, Center for Vocational and Technical Education, 1971.

LeFevre, C. The Mature Woman as Graduate Student. School Review, 1972, 80(2), 281-297.

Leland, C. The Case-Study Programs: Academic Misfits Which Lasted. In H.S. Astin (ed.), Some Action of Her Own: The Adult Woman and Higher Education. Lexington, MA: D.C. Heath, 1976, 23-42.

Levine, A.G. Marital and Occupational Plans of Women in Professional Schools: Law, Medicine, Nursing, Teaching. Unpublished doctoral dissertation, Yale University, 1968. Dissertation Abstracts International, 1969, 30(2-A), 829. Also available from ERIC (ADG69-13353), 1968.

Levitt, E.S. A Study of Four Career Patterns and Associated

Life History Characteristics Among Female Professional Librarians. Unpublished doctoral dissertation. Dissertation Abstracts International, 1971, January, 31(7-B), 4381.

Lipman-Blumen, J. and Leavitt, H. J. Vicarious and Direct Achievement Patterns in Adulthood. Counseling Psychologist, 1976, 6(1), 26-32.

Lloyd, B. J. Questionnaire Portrait of the Freshman Coed: After College, What? Journal of the National Association of Women Deans and Counselors, 1966, Summer, 29, 159-162.

Lunneborg, P. W. Vocational Indecision in College Graduates. Journal of Counseling Psychology, 1976, July, 23(4), 402-404.

Luria, Z. Recent Women College Graduates: A Study of Rising Expectations. American Journal of Orthopsychiatry, 1974, April, 44, 312-326.

Lutz, S. W. The Educational and Vocational Planning of Talented College-Bound Women. Unpublished doctoral dissertation, Texas Technical University. Dissertation Abstracts International, 1974, December, 35(6-A), 3427.

Lyon, E. R. Career Interests of Married Women with College Degrees. Unpublished doctoral dissertation, Northwestern University, 1967. Dissertation Abstracts, 1967, 28(6-A), 2097.

McCormack, T. Styles in Educated Females. The Nation, 1967, 204, 117-118.

McCullough, R. V. Professional Women Agree upon Traits Necessary for Success. Rough Notes, 1975, April, 118(4), 70-72.

_____. Goal Fulfillment Program Is Vital to Your Career. Rough Notes, 1976, October, 119(10), 68+.

McKinley, D. L. A Comparison of College Educated Working Mothers in Traditional and Nontraditional Occupations. Unpublished doctoral dissertation, Ohio State University, Columbus, 1970.

McLaughlin, C. Women of the Year: Great Changes, New Chances, Tough Choices. Time, 1976, 6-16.

McMillin, M. R. Vocational Commitment of College Women. Journal of the National Association for Women Deans, Administrators, and Counselors, 1974, 37(4), 158-160.

Marks, J. That Career Quandary. Seventeen, 1976, February, 35, 25.

Marple, D. J. Motivational Tendencies of Women Participants in Continuing Education. Unpublished doctoral dissertation, Columbia University. Dissertation Abstracts International, 1969, 30(5-A), 1824.

Masih, L. K. Career Saliency and Its Relation to Certain Needs, Interests, and Job Values. Personnel and Guidance Journal, 1967, March, 45(7), 653-658.

Matthews, E. E. The Marriage-Career Conflict in the Career Development of Girls and Young Women. Unpublished doctoral dissertation, Harvard University, 1960.

_____, and Tiedeman, D. V. Attitudes Toward Career and Marriage and the Development of Life Style in Young Women. Journal of Counseling Psychology, 1964, Winter, 11(4), 375-384.

Mayfield, B., and Nash, W. R. Career Attitudes of Female Professors. Psychological Reports, 1976, October, 39(2), 631-634.

Mears, G. L. Educational Motivation of Three Groups of Mature Women in a Metropolitan Area. Unpublished doctoral dissertation. Dissertation Abstracts International, 1972, 33(A), 2062-2063.

Mednick, M. T. S., Tangri, S. S., and Hoffman, L. W. Women and Achievement: Social and Motivational Analyses. New York: Halsted Press, 1975.

Meir, E. I. Relationship Between Intrinsic Needs and Women's Persistence at Work. Journal of Applied Psychology, 1972, August, 56(4), 293-296.

Meredith, J. C. Comparative Life Styles of Women: Secretarial Career Versus Career and Marriage. Unpublished doctoral dissertation, University of Southern California. Dissertation Abstracts, 1968, 28(7-B), 3063.

Metzger, S. M., Bollman, S. R., Hoeflin, R. M., and Schmalzreid, B. L. Comparison of Life Styles of Honors, Non-Honors Women. Personnel and Guidance Journal, 1969, 47, 671-674.

Miller, M. S. What Do You Want to Be When Your Kids Grow Up? American Home, 1977, 80, 52-53+.

Mishler, S. A. Barriers to the Career Development of Women. In S. H. Osipow (ed.), Emerging Women: Career Analysis and Outlooks. Columbus, OH: Charles E. Merrill, 1975, 117-146.

Moore, K. M., and Veres, H. C. Traditional and Innovative Career Plans of Two-Year College Women. Journal of College Student Personnel, 1976, 17, 34-38.

Morgan, D. Perception of Role Conflicts and Self Concepts Among

Career and Noncareer College Educated Women. Unpublished doctoral dissertation, Columbia University. Dissertation Abstracts, 1962, 23(5), 1816-1817.

Mowsesian, R. Educational and Career Aspirations of High School Females. Journal of the National Association of Women Deans and Counselors, 1972, 35(2), 65-70.

Mulvey, M. C. Psychological and Sociological Factors in Prediction of Career Patterns of Women. Genetic Psychology Monographs, 1963, 68(2), 309-386.

Nagely, D. L. A Comparison of College-Educated Working Mothers in Traditional and Nontraditional Occupations. Unpublished doctoral dissertation, Ohio State University. Dissertation Abstracts International, 1971, March, 31(9-A), 4556-4557.

_____. Traditional and Pioneer Working Mothers. Journal of Vocational Behavior, 1971, 1, 331-341.

Nevin, M. B. New Directions: Mid-Career Decisions for Women: Symposium. Educational Horizons, 1976, Summer, 54, 150-185.

Newcomb, T. M. Persistence and Change: Bennington College and Its Students After Twenty-Five Years. New York: John Wiley, 1967.

Nichols, R. C. , and Astin, A. W. Progress of the Merit Scholars: An Eight-Year Follow-Up. NMSC Research Reports 1. Evanston, IL: National Merit Scholarship Corporation, 1965.

Okun, B. F. Later Careers of Women College Graduates. Journal of the National Association of Women Deans and Counselors, 1972, Winter, 35(2), 83-89.

Oliver, L. W. Achievement and Affiliation Motivation in Career-Oriented and Home-Making-Oriented College Women. Journal of Vocational Behavior, 1974, June, 4(3), 275-281.

Osipow, S. H. (ed.). Emerging Woman: Career Analysis and Outlook. Columbus, OH: Charles E. Merrill, 1975.

Over-60 Achievers. New Woman, 1977, May-June, 7(3), 36-37.

Packer, A. B. , and Cage, B. N. Changing Attitudes of Mothers Toward Themselves and Education. Theory into Practice, 1972, June, 11, 196-201.

Parelius, A. P. Change and Stability in College Women's Orientations Toward Education, Family, and Work. Social Problems, 1975, February, 22(3), 420-432.

Parker, A. W. Career and Marriage Orientation in the Vocational

Development of College Women. Journal of Applied Psychology, 1966, 50, 232-235.

Parsons, H. D. Occupational Role Choices of Graduate-Educated Married Women. Unpublished doctoral dissertation, University of Missouri, Columbia, 1972. Dissertation Abstracts International, 1972, 33(9-A), 5319-5320. Also available from ERIC (ADG73-07070), 1973.

Paulsen, D. L. The Career Commitment of Twelfth Grade Girls. Unpublished doctoral dissertation, Yale University, 1967. Dissertation Abstracts International, 1968, 28(10-A), 4290. Also available from ERIC (ADG68-5200), 1967.

Perrucci, C. C. Minority Status and the Pursuit of Professional Careers: Women in Science and Engineering. Social Forces, 1970, 49(2), 245-259. Also in C. C. Perrucci and D. B. Targ (eds.), Marriage and the Family: A Critical Analysis and Proposals for Change. New York: David McKay, 1974, 376-397.

Powers, L., Wiesenfelder, H., and Parmelee, R. Practice Patterns of Women and Men Physicians. Preliminary report to the American Association of Medical Colleges, 1966, October.

Professional Come-Back: Housewives' Choice. The Times (London) Educational Supplement, 1964, September 18, 2574, 404.

Purvis, M. L. St. Louis Women of Achievement and Community. Unpublished doctoral dissertation, St. Louis University, 1973. Dissertation Abstracts International, 1974, 35(5-A), 2914. Also available from ERIC (ADG73-98760), 1973.

Rand, L. M., and Miller, A. L. A Developmental Cross-Sectioning of Women's Careers and Marriage Attitudes and Life Plans. Journal of Vocational Behavior, 1972, July, 2(3), 317-331.

Remarkable American Women 1776-1976: Life Special Report. New York: Time, 1976.

Reuter, B. A. The Career Development of the Professional Female Artist Compared to that of the Male. Dissertation Abstracts International, 1974, 35(6-A), 3597.

Rice, P. What Drives Professional Women. St. Louis Post-Dispatch, 1974, April, 3+.

Richardson, M. S. Self Concepts and Role Concepts in the Career Orientation of College Women. Unpublished doctoral dissertation, Columbia University. Dissertation Abstracts International, 1973, April, 33(10-B), 5001-5002.

_____. The Dimensions of Career and Work Orientation in College Women. Journal of Vocational Behavior, 1974, 5, 161-172.

_____. Self-Concepts and Role Concepts in the Career Orientation of College Women. Journal of Counseling Psychology, 1975, 22(2), 122-126.

_____, et al. Vocational Maturity and Career Orientation in College Women. Paper presented at the Eastern Psychological Association meeting, New York, 1976. Also available from ERIC (ED134911), 1977.

Riesman, D. Two Generations. Daedalus, 1964, Spring, 93(2), 711-735.

Roberts, M. L., and Ekstrom R. B. Goal Orientation and Commitment to Working of MBA Women. Paper presented at the American Psychological Association Convention, San Francisco, 1977.

Rosenfeld, R. A. Women's Employment Patterns and Occupational Achievements. Unpublished doctoral dissertation, University of Wisconsin, Madison. Dissertation Abstracts International, 1976, 37(9-A), 6095.

_____. Women's Employment Patterns and Occupational Achievements. Unpublished doctoral dissertation, University of Wisconsin, Madison, 1976. Also available from ERIC (ADG76-28935), 1976.

Rosenthal, E. R. Structural Patterns of Women's Occupational Choices. Unpublished doctoral dissertation. Dissertation Abstracts International, 1974, December, 35(6-A), 3901.

Rossi, A. S. Women in Science: Why So Few? Science, 1965, May 28, 148, 1196-1202. Discussion. 1965, August 13, 149, 707.

Rossman, J. E., and Campbell, D. P. Why College-Trained Mothers Work. Personnel and Guidance Journal, 1965, 43(10), 986-992.

Ryan, M. P. Personality Motives, Career Stages, and Work Status Among Nurses. Unpublished doctoral dissertation. Dissertation Abstracts International, 1971, October, 32(4-A), 2195.

Safilios-Rothschild, C. A Cross-Cultural Examination of Women's Marital, Educational and Occupational Options. Acta Sociologica, 1971, 14(1-2), 96-113.

_____. Towards the Conceptualization and Measurement of Work Commitment. Human Relations, 1971, 24, 489-493.

Saleh, S. D., and Lalljee, M. Sex and Job Orientation. Personnel Psychology, 1969, 22, 465-471.

Schletzer, V. M., and Stein, D. H. What Do Women Do with Advanced Degrees? The Experiences of One Department. Unpublished manuscript, University of Minnesota, n. d.

Schmidt, L. C. Sex-Roles and Life Styles of Professional Women. Unpublished doctoral dissertation, University of Alberta, Canada, 1973.

_____. Sex-Role Attitudes and Differing Life-Styles of Professional Married Women. Canadian Counsellor, 1974, June, 8(3), 197-206.

Sedlacek, C. G. Selected Factors Affecting Certainty and Persistence of Vocational Choice for College Women. Unpublished doctoral dissertation. Dissertation Abstracts, 1969, 29(11-A), 3843-3844.

Sedney, M. A., and Turner, B. F. A Test of Causal Sequences in Two Models for Development of Career-Orientation in Women. Journal of Vocational Behavior, 1975, 6, 281-291.

Seed, S. Saturday's Child: Thirty-Six Women Talk About Their Jobs. New York: Bantam Books, 1973.

Shab, F. Southern College Women: A Comparison of Arts and Science Majors with Education Majors. American Association of University Women Journal, 1967, 60(3), 142-144+.

Sharp, L. M. Education and Employment: The Early Careers of College Graduates. Baltimore: Johns Hopkins University Press, 1970.

Sheehy, G. Passages. New York: E. P. Dutton, 1974.

Shelton, P. B. Achievement Motivation in Professional Women. Dissertation Abstracts, 1968, 28(10-A), 4274.

Sherman, R. G., and Jones, J. H. Career Choices for Women: The New Determinants. Journal of College Student Personnel, 1976, July, 17(4), 289-294.

Sidlofsky, S., and Goodings, G. J. The Canadian Female Engineer: Role Confusion--Oh, No! Sociological Focus, 1973, Winter, 6(1), 14-29.

Simpson, R. L., and Simpson, I. H. Occupational Choice Among Career-Oriented College Women. Journal of Marriage and Family Living, 1961, 23, 377-383.

Smith, H. C. An Investigation of the Attitudes of Adolescent Girls Toward Combining Marriage, Motherhood, and a Career. Unpublished doctoral dissertation, Columbia University. Dissertation Abstracts, 1969, 29(11-A), 3883.

Smith, K. S. The Characteristics and Motivation of American Women Who Seek Positions of Political Leadership. Unpublished doctoral dissertation. Dissertation Abstracts International, 1976, 37(2-A), 1203.

Smith, M. Mom Goes to Law School. Ms., 1977, September, 6(3), 16-18.

Sobol, M. G. Commitment to Work. In F. I. Nye and L. W. Hoffman (eds.), The Employed Mother in America. Chicago: Rand McNally, 1963.

Solomon, L. D. Female Doctoral Chemists: Sexual Discrepancies in Career Patterns. Unpublished doctoral dissertation, Cornell University, 1972. Dissertation Abstracts International, 1972, 33(7-A), 3803. Also available from ERIC (ADG73-00360), 1972.

Stafford, R. L. Study of the Process of Vocational Development in Professional Women. Journal of the National Association of Women Deans and Counselors, 1967, Summer, 30, 190-192.

──────. An Analysis of Consciously Recalled Motivating Factors and Subsequent Professional Involvement for American Women in New York State. Unpublished doctoral dissertation, New York University. Dissertation Abstracts, 1967, 28(4-A), 1218-1219.

Standley, K., and Soule, B. Women in Professions: Historic Antecedents and Current Lifestyles. In R. E. Hardy and J. G. Cull (eds.), Career Guidance for Young Women: Considerations in Planning Professional Careers. Springfield, IL: Charles C. Thomas, 1974, 3-16.

Stebbins, R. A. Career: The Subjective Approach. Sociological Quarterly, 1970, Winter, 11, 32-49.

Tangri, S. S. Role-Innovation in Occupational Choice Among College Women. Unpublished doctoral dissertation, University of Michigan, 1969.

──────. Implied Demand Character of the Wife's Future and Role-Innovation: Patterns of Achievement Orientation Among Women. JSAS Catalog of Selected Documents in Psychology, 1974, Winter, 4, 12. Also in M. T. S. Mednick et al. (eds.), Women and Achievement: Social and Motivational Analyses. New York: Halsted Press, 1975, 239-254.

Tennov, D. The 'Seven Ages' of the Professional Woman. Women Speaking, 1972, 2.

Treas, J. J. Occupational Attainment Processes of Mature American Women. Unpublished doctoral dissertation, University of California, Los Angeles, 1976. Dissertation Abstracts International, 1976, 37(1-A), 624. Also available from ERIC (ADG76-15963), 1976.

Turner, R. H. Some Aspects of Women's Ambition. American Journal of Sociology, 1964, 70(3), 271-285.

Vogel, S. R., Rosenkrantz, P. S., Broverman, I. K., Broverman, D. M., and Clarkson, F. E. Sex-Role Self-Concepts and Life Style Plans of Young Women. Journal of Consulting and Clinical Psychology, 1975, 43, 427.

Walsh, P. A. Career Patterns of Women Administrators in Higher Education Institutions in California. Unpublished doctoral dissertation. Dissertation Abstracts International, 1975, 36, 3323.

Wasserman, E. R. Changing Aspirations of College Women. Journal of the American College Health Association, 1973, 21(4), 333-335.

Watley, D. J. Stability of Career Choices of Talented Youth. National Merit Scholarship Corporation Research Reports, 1968, 4(2).

_____. Career Progress: A Longitudinal Study of Gifted Students. Journal of Counseling Psychology, 1969, 16, 100-108.

_____. Career or Marriage. A Longitudinal Study of Able Young Women. National Merit Scholarship Corporation Research Reports, 1969, 5(7). Also in A. Theodore (ed.), The Professional Women. Cambridge, MA: Schenkman, 1971.

_____, and Kaplan, R. Career or Marriage: Aspirations and Achievements of Able Young Women. Journal of Vocational Behavior, 1971, 1(1), 29-43.

_____, and Nichols, R. C. Career Decisions of Talented Youth: Trends Over the Past Decade. National Merit Scholarship Corporation Research Reports, 1969, 5(1).

Weil, M. W. An Analysis of the Factors Influencing Married Women's Actual or Planned Work Participation. American Sociological Review, 1961, 26, 91-102.

_____. Career-Homemaker Role: New Orientation for Analysis. Journal of Home Economics, 1962, April, 54, 294-296.

Weissman, E. I. The Relationship Between the Marital Status, Feminine Identity Conflict, and Self-Actualization of Women Doctoral Students. Dissertation Abstracts International, 1974, December, 35(6-A), 3441.

Werts, C. E., and Watley, D. J. Determinants of Changes in Career Plans During College. Sociology of Education, 1968, Fall 41, 401-405.

White, K. Relation of Career Involvement to Persistence in the

Teaching Profession Among Beginning Female Elementary Teachers. Journal of Educational Research, 1966, October, 60, 51-53.

_____. Social Background Variables Related to Career Commitment of Women Teachers. Personnel and Guidance Journal, 1967, March, 45(7), 648-652.

White, M. S. Women in the Professions: Psychological and Social Barriers to Women in Science. Science, 1970, October 23, 170, 413-416. Also in C. Safilios-Rothschild (ed.), Toward a Sociology of Women. Lexington, MA: Xerox College Publishing, 1972, 300-308; and in J. Freeman, (ed.), Women: A Feminist Perspective. Palo Alto, CA: Mayfield, 1975, 227-237.

Whitesel, L. S. Career Commitments of Women Art Students. Unpublished doctoral dissertation, University of California, Berkeley, 1974. Dissertation Abstracts International, 1974, 35(8-A), 5243. Also available from ERIC (ADG75-03673), 1974.

Wilson, K. M. Assessment of the Graduate Study and Career Plans of Seniors at Three Liberal Arts Colleges for Women: A Pilot Project. Unpublished manuscript, Vassar College, College Research Center, Poughkeepsie, NY, 1964.

_____, and Dunn, F. E. Review of Center Studies: IV--Some Concomitants of Withdrawal from College: Brief Report of a Questionnaire Survey. Research Memorandum RM 67-1, Vassar College, College Research Center, Poughkeepsie, NY, 1967.

Wolfe, H. B. Women in the World of Work. University of the State of New York, State Education Department, Division of Research, 1969.

Wolfson, K. T. P. Career Development of College Women. Unpublished doctoral dissertation, University of Minnesota. Dissertation Abstracts International, 1972, 22(A), 169.

_____. Career Development Patterns of College Women. Journal of Counseling Psychology, 1976, March, 23(2), 119-125.

Wolkon, K. Pioneer Versus Traditional: Two Distinct Vocational Patterns of College Alumnae. Journal of Vocational Behavior, 1972, 2, 275-282.

Women's Bureau. 15 Years After College: A Study of Alumnae of the Class of 1945. Washington, D. C.: U. S. Department of Labor, 1963.

_____. College Women Seven Years After Graduation. Resurvey of Women Graduates--Class of 1957. Washington, D. C.: U. S. Department of Labor, 1966.

518 / Career Development

_____. Women Workers Today. Washington, D. C. : U. S. Department of Labor, 1970.

Wyse, L. Mrs. Success. Cleveland: Garret Press, 1970.

Young, A. Going Back to School at 35. Monthly Labor Review, 1973, 96(10), 39-42.

Young, L. R. Career Commitment, Sex Roles, and College Education. Unpublished doctoral dissertation, State University of New York, Stoney Brook, 1976. Dissertation Abstracts International, 1976, 37(3-A), 1815. Also available from ERIC (ADG 76-19697), 1976.

Zapoleon, M. W. The Myth of the Marriage-Career Conflict. In L. C. Muller and O. G. Muller (eds), New Horizons for College Women. Washington, D. C.: Public Affairs Press, 1960, 79-84.

Zissis, C. A Study of the Life Planning of 550 Freshman Women at Purdue University. Journal of the National Association of Women Deans and Counselors, 1964, Summer, 27, 153-159.

B. CAREER CONTINGENCIES

Ancker-Johnson, B. Physicist. Educational Horizons, 1975, Spring, 53(3), 116-121.

Angrist, S. S., and Almquist, E. M. Female Futures and Educational Policy. In Careers and Contingencies. New York: Dunellen, 1975, 187-211.

Arnott, C. C. Husbands' Attitude and Wives' Commitment to Employment. Journal of Marriage and the Family, 1972, November, 34(4), 673-688.

Axelson, L. J. The Marital Adjustment and Role Definitions of Husbands of Working and Nonworking Wives. Journal of Marriage and the Family, 1963, 25(2), 189-195.

_____. Some Differences in the Perception of the Working Wife Between Husbands and Wives. Paper presented at the Southern Sociological Association meeting, Atlanta, 1970.

Bachtold, L. M. Women, Eminence, and Career-Value Relationships. Journal of Social Psychology, 1975, April, 95(2), 187-192.

Bailyn, L. Notes on the Role of Choice in the Psychology of Professional Women. Daedalus, 1964, Spring, 93, 2, 700-710.

Also in R. J. Lifton, (ed.), The Woman in America. Boston: Houghton Mifflin, 1965, 236-246.

_____. Career and Family Orientations of Husbands and Wives in Relation to Marital Happiness. Human Relations, 1970, 23(2), 97-113. Also in J. M. Bardwick (ed.), Readings on the Psychology of Women. New York: Harper & Row, 1972, 107-117.

_____. Family Constraints on Women's Work. Annals of the New York Academy of Science, 1973, 208, 82-90. Also in R. B. Kundsin (ed.), Women and Success: The Anatomy of Achievement. New York: William Morrow, 1974, 94-102. And in A. Theodore (ed.), The Professional Woman. Cambridge, MA: Schenkman, 1971, 545-567.

Baker, M. Women Who Work. International Socialist Review, 1962, Summer, 23(3), 80-83+.

Banta, P. Dealing with Dual Careers. Public Management, 1976, March, 58(3), 12-15.

Barclay, D. Tangled Case of the Working Mother. New York Times Magazine, 1961, May 14, 75.

Baruch, R. The Achievement Motive in Women: Implications for Career Development. Journal of Personality and Social Psychology, 1967, 5, 260-267.

_____, Segal, S., and Handrick, F. A. Constructs of Career and Family: A Statistical Analysis of Thematic Material. Journal of Counseling Psychology, 1968, 15(4), 308-316.

Bebbington, A. C. The Function of Stress in the Establishment of the Dual-Career Family. Journal of Marriage and the Family, 1973, August, 35, 530-537.

Beckman, L. J., and Houser, B. B. Employed Women's Attitudes Toward Women's Liberation, Family Decision Making and Tasks. Paper presented at the American Psychological Association Convention, Chicago, 1975.

Benitez, R. P. Thirty Retired Career Women: An Exploratory Study of Perceived Needs. Unpublished doctoral dissertation, University of Southern California, 1974. Dissertation Abstracts International, 1974, 35(5-A), 3116. Also available from ERIC (ADG74-23569), 1974.

Bennett, D. D. Selected Attributes Which Influence Commitment to Teaching of Female Elementary Teachers with Different Preparational Backgrounds. Unpublished doctoral dissertation, Indiana University. Dissertation Abstracts, 1968, 28(10-A), 4019-4020.

Bentar, J. Admissions: Notes from a Woman Psychiatrist. New York: Bantam Books, 1974.

Berger, M., Foster, M., Strudler, B., and Wright, L. You and Me Against the World: Dual-Career Couples and Joint Job Seeking. Journal of Research and Development in Education, 1977, 10(4), 31-37.

_____, _____, and Wallston, B. Dual-Career Couples: Job-Seeking Strategies and Family Structure. Paper presented at the American Psychological Association Convention, Chicago, 1975.

_____, _____, and _____. Dual Career Couples: Social Networks, Family Structure, and Job Seeking. Symposium presentation at the American Psychological Association Convention, Chicago, 1975.

_____, _____, and _____. Finding Two Jobs. In Rapoport, R., and Rapoport, R. (eds.), Working Couples. New York: Harper and Row, 1977.

Berman, E., Sacks, S., and Lief, H. The Two-Professional Marriage: A New Conflict Syndrome. Journal of Sex and Marital Therapy, 1975, Spring, 1(3), 242-253. Also in H. H. Frank (ed.), Women in the Organization. Philadelphia: University of Pennsylvania Press, 1977, 291-304.

Blakey, W. A. Everybody Makes the Revolution: Some Thoughts on Racism and Sexism. Civil Rights Digest, 1974, Spring, 6(3), 11-19.

Blaubergs, M. S. Overcoming the Sexist Barriers to Gifted Women's Achievement. In B. Johnson (ed.), Advantage/Disadvantage Gifted. Ventura, CA: Ventura County Superintendent of Schools Office, 1979.

Blood, R. O., Jr. The Husband-Wife Relationship. In F. I. Nye and L. W. Hoffman (eds.), The Employed Mother in America. Chicago: Rand McNally, 1963.

_____. Long-Range Causes and Consequences of the Employment of Married Women. Journal of Marriage and the Family, 1965, February, 27(1), 43-47.

Bolin, W. D. W. Past Ideals and Present Pleasures: Women, Work and the Family. Unpublished doctoral dissertation, University of Minnesota, 1976. Dissertation Abstracts International, 1976, 37(12-A), 7916. Also available from ERIC (ADG77-12784), 1976.

Bralove, M. Working Partners. The Wall Street Journal, 1975, May 13, 155, 93, 1.

Brook, P. Women Senior Registrars in Psychiatry: Background and Career Intentions. British Journal of Psychiatry, 1976, 128, 599-601.

Brown, S. W. A Comparative Study of Maternal Employment and

Nonemployment. Unpublished doctoral dissertation, Mississippi State University, 1970.

Bruch, C. B., and Morse, J. A. Initial Study of Creative (Productive) Women Under the Bruch-Morse Model. Gifted Child Quarterly, 1972, Winter, 16(4), 282-289.

Bryson, J. B., Bryson, R. B., and Licht, B. G. Professional Pairs: Relative Career Values of Wives and Husbands. Symposium presentation at the American Psychological Association Convention, Chicago, 1975.

Bryson, R. B., Bryson, J. B., and Licht, M. H. Professional Pairs! A Survey of Husband-Wife Psychologists. Symposium présentation at the American Psychological Association Convention, Chicago, 1975.

_____, _____, _____, and Licht, B. G. The Professional Pair: Husband and Wife Psychologists. American Psychologist, 1976, January, 31(1), 10-16.

Burke, R. J., and Weir, T. Relationship of Wives' Employment Status to Husband, Wife and Pair Satisfaction and Performance. Journal of Marriage and the Family, 1976, May, 38(2), 279-287.

_____, and _____. Some Personality Differences Between Members of One-Career and Two-Career Families. Journal of Marriage and the Family, 1976, August, 38(3), 453-459.

Carruth, E. Some Executives' Wives Are Executives Too. Fortune, 1973, December, 88, 114-119.

Cartwright, L. K. Career Satisfaction and Role Harmony in Young Women Physicians. Symposium presentation at the American Psychological Association Convention, San Francisco, 1977.

Centra, J. A. Women, Men, and the Doctorate. Princeton: Educational Testing Service, 1974.

_____. Women, Marriage, and the Doctorate. Findings, 1975, 2(4), 1-5.

Chafetz, J. S., and Polk, B. B. Room at the Top: Social Recognition of British and American Females Over Time. Social Science Quarterly, 1974, March, 54(4), 843-853.

Clark, L. N. Considerations for Married Career Women. Journal of the National Association for Women Deans, Administrators, and Counselors, 1976, 40(1), 18-21.

Cleland, V., Bass, A. R., McHugh, N., and Montano, J. Social and Psychologic Influences on Employment of Married Nurses. Nursing Research, 1976, March-April, 25(2), 90-97.

Cockburn, P., and Raymond, Y. R. Women University Graduates
in Continuing Education and Employment, An Exploratory Study
Initiated by the Canadian Federation of University Women 1966,
and La Femme Diplomée Face à L'Education Permante et au
Monde du Travail. Toronto: Canadian Federation of University Women, 1967.

Cohen, L. M. Women's Entry into the Professions in Columbia:
Selected Characteristics. Journal of Marriage and the Family,
1973, May, 35(2), 322-329.

Cohen, M. S. Married Women in the Labor Force: An Analysis
of Participation Rates. Monthly Labor Review, 1969, October,
92, 31-35.

Commission Sociale de la Fédération Belge des Femmes Diplomées
d'Université. Les Jeunes Femmes Diplomées d'Université,
Leur Menage, Leur Vie Professionnelle, Leurs Problemes
[Young Female University Graduates, Their Management, Their
Professional Life, Their Problems.] R. Inst. Sociol. Solvay,
1960, 33(1), 103-156.

Constantini, E., and Craik, K. Women as Politicians: The Social
Background, Personalities, and Political Careers of Female
Party Leaders. Journal of Social Issues, 1972, 28(2), 217-236.

Cooper, S. E. The Double Role Syndrome or from Sesame Street
to the Groves of Academe. Educational Horizons, 1975, Spring,
53(3), 122-124.

Cowan, R. S. A Case Study of Technological and Social Change:
The Washing Machine and the Working Wife. In M. S. Hartman, and L. Banner (eds.), Clio's Consciousness Raised: New
Perspectives on the History of Women. New York: Harper
& Row, 1974, 245-253.

Cristo, M. G. Factors Influencing Career Mobility and Career Attainment of Women in the Field of Education. Unpublished doctoral dissertation. Dissertation Abstracts International, 1975,
36(6-A), 4034.

Crowley, J. E. et al. Dual Careers. Manpower Research Monograph No. 21, Washington, D. C.: U. S. Department of Labor,
1973.

Cuca, A. Women Psychologists and Marriage: A Bad Match?
APA Monitor, 1976, January, 7(1), 13.

Cunningham, R. M. Women Who Made It Offer Insights (Some Unintended) into Their Problems. College and University Business, 1970, February, 48, 56-61.

Curtis, J. Working Mothers. New York: Doubleday, 1976.

Darley, S. A. Big-Time Careers for the Little Woman: A Dual-Role Dilemma. Journal of Social Issues, 1976, 32(3), 85-98.

David, D. S. Career Patterns and Values: A Study of Men and Women in Science and Engineering. Unpublished doctoral dissertation, Columbia University, 1972. American Doctoral Dissertations, 1972, 11(97). Also available from ERIC (ADG02-63001), 1972.

Davidson, L. R. Sex Roles, Affect, and the Woman Physician: A Comparative Study of the Impact of Latent Social Identity upon the Role of Women and Men Professionals. Unpublished doctoral dissertation, New York University, 1975.

Davis, B. H. New Look at Working Wives. America, 1962, August 18, 107, 616+. Discussion. 1962, September 22, 107, 782-785.

Deguire, K. S. Activity Choice, Psychological Functioning, Degree of Satisfaction, and Personality Factors in Educated, Middle-Aged Women. Unpublished doctoral dissertation. Dissertation Abstracts International, 1974, November, 35(5-B), 2424.

Denmark, F. L., Baxter, B. K., and Shirk, E. J. The Future Goals of College Women. In F. L. Denmark (ed.), Women--Volume I: A PDI Research Reference Work. New York: Psychological Dimensions, 1976, 133-140.

Dias, S. L. A Study of Personal, Perceptual, and Motivational Factors Influential in Predicting the Aspiration Level of Women and Men Toward the Administrative Roles in Education. Unpublished doctoral dissertation. Dissertation Abstracts International, 1975, September, 36(3-A), 1202.

Douvan, E. Two Careers and One Family: Potential Pitfalls and Certain Complexity. Unpublished manuscript, University of Michigan, Ann Arbor, n. d.

Dowdall, J. A. Structural and Attitudinal Factors Associated with Female Labor Force Participation. Social Science Quarterly, 1974, June, 55(1), 121-130.

Dreifus, C. Work. In Woman's Fate: Raps from a Feminist Consciousness-Raising Group. New York: Bantam Books, 1973, 169-190.

Ducker, D. G. The Effects of Two Sources of Role Strain on Women Physicians. Unpublished doctoral dissertation. Dissertation Abstracts International, 1975, January, 35(7-B), 3552.

Duncan, R. P. Dual Occupational Participation and Migration. Dissertation Abstracts International, 1975, 36(A), 1115.

Durchholz, P., and O'Connor, J. Why Women Go Back to College.

In Women on Campus: The Unfinished Liberation. New York: Change Magazine, 1975, 236-241.

Edgerton, H. A. Women in Science Careers. Journal of the National Association of Women Deans and Counselors, 1962, June, 25(4), 166-169.

Elder, G. H., Jr. Role Orientations, Marital Age, and Life Patterns in Adulthood. Merrill-Palmer Quarterly, 1972, January, 18, 3-24.

Epstein, C. F. Woman's Place: Options and Limits in Professional Careers. Berkeley: University of California Press, 1970.

———. Law Partners and Marital Partners: Strains and Solutions in the Dual-Career Family Enterprise. Human Relations, 1971, 24(6), 549-564.

Ericksen, J. A. Work Attachment and Home Role Among a Cohort of American Women. Unpublished doctoral dissertation, University of Pennsylvania, 1976. Dissertation Abstracts International, 1977, 37(11-A), 7341. Also available from ERIC (ADG 77-10161), 1976.

Falk, L. L. Occupational Satisfaction of Female College Graduates. Journal of Marriage and the Family, 1966, 28(2), 177-185.

Families and the Rise of Working Wives: An Overview. Monthly Labor Review, 1976, May, 99(5), 12-19.

Family Problems Are Worse for Women Doctors. Medical Economy, 1973, April 30, 191-202.

Farley, J. Graduate Women: Career Aspirations and Desired Family Size. American Psychologist, 1970, December, 25(12), 1099-1100.

———. Married Women's Name Styles and Interest in Continuing Education. Journal of Employment Counseling, 1975, June, 12(2), 91-95.

Farmer, H. S. Helping Women to Resolve the Home-Career Conflict. Personnel and Guidance Journal, 1971, 49, 795-801.

———. What Inhibits Achievement and Career Motivation in Women? The Counseling Psychologist, 1976, 6(2), 12-15.

———. Why Women Contribute Less to the Arts, Sciences, and Humanities. Paper presented at the American Educational Research Association meeting, San Francisco, 1976.

———, and Bohn, M. J., Jr. Home-Career Conflict Reduction and the Level of Career Interest in Women. Journal of Counseling Psychology, 1970, 17(3), 228-232.

Feldman, S. Impediment or Stimulant? Marital Status and Graduate Education. American Journal of Sociology, 1973, January, 78(4), 982-994. Also in J. Huber, (ed.), Changing Women in a Changing Society. Chicago: University of Chicago Press, 1973, 220-232.

Felson, M., and Knoke, D. Social Status and the Married Woman. Journal of Marriage and the Family, 1974, August, 36(3), 516-521.

Ferree, M. M. Confused American Housewife. Psychology Today, 1976, September, 10, 76-78+.

Fidell, L. S. Employment Status, Role Dissatisfaction and the Housewife Syndrome. Unpublished manuscript, California State University, Northridge, 1976.

Fleck, H. Changing Life Patterns for Women. Forecast for Home Economics, 1968, September, 14, 71+.

Fogarty, M. P., Allen, A. J., Allen I., and Walters, P. A. Women in Top Jobs. London: Allen and Unwin, 1971.

_____, Rapoport, R., and Rapoport, R. N. Women and Top Jobs. London: Political and Economic Planning, 1968.

_____, _____, and _____. Sex, Career and Family. Beverly Hills: Sage Publications, 1971.

Frank, H. H. (ed.). The Two-Career Family. In Women in the Organization. Philadelphia: University of Pennsylvania Press, 1977, 305-308.

Frank, M. E., and Kiser, C. V. Changes in the Social and Demographic Attributes of Women in "Who's Who." Milbank Memorial Fund Quarterly, 1965, 43(1), 55-75.

Friedan, B. Have American Women Traded Brains for Brooms. Ladies Home Journal, 1963, January, 80, 24+.

From Kitchens to Careers. Senior Scholastic, 1964, November 4, 85(8), 5.

Garland, T. N. Husbands of Professional Women: The Forgotten Man. Unpublished doctoral dissertation, Case Western Reserve University. Dissertation Abstracts International, 1971, 32(8-A), 4734.

_____. The Better Half? The Male in the Dual Profession Family. In C. Safilios-Rothschild (ed.), Toward a Sociology of Women. Lexington, MA: Xerox College Publishing, 1972, 199-215.

Gibbons, K. M. The Single Working Mother. Women's Work, 1976, September/October, 2(5), 13-14.

Ginzberg, E. The Development of Human Resources. New York: McGraw-Hill, 1966.

_____, Berg, I. E., Brown, C. A., Herma, J. L., Yohalem, A. M., and Gorelick, S. Life Styles of Educated Women. New York: Columbia University Press, 1966.

_____, and Yohalem, A. M. Educated American Women: Life Styles and Self-Portraits. New York: Columbia University Press, 1966.

Giuliani, B., and Centra, J. A. The Woman Veterinarian. Personnel and Guidance Journal, 1968, 46(10), 971-975.

Goode, W. Family Life of the Successful Woman. In E. Ginzberg and A. M. Yohalem (eds.), Corporate Lib: Women's Challenge to Management. Baltimore: Johns Hopkins University Press, 1973, 97-117.

Goodwin, G. C. The Woman Doctoral Recipient: A Study of the Difficulties Encountered in Pursuing Graduate Degrees. Unpublished doctoral dissertation. Dissertation Abstracts International, 1967, 27(A), 4038.

Gray-Shellberg, L., Villareal, S., and Stone, S. Resolution of Career Conflicts: The Double Standard in Action. Paper presented at the American Psychological Association Convention, Honolulu, 1972.

Greenwald, C. Who Says a Woman Can't Raise a Family and Teach, Too? The Chronicle of Higher Education, 1974, September, 7(42), 16.

Grosgebauer, C. H. Volunteer to Career. Women's Work, 1976, July/August, 2(4), 17-19.

Gross, E. E. Patterns of Achievement Gratification and Felt Distress in Mothers of Preschool-Age Children. B. A. Honors thesis, University of Michigan, Ann Arbor, 1969.

Grossman, A. S. Almost Half of All Children Have Mothers in the Labor Force. Monthly Labor Review, 1977, June, 100, 41-44.

Gullahorn, J. E. Equality and Social Structure. In E. Donelson and J. E. Gullahorn (eds.), Women: A Psychological Perspective. New York: John Wiley, 1977, 266-281.

Hall, D. T. A Model of Coping with Role Conflict: The Role Behavior of College Educated Women. Administrative Science Quarterly, 1972, December, 17(4), 471-485.

_____. Pressures from Work, Self, and Home in the Life Stages of Married Women. Journal of Vocational Behavior, 1975, February, 6(1), 121-132.

_____, and Gordon, F. E. Effects of Career Choices on Married Women. Journal of Applied Psychology, 1973, 58(1), 42-48. Also in F. L. Denmark (ed.), Women--Volume I: A PDI Research Reference Work. New York: Psychological Dimensions, 1976, 175-182.

Haller, M., and Rosenmayer, L. The Pluridimensionality of Work Commitment: A Study of Young Married Women in Different Social Contexts of Occupational and Family Life. Human Relations, 1971, December, 24(6), 501-518.

Harbeson, G. E. Choice and Challenge for the American Woman. Cambridge, MA: Schenkman, 1967.

Harris, R. D. Coping with Role Conflict: My Story. Illinois Teacher of Home Economics, 1975, May/June, 18(5), 280-284.

Hatch, M. G., and Hatch, D. L. Problems of Married Working Women as Presented by Three Popular Women's Magazines. In M. Glazer-Malbin and H. Y. Waehrer (eds.), Woman in a Man-Made World. Chicago: Rand McNally, 1972, 183-186.

Haug, M. Social Class Measurement and Women's Occupational Roles. Social Forces, 1973, September, 52(1), 86-98.

Havens, E. M. Women, Work, and Wedlock: A Note on Female Marital Patterns in the United States. American Journal of Sociology, 1973, January, 78, 975-981.

Heer, D. M. Dominance and the Working Wife. In F. I. Nye and L. W. Hoffman (eds.), The Employed Mother in America. Chicago: Rand McNally, 1963.

Herman, J. B., and Gyllstrom, K. K. Working Men and Women: Inter- and Intra-Role Conflict. Psychology of Women Quarterly, 1977, Summer, 1(4), 319-333.

Hilberman, E., Gispert, M., and Harper, J. Impact of a District Branch Task Force on Women. American Journal of Psychiatry, 1976, October, 133(10), 1159-1164.

Hoffman, L. W. Effects of Maternal Employment on the Child. Child Development, 1961, March, 32, 187-197.

_____. The Decision to Work. In F. I. Nye and L. W. Hoffman (eds.), The Employed Mother in America. Chicago: Rand McNally, 1963, 18-39.

_____. Mother's Enjoyment of Work and Effects on the Child. In

F. I. Nye and L. W. Hoffman (eds.), The Employed Mother in America. Chicago: Rand McNally, 1963.

_____. Parental Power Relations and the Division of Household Tasks. In F. I. Nye and L. W. Hoffman (eds.), The Employed Mother in America. Chicago: Rand McNally, 1963.

_____. The Professional Woman as Mother. Annals of the New York Academy of Sciences, 1973, 208, 211-217. Also in R. B. Kundsin (ed.), Woman and Success: The Anatomy of Achievement. New York: William Morrow, 1974, 222-228.

_____. Effects of Maternal Employment on the Child--A Review of the Research. Developmental Psychology, 1974, 10, 204-228. Also in A. G. Kaplan and J. P. Bean (eds.), Beyond Sex-Role Stereotypes: Readings Toward a Psychology of Androgyny. Boston: Little, Brown, 1976, 293-318.

_____. The Employment of Women, Education, and Fertility. Merrill-Palmer Quarterly, 1974, April, 20(2), 99-119.

_____, and Nye, F. I. Working Mothers: An Evaluative Review of the Consequences for Wife, Husband and Child. San Francisco: Jossey-Bass, 1974.

Holmstrom, L. L. Career Patterns of Married Couples. In A. Theodore (ed.), The Professional Woman. Cambridge, MA: Schenkman, 1971, 516-524.

_____. The Two Career Family. Cambridge, MA: Schenkman, 1972.

Hunt, J. G., and Hunt, L. L. Dilemmas and Contradictions of Status: The Case of the Dual-Career Family. Paper presented at the Southern Sociological Society meeting, Washington, D. C., April 1975.

Hunter-Holmes, J. C. Factors Discriminating Among Occupational Groups of 230 Married Women with Children. Unpublished doctoral dissertation, University of Illinois, Urbana-Champaign, 1977. Dissertation Abstracts International, 1977, 38(1-B), 150. Also available from ERIC (ADG77-14962), 1977.

Huser, W. R. Certain Personality Characteristics and Self-Perceptions of Husbands and Wives in Traditional and Dual-Career Families. Unpublished doctoral dissertation, University of Utah. Dissertation Abstracts International, 1975, October, 36(4-B), 1968.

Kaley, M. M. Attitudes Toward the Dual Role of the Married Professional Woman. American Psychologist, 1967, 22, 301-306.

Kapur, R. Role-Conflict Among Employed Housewives. Indian Journal of Industrial Relations, 1969, July, 5(1), 39-67.

Kosa, J., and Coker, R. E., Jr. The Female Physician in Public Health: Conflict and Reconciliation of the Sex and Professional Roles. Sociology and Social Research, 1965, 49(3), 294-305. Also in A. Thedore (ed.), The Professional Woman. Cambridge, MA: Schenkman, 1971, 195-206.

Kreps, J. Sex, Age, and Work. New York Times, 1976, April 19, 125, 27.

Krohn, M. H. Planning for Work. New York: Catalyst, 1973.

Kuhlen, R. G. Needs, Perceived Need Satisfaction Opportunities and Satisfaction with Occupation. Journal of Applied Psychology, 1963, 47(1), 56-64.

Kundsin, R. B. (ed.). Women and Success: The Anatomy of Achievement. New York: William Morrow, 1974.

LaBarthe, E. R. A Study of the Motivation of Women in Administrative and Supervisory Positions in Selected Unified School Districts in Southern California. Unpublished doctoral dissertation. Dissertation Abstracts International, 1974, 34, 3695-3696.

Lake, B. Dual-Career Marriages: Can Two Work Better than One? Passages, 1977, November, 8(8), 20-24.

Laudicina, E. V. Toward New Forms of Liberation: A Mildly Utopian Proposal. Social Theory and Practice, 1973, Spring, 2(3), 275-288.

Lee, A. M. A Study of Married Women College Students. Journal of the National Association of Women Deans and Counselors, 1961, April, 24(3), 132-137. Also in The Teachers College Journal, 1960, March, 31(5), 118-119.

Lein, L., Durham, M., Pratt, M., Schedson, M., Thomas, R., and Weiss, H. Final Report: Work and Family Life. National Institute of Education Project. Cambridge, MA: Center for the Study of Public Policy, 1974.

Leland, C. A. Women-Men-Work: Women's Career Aspirations as Affected by the Male Environment. Unpublished doctoral dissertation, Stanford University, 1966.

Letchworth, G. E. Women Who Return to College: An Identity-Integrity Approach. Journal of College Student Personnel, 1970, March, 11(2), 103-106.

Levine, R. When a Married Woman Returns to College. Catholic School Journal, 1964, October, 64, 64.

_____, and Rolwing, R. H. Reasons Why Qualified Women Do Not

Pursue Mathematical Careers. Delta Kappa Gamma Bulletin, 1977, Winter, 43, 40-48.

Levitt, E. S. Vocational Development of Professional Women. Journal of Vocational Behavior, 1971, October, 1(4), 375-385.

Lewin, T. F. The Employment Experience of Married Women Social Caseworkers: A Study of One Hundred Graduates of the New York School of Social Work, Columbia University. Unpublished doctoral dissertation. American Doctoral Dissertations, 1962, 16(96), 203.

Londoner, C. A. Occupational Change and the Choice of Teaching as a New Career. Unpublished doctoral dissertation, Indiana University, Bloomington, 1971.

Lopate, C. Women in Medicine. Baltimore: Johns Hopkins University Press, 1968.

_____. Marriage and Medicine. In A. Theodore (ed.), The Professional Woman. Cambridge, MA: Schenkman, 1971.

McLean, K. Give Me Liberty and I'll Give You Guilt; How Working Women Cope with Success. American Home, 1976, August, 79, 30.

McMillan, M. R., Cerra, P. F., and Mehaffey, T. D. Opinions on Career Involvement of Married Women. Journal of the National Association of Women Deans and Counselors, 1971, Spring, 34(3), 121-124.

Manhardt, P. J. Job Orientation of Male and Female College Graduates in Business. Personnel Psychology, 1972, Summer, 25(2), 361-368.

Manis, J. D., and Hoffman, L. W. Fertility Motivations and Career Conflicts in Educated Women. In D. G. McGuigan (ed.), New Research on Women at the University of Michigan. Ann Arbor: University of Michigan, Center for Continuing Education of Women, 1974, 126-131.

Manpower Administration. Dual Careers: A Longitudinal Study of the Labor Experience of Women. Manpower Research and Development Monograph No. 21. Washington, D. C.: U. S. Department of Labor, 1972.

Martin, T. W., Berry, K. J., and Jacobsen, R. B. The Impact of Dual-Career Marriages on Female Professional Careers: An Empirical Test of a Parsonian Hypothesis. Journal of Marriage and the Family, 1975, November, 37(4), 734-742.

Maslin, A. Assessing and Reducing Housewives' Concerns About Vocational Reentry. Paper presented at the American Psychological Association Convention, Chicago, 1975.

Matteson, M. T., McMahon, J. T., and McMahon, M. Sex Differences and Job Attitudes: Some Unexpected Findings. Psychological Reports, 1974, December, 35(3), 1333-1334.

Meir, E. I., Carmon, A., and Sardi, Z. Prediction of Persistence at Work of Women Dentists. Personnel and Guidance Journal, 1967, November, 46, 247-251.

Michel, A. Needs and Aspirations of Married Women Workers in France. International Labor Review, 1966, 94(1), 39-53.

Mishler, S. A. Barriers to the Career Development of Women. In S. H. Osipow (ed.), Emerging Woman: Career Analysis and Outlooks. Columbus, OH: Charles E. Merrill, 1975, 117-146.

Miyahira, S. D. Marriage and the Employment of Women. In S. H. Osipow (ed.), Emerging Woman: Career Analysis and Outlooks. Columbus, OH: Charles E. Merrill, 1975, 69-90.

Moers, E. Money, the Job, and Little Women. Commentary, 1973, January, 55, 57-65.

Moore, B. M. Mothers, Homemakers and Wage Earners. NEA Journal, 1965, May, 54, 22-23.

Mortimer, J., Hall, R., and Hill, R. Husbands' Occupational Attitudes as Constraints on Wives' Employment. Paper presented at the American Sociological Association meeting, 1976.

Mostow, E., and Newberry, P. Work Role and Depression in Women: A Comparison of Workers and Housewives in Treatment. American Journal of Orthopsychiatry, 1975, July, 45(4), 538-548.

Motz, A. B. The Roles of the Married Woman in Science. Journal of Marriage and Family Living, 1961, November, 23(4), 374-376.

Myrdal, A., and Klein, V. Women's Two Roles: At Home and Work. Atlantic Highlands, NJ: Humanities Press, 1970.

Nemiroff, M. A. Ego Development, Sex-Role Attitudes, and the Domestic Division of Labor in Husbands of Professional Women. Unpublished doctoral dissertation, Catholic University of America. Dissertation Abstracts International, 1975, August, 36(2-B), 918.

Ngai, S. Y. A. Long-Distance Commuting as a Solution to Geographical Limitation to Career Choices of Two-Career Families. Unpublished master's thesis, Cornell University, 1974.

Nye, F. I., and Hoffman, L. W. The Employed Mother in America. Chicago: Rand McNally, 1963.

O'Leary, V. E. Some Attitudinal Barriers to Occupational Aspirations in Women. Psychological Bulletin, 1974, 81(11), 809-826.

Orden, S. R., and Bradburn, N. M. Working Wives and Marriage Happiness. American Journal of Sociology, 1969, January, 74(4), 392-407.

Osipow, S. H. (ed.). Perspective and Issues. In Emerging Woman: Career Analysis and Outlooks. Columbus, OH: Charles E. Merrill, 1975, 147-158.

―――― (ed.). Emerging Woman: Career Analysis and Outlook. Columbus, OH: Charles E. Merrill, 1975.

Papanek, H. Men, Women, and Work: Reflections on the Two-Person Career. American Journal of Sociology, 1973, January, 78(4), 852-872.

Parnes, H. S., Shea, J. R., Spitz, R. S., and Zeller, F. A. Dual Careers, Manpower Research Monograph, Vol. 1. Washington D. C.: U. S. Department of Labor, 1970.

Perrucci, C. C. Minority Status and the Pursuit of Professional Careers: Women in Science and Engineering. Social Forces, 1970, 49, 245-258.

Peters, J. R. Constituents of Experience in Job Happiness and Unhappiness in Employed Women. Unpublished doctoral dissertation, Duquesne University. Dissertation Abstracts International, 1970, September, 31(3-B), 1580-1581.

Peterson, E. Needs and Opportunities for Educated Women. In L. E. Dennis (ed.), Education and a Woman's Life: Proceedings of the Itasca Conference on the Continuing Education of Women. Washington, D. C.: American Council on Education, 1963, 64+.

――――. Outlook for Women. American Association of School Administrators Official Report, 1965, 62-74.

Piomelli, R. Pains and Pleasures of a Woman Architect. Educational Horizons, 1975, Spring, 53(3), 110-115.

Pleck, J. Work and Family Roles: From Sex-Patterned Integration to Segregation. Paper presented at the American Psychological Association Convention, San Francisco, 1977.

Pogrebin, L. C. Working Woman; Problems of Two-Career Professional Couples. Ladies Home Journal, 1974, January, 91, 50+.

――――. Working Woman: The Success Syndrome. Ladies Home Journal, 1974, July, 91, 42+.

_____. When She Earns More than He Does. Ladies Home Journal, 1976, February, 93, 70+.

Poloma, M. M. The Married Professional Woman: An Empirical Examination of Three Myths. Unpublished doctoral dissertation, Case Western Reserve University, 1970. Dissertation Abstracts International, 1971, 32(1-A), 564. Also available from ERIC (ADG71-19042), 1970.

_____. Role Conflict and the Married Professional Woman. In C. Safilios-Rothschild (ed.), Toward a Sociology of Women. Lexington, MA: Xerox College Publishing, 1972, 187-198.

_____, and Garland, T. N. Jobs or Careers? The Case of the Professionally Employed Married Woman in Europe and America. International Journal of Comparative Sociology, Part II, 1971.

_____, and _____. Jobs or Careers? The Case of the Professionally Employed Married Woman. In A. Michel (ed.), Family Issues of Employed Women in Europe and America. Leiden, Netherlands: E. J. Brill, 1971, 126-142.

_____, and _____. The Married Professional Woman: A Study in Tolerance of Domestication. Journal of Marriage and the Family, 1971, August, 33(3), 531-540.

_____, and _____. The Myth of the Egalitarian Family: Familial Roles and the Professionally Employed Wife. In A Theodore (ed.), The Professional Woman. Cambridge, MA: Schenkman, 1971, 741-761.

Pospisil, V. C. Problems of Dual Career Marriages. Industry Week, 1976, November 15, 191(4), 86-89.

Powell, B., and Reznikoff, M. Role Conflict and Symptoms of Psychological Distress in College Educated Women. Journal of Consulting and Clinical Psychology, 1976, June, 44(3), 473-479.

Powell, K. S. Maternal Employment in Relation to Family Life. Marriage and Family Living, 1961, 23, 350-355.

Powers, L., Weisenfelder, H., and Parmelee, R. Practice Patterns of Women and Men Physicians. Preliminary Report to the American Association of Medical Colleges, 1966.

Ramsey, G. V. Some Attitudes and Opinions of Employed Women. Journal of the National Association of Women Deans and Counselors, 1963, April, 26, 30-36.

Rapoport, R., and Rapoport, R. N. Work and Family in Contemporary Society. American Sociological Review, 1965, 30, 381-394.

534 / Career Contingencies

_____, and _____. The Dual Career Family: A Variant Pattern and Social Change. Human Relations, 1969, 22(1), 3-30. Also in C. Safilios-Rothschild (ed.), Toward a Sociology of Women. Lexington, MA: Xerox College Publishing, 1972, 216-244.

_____, and _____. Analysis of Dual-Career Families. In Dual-Career Families. New York: Penguin Books, 1971, 278-301.

_____, and _____. The Dual-Career Family and Its Environment: Contemporary Issues. In Dual-Career Families. New York: Penguin Books, 1971, 302-321.

_____, and _____. Dual-Career Families. New York: Penguin Books, 1971.

_____, and _____. Early and Later Experiences as Determinants of Adult Behavior: Married Women's Family and Career Patterns. British Journal of Sociology, 1971, March, 22(1), 16-30.

_____, and _____. Men, Women, and Equity. Family Coordinator, 1975, October, 24, 421-432.

Rappaport, A. F., Payne, D., and Steinmann, A. Marriage as a Factor in the Dyadic Perception of the Female Role. Psychological Reports, 1970, 27, 283-284.

Rice, R. W. Sex Role Definition--Attitudes Toward Marriage and Careers of Teacher-Trainees as Compared to Married Couples. Unpublished doctoral dissertation. Dissertation Abstracts International, 1973, 34(9-A), 6142.

Ritter, K. V., and Hargens, L. L. Occupational Positions and Class Identification of Married Working Women: A Test of the Asymmetry Hypothesis. American Journal of Sociology, 1975, 80(4), 934-948.

Rivers, C. Can a Woman Be Liberated and Married. New York Times Magazine, 1975, November, Section 6.

Roach, R. M. Honey, Won't You Please Stay Home. Personnel and Guidance Journal, 1976, October, 55(2), 86-89.

Roby, P. A. Shared Parenting: Perspectives from Other Nations. School Review, 1975, May, 83(3), 415-431.

Rollins, M. A. Monetary Contributions of Wives to Family Income in 1920 and 1960. Marriage and Family Living, 1963, May, 25(2), 226-227.

Rosen, B., Jerdee, T. H., and Prestwich, T. L. Dual-Career Marital Adjustment: Potential Effects of Discriminatory Managerial Attitudes. Journal of Marriage and the Family, 1975, August, 37(3), 565-572.

Rosenfeld, C., and Perrella, V. C. Why Women Start and Stop Working: A Study in Mobility. Monthly Labor Report, 1965, September, 88, 1077-1082.

Rosenthal, E. R. Structural Patterns of Women's Occupational Choice. Unpublished doctoral dissertation, Cornell University. Dissertation Abstracts International, 1974, 35(6-A), 3901.

Rossi, A. S. Ambivalence in Women: Should We Plan for the Real or the Ideal? Adult Leadership, 1967, 16, 100-102+.

_____. Women in Science: Why So Few? Science, 1965, May, 148, 1196-1202. Also in C. Safilios-Rothschild (ed.), Toward a Sociology of Women. Lexington, MA: Xerox College Publishing, 1972, 141-153.

Rostow, E. G. Conflict and Accommodation. Daedalus, 1964, Spring, 93(2), 736-760. Also in R. J. Lifton (ed.), The Woman in America. Boston: Houghton Mifflin, 1965, 211-235.

Rubin, L. Women in Middle Life: Work and Interpersonal Relationships. Symposium presentation at the American Psychological Association Convention, San Francisco, 1977.

Safilios-Rothschild, C. The Influence of the Wife's Degree of Work Commitment upon Some Aspects of Family Organization and Dynamics. Journal of Marriage and the Family, 1970, 32(4), 681-691.

_____. The Relationship Between Work Commitment and Fertility. International Journal of Sociology of the Family, 1972, 2(1), 64-71.

_____. Dual Linkages Between the Occupational and Family Systems: A Macrosociological Analysis. SIGNS: Journal of Women in Culture and Society, 1976, 1(3, Pt. 2), 51-60.

Saleh, S. E., Lee, R. J., and Prien, E. P. Why Nurses Leave Their Jobs: An Analysis of Female Turnover. Personnel Administration, 1965, January/February, 28(1), 25-28.

Salk, L. Can You Work and Be a Good Mother? Harper's Bazaar, 1977, August, 110, 88-89+.

Salo, K. E. Women's Views of Their Family and Work Roles. JSAS Catalog of Selected Documents in Psychology, 1977, 7(3), 69.

Sampson, J. M., et al. Employment Status of the Wife-Mother: Psychological, Social, and Socioeconomic Influences. Home Economics Research Journal, 1975, June, 3(4), 266-279.

Sartin, P. Real and Pseudo Problems of the Working Woman. UNESCO Courier, 1969, July, 22, 24-28.

Schiffler, R. J. Demographic and Social Factors in Women's Work Lives. In S. H. Osipow (ed.), Emerging Woman: Career Analysis and Outlooks. Columbus, OH: Charles E. Merrill, 1975, 10-22.

Seiberling, B. The Political Wife: What Are Her Career Options? Women's Work, 1976, March/April, 2(2), 10-11.

Seifer, N. Nobody Speaks for Me! Self Portraits of American Working Class Women. New York: Simon and Schuster, 1976.

Self, G. Women on the Move: Some Common Psychological Problems. Paper presented to the Governor's Commission on the Status of Women, Las Vegas, 1969.

Shaywitz, S. E. Catch 22 for Mothers. New York Times Magazine, 1973, March 4, 50+. Discussion. 1973, April 1, 69+.

Shea, J. R., Spitz, R. S., and Zeller, F. A. Dual Careers: A Longitudinal Study of Labor Market Experience of Women, Volume 1. Columbus, OH: Ohio State University, Center for Human Resource Research, 1970.

Shelton, B. Feminism: Implications for Employment Counselors. Journal of Employment Counseling, 1976, September, 13(3), 116-121.

Sherman, R. G., and Jones, J. H. Career Choices for Women--The New Determinants. Journal of College Student Personnel, 1976, July, 17(4), 289-294.

Siegel, A. E., and Haas, M. B. The Working Mother: A Review of the Research. Child Development, 1963, 34, 513-542.

Simmons, J. Why Do They Want to Stay Home? A Study of Career Oriented Mothers with Preschool Children. Cornell Journal of Social Relations, 1970, Spring, 5(1), 29-39.

Singh, K. P. Career and Family--Women's Two Roles (A Case Study in Role Conflict). Indian Journal of Social Work, 1972, October, 33(3), 277-281.

Smith, B. K. Who Am I? Dilemma of Professional Women. Unpublished address, University of Texas at Austin, 1974.

Smith, J. B. Separation Anxiety: A Personal Experience. American Journal of Nursing, 1975, June, 75(6), 972-973.

Smith, J. L. On Juggling a Family, A Home and A College Education. Mademoiselle, 1977, August, 83, 32+.

Sobol, M. B. G. Correlates of Present and Expected Future Work Status of Married Women. Unpublished doctoral dissertation, University of Michigan, 1969. Dissertation Abstracts International, 1961. 21(12), 3656. Also available from ERIC (ADG61-01791), 1961.

Southard, H. F. Mother's Dilemma: To Work or Not To. New York Times Magazine, 1960, July 17, 39.

Spiegel, J. Working Mothers. A Selected Annotated Bibliography. Washington: Business and Professional Women's Foundation, 1968.

Steinmann, A. The Vocational Roles of Older Married Women. Journal of Social Psychology, 1961, 54, 93-101.

Stolz, L. Effects of Maternal Employment on Children: Evidence from Research. Child Development, 1960, 31, 749-782.

Stoyr, M. W. Some Attitudes that Indicate Job Satisfaction in Vocational Home Economics Teachers Graduated from Two Different Curriculums at Michigan State University. Unpublished doctoral dissertation. Dissertation Abstracts, 1968, 28(10-A), 4033-4034.

Surprising Facts About Women, Work, Marriage. Science Digest, 1963, October, 54, 79-82.

Tangri, S. S. Effects of Background, Personality, College and Post-College Experiences on Women's Post-Graduate Employment. Washington, D. C.: U. S. Commission on Civil Rights, 1974.

Taylor, M. G., and Hartley, S. F. The Two-Person Career: A Classic Example. Sociology of Work and Occupations, 1975, November, 2(4), 354-375.

Taylor, P. Diary of An Out-of-Worker. Women's Work, 1975, March/April, 2(1), 12.

Thomas, J. L. Why Women Work--The Significance. Social Order, 1962, February, 12(2), 72-76.

Thomas, P., and Paolucci, B. Goals of Young Wives. Journal of Home Economics, 1966, 58(9), 720-723.

Thomopoulos, E. H. Parents of Preschool Children: The Work Status of the Mother as It Relates to Marriage Adjustment, Anxiety, and Egalitarianism. Unpublished doctoral dissertation, Illinois Institute of Technology. Dissertation Abstracts International, 1974, November, 35(5-B), 2486.

_____, and Huyck, M. H. Mother's Work Status as It Relates to Marriage Adjustment. Paper presented at the American Psychological Association Convention, Washington, D. C., 1976.

_____, and _____. Love and Labor: Maternal Work Status and Family Relationships. Paper presented at the American Psychological Association Convention, Washington, D. C., 1976.

Toporoff, R. Generating Role Types Concerning the Occupational Participation of Women in the Twentieth Century. Unpublished doctoral dissertation. Dissertation Abstracts International, 1972, 32(12-A), 7107.

Torrance, E. P. Creative Young Women in Today's World. Exceptional Children, 1972, April, 38(8), 597-603.

Treiman, D. J., and Terrell, K. Sex and the Process of Status Attainment: A Comparison of Working Women and Men. American Sociological Review, 1975, 40(2), 174-200.

Tyree, A., and Treas, J. The Occupational and Marital Mobility of Women. American Sociological Review, 1974, June, 39(3), 294-302.

'T Veld-Langeveld, H. M. Woman--Job--Society: Analysis of a Retarded Emancipation. Sociologia Neerlandica, 1972, 8(1), 64-81.

Veroff, J., and Feld, S. Marriage and Work in America: A Study of Motives and Roles. New York: Van Nostrand Reinhold, 1970.

Waite, L. J. Working Wives: 1940-1960. American Sociological Review, 1976, February, 41(1), 65-80.

_____, and Stolzenberg, R. M. Intended Child-Bearing and Labor Force Participation of Young Women: Insights from Nonrecursive Models. American Sociological Review, 1976, April, 41(2), 235-252.

Wallston, B. S., Foster, M., and Berger, M. I Will Follow Him: Myth, Reality, or Forced Choice? Psychology of Women Quarterly, 1978, Fall, 3(1), 9-21.

Wang, L. The Female Status Attainment Process and Occupational Mobility. Unpublished master's thesis, University of Wisconsin, 1973.

Weaver, C. N., and Holmes, S. L. Comparative Study of the Work Satisfaction of Females with Full-Time Employment and Full-Time Housekeeping. Journal of Applied Psychology, 1975, Fall, 60, 117-118.

Weil, M. W. An Analysis of the Factors Influencing Married Women's Actual or Planned Work Participation. American Sociological Review, 1961, 26(1), 91-96.

Welds, K. Voluntary Childlessness in Professional Women. Paper presented at the American Psychological Association Convention, San Francisco, 1977.

Westervelt, E. M. Woman as a Compleat Human Being. Journal of the National Association of Women Deans and Counselors, 1966, Summer, 29(4), 150-155.

Westoff, A. L. The Two-Career Couple. Princeton Alumni Weekly, 1973, November 27.

White, L. C. Maternal Employment and Anxiety over Mother Role. Louisiana State University Journal of Sociology, 1972, Spring.

White, M. S. Women in the Professions: Psychological and Social Barriers to Women in Science. Science, 1970, October 23, 170, 413-416. Also in C. Safilios-Rothschild (ed.), Toward a Sociology of Women. Lexington, MA: Xerox College Publishing, 1972, 300-308; and in J. Freeman (ed.), Women: A Feminist Perspective. Palo Alto: Mayfield 1975, 227-237.

Whitman, A. Problem that Plagues the Thoughtful Woman; Marriage-Versus-Career. Redbook, 1964, February, 122, 50-51+.

Whitmer, D. K. Sex Role Strain as a Factor in the Marital Adjustment and Academic Success of a Group of Married College Students. Unpublished doctoral dissertation, University of Florida, 1965. Dissertation Abstracts International, 1966, 27(1-A), 265. Also available from ERIC (ADG66-02062), 1965.

Why Women Work: What a Study Finds. U. S. News & World Report, 1971, August, 71, 66.

Winter, D. G., Stewart, A. J., and McClelland, D. C. Husband's Motives and Wife's Career Level. Journal of Personality and Social Psychology, 1977, 35(3), 159-166.

Wolf, W. C. Occupational Attainment of Married Women: Do Career Contingencies Matter. Unpublished doctoral dissertation, Johns Hopkins University, 1976. Dissertation Abstracts International, 1976, 37(2-A), 1258. Also available from ERIC (ADG 76-16837), 1976.

Woman's Loyalty: Work or Home First? The Times (London) Educational Supplement, 1964, November 6, 2581, 815.

Women's Bureau. Who Are the Working Mothers? Leaflet 37, Washington, D. C.: U. S. Department of Labor, 1970.

_____. Facts About Women Heads of Households and Heads of Families. Washington, D. C.: U. S. Department of Labor, 1973.

Women's Work Is Never Done. Transaction, 1969, June, 6, 8.

Wood, M. W. Homemakers Employed Outside the Home. American Vocational Journal, 1962, April, 37, 22-23.

Working Mothers. Special Issue. Parents Magazine, 1977, April, 52.

Working Wife and Mother. Changing Times, 1965, July, 19, 7-10.

Yarrow, M., Scott, P., De Leeuw, L., and Heinig, C. Child-Rearing in Families of Working and Non-Working Mothers. Sociometry, 1962, 25, 122-140.

Yehia, M. A. Attitudes Toward Women's Work Commitment: Changes from 1964 to 1975. Unpublished doctoral dissertation, Wayne State University, 1976. Dissertation Abstracts International, 1976, 37(5-A), 3125. Also available from ERIC (ADG76-26915), 1976.

Yockey, J. M. A Model of Contemporary Feminine Role Change and Family Size. Sex Roles: A Journal of Research, 1975, 1(1), 69-81.

Zapoleon, M. W. Occupational Planning for Women. Harper & Row, 1961.

Zissis, C. The Relationship of Selected Variables to Career-Marriage Plans of University Freshman Women. Unpublished doctoral dissertation, University of Michigan. Dissertation Abstracts International, 1962, 23(1), 128.

VIII

MINORITY WOMEN AND AMBITION

Black women have suffered cruelly in this society from living the phenomenon of being Black and female, in a country that is both racist and sexist.... [H]istory, past or present, rarely deals with the malicious abuse put upon the Black woman. We were seen as breeders by the master; despised and historically polarized from/by the master's wife; and looked upon as castraters by our lovers and husbands. The Black woman has had to be strong, yet we are persecuted for having survived. We have been called "matriarchs" by white racists and Black nationalists; we have virtually no positive self-images to validate our existence. Black women want to be proud, dignified and free from all those false definitions of beauty and womanhood that are unrealistic and unnatural. We, not white men or Black men, must define our own self-image as Black women and not fall into the mistake of being placed upon the pedestal which is even being rejected by white women. --Margaret Sloan.

Both Chicanos and gabachos have been guilty of the merciless stereotyping of females as docile, helpless, emotional, irrational, and intellectually inferior creatures who are best suited to be sex objects, domestic servants, and typists. --Patricia Cruz.

American Indian women have wisdoms and insights that are valuable, if not necessary, to the dialogue on women's rights--and the dialogue on human rights.... Today, as always, American Indian women well understand that there can be no liberation of Indian women as women until all Indian people are free of colonial oppression.--from a Native American woman, 1975.

A. MINORITY WOMEN--GENERAL

Alperson, E. D. The Minority Woman in Academe. Professional Psychology, 1975, August, 6(3), 252-256.

Bachelor's Degrees Awarded to Minority Students, 1973-74. Higher

542 / Minority Women

Education Panel Report No. 24. Washington, D. C.: American Council on Education, 1977.

Berg, P. A., and Hyde, J. S. Gender and Race Differences in Causal Attributions in Achievement Situations. Paper presented at the American Psychological Association Convention, Washington, D. C., 1976.

Bergmann, B. R. Occupational Segregation, Wages, and Profits When Employers Discriminate by Race or Sex. Eastern Economic Journal, 1974, April/July, 103-110.

Bernard, J. The Impact of Sexism and Racism on Employment Status and Earnings. In Women, Wives, Mothers: Values and Options. Chicago: Aldine, 1975, 200-212.

Birk, J. M., Cooper, J., and Tanney, M. Racial and Sex-Role Stereotyping in Career Information Illustration. Paper presented at the American Psychological Association Convention, Montreal, 1973.

Blake, J. The Changing Status of Women in Developed Countries. Scientific American, 1974, September, 231, 136-147.

Blakey, W. A. Everybody Makes the Revolution: Some Thoughts on Racism and Sexism. Civil Rights Digest, 1974, Spring, 6(3), 11-19.

Borich, G. D., and Peck, R. F. Achievement and Aptitude as a Function of Grade, Ethnicity, and Sex. Paper presented at the American Psychological Association Convention, Washington, D. C., 1976.

Borup, J. H. Validity of American College Test for Discerning Potential Academic Achievement Levels; Ethnic and Sex Groups. Journal of Educational Research, 1971, September, 65, 3-6.

Bradley, R. H. Sex, Race, Socioeconomic Status, Locus of Control, and Classroom Behavior Among Junior High School Students. Unpublished doctoral dissertation, University of North Carolina. Dissertation Abstracts International, 1974, December, 35(6-A), 3505-3506.

Brown, F. Title I: Is It Compensatory or Just a Partial Equalizer. Emergent Leadership, 1976, Fall, 1(1), 10-14.

_____, and Stent, M. D. Minority Representation in Higher Education in the United States. New York: Praeger, 1977.

Bryant, B. E. American Women Today and Tomorrow. Washington, D. C.: National Commission on the Observance of International Women's Year, 1977.

Bureau of the Census. Detailed Occupations of Employed Persons by Race and Sex for the United States: 1970. Washington, D. C.: U. S. Department of Commerce, 1973.

Butler, I. C. Self-Concept: Race and Social Class in Adolescent Females. Dissertation Abstracts International, 1974, February, 34(8-B), 4034.

Clark, Y. Y., and Abron-Robinson, L. A. Minority Women in Engineering Schools. IEEE Transactions on Education, 1975, February, E-18(1), 34-35.

Cole, N. S. Bias in Selection. Journal of Educational Measurement, 1973, 10, 237-255.

Cole, T. W., Sr. Opening Doors to Graduate School: Florida's Program for Minority Students. Carnegie Quarterly, 1976, Fall, 24(4), 6-7.

Coleman, J. S., and Staff. Equality of Educational Opportunity. Washington, D. C.: U. S. Department of Health, Education, and Welfare, 1966.

Commission on Human Resources, National Research Council. Minority Groups Among United States Doctorate-Level Scientists, Engineers, and Scholars, 1973. Washington, D. C.: National Academy of Sciences, 1974.

Counseling Girls and Women, A Guide for Jewish and Other Minority Women. Washington, D. C.: B'nai B'rith Career and Counseling Service, 1973.

Coursen, D. Women and Minorities in Administration. Arlington, VA: National Association of Elementary School Principals, 1975.

The Double Bind: The Price of Being a Minority Woman in Science. Paper presented at the American Association for the Advancement of Science Conference, December 1975.

Dyer, S. E. The Flow Through the System: Differential Levels of Educational Attainment for Women and Minorities. Symposium presentation at the American Psychological Association Convention, San Francisco, 1977.

El-Khawas, E. H., and Kinzer, J. L. Enrollment of Minority Graduate Students at PhD Granting Institutions. Higher Education Panel Reports, No. 19. Washington, D. C.: American Council on Education, 1974.

Equal Employment Opportunity Commission. Guidelines on Employment Selection Procedures. Federal Register, 1970, 35(149), 12333-12336.

Equal Employment Opportunity Coordinating Council. Uniform Guidelines on Employee Selection Procedures: A Discussion Draft. Washington, D. C. : EEOCC, August 23, 1973.

Flavin, J. R. Race and Sex of Experimenter and Subject as Possible Covariables Affecting Responses to Julian B. Rotter's Locus of Control Questionnaire. Unpublished doctoral dissertation, University of Houston. Dissertation Abstracts International, 1975, May, 35(11-B), 5662.

Forrest, K. S., and Chang, W. Affirmative Action and Equal Employment: A Bibliography. San Jose, CA: San Jose State University, Affirmative Action Office, n. d.

Freeman, H. R., Schockett, M. R., and Freeman, E. B. Effects of Gender and Race on Sex-Role Preferences of Fifth-Grade Children. Journal of Personality and Social Psychology, 1975, 95, 105-108.

Fricker, S. K., and Werner, E. E. Achievement Orientation of Adolescent Women of Hawaiian-, Japanese-, and Philipino-American Descent. JSAS Catalog of Selected Documents in Psychology, 1976, August, (7), 69.

Fujitomi, I., and Wong, D. The New Asian-American Women. In S. Cox (ed.), Female Psychology: The Emerging Self. Chicago: Science Research Associates, 1976, 236-248.

Gallimore, R. Affiliation Motivation and Hawaiian-American Achievement. Journal of Cross-Cultural Psychology, 1974, December, 5(4), 481-491.

Gery, G. J. Equal Opportunity--Planning and Managing the Process of Change. Personnel Journal, 1977, April, 56(4), 184-191+.

_____. Hiring Minorities and Women--The Selection Process. Personnel Journal, 1974, December, 53(12), 906-909.

Gitter, A. G., Altavela, J., and Mostofsky, D. I. Effect of Sex, Religion, and Ethnicity on Occupational Status Perception. Journal of Applied Psychology, 1974, February, 59, 96-98.

Gordon, N. M., Morton, T. E., and Braden, I. C. Faculty Salaries: Is There Discrimination by Sex, Race and Discipline? American Economic Review, 1974, June, 64(3), 419-427.

Green, D. R. Racial and Ethnic Bias in Test Construction. New York: McGraw-Hill, 1972.

Gump, J., and Rovers, L. The Consideration of Race in Efforts to End Sex Bias. In E. E. Diamond (ed.), Issues of Sex Bias and Sex Fairness in Career Interest Measurement. Washington, D. C.: U. S. Department of Health, Education, and Welfare, 1975, 123-139.

Haefner, J. E. Race, Age, Sex, and Competence as Factors in Employer Selection of the Disadvantaged. Journal of Applied Psychology, 1977, April, 62, 199-202.

Hare, B. R. The Relationship of Social Background to the Dimensions of Self-Concept. Unpublished manuscript, University of Chicago, 1969.

Hauser, R. H., Featherman, D. L., and Hogan, D. P. Race and Sex in the Structure of Occupational Mobility in the United States, 1962. Paper presented at the World Congress of Sociology, Toronto, Canada, 1974.

Hendrick, H. W. The White Male Club: Experimental Explorations of Racism and Sexism. Presented at the American Psychological Association Convention, Chicago, 1975.

Hernton, C. Sex and Racism in America. New York: Doubleday, 1965.

Hess, R. D. Social Class and Ethnic Influences Upon Socialization. In P. H. Mussen (ed.), Carmichael's Manual of Child Psychology, Volume 2. New York: John Wiley, 1970, 457-557.

Higa, G. Ethnic Scholarships and the 14th Amendment. Journal of College Student Personnel, 1977, November, 18(6), 511-517.

Howe, F. Sexism, Racism and the Education of Women. Today's Education, 1973, May, 62, 47B.

Hsieh, T. T., Shybut, J., and Lotsof, E. J. Internal Versus External Control and Ethnic Group Membership. Journal of Consulting and Clinical Psychology, 1969, 33(1), 122-124.

Jaeger, R. M., and Feijo, T. D. Race and Sex as Concomitants of Composite Halo in Teachers' Evaluative Rating of Pupils. Journal of Educational Psychology, 1975, April, 67, 226-237.

Johnson, D. G., and Sedlacek, W. E. Retention by Sex and Race of the 1968-1972 U. S. Medical School Entrants. Journal of Medical Education, 1975, 50(10), 925-933.

_____, Smith, V. C., Jr., and Tarnoff, S. L. Recruitment and Progress of Minority Medical School Entrants, 1970-1972: A Cooperative Study by the SNMA and the AAMC. Journal of Medical Education, 1975, 50, 711-755.

Knowles, L. L., and Prewitt, K. Institutional Racism in America. Englewood Cliffs, NJ: Prentice-Hall, 1969.

Kohen, A. I., and Roderick, R. D. The Effects of Race and Sex Discrimination on Early-Career Earnings. Columbus: Ohio State University, Center for Human Resource Research, College of Administrative Science, 1975.

Kranz, H. Are Merit and Equity Compatible. Public Administration Review, 1974, September/October, 34(5), 434-439.

Leggett, D. C. Retention of Minority Graduate Students. Symposium presentation at the American Psychological Association Convention, Washington, D. C., 1976.

Lockentz, L. Careers in Action: Minorities in Focus. St. Paul, MN: St. Paul Schools, 1977.

Lower, D., and Krain, M. Minorities and Women in the Health Fields. Washington, D. C.: U. S. Government Printing Office, 1976.

McCarthy, J. L., and Wolfle, D. Doctorates Granted to Women and Minority Group Members. Science, 1975, 189, 856-859.

Maehr, M. L. Sociocultural Origins of Achievement. Monterey, CA: Brooks/Cole, 1974.

Malik, H. M. A Study of Racism and Sexism in Career Counseling, Job Selection and Placement by Vocational Rehabilitation Counselors in Alaska, Idaho, and Oregon. Unpublished doctoral dissertation, University of Oregon. Dissertation Abstracts International, 1973, 34(9-A), 6146.

Martin, W. T., and Poston, D. L., Jr. The Occupational Composition of White Females: Sexism, Racism and Occupational Differentiation. Social Forces, 1972, March, 50(3), 349-355.

Mathis, M., and Jones, D. H. Finding More Women and Minorities for Management Level Jobs. Banking, 1974, March, 66, 94+.

Mednick, M. T. S., Tangri, S. S., and Hoffman, L. W. (eds.) Women and Achievement: Social and Motivational Analyses. New York: Halsted Press, 1975.

Medsger, B. Women at Work. Mission, KS: Sheed and Ward, 1975.

National Association of State Universities and Land-Grant Colleges. Office of Research and Information. Minority Enrollment at State Universities and Land Grant Colleges. Washington, D. C.: the Association, 1976.

National Board on Graduate Education. Minority Group Participation in Graduate Education: A Report with Recommendations of the National Board on Graduate Education, No. 5. Washington, D. C.: National Academy of Sciences, 1976.

National Organization for Women. Women and Minorities in Corporate Positions: The Shape of the Future. Unpublished manuscript, n. d.

Nelson, B. W., Bird, R. A., and Rodgers, G. M. Expanding Educational Opportunities in Medicine for Blacks and Other Minority Students. Journal of Medical Education, 1970, 45, 731-736.

Newman, P. Take a Good Look at Our Problems, 1970. In W. Martin (ed.), The American Sisterhood. New York: Harper & Row, 1972, 179-182.

Nieves, L. The Graduate Record Examinations and the Minority Student. Paper presented at the American Association for the Advancement of Science meeting, Boston, February 1976.

Norton, E. H. Affirmative Action for Both Minorities and Women: The Road to Real Reform. Contact, 1974, Fall, 5(4), 12-15.

O'Leary, V. E., and Harrison, A. O. Sex Role Stereotypes as a Function of Race and Sex. Paper presented at the American Psychological Association Convention, Chicago, 1975.

Pascal, A. Racial Discrimination in Economic Life. Lexington, MA: D. C. Heath, 1972.

Perry, A. R., Anderson, B. E., Rowan, R. L., and Northrup, H. R. The Impact of Government Manpower Programs, in General, and on Minorities and Women. Philadelphia: University of Pennsylvania, Wharton School, Industrial Research Unit, 1975.

Peterson, K., and Wilson, J. J. Women Artists. Harper & Row, 1976.

Phelps, E. S. The Statistical Theory of Racism and Sexism. American Economic Review, 1972, September, 62, 659-661.

Pinto, P. R., and Buchmeier, J. O. Problems and Issues in the Employment of Minority, Disadvantaged and Female Groups: An Annotated Bibliography. Minneapolis: University of Minnesota, Industrial Relations Center, No. 59, 1973. Also in JSAS Catalog of Selected Documents in Psychology, 1973, Winter, (3), 18.

Pottinger, J. S. Race, Sex and Jobs--The Drive for Equality. Change Magazine, 1972, October, 4(8), 24. Also in E. Wasserman, A. Y. Lewin, and L. H. Bleiweis (eds.), Women in Academia: Evolving Policies Toward Equal Opportunities. New York: Praeger, 1975, 37-44.

Project on the Status and Education of Women. Minority Women and Higher Education, No. 1. Washington D. C.: Association of American Colleges, 1974, November.

_____. Minority Women and Higher Education, No. 2. Washington D. C.: Association of American Colleges, 1975, March.

Raphael, E. E. Working Women and Their Membership in Labor Unions. Monthly Labor Review, 1974, May, 27-33.

Raymer, E. Race and Sex Identification in Preschool Children. Los Angeles: UCLA Center for Headstart Evaluation and Research, 1969. Also available from ERIC (ED041634), 1969.

Reich, M. The Economics of Racism. In L. Reynolds and M. Masters (eds.), Labor Economics and Labor Relations. Englewood Cliffs, NJ: Prentice-Hall, 1974.

Rowe, M. P. The Saturn's Rings Phenomenon: Microinequities and Unequal Opportunity for Women in the American Economy. Cambridge: Massachusetts Institute of Technology, 1975.

Russell, V. Racism and Sexism--A Collective Struggle--A Minority Woman's Point of View. United Church of Christ, Task Force on Women and Society, 1973. Reprint from KNOW, Inc., P.O. Box 86031, Pittsburgh, PA 15221, 1973.

Sargent, A. G. (ed.), Minority Women's Issues. In Beyond Sex Roles. St. Paul, MN: West, 1977, 256-258.

Schafer, C. L. Meeting Programs for Minorities. Sales Meeting Magazine, 1974, March, 23(3), 60-61+.

Schetlin, E. M. Sexism, Racism and the Crucial K-12 Years. Journal of the National Association for Women Deans, Administrators and Counselors, 1977, Spring, 40(3), 102-103.

Schiller, B. Class Discrimination Versus Racial Discrimination. Review of Economics and Statistics, 1971, August, 53, 263-269.

Schomburg, T. E. A Correlative Study of Body Concept, Academic Achievement, Level of Aspiration, Race and Sex. Unpublished doctoral dissertation, American University. Dissertation Abstracts International, 1975, June, 35(12-A, Pt. 1), 7662.

Schuman, H. Sociological Racism. Transaction, 1969, 7(2), 44-49.

Sedlacek, W. E., and Brooks, G. C., Jr. Racism in American Education: A Model for Change. Chicago: Nelson-Hall, 1977.

_____, _____, Christensen, K., Harway, M., and Merritt, M. S. Racism and Sexism: A Comparison and Contrast. Journal of the National Association for Women Deans, Administrators, and Counselors, 1976, Spring, 39(3), 120-127.

Sells, L. W. The Mathematics Filter and the Education of Women and Minorities. Paper presented at the American Association for the Advancement of Science meeting, Boston, February 1976.

Siiter, R., and Unger, R. K. Ethnic Differences in Sex-Role Stereotyping. Symposium presentation at the American Psychological Association Convention, Chicago, 1975.

Smith, M. A. (ed.). Minorities and the Health Professions: An Annotated Bibliography. Washington, D. C.: Association of American Medical Colleges, 1972.

Snyder, W. D. A Life History Approach to the Study of Social Mobility in Minority Females in Job Corps. Unpublished doctoral dissertation, University of Oregon, 1973. Dissertation Abstracts International, 1973, 34(9-A), 6128. Also available from ERIC (ADG74-06899), 1973.

Sorkin, A. L. Occupational Status and Unemployment of Nonwhite Women. Social Forces, 1971, March, 49(3).

Swartz, J. M., and Abramowitz, S. I. Effects of Psychiatrist Values and Patient Race and Sex on Clinical Judgment. Paper presented at the American Psychological Association Convention, New Orleans, 1974.

Szymanski, A. Race, Sex, and the United States Working Class. Social Problems, 1974, 21(5), 706-725.

_____. Racism and Sexism as Functional Substitutes in the Labor Market. Sociological Quarterly, 1976, Winter, 17(1), 65-73.

Takooshian, H. Ethnicity and Feminism. Symposium presentation at the American Psychological Association Convention, San Francisco, 1977.

Taylor, D. A. Recruitment and Training of Ethnic Minorities in Psychology. Personality and Social Psychology Bulletin, 1976, Spring, 2(2), 142-147.

Terry, R. The White Male Club. Civil Rights Digest, 1974, 6(3), 36-42.

Thomas, K. A. A Racial Comparison of Developmental Change in Marital-Family Status Projections of Teen Aged Girls. Paper presented at the Texas Academy of Science meeting, March 1971.

Thompson, A. R. Comparative Occupational Position of White and Non-White Females in the United States. Unpublished doctoral dissertation, University of Texas, Austin, 1973. Dissertation Abstracts International, 1973, 34(8-A), 4523. Also available from ERIC (ADG74-05338), 1973.

Thurow, L. The Economic Status of Minorities and Women. Civil Rights Digest, 1976, 8(2-3), 2-9.

Tsong, P. Z. Changing Patterns of Labor Force Participation Rates of Non-Whites in the South. Phylon, 1974, September, 35(3), 301-312.

Tulkin, S. Race, Class, Family and School Achievement. Journal of Personality and Social Psychology, 1968, 9, 31-37.

Turner, M. B. Women and Work. Los Angeles: Institute of Industrial Relations, University of California, 1964.

Vail, A. F. Dropout From Psychotherapy as Related to Patient-Therapist Discrepancies, Therapist Characteristics and Interaction in Race and Sex. Unpublished doctoral dissertation. Dissertation Abstracts International, 1974, November, 35(5-B), 2452.

Valley, J. A. The Influence of Race and Sex Upon a Counseling Interview Designed to Increase Need for Achievement in Upward Bound Students. Unpublished doctoral dissertation. Dissertation Abstracts International, 1976, May, 36(11-B), 5774-5775.

Vance, J. J., and Richmond, B. O. Cooperative and Competitive Behavior as a Function of Self-Esteem. Psychology in the Schools, 1975, April, 12, 225-229.

Vetter, B. M. Women and Minority Scientists. Science, 1975, September, 189, 751.

Waldman, E., and McEaddy, B. J. Where Women Work--An Analysis by Industry and Occupation. Monthly Labor Review, 1974, May, 3-13.

Walster, E., Cleary, T. A., and Clifford, M. M. The Effects of Race and Sex on College Admissions. Sociology of Education, 1971, 44, 237-244.

Welch, F. Education and Racial Discrimination. In O. Ashenfelter, and A. Rees (eds.), Discrimination in Labor Markets. Princeton, NJ: Princeton University Press, 1973.

Wise, H. D. (ed.). Special Feature on Equality: Racism, Sexism, Social Classism. Today's Education, 1974, March/April, 75-82.

Women and Minority Engineering Students. Report by the Engineering Manpower Commission of the Engineers' Joint Council, New York, 1974.

Women's Bureau, U. S. Department of Labor. Women Workers in Regional Areas and in Large States and Metropolitan Areas, 1971. Washington, D. C.: U. S. Gov. Printing Office, 1971.

_____. Facts on Women Workers of Minority Races. Washington, D. C.: U. S. Gov. Printing Office, 1972.

_____. Facts on Women Workers of Minority Races. Washington, D. C. : U. S. Gov. Printing Office, 1975, May (revised).

Women's Sports. San Mateo, CA: Women's Sports Publishing, Vol. 1 published 1974. Continuing monthly publication covering women in sports.

Wylie, R. C., and Hutchins, E. B. Schoolwork Ability Estimates and Aspirations as a Function of Socioeconomic Level, Race, and Sex. Psychological Reports, 1967, Monographic Supplement 3-V21.

Yawkey, T. D., and Jantz, R. K. Differential Effects of Intelligence, Race, SES, and Sex Variables on Arithmetic Achievement Test Performance. Journal of Instructional Psychology, 1974, Spring, 1(2), 2-10.

B. BLACK WOMEN

1. SOCIETAL FORCES

Abicht, M. Black Children and Their Environment. College Student Journal, 1976, Summer, 10(2), 142-152.

Adkins, D. C. Cross-Cultural Comparisons of the Motivation of Young Children to Achieve in School. Washington, D. C. : Office of Education, 1971. Also available from ERIC (ED060053), 1972.

_____, Payne, F. E., and Ballif, B. L. Motivation Factor Scores and Response Set Scores for 10 Ethnic-Cultural Groups of Preschool Children. American Educational Research Journal, 1972, 9, 557-572.

Alibaruho, G. L. The Attempt to Restructure Female Roles in the Afro-American Community. Humboldt Journal of Social Relations, 1975, Fall/Winter, 3(1), 44-47.

Almquist, E. M. Neither White nor Male: The Disadvantaged Position of Negro Women in the Labor Force. Paper presented at the Rocky Mountain Social Science Association meeting, Salt Lake City, 1972.

Amos, W. E. A Study of the Occupational Awareness of a Selected Group of Ninth Grade Students. Journal of Negro Education, 1960, 29, 500-503.

Anderson, M. H. Mostly Womenfolk and a Man or Two. Chicago: Third World Press, 1976.

The Arrogance of Social Science Research: Manipulating the Lives of Black Women and Their Infants. How Harvard Rules Women. Boston: New England Free Press, 1970.

Asbury, C. A. Sociological Factors Related to Discrepant Achievement of White and Black First Graders. Journal of Experimental Education, 1973, Fall, 42, 6-10.

_____. Maturity Factors Related to Discrepant Achievement of White and Black First Graders. Journal of Negro Education, 1975, Fall, 44(4), 493-501.

Ayella, M. E., and Williamson, J. B. The Social Mobility of Women: A Causal Model of Socioeconomic Success. Sociological Quarterly, 1976, Autumn, 17(4), 534-554.

Baehr, R. F. Need Achievement and Dialect in Lower-Class Adolescent Negroes. Proceedings of the 73rd Annual Convention of the American Psychological Association, 1965, 313-314.

Battle, E., and Rotter, J. Children's Feelings of Personal Control as Related to Social Class and Ethnic Group. Journal of Personality, 1963, 31, 482-490.

Baughman, E. E. Black Americans: A Psychological Analysis. New York: Academic Press, 1971.

_____, and Dahlstrom, W. G. Negro and White Children: A Psychological Study in the Rural South. New York: Academic Press, 1968.

Baumrind, D. An Exploratory Study of Socialization Effects on Black Children: Some Black-White Comparisons. Child Development, 1972, March, 43(1), 261-267.

Beal, F. Double Jeopardy: To Be Black and Female. New Generation, 1969, Fall, 51, 23-28. Also in T. Cade (ed.), The Black Woman. New York: New American Library, 1970, 90-101; and in R. Morgan (ed.), Sisterhood Is Powerful. New York: Random House, 1970, 340-353.

Bell, R. R. Lower Class Negro Mothers and Their Children. Integrated Education, 1965, December-January, 2(12), 23-27.

_____. The One Parent Mother in the Negro Lower Class. Paper presented to the Eastern Sociological Society meeting, April 1965.

_____. The Related Importance of Mother and Wife Roles Among Black Lower-Class Women. In R. Staples (ed.), The Black Family: Essays and Studies. Belmont, CA: Wadsworth, 1971.

Bennett, L., Jr. Negro Woman. Ebony, 1963, September, 18, 86-90+.

Bennett, W. S., and Gist, N. P. Class and Family Influences on Student Aspirations. Social Forces, 1964, 43, 167-173.

Berman, G. S., and Haug, M. R. Occupational and Educational Goals and Expectations: The Effects of Race and Sex. Social Problems, 1975, December, 23(2), 166-181.

Berman, Y. Occupational Aspirations of 545 Female High School Seniors. Journal of Vocational Behavior, 1972, April, 2(2), 173-177.

Bernard, J. Marriage and Family Among Negroes. Englewood Cliffs, NJ: Prentice-Hall, 1966.

Billingsley, A. Black Families in White America. Englewood Cliffs, NJ: Prentice-Hall, 1968.

_____. Family Functioning in the Low-Income Black Community. Social Casework, 1969, 50, 563-572.

_____. Black Families and White Social Science. Journal of Social Issues, 1970, Summer, 26(3), 127-142.

_____, and Billingsley, A. T. Negro Family Life in America. Social Service Review, 1965, September, 39, 310-319.

Bird, C. The Black Parallel. In Born Female. New York: Pocket Books, 1969, 110-125.

Black, M. T. The Effect of Race, Sex and Income on the Academic Performance and Aspirations of Black and White Freshmen Students. Unpublished doctoral dissertation, University of Michigan. Dissertation Abstracts International, 1975, April, 35(10-A), 6474.

The Black Woman. Special issue. The Black Scholar, 1971, December, 3.

The Black Woman. Special issue. Ebony, 1977, August, 32(10).

Black Women. Special issue. Journal of Social and Behavioral Sciences, 1975, Winter, 21(1).

Black Women's Liberation. Special issue. The Black Scholar, 1973, April, 3.

Blakey, W. A. Everybody Makes the Revolution--A Black Male View of Racism and Sexism. Civil Rights Digest, 1974, Spring, 6(3), 11-19. Reprint from KNOW, Inc., P. O. Box 86031, Pittsburgh, PA 15221.

Bond, H. M. Black American Scholars: A Study of Their Beginnings. Detroit: Balamp, 1972.

Bond, J. The Media Image of Black Women. Freedomways: A Quarterly Review of the Freedom Movement, 1975, 15, 34-37.

Bonner, F. B. Black Women and White Women: A Comparative Analysis of Perceptions of Sex Roles for Self, Ideal-Self, and the Ideal-Male. In W. D. Johnson and T. L. Green (eds.), Perspectives on Afro-American Women. Washington, D. C.: ECCA Publications, 1975.

Borth, A. M. Sex Differences in Coping and Defending in Two School Contexts. Paper presented at the American Psychological Association Convention, Chicago, 1975. Also available from ERIC (ED115528), 1976.

Brandes, P. D. The Effect of Role Playing by the Culturally Disadvantaged on Attitudes Toward Bidialectalism. Final report. Washington, D. C.: National Center for Educational Research and Development, 1971. Also available from ERIC (ED060001), 1972.

Bridgeman, B., and Burbach, H. J. Effects of Race of Successful Peer Models on Academic Expectations and Performance of Black and White Students. Paper presented at the American Educational Research Association meeting, Chicago, 1974, Also available from ERIC (ED090468), 1974.

Brief, A. P. Male-Female Differences in Occupational Attitudes within Minority Groups. Journal of Vocational Behavior, 1975, 6, 305-314.

Bright, M. V. Factors Related to the Traditionality or Innovativeness of Career Choices in Black College Women. Unpublished master's thesis, Howard University, 1970.

Brook, J., Whiteman, M., Peisach, E., and Deutsch, M. Aspiration Levels of and for Children: Age, Sex, Race, and Socioeconomic Correlates. Journal of Genetic Psychology, 1974, 124, 3-16.

Buck, M. R., and Austrin, H. R. Factors Related to School Achievement in an Economically Disadvantaged Group. Child Development, 1971, 42, 1813-1826.

Bullough, B. L. Alienation in the Ghetto. American Journal of Sociology, 1967, March, 72(5), 469-478.

Bureau of the Census. Black Women. In A Statistical Portrait of Women in the U. S. Washington, D. C.: U. S. Department of Commerce, 1976, 60-75.

_____. A Statistical Portrait of Women in the U. S. Washington, D. C.: U. S. Department of Commerce, 1976.

Butler, J. A., Jr. Athletic Behavior and Achievement Orientations of Female Adolescents: A Black-White Comparative Analysis. Unpublished master's thesis, Texas A & M University, 1976. Also available from ERIC (ED127106), 1976.

Cade, T. (ed.). The Black Woman. New York: New American Library, 1970.

_____. On the Issue of Roles. In The Black Woman. New York: New American Library, 1970, 101-110.

Cagle, L. T., and Beker, J. Social Characteristics and Educational Aspirations of Northern, Lower-Class, Predominantly Negro Parents Who Accepted and Declined a School Integration Opportunity. Journal of Negro Education, 1968, Fall, 37, 406-417.

Canavan, D. Field Dependence in Children as a Function of Grade, Sex, and Ethnic Group Membership. Paper presented at the American Psychological Association Convention, Washington, D. C., 1969.

Cantor, G. N. Sex and Race Effects in the Conformity Behavior of Upper-Elementary School-Aged Children. Developmental Psychology, 1975, 11(5), 661-662.

Careers for Negro Students. School and Society, 1965, October 16, 93, 364.

Carpenter, V. F. Motivational Components of Achievement in Culturally Disadvantaged Negro Children. Unpublished doctoral dissertation, Washington University. Dissertation Abstracts, 1968, 28(10-A), 3991-3992.

Carringer, D., and Wilson, C. S. Effects of Sex, Socioeconomic Class, Experimenter Race, and Kind of Verbal Reinforcement on the Performance of Black Children. Journal of Negro Education, 1974, Spring, 43, 212-220.

Carter, D. E., Little, C. A., and Barabasz, A. F. Comparative Study of Negro and White Attitudes Associated with Educational-Occupational Aspirations. Journal of Negro Education, 1972, Fall, 41(4), 361-364.

Chisholm, S. Racism and Anti-Feminism. Black Scholar, 1970, January-February, 1, 40-45.

_____. Sexism and Racism: One Battle to Fight. Personnel and Guidance Journal, 1972, October, 51(2), 123-125.

Cohen, M. B. You've Come a Long Way, Baby ... or Have You? Sexual Behavior, 1972, June, 2(6), 48-51.

Coleman, A. L. Occupational, Educational and Residence Plans of Negro High-School Seniors in Lexington and Fayette County,

Kentucky. Journal of Negro Education, 1960, Winter, 29(1), 73-79.

Comer, J. P. The Black Family: An Adaptive Perspective. New Haven, CT: Yale University, Child Study Center, 1970.

Cook, H., and Smothergill, D. Racial and Sex Determinants of Imitative Performance and Knowledge in Young Children. Journal of Educational Psychology, 1973, 65, 211-215.

Cottle, T. J. Black Children, White Dreams. New York: Dell, 1974.

Cowan, G. Achievement Motivation in Lower Class Negro Females as a Function of the Race and Sex of the Figure. Representative Research in Social Psychology, 1971, January, 2(1), 42-46.

Cramer, M. R., Bowerman, C. E., and Campbell, E. Q. Social Factors in Educational Achievement and Aspirations Among Negro Adolescents. Cooperative Research Project. Washington, D. C.: U. S. Office of Education, n. d.

Crawford, C. Status of Black Women. Ebony, 1975, March, 30, 26.

Cummings, S. Family Socialization and Fatalism Among Black Adolescents. Journal of Negro Education, 1977, Winter, 46, 62-75.

Curry, E. W. A Theoretical Model of Anticipatory Success: An Empirical Evaluation. Unpublished doctoral dissertation, Louisiana State University and Agricultural and Mechanical College, Baton Rouge, 1973. Also available from ERIC (ED087580), 1974.

Curtis, T., and Archibald, B. On Revering the Black Woman. Negro Digest, 1967, May, 76, 94-98.

Damico, S. B. Clique Membership and Its Relationship to Academic Achievement and Attitudes Toward School. Journal of Research and Development in Education, 1976, Summer, 9, 29-35.

Davis, A. Reflections on the Black Woman's Role in the Community of Slaves. Black Scholar, 1971, December, 3, 2-16.

———. The Myth of the Black Matriarch. In F. Klagsbrun (ed.), The First Ms. Reader. New York: Warner Books, 1973, 241-249.

Davis, J. A. Undergraduate Career Decisions: Correlates of Occupational Choice. Chicago: Aldine, 1965.

Davis, L. G. The Black Woman in American Society: A Selected Annotated Bibliography. Boston: G. K. Hall, 1975.

Deutsch, M. Minority Group and Class Status as Related to Social and Personality Factors in Scholastic Achievement. Monograph of the Society for Applied Anthropology, 1960, 2, 1-32.

Dixon-Altenor, C., and Altenor, A. Role of Occupational Status in the Career Aspirations of Black Women. Vocational Guidance Quarterly, 1977, March, 25, 211-215.

Dodd, J., and Randall, R. A Comparison of Negro Children's Drawings of a Man and a Woman. Journal of Negro Education, 1966, 35, 287-288.

Dodson, J. To Define Black Womanhood. Atlanta: Institute of the Black World, 1971.

Dole, A. A. Aspirations of Blacks and Whites for Their Children. Vocational Guidance Quarterly, 1973, 22(1), 24-31.

_____, and Passons, W. R. Life Goals and Plan Determinants Reported by Black and White High School Seniors. Journal of Vocational Behavior, 1972, July, 2(3), 209-222.

Educational and Occupational Goals of Men and Women at Black Colleges. Monthly Labor Review, 1976, June, 99, 10-16.

Eiszler, C. F., and Morrison, B. M. Task-Specific Self-Evaluation as a Measure of Achievement Motivation. Journal of Experimental Education, 1972, Spring, 40, 25-32.

Emphasis on Women. Special issue. Negro History Bulletin, 1976, May, 39, 583-604.

English, R. A. The Educational Aspirations of Black and White Youth. Unpublished doctoral dissertation, University of Michigan. Dissertation Abstracts International, June, 1971, 31(12-A), 6730.

Entwisle, D. R., and Greenberger, E. Adolescents' Views of Women's Work Role. American Journal of Orthopsychiatry, 1972, July, 42(4), 648-656. Also in J. Pottker and A. Fishel (eds.), Sex Bias in the Schools--the Research Evidence. Madison, NJ: Fairleigh Dickinson University Press, 1977, 207-216.

Epps, E. G. Family and Achievement: A Study of the Relation of Family Background to Achievement Orientation and Performance Among Urban Negro High School Students. Ann Arbor: University of Michigan, Institute for Social Research, 1969.

_____. Correlates of Academic Achievement Among Northern and Southern Urban Negro Students. Journal of Social Issues, 1969, Summer, 25(3), 55-70.

_____. Negro Academic Motivation and Performance: An Overview. Journal of Social Issues, 1969, Summer, 25(3), 5-11.

Erikson, E. Memorandum on Identity and Negro Youth. Journal of Social Issues, 1964, October, 20(4), 29-42.

Estes, M. F. A Bi-Racial Comparative Study of Expressed Role Preferences and Projected Life Plans of a Select Sample of Girls in Grades 9 and 12. Unpublished doctoral dissertation, Florida State University, 1971.

Feldman, J. M. Stimulus Characteristics and Subject Prejudice as Determinants of Stereotype Attribution. Journal of Personality and Social Psychology, 1972, 21(3), 333-340.

Fenelon, J. R., and Megargee, E. I. Influence of Race on the Manifestation of Leadership; Dominance in College Women. Journal of Applied Psychology, 1971, August, 55, 353-358.

Fichter, J. H. Career Preparation and Expectations of Negro College Seniors. Journal of Negro Education, 1966, Fall, 35(4), 322-335.

_____. Career Expectations of Negro Women Graduates. Monthly Labor Review, 1967, 90(11), 36-42. Also in A. Theodore (ed.), The Professional Woman. Cambridge, MA: Schenkman, 1971, 427-440.

_____. Marriage and Motherhood of Black Women Graduates. In N. Glazer-Malbin and H. Y. Waehrer (eds.), Woman in a Man-Made World. Chicago: Rand-McNally, 1972, 203-207.

Foster, J. A. Variations in Levels of Aspirations of Children Grouped by Class, Race, Sex and Grade Level. Unpublished doctoral dissertation, University of North Carolina, Greensboro. Dissertation Abstracts International, 1970, September, 31(3-B), 1517-1518.

Freeman, H. R., Schockett, M. R., and Freeman, E. B. Effects of Gender and Race on Sex-Role Preference of Fifth-Grade Children. Journal of Social Psychology, 1975, February, 95(1), 105-108.

Gaertner, S., and Bickman, L. Effects of Race on the Elicitation of Helping Behavior. Journal of Personality and Social Psychology, 1971, 20, 218-222.

Gaier, E. L., and Watts, W. A. Current Attitudes and Socialization Patterns of White and Negro Students Entering College. Journal of Negro Education, 1969, Fall, 38(4), 342-350.

Garner, M. E., and Silverstein, B. Childrearing Goals, Priorities, and Strategies: Assessing the World View of Low-Income Black Mothers. Unpublished manuscript, William Paterson College, Wayne, NJ, 1972.

Gist, N. P., and Bennett, W. S., Jr. Aspirations of Negro and White Students. Social Forces, 1963, 42(1), 40-48.

Gitter, A. G., Black, H., and Mostofsky, D. I. Race and Sex in Perception of Emotion. Journal of Social Issues, 1972, 28(4), 63-78.

Gold, A. R., and St. Ange, M. C. Development of Sex Role Stereotypes in Black and White Elementary School Girls. Developmental Psychology, 1974, May, 10(3), 461.

Gold, M. Achievement Motivation and the Child's Social Environment. Bethesda, MD: National Institute of Child Health and Human Development, 1976.

Gottlieb, D., and Heinsohn, A. L. Educational Goals of Black and White Youth in Segregated and Inter-Racial Schools. Final Report. Washington, D. C.: Office of Education, 1971. Also available from ERIC (ED057411), 1972.

Green, R. L., and Farquhar, W. W. Negro Academic Motivation and Scholastic Achievement. Journal of Educational Psychology, 1965, 56(5), 241-243.

Greenberg, J. W., and Davidson, H. H. Home Background and School Achievement of Black Urban Ghetto Children. American Journal of Orthopsychiatry, 1972, October, 42(5), 803-810.

_____, Gerver, J. M., Chall, J., and Davidson, H. H. Attitudes of Children from a Deprived Environment Toward Achievement-Related Concepts. Journal of Educational Research, 1965, 59(2), 57-62.

Grier, W. H., and Cobbs, P. M. Black Rage. New York: Basic Books, 1968.

Griggs, S. A. A Study of the Life Plans of Culturally Disadvantaged Negro Adolescent Girls with Father-Absence in the Home. Unpublished doctoral dissertation, Columbia University. Dissertation Abstracts, 1968, 28(12-A), 4950.

Gullahorn, J. E. Equality and Social Structure. In E. Donelson and J. E. Gullahorn (eds.), Women: A Psychological Perspective. New York: John Wiley, 1977, 266-281.

Gump, J. P. Comparative Analysis of Black Women's and White Women's Sex-Role Attitudes. Journal of Consulting and Clinical Psychology, 1975, 43, 858-863.

_____, and Rivers, W. The Consideration of Race in Efforts to End Sex Bias. In E. E. Diamond (ed.), Issues of Sex Bias and Sex Fairness in Career Interest Measurement. Washington,

D. C. : U. S. Department of Health, Education and Welfare, 1975, 123-139.

Gurin, P. Social Class Constraints on the Occupational Aspirations of Students Attending Some Predominantly Negro Colleges. Journal of Negro Education, 1966, Fall, 35(4), 336-350.

_____, and Epps, E. G. Black Consciousness, Identity, and Achievement. New York: John Wiley, 1975.

_____, and _____ (eds.). Aspirations. In Black Consciousness, Identity, and Achievement. New York: John Wiley, 1975, 39-67.

_____, and _____ (eds.). Individual Achievement: Summing Up. In Black Consciousness, Identity, and Achievement. New York: John Wiley, 1975, 181-188.

_____, and _____ (eds.). Precollege Family Background and Students' Aspirations, Motivation, and Performance. In Black Consciousness, Identity, and Achievement. New York: John Wiley, 1975, 103-141.

_____, and Gaylord, C. Educational and Occupational Goals of Men and Women at Black Colleges. Monthly Labor Review, 1976, June, 99(6), 10-16.

Hacker, H. M. Class and Race Differences in Gender Roles. In L. Duberman (ed.), Gender and Sex in Society. New York: Praeger, 1974, 134-183.

Hall, E. R. Motivation and Achievement in Negro and White Students. Final Report. Washington, D. C. : U. S. Department of Health Education and Welfare, 1971.

Halpern, S. The Relationship Between Ethnic Group Membership and Sex and Aspects of Vocational Choice of Pre-College Black and Puerto Rican High School Students. Unpublished doctoral dissertation. Dissertation Abstracts International, 1972, July, 33(1-A), 190-191.

Hare, N., and Hare, J. Black Women 1970. Transaction, 1970, November-December, 8, 65-68. Also in C. C. Perrucci and D. B. Targ (eds.), Marriage and the Family: A Critical Analysis and Proposals for Change. New York: David McKay, 1974, 98-107.

Harris, E. E. Personal and Parental Influences on College Attendance: Some Negro-White Differences. Journal of Negro Education, 1970, Fall, 39(4), 305-313.

Harris, M. B., and Ramsey, S. Stereotypes of Athletes. Perceptual and Motor Skills, 1974, October, 39(2), 705-706.

Harris, M. M. Personal Constructions of Sex-Typed Roles and Need Achievement Among Black and White Women. Unpublished doctoral dissertation, University of Pittsburgh. Dissertation Abstracts International, 1975, August, 36(2-B), 973-974.

Hernandez, E. Small Change for Black Women. Ms., 1974, August, 16-18.

Hernton, C. C. Sex and Racism in America. New York: Grove Press, 1965.

Hess, R., and Shipman, V. Early Experience and the Socialization of Cognitive Modes in Children. Child Development, 1965, 36, 869-885.

Hill, R. The Strengths of Black Families. New York: Emerson Hall, 1971.

Hobart, C. W. Underachievement Among Minority Group Students: An Analysis and a Proposal. Phylon, 1963, Summer, 24(2), 184-196.

Hobson, S. The Black Family: Together in Every Sense. Tuesday, 1971, April, 12-14+.

Hoffman, N. White Woman, Black Women: Inventing an Adequate Pedagogy. Women's Studies Newsletter, 1977, Winter/Spring, 5(1 and 2), 21-24.

Hyde, J. S., and Rosenberg, B. G. Black Women--And Women as a Minority Group. In The Psychology of Women: Half the Human Experience. Lexington, MA: D. C. Heath, 1976, 215-238.

Hyman, H. H., and Reed, J. S. 'Black Matriarchy' Reconsidered: Evidence from Secondary Analysis of Sample Surveys. Public Opinion Quarterly, 1969, 33(3), 346-354.

Inkeles, A. Social Structure and the Socialization of Competence. Harvard Educational Review, 1966, 36(3), 265-283. Also in Socialization and Schools. Cambridge, MA: President and Fellows of Harvard College, 1968, 50-68.

Iscoe, I., Williams, M., and Harvey, J. Age, Intelligence, and Sex as Variables in the Conformity Behavior of Negro and White Children. Child Development, 1964, 35, 451-460.

Jackson, J. J. Black Women in a Racist Society. In C. V. Willis, B. M. Kramer, and B. S. Brown (eds.), Racism and Mental Health. Pittsburgh: University of Pittsburgh Press, 1973.

_____. A Partial Bibliography on or Related to Black Women. Journal of Social and Behavioral Sciences, 1975, 21(1), 90-135.

Jackson, R. H. Aspirations of Lower Class Black Mothers. Journal of Comparative Family Studies, 1975, 6(2), 171-181.

Jones, R. L. (ed.). Black Psychology. New York: Harper & Row, 1972.

Jones, R. S. Proving Blacks Inferior: The Sociology of Knowledge. In J. A. Ladner (ed.), The Death of White Sociology. New York: Random House, 1973, 114-135.

Jordan, J. Second Thoughts of a Black Feminist. Ms., 1977, February, 5, 113-115.

Kamii, C. K. Socioeconomic Class Differences in the Preschool Socialization Practices of Negro Mothers. Unpublished doctoral dissertation, University of Michigan. Dissertation Abstracts, 1966, 26, 7157.

_____, and Radin, N. L. Class Differences in the Socialization Practices of Negro Mothers. Journal of Marriage and the Family, 1967, 29, 302-310.

Kandel, D. B. Race, Maternal Authority, and Adolescent Aspiration. American Journal of Sociology, 1971, 76(6), 999-1020.

Katz, I. The Socialization of Academic Motivation in Minority Group Children. Nebraska Symposium on Motivation, 1967, 15, 133-191.

Kelly, P. K., and Wingrove, C. R. Educational and Occupational Choices of Black and White, Male and Female Students in a Rural Georgia Community. Journal of Research and Development in Education, 1975, Fall, 9(1), 45-56.

Kim, K. H. The Social Context of Occupational and Educational Mobility Aspirations of Negro Adolescents. Unpublished doctoral dissertation, University of Maryland. Dissertation Abstracts, 1969, 29(12-A), 4564-4565.

King, H. The Black Woman and Women's Lib. Ebony, 1971, March, 26, 68-76.

King, K. Adolescent Perception of Power Structure in the Negro Family. Journal of Marriage and the Family, 1969, November, 31(4), 751-755.

_____, Abernathy, T. J., and Chapman, A. H. Black Adolescents' Views of Maternal Employment as a Threat to the Marital Relationship: 1963-1973. Journal of Marriage and the Family, 1976, November, 38(4), 733-737.

King, M. The Politics of Sexual Stereotypes. Black Scholar, 1973, 4, 4-12.

Kirchner, E. P., and Vondracek, S. I. What Do You Want to Be When You Grow Up? Vocational Choice in Children Aged Three to Six. Paper presented at the Society for Research in Child Development meeting, Philadelphia, 1973. Also available from ERIC (ED0762444), 1973.

Knebel, F. Identity, the Black Woman's Burden. Look, 1969, September 23, 33, 77-79.

Kovar, L. C. Faces of the Adolescent Girl. Englewood Cliffs, NJ: Prentice-Hall, 1968.

Kuvlesky, W. P., and Lever, M. Occupational Goals, Expectations, and Anticipatory Goal Deflection Experienced by Negro Girls Residing in Low-Income Rural and Urban Places. Proceedings of the Southwestern Sociological Association Meeting, 1967, March 18, 76-79.

_____, and Thomas, K. A. Social Ambitions of Negro Boys and Girls from a Metropolitan Ghetto. Journal of Vocational Behavior, 1971, April, 1(2), 177-187.

Ladner, J. A. Tomorrow's Tomorrow: The Black Woman. New York: Doubleday, 1972.

Langford, E. P. The Sex Role of the Female as Perceived by Anglo and Negro Children. Unpublished doctoral dissertation, East Texas State University. Dissertation Abstracts International, 1970, 30(7-A), 2803.

LaRue, L. J. M. Black Liberation and Women's Liberation. Transaction, 1970, November/December, 8($\frac{1}{2}$), 59-64.

_____. The Black Movement and Women's Liberation. Black Scholar, 1970, May, 1, 36-42. Also in S. Cox (ed.), Female Psychology: The Emerging Self. Chicago: Science Research Associates, 1976, 216-225.

Lerner, G. (ed.). Black Women in White America: A Documentary History. New York: Pantheon Books, 1972.

_____. Black Liberation--Women's Liberation: A Study in Ambivalence and Tension. Paper presented at the American Council on Education meeting, October 1972.

Lewis, H. The Changing Negro Family. In E. Ginzberg (ed.), The Nation's Children, Volume 1. New York: Columbia University Press, 1960, 103-137.

_____. Culture, Class, and Family Life Among Low-Income Urban Negroes. In A. Ross and H. Hill (eds.), Employment, Race, and Poverty. New York: Harcourt, Brace and World, 1967.

Lindsey, K. The Black Woman as a Woman. In T. Cade (ed.), The Black Woman. New York: New American Library, 1970, 85-89.

Long Thrust Toward Economic Equality; Negro Women Fastest Advancing Group. Ebony, 1966, August, 21, 38-40+.

Lystad, M. H. Family Patterns, Achievements, and Aspirations of Urban Negroes. Sociology and Social Research, 1961, April, 45(3), 281-288.

McBroom, P. The Black Matriarchy: Healthy or Pathological? Science News, 1968, October 19, 94, 394.

McDonald, R. L., and Gynther, M. D. Relationship of Self and Ideal-Self Descriptions with Sex, Race, and Class in Southern Adolescents. Journal of Personality and Social Psychology, 1965, 1, 85-88.

Mack, D. E. Where the Black-Matriarchy Theorists Went Wrong. Psychology Today, 1971, January, 4, 24+.

Mackie, J. B., Maxwell, A. D., and Rafferty, F. T. Psychological Development of Culturally Disadvantaged Negro Kindergarten Children: A Study of the Selective Influence of Family and School Variables. Paper presented at the American Orthopsychiatric Association meeting, Washington, D. C., 1967.

Madsen, M. Sub-Cultural Determinants of Cooperative and Competitive Behavior. Washington, D. C.: Office of Economic Opportunity, 1967. Also available from ERIC (ED057891), 1972.

Medley, M. L. Social Class, Family Structure, Academic Performance, Perceived Maternal Encouragement, and Academic Self-Concept as Determinants of College Plans Among Black, High School Seniors. Unpublished doctoral dissertation, Purdue University. Dissertation Abstracts International, 1975, August, 36(2-A), 1117.

Meissner, J. A., and Apthorp, H. Nonegocentrism and Communication Mode Switching in Black Preschool Children. Developmental Psychology, 1976, May, 12(3), 245-249.

Merbaum, A. D. Need for Achievement in Negro and White Children. Unpublished doctoral dissertation, University of North Carolina. Dissertation Abstracts, 1962, 23(2), 693-694.

Middleton, R., and Putney, S. Dominance in Decisions in the Family: Race and Class Differences. American Journal of Sociology, 1960, May, 65(6), 605-609.

Miller, E. W. The Negro in America: A Bibliography. Cambridge, MA: Harvard University Press, 1966.

Milne, C., Seefeldt, V., and Reuschlein, P. Relationship Between Grade, Sex, Race, and Motor Performance in Young Children. Research Quarterly, 1976, December, 47(4), 726-730.

Minigione, A. D. Need for Achievement in Negro and White Children. Journal of Consulting Psychology, 1965, 29(2), 108-111.

Moerk, E. L. Age and Epogenic Influences on Aspirations of Minority and Majority Group Children. Journal of Counseling Psychology, 1974, July, 21, 294-298.

Morrison, T. What the Black Woman Thinks About Women's Lib. New York Times Magazine, 1971, August 22, 14-15+. Discussion, 1971, September 5, 26.

Mulvihill, F. X. Sex Matriarchy and Academic Achievement of Black Students. Unpublished doctoral dissertation, Michigan State University. Dissertation Abstracts International, 1974, December, 35(6-A), 3916.

Murray, P. The Liberation of Black Women. In M. L. Thompson (ed.), Voices of the New Feminism. Boston: Beacon Press, 1970, 87-102. Also in J. Freeman (ed.), Women: A Feminist Perspective. Palo Alto: Mayfield Publishing Co., 1975, 351-363.

_____. The Negro Woman's Stake in the Equal Rights Amendment. Civil Liberties Law Review, 1972, March, 6(2), 253-259.

Musgrove, W. J. Follow-Up Study of Low Socio-Economic Negro and White Children on Scholastic Achievement. Journal of Negro Education, 1972, Winter, 41(1), 62-64.

Myers, L. W. Mothers from Families of Orientation as Role Models for Black Women. Northwest Journal of Africa and Black America Studies, 1973, Fall, 2, 7-9.

_____. A Study of the Self-Esteem Maintenance Process Among Black Women. Unpublished doctoral dissertation, Michigan State University. Dissertation Abstracts International, 1973, 34(3-A), 1375.

_____. Black Women and Self-Esteem. In M. Millman and R. M. Kanter (eds.), Another Voice: Feminist Perspectives on Social Life and Social Science. New York: Doubleday, 1975, 240-250.

National Black Feminist Organization. Statement of Purpose. In E. Lasky (ed.), Humanness: An Exploration into the Mythologies About Women and Men. New York: MSS Information Corporation, 1975, 410-414.

Negro Woman; Symposium with Introduction by J. H. Johnson. Ebony, 1966, August, 21, 25+.

Nelson, R. C. Interests of Disadvantaged and Advantaged Negro and White First Graders. Journal of Negro Education, 1968, 37, 168-173.

Noble, J. L. The American Negro Woman. In J. P. Davis (ed.), The American Negro Reference Book. Englewood Cliffs, NJ: Prentice-Hall, 1966, 522-547.

Nobles, W. W. Africanity: Its Role in Black Families. Black Scholar, 1974, June, 5(9), 10-17.

Norton, E. H. For Sadie and Maude. In R. Morgan (ed.), Sisterhood Is Powerful. New York: Random House, 1970, 353-360.

Nuttall, R. L. Some Correlates of High Need for Achievement Among Urban Northern Negroes. Journal of Abnormal and Social Psychology, 1964, 68(6), 593-600.

Oberle, W. H. Role Models of Black and White Rural Youth at Two Stages of Adolescence. Journal of Negro Education, 1974, Spring, 43, 234-244.

O'Leary, V. E. Black Women. In Toward Understanding Women. Monterey, CA: Brooks/Cole, 1977, 131-146.

_____, and Harrison, A. O. Sex Role Stereotypes as a Function of Race and Sex. Symposium presentation at the American Psychological Association Convention, Chicago, 1975.

Painter, D. H. Black Women in American Society. Current History, 1976, May, 70, 224-227+.

Pallone, N. J., Hurley, R. B., and Rickard, F. S. Further Data on Key Influences of Occupational Expectations Among Minority Youth. Journal of Counseling Psychology, 1973, 20, 484-486.

_____, Rickard, F. S., and Hurley, R. B. Key Influences of Occupational Preference Among Black Youth. Journal of Counseling Psychology, 1970, 17(6), 498-501.

Park, J. P. Black Nuns Relate to Black Power; National Black Sisters Conference. Christian Century, 1968, October 16, 85, 1320-1322.

Parker, S., and Kleiner, R. J. Characteristics of Negro Mothers in Single-Headed Households. Journal of Marriage and the Family, 1966, 28(4), 507-513.

Parsons, P. F. Research on Black Female Self-Concept: Origins, Issues, and Directions. Unpublished doctoral dissertation, Claremont Graduate School. Dissertation Abstracts International, 1975, February, 35(8-A), 5132.

Parsons, T., and Clark, K. (eds.). The Negro American. Boston: Beacon Press, 1966.

Picou, J. S. Black-White Variations in a Model of the Occupational Aspiration Process: Senior High School Students, Louisiana. Journal of Negro Education, 1973, Spring, 42, 117-122.

_____, and Curry, E. W. Structural, Interpersonal, and Behavioral Correlates of Female Adolescents' Occupational Choices. Adolescence, 1973, Fall, 8(31), 421-432.

Pierce, J. C., Avery, W. P., and Carey, A., Jr. Sex Differences in Black Political Beliefs and Behavior. In M. Githens and J. L. Prestage (eds.), A Portrait of Marginality. New York: David McKay, 1977, 66-74.

Powell, G. J. Self-Concept in White and Black Children. In C. Willie, B. Kramer, and B. Brown (eds.), Racism and Mental Health. Pittsburgh: University of Pittsburgh Press, 1973.

Presser, H. B. The Timing of the First Birth, Female Roles and Black Fertility. Milbank Memorial Fund Quarterly, 1971, July, 49(3, Pt. 1), 329-361.

Radin, N. Maternal Warmth, Achievement Motivation, and Cognitive Functioning in Lower-Class Preschool Children. Child Development, 1971, November, 42(5), 1560-1565.

Rainwater, L., and Yancey, W. J. The Moynihan Report and the Politics of Controversy. Cambridge, MA: M. I. T. Press, 1967.

Ramirez, M., and Price-Williams, D. R. Achievement Motivation in Children of Three Ethnic Groups in the United States. Journal of Cross-Cultural Psychology, 1976, March, 7(1), 49-60.

Reid, I. S. "Together" Black Women. New York: The Third Press, 1972.

Reid, W. M. Black Women's Struggle for Equality. New York: Pathfinder Press, 1976.

Rhoden, B. Fruitful Past but a Shaky Future. Ebony, 1977, August, 32(10), 60-62+.

Rhodes, B. The Changing Role of the Black Woman. In R. Staples (ed.), The Black Family. Belmont, CA: Wadsworth, 1971.

Richmond, B. O., Al-Rubaly, A., and Dalton, J. L. Guilt Among College Students as a Function of Race and Biological Sex. Journal of the National Association for Women Deans, Administrators, and Counselors, 1976, Spring, 39, 128-130.

_____, and Weiner, G. P. Cooperation and Competition Among

Young Children as a Function of Ethnic Grouping, Grade, Sex, and Reward Condition. Journal of Educational Psychology, 1973, June, 64, 329-334.

Richmond, D. M. Educational Horizons Among Lower Class Negro High School Students. Unpublished doctoral dissertation, University of Pittsburgh. Dissertation Abstracts International, 1969, 30(2-A), 835.

Rickman, G. A Natural Alliance: The New Role for Black Women. Civil Rights Digest, 1974, Spring, 6(3), 56-65.

Roberts, A., Mosley, K., and Chamberlain, M. W. Age Differences in Racial Self-Identity of Young Black Girls. Psychological Reports, 1975, December, 37(3, Pt. 2), 1263-1266.

Roberts, G. H. Relationship Between Self-Concept, Socioeconomic Status and Level of Academic Achievement of High School Students. Unpublished doctoral dissertation, University of Pittsburgh. Dissertation Abstracts International, 1975, March, 35(9-A), 5691-5692.

Robinson, P. Poor Black Women, and a Collective Statement. In B. Roszak and T. Roszak (eds.), Masculine/Feminine: Readings in Sexual Mythology and the Liberation of Women. New York: Harper & Row, 1969, 208-212.

_____, et al. Historical and Critical Essays for Black Women in the Cities. In T. Cade (ed.), The Black Woman. New York: New American Library, 1970, 198-210.

Rogers, C. Blacks and the Feminists. Christian Century, 1974, February 13, 91, 172-173.

Rooks, E. A Study of the Marriage Role Expectations of Black Adolescents. Adolescence, 1973, 8(31), 317-324.

Rychlak, J. F. Affective Assessment, Intelligence, Social Class, and Racial Learning Style. Journal of Personality and Social Psychology, 1975, 32, 989-995.

_____, Hewitt, C. W., and Hewitt, J. Affective Evaluations, Word Quality, and the Verbal Learning Styles of Black Versus White Junior College Females. Journal of Personality and Social Psychology, 1973, 27, 248-255.

Ryker, M. L., Rogers, E. C., and Beaujard, P. Six Selected Factors Influencing Educational Achievement of Children from Broken Homes. Education, 1971, February-March, 91(3), 200-211.

St. John, N. H. The Effect of Segregation on the Aspirations of Negro Youth. Harvard Educational Review, 1966, 36(3), 284-294.

Sampel, D. D., and Seymour, W. R. Prediction of Academic Success of Black Students: A Dilemma. Available from ERIC (ED040417), 1970.

_____, and _____. Academic Success of Black Students: A Dilemma. Journal of College Student Personnel, 1971, July, 12, 243-247.

Samuel, W., Soto, D., Parks, M., Ngissah, P., and Jones, B. Motivation, Race, Social Class, and IQ. Journal of Educational Psychology, 1976, June, 68(3), 273-285.

Scanzoni, J. The Black Family in Modern Society. Boston: Allyn and Bacon, 1971.

_____. Sex Roles, Economic Factors, and Marital Solidarity in Black and White Marriages. Journal of Marriage and the Family, 1975, February, 37(1), 130-144.

Schroth, M. L. Sex and Grade-Level Differences in Need Achievement Among Black College Students. Perceptual and Motor Skills, 1976, August, 43(1), 135-140.

Schulz, D. Coming Up Black: Patterns of Ghetto Socialization. Englewood Cliffs, NJ: Prentice-Hall, 1969.

Schwartz, M. Northern United States Negro Matriarchy: Status Versus Authority. Phylon, 1961, Spring, 261, 18-24.

Sciara, F. J., and Jantz, R. K. Father Absence and Its Apparent Effect on the Reading Achievement of Black Children from Low Income Families. Journal of Negro Education, 1974, Spring, 43(2), 221-227.

Scott, P. A Critical Overview of Sex Roles Research on Black Families. Women's Studies Abstracts, 1976, 5(2), 1-9.

_____. Teaching About Black Sex Roles: The Literature Approach. Paper presented at the National Council on Family Relations meeting, New York, 1976.

Scott, R., and Kobes, D. A. The Influence of Family Size on Learning Readiness Patterns of Socioeconomically Disadvantaged Preschool Blacks. Journal of Clinical Psychology, 1975, January, 31(1), 85-88.

Sedlacek, W. E., Brooks, G. C., Jr., Christensen, K., Harway, M., and Merritt, M. S. Racism and Sexism: A Comparison and Contrast. Journal of the National Association for Women Deans, Administrators, and Counselors, 1976, Spring, 39(3), 120-127.

Shade, B. J. The Modal Personality of Urban Black Middle-Class

Elementary School Children. Journal of Psychology, 1976, 92, 267-275.

Shaffer, R. A. Interracial Neighborhood Mix and Aspirations: The Influence of Contact. Unpublished doctoral dissertation, University of Notre Dame. Dissertation Abstracts International, 1976, May, 36(11-A), 7863.

Shockley, A. A. Negro Women in Retrospect; Blueprint for the Future. Negro History Bulletin, 1966, December, 29, 55-56+.

Silverstein, B., and Krate, R. Children of the Dark Ghetto: A Developmental Psychology. New York: Praeger, 1975.

_____, and _____. Cognitive-Linguistic Development. In Children of the Dark Ghetto: A Developmental Psychology. New York: Praeger, 1975, 143-169.

_____, and _____. Early Socialization: Micro Views. In Children of the Dark Ghetto: A Developmental Psychology. New York: Praeger, 1975, 40-60.

_____, and _____. Identification and Identity. In Children of the Dark Ghetto: A Developmental Psychology. New York: Praeger, 1975, 61-88.

_____, and _____. Socialization and Its Discontents: A Macro View. In Children of the Dark Ghetto: A Developmental Psychology. New York: Praeger, 1975, 14-39.

Slaby, A. E., and Sealy, J. R. Black Liberation, Women's Liberation. American Journal of Psychiatry, 1973, February, 130(2), 196-200.

Slaughter, D. T. Maternal Antecedents of the Academic Achievement Behaviors of Afro-American Head Start Children. Educational Horizons, 1969, Fall, 48(1), 24-28.

_____. Becoming an Afro-American Woman. School Review, 1972, 80(2), 299-318.

Smith, E. J. Reference Group Perspectives and the Vocational Maturity of Lower Socioeconomic Black Youth. Journal of Vocational Behavior, 1976, June, 8(3), 321-336.

Smith, H. P., and Abramson, M. Racial and Family Experience Correlates of Mobility Aspirations. Journal of Negro Education, 1962, Spring, 31(2), 117-124.

Smith, L. E. Androgyny, Sex Stereotypes, and Attitudes Among Black Americans. Symposium presentation at the American Psychological Association Convention, San Francisco, 1977.

Smitherman, G. On the Socialization of Black Girls. In B. E.

Chmaj (ed.), American Woman and American Studies. Pittsburgh: KNOW, Inc., 1971, 249.

Sommerville, R. Contemporary Family Materials--Black Family Patterns. Family Coordinator, 1970, July, 19, 279-286.

Sprey, J. Sex Differences in Occupational Choice Patterns Among Negro Adolescents. Social Problems, 1962, Summer, 10(1), 11-22.

Stabler, J. R., Johnson, E. E., and Jordan, S. E. The Measurement of Children's Self-Concepts as Related to Racial Membership. Child Development, 1971, 42, 2094-2097.

Stack, C. B. Sex Roles and Survival Strategies in an Urban Black Community. In M. Z. Rosaldo and L. Lamphere (eds.), Woman, Culture, and Society. Stanford: Stanford University Press, 1974, 113-128.

Stanfiel, J. D. Education and Income of Parents at Predominantly Black Colleges. Journal of Negro Education, 1972, Spring, 41(2), 170-176.

_____. Socioeconomic Status as Related to Aptitude, Attrition, and Achievement of College Students. Sociology of Education, 1973, Fall, 46, 480-488.

Staples, R. The Myth of the Black Matriarchy. Black Scholar, 1970, January-February, 1, 9-16.

_____. Towards a Sociology of the Black Family: A Decade of Theory and Research. Journal of Marriage and the Family, 1971, February, 33, 19-38.

_____ (ed.). The Black Family: Essays and Studies. Belmont, CA: Wadsworth, 1971.

_____. Some Comments on Black Women and Women's Liberation. Black Scholar, 1971, June, 1, 53-54.

_____. The Matricentric Family: A Cross-Cultural Examination. Journal of Marriage and the Family, 1972, February, 34, 156-165.

_____. The Black Woman's Burden: Racism and Sexism. Zena, 1972.

_____. The Black Woman in America: Sex, Marriage and the Family. Chicago: Nelson-Hall, 1973.

Steinmann, A., Crovitz, E., and Alshan, L. M. Black/White, Female/Male Undergraduates' Family-Role Attitudes, 1964-1965 - 1974-1975. Paper presented at the American Psychological Association Convention, Washington, D. C., 1976.

572 / Minority Women

_____, _____, and _____. A Decade Later: Black-White Attitudes Toward Women's Familial Roles. Symposium presentation at the American Psychological Association Convention, Washington, D.C., 1976.

_____, and Fox, D.J. Male-Female Perceptions of the Female Role in the United States. Journal of Psychology, 1966, 64(2), 265-276.

_____, and _____. Attitudes Toward Women's Family Role Among Black and White Undergraduates. Family Coordinator, 1970, October, 19(4), 363. Also in E. Lasky (ed.), Humanness: An Exploration into the Mythologies About Women and Men. New York: MSS Information Corporation, 1975, 415-420.

Sterling, D.H. The Experience of Being-Me for Black Adolescent Females: A Phenomenological Investigation of Black Identity. Unpublished doctoral dissertation, University of Pittsburgh. Dissertation Abstracts International, 1975, February, 35(8-A), 5039-5040.

Stokes, G. Black Woman to Black Man. Liberator, 1968, December, 8, 17.

Stresses and Strains on Black Women. Ebony, 1974, June, 29, 33-36.

Strickland, B.R. Aspiration Responses Among Negro and White Adolescents. Journal of Personality and Social Psychology, 1971, September, 19(3), 315-320.

Tanner, N. Matrifocality in Indonesia and Africa and Among Black Americans. In M.Z. Rosaldo and L. Lamphere (eds.), Women, Culture, and Society. Stanford, CA: Stanford University Press, 1974, 129-156.

Tatham, C.B., and Tatham, E.L. Academic Predictors for Black Students. Educational and Psychological Measurement, 1974, Summer, 34(2), 371-374.

Tatje, T.A. Mother-Daughter Dyadic Dominance in Black American Kinship. Dissertation Abstracts International, 1974, December, 35(6-A), 3202.

Teahan, J.E. Effect of Sex and Predominant Socioeconomic Class School Climate on Expectations of Success Among Black Students. Journal of Negro Education, 1974, Spring, 43, 245-255.

Teicher, J. Some Observations on Identity Problems in Children of Negro-White Marriages. Journal of Nervous and Mental Disease, 1968, 146(3), 249-265.

Tenhouten, W. The Black Family: Myth and Reality. Psychiatry, 1970, May, 145-173.

These Days Black Women Are Singing Strong. Vogue, 1969, May, 153, 169-173.

Thomas, C. L., and Stanley, J. C. Effectiveness of High School Grades for Predicting College Grades of Black Students: A Review and Discussion. Journal of Educational Measurement, 1969, 6(4), 203-215.

Thomas, K. A. Sex Differences in the Projections of Rural Negro and White Youth Toward Marriage and Procreation. Paper presented at the Southwestern Sociological Association meeting, Dallas, 1971.

_____. Unrealistic Development of Frames of Aspirational Reference of Rural Negro and White Girls: A Refutation of Popular Theory. Washington, D. C. Cooperative State Research, 1971. Also available from ERIC (ED091090), 1974.

Tibbetts, S. L. Sex-Role Stereotyping in the Lower Grades: Part of the Solution. Journal of Vocational Behavior, 1975, April, 6(2), 255-261.

Triandis, H. C. (ed.). Variations in Black and White Perceptions of the Social Environment. Urbana: University of Illinois Press, 1976.

Turner, B. F. Socialization and Career Orientation Among Black and White College Women. Paper presented at the American Psychological Association Convention, Honolulu, 1972.

_____, and McCaffery, J. H. Socialization and Career Orientation Among Black and White College Women. Journal of Vocational Behavior, 1974, 5(3), 307-319.

_____, and Turner, C. B. The Political Implications of Social Stereotyping of Women and Men Among Black and White College Students. Sociology and Social Research, 1974, January, 58(2), 155-162.

_____, and _____. Evaluations of Women and Men Among Black and White College Students. Sociological Quarterly, 1974, Summer, 15(3), 442-456.

_____, and _____. Race and Sex Differences in Evaluating Women. Paper presented at the American Psychological Association Convention, New Orleans, 1974.

_____, and _____. Race, Sex, and Perception of the Occupational Opportunity Structure Among College Students. Sociological Quarterly, 1975, Summer, 16(3), 345-360.

Turner, C. B., and Turner, B. F. Perception of the Occupational Opportunity Structure, Socialization to Achievement and Career

Orientation as Related to Sex and Race. Proceedings of the Annual Convention of the American Psychological Association, 1971, 6(Pt. 1), 243-244.

Walker, A. In Search of Our Mothers' Gardens: The Creativity of Black Women in the South. Ms., 1974, May, 2, 64-70.

Walker, B. Black Feminism--One Woman's View. Redbook, 1976, March, 146, 31+.

Ward, S. H., and Braun, J. R. Self-Esteem and Racial Preference in Black Children. American Journal of Orthopsychiatry, 1972, 42(4), 644-647.

Ware, C. The Relationship of Black Women to the Women's Liberation Movement. In Woman Power: The Movement for Women's Liberation. New York: Tower, 1970, 70-99.

_____. The Black Family and Feminism: A Conversation with Eleanor Holmes Norton. Ms., 1972, Spring, 95+. Also in F. Klagsbrun (ed.), The First Ms. Reader. New York: Warner Books, 1973, 36-41.

_____. Black Feminism. In A. Koedt, E. Levine, and A. Rapone (eds.), Radical Feminism. New York: Quadrangle/The New York Times Book Co., 1973, 81-84.

Watkins, M., and David, J. To Be a Black Woman: Portraits in Fact and Fiction. New York: William Morrow, 1970.

Watley, D. J. Black and Nonblack Youth: Does Marriage Hinder College Attendance? Research Reports, National Merit Scholarship Corporation, 1971, 7(5).

Watson, V. Self-Concept Formation and the Afro-American Woman. Journal of Afro-American Issues, 1974, Summer, 2(3), 226-236.

Webster, S. W. Some Correlates of Reported Academically Supportive Behaviors of Negro Mothers Toward Their Children. Journal of Negro Education, 1965, Spring, 34(2), 114-120.

Wells, T. T. The Effects of Discrimination upon Motivation and Achievement of Black Children in Urban Ghetto Schools. American Behavioral Scientist, 1969, March, 12(4), 26-33.

Whitaker, S. V. Comparative Study of Self-Esteem Among Black, White, and Latino Women. Paper presented at the American Psychological Association Convention, San Francisco, 1977.

White, K. Belief in Reinforcement Control Among Southern Negro Adolescents: The Effects of School Desegregation, Socioeconomic Status, and Sex of Student. Journal of Social Psychology, 1971, 85, 149-150.

_____, and Knight, J. H. School Desegregation, Socioeconomic Status, Sex and the Aspirations of Southern Negro Adolescents. Journal of Negro Education, 1973, Winter, 42(1), 71-78.

Whiteman, M., Brown, B. R., and Deutsch, M. Some Effects of Social Class and Race on Children's Language and Intellectual Abilities. In M. Deutsch (ed.), The Disadvantaged Child. New York: Basic Books, 1967, 319-335.

Wilcox, P. Positive Mental Health in the Black Community. The Black Liberation Movement. In C. Willie, B. Kramer, and B. Brown (eds.), Racism and Mental Health. Pittsburgh: University of Pittsburgh Press, 1973.

Williams, M. Why Women's Liberation Is Important to Black Women, 1970. In W. Martin (ed.), The American Sisterhood. New York: Harper & Row, 1972, 171-178.

Williams, O. American Black Women in the Arts and Social Sciences: A Bibliographic Survey. Metuchen, NJ: Scarecrow Press, 1973.

Willie, C. V. (ed.). The Family Life of Black People. Columbus, OH: Charles E. Merrill Books, 1970.

Wilson, M. T., and Koeski, G. F. Sex Stereotyping in a Selected Sample of Black American Adolescents. Available from ERIC (ED079656), 1971.

Winkler, K. J. Black Women's Career Goals Found Lower than Men's. The Chronicle of Higher Education, 1977, May, 15(7), 12.

Wispe, L. G., and Freshley, H. B. Race, Sex and Sympathetic Helping Behavior: The Broken Bag Caper. Journal of Personality and Social Psychology, 1971, 17, 59-65.

Wylie, R. C. Children's Estimates of Their Schoolwork Ability as a Function of Sex, Race, and Socio-economic Level. Journal of Personality, 1963, 31(2), 203-224.

_____, and Hutchins, E. B. Schoolwork-Ability Estimates and Aspirations as a Function of Socioeconomic Level, Race, and Sex. Psychological Reports, 1967, 21(3), 781-808.

Wyne, M. D., White, K. P., and Coop, R. H. Antecedent Conditions of the Development of Self-Concept in Black Americans. In The Black Self. Englewood Cliffs, NJ: Prentice-Hall, 1974, 15-43.

_____, _____, and _____. The Black Self. Englewood Cliffs, NJ: Prentice-Hall, 1974.

576 / Minority Women

_____, _____, and _____. The Social Context of the Black Self. In The Black Self. Englewood Cliffs, NJ: Prentice-Hall, 1974, 63-82.

Young, V. H. Family and Childhood in a Southern Negro Community. American Anthropologist, 1970, 72, 269-288.

_____. A Black American Socialization Pattern. American Ethnologist, 1974, May, 1(2), 405-413.

Zito, R. J., and Bardon, J. I. Negro Adolescents' Success and Failure Imagery Concerning Work and School. Vocational Guidance Quarterly, 1968, March, 16(3), 181-184.

B. BLACK WOMEN (continued)

2. SOCIAL-PSYCHOLOGICAL FORCES

Argyle, F. The Self-Concept of Negro and White School Beginners. Paper presented at the American Educational Research Association meeting, Chicago, 1968.

Banks, J. A., and Grambs, J. Black Self-Concept: Implications for Education and the Social Sciences. New York: McGraw-Hill, 1972.

Beglis, J. F., and Sheikh, A. A. Development of the Self Concept in Black and White Children. Journal of Negro Education, 1974, Winter, 43(1), 104-110.

Berg, P. A., and Hyde, J. S. Gender and Race Differences in Causal Attributions in Achievement Situations. Paper presented at the American Psychological Association Convention, Washington, D. C., 1976.

Bridgette, R. E. Self Esteem in Negro and White Southern Adolescents. Unpublished doctoral dissertation, University of North Carolina, Chapel Hill. Dissertation Abstracts International, 1970, 31(B), 2977.

Cameron, H. K. Nonintellectual Correlates of Academic Achievement. Journal of Negro Education, 1968, Summer, 37(3), 252-257.

Caplin, M. D. The Relationship Between Self Concept and Academic Achievement and Between Level of Aspiration and Academic Achievement. Unpublished doctoral dissertation, Columbia University. Dissertation Abstracts, 1966, 27(4-A), 979-980.

_____. Section B: Self Concept, Level of Aspiration, and Academic Achievement. Journal of Negro Education, 1968, Fall, 37(4), 435-439.

_____. Relationship Between Self Concept and Academic Achievement. Journal of Experimental Education, 1969, Spring, 37(3), 13-16.

Coleman, J. S., Campbell, E. Q., Hobson, C. J., McPartland, J., Mood, A. M., Weinfeld, F. D., and York, R. L. The Locus of Control and Academic Performance Among Racial Groups. In S. S. Guterman (ed.), Black Psyche: The Modal Personality Patterns of Black Americans. Berkeley: Glendessary Press, 1972, 271-288.

Cooper, H. M., Baron, R. M., and Lowe, C. A. The Importance of Race and Social Class Information in the Formation of Expectancies About Academic Performance. Journal of Educational Psychology, 1975, April, 67(2), 312-319.

Crain, R. L., and Weisman, C. S. Discrimination, Personality, and Achievement: A Survey of Northern Blacks. New York: Seminar Press, 1972.

Davidson, H. H., and Greenberg, J. W. Traits of School Achievers from a Deprived Background. Unpublished manuscript, City College of New York, 1967. Also available from ERIC (ED 013849), 1968.

Davis, J. A. Undergraduate Career Decisions: Correlates of Occupational Choice. Chicago: Aldine, 1965.

Deutsch, M. Minority Group and Class Status as Related to Social and Personality Factors in Scholastic Achievement. Monograph of the Society for Applied Anthropology, 1960, 2, 1-32.

DiCeasare, A., Sedlacek, W. E., and Brooks, G. C., Jr. Non-Intellectual Correlates of Black Student Attrition. University of Maryland Counseling and Personnel Services Journal, 1971, 2, 1-16. Also edited version in Journal of College Student Personnel, 1972, 13(4), 319-324.

Dole, A. A., and Passons, W. R. Life Goals and Plan Determinants Reported by Black and White High School Seniors. Journal of Vocational Behavior, 1972, July, 2(3), 209-222.

Drabick, L. W. Investigation of the Relationships Between Migration Intent and Vocational and Educational Expectations of North Carolina Rural Youth. Available from ERIC (ED042540), 1971.

DuCette, J., and Wolk, S. Locus of Control and Levels of Aspiration in Black and White Children. Review of Educational Research, 1972, Fall, 42(4), 493-504.

Ellis, D. P., and Wiggins, J. W. Cooperation, Aggression and

Learning in a Bi-Racial Classroom (The Socialization of Academic Behavior Among Negro Junior High School Students). Final Report. Washington, D.C.: Office of Education, 1968. Also available from ERIC (ED026442), 1969.

Ellis, J.T. Academic Performance and Selected Psychosocial Factors of Black Male and Female Students in a Higher Education Program. Unpublished doctoral dissertation, Fordham University. Dissertation Abstracts International, 1975, January, 35 (7-A), 4247-4248.

Entwistle, D.R., and Webster, M. Expectations in Mixed Racial Groups. Sociology of Education, 1974, Summer, 47(3), 301-318.

Eppes, J.W. The Effect of Varying the Race of the Experimenter on the Level of Aspiration of Externally Controlled Inner City School Children. Unpublished doctoral dissertation. Dissertation Abstracts International, 1970, 31(2-B), August, 912.

Epps, E.G. Correlates of Academic Achievement Among Northern and Southern Urban Negro Students. Journal of Social Issues, 1969, 25(3), 55-70.

Esposito, R.P. The Relationship Between the Motive to Avoid Success and Vocational Choice by Race and Sex. Unpublished doctoral dissertation, Fordham University. Dissertation Abstracts International, 1975, September, 36(3-A), 1302.

Farley, F.H., and Sewell, T. Attribution and Achievement Motivation Differences Between Delinquent and Non-Delinquent Black Adolescents. Adolescence, 1975, Fall, 10, 391-397.

Felton, G.S., and Biggs, B.E. Teaching Internalization Behavior to Collegiate Low Achievers in Group Psychotherapy. Psychotherapy: Theory, Research and Practice, 1972, Fall, 9(3), 281-283.

_____, and _____. Psychotherapy and Responsibility: Teaching Internalization Behavior to Black Low Achievers Through Group Therapy. Small Group Behavior, 1973, May, 4(2), 147-155.

Fenelon, J.R., and Megargee, E.I. Influence of Race on the Manifestation of Leadership; Dominance in College Women. Journal of Applied Psychology, 1971, August, 55, 353-358.

Fleming, J. Approach and Avoidance Motivation in Interpersonal Competition: A Study of Black Male and Female College Students. Unpublished doctoral dissertation, Harvard University, 1974.

_____. Fear of Success in Black Women. Paper presented at the Eastern Psychological Association meeting, New York, April, 1976.

Flynn, T. M., et al. Traits Related to Achievement Motivation in Migrant Pre-School Children. Washington, D. C.: Office of Education, 1970. Also available from ERIC (ED049870), 1971.

_____. Traits Related to Achievement Motivation in Migrant Pre-School Children. Unpublished doctoral dissertation, Florida State University. Dissertation Abstracts International, 1971, July, 32(1-A), 236.

Friend, R. M., and Neale, J. M. Children's Perception of Success and Failure: An Attributional Analysis of the Effects of Race and Social Class. Developmental Psychology, 1972, 7, 124-128.

_____, and _____. Perceptions of Success and Failure by Disadvantaged Elementary School Children. Final Report. Washington, D. C.: National Center for Educational Research and Development, 1972. Also available from ERIC (ED075554), 1973.

Gaier, E. L., and Wambach, H. S. Self-Evaluation of Personality Assets and Liabilities of Southern White and Negro Students. Journal of Social Psychology, 1960, February, 51, 135-143.

Garrett, A. M., and Willoughby, R. H. Personal Orientation and Reactions to Success and Failure in Urban Black Children. Developmental Psychology, 1972, July, 7(1), 92.

Greenberger, E., Campbell, P., Sorensen, A. B., and O'Connor, J. Toward the Measurement of Psychosocial Maturity. Report. Baltimore: Johns Hopkins University, Center for Social Organization of Schools, 1971.

Gurin, P., Gurin, G., Lao, R. C., and Beattie, M. Internal-External Control in the Motivational Dynamics of Negro Youth. Journal of Social Issues, 1969, Summer, 25(3), 29-53.

Guttentag, M., and Klein, I. Relationship Between Inner Versus Outer Locus of Control and Achievement in Black Middle School Children. Educational and Psychological Measurement, 1967, Winter, 36, 1101-1109.

Hall, E. R., Joesting, J., and Woods, M. J. Relationships Among Measures of Locus of Control for Black and White Students. Psychological Reports, 1977, February, 40(1), 59-62.

Harrison, A. O. Locus of Control and Problem-Solving Abilities in Young Black Children. Revised version of paper presented at the Conference on Empirical Research in Black Psychology II. New York, 1975. Also available from ERIC (ED114446), 1976.

Hays, E. J. Environmental Press and Psychological Need as Related to Academic Success of Minority Group Students. Journal of Counseling Psychology, 1974, July, 21(4), 299-304.

Healey, G. W., and DeBlassie, R. R. A Comparison of Negro, Anglo, and Spanish-American Adolescents' Self Concepts. Adolescence, 1974, Spring, 9, 33, 15-24.

Henderson, E. H., and Long, B. H. Personal-Social Correlates of Academic Success Among Disadvantaged School Beginners. Journal of School Psychology, 1971, 9(2), 101-113.

Henderson, G. G. The Academic Self-Concept of Black Female Children Within Differential School Settings. Journal of Afro-American Issues, 1974, Summer, 2(3), 248-266.

Hobart, C. W. Underachievement Among Minority Group Students: An Analysis and a Proposal. Phylon, 1963, Summer, 24(2), 184-196.

Hohmuth, A. V., and Ramos, R. A. Locus of Control, Achievement, and Failure Among Disadvantaged College Students. Psychological Reports, 1973, 33, 573-574.

Holley, J. L. An Analysis of Personality Needs and Certain Background Factors Which May Influence Career Choice of Women Business Education Majors. Unpublished doctoral dissertation, University of Mississippi. Dissertation Abstracts International, 1970, July, 30(1-A), 223-224.

Jameson, A. S. An Analysis of Self-Esteem and Academic Achievement of Tri-Racial Isolate, Negro and Caucasian Elementary and Middle School Boys and Girls. Unpublished doctoral dissertation, University of Maryland. Dissertation Abstracts International, 1974, August, 35(2-A), 722.

Jensen, A. R. Personality and Scholastic Achievement in Three Ethnic Groups. British Journal of Educational Psychology, 1973, June, 43(2), 115-125.

Jones, R. L. (ed.). Black Psychology. New York: Harper & Row, 1972.

Jorgensen, C. C. The Socialization and Meaning of Sense of Internal Versus External Control Among Black High School Students. Unpublished doctoral dissertation, University of Michigan. Dissertation Abstracts International, 1972, 32(A), 4106.

———. Internal-External Control in the Academic Achievement of Black Youth: A Reappraisal. Integrated Education, 1976, November, 14(6), 84, 20-23.

Kardiner, A., and Ovesey, L. The Mark of Oppression: Explorations in the Personality of the American Negro. Cleveland: World, 1966.

Katz, I. A Critique of Personality Approaches to Negro Performance, with Research Suggestions. Journal of Social Issues, 1969, July, 25(3), 13-27.

_____. A Catalog of Personality Approaches to Negro Performance with Research Suggestions. Journal of Social Issues, 1969, 30, 13-28.

Kaul, T. J. Counselor Race and Power Base: Effects on Attitudes and Behavior. Journal of Counseling Psychology, 1977, 24(5), 430-436.

Kinder, D. R., and Reeder, L. G. Ethnic Differences in Beliefs About Control. Sociometry, 1975, 38(2), 261-272.

Larson, J. C., and Royster, E. C. Self-Concept Correlates of Achievement in Blacks and Whites. Paper presented at the American Psychological Association Convention, Washington, D. C., 1976.

Lawrence, W. W. The Relationship of Intelligence, Self Concept, Socio-Economic Status, Race and Sex to Level of Career Maturity of Twelfth-Grade Students. Unpublished doctoral dissertation, University of North Carolina, Chapel Hill. Dissertation Abstracts International, 1974, December, 35(6-A), 3426-3427.

_____, and Brown, D. An Investigation of Intelligence, Self-Concept, Socioeconomic Status, Race and Sex as Predictors of Career Maturity. Journal of Vocational Behavior, 1976, August, 9(1), 43-52.

Lessing, E. E. Racial Differences in Indices of Ego Functioning Relevant to Academic Achievement. Journal of Genetic Psychology, 1969, 115, 153-167.

Levy, N., et al. Personality Types Among Negro College Students. Educational and Psychological Measurement, 1972, August, 32(3), 641-653.

Littig, L. W. A Study of Certain Personality Correlates of Occupational Aspirations of Black and White College Women. Final Report. Washington, D. C.: Office of Education, 1971. Also available from ERIC (ED056242), 1972.

Logan, D. D. Sex X Race Differences in Fear of Success. Unpublished doctoral dissertation, University of California, Berkeley. Dissertation Abstracts International, 1974, December, 35(6-B), 3066.

Lourenso, S. V., Greenberg, J. W., and Davidson, H. H. Personality Characteristics Revealed in Drawings of Deprived Children Who Differ in School Achievement. Journal of Educational Research, 1965, 59(2), 63-67.

Love, B. B. Self-Esteem in Women Related to Occupational Status: A Biracial Study. Unpublished doctoral dissertation, Northwestern University. Dissertation Abstracts International, 1974, December, 35(6-A), 3427.

McClain, E. W. Personality Characteristics of Negro College Students in the South. Journal of Negro Education, 1967, Summer, 36(3), 320-325.

Malpass, R. S., and Symonds, J. D. Value Preferences Associated with Social Class, Sex, and Race. Journal of Cross-Cultural Psychology, 1974, September, 5(3), 282-300.

Marx, R. W., and Winne, P. H. Self-Concept and Achievement: Implications for Educational Programs. Integrated Education, 1975, January/February, 13(1), 30-31.

Medley, M. L. Social Class, Family Structure, Academic Performance, Perceived Maternal Encouragement, and Academic Self-Concept as Determinants of College Plans Among Black, High School Seniors. Dissertation Abstracts International, 1975, August, 36(2-A), 1117.

Mednick, M. T. S. Motivational and Personality Factors Related to Career Goals of Black College Women. Washington, D. C.: U. S. Department of Labor, Manpower Administration, 1973.

_____, and Puryear, G. R. Motivational and Personality Factors Related to Career Goals of Black College Women. Journal of Social and Behavioral Sciences, 1975, 21, 1-30.

_____, and _____. Race and Fear of Success in College Women: 1968 and 1971. Journal of Consulting and Clinical Psychology, 1976, October, 44(5), 787-789.

Milgram, N. A. Locus of Control in Negro and White Children at Four Age Levels. Psychological Reports, 1971, October, 29(2), 459-465.

Miller, D. M., and O'Connor, P. Achiever Personality and Academic Success Among Disadvantaged College Students. Journal of Social Issues, 1969, Summer, 25(3), 103-116.

Mitchell, D. C. Urban Community College Students' Beliefs in Internal-External Control. Unpublished doctoral dissertation, Case Western Reserve University. Dissertation Abstracts International, 1971, 32(1-A), 203.

Money, J. Small Change for Black Women. Ms., 1974, August, 3(2), 16-18.

Morris, J. Personal Adjustment of the High Achieving Negro Student. Unpublished doctoral dissertation, University of Michigan. Dissertation Abstracts International, 1969, 30(1-A), 173.

Murray, S. R., and Mednick, M. T. S. Perceiving the Causes of Success and Failure in Achievement: Sex, Race, and Motivational Comparisons. Journal of Consulting and Clinical Psychology, 1975, 43, 881-885.

_____, and _____. Black Women's Achievement Orientation: Motivational and Cognitive Factors. Psychology of Women Quarterly, 1977, Spring, 1(3), 247-259.

Musgrove, W. J. A Follow-Up Study of Black and White Kindergarten Children on Academic Achievement and Social Adjustment. Academic Therapy, 1971-72, Winter, 7, 123-129.

Myers, L. W. A Study of the Self-Esteem Maintenance Process Among Black Women. Unpublished doctoral dissertation, Michigan State University. Dissertation Abstracts International, 1973, 34(3-A), 1375.

_____. Black Women and Self-Esteem. In M. Millman and R. M. Kanter (eds.), Another Voice: Feminist Perspectives on Social Life and Social Science. New York: Doubleday, 1975, 240-250.

Okediji, P. A. The Occupational Aspirations of Black and White College Females and Their Personality Correlates. Unpublished masters' thesis, Howard University, 1971.

Pandey, R. E. Personality Characteristics of Successful, Dropout, and Probationary Black and White University Students. Journal of Counseling Psychology, 1972, September, 19, 382-386.

_____. A Comparative Study of Dropout at an Integrated University: The 16 Personality Factor Test. Journal of Negro Education, 1973, Fall, 42(4), 447-451.

Paretti, J. P. The Effects of Examiner Race and Sex Factors on Anxiety Among Black School Children in a Group Test-Taking Situation. Unpublished doctoral dissertation, Boston University. Dissertation Abstracts International, 1974, July, 35(1-A), 266.

Parsons, P. F. Research on Black Female Self-Concept: Origins, Issues, and Directions. Unpublished doctoral dissertation, Claremont Graduate School. Dissertation Abstracts International, 1975, February, 35(8-A), 5132.

Paschal, B. J. The Role of Self Concept in Achievement. Journal of Negro Education, 1968, Fall, 37(4), 392-396.

Powell, G. J. Self-Concept in White and Black Children. In C. Willie, B. Kramer, and B. Brown (eds.), Racism and Mental Health. Pittsburgh: University of Pittsburgh Press, 1973.

Puryear, G. R. Fear of Success in Black College Women as It Relates to Militancy and Affective Attachment. Unpublished master's thesis, Howard University, 1971.

_____, and Mednick, M. T. S. Black Militancy, Affective Attachment, and the Fear of Success in Black College Women. Journal of Consulting and Clinical Psychology, 1974, April, 42, 263-266. Also in E. Lasky (ed.), Humanness: An Exploration into the Mythologies About Women and Men. New York: MSS Information Corp., 1975, 406-409.

Rhine, W. R., and Spencer, L. M. Effects of Follow Through on School Fearfulness Among Black Children. Journal of Negro Education, 1975, Fall, 44(4), 446-453.

Roberts, G. H. Relationship Between Self-Concept, Socioeconomic Status and Level of Academic Achievement of High School Students. Dissertation Abstracts International, 1975, March, 35 (9-A), 5691-5692.

Rotter, J. B. External Control and Internal Control. Psychology Today, 1971, June, 5(1), 37-42+.

Royer, G. W. Relationship of Internal, Powerful Others, and Chance Locus of Control to Race, Socioeconomic Class, Sex and Perceived Teacher Behavior. Unpublished doctoral dissertation, Ohio State University. Dissertation Abstracts International, 1976, May, 36(11-A), 7309.

Rychlak, J. F. Affective Assessment, Intelligence, Social Class, and Racial Learning Style. Journal of Personality and Social Psychology, 1975, 32, 989-995.

Samuel, N., and Laird, D. S. Self Concepts of Two Groups of Black Female College Students. Journal of Negro Education, 1974, Spring, 43, 228-233.

Schroth, M. L. Sex and Grade-Level Differences in Need Achievement Among Black College Students. Perceptual and Motor Skills, 1976, August, 43(1), 135-140.

Scott, R., and Ford, J. A. An Assessment of the Differences Between High and Low Achieving Students. Final Report. Washington, D. C.: National Center for Educational Research and Development, 1972. Also available from ERIC (ED068890), 1973.

Sewell, T. E., and Severson, R. A. Learning Ability and Intelligence as Cognitive Predictors of Achievement in First-Grade Black Children. Journal of Educational Psychology, 1974, December, 66, 948-955.

Shade, B. J. The Modal Personality of Urban Black Middle-Class Elementary School Children. Journal of Psychology, 1976, 92, 267-275.

Shaw, M. E. The Self-Image of Black and White Pupils in an Integrated School. Journal of Personality, 1974, March, 42(1), 12-22.

Shaw, R. L., and Uhl, N. P. Control of Reinforcement and Academic Achievement; Bialer-Cromwell Children's Locus of Control Scale. Journal of Educational Research, 1971, January, 64(5), 226-228.

Simpson, W. A. Self Concept and Career Choice Among Black Women. Unpublished doctoral dissertation, Oklahoma State University. Dissertation Abstracts International, 1976, May, 36(11-A), 7220.

Solomon, D. The Generality of Children's Achievement-Related Behavior. Journal of Genetic Psychology, 1969, 114(1), 109-125.

_____, Houlihan, K. A., and Parelius, R. J. Intellectual Achievement Responsibility in Negro and White Children. Psychological Reports, 1969, 24(2), 479-483.

Swinger, H. K., and Friendly, F. Race and Motive to Avoid Success. Symposium presentation at the American Psychological Association Convention, Washington, D. C., 1976.

Wen, S. S., and McCoy, R. E. Relationships of Selected Nonacademic and Academic Variables to the Grade Point Average of Black Students. Educational and Psychological Measurement, 1975, 35(4), 935-939.

_____, and _____. Personal Concerns and Manifest Anxiety in Black Students. Journal of Clinical Psychology, 1976, January, 32(1), 64-66.

Weston, P. J., and Mednick, M. T. S. Race, Social Class, and the Motive to Avoid Success in Women. Journal of Cross-Cultural Psychology, 1970, September, 1(3), 284-291. Also in J. Bardwick (ed.), Readings on the Psychology of Women. New York: Harper & Row, 1972, 68-71; And in M. T. S. Mednick, et al. (eds.), Women and Achievement: Social and Motivational Analyses. New York: Halsted Press, 1975, 231-238.

Whisenton, J. T., and Loree, M. R. Comparison of the Values, Needs, and Aspirations of School Leavers with Those of Non-School Leavers. Journal of Negro Education, 1970, Fall, 39(4), 325-332.

White, K. Belief in Reinforcement Control Among Southern Negro Adolescents: The Effects of School Desegregation, Socio-economic Status, and Sex of Student. Journal of Social Psychology, 1971, 85, 149-150.

Williams, J. G., and Stack, J. J. Internal-External Control as a Situational Variable in Determining Information Seeking by Negro Students. Journal of Consulting and Clinical Psychology, 1972, October, 39(2), 187-193.

Wood, F. H. The Relationship of Measures of Attainment Value and

Achievement Expectancy to the Reading Achievement of First-Grade Children from Low-Income Families. Unpublished manuscript, University of Minnesota, 1967. Also available from ERIC (ED016601), 1968.

Wyne, M. D., White, K. P., and Coop, R. H. Personal Control and the Black Self. In The Black Self. Englewood Cliffs, NJ: Prentice-Hall, 1974, 45-61.

Zytkoskee, A., Strickland, B. R., and Watson, J. Delay of Gratification and Internal Versus External Control Among Adolescents of Low Socioeconomic Status. Developmental Psychology, 1971, January, 4(1, Pt. 1), 93-98.

B. BLACK WOMEN (continued)

3. COUNSELING, EDUCATIONAL, OCCUPATIONAL FORCES

Adenika, T. J., and Berry, G. L. Teachers' Attitudes Toward the Education of the Black Child. Education, 1976, Winter, 97(2), 102-114.

Allen, J. G. The Effects of an Achievement Motivation Program on the Self-Concepts of Selected Ninth-Grade Students Representing Three Ethnic Groups. Unpublished doctoral dissertation, North-Texas State University. Dissertation Abstracts International, 1973, May, 33(11-A), 6048.

Almquist, E. M. The Income Losses of Working Black Women: Product of Race and Sex Discrimination. Paper presented at the American Sociological Association meeting, New York City, 1973.

_____. Black Women in the Labor Force: The Experience of a Decade. Unpublished manuscript, North Texas State University, Denton, TX, n. d.

Alpha Kappa Alpha Sorority, Inc., Heritage Series #1. Negro Women in the Judiciary, 1968. #2, Women in Politics, 1969. #3, Women in Business, 1970. #4, Women in Medicine, 1971. #5, Women in Dentistry, 1972. Chicago: Alpha Kappa Alpha Sorority, Inc.

Antonovsky, A. A Study of Some Moderately Successful Negroes in New York City. Phylon, 1967, Fall, 28(3), 246-260.

Astin, A. W. Racial Considerations in Admissions. In D. C. Nichols and O. Mills (eds.), The Campus and the Racial Crisis. Washington, D. C.: American Council on Education, 1970, 113-141.

Baird, L. L. The Graduates. Princeton, NJ: Educational Testing Service, 1973.

_____. A Portrait of Blacks in Graduate Studies. Findings, 1974, 1(2), 1-4.

Ball, H. W. Racial Attitudes of White Educators in a Situational Context. Unpublished master's thesis, University of Maryland, 1971.

Bayer, A. E. The Black College Freshman: Characteristics and Recent Trends. ACE Research Reports, 1972, 7(3).

_____. The New Student in Black Colleges. School Review, 1973, May, 81, 415-526.

_____, and Boruch, R. F. Black and White Freshmen Entering Four-Year Colleges. Educational Record, 1969, 50, 371-386.

_____, and _____. The Black Student in American Colleges. ACE Research Reports, 1969, 4(2).

Beatty, R. W. Blacks as Supervisors: A Study of Training, Job Performance, and Employees' Expectations. Academy of Management Journal, 1973, 16(2), 196-206.

Beckett, J. O. Working Wives: A Racial Comparison. Social Work, 1976, November, 463-471.

Bergen, M. They Are Owners, Bosses, Workers. Ebony, 1977, August, 32(10), 122-128.

Bigoness, W. J. Effect of Applicant's Sex, Race, and Performance on Employers' Performance Ratings: Some Additional Findings. Journal of Applied Psychology, 1976, 61(1), 80-84.

Bird, C. Black Womanpower. New York Magazine, 1969, March, 2(10), 36+.

Bock, E. W. Farmer's Daughter Effect: The Case of the Negro Female Professionals. Phylon, 1969, 30(1), 17-26.

Bond, H. M. The Negro Scholar and Professional in America. In J. P. Davis (ed.), The American Negro Reference Book. Englewood Cliffs, NJ: Prentice-Hall, 1966, 548-589.

Bridgeman, B., and Burbach, H. J. Effects of Race of Successful Peer Models on Academic Expectations and Performance of Black and White Students. Paper presented at the American Educational Research Association meeting, Chicago, April 1974.

Brookover, W., Peterson, A., and Thomas, S. Self-Concept of Ability and School Achievement. Final Report. Cooperative

Research Project. East Lansing: Michigan State University, Office of Research and Publications, 1967.

Brown, H. A., and Ford, D. L., Jr. An Exploratory Analysis of Discrimination in the Employment of Black MBA Graduates. Journal of Applied Psychology, 1977, 62(1), 50-56.

Brown, N. W. An Investigation of Personality Characteristics of Negroes Attending a Predominately White University and Negroes Attending a Predominately Black College. Personality and Social Psychology Bulletin, 1974, 1(1), 321-323.

Bryant, J. W. A Survey of Black American Doctorates. New York: Ford Foundation, 1969.

Bryson, S., and Bardo, H. Race and the Counseling Process: An Overview. Journal of Employment Counseling, 1976, June, 13(2), 68-77.

Buck, M. R., and Austrin, H. R. Factors Related to School Achievement in an Economically Disadvantaged Group. Child Development, 1971, 42, 1813-1826.

Burke, Y. B. Black Women in Politics, Today. Contact, 1974, Fall, 5(4), 20.

Burrell, L., and Rayder, N. F. Black and White Students' Attitudes Toward White Counselors. Journal of Negro Education, 1971, 20, 48-52.

Campbell, D. N. On Being Number One: Competition in Education. Phi Delta Kappan, 1974, October, 56, 143-146.

Careers for Negro Students. School and Society, 1965, October, 93, 364.

Carrington, C. H., and Sedlacek, W. E. Attitudes and Characteristics of Black Graduate Students. Journal of College Student Personnel, 1977, November, 18(6), 467-471.

Carroll, C. M. Three's a Crowd: The Dilemma of the Black Woman in Higher Education. In A. S. Rossi and A. Calderwood (eds.), Academic Women on the Move. New York: Russell Sage Foundation, 1973, 173-186.

Carter, D. E., et al. School Integration: An Attempt to Predict Peer Acceptance. Paper presented at the American Educational Research Association meeting, Chicago, April 1974. Also available from ERIC (ED096364), 1975.

Cascio, W. F., and Bass, B. M. The Effects of Role Playing in a Program to Modify Attitudes Toward Black Employees. Journal of Psychology, 1976, March, 92(2), 261-266.

Changing Status of Negro Women Workers. Monthly Labor Review, 1964, June, 87, 671-673.

Christensen, K. C., and Sedlacek, W. E. Differential Faculty Attitudes Toward Blacks, Females and Students in General. Counseling Center Research Report #13-72. College Park: University of Maryland, 1972. Also in Journal of the National Association for Women Deans, Administrators, and Counselors, 1974, Winter, 37(2), 78-83.

Claerbaut, D. P. A Study of Black Student Alienation at Small Private Liberal Arts Colleges. Unpublished doctoral dissertation, Loyola University. Dissertation Abstracts International, 1976, May, 36(11-A), 7682.

Clark, E. T., and Misa, K. F. Peers' Perceptions of Negro and White Occupational Preferences. Personnel and Guidance Journal, 1967, November, 46(3), 288-291.

Clift, V. A. Educating the American Negro. In J. P. David (ed.), The American Negro Reference Book. Englewood Cliffs, NJ: Prentice-Hall, 1966, 360-397.

Coleman, A. L. Occupational, Educational and Residence Plans of Negro High-School Seniors in Lexington and Fayette County, Kentucky. Journal of Negro Education, 1960, Winter, 29(1), 73-79.

Comer, J. P. Black Education: A Holistic View. Urban Review, 1975, Fall, 8(3), 162-170.

Commission on Civil Rights. Last Hired, First Fired: Layoffs and Civil Rights. Washington, D. C.: U. S. Commission on Civil Rights, 1977.

Cooper, H. The Effects of Information About a Student's Race and Social Class on Others' Expectancies of Academic Success and Responsibility. Unpublished masters thesis, University of Connecticut, 1974.

Copeland, E. J. Counseling Black Women with Negative Self-Concepts. Personnel and Guidance Journal, 1977, March, 55, 397-400.

Davis, J. A. Undergraduate Career Decisions: Correlates of Occupational Choice. Chicago: Aldine, 1965.

Davis, J. P. (ed.). The American Negro Reference Book. Englewood Cliffs, NJ: Prentice-Hall, 1966.

Davis, J. S. The Effects of an Enriched Summer Program and Prior Experience with White Persons on Academic Success of Incoming Black Students and the Continuing Effects in the Following Semester. Washington, D. C. : National Center for Educational Research and Development, 1976. Also available from ERIC (ED095244), 1974.

DeJoie, C. M. Black Woman in Alienation in White Academia. Negro Educational Review, 1977, January, 28, 4-12.

Dixon-Altenor, C., and Altenor, A. Role of Occupational Status in the Career Aspirations of Black Women. Vocational Guidance Quarterly, 1977, March, 25, 211-215.

Educational and Occupational Goals of Men and Women at Black Colleges. Monthly Labor Review, 1976, June, 99, 10-16.

Edwards, O. L. Cohort and Sex Changes in Black Educational Achievement. Sociology and Social Research, 1975, January, 59(2), 110-120.

Eltzroth, M. Vocational Counseling for Ghetto Women with Prostitution and Domestic Service Backgrounds. Vocational Guidance Quarterly, 1973, 22(1), 32-38.

Enrollment of Black Freshmen Slowed This Year Study Indicates. The Chronicle of Higher Education, 1974, February 11, 8(19), 1+.

Epps, E. G. Negro Academic Motivation and Performance: An Overview. Journal of Social Issues, 1969, Summer, 25(3), 5-11.

Epstein, C. F. Positive Effects of the Multiple Negative: Explaining the Success of Black Professional Women. American Journal of Sociology, 1973, January, 78(4), 912-935. Also in F. L. Denmark (ed.), Women--Volume I: A PDI Research Reference Work. New York: Psychological Dimensions, Inc. , 1976, 183-206.

_____. Black and Female: The Double Whammy. Psychology Today, 1973, August, 7(3), 57-61.

Evans, C. L. The Immediate Effects of Classroom Integration on the Academic Progress, Self-Concept and Racial Attitude of Negro Elementary Children. Unpublished doctoral dissertation. Dissertation Abstracts International, 1970, May, 30(11-A), 4825-4826.

Farver, A. S. , Sedlacek, W. E. , and Brooks, G. C. Longitudinal Predictions of University Grades for Blacks and Whites. Measurement and Evaluation in Guidance, 1975, January, 7(4), 243-250.

Fichter, J. H. Neglected Talents: Background and Prospects of Negro College Graduates. Report No. 112. Chicago: National Option Research Center, 1966.

_____. Career Preparation and Expectations of Negro College Seniors. Journal of Negro Education, 1966, Fall, 35(4), 322-335.

_____. Career Expectations of Negro Women Graduates. Monthly Labor Review, 1967, 90(11), 36-42. Also in A. Theodore (ed.), The Professional Woman. Cambridge, MA: Schenkman, 1971, 427-440.

_____. Marriage and Motherhood of Black Women Graduates. In N. Glazer-Malbin and H. Y. Waehrer (eds.), Woman in a Man-Made World. Chicago: Rand-McNally, 1972, 203-207.

Fisher, R. Black, Female--and Qualified. In Women on Campus: The Unfinished Liberation. New York: Change Magazine, 1975, 160-166.

Freeman, R. B. Black Elite: The New Market for Highly Educated Black Americans. New York: McGraw-Hill, 1977.

Frost, D. White Women Only. Do It Now, 1976, April, 9(3), 11.

Fugita, S. S., Wexley, K. N., and Hillery, J. M. Black-White Differences in Nonverbal Behavior in an Interview Setting. Journal of Applied Social Psychology, 1974, October/December, 4(4), 343-350.

Garfinkle, S. H. Occupations of Women and Black Workers, 1962-1974. Monthly Labor Review, 1975, November, 98, 25-34.

Gay, G. Teachers' Achievement Expectations of and Classroom Interactions with Ethnically Different Students. Contemporary Education, 1975, Spring, 46, 166-172.

Ginzberg, E. The Development of Human Resources. New York: McGraw-Hill, 1966.

_____, and Hiestand, D. L. Employment Patterns of Negro Men and Women. In J. P. Davis (ed.), American Negro Reference Book. Englewood Cliffs, NJ: Prentice-Hall, 1966, 205-250.

Giovanni, N. One Day I Fell Off the Roof (A View of the Black University). In T. Cade (ed.), The Black Woman. New York: New American Library, 1970, 132-136.

Goldman, R. D., and Hewitt, B. N. Predicting the Success of Black, Chicano, Oriental and White College Students. The Journal of Educational Measurement, 1976, Summer, 13(2), 107-117.

Gottlieb, D., and Heinsohn, A. L. Educational Goals of Black and White Youth in Segregated and Inter-Racial Schools. Final Report. Available from ERIC (ED057411), 1972.

_____, and Tenhouten, W. D. Racial Composition and the Social

System of Three High Schools. Journal of Marriage and the Family, 1965, May, 27, 204-212.

Gould, S. H., and van den Berghe, P. L. Particularism in Sociology Departments' Hiring Practices. Race, 1973, July, 15(1), 106-111.

Grainger, B., Kostick, B., and Staley, Y. A Study of Achievement Motivation of Females in Two Southern, Non-Coeducational Segregated Colleges. Unpublished manuscript, 1970.

Granson, M. R. A Slave Woman Runs a Midnight School. In G. Lerner (ed.), Black Women in White America. New York: Random House, 1973, 32-33.

Grantham, R. J. Effects of Counselor Sex, Race, and Language Style on Black Students in Initial Interviews. Journal of Counseling Psychology, 1973, November, 20(6), 553-559.

Gurin, P., and Epps, E. G. (eds.). College and Its Impact on Motivation and Aspirations. In Black Consciousness, Identity, and Achievement. New York: John Wiley, 1975, 143-179.

_____, and _____ (eds.). Individual Achievement: Summing Up. In Black Consciousness, Identity, and Achievement. New York: John Wiley, 1975, 181-188.

_____, and Gaylord, C. Educational and Occupational Goals of Men and Women at Black Colleges. Monthly Labor Review, 1976, June, 99, 10-16.

_____, and _____. Sex Role Constraints: The College-Educated Black Woman. Unpublished manuscript, University of Michigan, Ann Arbor, n. d.

_____, and Kate, D. Motivation and Aspiration in the Negro College. Final Report. Ann Arbor: University of Michigan, Institute for Social Research, 1966.

_____, and Pruitt, A. Counseling Implications of Black Women's Market Position, Aspirations and Expectancies. Paper presented at the Conference on the Educational and Occupational Needs of Black Women, Washington, D. C., December 1975.

Guthrie, R. V. Early Black Psychologists. In Even the Rat Was White: A Historical View of Psychology. New York: Harper & Row, 1976, 120-174.

_____. Psychology and Race. In Even the Rat Was White: A Historical View of Psychology. New York: Harper & Row, 1976, 29-46.

Hall, E. R. Motivation and Achievement in Negro and White Students, Final Report. Washington, D. C. : U. S. Department of Health, Education and Welfare, 1971.

Halleck, S. L. The Uses of Abnormality. In Politics of Therapy. New York: Harper & Row, 1971, 99-118.

Halpern, S. The Relationship Between Ethnic Group Membership and Sex and Aspects of Vocational Choice of Pre-College Black and Puerto Rican High School Students. Unpublished doctoral dissertation. Dissertation Abstracts International, 1972, July, 33(1-A), 190-191.

Hammer, W. C. , Kim, J. S. , Baird, L. , and Bigoness, W. J. Race and Sex as Determinants of Ratings by Potential Employers in a Simulated Work-Sampling Task. Journal of Applied Psychology, 1974, December, 59(6), 705-711.

Harwood, E. , and Hodge, C. C. Jobs and the Negro Family: A Reappraisal. The Public Interest, 1971, Spring, 23, 125-131.

Hauenstein, L. S. , Kasl, S. V. , and Harburg, E. Work Status, Work Satisfaction, and Blood Pressure Among Married Black and White Women. Psychology of Women Quarterly, 1977, Summer, 1(4), 334-349.

Haynes, H. Ethnic Woman--And We Hope and Dream Too. In D. Wark and E. G. Joselyn (eds.), Student Counseling Bureau Review: Women in Transition. Minneapolis: University of Minnesota, Student Counseling Bureau, 1975, September, 26(1), 47-50.

Hedegard, J. M. , and Brown, D. R. Encounters of Some Negro and White Freshmen with a Public Multiversity. Journal of Social Issues, 1969, Summer, 25(3), 131-144.

Hernandez, E. Small Change for Black Women. Ms. , 1974, August, 16-18.

Houzer, S. Black Women in Athletics. Physical Educator, 1974, December, 31, 208-209.

Huck, J. R. , and Bray, D. W. Management Assessment-Center Evaluations and Subsequent Job-Performance of White and Black Females. Personnel Psychology, 1976, Spring, 29(1), 13-30.

Institute for the Study of Educational Policy. Equal Educational Opportunity for Blacks in U. S. Higher Education: An Assessment. Washington, D. C. : Howard University Press, 1976.

Jackson, B. D. Social Acceptance and Personal and Social Adjustment Among Integrated Black and White Elementary and Junior High School Students. Unpublished doctoral dissertation, California School of Professional Psychology. Dissertation Abstracts International, 1976, May, 36(11-A), 7683.

Jackson, J. J. But Where Are the Men? The Black Scholar, 1971, December, 3(4), 30-41.

_____, and Huber, J. So You Really Want to Hire Blacks and Women? Sociological Abstracts, 1973, December, 21(7), 227-228, Supplement 37.

Jaffe, A. J., Adams, W., and Meyers, S. G. Negro Higher Education in the 1960's. New York: Praeger, 1968.

Jefferies, D. Counseling for the Strengths of the Black Woman. The Counseling Psychologist, 1976, 6(2), 20-22.

Jencks, C., and Brown, M. Effects of Desegregation on Student Achievement: Some New Evidence from the Equality of Educational Opportunity Survey. Sociology of Education, 1975, Winter, 48(1), 126-140.

Jensen, B. Black and Female Too: Career Women Find that the Road up to the Top May Be Paved with Racism, Sexism, and Sometimes Both (Experiences of Several Black Women Executives). Black Enterprise, 1976, July, 6, 26-29.

Johnson, K. R. The Language of Black Children: Instructional Implications. In R. L. Green (ed.), Racial Crisis in American Education. Chicago: Follett, 1969.

Jones, A., and Seagull, A. A. Dimensions of the Relationship Between the Black Client and the White Therapist. American Psychologist, 1977, October, 32(10), 850-855.

Jones, B. A. P. The Contribution of Black Women to the Incomes of Black Families: An Analysis of the Labor Force Participation Rates of Black Wives. Unpublished doctoral dissertation, Georgia State University, 1973. Dissertation Abstracts International, 1973, 34(6-A), 2856. Also available from ERIC (ADG 73-31454), 1973.

Jones, H. The Effects of Pre-College Counseling on the Educational and Career Aspirations of Blacks and Women Enrolled at the University of Pittsburgh. Unpublished manuscript, University of Pittsburgh, 1973.

Jones, J. C., Harris, L. J., and Hauck, W. E. Differences in Perceived Sources of Academic Difficulties: Black Students in Predominantly Black and in Predominately White Colleges. Journal of Negro Education, 1975, Fall, 44(4), 519-529.

Jones, R. S. Proving Blacks Inferior: The Sociology of Knowledge. In J. A. Lader (ed.), The Death of White Sociology. New York: Random House, 1973, 114-135.

Katz, M. W. End Racism in Education: A Concerned Parent Speaks.

In T. Cade (ed.), The Black Woman. New York: New American Library, 1970, 124-131.

Kaul, T. J. Counselor Race and Power Base: Effects on Attitudes and Behavior. Journal of Counseling Psychology, 1977, 24(5), 430-436.

Kiehle, T. J., Bramble, J., and Mason, E. J. Teachers' Expectations: Ratings of Student Performance as Biased by Student Characteristics. Journal of Experimental Education, 1974, Fall, 43(1), 54-60.

Kleinfeld, J. Relative Importance of Teachers and Parents in the Formation of Negro and White Students' Academic Self-Concept. Journal of Educational Research, 1972, January, 65(5), 211-212.

Lamb, R. R. Concurrent Validity of the American College Testing Interest Inventory for Minority Group Members. Unpublished doctoral dissertation. Dissertation Abstracts International, 1975, 35(7-A), 4161.

Lee, J. M. Studies of Economically Deprived Elementary Children in Southern Illinois: A Summary of Four Doctoral Dissertations. Available from ERIC (ED021886), 1969.

Leggon, C. B. The Black Female Professional: Role Strains and Status Inconsistencies. Unpublished doctoral dissertation, University of Chicago, 1975. Dissertation Abstracts International, 1975, 36(7-A), 4776. Also available from ERIC (ADG02-83749), 1975.

Lewis, H., et al. Improving Employment Possibilities for Female Black Teenagers in New York City. Final Report. Washington D.C.: U.S. Department of Labor, Manpower Administration, 1976. Also available from ERIC (ED130032), 1977.

Lewis, S. D. Professional Woman: Her Fields Have Widened. Ebony, 1977, August, 32, 114-116+.

Long Thrust Toward Economic Equality: Negro Women Fastest Advancing Group. Ebony, 1966, August, 21, 38-40+.

Lott, A. S., and Lott, B. E. Negro and White Youth: A Psychological Study in a Border-State Community. New York: Holt, Rinehart, and Winston, 1963.

Low, W. The Education of Negroes Viewed Historically. In V. Clift, et al. (eds.), Negro Education in America. New York: Harper & Row, 1962, 16, 27-59.

McCandless, B. R., Roberts, A., and Starnes, T. Teachers' Marks, Achievement Test Scores, and Aptitude Relations with Respect to Social Class, Race, and Sex. Journal of Educational Psychology, 1972, April, 63, 153-159.

McCormick, M. K., and Williams, J. H. Effects of a Compensatory Program on Self-Report, Achievement and Aspiration Level of Disadvantaged High School Students. Journal of Negro Education, 1974, Winter, 43(1), 47-52.

Mack, G. E. The Black Woman Graduate Student. Women on Campus: 1970--A Symposium. Ann Arbor: University of Michigan, 1970, 42-45.

Mackie, J. B., Maxwell, A. D., and Rafferty, F. T. Psychological Development of Culturally Disadvantaged Negro Kindergarten Children: A Study of the Selective Influence of Family and School Variables. Paper presented at the American Orthopsychiatric Association meeting, Washington, D. C., March 1967.

Mackler, B. Blacks Who Are Academically Successful. Urban Education, 1970, 5(3), 210-237.

Marshall, J. S. The Effects of Project BIG on Self Concept and Black Pride of Urban Black Children at the Fourth Grade Level. Unpublished doctoral dissertation, Ball State University. Dissertation Abstracts International, 1974, August, 35(2-A), 804-805.

Massey, G. C., Scott, M. V., and Dornbusch, S. M. Racism Without Racists: Institutional Racism in Urban Schools. Black Scholar, 1975, November, 7(3), 10-19.

Miller, B. J. Inner City Women in White Schools. Journal of Negro Education, 1973, Summer, 42, 392-413.

Molina, J. C. The Influence of Experiences as Teacher Aids on the Level and Direction of Occupational Aspirations of Selected Disadvantaged High-School Girls. Unpublished doctoral dissertation, United States International University. Dissertation Abstracts, 1969, 29(8-A), 2805-2806.

Mommsen, K. G. Professionalism and the Racial Context of Career Patterns Among Black American Doctorates: A Note on the Brain Drain Hypothesis. Unpublished manuscript, 1972.

Moore, W. The Black Woman in Higher Education. In W. Moore and L. Wagstaff (eds.), Black Educators in White Colleges. San Francisco: Jossey-Bass, 1974.

Morton, C. A. Black Women in Corporate America. Ebony, 1975, November, 31, 106-108+.

Negro Women in the Judiciary. Alpha Kappa Sorority, Heritage Series #1, 1968, August, 1-24.

Nelson, B. W., Bird, R. A., and Rodgers, G. M. Expanding Educational Opportunities in Medicine for Blacks and Other Minority Students. Journal of Medical Education, 1970, 45, 731-736.

Newell, B. W. Parallels of Negro and Women's Education. School and Society, 1970, October, 98, 357-359.

Newsday Improves Status of Women and Minorities. Editor and Publisher, 1975, March 22, 108(12), 13.

Occupations of Women and Black Workers, 1962-74. In Monthly Labor Review, 1975, November, 25-35.

Olsen, H. D. Effects of Changes in Academic Roles on Self-Concept-of-Academic Ability of Black and White Compensatory Education Students. Journal of Negro Education, 1972, Fall, 41(4), 365-369.

Park, J. P. Black Nuns Relate to Black Power; National Black Sisters Conference. Christian Century, 1968, October, 85, 1320-1322.

Payne, E. L. Black Women in Business. Contact, 1974, Fall, 5(4), 16-19.

Pendergrass, V., Kimmel, E., Joesting, J., Petersen, J., and Bush, E. Sex Discrimination Counseling. American Psychologist, 1976, January, 31(1), 36-46.

Persons, W. E., III. Occupational Prediction as a Function of the Counselor's Racial and Sexual Bias. Unpublished doctoral dissertation. Dissertation Abstracts International, 1973, 34(A), 139-140.

Peterson, M. T. Status and Trends in the Promotion of Women to Secondary School Principal-ships with Special Reference to Black Women. Unpublished doctoral dissertation. Dissertation Abstracts International, 1973, 33(A), 6915.

Pettigrew, T. F. The Negro and Education. In I. Katz and P. Gurin (eds.), Race and the Social Sciences. New York: Basic Books, 1969.

Pfeifer, C. M., Jr. The Validity of Academic Predictors for Black and White Students at a Predominantly White University. Journal of Educational Measurement, 1971, 8, 253-261.

Pressman, S. Job Discrimination and the Black Woman. NAACP: The Crisis, 1970, March.

Richer, J. Career Expectations of Negro Women Graduates. Monthly Labor Review, 1967, 90, 36-42.

Richmond, B. O., and Weiner, G. P. Cooperation and Competition Among Young Children as a Function of Ethnic Grouping, Grade, Sex, and Reward Condition. Journal of Educational Psychology, 1973, June, 64, 329-334.

Rickman, G. Continuing the Search for Greater Horizons: Black Women in Business. Contact, 1972, Fall, 3(6), 26-29.

Rist, R. C. The Self-Fulfilling Prophecy in Ghetto Education. In J. M. Hunt (ed.), Human Intelligence. New Brunswick, NJ: Transaction Books, 1972, 123-162.

Roark, A. C. Business Graduates Find It Helps to Be Female or Black--or Both. The Chronicle of Higher Education, 1977, August, 14(21), 5-6.

Robinson, J. W., and Preston, J. D. Equal-Status Contact and Modification of Racial Prejudice: A Reexamination of the Contact Hypothesis. Social Forces, 1976, June, 54(4), 911-924.

Rubovits, P. C., and Maehr, M. L. Pygmalion Black and White. Journal of Personality and Social Psychology, 1973, 25(2), 210-218.

Rush, T. G., Meyers, C. F., and Arata, E. S. Black American Writers Past and Present: A Biographical and Bibliographical Dictionary. Metuchen, NJ: Scarecrow Press, 1975.

Schmedinghoff, G. J. Counseling the Black Student in Higher Education: Is It a Racial, Socioeconomic, or Human Question? Journal of College Student Personnel, 1977, November, 18(6), 472-477.

Schroth, M. L. Sex and Grade-Level Differences in Need Achievement Among Black College Students. Perceptual and Motor Skills, 1976, August, 43(1), 135-140.

Scott, P. Preparing Black Women for Nontraditional Professions: Some Considerations for Career Counseling. Journal of the National Association for Women Deans, Administrators, and Counselors, 1977, Summer, 40(4), 135-139.

_____, and Horhn, M. A Pilot Study of Black Female Undergraduates Enrolled as Majors in Nontraditional Curricula at the University of Tennessee, Knoxville. Unpublished manuscript, 1975.

Sedlacek, W. E., Lewis, J. A., and Brooks, G. C., Jr. Black and Other Minority Admissions to Large Universities: A Four Year National Survey of Policies and Outcomes. Research in Higher Education, 1974, 2, 221-230.

Shaw, M. E. The Self-Image of Black and White Pupils in an Integrated School. Journal of Personality, 1974, March, 42(1), 12-22.

She's a Fighter on Three Fronts: Addie Wyatt Is Black, Female, and International Vice President of the Amalgamated Meat Cutters and Butcher Workmen of North America. Ebony, 1977, August, 32(10), 70.

Siegel, A. I., and Federman, P. J. Employment of Black Philadelphians. JSAS Catalog of Selected Documents in Psychology, 1975, Fall, 5, 328.

Silverstein, B., and Krate, R. Children in School: Toward a Typology of Behavior Patterns. In Children of the Dark Ghetto: A Developmental Psychology. New York: Praeger, 1975, 170-201.

_____, and _____. Cognitive-Linguistic Development. In Children of the Dark Ghetto: A Developmental Psychology. New York: Praeger, 1975, 143-169.

_____, and _____. Competence and Performance: The Politics of Intelligence. In Children of the Dark Ghetto: A Developmental Psychology. New York: Praeger, 1975, 123-142.

_____, and _____. The Interaction of Teachers and Students. In Children of the Dark Ghetto: A Developmental Psychology. New York: Praeger, 1975, 202-227.

Smith, A. G. The Negro Professional Woman: A Study in Continuity and Change, 1945-1970. Unpublished manuscript, Agnes Scott College, n. d.

Smith, M. Black Girls in Uniform. Ebony, 1968, August, 23, 68-70+.

Snyder, D., and Hudis, P. M. Occupational Income and the Effects of Minority Competition and Segregation: A Reanalysis and Some New Evidence. American Sociological Review, 1976, April, 41(2), 209-234.

Solomon, D. The Generality of Children's Achievement-Related Behavior. Journal of Genetic Psychology, 1969, 114(1), 109-125.

Sorkin, A. L. Education, Occupation and Income of Non-White Women. Journal of Negro Education, 1972, Fall, 41(4), 343-351.

Sowell, T. Black Excellence: The Case of Dunbar High School. Public Interest, 1974, Spring, 35, 3-21.

Stanley, J. C., and Porter, A. C. Correlation of Scholastic Aptitude Test Scores with College Grades for Negroes Versus Whites. Journal of Educational Measurement, 1967, 4(4), 199-218.

Stewart, D. G. The Social Adjustment of Black Females of a Predominantly White University. Unpublished doctoral dissertation, University of Connecticut. Dissertation Abstracts International, 1972, May, 32(11-A), 6541.

Thompson, J. On Being Black and Female and an Accountant. In

H. H. Frank (ed.), Women in the Organization. Philadelphia: University of Pennsylvania Press, 1977, 266-270.

Tolbert-Stroud, S. Working Black Women. In D. Jongeward and D. Scott (eds.), Affirmative Action for Women: A Practical Guide. Reading, MA: Addison-Wesley, 1973, 121-138.

Toldson, I. L., and Pasteur, A. B. Beyond Rhetoric: Techniques for Using the Black Aesthetic in Group Counseling and Guidance. Journal of Non-White Concerns in Personnel and Guidance, 1976, April, 4(3), 142-151.

Tribble, I. Motivational Counseling: A Black Educational Imperative. Educational Leadership, 1970, December, 28(3), 297-301.

Veroff, J., and Peele, S. Initial Effects of Desegregation on the Achievement Motivation of Negro Elementary School Children. Journal of Social Issues, 1969, 25(3), 71-91.

Vetter, B. M. Women and Minority Scientists. Science, 1975, September, 189, 751.

Vontress, C. E. Counseling Negro Students for College. Journal of Negro Education, 1968, Winter, 37(1), 37-44.

Walster, E., Cleary, T. A., and Clifford, M. The Effect of Race and Sex on College Admission. Sociology of Education, 1971, 44(2), 237-244.

What's a Nice Girl Like You Doing in a Place Like This? Ebony, 1977, June, 32(8), 103-104+.

White, K., and Knight, J. H. School Desegregation, Socioeconomic Status, Sex and the Aspirations of Southern Negro Adolescents, Journal of Negro Education, 1973, Winter, 42(1), 71-78.

Whiting, F. S. Selected Effects of Busing on Black Students. Unpublished doctoral dissertation, Indiana University. Dissertation Abstracts International, 1975, March, 35(9-A), 5702.

Williams, H. The Black Social Workers' Dilemma. In T. Cade (ed.), The Black Woman. New York: New American Library, 1970, 170-179.

Williams, J. E., and Stabler, J. R. If White Means Good, then Black--. Psychology Today, 1973, July, 7, 50-54.

Williams, O. American Black Women in the Arts & Social Sciences: A Bibliographic Survey. Metuchen, NJ: Scarecrow Press, 1973.

Wilson, K. M. Black Students Entering College Research Center Colleges: Their Characteristics and Their First-Year Academic Performance. Research Memorandum 69-1. Poughkeepsie, NY: Vassar College, College Research Center, 1969.

Women in Business. Alpha Kappa Alpha Sorority, 1970, April, Heritage Series # 3.

Women in Dentistry. Alpha Kappa Alpha Sorority, 1972, Heritage Series # 5.

Women in Medicine. Alpha Kappa Alpha Sorority, 1971, Heritage Series # 4.

Women in Politics. Alpha Kappa Alpha Sorority, 1969, July, Heritage Series #1.

Women in the Service Academies. Ebony, 1976, November, 32(1), 31-34+.

Wright, S. J. Redressing the Imbalance of Minority Groups in the Professions. Journal of Higher Education, 1972, March, 43(3), 239-248.

Yee, A. H., and Fruth, M. J. Do Black Studies Make a Difference in Ghetto Children's Achievement and Attitudes? Journal of Negro Education, 1973, Winter, 42(1), 33-38.

B. BLACK WOMEN (continued)

4. CAREER DEVELOPMENT, ORIENTATION, CONTINGENCIES

Antonovsky, A. A Study of Some Moderately Successful Negroes in New York City, Phylon, 1967, Fall, 28(3), 246-260.

Axelson, L. J. The Working Wife: Differences in Perception Among Negro and White Males. Journal of Marriage and the Family, 1970, August, 32, 457-464.

Beckett, J. O. Working Wives: A Racial Comparison. Social Work, 1976, November, 21(6), 463-471.

Bond, H. M. Black American Scholars: A Study of Their Beginnings. Detroit: Balamp, 1972.

Davis, L. G. Black Women in the Cities, 1872-1975: A Bibliography of Published Works on the Life and Achievement of Black Women in Cities in the United States. Monticello, IL: Council of Planning Librarians, 1975.

Dixon-Altenor, C., and Altenor, A. Role of Occupational Status in the Career Aspirations of Black Women. Vocational Guidance Quarterly, 1977, March, 25, 211-215.

Epstein, C. F. Positive Effects of the Multiple Negative: Explaining the Success of Black Professional Women. American Journal of Sociology, 1973, January, 78(4), 912-935. Also in F. L. Denmark (ed.), Women--Volume I: A PDI Research Reference Work. New York: Psychological Dimensions, 1976, 183-206.

──────. Black and Female: The Double Whammy. Psychology Today, 1973, August, 7(3), 57-61.

Fichter, J. H. Career Expectations of Negro Women Graduates. Monthly Labor Review, 1967, 90(11), 36-42. Also in A. Theodore (ed.), The Professional Woman. Cambridge, MA: Schenkman, 1971, 427-440.

──────. Marriage and Motherhood of Black Women Graduates. In N. Glazer-Malbin and H. Y. Waehrer (eds.), Woman in a Man-Made World. Chicago: Rand-McNally, 1972, 203-207.

Hauenstein, L. S., Kasl, S. V., and Harburg, E. Work Status, Work Satisfaction, and Blood Pressure Among Married Black and White Women. Psychology of Women Quarterly, 1977, 1(4), 334-349.

Himes, J. S. Interrelation of Occupational and Spousal Roles in a Middle Class Negro Neighborhood. Marriage and Family Living, 1960, November, 22, 262-263.

Holley, J. L. An Analysis of Personality Needs and Certain Background Factors Which May Influence Career Choice of Women Business Education Majors. Unpublished doctoral dissertation. Dissertation Abstracts International, 1970, July, 30(1-A), 223-224.

Leggon, C. B. The Black Female Professional: Role Strains and Status Inconsistencies. Unpublished doctoral dissertation. Dissertation Abstracts International, 1975, 36(7-A), 4776.

Mommsen, K. G. Professionalism and the Racial Context of Career Patterns Among Black American Doctorates: A Note on the "Brain Drain" Hypothesis. Unpublished manuscript, 1972.

Pierce, P. Marriage and the Educated Black Woman. Ebony, 1973, August, 28, 160-162+.

Reed, J. Marriage and Fertility in Black Female Teachers. Black Scholar, 1970, January/February, 1, 22-28.

Rhodes, L. G. A Critical Analysis of the Career Backgrounds of Selected Black Female Librarians. Unpublished doctoral dissertation, Florida State University, 1975. Dissertation Abstracts International, 1975, 36(6-A), 3190. Also available from ERIC (ADG75-26810), 1975.

Richer, J. Career Expectations of Negro Women Graduates. Monthly Labor Review, 1967, 90, 36-42.

Rush, T. G., Meyers, C. F., and Arata, E. S. Black American Writers Past and Present: A Biographical and Bibliographical Dictionary. Metuchen, NJ: Scarecrow Press, 1975.

Scanzoni, J. Sex Roles, Economic Factors, and Marital Solidarity in Black and White Marriages. Journal of Marriage and the Family, 1975, February, 37(1), 130-144.

She's a Fighter on Three Fronts: Addie Wyatt Is Black, Female, and International Vice President of the Amalgamated Meat Cutters and Butcher Workmen of North America. Ebony, 1977, August, 32(10), 70.

Turner, B. F. Socialization and Career Orientation Among Black and White College Women. Paper presented at the American Psychological Association Convention, Honolulu, 1972.

_____, and McCaffery, J. H. Socialization and Career Orientation Among Black and White College Women. Journal of Vocational Behavior, 1974, 5(3), 307-319.

Wilson, K. M. Black Students Entering College Research Center Colleges: Their Characteristics and Their First-Year Academic Performance. Research Memorandum 69-1. Poughkeepsie, NY: Vassar College, College Research Center, 1969.

C. LATIN WOMEN

1. SOCIETAL FORCES

Adkins, D. C., Payne, F. E., and Ballif, B. L. Motivation Factor Scores and Response Set Scores for 10 Ethnic-Cultural Groups of Preschool Children. American Educational Research Journal, 1972, 9, 557-572.

Aguirre, B. E. Women in the Cuban Bureaucracies: 1968-1974. Journal of Comparative Family Studies, 1976, Spring, 7(1), 23-40.

Almazol, C. La Chicana and the Catholic Religion. Unpublished manuscript, University of California, Berkeley, 1971.

The American Woman. Special Issue. Transaction, 1970, November-December, 8(1-2).

Anderson, J. G., and Evans, F. B. Family Socialization and Educational Achievement in Two Cultures: Mexican-American and Anglo-American. Sociometry, 1976, September, 39(3), 209-222.

_____, and Johnson, W. H. Stability and Change Among Three Generations of Mexican-Americans: Factors Affecting Achievement. American Educational Research Journal, 1971, March, 8, 285-309.

Angelini, A. L. Measuring the Achievement Motive in Brasil. Journal of Social Psychology, 1966, 68(1), 35-40.

Anquiano, L. World Women's Challenge--A New Society Based on Justice and Peace. Comunidad. San Antonio: Southwest Regional Office for the Spanish Speaking, November-December, n. d., 1-4.

Antonovsky, A. Aspiration, Class and Racial-Ethnic Membership. Journal of Negro Education, 1967, 36(4), 385-393.

Aquilar, L. P. The Barrio Experience from a Different Perspective. La Luz, 1973, January, 1(9), 16-17.

Aramoni, A. Machismo. Psychology Today, 1972, January, 69-72.

Arellano, J. Victims of Machismo. El Grito del Norte, 1971, June 5, 4(4-5).

Arnold, M. Mexican Women: The Anatomy of a Stereotype in a Mestizo Village. Unpublished doctoral dissertation, University of Florida. Dissertation Abstracts International, 1974, May, 34(11-B), 5295-5296.

Baca, G. Reversal of Roles. Unpublished student paper, Chicano Studies, University of California, Berkeley, 1972.

Barberio, R. The Relationship Between Achievement Motivation and Ethnicity in Anglo-American and Mexican-American Junior High School Students. Psychological Record, 1967, 17(2), 263-266.

Barrio, R. Macho--A Pitiful Effort. El Tecolote, 1974, February 22, 4(3).

Bender, P. S., and Ruiz, R. A. Race and Class as Differential Determinants of Underachievement and Underaspiration Among Mexican-Americans and Anglos. Journal of Educational Research, 1974, October, 68(2), 51-55.

Bernal, L. Future of the Latina in the United States. Speech presented at the Spanish Speaking Women's Conference, August 1975.

Betancourt, R. Sex Differences in Language Proficiency of Mexican-American Third and Fourth Graders. Journal of Education, Boston, 1976, May, 158(2), 55-65.

Blough, W. J. Political Participation in Mexico: Sex Differences in Behavior and Attitudes. Unpublished doctoral dissertation,

University of North Carolina. Dissertation Abstracts, 1968, May 28 (11-A), 4972.

Britain, S. D., and Abad, M. Field-Independence: A Function of Sex and Socialization in a Cuban and an American Group. Personality and Social Psychology Bulletin, 1974, 1(1), 319-320.

Bronson, L., and Meadow, A. The Need Achievement Orientation of Catholic and Protestant Mexican-Americans. Revista Interamericana de Psicologia, 1968, 2(3), 159-168.

Bryant, B., and Meadow, A. School-Related Problems of Mexican-American Adolescents. Journal of School Psychology, 1976, Summer, 14(2), 139-150.

Bureau of the Census. Spanish Women. A Statistical Portrait of Women in the U. S. Washington, D. C.: U. S. Department of Commerce, 1976, 76-82.

Buriel, R. Cognitive Styles Among Three Generations of Mexican American Children. Journal of Cross-Cultural Psychology, 1975, December, 6(4), 417-429.

Burma, J. H. (ed.). Mexican-Americans in the United States. Cambridge, MA: Schenkman, 1970.

Burton, R. V. Cross-Sex Identity in Barbados. Developmental Psychology, 1972, 6, 365-374.

Buys, C. J., Field, T. K., and Schmidt, M. M. A Comparison of Low Socio-Economic Mexican American Students' and Parents' Attitudes Toward College Education. Personality and Social Psychology Bulletin, 1976, Summer, 2(3), 294-298.

Cabello-Argandona, R., Gomez-Quinones, J., and Duran, P. H. The Chicana: A Comprehensive Bibliographic Study. Los Angeles: University of California, Bibliographic Research Division, 1975.

Cabeza de Vaca, F. The Pioneer Woman in Aztlan. In L. Valdez and S. Steiner (eds.), Aztlan, An Anthology of Mexican-American Literature. New York: Random House, 1972.

Cabrera, Y. A. A Study of American and Mexican-American Culture Values and Their Significance in Education. Unpublished doctoral dissertation. Dissertation Abstracts, 1964, 25, 309.

_____. Beside Every Man Stands a Woman. Hijas de Cuahtemoc, 1971, April, 1, 9.

Cain, M. A. A Study of Relationships Between Selected Factors and the School Achievement of Mexican-American Migrant Children. Unpublished doctoral dissertation, Michigan State University.

Dissertation Abstracts International, 1971, February, 31(8-A), 3947.

Canavan, D. Field Dependence in Children as a Function of Grade, Sex, and Ethnic Group Membership. Paper presented at the American Psychological Association Convention, Washington, D.C., 1969.

Cardozo-Freeman, I. Games Mexican Girls Play. Journal of American Folklore, 1975, January-March, 88(347), 12-24.

Casilla, R.J. A Re-examination of the Role of Mexican-American Women. Mano a Mano, 1974, October, 3(5), 2.

La Causa Chicana, Una Familia Unida. The Journal of Social Casework: Contemporary Social Work, 1971, May, 52(5).

Chabran, M. (ed.). La Chicana, Reader. Berkeley: Chicano Studies, University of California, 1974.

Chapa, E. Chicana Bibliography. Austin, TX: Chicana Research and Learning Center, in press.

Chavez, H. Las Chicanas. Regeneracion, 1971, 1(10).

Chavez, J.V. Women of the Mexican-American Movement. Mademoiselle, 1972, April, 74, 82+.

The Chicana. Special Issue. El Grito Del Norte. Espanola, NM: 1971.

Chicana Caucus, National Chicano Political Conference. Women of La Raza Unite! Ms., 1972, December, 1(6).

A Chicana Idea. El Popo, 1972, December, 1-3.

Chicana Rights Project Year End Report. San Francisco: M.A.L.D.E.F., 1975, May, 1-14.

Chicana Service Action Center. Chicana Studies and Concerns. Los Angeles: Comision Femenil Mexicana Nacional, 1974.

Christensen, E.W. The Puerto Rican Woman: The Challenge of a Changing Society. Character Potential, 1975, March, 7(2), 89-96.

Cohen, L.M. Colombian Professional Women as Innovators of Culture Change. Unpublished doctoral dissertation, Catholic University of America. Dissertation Abstracts, 1966, 27(12-B).

Colman, H. Chicano Girl. New York: William Morrow, 1973.

Comision Feminil Holds First National Constitutional Convention. El Chicano, 1973, May 24, 7(51).

Cordova, I. The Relationship of Acculturation, Achievement, and Alienation Among Spanish American Sixth Grade Students. Las Cruces: New Mexico State University, 1971.

Cotera, M. Chicana Caucus. Magazin, 1972, August, 1(6), 24-26.

_____. A Reading List for Chicanas. Austin, TX: Information Systems Development, 1973.

_____. La Mujer. Magazin, 1973, September, 1(9), 30-34.

_____. When Women Speak. Event, 1974, January, 14(1), 22-25.

_____. La Chicana and la Familia. In Profile on the Mexican American Woman. Austin, TX: National Educational Laboratory Publishers, 1976, 140-156.

_____. La Chicana Today, Posture and Accomplishments. In Profile on the Mexican American Woman. Austin, TX: National Educational Laboratory Publisher's, 1976, 157-196.

_____. Diosa y Hembra. Austin, TX: Information Systems Development, 1976.

_____. Profile on the Mexican American Woman. Austin, TX: National Educational Laboratory Publishers, 1976.

Davidson, E. W. The Assimilation of Mexican Americans: A Personal Documentary of a Chicana and How She Relates to the Educational System. Unpublished student paper, Chicano Studies, University of California, Berkeley, 1972.

Del Drago, M. The Pride of Inez Garcia. Ms., 1975, May, 54.

Delgado, S. Chicana: The Forgotten Woman. Regeneracion, 1971, 2(1), 2-4.

_____. Young Chicana Speaks on Problems Faced by Young Girls. Regeneracion, 1971, 1(10).

Diaz-Guerrero, R. Psychology of the Mexican: Culture and Personality. Austin: University of Texas Press, 1975.

_____. A Mexican Psychology. American Psychologist, 1976, 32(11), 934-944.

Dumas, N. La Chicana and Women's Liberation. Unpublished student paper. Chicano Studies, University of California, Berkeley, 1971.

Duran, P. H., and Cabello-Argandona, R. The Chicana: A Bibliographic Study. Los Angeles: University of California Chicano Studies Program, 1974. Also available from ERIC (ED 076305), 1973.

Dworkin, A. G. National Origin and Ghetto Experience as Variables in Mexican American Stereotype. In C. A. Hernandez, M. J. Haug, and N. N. Wagner (eds.), Chicanos: Social and Psychological Perspectives (2nd ed.). St. Louis: C. V. Mosby, 1976, 136-139.

Espinosa, L. A. Machismo, Another View. La Luz, 1974, August, 1(4).

Flores, F. Conference of Mexican Women. Regeneracion, 1971, 1(10).

Flynn, B. Chicano: A Selected Bibliography. San Bernardino and Riverside Counties, CA: Inland Library System, 1971.

Garcia, M., and Dingman, J. A. Sex-Role Stereotypes Among Latinos. Symposium presentation at the American Psychological Association Convention, Chicago, 1975.

Garcia-Hancock, V. La Chicana, Chicano Movement and Women's Liberation. Chicano Studies Newsletter, University of California, Berkeley, 1971, February/March, 1(4-5), 1+.

Gill, L. J., and Spilka, B. Some Non-Intellectual Correlates of Academic Achievement Among Mexican-American Secondary School Students. Journal of Educational Psychology, 1962, 53(3), 144-149. Also in M. Kornrich (ed.), Underachievement. Springfield, IL: Charles C. Thomas, 1965, 102-110.

Goebel, J. B., and Cole, S. G. Mexican-American and White Reactions to Stimulus Persons of Same and Different Race: Similarity and Attraction as a Function of Prejudice. Psychological Reports, 1975, 36, 827-833.

Goldman, R. D., and Hewitt, B. N. Predicting the Success of Black, Chicano, Oriental and White College Students. Journal of Educational Measurement, 1976, Summer, 13(2), 107-117.

Gonzales, J. Sex Role Stereotypes. La Luz, 1973, January, 1(9), 21.

Gonzalez, S. A. La Chicana Piensa: The Socio-Cultural Conscience of a Mexican-American Woman. San Antonio, TX: Cultural Distribution Center, 1974.

⸻. The Chicana Perspective: A Design for Self-Awareness. San Jose, CA: San Jose State University, Spartan Bookstore, 1977.

Goodman, M. E., and Beman, A. Child's Eye-View of Life in an Urban Barrio. In N. Wagner and M. J. Haug (eds.), Chicanos: Social and Psychological Perspectives. St. Louis: C. V. Mosby, 1971.

Grant, T. E., and Renzulli, J. S. Identifying Achievement Potential in Minority Group Students. Exceptional Children, 1975, January, 41(4), 255-259.

Gray, T. C. A Bicultural Approach to the Issue of Achievement Motivation, 1975. Xerox University Microfilm, P. O. Box 1764, Ann Arbor, MI 48106. Order No. 75-25, 536.

Green, H. B. Comparison of Nurturance and Independence Training in Jamaica and Puerto Rico, with Consideration of the Resulting Personality Structure and Transplanted Social Patterns. Journal of Social Psychology, 1960, 51, 27-63.

Gutierrez, L. A. Bibliography on La Mujer Chicana. Austin, TX: Center for the Study of Human Resources and the Minority Women's Employment Program, 1975.

Hancock, V. G. La Chicana, Chicano Movement and Women's Liberation. Chicano Studies Newsletter (Berkeley), 1971, February/March, 1-6.

Harris, M. B., and Ramsey, S. Stereotypes of Athletes. Perceptual and Motor Skills, 1974, October, 39(2), 705-706.

Hart, D. Enlarging the American Dream. American Education, 1977, May, 13(4).

Hawkes, G. R., and Taylor, M. Power Structure in Mexican and Mexican-American Farm Labor Families. Journal of Marriage and the Family, 1975, November, 37(4), 807-811.

Hepburn, R. A., Gonzalez, V., and De Burciaga, C. P. The Chicana as Feminist. In A. G. Sargent (ed.), Beyond Sex Roles. St. Paul, MN: West, 1977, 266-273.

Hernandez, C. A., Haug, M. J., and Wagner, N. N. (eds.), Chicanos: Social and Psychological Perspectives. (2nd Ed.). St. Louis: C. V. Mosby, 1976.

Herrera-Duran, P. The Chicana: A Preliminary Bibliographic Study. Chicano Studies Center, University of California, Los Angeles, 1974.

Hispanic American Women Honored. Noticias de la Semana, 1975, December 15.

Hobart, C. W. Underachievement Among Minority Group Students: An Analysis and a Proposal. Phylon, 1963, Summer, 24(2), 184-196.

Interview with Delia Alvarez, POW Sister. La Raza, 1973, February, 1(10), 36-37.

Javier, M. C. La Chicana. Unpublished manuscript, Chicano Studies, University of California, Berkeley, 1971.

Johnson, A. G. Modernization and Social Change Attitudes Toward Women's Roles in Mexico City. Unpublished doctoral dissertation, University of Michigan. Dissertation Abstracts International, 1973, May, 33(11-A), 6471.

Jurado, M. Lack of Communication. Regeneracion, 1971, 1(10), 8.

Kagan, S., and Ender, P. B. Maternal Response to Success and Failure of Anglo-American, Mexican-American, and Mexican Children. Child Development, 1975, June, 46(2), 452-458.

Kimball, W. L. Parent and Family Influences on Academic Achievement Among Mexican American Students. Unpublished doctoral dissertation, University of California, Los Angeles. Dissertation Abstracts, 1968, 29(6-A), 1965.

King, L. M. Puertorriquenas in the United States. Civil Rights Digest, 1974, 6(3), 20-28.

Knaster, M. Women in Latin America: The State of Research. Latin American Research Review, 1976, 11(1), 3-74.

_____. Women in Spanish America: An Annotated Bibliography from Pre-Conquest to Contemporary Times. Boston: G. K. Hall, 1977.

Kovar, L. C. Faces of the Adolescent Girl. Englewood Cliffs, NJ: Prentice-Hall, 1968.

Krasno, F. Organizing the Unorganized. Black Maria, 1974, Spring, 2, 27-39.

Kuvlesky, W. P., and Patella, V. M. Degree of Ethnicity and Aspirations for Upward Social Mobility Among Mexican-American Youth. Journal of Vocational Behavior, 1971, 1(3), 231-244.

LaBelle, T. J. Attitudes and Academic Achievement Among Male and Female Anglo and Spanish American Fifth Grade Students. Unpublished doctoral dissertation, University of New Mexico. Dissertation Abstracts International, 1970, October, 31(4-A), 1624.

Leyva, R. Educational Aspirations and Expectations of Chicanos, Non-Chicanos and Anglo-Americans. California Journal of Educational Research, 1975, January, 26, 27-39.

Longauex y Vasquez, E. The Mexican-American Woman. In R. Morgan (ed.), Sisterhood Is Powerful. New York: Random House, 1970, 379-384.

Longeau, E. V.   La Chicana.   Magazin, 1972, April, 1(4), 66-68.

Lorenzana, N.   La Chicana: Transcending the Old and Carving Out a New Life and Self-Image.   De Colores, 1975, 2(3), 6-14.   Also available from ERIC (EJ134959), 1976.

Lurie, N. O.   Indian Women, A Legacy of Freedom.   The American Way, 1973, March.

McClintock, C. G.   Development of Social Motives in Anglo-American and Mexican-American Children.   Journal of Personality and Social Psychology, 1974, 29(3), 348-354.   Also in C. A. Hernandez et al. (eds.), Chicanos: Social and Psychological Perspectives. (2nd Ed.).   St. Louis, MO: C. V. Mosby, 1976, 126-132.

Machismo.   Inside the Beast, 1973, June 8, 1(13), 34-37.

MacLachlan, C. M.   Modernization of Female Status in Mexico: The Image of Woman's Magazines.   Revista/Review Interamericana, 1974, 4(2), 246-257.

Madsen, M. C.   Sub-Cultural Determinants of Cooperative and Competitive Behavior.   Available from ERIC (ED057891), 1972.

_____, and Shapira, A.   Cooperative and Competitive Behavior of Urban Afro-American, Anglo-American, Mexican-American, and Mexican Village Children.   Developmental Psychology, 1970, 3(1), 16-20.

Magón, R. F.   A La Mujer.   Oakland, CA: Prensa Sembrado, 1974.

Major, L. B.   The Psyche: Changing Role Creates Latina's World of Conflict.   Agenda, 1974, Spring, 6-7.

Mannino, F. V., and Shore, M. F.   Perceptions of Social Supports by Spanish-Speaking Youth with Implications for Program Development.   Journal of School Health, 1976, October, 46(8), 471-474.

Mariscal, L.   Index to Material on La Chicana Appearing in El Grito del Norte.   Berkeley, CA: Chicano Studies Library, 1976.

Marotz, R.   Sex Differentiation and Inequality: A Mexican-United States Comparison of Parental Aspirations for Daughters.   Journal of Comparative Family Studies, 1976, Spring, 7(1), 41-53.

Martinez, E.   La Chicana.   Ideal, 1972, September, 5-20.

Mayo, A.   Mexico: Mucho Macho.   Ms., 1972, December, 1(6).

Meadow, A., Lennhoff, S., Satterfield, D., and Tharp, R. G.

Changes in Marriage Roles Accompanying the Acculturation of the Mexican-American Wife. Journal of Marriage and the Family, 1968, August, 30(3), 404-412.

Mittelback, F. G., Moore, J., and McDaniel, R. Intermarriage of Mexican-Americans. Graduate School of Business Administration, University of California, Los Angeles, 1966.

Moerk, E. L. Age and Epogenic Influences on Aspirations of Minority and Majority Group Children. Journal of Counseling Psychology, 1974, July, 21, 294-298.

Montiel, M. The Social Science Myth of the Mexican-American Family, El Grito del Norte, 1970, Summer, 3(4), 56-63.

———. The Chicano Family: A Review of Research. Social Work, 1973, March, 22-31.

Morales, R. The Chicana Women Yesterday and Today. Renascimiento, 1973, September, 4(65), 1-2.

Moreno, D. (ed.). La Mujer--En Pie de Lucha. Mexico City: Espiña del Norte Publications, 1973.

Morner, M. The Conquest of Women. In L. Hanke (ed.), History of Latin American Civilization. Boston: Little, Brown, 1973.

Morton, W. M. Women Suffrage in Mexico. Gainsville: University of Florida Press, 1962.

Murillo, N. The Mexican American Family. In C. A. Hernandez et al. (eds.), Chicanos: Social and Psychological Perspectives. (2nd Ed.). St. Louis: C. V. Mosby, 1976, 15-25.

Nash, J., and Safa, H. I. (eds.). Sex and Class in Latin America. New York: Praeger, 1976.

Native Women. El Grito del Norte, 1971, June 5, 4(4-5), J.

Navar, I. La Mexicana, An Image of Strength. Agenda, 1974, Spring, 3-5.

Nelson, J. F. Some Causes and Consequences of Female Liberation Attitudes in Two Latin American Metropolises: A Causal Analysis of Non-Interval Data. Unpublished doctoral dissertation, University of Chicago. Dissertation Abstracts International, 1975, 36(7-A), 4779.

Nielo, C. The Chicana and the Women's Rights Movement: A Perspective. Civil Rights Digest, 1974, Spring, 6(3), 36-42.

Nieto, N. Macho Attitudes. Hijas de Cuahtomoc, 1971, April, 1, 9.

Nieto-Gomez, A. Chicanas Identity. Regeneracion, 1971, 1(10), 9.

―――― (ed.). Encuentro Feminil, 1973, Spring, 1(1).

――――. Colonial Women in Mexico. Regeneracion, 1974, 2(4), 18-19.

――――. Heritage of La Hembra. In S. Cox (ed.), Female Psychology: The Emerging Self. Chicago: Science Research Associates, 1976, 226-235.

Noel, R. C., and Allen, M. J. Sex and Ethnic Bias in the Evaluation of Student Editorials. Journal of Psychology, 1976, September, 94(1), 53-58.

Nuttall, R. L. Do the Factors Affecting Academic Achievement Differ by the Socio-Economic Status or Sex of the Student? A Puerto Rican Secondary School Sample. Final Report. Washington, D. C.: National Center for Education Research and Development, 1972. Also available from ERIC (ED064465), 1972.

Pallone, N. J., Hurley, R. B., and Rickard, F. S. Further Data on Key Influencers of Occupational Expectations Among Minority Youth. Journal of Counseling Psychology, 1973, 20, 484-486.

Paredes, F. Acculturation and Androgyny Among Mexican-Americans. Symposium presentation at the American Psychological Association Convention, San Francisco, 1977.

Pena, V. The Effect of Urbanization on the Traditional View/Role of the Chicana. Unpublished student paper, Chicano Studies, University of California, Berkeley, 1972.

Peñalosa, F. Mexican Family Roles. Journal of Marriage and the Family, 1968, November, 30, 680-689.

Perez-Solis, M. A Study of the Part-Time Employed Chicanas, Their Relation to the Women's Liberation Movement and the Chicano Movement. Unpublished manuscript, Chicano Studies, University of California, Berkeley, 1971.

Pesquera, B. M. La Raza Women as Revolutionaries. Unpublished student paper, Chicano Studies, University of California, Berkeley, 1971.

Pick, G. M. de. Refleccioners Sobre el Feminismo y la Raza. La Luz, 1972, August.

Portillo, C., Rios, G., and Rodriguez, M. Bibliography of Writings on La Mujer. Berkeley: University of California, Chicano Studies Library, 1976.

Pritikin, R. Raza Women Struggle. Berkeley Barb, 1974, November, 15.

Pulido, M. L. From the Past to the Present on to the Future. Unpublished student paper, Chicano Studies, University of California, Berkeley, 1971.

Ramirez, M., III. Identification with Mexican Family Values and Authoritarianism in Mexican Americans. Journal of Social Psychology, 1967, October, 73, 3-11.

_____, and Price-Williams, D. R. Achievement Motivation in Children of Three Ethnic Groups in the United States. Journal of Cross-Cultural Psychology, 1976, March, 7(1), 49-60.

Randall, M. Cuban Women Now. Toronto: The Women's Press, 1974.

Raza Unida Party. Party Platform on Chicanas. El Grito del Norte, 1971, June 5, 4(44), J.

La Raza Women Bibliography. San Francisco: Concilio Mujeres, 1975.

Raza Women's Platform. Rasca Tripas, La Raza Unida Party, Oakland, CA.

Regeneracion. Special issue on Chicana liberation. Available from Box 54624, Los Angeles, CA 90054.

Reyes de Garmo, E. An Exploratory Study of Mexican-American Women in an Urban Community. Unpublished doctoral dissertation, University of California, Berkeley, 1975.

Rincón, B. La Chicana, Her Role in the Past and Her Search for a New Role in the Future. Regeneracion, 1971, 1(10), 15-18. Also in F. Flores (ed.), Regnor Regeneracion, 1974, II(4), 39.

Rivera, A., and Duran, M. The Struggle for Women's Liberation in Puerto Rico Today. Intercontinental Press, 1975, April 21, 3(2), 534-536.

Rodarte, I. Machismo Vs. Revolucion. Chicanismo, 1972, April 14, 3(2), 3+.

Rodríquez, A. Message to My Sisters. El Grito del Norte. 1971, June 5, 4(45), J.

Roybal, R. M. Hispano Women Are Organized: Chicanas Unidas. La Luz, 1974, April, 3(1), 22.

Rucabo, G. La Chicana. Unpublished student paper, Chicano Studies, University of California, Berkeley, 1971.

Sanchez, R. (ed.). Mujer de la Raza. Unpublished anthology. Stanford: Chicano Fellows, 1974.

Saragoza, E. La Mujer in the Chicano Movement. Bronce Magazine, 1969, June, 1(4), 13.

Satterfield, D. M. Acculturation and Marriage Role Patterns: A Comparative Study of Mexican-American Women. Unpublished doctoral dissertation, University of Arizona. Dissertation Abstracts, 1967, 27(7-B), 2517.

Sepulveda, B. R. The Hispanic Woman Responding to the Challenges that Affect Us All. La Luz, 1972, November, 1(7).

Sister of Longest Held POW Starts Protest. Regeneracion, 1971, 1(10).

Smith, P. Daughters of the Promised Land: Women in American History. Boston: Little, Brown, 1970.

Southard, H. The Mexican American Woman--Her Rights. Y. W. C. A., 1972, January, 66, 17.

Stedman, J. M., and Adams, R. L. Achievement as a Function of Language Competence, Behavior Adjustment, and Sex in Young, Disadvantaged Mexican-American Children. Journal of Educational Psychology, 1972, October, 63, 411-417.

_____, and McKenzie, R. E. Family Factors Related to Competence in Young Disadvantaged Mexican-American Children. Child Development, 1971, November, 42(5), 1602-1607.

Stone, P. C., and Ruiz, R. A. Race and Class as Differential Determinants of Underachievement and Underaspiration Among Mexican-Americans. Paper presented at the American Psychological Association Convention, 1971.

Suarez, C. F. Sexual Stereotypes--Psychological and Cultural Survival. In Non-Sexist Education for Survival. Washington, D. C.: National Education Association, 1973, 18-20.

Sutherland, E. Colonized Women: The Chicana: An Introduction. In R. Morgan (ed.), Sisterhood Is Powerful. New York: Random House, 1970, 376-378.

Swartzbaugh, R. G. Machismo: A Value System of a Mexican Peasant Class. Unpublished doctoral dissertation, Ohio State University. Dissertation Abstracts International, 1970, August, 31(2-B), 493.

A Talk with PFLP Women on the Women's Role in the Struggle. Sada Al-Thawra, 1971, May, 1-7.

Torres, D. C. La Chicana and Her Search for Identity. Unpublished student paper, Chicano Studies, University of California, Berkeley, 1971.

Torres-Matrullo, C. Acculturation and Psychopathology Among Puerto Rican Women in Mainland United States. Unpublished doctoral dissertation, Rutgers State University. Dissertation Abstracts International, 1974, December, 35(6-B), 3041.

Tovor, F. R. The Puerto Rican Woman. New York: Plus Ultra Press, 1972.

Trujillo, M. The Colorado Chiaca and the Sixteenth Century Concept of Honor. Denver: El Valle, 1973.

_____. The Terminology of Machismo. Paper presented at the Chicano Conference, Colorado State University, Fort Collins, 1974.

Vangie, M. Women at Frontera, California. Regeneracion, 1971, 1(10).

Vasquez, M. La Chicana from Silence to Voiced Opinion. Unpublished student paper, Mexican-American Studies, California State University, 1972.

Vidal, M. Women: New Voice of LaRaza! In Chicanas Speak Out. New York: Pathfinder Press, 1971.

Viva la Chicana and All Brave Women of la Causa. El Grito del Norte, 1971, June 5, 4(4/5), A-B.

Ward, M. M. Woman Suffrage in Mexico. Gainesville: University of Florida Press, 1962.

Women and the Cuban Revolution. Merit Pamphlet. New York: Pathfinder Press, 1970.

Women's Action Program. Spanish Speaking Women's Concerns Group, Recommendations and Implementations. Washington, D. C.: Department of Health, Education and Welfare, 1972.

Women's Bureau. Fact Sheet on Women of Spanish Origin in the United States, 1971. Washington, D. C.: U. S. Department of Labor, 1971.

_____. Women of Spanish Origin in the United States. Washington, D. C.: U. S. Department of Labor, 1976.

_____. Women of Puerto Rican Origin in the Continental United States. Washington, D. C.: U. S. Department of Labor, 1977.

The Women Unite. Hijas de Cuahtemoc, 1971, April, 1, 7.

Workshop Resolutions--First National Chicana Conference. In Chicanas Speak Out. New York: Pathfinder Press, 1971.

C. LATIN WOMEN (continued)

2. SOCIAL-PSYCHOLOGICAL FORCES

Allen, J. G. The Effects of an Achievement Motivation Program on the Self-Concepts of Selected Ninth-Grade Students Representing Three Ethnic Groups. Unpublished doctoral dissertation. Dissertation Abstracts International, 1973, May, 33(11-A), 6048.

Berman, Y. Occupational Aspirations of 545 Female High School Seniors. Journal of Vocational Behavior, 1972, April, 2(2), 173-177.

Brennis, C., and Roll, S. Ego Modalities in the Manifest Dreams of Male and Female Chicanos. Psychiatry, 1975, 38(2), 172-185.

Bruckman, I. R. Vocational Expectations and Aspirations in Mexican-American Schoolchildren. Revista Interamericana de Psicologia, 1971, 5(1-2), 39-46.

Carrillo-Beron, C. Traditional Family Ideology in Relation to Locus of Control: A Comparison of Chicano and Anglo Women. Unpublished doctoral dissertation, University of California, Berkeley, 1971.

Cole, D., and Cole, S. Locus of Control and Cultural Conformity: On Going Against the Norm. Personality and Social Psychology Bulletin, 1974, 1(1), 351-353.

Evans, F. B., and Anderson, J. G. The Psychocultural Origins of Achievement and Achievement Motivation: The Mexican-American Family. Sociology of Education, 1973, Fall, 46(4), 396-416.

Garza, R. T., and Amers, R. E., Jr. A Comparison of Chicanos and Anglos on Locus of Control. In C. A. Hernandez et al. (eds.), Chicanos: Social and Psychological Perspectives. (2nd Ed.). St. Louis: C. V. Mosby, 1976, 133-135.

Grossman, B. Children's Ideal Self--Which Sex? Drawings from Two Mexican Subcultures. Paper presented at the American Psychological Association Convention, San Francisco, 1977.

Hale, J. M. Effects of Image-Enhancement Indoctrination on the Self-Concept, Occupational Aspiration Level, and Scholastic Achievement of Mexican-American Model Neighborhood Area Students. Unpublished doctoral dissertation, East Texas State University. Dissertation Abstracts International, 1973, February, 33(8-A), 4087-4088.

Hall, L. H. Personality Variables of Achieving and Non-Achieving

Mexican-American and Other Community College Freshmen. Journal of Educational Research, 1972, January, 65(5), 224-228.

Halpern, S. The Relationship Between Ethnic Group Membership and Sex and Aspects of Vocational Choice of Pre-College Black and Puerto Rican High School Students. Unpublished doctoral dissertation. Dissertation Abstracts International, 1972, July, 33(1-A), 190-191.

Healey, G. W., and DeBlassie, R. R. Comparison of Negro, Anglo, and Spanish-American Adolescents' Self Concepts. Adolescence, 1974, Spring, 9(33), 15-24.

Hishiki, P. C. The Self-Concepts of Sixth Grade Girls of Mexican-American Descent. California Journal of Educational Research, 1969, March, 20(2), 56-62.

Holtzman, W. H., Diaz-Guerrero, R., and Swartz, J. D. Personality Development in Two Cultures: A Cross-Cultural Longitudinal Study of School Children in Mexico and the United States. Austin: University of Texas Press, 1975.

Kagan, S., and Madsen, M. C. Cooperation and Competition of Mexican, Mexican-American, and Anglo-American Children of Two Ages Under Four Instructional Sets. Developmental Psychology, 1971, 5, 32-39.

_____, and _____. Rivalry in Anglo-American and Mexican Children of Two Ages. Journal of Personality and Social Psychology, 1972, 24(2), 214-220.

Linton, T. H. A Study of the Relationship of Global Self-Concept, Academic Self-Concept and Academic Achievement Among Anglo and Mexican-American Sixth Grade Students. Paper presented at the American Educational Research Association meeting, Chicago, 1972. Also available from ERIC (ED063053), 1972.

Major, L. B. The Psyche: Changing Role Creates Latina's World of Conflict. Agenda, 1974, Spring, 6-7.

Mason, E. P. Comparison of Personality Characteristics of Junior High Students from American Indian, Mexican, and Caucasian Ethnic Backgrounds. Journal of Social Psychology, 1967, 73(2), 145-155.

Mebane, D. F., Johnson, D. L., and Mebane, M. Manifest Anxiety in Mexican, Japanese, Israeli, and American Children. JSAS Catalog of Selected Documents in Psychology, 1976, May, 6, 40.

Morrison, K. E. An Examination of Self-Concept as It Relates to the Selected School Behaviors of Puerto Rican, Black, and White

Senior High School Students in Camden, New Jersey: An Experimental, Interdisciplinary Study in Education, Sociology, and Psychology. Unpublished doctoral dissertation, Rutgers University. Dissertation Abstracts International, 1975, October, 36 (4-A), 2108-2109.

Padilla, A. M. Psychological Research and the Mexican-American. In C. A. Hernandez et al. (eds.), Chicanos: Social and Psychological Perspectives. (2nd Ed.). St. Louis: C. V. Mosby, 1976, 152-159.

Ramirez, M., III. Cognitive Styles and Cultural Democracy in Education. In C. A. Hernandez et al. (eds.). Chicanos: Social and Psychological Perspectives. (2nd Ed.). St. Louis: C. V. Mosby, 1976, 196-210.

Rogers, D. P. Personality Traits and Academic Achievement Among Mexican-American Students. Unpublished doctoral dissertation, University of Texas, Austin. Dissertation Abstracts International, 1972, 33(5-A), 2179-2180.

Sanders, M., Scholz, J. P., and Kagan, S. Three Social Motives and Field Independence-Dependence in Anglo American and Mexican American Children. Journal of Cross-Cultural Psychology, 1976, December, 7(4), 451-462.

Schwartz, A. J. Comparative Values and Achievement of Mexican-American and Anglo Pupils. Washington, D. C.: Office of Education, 1969. Also available from ERIC (ED028873), 1969.

———. A Comparative Study of Values and Achievement: Mexican-American and Anglo Youths. Sociology of Education, 1971, Fall, 44, 438-462.

Valenzuela-Crocker, E. Chicana Business Women, Forging Paths in Power and Profit. Agenda, 1974, Spring, 16-21.

Vasquez, A. G., and Uhlig, G. E. The Spanish-Speaking of Chicago: Educational Issues. Journal of Instructional Psychology, 1971, 2(3), 2-8.

Vela, J. E. A Comparison of Chicano and Anglo Perceptions of the University Environment. Journal of College Student Personnel, 1977, November, 18(6), 462-466.

C. LATIN WOMEN (continued)

3. COUNSELING, EDUCATIONAL, OCCUPATIONAL FORCES

Anderson, J. G., and Safar, D. The Influence of Differential Community Perceptions on the Provision of Equal Educational Opportunities. Sociology of Education, 1967, 40(3), 219-230.

Aquilar, L. P. Unequal Opportunity and the Chicana. Civil Rights Digest, 1973, Spring, 5(4), 30-33.

Brawner, M. R. Migration and Educational Achievement of Mexican Americans. Social Science Quarterly, 1973, March, 53(4), 727-737.

Carrillo, G. A. Rural Chicanas in the Labor Force. Unpublished student paper, Chicano Studies, University of California, Berkeley, 1971.

Chapa, E. Report from the National Women's Political Caucus. Magazin, 1973, September, 1(9), 37-39.

Chavez, M. Chicana on Campus. Hijas de Cuahtemoc, 1971, April, 1, 8.

Chicana Service Action Center. Chicana Status and Concerns. Los Angeles: Comision Femenil Mexicana Nacional, 1974.

Comision Feminil Holds First National Constitutional Convention. El Chicano, 1973, May 24, 7(51).

Cotera, M. La Chicana Today, Posture and Accomplishments. In Profile on the Mexican-American Woman. Austin, TX: National Educational Laboratory Publishers, 1976, 157-196.

_____. Chicanas in the U.S., A Socioeconomic Profile. In Profile on the Mexican American Woman. Austin, TX: National Educational Laboratory Publishers, 1976, 120-139.

De Garcia, N. V. Education and the Spanish Speaking Woman: A Sad Reality. Journal of the National Association for Bilingual Education, 1976, May.

Delgado, S. Young Chicana Speaks on Problems Faced by Young Girls. Regeneracion, 1971, 1(10).

Esquer, R. J. Sexism in Education: The University. Unpublished student paper, Chicano Studies, University of California, Berkeley, 1970.

Gay, G. Teachers' Achievement Expectations of and Classroom Interactions with Ethnically Different Students. Contemporary Education, 1975, Spring, 46, 166-172.

Gonzales, A. Analysis of a Challenge Program in Relation to Entry and Success of Mexican-American Students in Higher Education and the Effect on Their Self-Image, Attitude Toward Education and Degree of Community Participation. Unpublished doctoral dissertation, University of Michigan. Dissertation Abstracts International, 1975, January, 35(7-A), 4284.

Gonzalez, R. M. A Review of the Literature on Mexican-American Women Workers in the United States Southwest 1900-1975. Unpublished manuscript, University of California, Irvine, 1976.

Goodman, P. W., and Brooks, B. S. A Comparison of Anglo and Mexican-American Students Attending the Same University. Kansas Journal of Sociology, 1974, Fall, 10(2), 181-203.

Gouveia, A. J. Student-Teachers in Brazil: A Study of Young Women's Career Choices. Unpublished doctoral dissertation, University of Chicago, 1962. American Doctoral Dissertations, 1962, 11(96), 204. Also available from ERIC (ADG02-61504), 1962.

Hall, P. Q., Malcolm, S. M., and Posner, S. E. Conference on Minority Women Scientists. Science, 1976, February 6, 191, 457.

Hernandez, D. Mexican-American Challenge to a Sacred Cow, A Critical Review and Analysis Focusing on Two UCLA Graduate School of Education Research Studies About Mexican American "Values" and Achievement. Los Angeles: Mexican Cultural Center, 1970.

Hispanic American Women Honored. Noticias de la Semana, 1975, December 15.

Hurstfield, J. The Educational Experiences of Mexican Americans: Cultural Pluralism or Internal Colonialism? Oxford Review of Education, 1975, 1(2), 137-149.

Kuvlesky, W. P., and Patella, V. M. Aspirations of Chicano Youth from the Texas Border Region: A Metropolitan-Non-Metropolitan Comparison. Washington, D. C.: Cooperative State Research Service, 1974. Also available from ERIC (ED091093), 1974.

Lamb, R. R. Concurrent Validity of the American College Testing Interest Inventory for Minority Group Members. Unpublished doctoral dissertation. Dissertation Abstracts International, 1975, 35(7), 4161.

Legislatures $25 Million Staff: Women and Minorities. California Journal, 1974, August, 273.

Lowman, R. P., and Spuck, D. W. Predictors of College Success for the Disadvantaged Mexican-American. Journal of College Student Personnel, 1975, January, 16(1), 40-48.

Massey, G. C., Scott, M. V., and Dornbusch, S. M. Racism Without Racists: Institutional Racism in Urban Schools. Black Scholar, 1975, November, 7(3), 10-19.

Maymi, C. R. Business/Women Fighting to Open the Doors to Opportunity. Agenda, 1974, Spring, 8-10.

Medina, C., and Reyes, M. R. Dilemmas of Chicana Counselors. Social Work, 1976, November, 21(6), 515-517.

Molina, J. C. The Influence of Experiences as Teacher Aides on the Level and Direction of Occupational Aspirations of Selected Disadvantaged High School Girls. Unpublished doctoral dissertation. Dissertation Abstracts, 1969, 29(8-A), 2805-2806.

Moore, B. E. A. Some Working Women in Mexico: Traditionalists and Modernists. Unpublished doctoral dissertation, Washington University. Dissertation Abstracts International, 1970, 31(7-A), 3659.

Nava, Y. Employment Counseling and the Chicana. Encuentro Femenil, 1973, Spring, 1.

Newcomb, H. Do You Know Frontera? Or a Brief History of the California Institute for Women. Unpublished student paper, Chicano Studies, University of California, Berkeley, 1974.

Nieto-Gomez, A. The Needs of the Spanish Speaking Mujer (Women) in Woman-Manpower Training Programs. Available from ERIC (ED096044), 1974.

Poblano, R. Ghosts in the Barrio: Issues in Bilingual-Bicultural Education. California: Lewsing Press, 1973.

Project on the Status and Education of Women. Minority Women and Higher Education #2. Washington, D.C.: Association of American Colleges, 1975, March.

Rios, G. E. The Chicana College Student. Unpublished student paper, Chicano Studies, University of California, Berkeley, 1975.

Ross, C. S. Identification of Cultural Characteristics of Young Puerto Rican Children in Mainland Schools: A Survey of the Reference Literature, and a Study and Analysis of Teachers' Perceptions. Unpublished doctoral dissertation, Rutgers University. Dissertation Abstracts International, 1974, December, 35(6-A), 3414-3415.

Sanchez, C. Chicanas in Higher Education. Encuentro Femenil, 1973, Spring, 1, 27-33.

Sanchez, G. I. Bilingualism and Mental Measures: A Word of Caution. In C. A. Hernandez et al. (eds.), Chicanos: Social and Psychological Perspectives. (2nd Ed.). St. Louis: C. V. Mosby, 1976, 169-173.

Sedlacek, W. E., Lewis, J. A., and Brooks, G. C., Jr. Black and Other Minority Admissions to Large Universities: A Four Year National Survey of Policies and Outcomes. Research in Higher Education, 1974, 2, 221-230.

Sharma, P. C. Female Working Role and Economic Development: A Selected Research Bibliography, Monticello, IL: Council of Planning Librarians, 1974.

Smith, M. L. Influence of Client Sex and Ethnic Group on Counselor Judgments. Journal of Counseling Psychology, 1974, 21, 516-521.

Stewart, J. En Expaña--Un Banco para las Mujeres. Burroughs Clearing House, 1975, February, 59(5), 20-21+.

Vangie, M. Women at Frontera, California. Regeneracion, 1971, 1(10).

Wanted: Chicano and Chicano Nurses. National Chicano Health Organization, 1709 W. 8th St., Los Angeles, CA.

Women and Labor in 19th Century Mexico. Paper presented at the Pacific Coast Council on Latin American Studies Conference, California, MT, October 1972.

Women's Action Program. Spanish Speaking Women's Concerns Group, Recommendations and Implementations. Washington, D. C.: Department of Health, Education and Welfare, 1972.

Wright, S. J. Redressing the Imbalance of Minority Groups in the Professions. Journal of Higher Education, 1972, March, 43(3), 239-248.

C. LATIN WOMEN (continued)

4. CAREER DEVELOPMENT, ORIENTATION, CONTINGENCIES

Contreras, E., and Winter, R. La Chicana, Changing Perspectives On Marriage, Family and Careers. Unpublished manuscript, Chicano Studies, University of California, Berkeley, 1971.

Garcia-Hancock, V. (ed.). La Chicana: Changing Perspectives on Marriage, Family and Career. Reading List, Chicano Studies, University of California, Berkeley, n. d.

Kao, R. S. Sharing of Homemaking Tasks Between New York City Puerto Rican Working Class Husbands and Wives as Related to the Wife's Family Life Attitudes and Her Employment or

Non-Employment. Unpublished doctoral dissertation, New York University. Dissertation Abstracts International, 1974, August, 35(2-B), 924.

Nuttall, E., and Nuttall, R. L. Coping Patterns for Puerto Rican Mothers Heading Single-Family Households. Paper presented at the American Psychological Association Convention, Washington, D. C., 1976.

Perez-Solis, M. A Study of the Part-Time Employed Chicanas, Their Relation to the Women's Liberation Movement and the Chicano Movement. Unpublished manuscript, Chicano Studies, University of California, Berkeley, 1971.

Richmond, M. L. Beyond Resource Theory: Another Look at Factors Enabling Women to Affect Family Interaction. Journal of Marriage and the Family, 1976, May, 38(2), 257-266.

Steinmann, A., Levi, J., and Fox, D. J. A Cross-Cultural Study: Women's Attitudes Towards Career and Family Roles. International Journal of Health Education, 1963, 8(4), 1-8.

Weller, R. H. The Employment of Wives, Dominance, and Fertility. Journal of Marriage and the Family, 1968, 30(3), 437-442.

_____. The Employment of Wives, Role Incompatibility and Fertility: A Study of Middle Class Residents of Puerto Rico. Milbank Memorial Fund Quarterly, 1968, 46, 507-526.

D. NATIVE-AMERICAN WOMEN

Abu-Laban, B. The Impact of Ethnicity and Occupational Background on the Aspirations of Canadian Youth. Sociological Inquiry, 1966, Winter, 36(1), 116-123.

Adkins, D. C., Payne, F. E., and Ballif, B. L. Motivation Factor Scores and Response Set Scores for 10 Ethnic-Cultural Groups of Preschool Children. American Educational Research Journal, 1972, 9, 557-572.

Anderson, J. G., and Safar, D. The Influence of Differential Community Perceptions on the Provision of Equal Educational Opportunities. Sociology of Education, 1967, 40(3), 219-230.

Bahr, H. M., Chadwick, B. A., and Day, R. C. (eds.). Native Americans Today: Sociological Perspectives. New York: Harper & Row, 1972.

Beuf, A. H. The Home of Whose Brave? Problems Confronting Native Americans in Education. Journal of the National Association for Women Deans, Administrators, and Counselors, 1976, Winter, 39(2), 70-80.

Campbell, D. N. On Being Number One: Competition in Education. Phi Delta Kappan, 1974, October, 56, 143-146.

Comer, A. Hokahe! A Look at the Young Indian Woman. Mademoiselle, 1970, October, 71, 158-159+.

Delk, J. L., et al. Drop-Outs from an American Indian Reservation School: A Possible Prevention Program. Journal of Community Psychology, 1974, January, 2(1), 15-17.

Downs, J. F. The Cowboy and the Lady: Models as a Determinant of the Rate of Acculturation Among the Piñon Navajo. In H. M. Bahr et al. (eds.), Native Americans Today: Sociological Perspectives. New York: Harper & Row, 1972, 275-291.

Edington, E. D. Academic Achievement of American Indian Students --Review of Recent Research. Paper presented at Rural Sociological Society meeting, San Francisco, 1969. Also available from ERIC (ED032168), 1970.

Ewers, J. C. Deadlier Than the Male. American Heritage, 1965, June, 16(4), 10-13.

French, L. Social Problems Among Cherokee Females: A Study of Cultural Ambivalence and Role Identity. American Journal of Psychoanalysis, 1976, Summer, 36(2), 163-169.

Gay, G. Teachers' Achievement Expectations of and Classroom Interactions with Ethnically Different Students. Contemporary Education, 1975, Spring, 46, 166-172.

Graves, T. D., and Chance, N. A. Culture Change and Psychological Adjustment: The Case of the American Indian and Eskimo. Paper presented at the International Congress of Anthropological and Ethnological Sciences, Tokoyo and Kyoto, Japan, 1968.

_____, Powers, J. F., and Michener, B. P. Socio-Cultural and Psychological Factors in American Indian High School Classroom Performance and Post-Graduation Success: Theory and Methodology. Indian Education Research Report No. 1. Boulder: University of Colorado, 1967.

Gridley, M. American Indian Women. New York: Hawthorn Books, 1974.

Hall, P. Q., Malcolm, S. M., and Posner, S. E. Conference on Minority Women Scientists. Science, 1976, February, 191, 457.

Harris, L. D. Americans for Indian Opportunity, Washington, D. C.,

Go Back to Where?--Notes of Feminine Indian Activist. Invited address at the American Psychological Association Convention, Chicago, 1975.

Havighurst, R., and Fuchs, E. To Live on This Earth: American Indian Education. New York: Doubleday, 1972.

Hoylan, R. Indian Women and the Movement. HUD Challenge, 1975, September.

Just, G. A. American Indian Attitudes Toward Education in Select Areas of South Dakota. Unpublished master's thesis, South Dakota State University, 1970.

Katz, J. B. (ed.). I Am the Fire of Time: The Voices of Native American Women. New York: E. P. Dutton, 1977.

Kersey, Jr., H. A., and Greene, H. R. Educational Achievement Among Three Florida Seminole Reservations. School and Society, 1972, January, 100, 25-28.

Knill, W. D. Occupational Aspirations of Northern Saskatchewan Students. Alberta Journal of Educational Research, 1964, 10(1), 3-16.

Lamb, R. R. Concurrent Validity of the American College Testing Interest Inventory for Minority Group Members. Unpublished doctoral dissertation. Dissertation Abstracts International, 1975, 35(7), 4161.

Landes, R. The Ojibwa Woman. New York: W. W. Norton, 1971.

Lefley, H. P. Social and Familial Correlates of Self-Esteem Among American Indian Children. Child Development, 1974, September, 45(3), 829-833.

_____. Differential Self-Concept in American Indian Children as a Function of Language and Examiner. Journal of Personality and Social Psychology, 1975, 31(1), 36-41.

Lewis, A. Separate Yet Sharing; Role of Iroquoian Women. Conservationist, 1976, January/February, 30(4), 17.

Livingston, K. S. Contemporary Iroquois Women and Work: A Study of Consciousness of Inequality. Unpublished doctoral dissertation, Cornell University, 1974. Dissertation Abstracts International, 1974, December, 35(6-A), 3194-3195. Also available from ERIC (ADG74-26284), 1974.

Lurie, N. (ed.). Indian Women: A Legacy of Freedom. In R. I. Acopi (ed.), Look to the Mountain Top. San Jose, CA: H. M. Gousha, 1972.

McDonald, T. Group Psychotherapy with Native-American Women.

International Journal of Group Psychotherapy, 1975, October, 25(4), 410-420.

McNickle, D. The Sociocultural Setting of Indian Life, the Mental Health of the American Indian. American Journal of Psychiatry, 1968, 125(2), 219-223.

Metcalf, A. From Schoolgirl to Mother: The Effects of Education on Navajo Women. Social Problems, 1967, June, 23(5), 535-544.

Native American Women. New York: American Indian Treaty Council Information Center, 1975.

Niethammer, C. Daughters of the Earth. New York: P. F. Collier, 1977.

Reboussin, R., and Goldstein, J. W. Achievement Motivation in Navaho and White Students. American Anthropologist, 1966, 68(3), 740-745. Also in H. M. Bahr et al. (eds.), Native Americans Today: Sociological Perspectives. New York: Harper & Row, 1972, 172-177.

Rosenthal, B. Development of Self-Identification in Relationship to Attitudes Towards the Self in the Chippewa Indians. Genetic Psychology Monographs, 1974, August, 90, 43-141.

Ryan, R. A. An Investigation of Personality Traits of Native American College Students at the University of South Dakota. Unpublished doctoral dissertation, University of South Dakota. Dissertation Abstracts International, 1974, July, 35(1-A), 198-199.

Sedlacek, W. E., Lewis, J. A., and Brooks, G. C., Jr. Black and Other Minority Admissions to Large Universities: A Four Year National Survey of Policies and Outcomes. Research in Higher Education, 1974, 2, 221-230.

Senior, W. B. Relation of Self-Concept and Values and Public School Achievement for Selected American Pueblo Indian Students Attending Public School in the State of New Mexico. Unpublished doctoral dissertation, University of New Mexico. Dissertation Abstracts International, 1974, August, 35(2-A), 828.

Sharma, S. Manifest Anxiety and School Achievement of Adolescents. Journal of Consulting and Clinical Psychology, 1970, June, 34(3), 403-406.

Swanson, R., and Henderson, R. W. Achieving Home-School Continuity in the Socialization of an Academic Motive. Journal of Experimental Education, 1976, Spring, 44, 38-44.

Thurber, S. Changes in Navajo Responses to the Draw-A-Man Test. Journal of Social Psychology, 1976, June, 99(1), 139-140.

Witt, S. H. Native Women Today: Sexism and the Indian Woman. Civil Rights Digest, 1974, 6, 43-45. Also in S. Cox (ed.), Female Psychology: The Emerging Self. Chicago: Science Research Associates, 1976, 249-259.

Women's Bureau. American Indian Women. Washington, D. C.: U. S. Department of Labor, 1977.

Wright, S. J. Redressing the Imbalance of Minority Groups in the Professions. Journal of Higher Education, 1972, March, 43(3), 239-248.

AUTHOR AND COAUTHOR INDEX

Abramowitz, C. V. 264, 338
Abramowitz, S. I. 264, 338, 549
Abrams, M. S. 232
Abramson, J. 303, 368
Abramson, L. M. 89
Abramson, M. 570
Abramson, P. 384
Abramson, P. R. 55, 89
Abron-Robinson, L. A. 543
Abu-Laban, B. 624
Abzug, B. S. 397
Acker, J. 5, 451
Acopi, R. I. 626
Adams, B. N. 146
Adams, E. 42, 119, 226
Adams, E. B. 146
Adams, G. R. 248, 335, 338
Adams, J. F. 264
Adams, K. A. 451
Adams, M. 42
Adams, P. W. 338
Adams, R. L. 146, 615
Adams, W. 594
Adelson, J. 13
Adenika, T. J. 586
Adilman, P. H. 146
Adkins, D. C. 551, 603, 624
Adler, S. 255
Agel, J. 300
Aguirre, B. E. 603
Aguren, C. T. 174, 242
Ahammer, I. M. 5, 42
Ahern, D. D. 451
Ahlum, C. 303
Ahluwalia, S. P. 192
Ahluwalia, R. B. 111
Ahrons, C. 264
Aiken, L. H. 372, 476
Akhtar, S. 79
Akhter, M. 192
Alberti, J. M. 42, 79, 109, 174, 318, 423
Alberti, R. E. 264

Albino, J. E. 79
Albjerg, M. H. 79, 338
Albrecht, S. L. 5, 42, 79
Albright, D. 42
ALC Commission on Women in Church and Society 493
Alciatore, R. T. 358, 432
Aldous, J. 5
Alexander, A. 42
Alexander, K. L. 79, 338
Alexander, R. A. 399, 452
Alexander, S. 303, 397
Ali, S. N. 192
Alibaruho, G. L. 551
Alker, H. 252
Allen, A. J. 456, 504, 525
Allen, B. P. 59
Allen, D. B. 303
Allen, D. V. 360
Allen, G. J. 242
Allen, I. H. 456, 485, 504, 525
Allen, J. G. 586, 617
Allen, J. L. 220
Allen, M. J. 613
Allgeier, E. R. 5
Allison, R. B. 5
Allison, S. N. 238
Almazol, C. 603
Almquist, C. 251
Almquist, E. M. 79, 146, 147, 265, 397, 500, 501, 518, 551, 586
Alonso, R. C. 192
Alpander, G. G. 451
Alpaugh, P. K. 79
Alpenfels, E. J. 498
Alper, T. G. 79, 80, 147, 192
Alperson, E. D. 541
Alpert, J. L. 69, 127, 303
Alpert, J. L. 42, 43, 80, 338
Alpert, R. 19, 35, 71
Al-Rubaly, A. 567

Alshan, L. M. 73, 571, 572
Altavela, J. 101, 154, 544
Altenor, A. 557, 590, 601
Althof, S. E. 220
Altman, S. L. 147, 500
Altschule, M. D. 80
Altshuler, R. J. 238
Altucher, N. 30
Alutto, J. A. 192
Alves, G. J. 188
Alvord, D. J. 174
Amatea, E. S. 265
AMEG Commission Report on Sex Bias in Measurement 265
American Association of University Professors 368
American Association of University Women Educational Foundation 265
American Federation of Teachers 303
American Historical Association 480
American Political Science Association 480
American Psychological Association Task Force 265
Amers, R. E., Jr. 617
Ames, C. 256
Ames, R. 256
Amidjaja, I. R. 80
Amidon, A. 135
Amira, S. 264
Amos, W. E. 551
Amundsen, K. 43, 397
Anastasi, A. 80, 147, 398
Anastasiow, M. 344
Ancker-Johnson, B. 467, 518
Anderson, B. E. 547
Anderson, C. 43
Anderson, D. 115
Anderson, J. G. 603, 617, 619, 624
Anderson, L. B. 193
Anderson, M. 265
Anderson, M. H. 551
Anderson, P. E. 414
Anderson, P. R. 304
Anderson, P. S. 485
Anderson, R. 5
Anderson, R. C. 147
Anderson, R. E. 398

Anderson, R. P. 213
Anderson, S. 332
Anderson, T. B. 174
Andreas, C. 5, 304, 398
Andreasen, V. K. 128
Andres, D. 18
Andrews, H. B. 184
Andrews, J. A. 81
Aneshensel, C. S. 33
Angelini, A. L. 604
Angrist, S. S. 43, 80, 146, 147, 193, 265, 338, 500, 501, 518
Annerblom, M. L. 5
Anquiano, L. 604
Anthony, S. B. 43
Antonovsky, A. 586, 601, 604
Anttonen, R. G. 364
Antwisle, D. R. 80
Apostal, R. A. 193
Appleton, H. L. 80
Appley, D. 80
Apthorp, H. 564
Aquilar, L. P. 604, 620
Aramoni, A. 604
Arata, E. S. 598, 603
Arber, S. 65
Arbuckle, D. S. 81
Arbuthnot, J. 81
Archer, J. 39, 63, 75, 112
Archer, J. 43
Archibald, B. 556
Arellano, J. 604
Argote, L. M. 220
Argyle, F. 576
Arkava, M. L. 265
Arlow, P. 338
Armanda, A. 6
Armenakis, A. A. 399, 452, 453
Arnold, M. 604
Arnold, M. R. 100
Arnold, R. D. 338
Arnott, C. C. 518
Aronew, E. 107
Aronoff, J. 6
Aronson, H. 399
Arter, M. H. 384
Arvey, R. 409
Arvis, P. F. 451
Asbury, C. A. 552
Asche, M. 174
Ashbaugh, J. A. 265

Ashburn, E. A. 398, 451
Ashenfelter, O. 434, 550
Asher, J. 265
Asher, S. R. 339
Askins, J. 304
Aslin, A. L. 265
Asper, L. B. 384
Association for Women in Mathematices (Philadelphia Chapter) 467
Association of American Medical Colleges 368
Ast, S. 129
Astin, A. H. 43, 368, 502
Astin, A. W. 147, 193, 339, 384, 501, 511, 586
Astin, H. S. 6, 81, 147, 193, 214, 280, 304, 305, 313, 339, 340, 369, 398, 467, 480, 498, 501, 502, 508
Astin, N. 290
Athanassiades, J. C. 398, 451
Atkinson, J. 6
Atkinson, J. W. 228
Atlanta, Georgia, NOW Chapter 398
Attwood, C. L. 339
Auburn, P. N. 118
Augustine, M. 86
Aulette, J. R. 43
Austrin, H. R. 554, 588
Avery, W. P. 567
Avila, D. L. 193
Axelson, L. J. 518, 601
Ayella, M. E. 398, 552

Babchuk, N. 480
Babcock, R. J. 265, 304
Baca, G. 604
Bach, L. 384
Bachtold, L. M. 174, 193, 212, 214, 502, 518
Backer, T. E. 274, 413, 504
Bacon, P. A. 384
Badaracco, M. R. 38, 43, 73
Badner, G., Jr. 339
Baefsky, P. M. 81
Baehr, R. F. 552
Baer, J. 274
Baer, M. F. 398, 487
Baer, R. M. 157

Index / 631

Baetjer, A. M. 399
Baggett, L. R. 339, 468
Bagley, M. T. 339
Bahr, H. M. 624, 625, 627
Baier, K. 505
Bailey, J. T. 194
Bailey, K. G. 81, 175
Bailey, L. J. 214
Bailey, M. M. 3, 37
Bailey, P. 502
Bailey, R. C. 81, 174, 175
Bailyn, L. 452, 498, 518, 519
Baine, E. V. 385
Baird, A. W. 150
Baird, J. E. 81
Baird, L. L. 81, 175, 339, 587, 593
Bakan, D. 6, 43
Baker, B. J. 43
Baker, C. C. 81
Baker, C. T. 161, 202
Baker, E. C. 491
Baker, M. 368, 519
Baker, T., and Fitzgerald, W. 304
Balasuriya, T. 493
Balazs, E. K. 147, 148, 175, 194
Baldwin, J. M. 175
Balkin, J. 55
Ball, H. W. 587
Ball, P. G. 387
Ballif, B. L. 551, 603, 624
Balter, L. 12
Baltes, P. B. 6, 14
Bancke, L. L. 148
Banducci, R. 148
Banerjee, D., and Pereek, U. 81
Banikiotes, F. G. 43
Banikiotes, P. G. 43
Banker, J. 148
Banks, J. A. 576
Banner, L. W. 491, 522
Bannon, M. M. 160
Banreti-Fuchs, K. M. 214
Banta, P. 519
Barabasz, A. F. 555
Barachie, D. 86
Barbash, J. 399
Barberio, R. 604
Barbier, M. N. 265
Barcelona, C. T. 452

632 / Index

Barclay, D. 519
Bard, J. F. 304
Bardo, H. 588
Bardon, J. I. 576
Bardwick, J. M. 6, 13, 19, 24, 33, 41, 43, 44, 51, 63, 81, 117, 128, 156, 175, 200, 227, 441, 473, 502, 519, 585
Barfield, V. M. 38
Barger, B. 194
Barker, L. W. 175
Barnal, L. 399
Barnard, T. M. 399
Barnard, W. A. 28
Barnes, M. 452
Barnes, R. D. 247
Barnes, W. F. 81
Barnett, J. 420
Barnett, M. A. 81
Barnett, R.C. 6, 82, 194
Baron, A. S. 368
Baron, R. M. 577
Barr, M. 68
Barrett, C. 6, 304
Barrett, C. J. 266
Barrio, R. 604
Barron, P. S. E. 399
Barry, H., III 6
Barry, K. 44
Barsaloux, J. 85
Bart, P. 44, 82
Bar-Tal, D. 44, 256
Bartnoff, J. 399
Bartol, K. M. 82, 209, 399, 452
Bartol, R. A. 452
Barton, C. 145
Baruch, G. K. 6, 44, 82, 148, 175, 220
Baruch, R. W. 82, 502, 519
Bass, A. R. 521
Bass, B. A. 242
Bass, B. M. 399, 452, 588
Basualdo, E. A. 368
Batcock, A. 11
Bates, M. 452, 480
Batlis, N. C. 239, 242
Batt, R. 452
Batterberry, A. 490
Batterberry, M. 490
Battle, E. S. 11, 83, 239 242, 552

Battle-Sister, A. 6
Bauer, R. A. 178
Baughman, E. E. 552
Baum, O. E. 266, 339
Baumel, E. 255
Baumrind, D. 7, 44, 148, 552
Baxter, B. K. 504, 523
Bayer, A. E. 44, 83, 149, 313, 368, 369, 587
Beach, D. R. 266
Beal, F. 552
Bean, J. P. 29, 37, 45, 56, 60, 61, 157, 283, 528
Beardslee, C. 7
Beattie, M. 479
Beatty, R. W. 587
Beaujard, P. 568
Beaven, M. 44
Bebbington, A. C. 519
Beck, B. H. 83
Beck, E. L. 452
Becker, G. 83
Becker, G. S. 399
Becker, M. 339
Becker, W. C. 7
Becker, W. M. 243
Beckett, J. O. 587, 601
Beckham, B. 399
Beckman, L. J. 256, 519
Bedeian, A. G. 452, 453
Bedell, J. 83
Bee, H. 69, 187, 472
Beeken, D. 247
Beesly, M. G. 266
Beeson, T. 493
Begley, P. J. 244
Beglis, J. F. 576
Behrman, J. A. 21, 59
Beier, E. G. 145
Beier, P. 145
Beker, J. 555
Belin, S. B. 266
Bell, C. S. 399, 453
Bell, D. 400
Bell, H. M. 188
Bell, M. L. 505
Bell, R. R. 552
Belletterie, G. 112
Belli, D. 34
Bellucci, G. 175
Below, H. I. 44
Belson, B. A. 266

Bem, D. J. 7, 45, 83, 400
Bem, S. J. 7, 44, 45, 83, 400
Beman, A. 608
Bender, M. 453
Bender, P. S. 604
Bendo, A. A. 175
Benedek, E. P. 339
Benedetti, C. R. 194
Benetar, J. 480, 502
Bengelsdorf, W. 340
Benitez, R. P. 519
Bennett, D. D. 519
Bennett, L., Jr. 552
Bennett, S. M. 77
Bennett, W. S. 149, 553, 559
Bennett, W. W. 453
Benreti-Fuchs, K. M. 194
Benson, P. 114
Benston, M. 400
Bentar, J. 519
Bentler, P. M. 14, 52
Benton, A. A. 83
Benton, R. 433
Bentzen, F. 83
Berberian, V. 178, 244
Bèreaud, S. 36, 44, 135, 227, 304, 332
Bereus, A. E. 7, 83, 228
Berg, I. E. 154, 526
Berg, P. 266
Berg, P. A. 256, 542, 576
Berg, P. I. 266
Bergen, M. 587
Berger, C. R. 175
Berger, G. 7, 83
Berger, M. 520, 538
Berger, S. E. 45, 81, 103
Berglund, G. W. 107, 157
Bergmann, B. 400
Bergmann, B. R. 542
Berk, R. A. 402
Berkan, J. 220
Berlew, D. C. 453
Berlyne, D. E. 227
Berman, E. 480, 520
Berman, G. 149, 194
Berman, G. S. 83, 553
Berman, M. R. 266
Berman, V. A. 83, 221
Berman, Y. 553, 617
Bernal, L. 604

Bernard, J. S. 8, 45, 46, 59, 83, 304, 305, 328, 340, 369, 385, 400, 453, 468, 474, 498, 542, 553
Bernard, M. 266
Bernard, S. 400
Bernstein, A. W. 221
Bernstein, B. E. 149
Bernstein, J. 8, 340
Bernstein, M. C. 400
Bernstein, M. D. 480
Bernstein, V. 373
Berreman, G. D. 468
Berry, G. L. 586
Berry, J. 27, 28, 287, 305, 369, 401, 502
Berry, J. B. 266, 287
Berry, K. J. 530
Berry, M. 369
Berry, T. 27, 28
Berscheid, E. 46, 51
Bert, C. V. 83
Bertsch, D. P. 149
Berwald, H. 369
Besdine, M. 149
Berzins, J. I. 46
Bessmer, M. 203
Best, D. L. 77
Betancourt, J. 453
Betancourt, R. 604
Bettelheim, B. 401
Betz, N. E. 84
Beuf, A. H. 84, 624
Beymer, L. 293
Bezler, A. G. 194
Bhanthumavin, D. L. 27
Bibb, J. J. Jr. 209
Biber, H. 8, 340
Bickel, H. E. 266
Bickel, P. J. 340
Bickman, L. 84, 558
Bickner, M. L. 401
Bieliauskas, V. J. 46
Bieri, J. 149
Biggar, J. C. 46
Biggerstaff, M. A. 267
Biggs, B. E. 578
Bigoness, W. J. 401, 587, 593
Bikman, M. 340, 369
Biller, H. B. 8, 46, 149
Billings, V. 46, 47, 305, 401
Billingsley, A. 553

Billingsley, A. T. 553
Billingsley, P. 267
Bing, E. 8, 149, 401
Bingham, G. 84
Bingham, S. 84
Bingham, W. C. 267
Binyon, M. 84
Biondo, J. 243
Bird, A. M. 84
Bird, C. 47, 84, 305, 401, 453, 497, 553, 587
Bird, R. A. 547, 596
Birk, J. M. 267, 297, 340, 542
Birnbaum, J. A. 8, 176, 194, 502
Birns, B. 8
Birren, J. E. 79, 210
Bisconti, A. S. 340
Bishop, J. D. 221
Bishop, J. F. 340, 401
Bisseret, N. 10
Bitton, D. 48
Bjorkquist, D. C. 340
Black, A. E. 7
Black, H. 559
Black, M. 76
Black, M. T. 553
Black, T. E. 84
Blackburn, M. 367
Blackledge, E. H. 305
Blackmore, J. 460
Blackwell, G. W. 305, 502
Blai, B., Jr. 503
Blake, C. H., Jr. 503
Blake, J. 8, 542
Blake, K. A. 44, 116, 309, 400, 427
Blakey, W. A. 47, 520, 542, 553
Blanchard, F. 16
Blank, S. 195
Blankenbaker, J. 87
Blankstein, K. R. 195
Blaska, B. 340, 369
Blau, F. D. 401
Blau, Z. S. 149
Blaubergs, M. S. 8, 84, 149, 176, 195, 221, 305, 401, 520
Blaufarb, M. 340
Blaxall, M. 62, 115, 321, 400, 401, 418, 428, 437, 508

Bledsoe, J. C. 9, 84, 149, 176
Bleiweis, L. H. 335, 383, 436, 547
Blimline, C. A. 47, 84, 268, 287
Blitz, R. C. 401, 499
Block, J. 9, 300
Block, J. H. 9, 47
Block, J. S. 468
Blood, R. O., Jr. 520
Bloom, A. R. 84, 149
Bloom, L. Z. 47, 268
Bloom, V. 126
Blough, W. J. 604
Bloustein, E. J. 402
Blum, L. 340
Blum, S. H. 83
Blumberg, H. 81
Blumberg, R. D. 9
Blumen, J. L. 85
Boalt Hall Women's Association of the School of Law at the University of California 486
Bobbe, C. N. 85
Bobowski, R. C. 268, 305
Bobson, S. 176
Bock, E. W. 493, 587
Boddez, M. 176
Boehm, V. R. 432, 453
Bogan, F. A. 402
Bogie, C. E. 268
Bogie, D. W. 85, 268
Bohan, J. S. 176
Bohannon, W. E. 47
Bohn, M. J., Jr. 524
Boivin, M. R. 220
Bolen, L. M. 243
Bolin, W. D. W. 520
Bollman, S. R. 510
Bolt, M. 41
Bolt, R. H. 468
Bolton, E. B. 453
Bon, R. J. 453
Bond, H. M. 553, 586, 601
Bond, J. 554
Bond, J. R. 85, 141
Bone, R. N. 23
Boneau, C. A. 480
Bongort, K. J. 221
Bonjean, C. M. 372, 476
Bonk, E. C. 353

Bonner, F. B.   554
Bonno, B.   114
Bonz, M. H.   221
Boocock, S.   437
Boodish, H. M.   305, 402
Boor, M.   243
Booth, A. N.   453
Boots, M.   73
Borchert, J.   85
Bordua, D. J.   150
Borgers, S. B.   268, 291, 305
Borich, G. D.   85, 542
Boring, P. Z.   268
Borislow, B.   176
Borow, H.   268
Borth, A. M.   554
Boruch, R. F.   587
Borup, J. H.   268, 542
Bosdell, B.   335
Bose, C. E.   85, 402
Boss, D. L.   85
Bott, M. M.   85
Botwinick, J.   213, 220
Bouchard, T. J.   85
Boulding, E.   47
Boulding, K.   85, 402
Boutwell, W. D.   340
Bouvier, L. F.   437
Bowden, J. D.   76
Bowden, S. S.   214
Bowen, L.   52
Bower, W. S.   85
Bowerman, C. E.   556
Bowers, J. J.   475
Bowers, T. A.   503
Bowles, R. T.   133
Bowman, G. W.   402, 453
Bowman, P. H.   125
Boyd, B.   268
Boyd, B. J.   503
Boyd, M.   47
Boyer, E.   402
Boyer, J. L.   85
Boyer, P. S.   507
Boyle, B. M.   402
Boyle, R. P.   9
Bozeman, B.   47
Brabant, S.   9, 86
Bradburn, N. M.   532
Braden, I. C.   372, 544
Bradford, D. L.   454
Bradley, J.   205

Bradley, R. H.   86, 243, 542
Bradway, K.   111
Brady, P. J.   176
Brager, G.   86, 341
Bragg, B. W. E.   150
Brainard, S.   376
Braito, R.   12, 50
Bralove, M.   520
Bramble, J.   354, 595
Brandenburg, J. B.   268, 340
Brandes, P. D.   554
Brandon, G. L.   306
Brandt, D. A.   221
Brandt, J. D.   243
Brandt, L. J.   341, 369
Brannigan, G. G.   86, 176, 243
Brannon, R.   47
Brashear, D. B.   268
Braun, J. R.   574
Braun, J. S.   164, 206
Braunagel, J. S.   490
Brawer, M. J.   408
Brawner, M. R.   620
Bray, D. W.   306, 402, 593
Bray, H.   351
Brebner, R. A.   268
Breeding, B.   306
Breedlove, C.   221
Breen, L. J.   252
Brehony, K. A.   86
Breinich, S. C.   426
Bremer, T. H.   221
Brennan, P.   284
Brenner, M. H.   454
Brennis, C.   617
Brenton, M.   221
Breogh, H.   60
Brew, A. P.   268
Breytspraak, C. H.   9
Brickman, P.   239
Brico, A.   397, 490
Bridgeman, B.   554, 587
Bridges, W. P.   402
Bridgette, R. E.   576
Brief, A. P.   402, 454, 554
Brierley, J.   86
Bright, M. H.   221
Bright, M. V.   554
Brigman, S. L.   344
Brinker, D. B., Jr.   19
Brinkerhoff, M. B.   86
Brinkerhoff, R.   176

Briscoe, M. L.   42, 119, 226
Brissett, M.   243
Britain, S. D.   605
Brittain, C. V.   153
Britton, G. E.   86
Britton, J. H.   155
Broad, M.   402
Brockway, B. S.   195, 268
Brodsky, A. M.   269, 341
Brody, C. M.   306, 341
Brogan, C. L.   9
Brogan, D.   43, 62, 150, 320
Broghton, A.   167, 253
Bromhead, E.   306
Bronfenbrenner, U.   306
Bronson, G. F.   402
Bronson, L.   605
Bronzaft, A. L.   52, 95
Brook, J. S.   86, 150, 554
Brook, P.   520
Brooke, M. H.   499
Brooke, M. J.   86
Brookhart, R. A.   341
Brookover, W. B.   176, 586
Brooks, B.   269, 503
Brooks, B. S.   621
Brooks, G. C.   71, 548, 569, 577, 590, 598, 623, 627
Brooks, L. P.   86, 269, 503
Brooks, M.   243
Brooks, T. R.   403
Brookshire, M. L.   341
Brophy, B.   48
Brophy, J. E.   24, 306, 350
Brose, C.   300
Bross, D. R.   306
Brothers, J.   221, 403
Broughton, A.   167
Broverman, D. M.   9, 40, 48, 69, 86, 124, 186, 269, 515
Broverman, I. K.   9, 40, 48, 69, 187, 269, 516
Brown, B.   257
Brown, B. A.   48
Brown, B. R.   575
Brown, B. S.   561, 567, 575, 583
Brown, C. A.   154, 526
Brown, C. R.   269
Brown, D.   581, 593
Brown, F.   48, 542
Brown, G. D.   403
Brown, H. A.   588

Brown, H. G.   403
Brown, J. M.   468, 496
Brown, L. S.   48
Brown, M.   213, 221, 594
Brown, N.   93
Brown, N. W.   214, 588
Brown, R. H., III   403
Brown, S. W.   520
Brownlee, J.   486
Bruce, J. A.   150
Bruce, J. D.   369
Bruce, P.   86
Bruch, C. B.   87, 195, 521
Bruckman, I. R.   48, 617
Bruder, R. A.   110, 229, 259
Bruemmer, L.   48
Bruker, R.   385, 454
Brunclik, H. L.   211
Brunner, T.   322
Bruton, B.   12, 50
Bryan, W. E.   150, 177, 214
Bryant, B.   605
Bryant, B. E.   9, 403, 542
Bryant, B. K.   243
Bryant, J. W.   588
Bryant, N. D.   108
Bryce, R. A.   454
Bryn, K.   468
Bryne, K. M.   70, 129
Bryson, J. B.   66, 481, 521
Bryson, R. B.   481, 521
Bryson, S., and Bardo, H.   588
Buccieri, C.   306
Buchanan, H. T.   87
Bucher, C. H.   87
Buchmeier, J. O.   547
Buck, M. R.   554, 588
Buckey, A.   306
Buckley, J. E.   403
Budner, S.   369
Buehlmann, B. B.   222
Buek, A. P.   306
Buescher, R. M.   87
Bull, J.   341
Bullard, D. G.   269
Bullough, B.   9, 48, 475, 554
Bullough, V. L.   9, 48, 475
Bumpass, L. L.   50, 65, 503
Bundy, D. A.   269
Bunker, B. B.   403
Bunker, G. L.   48

Bunker, J. P.   341
Bunker, K. A.   405
Bunting, J. W.   306
Bunting, M. I.   306, 369, 403, 468
Burbach, H. J.   554, 587
Bureau of Guidance   269
Bureau of the Census   306, 403, 542, 554, 605
Burford, B.   114
Burger, L. J.   484
Burghardt, N. R.   87, 222
Burhenne, D. P.   48
Buriel, R.   605
Burk, D.   403
Burke, B. W.   222
Burke, M.   457
Burke, R. J.   87, 454, 521
Burke, Y. B.   588
Burlin, F. D.   87, 150, 243, 244
Burma, J. H.   605
Burnett, P.   129
Burns, D. M.   385
Burns, D. S.   404
Burnstein, E.   30, 222
Burrell, L.   588
Burstyn, J.   341
Burtle, V.   274, 275, 287, 289, 290, 296
Burton, E. C.   195
Burton, G.   10, 48
Burton, R. V.   605
Burzynski, H. G.   306
Bush, C.   26
Bush, E.   290, 597
Bushnell, J. H.   341
Business and Professional Women's Foundation   269, 454
Busse, T. V.   169, 210
Butcher, H. J.   87
Butler, I. C.   177, 543
Butler, J. A., Jr.   554
Butler, M.   481
Butter, R. R.   150
Butterfield, D. A.   82, 87
Butterfield, E. C.   244
Butterfield, R.   107
Buys, C. J.   605
Buzenberg, M. E.   454
Byham, W. C.   204, 406, 410, 418, 420, 424, 446

Caballero, C. M.   222
Cabello-Argandona, R.   605, 607
Cabeza de Vaca, F.   605
Cabrera, Y. A.   605
Cadden, V.   49
Cade, T.   552, 555, 564, 568, 591, 595, 600
Cage, B. N.   511
Cagle, L. T.   555
Cahill, N. J.   342, 469
Cain, G. G.   404
Cain, M. A.   605
Calder, B.   404
Calderwood, A.   315, 328, 329, 330, 359, 360, 362, 368, 378, 380, 381, 392, 501, 588
Caldwell, M. D.   87
Caldwell, O. J.   404
Caldwell, T.   49
Calef, S. R.   222
Calia, V. P.   269
California State Advisory Commission on the Status of Women   269
Callahan, C. M.   120, 431
Callard, E. D.   150
Calsyn, R. J.   177
Cameron, H. K.   576
Campbell, D. N.   588, 625
Campbell, D. P.   87, 214, 269, 279, 404, 469, 513
Campbell, E. Q.   308, 556, 577
Campbell, J.   307
Campbell, J. T.   404
Campbell, M. A.   342, 475
Campbell, P.   579
Campbell, P. B.   10, 88
Campbell, R. E.   269
Campbell, R. R.   49
Campbell, W. W., Jr.   223
Canady, R. L.   393
Canary, B.   49
Canavan, D.   88, 555, 606
Cancian, F.   342, 370
Cannon, W. M.   218
Canter, R. J.   88
Cantor, G. N.   555
Cantor, M. G.   412, 443, 475, 490, 495

Cantwell, M. 404
Canty, E. M. 342
Caplan, P. J. 88
Caple, R. B. 188
Caplin, M. D. 576, 577
Carden, A. I. 26
Cardi, M. W. 88
Cardozo-Freeman, I. 606
Carey, A. Jr. 567
Carey, E. A. 270
Carlsen, M. L. 342
Carlson, E. 454
Carlson, H. 72, 495
Carlson, N. L. 150
Carlson, R. 49, 177
Carment, P. W. 88
Carmody, J. F., Fenske, R. H., and Scott, C. S. 88
Carmon, A. 531
Carnegie Commission on Higher Education 307, 342, 370
Carney, R. E. 10, 151, 195
Carpenter, M. 49
Carpenter, R. L. 404, 490
Carpenter, V. F. 555
Carper, J. 487
Carr, B. C. 467
Carr, D. L. 170
Carr, R. G. 363
Carrigan, W. C. 88, 151
Carrillo, G. A. 620
Carrillo-Beron, C. 617
Carringer, D. 555
Carrington, C. H. 588
Carroll, C. M. 588
Carroll, J. S. 88
Carroll, M. A. 385
Carruth, E. 454, 521
Carsello, C. 272
Carter, C. A. 481
Carter, D. 10, 270, 279, 282
Carter, D. E. 555
Carter, N. 88
Cartwright, L. K. 88, 151, 195, 214, 475, 521
Cary, E. 307, 404
Cascario, E. F. 342
Cascio, W. F. 588
Casey, T. J. 270
Cash, T. F. 244, 404
Cashdan, S. 195

Casilla, R. J. 606
Cassara, B. 49, 498
Cassell, P. 286
Casserly, P. L. 342
Castleman, J. 70
Cater, L. A. 10, 37, 49, 68, 277, 307, 443
Cates, J. N. 481
Caudill, M. S. 61
Cavanagh, B. K. 404
Cecil, E. A. 88, 404
Cegelka, P. T. 89, 307
Centa, D. 252
Center for Law and Education 307
Center for Women in Medicine 475
Centers, R. 49, 89
Centra, J. A. 342, 476, 505, 521, 526
Cerra, P. F. 530
Chabassol, D. J. 196
Chabran, M. 606
Chadwick, B. A. 624
Chafe, W. H. 10, 49, 405
Chafetz, J. S. 49, 307, 405, 521
Chall, J. 559
Chalmers, E. L., Jr. 307, 342, 370
Chamberlain, M. W. 568
Chambers, J. L. 89
Chammah, A. M. 127
Chan, J. 469
Chananie, J. D. 355
Chance, J. E. 151, 196, 244
Chance, N. A. 625
Chandler, T. A. 244
Chandler, T. M. 343
Chang, A. 42
Chang, T. S. 177, 343
Chang, W. 313, 414, 544
Charters, W. W. 357
Chapa, E. 606, 620
Chapman, A. H. 562
Chapman, J. B. 405, 454
Chapman, J. R. 405
Charters, W. W. 357
Chasen, B. 10, 270, 307, 343
Chavez, H. 606

Chavez, J. V.   606
Chavez, M.   620
Chayes, A. H.   49
Cheney, T.   249
Cherney, R. J.   242
Chernik, D. A.   454
Cherniss, C.   10, 49, 270
Chernovetz, M. E.   19
Cherry, F.   222
Cherry, K.   270
Cherry, L.   343
Cherry, R.   270
Chesler, P.   270, 271, 481
Chicana Service Action Center
   606, 620
Chinas, B. L.   370
Chisholm, S.   307, 405, 555
Chitayat, D.   138
Chmaj, B. E.   307, 570
Chobot, D. S.   89
Chodorow, N.   10, 151
Chombart de Leuwe, M. J.
   10
Chow, E. N. L.   114
Christen, S. R.   405
Christensen, E. W.   606
Christensen, H. T.   89
Christensen, K. C.   71, 343,
   548, 569, 589
Christensen, S.   343
Christopher, S. A.   151
Christy, M. D.   100
Chu, D.   308, 343
Chung, K. H.   454
Churchill, N. C.   405
Cicirelli, V. G.   221
Cimons, M.   405
Citizens' Advisory Council on
   the Status of Women   405
Citron, M.   40
Claebaut, D. P.   589
Clarenbach, K. F.   308
Clark, E. T.   89, 151, 177,
   186, 589
Clark, K.   567
Clark, L.   370
Clark, L. N.   521
Clark, M. A.   244
Clark, R. A.   107
Clark, S. M.   363, 381, 441
Clark, Y. Y.   543
Clarke, E.   271
Clarke, E. A.   385

Clarke, G. F.   343
Clarke, P.   405
Clarke, R. R.   124, 359
Clarkson, F. E.   40, 48, 269,
   516
Claus, K. E.   194
Clautour, S. E.   49
Clawson, A. H.   405
Clay, J. T.   196
Cleary, T. A.   244, 246, 366,
   550, 600
Cleland, V.   521
Clements, K.   196
Clementson, J.   29
Cless, E. L.   308, 330
Cleveland, S.   196
Clifford, M. M.   244, 343,
   366, 550, 600
Clift, V. A.   589, 595
Clifton, A. K.   49, 50
Clifton, M. A.   173, 189
Cline-Naffziger, C.   271
Clock, J. H.   10
Clopton, J. R.   196
Clutterbuck, D.   455
Coakley, J.   271
Coates, S.   11
Coates, T. J.   89
Cobb, B. B.   430
Cobb, S.   168
Cobbley, L. O.   385
Cobbs, P. M.   559
Coburn, K.   47, 268
Cochran, D.   50
Cochran, D. J.   271
Cochrane, D. G.   490
Cockburn, P.   522
Cohen, A.   211, 308
Cohen, L.   11, 127, 252
Cohen, L. M.   522, 606
Cohen, M. B.   50, 555
Cohen, M. S.   405, 522
Cohen, N. E.   222
Cohen, R. S.   31
Cohen, S.   244
Cohen, S. L.   125, 154, 405
Cohn, E.   112, 481
Coker, D. R.   11
Coker, R. E., Jr.   477, 529
Cole, C. W.   215
Cole, D.   89, 239, 343, 617
Cole, J.   481
Cole, N. A.   271

Cole, N. S. 271, 291, 351, 543
Cole, S. G. 608, 617
Cole, T. W., Sr. 543
Coleman, A. L. 555, 589
Coleman, J. S. 11, 89, 162, 308, 543, 577
Coleman, M. A. 21, 25, 89, 322
Coleman, N. C. 222
Coles, B. K. 222
Coles, F. S. 486
Colker, R., and Widom, C. S. 89
College and University Personnel Association 385
Collier, H. V. 89
Collins, A. M. 120, 271, 287, 431
Collins, G. 14
Collins, J. A. 89
Collins, L. 385
Collins, W. E. 430
Colman, D. 109
Colman, H. 606
Colson, E., and Scott, E. 370
Comer, A. 625
Comer, J. P. 556, 589
Comer, N. A. 90
Comisarow, R. W. 475
Commission on Civil Rights 308, 406, 589
Commission on Human Resources, National Research Council 543
Commission on the Status of Women 406
Commission Sociale de la Fédération Belge des Femmes Diplomees d'Université 522
Committee on Education and Employment of Women 308
Committee to Eliminate Sexual Descrimination in the Public Schools 308
Committee to Eliminate Sexual Discrimination in the Public Schools, and the Discrimination in Education Committee of NOW, Ann Arbor Chapter 308
Comstock, P. 508

Conaway, C. Y. 503
Condelli, L. 109
Condran, G. A. 406
Condry, J. 222
Conn, L. K. 11, 152
Connell, D. M. 90, 177
Constantini, E. 196, 488, 522
Constantinople, A. 50, 151
Contreras, E. 623
Conway, J. 11
Conyers, J. E. 406
Cook, A. H. 308
Cook, B. I. 151, 196, 271
Cook, H. 556
Cook, K. V. 32
Cook, R. E. 263
Cook, T. D. 104
Cooley, F. R. 343
Cooley, R. P. 455
Cooney, R. S. 406
Coonrod, C. 455
Coop, R. H. 575, 576, 586
Cooper, C. R. 100
Cooper, G. 271, 309, 406
Cooper, H. 589
Cooper, H. M. 577
Cooper, J. F. 267, 272, 542
Cooper, S. 332
Cooper, S. E. 522
Cooperman, I. G. 503
Cope, R. G. 90
Copeland, E. J. 589
Coplan, V. 301
Corazzini, J. G. 375, 483
Corbin, C. B. 196
Corby, N. 266
Cordova, I. 607
Corning, W. C. 21
Corrallo, S. B. 309
Corsini, D. A. 215
Corwin, B. J. 113
Corwin, R. G. 177
Cosby, A. G. 413
Cosentino, F. 50, 90
Coser, R. L. 406
Cosper, W. B. 481
Costar, J. W. 273
Costello, T. 406
Costrich, N. 50
Cotera, M. 607, 620
Cotier, S. 90, 177, 196
Cotten, D. 87
Cottle, T. J. 90, 151, 309,

344, 556
Council for University Women's Progress at the University of Minnesota 309
Counselman, E. F.   177, 503
Coursen, D.   385, 543
Cousins, M.   406
Cousins, R. B.   239
Covington, M. V.   120
Cowan, G.   90, 178, 556
Cowan, J.   406
Cowan, R. S.   522
Cowley, S. C.   407, 494
Cox, D. F.   178
Cox, S.   7, 17, 45, 141, 270, 544, 563, 613, 628
Coyle, J. M.   407
Cozy, H. M.   215
Craiglow, J. H.   309
Craik, K. H.   196, 488, 522
Craik, M.   50
Crain, R. L.   577
Cramer, B.   11
Cramer, M. R.   556
Crandall, V. C.   11, 90, 159, 196, 239, 244, 248, 250, 256
Crandall, V. J.   11, 90, 151, 152, 159, 161, 202, 239
Crano, W. D.   6, 90
Crase, D.   309, 344
Crawford, C.   556
Crawford, J. D.   91, 113
Creaser, J.   272
Crescimbeni, J.   152
Cristall, L.   91
Cristo, M. G.   152, 309, 522
Crockett, H.   141
Crockford, R. E.   309
Crofoot, A. P.   180, 350
Croke, J. A.   70, 239, 256
Cronkhite, B. B.   309
Crooks, L. A.   398, 404, 407
Crooks, M. M.   508
Cropley, A. J.   91, 98
Crosby, J. W.   385
Crosman, A. M.   344
Cross, K. P.   309, 344
Cross, S. L.   272
Crothers, D.   333
Crouch, D. R.   407
Crouch, J. G.   91, 196
Crovitz, E. K.   104, 196, 344, 571, 572

Crowe, D. H.   260
Crowe, K. P.   309
Crowell, S.   400
Crowley, J. E.   407, 522
Crowne, D. P.   11, 152
Crumrine, J.   230
Cruz, P.   541
Cuca, A.   522
Cuca, J. M.   480
Cull, J. G.   36, 277, 331, 351, 457, 461, 494, 515
Cullen, D. M.   319, 374, 375, 425
Culver, C.   93
Cummings, L.   272
Cummings, S.   556
Cunningham, J. D.   259
Cunningham, R. M.   407, 522
Cunningham, T.   178, 244
Curacar, G.   134
Curry, E. W.   165, 186, 556, 567
Curtis, E. A.   169
Curtis, J.   522
Curtis, R. C.   223
Curtis, T.   556
Cutler, M. H.   309
Cymerman, S.   282, 319
Czajka, J.   65

Daddio, S.   455
Dahlstrom, E.   11, 50
Dahlstrom, W. G.   552
Dainton, P. M.   455
Dale, C. T.   385, 455
Dale, R. R.   344
Dalgleish, L.   481
Dalsimer, K.   223
Dalton, J. L.   567
Dalton, S.   344
Daly, E. M.   272
Daly, J. T.   351
Daly, M.   494
Damico, S. B.   12, 66, 185, 556
D'Amorim, M. A.   178
Dana, C. M.   407
D'Andrade, R. G.   12
Daniels, A. K.   12, 309, 370, 407
Daniels, J.   36, 44, 135, 227, 304, 332

Dansker, M. M. 272
Darden, E. 310
Darian, J. C. 407
Darley, J. G. 344
Darley, S. A. 523
Darling, R. W. 344
Darmofall, S. H. 1, 2, 26
Darte, E. 195
Datrin, S. 272
Daughtry, T. 255
Dauterive, J. W. 407
Dauw, D. C. 91
David, D. S. 469, 503, 523
David, J. 574
Davids, A. 197
Davidson, E. W. 607
Davidson, H. H. 178, 344, 559, 577, 581
Davidson, L. R. 91, 523
Davidson, S. 407
Davis, A. 556
Davis, A. E. 310, 370
Davis, A. J. 178
Davis, B. H. 523
Davis, D. 491
Davis, D. A. 91
Davis, D. E. 245, 256
Davis, E. C. 50, 91
Davis, F. 178, 370, 408, 503
Davis, J. 345
Davis, J. A. 91, 152, 197, 215, 556, 577, 589
Davis, J. L. 286
Davis, J. P. 566, 587, 589, 591
Davis, J. S. 589
Davis, L. 114, 345
Davis, L. G. 556, 601
Davis, L. S. 91
Davis, N. J. 50, 503
Davis, O. 345
Davis, S. A. 310
Davis, S. O. 272, 345
Davis, W. 111, 408
Davis, W. L. 12, 245, 256
Dawes, A. S. 249
Dawis, R. V. 158
Dawkins, L. B. 455
Day, D. R. 91, 455
Day, H. I. 227
Day, R. C. 624
Deabler, H. L. 57

Dean, D. G. 12, 50
Dean, R. S. 91
Dearden, J. 92
Deaux, K. 51, 92, 138, 178, 222, 256, 257, 262, 455
DeBellefonds, J. 469
DeBlassie, R. R. 579, 618
DeBurciaga, C. P. 609
DeCecco, J. P. 71
deCharms, R. 245
Deckard, B. S. 51, 310, 408
DeCrow, K. 12, 310, 345, 408
Decter, M. 51
Deering, A. 482
Deever, S. G. 240
Defabaugh, G. L. 92
DeFazio, M. 408
DeGarcia, N. V. 620
DeGarma, E. G. 6
Degler, C. N. 51
Deguire, K. S. 523
Deichmann, J. 112
DeJoie, C. M. 590
DeJong, P. Y. 408
DeLamater, J. 414, 499
DelDrago, M. 607
DeLeeuw, L. 173, 540
Delgado, J. 408
Delgado, S. 607, 620
DeLisser, O. 252
Delk, J. L. 272, 625
Dell, D. M. 112
Dellas, M. 12, 92
Delworth, U. 51, 310
Dement, A. L. 345
Denebrink, J. 272
Denham, S. A. 215
Denise, S. M. 92, 345
Denker, E. R. 333
Denmark, F. L. 3, 10, 29, 33, 39, 45, 47, 65, 75, 77, 92, 102, 130, 140, 157, 163, 178, 227, 235, 239, 258, 262, 319, 332, 345, 350, 371, 375, 398, 408, 409, 411, 412, 425, 442, 464, 481, 482, 491, 504, 523, 527, 590, 602
Dennis, L. E. 310, 324, 328, 435, 502, 532
Department of Labor 409
Depner, C. 67, 92, 223

Depree, S. 152
Dermer, M. 51
Desiderato, O. 197
Detterbeck, J. L. 225
Deutsch, C. J. 92
Deutsch, M. 86, 124, 150, 361, 554, 557, 575, 577
Deutsch, R. 409
Dewey, C. R. 273
Dewey, R. 151
DeWolf, V. A. 92, 279, 504
Dexter, E. W. 504
Diamond, E. E. 92, 267, 271, 273, 288, 297, 409, 544, 559
Diamond, H. 456
Diamond, I. 488
Dias, S. L. 92, 178, 385, 386, 504, 523
Diaz-Guerrero, R. 607, 618
DiCeasare, A. 577
Dicerkson, K. G. 345
Dickstein, L. S. 93
Diesler, S. B. 409, 456
Diggory, J. C. 92
DiMarco, N. 197, 456, 488
Dimitri, O. 166, 218
Dinerman, B. 310
Dingman, J. A. 608
Dinneiman, B. 491
Dion, K. L. 51, 93
Dipboye, R. L. 93, 257, 409
Dipietro, A. E. 409
DiSabatino, M. 93, 178, 197, 223, 273
Discrimination in Education Committee of NOW, Ann Arbor Chapter 308
Dissinger, J. K. 245
Ditzian, J. L. 118
Dixit, R. C. 12
Dixon, P. W. 152
Dixon, R. B. 51, 93
Dixon-Altenor, C. 557, 590, 601
Doan, B. 475
Dobbert, M. L. 345
Dobbins, M. P. 410
Doctor, R. 245
Dodd, J. 557
Dodge, K. A. 19, 104
Dodge, N. 445
Dodson, E. A. 152

Dodson, J. 557
Doely, S. B. 494
Doherty, E. G. 43, 93
Doherty, W. J. 215
Dolan, E. F. 310
Dole, A. A. 93, 557, 577
Doll, P. A. 456
Domash, L. 12
Domingues, P. M. 12
Domino, G. 137
Donady, B. 298
Donahue, T. J. 273
Donaldson, P. 195
Donelson, E. 2, 13, 16, 56, 104, 418, 498, 526, 559
Donlon, M. H. 410
Donnalley, M. J. 346
Donnan, H. H. 197
Donnelly, C. 456
D'Orazio, D. E. 55, 100
Dorman, L. 13
Dorn, R. S. 223
Dornbusch, S. M. 596, 621
Dorros, K. 51, 202
Dorsen, N. 66, 410
Doss, C. 152
Doty, B. A. 346, 504
Doty, C. N., and Hoeflin, R. M. 197
Doubrovsky, C. P. 310
Douvan, E. 6, 13, 19, 44, 51, 93, 152, 179, 227, 346, 523
Dowdall, J. A. 523
Downs, J. F. 625
Doyle, D. C. 126
Doyle, J. A. 51
Doyle, K. O., Jr. 117, 383
Drabick, L. W. 577
Dragastin, S. E. 8, 44
Draper, P. 13
Drauden, G. 85
Draznin, J. N. 456
Dreifus, C. 13, 523
Dresselhaus, M. S. 346, 410
Drew, D. 93
Drews, E. M. 273, 410
Droege, R. C. 93
Drucker, J. 415
Dua, P. S. 197
Dube, W. F. 346

Dubeck, P. J.   488
Duberman, L.   560
DuBrin, A. J.   13, 51
DuCette, J.   245, 249, 255, 577
Duchan, L.   376
Duchnowski, A. J.   176
Ducker, D. G.   93, 475, 523
Dudar, H.   51
Duff, F.   410
Duffly, P. R.   93
Dufresne, M. J.   51
Duke, M. P.   245, 251
Dukes, R. L.   94
Dulaney, D. D.   275
Dumas, N.   607
Dunahoo, K. L.   427
Dunbar, D. S.   94
Duncan, B.   94, 410
Duncan, R. P.   523
Dunkle, M. C.   310, 346
Dunlap, S. M.   94
Dunn, C. J.   386
Dunn, F. E.   517
Dunn, N. E.   310
Dunteman, G. H.   197, 215, 273
DuPont, H.   410, 456
Duquin, M. E.   13, 179, 258
Duran, M.   614
Duran, P. H.   605, 607
Durand, D.   245
Durchholz, P.   504, 523
Durflinger, G. W.   197
Durham, M.   529
Durka, D. W.   245
Durning, K. P.   498
Durrant, S. A.   469
Dusek, J. B.   107, 200, 240, 346
Dutton, R. E.   94, 410
Dweck, C. S.   94, 240, 257
Dweck, S.   304, 398, 502
Dworkin, A. G.   51, 608
Dwyer, C. A.   94
Dyal, J. A.   21
Dyer, J. L.   8, 340
Dyer, S.   222
Dyer, S. E.   346, 543
Dyer, W. W.   51
Dyrud, J.   273

Eason, J.   273
East, C.   410
Easton, B.   13
Eaton, C.   318
Eaton, D.   314
Eaton, E. M.   266
Eaton, G.   326
Eaton, L. L.   386
Eberly, M.   456
Ebert, P. C.   410
Eckland, B. K.   79, 338
Eddy, J.   335
Edgar, R.   81
Edgerton, H. A.   469, 504, 524
Edington, E. D.   625
Edson, K.   188
Education Committee. N.Y.C. Chapter, National Organization for Women   311
Edwards, C. N.   11, 94, 152, 197
Edwards, C. P.   41
Edwards, J. N.   23, 160
Edwards, O. L.   590
Edwards, R. C.   410, 411
Effertz, J.   109, 423
Egelston, J. C.   370
Egin, A. W.   346
Ehrenreich, B.   475
Ehrensaft, D. R.   14
Ehrhardt, A. A.   29, 66
Ehrlich, C.   370
Eiden, L. J.   346
Ein, P. L.   94
Einstein, H.   311, 411
Eisen, S. V.   26, 117
Eisenberg, J.   130
Eisenberg, M.   149, 194
Eisenman, R.   165, 252
Eisenmann, R.   94, 152, 245
Eisenstein, H.   129
Eister, D. Z.   80
Eiszler, C. F.   557
Ekberg-Jordan, S.   456
Eklund, C. G.   456
Ekstrom, R. B.   311, 321, 356, 463, 513
El-Assal, M. M.   34, 168, 253
Elbe, K. E.   370

Elbert, S. 311
Elder, G. H. 8, 44, 95, 153, 524
Elder, P. 311
Elias, M. 273
Eliasberg, A. 153
El-Khawas, E. H. 543
Ellinger, N. 140
Elliott, E. D. 14, 153
Ellis, D. L. 311, 411
Ellis, D. P. 577
Ellis, J. R. 95, 346
Ellis, J. T. 578
Ellis, L. J. 14, 52
Ellman, M. 14, 51, 370, 411
Ellsberg, H. 469
Elman, J. B. 95
Elmore, P. B. 347
Elovson, A. C. 347
Elton, C. F. 95, 128, 197, 208, 219, 273, 293
Eltzroth, M. 590
Eme, R. 223
Emerick, R. 34, 168, 253
Emerson, T. I. 48, 411
Emig, J. 371
Emma Willard Task Force on Education 311
Emmerich, W. 14
Emmons, M. L. 264
Emswiller, T. 257
Ender, P. B. 610
Endicott, J. 122
Endman, M. 113
Endsley, R. C. 6
Engelhard, P. A. 273
Engineering Manpower Commission of the Engineers' Joint Council 469
English, D. 475
English, P. 223
English, R. A. 557
Entine, A. D. 274, 311, 411, 504
Entwistle, D. R. 95, 108, 153, 557, 578
Entwistle, N. J. 198
Eppes, J. W. 578
Epps, E. G. 557, 560, 578, 590, 592
Epstein, A. S. 153
Epstein, C. F. 2, 14, 52, 95, 311, 312, 371, 411, 412, 469, 486, 499, 524, 590, 601, 602
Epstein, R., and Liverant, S. 14
Epstein, S. 63, 137, 185
Equal Employment Opportunity Commission 412, 543
Equal Employment Opportunity Coordinating Council 543
Erb, E. D. 95, 198
Ericksen, J. A. 524
Erickson, L. G. 95
Erickson, V. L. 14, 52, 95, 274, 312
Erikson, E. 52, 558
Erkut, S. 257
Ernest, J. 96
Erskine, C. G. 52
Erskine, H. 488
Eskilson, A. 96
Espinosa, L. A. 608
Esposito, R. P. 578
Esposito, V. 405
Esquer, R. J. 620
Estep, M. 21, 25, 322
Estes, M. F. 558
Estler, S. E. 386
Estrin, T. 469
Etaugh, C. 14, 52, 96, 179, 257, 413
Etzioni, A. 441
Etzkowitz, M. 413
Evans, C. 52
Evans, C. L. 590
Evans, F. B. 603, 617
Evans, V. M. 413
Evenbeck, S. 259
Evers, M. 94, 410
Ewers, J. C. 625
Exline, R. V. 96
Eyde, L. D. 153, 215, 274, 488, 504
Ezorosky, G. 371

Fabian, J. J. 481, 499
Fabrikant, B. 274
Facos, T. 53
Fader, S. S. 413
Fagerburg, J. F. 179, 198
Fagerlind, L. 108
Faggen-Steckler, J. 274
Fagot, B. I. 14, 15, 89

Faguiri, R. 82
Fairlie, H. 53
Fakouri, M. E. 15
Falbo, T. 96, 347
Falk, G. 48
Falk, L. L. 524
Falk, W. W. 413
Fallon, B. J. 96
Fanelli, G. C. 245
Fanshel, D. 481
Farber, S. M. 29, 53, 57, 96, 104, 117, 119, 312, 322
Farell, J. 483
Farley, F. H. 153, 578
Farley, J. 153, 312, 347, 413, 524
Farmer, H. S. 15, 96, 153, 179, 223, 274, 413, 481, 504, 524
Farooqi, F. 79
Farquar, N., and Mohlmar, C. 312
Farquhar, W. W. 211, 559
Farrell, W. 15, 413
Farris, E. 257
Farris, J. A. 37
Farver, A. S. 590
Fassberg, S. 60
Fauble, M. L. 187
Faunce, P. S. 15, 53, 97, 198, 215, 347, 413, 504
Fava, S. F. 371
Fay, M. 475
Fay, T. L. 15, 53, 76
Fazio, R. T. 275
Feather, N. T. 97, 179, 223, 240, 245, 246, 257, 258, 262
Featherman, D. L. 413, 545
Fecher, A. A. R. 386
Federbush, M. 312
Federman, P. J. 599
Fedor, I. 274
Feigenbaum, L. 290
Feij, J. A. 97, 224
Feijo, T. D. 353, 545
Feilke, J. F. 456
Fein, G. 15
Fein, L. G. 15, 481
Feingold, S. N. 27, 28, 287, 312, 413, 414
Feinman, S. 53, 97
Feinstein, J. 50

Fekart, M. A. 179
Feld, S. C. 171, 198, 538
Feldhusen, J. F. 98, 211
Feldman, D. H. 362
Feldman, H. 53, 175
Feldman, J. M. 558
Feldman, K. A. 312, 347
Feldman, M. 53
Feldman, R. S. 157
Feldman, S. D. 347, 525
Feldman-Summers, S. 64, 258
Felker, D. W. 190, 210, 256
Felshin, J. 496
Felson, M. 525
Felton, G. S. 578
Feminist Business Association 456
Feminist Psychology Group 265
Fenelon, J. R. 558, 578
Fennema, E. 16, 98, 132, 198, 347, 348
Fenner, B. J. 105
Fenner, M. 491
Fenske, R. H. 88, 131
Fensterhaim, H. 274
Fenwick-Naditch, S. 16
Ferber, M. A. 348, 371, 376, 414
Ferdinand, W. 153
Ferdman, J. 16
Ferguson, L. R. 19
Ferree, M. M. 414, 525
Ferrell, M. 233
Ferrer, D. 238
Ferriss, A. L. 414
Feshback, N. D. 312, 414
Feulner, P. N. 198, 371, 475, 486
Fibel, B. 53
Fichter, J. H. 558, 590, 591, 602
Fidell, L. 59, 371, 482, 491
Fidell, L. S. 414, 481, 499, 525
Fidler, D. S. 54
Fiedler, L. 274
Field, R. S. 198
Field, T. K. 605
Field, T. W. 91, 98
Fields, C. M. 313, 348
Fields, R. M. 275, 313, 482

Figes, E. 16, 53
Filene, P. G. 53
Fincher, C. 275
Fink, A. 98
Finkelstein, C. S. 205
Finlayson, D. S. 153
Finley, C. J. 336, 447
Finn, J. A. 246
Fiorenzo, B. 49
Firestone, S. 16, 54
Fischer, A. 153
Fischer, E. H. 154
Fischer, J. 275
Fischer, P. L. 16
Fish, J. A. 191
Fishel, A. 11, 22, 56, 60, 95, 130, 133, 298, 313, 314, 327, 343, 351, 379, 386, 394, 474, 557
Fisher, A. 43, 153
Fisher, J. E. 98, 220, 258, 260
Fisher, J. K. 179
Fisher, R. 591
Fisher, W. R. 205
Fitzgerald, B. J. 98
Fitzgerald, H. E. 16
Fitzgerald, L. 369
Fitzgerald, L. E. 275, 414
Fitzgerald, L. F. 98, 224
Fitzgerald, N. M. 99
Fitzgerald, W. 304
Fitzpatrick, B. 313
Fitzpatrick, J. L. 99
Fixter, D. 336
Flaherty, M. R. 211
Flammer, D. P. 16
Flanagan, J. C. 348
Flanders, D. P. 414
Flaugher, R. L. 275
Flavin, J. R. 246, 544
Fleck, H. 525
Fleming, E. S. 364
Fleming, G. J. 488
Fleming, J. 224, 578
Fleming, J. T. 386
Flerx, V. C. 54
Fley, J. 248, 371, 414
Fling, S. 16
Flores, F. 608, 614
Flynn, B. 608
Flynn, T. M. 579
Fodor, I. G. 302, 346

Fogarty, M. P. 456, 457, 504, 525
Folger, J. K. 313
Foliet, J. 51
Follett, C. F. 348
Follingstad, D. R. 275
Fontana, G. L. 16, 54, 154, 179
Foote, F. L. 488
Ford, D. L., Jr. 588
Ford, E. G. 244
Ford, J. A. 584
Forest, C. A. 371, 494
Forisha, B. 99
Forrest, K. S. 313, 414, 544
Forslund, M. A. 99, 348
Fortner, M. L. 99
Foster, A. 154
Foster, D. A. 171
Foster, G. H. 457
Foster, J. A. 558
Foster, J. M. 210
Foster, M. 520, 538
Foster, N. J. 54, 246
Fournet, G. P. 100, 180
Fowler, M. G. 54
Fox, B. 414
Fox, D. J. 73, 136, 190, 572, 624
Fox, G. L. 54, 348
Fox, H. W. 414
Fox, J. H. 414
Fox, L. H. 99, 215, 275, 348, 349
Fox, R. B. 99, 154
Fralley, J. 303
Francis, A. 415
Francis, B. R. 16, 154
Francke, C. A. 457
Frank, A. C. 275
Frank, C. E. 138, 219
Frank, F. D. 415
Frank, H. H. 59, 76, 142, 228, 236, 275, 349, 374, 402, 415, 427, 447, 491, 520, 525, 600
Frank, M. E. 525
Frankel, P. M. 99
Frankel, P. S. 99, 179
Franken, R. E. 100
Franklin, B. M. 313
Franks, V. 274, 275, 287, 289, 290, 296

Franson, M. H. 469
Frazier, N. 313, 329, 349
Franzini, L. R. 16
Franzwa, H. 415
Frasch, C. 250
Fraser, S. C. 109
Freeark, K. 306
Freedberg, S. 224
Freedman, A. E. 48
Freedman, B. E. 100
Freedman, M. B. 54, 349
Freeman, E. B. 544, 558
Freeman, H. R. 544, 558
Freeman, J. 17, 40, 41, 54, 57, 313, 328, 367, 372, 378, 383, 400, 401, 415, 474, 517, 539, 565
Freeman, M. 22
Freeman, R. B. 591
Freiberg, P. 17
Freidl, E. 17
French, E. 100
French, J. R. 168
French, L. 625
French, P. 457
Frerichs, M. 179
Frerking, R. A. 154
Freshley, H. B. 575
Fretz, B. R. 288
Fretz, C. F. 415
Fricker, S. K. 17, 544
Fried, F. E. 349
Fried, M. G. 415
Friedan, B. 17, 100, 313, 525
Friedersdorf, N. W. 276
Friedland, S. J. 129
Friedlander, F. 17
Friedle, R. 236
Friedman, A. F. 76
Friedman, B. 415
Friedman, J. S. 17, 54
Friedman, M. 184, 322
Friedman, R. J. 180
Friedman, S. T. 119, 203
Friedrich, L. K. 100
Friedrich, N. M. 313
Friedrichs, A. G. 100
Friend, J. G. 505
Friend, R. M. 258, 579
Friendly, F. 585
Frieze, I. H. 54, 67, 70, 128, 198, 207, 240, 242, 256, 258, 259, 260, 262, 263, 450, 469
Friskey, E. A. 349, 505
Frohreich, D. S. 349
Fromkin, H. L. 93, 409
Froomkin, J. 314
Froschl, M. 17, 314, 338
Frost, B. P. 199
Frost, D. 591
Frueh, T. 17
Fruen, M. A. 100, 199
Fruth, M. J. 601
Fry, B. J. 314
Fry, L. 431
Fry, P. S. 100, 180
Fuchs, E. 626
Fuchs, R. 505
Fuchs, V. R. 415
Fugita, S. S. 591
Fujitomi, I. 17, 544
Fukuda, N. K. 152
Fuller, F. F. 276
Fullmer, D. W. 54
Furman, L. 491
Furniss, W. T. 314, 316, 328, 344, 355, 360
Furst, E. J. 180, 350
Furugori, T. 415

Gable, R. K. 246
Gabriel, M. E. 125
Gackenbach, J. I. 457
Gadbois, C. 154
Gadzella, B. M. 100, 180, 246
Gaedert, W. P. 241, 259
Gaertner, S. 558
Gaffga, R. H. 314
Gager, N. 314, 316
Gahagan, J. P. 138
Gaier, E. L. 12, 92
Gaines, S. 45
Galenson, M. 416
Gallagher, J. J. 100
Gallese, L. R. 416
Galliano, G. 272
Gallimore, R. 17, 544
Galloway, J. M. 314
Galvin, R. 416
Galway, K. 363, 381, 441
Gander, M. J. 314
Gaier, E. L. 558, 579

Gannon, M. J.   505
Garbin, A. P.   9, 86
Garcia, M.   608
Garcia-Hancock, V.   608, 623
Gardiner, H. W.   55, 100, 199
Gardner, G. H. F.   469
Gardner, H. R.   386
Gardner, J.   276
Gardner, J. A. E.   314
Gardner, J. E.   372
Gardner, L. I.   31
Garfinkle, S. H.   416, 591
Garland, H.   101, 259, 457
Garland, T. N.   525, 533
Garner, M. E.   558
Garrett, A. M.   246, 579
Garrett, C. S.   17
Garrison, D.   491
Garske, J. P.   224
Garskof, M. H.   17, 55, 70, 227, 400
Garvin, A. D.   138
Garza, R. T.   617
Gaskell, J. S.   101
Gass, S.   302
Gasser, M. H.   386
Gastorf, J. W.   136
Gaudreau, P. A.   55, 416
Gay, G.   591, 620, 625
Gaylin, J.   416
Gaylord, C.   560, 592
Gearty, J. Z.   224
Gehlen, F. L.   488
Geis, F. L.   416
Gelb, L.   276
Gelso, C.   266
George, E. L.   416
Gerard, G. B.   416
Gerber, G. L.   55
Gershon, A.   205
Gersick, K. E.   88
Gerson, A.   14, 52
Gerson, M.   55
Gersoni-Stavn, D.   7, 17, 18, 45, 143, 298, 303, 308, 311, 324, 330
Gerstl, J. E.   472
Gerver, J. M.   559
Gery, G. J.   416, 544
Getz, S. K.   55
Ghei, S. N.   18
Giat, L.   242

Gibbons, A. R.   314
Gibbons, K. M.   475, 488, 526
Gickling, E. E.   101
Giele, J. Z.   2, 18
Gilbert, B.   496
Gilbert, D.   55
Gilbert, L. A.   55, 92
Gilbert, M.   475
Giles, P.   222
Gilfeather, K.   494
Gill, D. L.   204
Gill, L. J.   608
Gill, M. K.   101
Gillard, B. J.   156
Gillen, B.   404
Gillespie, D. L.   376
Gilliard, D.   94, 240
Gillie, A. C.   180
Gillies, J.   387
Gilligan, M. B.   482
Gilliland, L. L.   246, 350
Gillman, D. C.   356
Gilmore, B.   101, 224
Gilroy, F. D.   135
Gingles, R.   146
Ginn, F. W.   154
Ginn, R. O.   55, 101
Ginorio, A. B.   140, 445
Ginzberg, E.   154, 314, 416, 457, 505, 526, 563, 591
Giovanni, N.   591
Girard, K. L.   314
Gispert, M.   482, 527
Gist, N. P.   149, 553, 559
Githeus, M.   31, 47, 61, 567
Gittell, M.   314
Gitter, A. G.   101, 154, 544, 559
Giuliani, B.   476, 505, 526
Giventer, L. L.   372
Gjesme, T.   101, 180
Glad, D.   299
Glancy, D. J.   224, 486
Glanstein, P. J.   246
Glass, L. W.   174
Glasser, K. J.   101, 240
Glazer-Malbin, N.   55, 57, 64, 65, 290, 315, 415, 416, 417, 418, 432, 446, 448, 480, 527, 558, 591, 602
Glenn, H. M.   55, 315, 417
Glenn, N. D.   505
Glick, R.   505

Glidewell, J. C. 18
Gloeckner, M. L. 476
Glogowski, D. 216
Goad, R. 290, 326, 350
Goebel, J. B. 608
Goebes, D. D. 350
Goering, M. L. 283
Goerss, K. V. W. 199, 276, 387
Goethals, G. P. 146
Goetz, T. E. 417
Golann, S. E. 483
Gold, A. R. 101, 559
Gold, D. 18
Gold, M. 18, 559
Gold, S. S. 327, 505
Goldberg, B. J. 276
Goldberg, C. 102, 259
Goldberg, L. H. 276
Goldberg, P. A. 55, 89, 102, 125
Goldberg, R. E. 102
Goldberg, S. 18, 56
Golden, G. A. 102
Golden Gate Law School Women's Association 486
Goldgield, R. J. 457
Goldman, E. K. 199
Goldman, F. H. 315
Goldman, P. R. 122
Goldman, R. D. 60, 102, 107, 591, 608
Goldsmith, N. F. 470
Goldstein, A. G. 244
Goldstein, J. W. 627
Goldstein, M. Z. 350
Goldstein, R. L. 154
Goldston, J. 246
Gomes, B. 264
Gomez-Quinones, J. 605
Gonzales, A. 620
Gonzales, J. 608
Gonzalez, A. E. 120
Gonzalez, A. E. J. 120, 231
Gonzalez, R. M. 621
Gonzalez, S. A. 608
Gonzalez, V. 609
Good, K. C. 224
Good, L. R. 224
Good, S. 159, 248
Good, T. L. 306, 350
Goodale, J. G. 155
Goode, W. 526

Goode, W. J. 52
Goodings, G. J. 473, 514
Goodman, J. 102, 130, 294
Goodman, M. E. 608
Goodman, N. C. 457
Goodman, P. W. 621
Goodman, W. 56
Goodmonson, C. W. 224
Goodstein, L. D. 56
Goodwin, G. C. 350, 526
Gordon, C. W. 480
Gordon, F. E. 18, 102, 180, 443, 453, 457, 459, 465, 527
Gordon, G. E. 109, 412
Gordon, L. K. 327, 463
Gordon, M. 410, 411
Gordon, M. S. 417
Gordon, N. M. 372, 417, 544
Gordon, R. S. 387
Gorelick, S. 154, 526
Gorfein, D. 58
Gornick, V. 3, 6, 10, 224, 225, 270, 467, 492
Goslin, D. 30
Gossmann, I. 113
Gosswiller, R. 103
Gottesdiener, M. 55
Gottfredson, G. D. 103, 276, 281, 417
Gottfredson, L. S. 281, 417, 276
Gottfries, I. 64
Gottlieb, D. 129, 505, 559, 591
Gottman, J. M. 339
Gottsdanker, J. S. 199, 216
Gottsegen, A. J. 168
Gottsegen, G. B. 372, 482
Gottsegen, M. G. 372, 482
Gough, H. G. 18, 216
Gould, C. C. 324, 377, 415, 433, 444, 445
Gould, J. S. 103, 315, 417
Gould, K. 417, 459
Gould, L. J. 23, 276
Gould, R. E. 43
Gould, S. H. 372, 592
Gouveia, A. J. 621
Gove, W. R. 18, 56, 103, 277
Gover, R. 40
Gozali, H. 246

Gozali, J. 246
Grabe, M. D. 103, 180
Grafton, S. 488
Graham, E. 315, 377, 432, 458
Graham, J. M. 180
Graham, L. 417
Graham, P. 315
Graham, P. A. 314, 316, 328, 344, 355, 360, 369, 372
Graham, S. 417
Grainger, B. 103, 225, 592
Grambs, J. D. 56, 149, 387, 576
Grandjean, B. D. 372, 476
Grandy, T. G. 155
Granson, M. R. 592
Grant, T. E. 609
Grant (West), A. 56
Grantham, R. J. 592
Grasmuck, S. 31
Graves, K. 311, 411
Graves, T. D. 625
Gravitz, M. A. 130
Gray, B. 103
Gray, B. M. 417
Gray, M. 400, 470
Gray, T. C. 609
Gray-Shellberg, L. 526
Grebner, F. 350
Grebow, H. 155
Green, D. R. 544
Green, E. 103, 225, 315, 417
Green, F. 356
Green, H. B. 609
Green, L. B. 155
Green, L. H. 199, 246
Green, M. 36
Green, M. L. 316
Green, R. G. 246
Green, R. L. 559, 594
Green, T. L. 554
Greenawalt, J. P. 124
Greenberg, J. W. 559, 577, 581
Greenberg, R. P. 56
Greenberg, S. 56
Greenberger, E. 80, 95, 1 557, 579
Greendorfer, S. L. 18, 10

Greene, C. N. 251
Greene, H. R. 626
Greene, M. 315
Greenfeig, B. 266
Greenfeld, S. T. 238
Greenhouse, P. 56
Greenspan, L. J. 225
Greenstein, M. 18
Greenwald, C. 372, 417, 526
Greenwald, E. R. 103
Greenwald, J. A. 33
Greer, G. 56
Greif, A. C. 277
Grelsch, J. R. 494
Grenell, G. 103
Greyser, S. A. 453
Gribbons, W. D. 277
Gridley, M. 625
Grier, W. H. 559
Grieve, N. 482
Griggs, S. A. 559
Griffith, M. E. 268
Griffiths, M. W. 418
Griffin, F. C. 43
Grigg, C. M. 18
Grimm, J. W. 418
Grimstad, K. 311, 411
Grindle, E. S. 494
Gronau, R. 418
Groot, H. 482
Gropper, N. B. 320
Groseclose, E. 315
Grosgebauer, C. H. 418, 475, 526
Gross, A. 418, 505
Gross, E. 418, 526
Gross, H. J. 225
Gross, N. 315, 387
Gross, R. 506
Gross, W. 104
Grossblat, M. 486
Grossman, A. S. 418, 526
Grossman, B. 617
Grossman, F. K. 500
Grossman, M. L. 19
Grossnickle, W. F. 113
Groszko, M. G. 104, 225, 315, 350
Grote, B. H. 25
Groth, N. J. 104, 155, 372
Group for the Advancement of Psychiatry 104, 315, 350

652 / Index

Groves, R. 351
Gruber, M. 488
Gruber, S. 225
Gruchow, N. 315
Gruder, C. L. 104
Grumbine, C. 277, 351
Grundy, B. L. 277, 351
Grusec, J. E. 19
Gubbels, R. 418
Guber, S. 19, 56
Gubernick, D. 140
Gue, L. R. 378, 391
Guidance Associates Inc. 418
Gullahorn, J. E. 13, 16, 56, 104, 418, 499, 526, 559
Gumbach, D. 104
Gump, J. P. 57, 104, 180, 544, 559
Gumperz, E. 57, 418
Gunderson, B. B. 57, 104
Gupta, A. K. 104
Gurin, G. 171, 579
Gurin, M. G. 277
Gurin, P. 418, 560, 579, 592, 597
Gurman, A. S. 155
Gurwitz, S. B. 19, 80, 104
Gust, T. 155, 199
Gustav, A. 344
Gutek, B. A. 433
Guterman, S. S. 577
Guthrie, R. V. 592
Gutierrez, L. A. 609
Gutman, N. D. 6, 44
Gutmann, J. E. 451
Guttentag, M. 57, 178, 277, 315, 345, 351, 579
Guttman, M. A. J. 277, 284, 285, 292, 315, 316, 320, 351, 372, 373, 387, 482
Guttmann, D. 19, 180
Gwartney, J. 418
Gyllstrom, K. K. 527
Gynther, M. D. 564
Gysbers, N. C. 155, 199

Haan, N. 57
Haarman, G. B. 167
Haas, M. B. 155, 536
Haavio-Mannila, E. 104, 476, 488
Haber, S. 506

Hackamack, L. C. 457
Hacker, H. M. 57, 560
Hacker, S. 330, 506
Hackett, C. W. 458
Hackman, J. R. 367
Hadley, T. 257
Haefner, J. E. 545
Haener, D. 277, 418
Hagan, N. 91
Hagen, R. L. 105, 419
Hagey, S. J. 180
Hahn, M. C. 277
Haimowitz, M. L. 225
Haimowitz, N. R. 225
Haines, J. R. 317, 421
Halas, C. M. 19
Hale, J. M. 617
Hales, L. W. 105, 181
Hall, D. T. 18, 102, 105, 155, 180, 453, 526, 527
Hall, E. 194
Hall, E. B. 316
Hall, E. R. 57, 560, 579, 592
Hall, G. 419
Hall, K. P. 105, 116, 373, 428
Hall, L. H. 617
Hall, M. 181
Hall, O. 419
Hall, P. Q. 621, 625
Hall, R. 531
Halleck, S. L. 593
Haller, A. O. 123, 165
Haller, L. M. 387
Haller, M. 527
Halperin, M. S. 19, 105
Halpern, S. 560, 593, 618
Halpin, G. 19, 155
Halprin, R. 225
Ham, M. H. 45
Hamilton, M. G. 419
Hamilton, M. T. 419
Hammack, B. 233
Hammel, E. A. 340
Hammer, W. C. 593
Hammes, R. G. 181
Hammond, E. H. 277
Hanan, D. O. 419
Hancock, V. G. 609
Hancock, W. L. B. 419
Handley, A. 316
Handlon, J. H. 460

Handrich, M. 76
Handrick, F. A. 519
Hands, S. L. 351
Haney, R. 205
Hanisch, C. 56
Hanke, L. 612
Hanley, M. A. 105
Hannah, W. 199
Hansan, J. F. 316
Hansen, A. H. 155
Hansen, A. S. 251
Hansen, D. 419
Hansen, G. R. 506
Hansen, J. C. 23, 39, 186, 187, 278, 290, 445
Hansen, L. S. 181, 278, 284, 303, 316, 320, 419, 506
Hansen, P. 105, 458
Hansen, R. A. 105, 470
Hansen, R. D. 259
Hanson, D. E. 105
Hanson, G. R. 271, 278, 291, 351
Hanson, J. T. 155
Hansson, R. O. 19
Hanusa, B. 258
Harasymiw, S. J. 254
Harback, E. 70, 129
Harbeson, G. E. 527
Harburg, E. 593, 602
Hardee, M. D. 278
Hardesty, F. P. 58
Harding, J. 100
Hardy, R. E. 36, 277, 331, 351, 457, 461, 494, 515
Hare, B. R. 545
Hare, J. 560
Hare, N. 387, 560
Harford, T. C. 57
Hargens, L. L. 437, 534
Harkleroad, M. A. 351
Harlan, A. 373
Harlow, D. N. 506
Harmatz, M. G. 199
Harmon, L. 373
Harmon, L. A. 316
Harmon, L. W. 155, 216, 275, 278, 279, 351, 506
Harnsberger, S. 109
Harper, J. 105, 482, 527
Harper, M. A. 494
Harragan, B. L. 419

Harrell, S. N. 156
Harrington, T. F. 289
Harris, A. 321
Harris, A. S. 373
Harris, B. 247
Harris, B. F. 373
Harris, C. 458
Harris, C. L. 188
Harris, C. M. 216, 316
Harris, D. 166, 192
Harris, D. V. 497
Harris, E. E. 560
Harris, G. G. 289
Harris, J. 57
Harris, L. D. 625
Harris, L. H. 57
Harris, L. J. 594
Harris, M. B. 373
Harris, M. B. 560, 609
Harris, M. J. 105
Harris, M. M. 561
Harris, P. R. 316
Harris, R. D. 373, 527
Harris, S. R. 279
Harrison, A. O. 547, 566, 579
Harrison, B. G. 316, 317
Harrison, E. 419
Harrison, F. 156
Harrison, J. 57
Harrison, P. 317
Harrower, M. 482
Hart, D. 609
Hart, L. B. 419
Hart, M. 496
Hart, R. 129
Harter, S. 105
Hartley, R. E. 19, 58
Hartley, S. F. 537
Hartman, E. A. 106
Hartman, M. 491, 522
Hartmann, H. I. 420
Hartsook, J. E. 279
Hartup, W. W. 19, 58, 90
Harvard University 351
Harvey, A. L. 106, 225
Harvey, D. W. 279
Harvey, J. 561
Harvey, J. H. 247, 256, 257
Harway, M. 71, 279, 280, 548, 569
Harwood, E. 593
Harwood, K. 492

Hasak, P. 247
Haskell, M. 491
Haskins, M. J. 216
Haslett, B. 140, 373
Hasslocher, P. 166
Hatch, D. D. 351
Hatch, D. L. 527
Hatch, M. G. 527
Hatfield, J. S. 19
Hathorn, S. 61
Hauch, W. E. 594
Hauenstein, L. S. 593, 602
Haug, M. 527
Haug, M. J. 608, 609
Haug, M. R. 83, 106, 553
Haun, H. T. 387
Hauser, R. H. 545
Hauser, R. M. 413
Haven, E. W. 106, 156
Havens, E. M. 527
Havighurst, R. J. 6, 280, 628
Hawkes, G. R. 609
Hawkins, H. L. 125
Hawkins, R. R. 317
Hawley, M. J. 106
Hawley, P. J. 280
Hayden, M. E. 341, 369
Hayduk, L. A. 153
Hayes, M. 67
Hayghe, H. 423
Hayman, J. 415
Haynes, H. 593
Hayrynen, Y. P. 280, 351
Hays, E. J. 579
Hays, J. R. 226
Headley, D. 295
Healey, G. E. 579, 618
Healey, R. E. 156
Health Resources Administration 476
Heath, B. R. 163
Heath, K. G. 420
Herbert, D. J. 269
Hechinger, F. M. 363
Hechinger, G. 363
Heckhausen, H. 263
Hedegard, J. M. 593
Hedges, E. 310
Hedges, J. N. 420
Heer, D. M. 527
Hefner, R. 28, 32, 58, 68, 127, 317

Heide, W. S. 420, 496
Heilbrun, A. B. 20, 50, 58, 90, 106, 156, 199, 226, 280
Heilman, M. 373, 420
Heinemann, S. H. 368
Heinen, J. S. 463
Heinig, C. 173, 450
Heinsohn, A. L. 106, 559, 591
Heinzelmann, G. 494
Heist, P. A. 352, 506
Hellinger, M. L. 269
Helmich, D. L. 458
Helmreich, R. 72, 113, 134, 190
Helms, J. E. 296
Helso, H. 216
Helson, R. M. 20, 106, 107, 156, 199, 200, 216, 420, 470, 505
Helwig, A. A. 280
Hembrough, B. L. 317
Hendel, D. D. 70, 280, 317, 348
Hender, J. 322
Henderson, E. H. 580
Henderson, G. G. 580
Henderson, R. W. 627
Hendrick, H. W. 420, 545
Hendricks, M. 239
Hendrickson, D. H. 505
Hendrix, J. C. 268
Henken, V. 107
Henley, N. 38, 107, 317, 343, 420
Hennessee, D. 491
Hennig, M. M. 157, 181, 458
Henning, C. M. 494
Henninger, M. 145, 263
Henry, P. 10
Henschel, B. J. S. 200, 373, 387
Hepburn, R. A. 609
Heppner, P. P. 107
Herb, T. R. 18
Herberg, D. M. C. 482, 507
Heretick, D. M. L. 157
Herma, J. L. 154, 526
Herman, D. D. 420
Herman, J. B. 55, 417, 527
Herman, M. H. 58, 352, 507
Hermans, H. J. 157, 226

Hernandez, C. A. 608, 609, 611, 612, 617, 619, 622
Hernandez, D. 621
Hernandez, E. 561, 593
Hernton, C. C. 545, 561
Herrera-Duran, P. 609
Herricks, J. S. 216, 458
Herring, C. 266, 339
Herron, E. W. 200
Herschberger, R. 58
Hertz, T. W. 100
Hertzog, J. 226
Herzfeld, N. K. 420
Hess, D. T. 132
Hess, R. D. 20, 157, 545, 561
Hess, T. B. 491
Hesselbart, S. 181, 200
Hetherington, E. M. 20
Hetherington, M. 157
Hewer, V. H. 107
Hewitt, B. N. 102, 107, 591, 608
Hewitt, C. W. 568
Hewitt, J. 568
Hewitt, L. S. 107
Hicks, L. 373, 387, 482
Hicks, N. 317
Hieronymus, B. 458
Hiestand, D. L. 507, 591
Higa, G. 545
Higbee, K. L. 84
Higgins, E. T. 128
Higginson, M. 421
Hilberman, E. 352, 482, 527
Hill, A. H. 157
Hill, A. J. 317, 352
Hill, C. E. 280
Hill, C. T. 67, 125
Hill, G. 76
Hill, H. 563
Hill, J. F. 146
Hill, J. P. 11
Hill, J. W. 280
Hill, K. T. 107, 122, 200, 240, 241
Hill, R. 531, 561
Hill, R. E. 476
Hillery, J. M. 591
Hills, D. T. 288
Hilpert, F. P. 107
Hilton, I. 35, 421

Hilton, M. E. 281
Hilton, M. J. 458
Hilton, T. L. 107, 157
Hiltunen, W. A. 281
Himes, J. S. 602
Hindsman, E. 207
Hipple, J. L. 58, 107, 281, 317, 352
Hiroto, D. S. 247
Hirsch, R. 266
Hishiki, P. C. 618
Hitchman, G. S. 352
Hixon, D. L. 491
Hjelle, L. A. 107, 157, 247
Hoban-Hopkins, F. T. 200
Hobart, C. W. 561, 580, 609
Hobson, C. J. 577
Hobson, S. 561
Hochman, L. M. 352
Hochreich, D. J. 58, 247
Hochschild, A. R. 59, 421
Hodge, C. C. 593
Hodges, K. 240
Hodges, K. L. 124, 241
Hoeflin, R. M. 108, 197, 352, 510
Hoepner, B. J. 213
Hofer, B. 352
Hoffer, W. 421
Hoffman, B. H. 352
Hoffman, D. 59
Hoffman, D. S. 108, 352,
Hoffman, D. T. 482
Hoffman, L. R. 108
Hoffman, L. W. 7, 8, 18, 20, 22, 28, 38, 48, 49, 57, 65, 104, 107, 120, 137, 157, 170, 176, 194, 211, 226, 227, 240, 258, 323, 510, 515, 520, 527, 528, 530, 531, 546
Hoffman, M. L. 7, 18, 20, 22
Hoffman, N. 561
Hoffman, R. 476
Hoffman, R. L. 20
Hoffmann, L. 379
Hogadone, E. B. 458
Hogan, D. P. 545
Hogan, P. 421
Hogan, R. 171
Hohenshil, T. H. 281, 507
Hohman, D. W. 158

Hohmuth, A. V.   580
Holbrook, J. E.   226
Holden, C.   373
Holden, J. D.   445
Holder, R. L.   158
Hole, J.   59, 317, 374, 476, 486, 488, 491, 494
Holland, J. L.   103, 276, 281, 388, 417
Hollander, E. P.   96
Hollander, H. E.   317, 421
Hollenbeck, G. P.   158
Hollender, J.   20, 181
Holley, J. L.   580, 602
Holliday, F. G. T.   352
Hollis, R. E.   247
Holm, J. M.   421
Holmberg, J. J.   421
Holme, A.   42, 173
Holmes, D. S.   108
Holmes, S. L.   538
Holmstrom, E. I.   340, 352, 353
Holmstrom, L. L.   507, 528
Holmstrom, R. W.   353
Holroyd, J.   281, 482
Holstein, R.   421
Holstrom, E.   59, 340
Holt, L.   331
Holter, H.   21, 59
Holtzman, W. H.   618
Homall, G. M.   181
Hong, L. K.   21
Honigfeld, G.   200
Honigman, R.   470
Honomichl, J. J.   458
Honzik, M. P.   158
Hood, K. E.   421
Hooks, K.   415
Hopkins, E. B.   374
Hopkins, L. B.   226
Horai, J.   138
Horhn, M.   330, 598
Horing, L. S.   374
Horn, E. L.   497
Horn, M. T.   421
Hornaday, J. A.   281
Horne, M. D.   254
Horner, M. S.   6, 13, 19, 44, 51, 224, 226, 227, 228
Horney, K.   264
Horst, L.   353

Horwitz, S.   494
Hosford, R. E.   281
Hosinski, M.   186
Hotchkiss, L.   292
Hottes, J.   111
Hottes, J. H.   108
Hough, K. S.   59
Houlihan, K. A.   169, 210, 585
Hounshell, P. B.   243
House, E. W.   84, 267
House, G. F.   158, 228
House, W. C.   241, 247
Houser, B. B.   519
Houts, P. S.   108
Houzer, S.   593
Howard, S.   388
Howard, T. M.   317
Howe, F.   21, 108, 318, 327, 353, 366, 374, 421, 422, 545
Howe, K. G.   108, 228
Howell, M. C.   108, 353, 422
Howell, R. J.   22
Hoyer, W. J.   175
Hoylan, R.   626
Hoyle, J.   388
Hoyt, D.   201, 216
Hoyte, S. K.   422
Hrebiniak, L. G.   192
Hrycenko, I.   247
Hrynyk, N. P.   391
Hsieh, T. T.   247, 545
Huang, A. S.   470
Huber, J.   21, 59, 277, 371, 422, 444, 525, 594
Huber, J. A.   348, 371
Huck, J. R.   593
Hudark, M. T.   275
Hudgins, A. L.   207
Hudis, P. M.   599
Huebner, L. A.   375, 483
Hughes, H. M.   374
Hughes, M. M.   422
Huguet, M.   10
Huit, J.   322
Hulbert, T.   108
Hulett, S. A.   388
Hulicka, I. M.   67
Hulin, C. L.   422
Hull, R. E.   99, 108, 348
Hult, J.   318
Hummel-Rossi, B.   338

Humphrey, F. G.   281
Humphreys, L. W.   453
Hummer, P. M.   422
Hundert, J.   228
Hunt, C. L.   422
Hunt, D. E.   227
Hunt, J. G.   108, 528
Hunt, J. M.   598
Hunt, K.   473
Hunt, L. L.   108, 528
Hunt, P.   143
Hunt, P. J.   458
Hunt, W. K.   162
Hunter, E.   59, 89
Hunter, F. C.   158
Hunter, J. B.   164
Hunter, J. E.   21, 59
Hunter, K.   281
Hunter, R.   352
Hunter-Holmes, J. C.   528
Hurley, R. B.   566, 613
Hurstfield, J.   621
Hurwitz, R. E.   108
Husbands, S. A.   318
Husen, T.   108
Huser, W. R.   528
Hutchins, E. B.   145, 173, 354, 551, 575
Huth, C. M.   282
Huyck, M. H.   59, 537, 538
Hyde, J. S.   2, 21, 59, 256, 542, 561, 576
Hyman, H. H., and Reed, J. S.   561

Iacobacci, R. F.   374
Ibrahim, H.   181
Ickes, W.   260
Ickes, W. J.   256
Iglitzin, L. B.   59, 60
Ignacio, R.   152
Ilgen, D. R.   219, 262, 444, 466
Ingraham, M.   388
Ingram, B.   103, 109
Inkeles, A.   561
Insel, P. M.   10, 60, 86, 361
Institute for the Study of Educational Policy   593
Isaacs, A. F.   109, 201
Isaacson, R. L.   118, 201

Iscoe, I.   561
Istiphan, I.   353
Izard, C. E.   201, 241

Jaackkola, R.   476
Jackaway, R.   228, 241, 259
Jacklin, C. N.   27, 63, 109, 118, 184, 329, 361, 459
Jackson, A.   482
Jackson, B. D.   593
Jackson, C.   264
Jackson, D. W.   21
Jackson, J. J.   21, 422, 561, 594
Jackson, P.   353
Jackson, P. W.   158
Jackson, R. H.   562
Jackson, T.   254
Jackson-White, R.   109, 110, 229, 259
Jacob, N. L.   459
Jacobs, A. D.   353
Jacobs, C.   318, 326
Jacobs, F.   462
Jacobs, J. C.   21
Jacobs, J. E.   109, 318, 423
Jacobs, K. F.   374
Jacobs, K. W.   247
Jacobs, S.   89
Jacobs, S. E.   21
Jacobs, S. L.   2
Jacobsen, R. B.   530
Jacobson, C. J.   423
Jacobson, L. F.   10, 43, 60, 86, 361
Jacobson, M. B.   109, 423
Jacoby, G.   228
Jacoby, S.   318
Jaeger, R. M.   353, 545
Jaffe, L.   318, 374
Jaghelian, A.   282
Jain, D. C.   158
Jain, K. C.   109
Jakobovics, E.   11
Jakubowski, P. A.   282
James, E. T.   507
James, J. W.   507
James, R. J.   109, 201
Jameson, A. S.   580
Jancura, E. G.   459
Janes, G. D.   158, 181, 353
Janeway, E.   21, 109, 318, 459

Jankowska, H. 21
Jansen, D. G. 353
Jantz, R. K. 551, 569
Jantzen, A. C. 201, 217, 476, 507
Janzen, H. L. 247
Jaquette, J. S. 413, 488
Jardim, A. 458
Jardine, L. L. 110
Jass, R. 385, 454
Javier, M. C. 610
Jay, W. T. 318
Jayaratne, T. E. 442
Jefferies, D. 594
Jellison, J. M. 110, 229, 259
Jencks, C. 319, 594
Jenkin, N. 60, 76
Jenkins, E. K. 353
Jenkins, W. J. 388
Jennings, J. 221
Jennings, S. A. 22
Jensen, A. R. 361, 580
Jensen, B. 594
Jerdee, T. H. 69, 128, 438, 463, 464, 507, 534
Joe, V. C. 247, 248
Joesting, J. 60, 110, 201, 290, 579, 597
Joesting, R. 110
Joffe, C. 22, 319
Johanson, A. J. 158
Johns Hopkins University 353
Johnsgard, K. W. 497
Johnson, A. C. 458
Johnson, A. G. 610
Johnson, B. 9, 84, 127, 149, 176, 195, 221, 305, 401, 520
Johnson, B. L., and Kilmann, P. R. 22, 158, 181, 248, 423
Johnson, C. 73
Johnson, D. 15, 388
Johnson, D. E. 201
Johnson, D. G. 354, 545
Johnson, D. H. 282
Johnson, D. L. 618
Johnson, E. E. 262, 571
Johnson, G. E. 374
Johnson, H. N. 248
Johnson, J. E. 73, 90, 136, 177, 190
Johnson, J. L. 388
Johnson, K. R. 594
Johnson, M. 437, 488, 489
Johnson, M. A. 282
Johnson, M. M. 22
Johnson, P. 54
Johnson, P. A. 201
Johnson, P. B. 110, 142, 423
Johnson, R. W. 110, 158, 201, 282
Johnson, T. J. 110
Johnson, T. P. 354
Johnson, W. D. 554
Johnson, W. H. 603
Johnson, Z. C. 159
Johnston, H. S. 110
Johnston, J. A. 155, 199
Johnston, J. R. 159
Johnston, R. L. 319
Johnston, S. 259
Johnstone, E. 423
Jones, A. 594
Jones, A. R. 495
Jones, B. 569
Jones, B. A. P. 594
Jones, B. J. 317
Jones, D. H. 546
Jones, E. B. 81
Jones, H. 594
Jones, J. B. 159
Jones, J. C. 594
Jones, J. G. 507
Jones, J. H. 514, 536
Jones, K. O. 273
Jones, L. J. 229
Jones, R. H. 111, 374
Jones, R. L. 562, 580
Jones, R. S. 562, 594
Jones, W. H. 19
Jong, E. 423
Jongeward, D. 111, 423, 425, 459, 490, 496, 600
Jordan, E. P. 45
Jordan, J. 229, 562
Jordan, S. E. 57
Jordan-Viola, E. 60
Jorgensen, C. C. 580
Jorgensen, E. C. 22
Joselyn, E. G. 103, 267, 345, 593

Joseph, J. 507
Josephine, H. B. 491
Josephson, L. 6
Juhasz, J. 181
Julian, J. B. 151
Julian, J. W. 88, 151
Jurado, M. 610
Juran, S. H. 111, 229
Just, G. A. 626

Kaczkowski, H. R. 170
Kagan, J. 22, 30, 60, 111, 161, 202
Kagan, S. 610, 618, 619
Kahan, J. P. 260
Kahn, A. 105, 108, 111, 144, 184, 241, 259, 419
Kahn, D. 60
Kahn, O. L. 498
Kahn, R. L. 463
Kahn, S. E. 423
Kahne, H. 423, 499
Kahoe, R. D. 60
Kaley, M. M. 423, 499, 528
Kalka, B. S. 60
Kalunian, P. 282, 319
Kamii, C. K. 562
Kaminski, D. M. 159
Kammeyer, K. 22
Kanareff, V. T. 111
Kandel, D. B. 159, 562
Kane, J. E. 497
Kane, R. D. 111, 159, 282, 319
Kanekar, S. 111
Kangas, J. 111
Kanouse, D. E. 259
Kanowitz, L. 486
Kanter, R. M. 29, 75, 121, 321, 324, 370, 424, 431, 565, 583
Kantor, M. B. 18
Kao, R. S. 623
Kaplan, A. G. 29, 37, 45, 56, 60, 61, 157, 282, 283, 528
Kaplan, F. 65, 120, 431
Kaplan, H. I. 476
Kaplan, J. 497
Kaplan, R. M. 60, 102, 516

Kapur, R. 528
Karabenick, J. D. 229
Karabenick, S. A. 111, 229, 231, 254
Kardiner, A. 580
Karelius-Schumacher, K. L. 283
Karman, F. J. 23, 159, 201, 217
Karmel, B. 111
Karmens, L. 116
Karre, I. 182
Kaser, J. 424
Kashket, E. R. 470
Kasl, S. V. 593, 602
Kass, N. 201
Kassinove, H. 238
Katasaky, M. 339
Katcher, A. H. 349
Kate, D. 592
Katkovsky, W. 11, 90, 151, 152, 159, 229, 239, 248
Katz, J. 201, 508
Katz, J. B. 626
Katz, J. C. 374
Katz, K. 319, 361, 562, 580, 581, 597
Katz, M. W. 594
Katz, P. A. 35, 61, 78
Katzell, M. E. 84, 204, 410, 418, 420, 424, 447
Kaufman, M. A. 265, 304
Kaufmann, S. 388
Kaul, T. J. 581, 595
Kay, J. H. 491
Kay, M. J. 424, 459
Kayden, X. 319
Kaye, B. I. 283
Kaye, B. W. 388
Kaye, C. 93
Kazickas, J. 283
Kearney, J. F. 248
Kearney, M. 248
Keating, D. P. 99, 111, 147, 215
Keating, L. A. 356
Keefer, K. E. 182
Keiffer, M. G. 319, 374, 375
Keil, W. 159
Keil-Specht, H. 159
Keith-Spiegel, P. 210, 483
Kellen, K. 242
Keller, J. M. 248

Keller, S. 112, 424
Kelley, J. 459
Kellogg, R. L. 23
Kelly, B. R. 74
Kelly, J. 413
Kelly, J. A. 23, 41, 61
Kelly, P. K. 562
Kelly, S. 495
Kemer, B. J. 354
Kemp, B. W. 399, 543
Kemper, T. D. 23
Keniston, E. 424
Keniston, K. 61, 424
Kenkel, M. B. E. 229
Kennedy, C. 201, 216
Kenny, D. A. 177
Kent, M. 23, 319
Kent, R. N. 363
Kenworthy, J. A. 283, 354, 483
Kenyon, G. S. 159, 354
Kerlin, L. 433
Kerr, B. A. 112
Kerr, S. 373
Kerr, W. D. 319
Kersey, H. A., Jr. 626
Kessler, S. 61
Kestenbaum, J. M. 202
Keyserling, M. D. 424
Khan, S. B. 160, 202
Kibler, M. O. 210
Kidd, R. F. 256
Kidd, T. R. 112, 354
Kidder, L. 50, 481
Kidder, L. H. 112
Kieffer, M. G. 425
Kiehle, T. J. 354, 595
Kiesler, S. B. 61, 125, 258
Kievit, M. B. 425
Kilby, J. E. 283
Killian, J. R., Jr. 470, 483
Kilmann, P. R. 22, 158, 181, 248
Kilpatrick, D. G. 134
Kim, J. S. 593
Kim, K. H. 562
Kimball, B. 229
Kimball, M. M. 23, 229, 425
Kimball, W. L. 610
Kimmel, E. 266, 290, 483, 597

Kinder, D. R. 581
King, A. G. 425
King, H. 562
King, K. 239, 562
King, L. M. 610
King, M. 237, 562
King, M. C. 61
King, M. E. 23
King, P. 161, 425
Kinnane, J. E. 160
Kinsell-Rainey, L. W. 61, 112
Kinsolving, D. L. 23
Kinzer, J. L. 543
Kipnis, D. M. 23, 112, 248
Kirchner, E. P. 563
Kirk, B. A. 112, 275
Kirk, K. W. 476
Kirkbride, V. R. 283, 354
Kirkpatrick, J. J. 425, 489
Kirkpatrick, W. J. 319
Kirschner, B. F. 61
Kirsch, S. 166, 218
Kirshstein, R. J. 375, 425
Kiser, C. V. 525
Kitchener, K. S. 375, 483
Kitching, J. C. 182
Kivlin, J. E. 134, 189
Klagsbrun, F. 225, 429, 556, 574
Klaiber, E. L. 9, 86, 124
Klarke, L. S. 459
Klarreich, S. F. 283
Kleemeier, C. 20, 106, 156, 226
Klein, D. P. 425
Klein, E. A. 61
Klein, E. B. 23
Klein, F. L. 182
Klein, I. 579
Klein, M. H. 283
Klein, R. B. 160
Klein, R. R. 283
Klein, V. 2, 66, 425, 531
Kleiner, R. J. 566
Kleinfeld, J. 595
Klemmack, D. L. 23, 160
Kline, C. 23
Kline, K. H. 221
Klocke, R. A. 299, 365
Kloedt, A. 283
Kloh, W. L. A. 348

Knafle, J. D. 202
Knapp, J. J. 230
Knaster, M. 610
Knebel, F. 563
Knefelkamp, L. L. 283, 284, 320
Knight, G. F. 118
Knight, J. H. 575, 600
Knight, L. W. 394
Knill, W. D. 626
Knoke, D. 525
Knott, T. C. 182
Knotts, R. E. L. 425, 459
Knowles, L. L. 545
Knowles, L. W. 354
Knox, B. S. 283
Knudsen, D. D. 112, 319, 425
Knudsen, K. 459
Knudson, E. G. 160
Kobayashi, K. 388
Kobayashi, Y. 9, 86, 124
Kobes, D. A. 569
Koedt, A. 3, 574
Koehler, V. 112
Koehn, H. E. 459
Koenig, F. 112
Koenig, R. 425
Koeske, G. F. 61, 140
Koeske, R. K. 61
Koeski, G. F. 575
Koff, L. A. 460
Kogan, N. 113, 202
Kohen, A. I. 423, 426, 545
Kohlberg, L. A. 23, 61
Kohr, R. L. 182
Komarita, N. I. 182, 354
Komarovsky, M. 24
Komisar, L. 62, 319
Konanc, J. T. 283, 352
Koontz, E. D. 284, 388, 389, 426
Koral, A. 24
Korda, M. 426
Korman, A. K. 182
Kornrich, M. 11, 89, 138, 129, 608
Korr, W. 230
Kosa, J. 217, 477, 529
Kosecoff, J. 98
Koskinen, P. 197
Kosson, N. 15
Kostich, B. 103, 225, 592

Kotel, J. 470
Kott, E. 482
Kotzin, M. 62
Koufacos, C. 354
Kovar, L. C. 563, 610
Kraig, K. 343
Krain, M. 26, 477, 546
Kraines, R. J. 39
Krakauer, A. 284
Krall, V. 202
Kramer, B. M. 561, 567, 575, 583
Kramer, C. 107
Kramer, M. 477
Kramer, N. A. 354
Kranz, H. 426, 546
Krasno, F. 610
Krate, R. 570, 599
Krause, J. L. 329
Kravetz, D. F. 62, 284
Krawitz, R. N. 114
Krech, H. S. 62
Kremnitzer, S. 211
Kreps, J. 320, 375, 426, 427, 529
Kresojevich, I. Z. 230
Kreuter, G. 320
Kriebel, C. 460
Krieger, S. F. 160
Krieger, W. G. 24
Kriesberg, L. 160
Krippner, S. 160
Krishnan, A. 230
Kristal, J. 113
Krohn, B. 389
Krohn, M. H. 529
Krohn, M. J. 284
Kronsky, B. J. 284
Krooth, D. M. 140, 237
Krosky, B. J. 375
Krovetz, M. L. 248
Krumboltz, J. D. 298
Krusell, J. 399, 452
Krussell, J. L. 230, 259
Kuder, G. F. 281
Kuhlems, R. 357
Kuhlen, R. G. 375, 529
Kuhlmann, H. G. 460
Kuhn, D. 232
Kukla, A. 260, 263
Kukla, K. J. 182, 260
Kumlien, C. D. 495

Kundsin, R. B.   24, 113, 157, 160, 161, 181, 202, 228, 306, 320, 338, 368, 412, 463, 470, 508, 519, 528, 529
Kunz, P. R.   86
Kurth, S.   62
Kuruvilla, T. C.   166
Kushner, R.   305, 369
Kutner, N. G.   47, 62, 150, 320
Kuvlesky, W. P., and Lever, M.   113, 563, 610, 621

LaBarthe, E. R.   389, 508, 529
Labbie, S.   206
LaBelle, T. J.   610
Labovitz, S.   431
Lacey, B. W.   244
Lacher, M.   182
Lacher, M. R.   182
Lacks, P. B.   282
Ladan, C. J.   508
Ladd, E. C., Jr.   375
Ladner, J. A.   562, 563, 594
Lafevre, C.   355
Lahaderne, H.   353
Laird, D. S.   584
Lake, B.   529
Lakky, E.   30
Lakshminarayana, H. D.   160
Lalljee, M.   129, 513
Lamb, R. R.   351, 595, 621, 626
Lambert, R. D.   62
Lamel, L.   320
Lampshere, L.   10, 33, 151, 571, 572
Lancaster, J. B.   113
Lancaster, S. L.   248
Land, K. S.   94, 410, 445
Landau, D.   274
Landau, E. A.   427
Landers, D. A.   113, 160
Landes, R.   626
Landisberg, S.   24
Landman, L.   43
Lando, H. A.   113
Landon, D. D.   460
Landon, G. L.   375, 389

Lane, D. W.   115
Lang, G.   178, 344
Lange, J.   284
Langer, M.   6
Langford, E. P.   563
Langmeyer, D.   133
Langsam, I.   113
Lanier, H. B.   230
Lanning, W.   216
Lansky, K. K.   161
Lansky, L. B.   24
Lansky, L. M.   62, 161, 202
Lantier, F.   427
Lanzafame, L. J.   230
Lanzetta, J. T.   111
Lao, R. C.   113, 579
Laosa, L. M.   24
Lapidus, D.   24
LaPointe, K. A.   347
Larimore, D. L.   89
Larney, V. H.   470
Larsen, M. S.   161
Larsen, W.   41
Larson, D.   119, 203
Larson, G. L.   230
Larson, J. C.   581
Larson, R.   284
Larson, W. R.   71
LaRue, L. J. M.   563
Larum, H.   111
LaRussa, G. W.   161, 202, 217, 486, 508
Larwood, L.   113, 284, 460
Lasky, E.   13, 20, 48, 183, 227, 565, 572, 583
LaSorte, M. A.   375
Lasswell, H. D.   525
Latorre, R. A.   113
Laudicina, E. V.   529
Lauer, E. M.   6
Lavach, J.   230
Lavine, T. Z.   355
Lavoie, J. C.   248, 338, 355
Lawlis, G. F.   113, 213
Lawrence, G. L.   24
Lawrence, L.   223
Lawrence, R.   290
Lawrence, W. W.   581
Laws, J. L.   24, 202, 375, 427, 508
Layden, M. A.   260
Leahy, R. L.   229
Lear, F.   427

Leavitt, H. J.   25, 85, 115, 402, 509
Lecht, L. A.   427
Ledbetter, R. B.   460
Leder, G. C.   113
Lederer, M.   427
Lederer, W.   62
Lee, A. M.   529
Lee, B. L.   161
Lee, D.   144, 367
Lee, D. E.   355
Lee, G. K.   435
Lee, J. M.   595
Lee, M. D.   427
Lee, P. C.   320
Lee, R. J.   478, 535
Lee, S.   260
Lee, S. L.   508
Lefcourt, H. M.   249
Lefevre, C.   183, 508
Leffler, A.   376
Lefkowitz, M. M.   24
Lefley, H. P.   626
Legault, J.   460
Legerski, A.   34
Leggett, D. C.   546
Leggon, C. B.   595, 602
Legoux, Y.   114
Lehmann, P.   320
Leidig, M. S.   62
Leifer, A.   355
Leiman, A. H.   169
Lein, L.   529
Leita, C.   491
Leive, L.   470
Leland, C.   114, 355, 508, 529
Lelievre, C. C.   452
Lelievre, T. W.   452
LeMay, M. L.   161, 183
Lemon, D. K.   389
Lenney, E.   183
Lennhoff, S.   183
Lenning, O. T.   114, 183, 202
Leo, E. S.   114
Leon, G. R.   376
Leonard, L. C.   201
Leonard, M. M.   114, 280, 284, 320
Leonard, T. H.   171, 300
Leppaluoto, J.   346
Lerch, H. A.   202

Lerner, G.   62, 114, 563, 592
Lerner, H. E.   62
Lernern, R. M.   114
Leserman, J. P.   114
Lesser, G. S.   100, 114, 159, 355
Lessing, E. E.   581
Lester, R. A.   376
Letchworth, G. E.   163, 284, 320, 529
Levenberg, L. H.   183
Levenson, H.   114, 249
Leventhal, D. B.   114
Leventhal, G. S.   115
Lever, J.   330, 362
Lever, J. R.   24, 25
Lever, M.   563
Levi, J.   190, 624
Levin, C.   265
Levin, P.   146
Levine, A.   25, 115, 161, 230, 355, 508
Levine, D. M.   143, 366
Levine, E.   3, 59, 317, 374, 476, 486, 488, 491, 494, 574
Levine, R.   230, 470, 529
LeVine, R. A.   12, 161
Levine, R. V.   249, 260
Levine, S.   25
Levine, S. E.   320
Levine, S. M.   75, 140
Levinger, G.   172
Levinson, R. M.   427
Levitin, T. E.   355, 407, 427, 428
Leviton, H.   183
Levitt, E. S.   25, 161, 217, 508, 530
Levitt, M. J.   428
Levy, B. B.   25, 320, 355, 376
Levy, D. R.   475
Levy, J.   475
Levy, L.   320
Levy, N.   581
Levy, R.   428
Lewin, A. Y.   335, 376, 383, 547
Lewin, T. F.   483, 530
Lewis, A.   428, 436, 626
Lewis, E. C.   25, 212, 219,

284, 320, 355, 356
Lewis, G. J. 285
Lewis, H. 563, 595
Lewis, H. B. 25, 115
Lewis, J. 115, 198, 598
Lewis, J. A. 284, 285, 623, 627
Lewis, M. 18, 25
Lewis, P. 249
Lewis, R. O. 115
Lewis, S. A. 447
Lewis, S. D. 595
Lewko, J. H. 363
Ley, K. 320
Leyva, R. 610
Liberty, P. G. 30
Libow, J. A. 260
Licht, B. G. 481, 521
Licht, M. H. 481, 521
Lichtenstein, K. 249
Lichtenstein, P. 118
Lickamyer, A. R. 63
Liddicoat, J. P. 202
Liebman, J. S. 356
Lief, H. 520
Lifton, R. J. 62, 63, 115, 428, 452, 498, 519, 535
Lightfoot, S. L. 321
Lightner, J. 373
Liljefois, R. 108
Lillie, C. 356
Lin, Y. G. 118, 203
Lindbloom, C. G. 285
Lindsey, K. 428, 564
Lindskold, S. 138
Linn, R. L. 285
Linner, B. 62
Linsenmeier, J. A. W. 239
Lintner, A. C. 249
Linton, D. L. 389
Linton, T. H. 618
Lipinski, B. 115
Lipman-Blumen, J. 25, 62, 63, 115, 320, 376, 428, 509
Lippman, M. Z. 25
Lipset, S. M. 375
Lipsitt, P. D. 116
Lirtzman, S. I. 116
Lisles, L. 494
Liss-Levinson, N. 116
Litrownik, A. J. 16
Littig, L. W. 116, 581

Little, C. A. 555
Little, D. M. 285, 428
Littman, I., 15
Liu, P. Y. 203
Liverant, S. 14
Liversidge, W. 26
Livingston, J. 285
Livingston, K. S. 626
Livson, N. 57
Lloyd, B. B. 43, 63, 75, 112
Lloyd, B. J. 428, 509
Lloyd, C. B. 374, 428, 430, 436, 443, 451
Lloyd, M. A. 285, 320
Lloyd-Jones, E. M. 116
Locke, E. A. 116
Lockentz, L. 546
Lockheed, M. E. 295, 311, 321, 349, 356, 363, 373, 428
Lockheed-Katz, J. 231
Lockheed-Katz, M. E. 116
Loeb, J. W. 371, 376
Loeffler, D. L. 330
Loeffler, M. 321
Lofft, V. M. 428
Lofquist, L. H. 158
Logan, D. D. 581
Logan, J. 123
Lohnes, P. R. 277
Lomax, R. M. 183
London, J. 321
Londoner, C. A. 530
Long, B. H. 580
Long, C. K. 116
Long, J. M. 203, 217
Long, T. E. 376, 389
Longauex y Vasquez, E. 610
Longeau, E. V. 611
Long-Laws, J. 321
Longstreth, C. A. 389
Looft, W. R. 116, 117
Lopata, H. Z. 321, 376, 429, 483
Lopate, C. 477, 530
Lopatich, G. 282, 319
Lorber, J. 26
Lord, E. 483
Lord, M. 11, 407
Loree, M. R. 585
Lorenzana, N. 611
Loring, R. 26, 117, 305, 460
Lorr, M. 37

Losco, J. 63
Lotsaf, E. J. 247, 545
Lott, A. S. 595
Lott, B. E. 595
Louisa, V. 210
Lourenso, S. V. 581
Lovano-Kerr, J. 376
Love, B. B. 183, 581
Lovett, S. L. 203
Low, W. 595
Lowe, C. A. 577
Lowenthal, H. 492
Lower, D. 26, 477, 546
Lowman, R. P. 621
Lowrey, B. 356
Lowry, H. M. 414
Loyd, B. B. 39
Loyd, D. F. 285
Loyd, L. L. 203
Lozoff, M. M. 63, 161, 355, 508
Lubetkin, A. I. 116
Lubetkin, B. S. 116
Lubkin, G. B. 471
Lublin, J. S. 460
Lucas, M. E. 57
Luce, C. B. 429
Luchins, E. H. 321, 471
Ludeman, W. W. 356
Ludovici, L. J. 321, 489
Lueptow, L. B. 161
Luginbuhl, J. E. R. 260
Lum, M. K. M. 183
Lumsden, H. H. 341
Lundgren, D. 133
Lundgren, D. C. 183
Lundsteen, S. W. 159
Lundy, M. A. W. 63
Lunneborg, C. E. 117
Lunneborg, P. W. 63, 117, 285, 356, 509
Lupini, D. 389
Luria, Z. 34, 509
Lurie, N. O. 611, 626
Lussier, R. J. 252
Luthans, F. 405
Lutz, S. W. 509
Lutzker, D. R. 117
Lyell, R. G. 26
Lyle, J. R. 429, 460
Lynch, E. M. 460
Lynn, D. B. 26, 161
Lynn, N. B. 477

Lyon, C. 376
Lyon, E. R. 509
Lyon, R. 321
Lystad, M. H. 564

McAffee, N. 471
McAllister, A. B. 285, 321
McArthur, L. Z. 26, 117, 260
Macaulay, J. R. 322
McBee, M. I. 44, 116, 184, 309, 356, 400, 427, 429
McBee, S. 429, 492
MacBrayer, C. T. 63
McBride, K. D. 26
McBroom, P. 564
McCaffery, J. H. 573, 603
McCallon, E. L. 184
McCandless, B. R. 26, 595
McCanne, L. 356
McCanne, T. 356
McCarbery, R. J. 26
McCareins, A. G. 239
McCarthy, J. L. 546
McCarthy, K. 298, 473
McCarthy, K. A. 274
McCarthy, P. A. 250
McCary, J. L. 127
McCelland, D. C. 63
Maccia, E. S. 21, 25, 322, 324, 327, 373
McClain, E. W. 184, 285, 582
McClelland, D. C. 227, 539
McClelland, L. 3, 237
McClendon, M. J. 429
McClintock, C. G. 117, 119, 611
McCloud, T. E. 217
McClure, R. F. 162
Maccoby, E. E. 12, 23, 27, 29, 33, 63, 109, 117, 118, 184, 322, 459, 471
McComb, A. 63, 285
McConnell, J. 143
McConnell, W. A. 118
McCord, B. 460
McCorkle, E. M. 389
McCormack, T. 509
McCormick, M. K. 596
McCormick, N. 482
McCowan, R. J. 162

McCoy, R. E. 585
McCoy, V. 286
McCuen, J. R. 132
McCulloch, D. H. 323
McCullough, R. V. 184, 461, 509
McCune, C. W. 330
McCune, S. D. 322, 377
McCurdy, D. W. 479
McDaniel, R. 612
McDavid, J. W. 133
McDermott, M. 118
McDill, E. L. 162
MacDonald, A. P. 27, 162, 243, 250
MacDonald, C. 356
McDonald, F. J. 135, 382
McDonald, P. J. 98, 220
McDonald, R. L. 564
McDonald, T. 626
McDonnell, C. 182, 477
MacDonnell, J. 110
McDonnell, J. J. 489
McEaddy, B. J. 429, 446, 550
McElroy, D. K. 89
McEwen, M. 377
McEwen, M. K. 286
McFadden, J. R. 27
McFadden, K. 442
McFarland, W. J. 118
McFarlane, L. 64
McGhee, P. E. 17, 170, 250
McGinley, P. 70, 129
McGinnies, E. 27
McGovern, L. P. 118
McGowan, B. 203
McGrath, D. 50
McGrath, E. M. 356
McGrath, P. L. 322
McGuigan, D. G. 226, 428, 507, 530
McGuinness, E. 231
McGuire, C. 207
McGuire, J. M. 118
Machacek, L. 322
McHugh, M. 258
McHugh, M. C. 260
McHugh, N. 521
McHugh, W. T. 184
McIntosh, G. R. 377
McIntosh, J. C. 377, 390

Mack, D. 118
Mack, D. E. 564
Mack, G. E. 596
McKain, A. E. 10
McKay, B. J. 118
McKay, G. 62
McKeachie, W. J. 10, 118, 151, 195, 203
McKemi-Belt, V. L. 461
McKenzie, R. E. 615
McKenzie, S. P. 118, 203
Mackie, J. B. 564, 596
Mackie, M. 377
McKim, J. 429
McKinley, D. L. 509
McKinney, M. 47
Mackler, B. 596
McKnight, D. 322
Maclachlan, C. M. 611
McLaughlin, C. 509
McLaughlin, G. W. 162
McLaughlin, S. D. 429
McLean, K. 530
Maclennan, L. 461
Macleod, J. 429
McLure, G. T. 322, 323, 390
McLure, J. W. 323, 390
McMahan, I. D. 119, 241, 260
McMahon, J. T. 120, 531
McMahon, M. 120, 531
McManus, M. L. 64
McMillan, M. R. 119, 509, 530
McMurray, G. L. 483
McNally, G. B. 429
McNamara, W. A. 323
McNeel, S. P. 119, 377
McNickle, D. 627
McPartland, J. 308, 577
McPherson, L. I. 161
McReynolds, M. 121
Macy, J. W., Jr. 119, 430
Madaus, G. F. 218
Madden, J. F. 430
Madsen, M. C. 564, 611, 618
Maehr, M. L. 27, 546, 598
Maes, P. C. J. M. 157, 226
Magelsdorff, A. D. 94
Magón, R. F. 611
Magoon, T. M. 483
Magruder, H. 300, 335

Mahler, I. 249
Mahoney, J. 64
Mahoney, M. H. 404
Mahood, W. 430
Mai-Dalton, R. 64
Maides, S. 64
Maier, N. R. F. 20, 108, 119, 130
Maimon, P. D. 162
Major, B. N. 231
Major, L. B. 611, 618
Makosky, V. P. 231
Malan, M. 461
Malcolm, S. M. 621, 625
Malik, H. M. 286, 546
Malinowski, C. 145
Malkiel, B. G. 430
Malkiel, J. A. 430
Malmaud, R. K. 64
Malone, M. 231
Malpass, R. S. 582
Malumphy, T. M. 203, 356
Manaster, G. J. 119, 203
Mandel, S. L. 27
Mandel, W. M. 430, 499
Mander, A. V. 286
Mandle, J. D. 27, 64, 430
Mangieri, J. N. 184
Mangiore, T. W. 442
Manhardt, P. J. 461, 530
Manis, J. D. 530
Manis, L. G. 286
Manley, R. O. 162
Mannes, M. 27, 119, 203
Manning, P. K. 360
Manning, T. T. 64
Mannino, F. V. 611
Manoogian, S. T. 5
Manosevitz, M. 16
Manpower Administration 430, 530
Mantini, B. K. 330
Maquire, U. 203
Marcia, J. E. 184
Marconi, K. M. 430
Marcotte, D. B. 134
Marcus, G. H. 471
Marcus, L. R. 377
Marecek, J. 50, 64, 119, 184, 250, 286, 323
Margolin, G. 27
Marino, C. D. 162

Marion, S. P. 238
Mariscal, L. 611
Marjoribanks, K. 119
Markes, S. 64
Marks, D. 311, 411
Marks, J. 509
Marlowe, D. 11, 152
Marlowe, L. 203
Marmor, J. 27, 64
Marotz, R. 611
Marple, B. L. N. 204
Marple, D. J. 509
Marquis, K. 237
Marrett, C. B. 430
Marsalis, L. W. 356, 377
Marsden, G. 32
Marshak, W. P. 356
Marshall, C. 6
Marshall, J. 231
Marshall, J. S. 596
Marshall, K. K. 430
Martens, J. L. 253
Martens, R. 204
Martin, A. G. 323
Martin, A. M. 323
Martin, C. R., Jr. 461
Martin, D. 119, 162
Martin, J. C. 119
Martin, M. 377
Martin, P. Y. 67
Martin, R. R. 126
Martin, S. 162
Martin, T. W. 530
Martin, W. 73, 153, 547, 575
Martin, W. T. 430, 546
Martinez, E. 611
Martyna, W. 10, 37, 45, 49, 110, 229, 231, 259, 277, 307, 404
Marwell, G. 119
Marx, R. W. 582
Masendorf, F. 85
Masih, L. K. 119, 204, 217, 510
Maslin, A. 286, 530
Maslow, A. P. 489
Mason, E. J. 354, 357, 595
Mason, E. P. 618
Mason, K. O. 65, 85, 402
Massari, D. J. 250
Massey, G. C. 596, 621
Massey, R. 480
Masterman, M. 377

Masters, M. 548
Masters, R. J. 461
Matheny, P. H. P. 390
Mathes, E. W. 184
Mathews, J. J. 430
Mathews, M. R. 357, 477
Mathies, L. 323
Mathis, L. R. 357
Mathis, M. 546
Mathison, M. A. 323
Mathur, M. B. 12
Mathys, N. 461
Matis, E. E. 204
Matossian, J. 140
Matson, P. L. 461
Mattes, L. 390
Matteson, M. T. 120, 461, 531
Mattfeld, J. A. 369, 468, 470, 471, 472, 473, 483
Matthews, E. E. 27, 28, 204, 286, 287, 299, 300, 305, 431, 510
Matthies, M. T. 431
Mausner, B. 222, 232
Mausner, J. S. 483
Mawardi, B. H. 217
Mawby, R. G. 147
Maxey, A. 32
Maxey, E. J. 131
Maxted, M. C. 120
Maxwell, A. D. 564, 596
Maxwell, P. G. 120, 231
Mayer, W. K. 204
Mayfield, B. 510
Maymi, C. R. 431, 622
Mayo, A. 611
Mead, M. 65, 120, 289, 431
Meade, C. 357
Meade, R. D. 28
Meadow, A. 605, 611
Meadow, M. J. 60
Meadows, W. M. 194, 214
Mears, G. L. 510
Mears, J. 377
Mebane, D. F. 618
Mebane, M. 618
Meda, R. 28, 317
Medalen, J. I. 471
Medina, C. 622
Medley, M. L. 564, 582
Mednick, M. T. S. 8, 20, 28, 38, 48, 49, 57, 65, 104, 107, 120, 137, 170, 176, 194, 211, 226, 227, 231, 240, 258, 261, 321, 323, 344, 368, 381, 420, 427, 434, 441, 502, 510, 515, 546, 582, 583, 585
Medsger, B. 431, 546
Medsker, L. L. 139, 170, 211
Medvene, A. M. 120, 162, 287, 431
Meehan, W. J. 204
Meeker, B. F. 120
Megargee, E. I. 120, 431, 558, 578
Mchaffey, T. D. 530
Mehl, D. 138, 170
Mehnert, I. B. 287
Mehrabian, A. 142
Mehrens, W. A. 184
Mehryar, A. H. 15
Meidam, M. T. 146
Meier, H. C. 28
Meier, R. P. 123, 165
Meir, E. I. 204, 510, 531
Meissner, J. A. 564
Meixal, C. A. 28
Melchionne, T. M. 486
Melder, J. 343
Menaker, E. 287
Mendelsohn, M. 323
Mendenhall, T. C. 323
Menninger, K. 477
Menoff, B. R. 204
Mepham, G. J. 431
Merbaum, A. D. 564
Meredith, C. 205
Meredith, E. 323
Meredith, J. C. 510
Meredith, R. 323
Merenda, P. F. 357
Merriam, E. 431
Merrirr, K. 323
Merritt, D. H. 461
Merritt, E. 497
Merritt, M. S. 71, 548, 569
Merritt, R. 185
Merritt, S. A. 489
Merry, P. E. 357
Mesrop, A. 308
Messe, L. A. 120, 431
Messer, S. B. 250

Metcalf, A. 627
Metee, D. R. 184
Metzger, S. M. 510
Meyer, J. 369
Meyer, J. W. 28
Meyer, M. I. 65
Meyer, M. M. 120
Meyer, P. 461
Meyer, W. 263
Meyer, W. J. 357
Meyers, C. F. 598, 603
Meyers, S. G. 594
Mezzano, J. 387
Michael, A. 442, 531, 533
Michael, J. A. 86, 341, 390
Michael, W. B. 159, 205
Michaels, J. W. 323
Michaelson, B. L. 121, 185
Michaelson, E. J. 65
Michener, B. P. 625
Mickish, G. 390
Middleton, R. 18, 564
Midgley, N. 232
Midlarsky, E. 287, 477
Mikula, G. 121
Milanovich, A. 390
Miles, B. 28, 357
Miles, C. 431
Miles, M. B. 357
Milgram, N. A. 185, 357, 582
Milgram, R. M. 185, 357
Milholland, J. E. 118
Miljus, R. 435
Miller, A. L. 512
Miller, B. 86
Miller, B. J. 596
Miller, B. S. 121, 232
Miller, C. D. 215, 217
Miller, D. M. 582
Miller, E. W. 564
Miller, F. L. 431
Miller, G. P. 294, 362
Miller, G. R. 121
Miller, H. P. 443
Miller, J. 431
Miller, J. A. 147
Miller, J. B. 73, 276, 288, 295
Miller, K. 323
Miller, L. B. 8, 340
Miller, M. H. 477

Miller, M. M. 377
Miller, M. S. 510
Miller, P. M. 344
Miller, R. H. 18
Miller, R. L. 121
Miller, S. B. 377
Miller, S. J. 163, 255
Miller, S. M. 28, 185
Miller, S. R. 28, 163, 250
Miller, T. W. 28, 65
Millett, K. 65, 121, 324, 431
Millman, M. 29, 65, 75, 121, 321, 324, 370, 431, 583
Mills, C. J. 47
Mills, O. 586
Milne, C. 565
Milner, J. S. 224
Mincer, J. 432
Miner, J. B. 121, 357, 390, 461
Minigione, A. D. 565
Minnigerode, F. A. 65, 250
Minton, H. L. 247
Mintz, E. 29, 163
Mintz, R. S. 121
Minuchin, P. 29, 121, 324
Mirels, H. L. 250
Misa, K. F. 589
Mischel, H. N. 378, 432
Mischel, W. 29
Mischell, H. 121
Mishler, S. A. 29, 288, 510, 531
Mitchell, B. A. 205
Mitchell, D. C. 582
Mitchell, E. 29, 288, 324
Mitchell, J. 29, 324, 432
Mitchell, J. M. 378
Mitchell, J. S. 65, 66
Mitchell, S. B. 357, 358, 432
Mittelback, F. G. 612
Mitzner, P. L. 462
Miyahira, S. D. 531
Mochizuki, J. 286
Modern Language Association, Commission on Status of Women 492
Moerk, E. L. 565, 612
Moers, E. 531
Mogar, R. E. 205
Mogy, R. B. 260
Mohlmar, C. 312
Mohr, D. 29

Molina, J. C. 596, 622
Mommsen, K. G. 596, 602
Monahan, L. 232
Money, J. 29, 66, 582
Monge, R. H. 185
Monson, R. G. 163
Monsour, K. J. 324
Montagu, A. 121
Montague, A. C. 217
Montanelli, D. S. 122, 241
Montanto, J. 521
Montemayor, R. 122
Montgomery, J. 462
Montgomery, J. R. 162
Montiel, M. 612
Monts, E. A. 484
Mood, A. M. 308, 577
Moody, D. L. 213
Mooney, J. D. 358
Mooney, R. F. 217
Moore, B. E. A. 622
Moore, B. M. 531
Moore, J. 612
Moore, K. A. 232
Moore, K. M. 358
Moore, K. M. 510
Moore, L. 90, 178
Moore, L. L. 232
Moore, S. F. 288
Moore, S. G. 58
Moore, S. L. 288
Moore, T. W. 49
Moore, W. 596
Moose, M. E. 358
Morales, R. 612
Moran, B. K. 6, 10, 270, 467, 492
More, D. M. 136, 365
Moreland, J. R. 66
Moreno, D. 612
Morgan, D. D. 185, 510
Morgan, R. 3, 295, 384, 475, 491, 492, 498, 552, 566, 610, 615
Morgan, S. W. 232
Morgan, W. P. 497
Morgenstern, R. 104, 225, 315, 350
Morgenthaler, E. 432
Morlock, L. L. 142, 366, 378
Morneau, R. H., Jr. 487
Morner, M. 612

Morphy, D. R. 100
Morrill, W. H. 217
Morris, E. 205
Morris, J. 432, 582
Morris, L. D. 29, 163
Morris, L. W. 205
Morris, R. 432
Morrison, B. M. 557
Morrison, K. E. 618
Morrison, N. 181
Morrison, R. F. 185, 205
Morrison, T. 565
Morse, J. 205
Morse, J. A. 87, 122, 195, 521
Morse, J. J. 185
Morse, J. L. 462
Morse, S. J. 124
Morsink, H. A. 390
Mortimer, J. 531
Morton, C. A. 596
Morton, T. E. 372, 417, 544
Morton, W. M. 612
Moser, C. H. 432
Moses, J. L. 432
Moskalski, D. D. 165
Moskowitz, J. M. 117
Mosley, K. 568
Moss, H. A. 22, 30
Mostofsky, D. I. 101, 154, 544, 559
Mostow, E. 531
Mott, F. L. 288
Motta, R. W. 358
Motz, A. B. 471, 531
Moulton, R. 38, 73
Moulton, R. W. 30
Mowder, B. 66
Mowsesian, R. 163, 511
Moynahan, E. D. 100
Mueller, E. 135, 242
Mueller, K. H. 324
Muhlenkamp. A. F. 163, 205, 218
Mukhergee, B. N. 122
Mullaney, T. R. 358
Muller, L. C. 72, 324, 333
Muller, O. G. 72, 324, 333, 518
Mulligan, K. 324
Mullins, C. J. 498
Mullis, I. V. S. 324
Mulvey, M. C. 205, 511

Mulvey, R. B. 288
Mulvihill, F. X. 565
Munday, D. A. 163
Munger, M. O. 30
Munley, P. H. 218, 288
Munnell, B. 433
Munz, D. C. 163
Murillo, N. 612
Murlidharan, R. 163
Murphy, B. M. 270
Murphy, G. 288, 301
Murphy, L. 508
Murphy, L. K. 433
Murphy-Berman, V. 122, 232
Murray, H. B. 250
Murray, P. 66, 565
Murray, R. 184, 429
Murray, S. R. 122, 260, 261, 582, 583
Murtagh, R. 492
Musella, D. F. 390
Musgrove, W. J. 565, 582
Mushier, C. L. 205
Mussen, P. H. 20, 29, 30, 545
Muth, P. 163
Muzio, N. R. 42
Myers, A. E. 206
Myers, C. H. 358
Myers, L. W. 565, 582
Myerson, B. 433
Myint, T. 502
Myrdal, A. 66, 531

Nachmann, B. 277
Nadelson, C. C. 122, 358, 477
Nader, L. 484
Naffziger, C. C. 30
Naffziger, K. G. 30, 288
Nagely, D. L. 288, 511
Nagy, J. 82
Naiman, A. 324
NAIW 462
Nakamura, C. Y. 30, 128, 167, 189, 336
Nash, J. 612
Nash, J. M. 164
Nash, S. C. 122
Nash, W. R. 510
National Association of State Universities and Land-Grant Colleges. Office of Research and Information 546
National Black Feminist Organization 565
National Board of Graduate Education 546
National Council of Administrative Women in Education 390
National Institute of Education, Career Education Program 288
National Organization for Women 358, 462, 546
National Research Council 471
Nava, Y. 622
Navar, I. 612
Navarro, V. 477
Navin, S. 288
Naylor, H. H. 324
NEA, DuShane Emergency Fund Division 378
Neale, J. M. 579
Neidig, M. B. 391
Nell, O. 324, 433
Nelson, B. W. 547, 596
Nelson, C. 484
Nelson, D. D. 30
Nelson, H. Y. 122
Nelson, I. M. 206, 218
Nelson, J. F. 612
Nelson, L. D. 356
Nelson, M. C. W. 433
Nelson, R. C. 566
Nelson, R. E. 111, 241, 259
Nelson, S. 433
Nemeroff, W. F. 466
Nemeth, C. 122
Nemeth, S. E. 462
Nemiroff, M. A. 531
Nesselroade, J. R. 6
Nettl, P. 492
Neubeck, G. 107
Neugarten, B. L. 39, 324, 325, 378
Neujahr, J. L. 105, 470
Neulinger, J. 289
Neuman, R. R. 289
Neuringer, C. 196, 209
Nevill, D. 66, 185
Nevin, M. 122, 511
Newberry, P. 531

Newcomb, A. 239, 343
Newcomb, H. 622
Newcomb, T. M. 312, 347, 511
Mewcomer, M. 325
Newell, B. W. 597
Newland, J. E. 433
Newman, D. 433
Newman, J. E. 358
Newman, P. 547
Newton, H. 358
New York Board of Regents 325
Nezzer, M. 433
Ngai, S. Y. A. 531
Ngissah, P. 569
Nicholls, J. G. 185, 250, 261
Nichols, C. 289, 358
Nichols, I. A. 185
Nichols, R. C. 164, 501, 511, 516
Nickerson, E. 194
Nicoll, T. L. 66
Nieboer, N. A. 391
Nielo, C. 612
Niemi, B. 433
Nietfeld, C. R. 352
Niethammer, C. 627
Nieto, N. 612
Nieto-Gomez, A. 613, 622
Nieva, V. F. 433
Nieves, L. 547
Nikkari, J. G. 206
Niple, M. L. 503
Nixon, M. 378, 391
Noble, J. L. 566
Nobles, W. W. 566
Nochlin, L. 492
Noel, R. C. 613
Noeth, R. J. 278, 291, 506
Nolfi, S. L. 485
Nolte, M. C. 325
Nordholm, L. A. 27
Nordin, M. L. 95
Nordin, V. D. 127, 317
Nordlie, D. A. 30
Nordlie, P. G. 325
Norfleet, M. A. 206
Norman, B. 391
Norman, R. 66, 289
Norman, R. D. 30
Northcott, C. 495

Northrup, H. R. 547
Norton, D. 32, 68, 126
Norton, E. H. 547, 566
Norton, S. D. 462
Notestine, E. B. 433
Notman, M. T. 122, 358, 477
Novak, M. 495
Nowakiwska, M. 368
Nowicki, S. 30, 164, 241, 243, 245, 250, 251
Nunn, C. Z. 164
Nurkhart, M. Q. 31
Nuthall, G. A. 123
Nuttall, E. V. 164, 624
Nuttall, R. L. 123, 164, 566, 613, 624
Nuttin, J. M., Jr. 119
Nuttin, J. R. 178
Nuzum, R. E. 164
Nye, F. I. 157, 515, 520, 527, 528, 531
Nystrand, P. M. 332

Oaxaca, R. 433, 434
O'Barr, J. 306
Oberle, W. H. 566
O'Brien, C. G. 61
O'Brien, E. J. 185
O'Brien, G. M. 391
O'Brien, J. E. 471
O'Brien, M. 462
O'Carroll, M. 123
O'Connell, A. 232
O'Connell, A. A. 31
O'Connell, A. N. 123
O'Connell, E. 165
O'Connell, E. J. 346
O'Connell, J. W. 340
O'Connor, H. A. 124
O'Connor, J. 504, 523, 579
O'Connor, K. A. 206
O'Connor, P. 582
Odarenko, D. J. 314
Odell, M. Q. 206
Oden, S. 244
Odiorne, G. S. 434
Oetzel, R. 123
Office of Experimental Projects and Programs 471
Offir, C. 38, 123, 137, 444
Ogilvie, B. C. 213, 497

Oglesby, C. A. 359, 496, 497
O'Hara, R. 123
Ohlbaum, J. S. 186, 218
Ohlsen, M. M. 289
Okediji, P. A. 583
Okun, B. F. 511
Olch, D. R. 279
O'Leary, J. A. 123
O'Leary, K. D. 363
O'Leary, V. E. 2, 66, 67, 123, 164, 186, 206, 232, 233, 259, 261, 434, 484, 532, 547, 566
Olesen, V. L. 178, 359, 370, 408, 434, 503
Oleshansky, B. 28, 32, 58, 68, 127, 317, 325
Olins, R. A. 88, 404
Olive, H. 123
Oliver, L. W. 164, 206, 289, 511
Oliver, R. L. 454
Olivers, T. C. 289
Ollison, L. 31
Olsen, H. D. 184, 597
Olsen, L. C. 174
Olsen, N. J. 164, 225
Olson, A. L. 147
Olson, L. A. 241
Oltman, R. M. 325, 359, 378, 391, 434, 489
O'Mahoney, M. T. 206
Omvig, C. 89
O'Neal, E. 284
O'Neal, E. C. 98, 220
O'Neil, P. M. 218
O'Neill, P. 434
O'Neill, W. L. 11, 434
Oppenheimer, V. K. 434
Orbach, N. R. F. 477
Orden, S. R. 532
Orenstein, A. M. 168
Organ, D. W. 251, 446
Orleans, J. H. 306
Ornstein, A. C. 326
O'Rourke, M. C. 359
Orr, H. K. 20
Orso, D. P. 123
Orth, C. D., III 462
Ortner, S. B. 67
Orton, J. 124
Orum, A. M. 31

Orum, A. W. 31
Osawa, M. 123
Osborn, J. 289, 325
Osborn, M. E. 164
Osborn, M. O. 210
Osborn, R. H. 325
Osborn, S. M. 289
Osen, L. 123, 471
O'Shea, A. J. 289
Osipow, S. H. 29, 102, 123, 169, 186, 187, 192, 213, 218, 220, 288, 378, 435, 510, 511, 531, 532, 536
Oslooper, T. 67
Osmond, H. 289
Osmond, M. W. 67
Osofsky, H. J. 67
Osofsky, J. D. 67, 165
Otten, A. L. 435
Otto, K. M. 289
Otto, L. B. 123, 165
Overman, S. J. 326
Ovesey, L. 580
Ozehosky, R. J. 186

Pack, S. J. 78
Packard, R. 114
Packard, S. 378
Packer, A. B. 511
Packer, H. L. 363
Padilla, A. M. 619
Pagano, A. 103, 315, 417
Page, M. U. 206, 218
Page, R. 72
Page, R. H. 124
Paige, K. 200
Painter, D. H. 566
Painter, E. G. 124, 326, 378, 391
Paisios, J. 462
Paisley, W. 481
Palfrey, C. F. 359
Pallone, N. J. 186, 566, 613
Palmer, A. B. 186
Palmer, R. J. 90, 177, 196
Palmer, P. 391
Pandey, R. E. 583
Panek, P. E. 124
Paolucci, B. 537
Papalia, D. E. 124
Papanek, H. 532
Pappo, M. 233

Paredes, F. 613
Pareek, U. 81
Parelius, A. P. 67, 511
Parelius, R. J. 169, 210, 585
Parelman, A. 43
Paretti, J. P. 583
Pargman, D. 182
Park, C. C. 124
Park, J. P. 566, 597
Parke, R. 424
Parker, A. 30
Parker, A. W. 511
Parker, H. J. 155
Parker, S. 566
Parker, V. J. 233
Parks, B. J. 336, 447
Parks, M. 569
Parlee, M. B. 124
Parmelee, R. 478, 512, 533
Parnes, 435, 523
Parrish, J. B. 289, 379, 410, 435, 468, 471, 472
Parsley, K. M., Jr. 124
Parsons, H. D. 512
Parsons, J. 31, 54, 70, 128, 198, 241, 261
Parsons, J. E. 67, 124, 207, 241, 261
Parsons, J. L. 163, 205, 218, 269
Parsons, O. A. 251, 254
Parsons, P. F. 566, 583
Parsons, T. 31, 326, 567
Pascal, A. 547
Pascale, L. 50
Pascarella, E. T. 359
Paschal, B. J. 583
Paschall, N. 261
Pascoe, E. J. 359
Pasewark, R. A. 98
Pasquella, M. 261
Passer, M. W. 259
Passon, W. R. 557, 577
Pasternak, S. 99
Pasteur, A. B. 600
Patai, R. 31
Pate, B. 67
Pate, M. A. 141
Patella, V. M. 610, 621
Paterson, A. 176
Patigalia, S. 68

Patrick, T. A. 165, 207
Patten, F. G. 379
Patterson, A. R. 484
Patterson, C. H. 121
Patterson, G. R. 15, 27
Patterson, L. E. 186
Patterson, M. 93, 350, 379
Patterson, T. W. 212
Patton, R. G. 31
Patty, R. S. A. 233
Paul, R. J. 88, 404, 435
Paulsen, D. L. 512
Pavalko, R. M. 124
Pawlicki, R. E. 251
Paxton, K. 326
Payne, D. 68, 186, 534
Payne, D. A. 124, 359
Payne, E. L. 597
Payne, F. E. 551, 603, 624
Pearlman, J. 47, 368, 389
Pearson, K. G. 462
Peck, R. F. 85, 542
Peden, I. C. 124, 379, 472, 473
Pedhazur, E. J. 74
Peele, S. 124, 600
Peisach, E. 86, 150, 554
Peiser, G. L. 125, 359
Pena, V. 613
Penalosa, F. 613
Pender, A. 326, 435
Pendergrass, V. 290, 484, 597
Pendleton, C. 472
Pengelly, R. S. 125
Penk, W. E. 251
Penman, R. 67
Penn, J. R. 125
Penn, L. 67
Pennell, M. 477, 478
Penner, L. A. 125
Penney, S. 317, 421
Pennsylvania Department of Education 326
Pepe, E. A. 67
Peplau, L. A. 67, 125, 233, 234
Peratus, K. W. 307, 404
Peretti, P. O. 125
Perez-Reyes, M. 352
Perez-Solis, M. 613, 624
Perham, J. 462
Perlman, D. 39, 211

Perlmutter, B.   43, 80
Perney, L. R.   125
Perney, V.   241, 247
Perella, V. C.   435, 535
Perrone, P. A.   125, 165, 218
Perroy, E.   10
Perucci, C. C.   31, 33, 43, 67, 472, 512, 532, 560
Perry, A. R.   547
Perry, D. G.   31
Perry, D. K.   218
Perry, L. C.   31
Persons, W. E., III   597
Perun, P. J.   379
Pesquera, B. M.   613
Pestonjee, D.   79
Peters, A.   31
Peters, H. J.   23, 39, 186, 278, 290, 445
Peters, J.   68
Peters, J. R.   532
Peters, L. H.   462, 466
Petersen, J.   290, 597
Peterson, A.   587
Peterson, C. C.   32
Peterson, E.   435, 532
Peterson, E. H.   165
Peterson, E. T.   32
Peterson, I.   379
Peterson, J. L.   32, 95, 346
Peterson, K.   492, 547
Peterson, M.   392
Peterson, M. J.   68
Peterson, M. T.   597
Peterson, R. A.   218
Peterson, R. E.   125, 165
Petit, Sister R. M.   379
Pettigrew, T. F.   597
Petty, M. M.   435
Pew, S.   197
Pfeifer, C. M. Jr.   597
Pfiffner, V. T.   207, 392
Phares, E. J.   12, 245, 251, 252
Phelan, J. G.   454
Phelps, C. E.   478
Phelps, E. S.   547
Phelps, S.   290
Pheterson, G. L.   125
Phillips, B. N.   146, 207
Phillips, F. L.   68
Phillips, P. B.   290

Phillips, V. K.   207
Phillips, W. E.   125
Phipps-Sanger, S.   53, 97, 252
Piacente, B. S.   125
Piccola, G.   20, 106, 156, 226
Pick, A. D.   148
Pick, G. M. de   613
Picou, J. S.   567
Piel, E. R.   290
Pierce, J. C.   567
Pierce, J. V.   125, 165
Pierce, P.   602
Pietrofesa, J. J.   207, 290, 294, 326, 436
Pifer, A.   326, 436
Piliavin, J. A.   126
Pincus, C.   290
Pines, A.   135
Pinsker, S.   290
Pinto, L. R.   290
Pinto, P. R.   547
Piomelli, R.   492, 532
Pirsig, N.   326
Plant, W. T.   126
Platt, B. B.   102
Platt, J. J.   94, 152, 165, 245, 252
Pleck, J. H.   68, 75, 126, 234, 237, 359, 532
Plog, S. C.   498
Plost, M.   165, 326
Plotsky, F. A.   290, 326, 350, 359, 360
Plovsky, G.   157
Poblano, R.   622
Podis, E.   492
Poffenberger, T.   32, 68, 126
Poggio, J. P.   209
Pogrebin, L. C.   126, 290, 436, 532, 533
Pohly, S. R.   135, 242
Polacheck, S. W.   432, 436
Poland, N.   489
Polit, D.   164
Polk, B. B.   32, 68, 436, 521
Pollack, F.   311, 411
Pollis, N. P.   126
Poloma, M. M.   436, 533
Polowy, C. I.   326
Polster, M.   290

Pomeranz, D. 252
Pomeroy, E. L. 266
Pont, H. B. 87
Ponzo, Z. 186
Pool, J. G. 341
Pope, S. K. 165
Popp, A. L. 115
Poppleton, P. K. 166
Porjesz, Y. R. 234
Porter, A. C. 599
Porter, J. 126, 186
Porter, J. B. 166, 207
Portillo, C. 613
Portz, E. 166
Posner, S. E. 621, 625
Pospisil, V. C. 533
Postl, B. 166, 218
Poston, D. L., Jr. 430, 546
Potepan, P. A. 212, 263
Potter, B. A. 290
Potter, E. F. 360
Potter, N. D. 32
Pottinger, J. S. 436, 547
Pottker, J. 11, 22, 56, 60, 95, 130, 133, 298, 313, 314, 327, 343, 351, 379, 386, 394, 474, 557
Potvin, R. 255
Poulous, R. 291
Poulsen, S. B. 212
Powell, A. 252, 482
Powell, B. 291, 533
Powell, G. J. 567, 583
Powell, G. N. 436
Powell, K. S. 533
Powell, M. 126
Powers, E. A. 12, 50
Powers, J. F. 625
Powers, L. 478, 512, 533
Poznanski, E. 32
Prather, J. E. 126, 436, 462, 499
Pratt, A. B. 126, 290
Pratt, L. 166
Pratt, L. V. 327
Pratt, M. 529
Prediger, D. J. 278, 291
Prenter, I. L. 126, 166
Prescott, D. 234
President's Commission on the Status of Women 436
Press, A. 95

Presser, H. B. 567
Pressman, S. 436, 597
Prestage, J. L. 31, 47, 61, 567
Preston, A. 11, 90, 151, 152, 159, 239
Preston, J. D. 598
Preston, T. 482
Prestwich, T. L. 464, 534
Prewitt, K. 545
Price, B. R. 487
Price, G. E. 268, 291
Price, K. H. 259, 457
Price-Williams, D. R. 567
Prien, E. P. 478, 535
Primavera, A. M. 187
Primavera, L. H. 187
Princc, J. S. 294, 362
Pringle, M. B. 292
Pritikin, R. 613
Prociuk, T. J. 252
Profant, P. M. 126
Professional Women's Caucus 437
Project on the Status and Education of Women 327, 497, 547, 622
Provenzano, F. J. 34
Pruitt, A. 592
Pruitt, G. S. 392
Pryor, S. 234
Psathas, G. 292
Puddefoot, S. 437
Pugh, M. D. 141, 275
Pugh, R. C. 248
Pulido, M. L. 614
Pullen, D. L. 327
Pullum, C. A. 478
Punk, H. H. 327
Puri, P. 208
Purvis, M. L. 512
Puryear, G. R. 231, 582, 583
Putnam, B. A. 187
Putnam, L. 463
Putney, S. 564
Pyke, S. W. 292, 360

Quadango, J. 463, 478
Quarter, J. 166, 218
Query, J. M. 166
Quimby, V. 187

Quinn, F. X. 437
Quinn, R. P. 327, 407, 427, 428, 442, 463
Quinn, S. 68
Quisenberry, D. J. 144, 355, 367

Raban, R. 242
Rabinowitz, C. 4, 41, 78
Rabson, A. 90, 152
Rachiele, L. 217
Radcliffe Institute 360
Radding, N. 290
Rader, H. B. 392
Raderman, R. 360
Radi, S. 68
Radin, N. L. 153, 562, 567
Raffel, N. K. 327
Rafferty, F. T. 564, 596
Rafferty, J. E. 171
Rago, J. J., Jr. 464
Rainwater, L. 567
Rall, M. 489
Ralston, Y. L. 392
Ramaley, J. A. 258, 469
Ramanaiah, N. V. 252
Ramey, E. R. 437, 463
Raming, I. 495
Ramirez, F. O. 446
Ramirez, M., III 567, 614, 619
Ramos, R. A. 580
Ramsey, G. V. 533
Ramsey, S. 560, 609
Ramsey, S. E. 292
Ramsey, S. J. 54
Rand, L. M. 126, 207, 512
Randall, M. 614
Randall, R. 557
Randolph, C. 292
Randolph, K. S. 360
Randour, M. L. 379, 484
Raphael, E. E. 548
Raphelson, A. C. 223
Rapone, A. 3, 574
Rapoport, A. 127
Rapoport, R. 127, 457, 504, 520, 525, 533, 534
Rapoport, R. N. 127, 457, 504, 520, 525, 533, 534
Rapoza, R. S. 278

Rappaport, A. F. 68, 136, 187, 534
Rascovsky, A. 6
Raskin, B. L. 292
Ratner, E. L. 376
Rau, L. 35, 71
Rawlings, E. 270, 279, 282
Ray, C. D. 472, 478
Ray, E. M. 290, 508
Rayder, N. F. 588
Raygor, A. W. 18, 350
Rayman, J. 278, 292
Raymer, E. 548
Raymand, B. J. 75, 140
Raymond, Y. R. 522
Raynor, J. O. 207, 228
Raza Unida Party 614
Reagan, D. B. 62, 115, 321, 400, 401, 418, 428, 437, 508
Rebecca, M. 32, 58, 68, 127
Reboussin, R. 627
Recruitment, Leadership and Training Institute 392
Red, S. B. 127
Reed, H. B. 218, 360
Reed, J. L. 182, 477
Reed, J. S. 561, 602
Reed, L. 263
Reeder, L. G. 581
Reeling, P. A. 360
Rees, A. 434, 550
Rees, M. 360
Reeves, E. T. 368
Reeves, M. E. 392
Reeves, N. 32, 68, 308, 437, 463
Regan, C. A. 166
Rehberg, R. 292
Reich, A. 379
Reich, M. 548
Reid, I. S. 127, 252, 567
Reid, P. T. 69
Reid, W. M. 567
Reilly, D. E. 207
Reilly, M. E. 437
Reilly, R. 357
Reilly, T. M. 392
Reimanis, G. 166, 252, 253
Reis, H. T. 230
Reisman, D. 319, 360
Reiter, H. H. 208

Reiter, R. G. 32, 127
Reitz, H. J. 218
Renas, S. R. 414
Renee, A. 109
Renner, H. L. 208
Renshaw, J. E. 477, 478
Renzulli, J. S. 609
Reppucci, N. D. 257
Rescher, N. 505
Reschly, D. J. 127
Reskin, B. F. 472
Resnick, H. 187
Resource Center on Sex Roles in Education 327
Resources Analysis Branch 360
Rest, S. 263
Rettig, J. L. 208
Reuben, E. 333, 379
Reuschlein, P. 565
Reuter, B. A. 492, 512
Reuter, M. 492
Rey, L. D. 127
Reyes, M. R. 622
Reyes de Garmo, E. 614
Reynolds, D. H. 113
Reynolds, L. 548
Reynolds, M. K. 231
Rezier, A. G. 219
Rezler, A. G. 208
Reznick, J. S. 5
Reznikoff, M. 533
Rheingold, H. L. 32
Rhine, W. R. 166, 584
Rhoden, B. 567
Rhodes, L. G. 602
Rhoem, W. 228
Rhude, B. E. 208
Ribal, J. E. 32
Ribich, F. D. 252
Rice, D. G. 293
Rice, J. K. 293, 360
Rice, P. 437, 512
Rice, R. P. 127, 534
Rich, A. 327
Rich, N. A. 127
Richards, C. V. 69
Richards, J. M., Jr. 127
Richards, R. 70
Richardson, B. 327
Richardson, M. S. 42, 43, 69, 80, 127, 187, 512, 513

Richer, J. 597, 602
Richmond, B. O. 550, 567, 597
Richmond, D. M. 568
Richmond, M. L. 624
Rickard, F. S. 566, 613
Rickman, G. 568, 598
Ricks, F. A. 292, 360
Rideout, A. H. 392
Rider, E. A. 234
Ridgeway, C. L. 32, 166
Ridley, R. 261
Rieder, C. H. 327
Riegel, K. 58
Ries, K. 322
Riesche, D. L. 32
Riesman, D. 327, 513
Riley, M. 437
Riley, S. B. 380
Rincon, B. 614
Ring, S. I. 368
Ringness, T. A. 166, 167
Ringo, M. 462
Riordan, R. J. 293
Rios, G. E. 613, 622
Ripley, T. M. 437
Risch, C. 293
Rist, R. C. 598
Ritchie, J. W. 380
Ritschel, S. 109
Ritter, K. V. 437, 534
Rivera, A. 614
Rivers, C. 534
Rivers, W. 559
Riverside California NOW Education Task Force 361
Rizzo, A. M. 489
Roach, A. J. 285, 428
Roach, R. M. 534
Roark, A. C. 463, 598
Robb, G. P. 353
Robbins, E. 234
Robbins, L. 234
Robbins, M. L. 470
Robbins, P. F. 437
Robbins, R. B. 234
Roberts, A. 568, 595
Roberts, D. F. 69
Roberts, G. C. 69, 208
Roberts, G. H. 568, 584
Roberts, J. 380
Roberts, J. E. 496
Roberts, J. I. 323, 328,

348, 484
Roberts, M. L. 463, 513
Robertson, W. 463
Robin, S. S. 408, 472
Robinson, E. A. 275
Robinson, J. A. 463
Robinson, J. W. 598
Robinson, L. H. 328, 380
Robinson, P. 568
Robison, K. A. 234
Robitaille, D. F. 187
Roby, P. 328, 361, 380, 437, 534
Rock, D. A. 404
Rodarte, I. 614
Rodda, W. C. 253
Roderick, R. D. 426, 545
Rodger, W. 492
Rodgers, G. M. 547, 596
Rodin, J. 128
Rodriguez, M. 613
Rodriguez, A. 614
Roe, A. 361
Roebling, M. G. 438
Roesch, R. 438
Roeske, N. A. 478
Rogers, C. 568
Rogers, D. P. 619
Rogers, E. C. 568
Rogers, J. D. 97
Rogers, M. M. 30
Rogers, P. A. 264
Rogers, R. W. 54
Rohfeld, R. W. 293
Rohlen, J. M. 128
Rohner, R. P. 32
Rohrilich, L. T. 438
Roiphe, A. 293
Rokoff, G. 406
Roll, S. 617
Rollenhagen, J. 274
Rollesson, C. K. 484
Rollins, M. A. 534
Rolwing, R. H. 470, 529
Romano, N. C. 69
Romer, N. 234
Romine, B. H. 208
Roodin, P. A. 167, 253
Rooks, E. 568
Rooney, J. F. 141
Roper, Inc. 69
Ropp, J. 179, 257

Rosaldo, M. Z. 10, 33, 151, 571, 572
Rose, C. 69, 187, 328, 361
Rose, H. A. 95, 128, 197, 208, 219, 273, 293
Rose, S. 96
Rosen, B. 33, 69, 128, 438, 463, 464, 507, 534
Rosen, D. 337
Rosen, J. 128
Rosen, J. L. 208
Rosen, M. 165, 326, 492
Rosen, R. 128, 328, 380, 484
Rosenbaum, G. 181
Rosenbaum, R. M. 263
Rosenberg, B. G. 2, 21, 33, 59, 561
Rosenberg, D. 438
Rosenberg, F. R., and Simmons, R. G. 187
Rosenblatt, A. 484
Rosenbluh, E. S. 167
Rosenblum, D. C. 250
Rosenfeld, C. 535
Rosenfeld, E. F. 33
Rosenfeld, H. M. 167
Rosenfeld, R. A. 513
Rosenfield, D. 190, 261
Rosenhan, D. 33
Rosenkrantz, P. S. 40, 48, 69, 95, 141, 187, 269, 516
Rosenmayer, L. 527
Rosenthal, B. 627
Rosenthal, E. R. 56, 167, 513, 535
Rosenthal, J. C. 187
Rosenthal, R. 361
Rosenwood, L. M. 117
Roskam, A. H. 208
Rosow, J. M. 438
Ross, A. 563
Ross, C. 622
Ross, D. R. 380
Ross, J. 261, 429, 460
Ross, M. 404
Ross, M. B. 361
Ross, S. C. 328, 438
Rossi, A. S. 33, 69, 128, 167, 234, 315, 328, 329, 330, 359, 360, 361, 362, 368, 376, 378, 380, 381, 392, 438, 472, 473, 480,

680 / Index

501, 513, 535, 588
Rossiter, M. W.   473
Rossman, J. E.   513
Ross-Skinner, J.   464
Rostow, E. G.   535
Roszak, B.   57, 69, 70, 568
Roszak, T.   57, 69, 70, 568
Roth, J. D.   291
Roth, R. M.   208
Rothbart, M. K.   33, 64, 167
Rothchild, N.   328
Rothenberg, S.   452
Rothman, A. I.   100, 199
Rothney, J. W.   163
Rothwell, C. E.   382
Rotter, J. B.   242, 253, 552, 584
Rotter, N. G.   438
Rounds, J. B., Jr.   158
Roundtree, J.   251
Roussell, C.   392
Rovers, L.   544
Rowan, R. L.   547
Rowbotham, S.   34
Rowe, M. P.   548
Royal Commission   438
Roybal, R. M.   614
Royer, G. W.   584
Royster, E. C.   581
Rozsnafszky, J.   70
Rubin, D.   167
Rubin, G.   70
Rubin, J. Z.   34
Rubin, L.   535
Rubin, Z.   67, 125
Rubin-Rabson, G.   329, 438, 484
Ruble, D. N.   54, 67, 70, 124, 128, 167, 189, 198, 207, 241, 261
Rubovits, P. C.   598
Rucabo, G.   614
Rudd, M. H.   361
Rudikoff, S.   235, 438, 439
Rudolph, J. R.   71
Rudy, A. J.   70
Ruether, R. R.   495
Ruffer, W. A.   209
Ruhland, D.   3

Ruina, E.   473
Ruiz, R. A.   604, 615
Rumbarger, M. L.   329
Rush, A. K.   286
Rush, M. C.   124
Rush, T. G.   598, 603
Rushing, W. A.   167
Russell, V.   548
Russin, J. M.   361
Russo, N. F.   34, 480
Ruth, S.   70
Rutherford, E.   30
Rutherford, M.   329
Rutledge, C.   128
Ryan, M. P.   209, 478, 513
Ryan, R. A.   627
Ryan, S. M.   70
Ryan, T. T.   272
Ryback, D.   209
Rychlak, J. F.   34, 568, 584
Ryckman, R. M.   188, 253
Ryker, M. L.   568
Rytina, N. F.   439
Ryten, E.   329

Saario, T. N.   329, 333, 361, 376
Saarni, C. I.   70
Sachdeva, D.   362
Sack, D. G.   142, 366
Sacks, K.   70
Sacks, S.   520
Sacks, S. R.   129
Sader, M.   129
Sadker, D.   329
Sadker, M.   311, 329, 349
Saegert, S.   129
Safa, H. I.   612
Safar, D.   619, 624
Safford, S. F.   233
Safilios-Rothschild, C.   21, 34, 59, 68, 69, 102, 129, 328, 329, 361, 367, 372, 380, 383, 473, 474, 487, 488, 497, 513, 517, 525, 533, 535, 539
Safran, C.   439
St. Ange, M. C.   559
St. John, N. H.   568
St. Peter, S.   129
Salastin, S.   277
Saleh, S. D.   129, 513

Saleh, S. E.   478, 535
Salk, L.   535
Salkind, N. J.   209
Salo, K. E.   535
Salter, A.   329
Saltzstein, H. D.   129
Salvia, J.   361
Salwen, L. H.   293
Salzman-Webb, M.   70
Samara, B. M.   362
Sampel, D. D.   569
Sampson, E. E.   129, 167
Sampson, J. M.   535
Samson, D. F.   253
Samuel, N.   584
Samuel, W.   569
Samuels, C.   489
Sanchez, C.   622
Sanchez, G. I.   622
Sanchez, R.   614
Sanday, P. R.   34
Sandell, S.   473
Sanders, D.   113
Sanders, E. B.   129
Sanders, M.   619
Sanders, M. K.   70, 129
Sanders, S.   96, 352
Sandidge, S.   129
Sandis, E. E.   34, 167
Sandler, B.   293, 310, 329, 346, 381, 439
Sandler, B. E.   167
Sands, B. L.   188
Sang, B.   291
Sangerman, H.   439
Santrock, H.   34
Sappenfield, B. R.   188
Saragoza, E.   615
Sarason, I. G.   146
Sarason, S. B.   200
Sardi, Z.   531
Saretsky, L.   293
Sargent, A. G.   45, 56, 70, 80, 351, 403, 424, 448, 454, 548, 609
Sartin, P.   536
Sarup, G.   70
Sarvas, A. F.   381, 393
Sasek, J.   76
Sasfy, J. H.   261
Sashkin, M.   130
Sassower, D. L.   330
Satterfield, D. M.   611, 615

Sattler, J. M.   209
Saunders, T. R.   130
Savasta, M.   137
Sawhill, I. V.   439
Sawrey, W. L.   26
Saxe, L.   44
Scagnelli, J.   352
Scally, B.   482
Scalia, F. A.   167
Scanzoni, J.   34, 569, 603
Scarf, M.   70
Scates, A. Y.   439
Schab, F.   362
Schaefer, C. E.   147, 167, 188
Schaeffer, D. L.   22, 26, 63, 102, 130, 133
Schaeffer, R. G.   362, 439
Schafer, C. L.   548
Schaie, K. W.   14
Schallberger, B.   64
Schearer, M.   130
Scheck, D. C.   34, 168, 253
Schedson, M.   529
Scheele, A. M.   283
Scheflbein, B.   385, 454
Schein, V. E.   130, 464, 484
Scheirer, E. A.   85
Schell, A.   68
Schell, D. M.   130
Schell, R. E.   70, 130
Scher, M.   293, 484
Schersky, R.   130
Schetlin, E. M.   330, 393, 548
Schien, V.   439
Schiffler, R. J.   536
Schiller, B.   548
Schilling, G. F.   473
Schissel, R. F.   219
Schlack, M. J.   393
Schlacter, G.   34
Schleman, H. B.   293
Schleman, H. G.   330
Schletzer, V. M.   330, 513
Schlossberg, N. K.   102, 130, 290, 293, 294, 330
Schmaljohn, P. J.   294
Schmalzreid, B. L.   510
Schmeck, R. R.   252
Schmedinghoff, G. J.   598
Schmidt, J. A.   188
Schmidt, L. C.   130, 514

Schmidt, M. M.   605
Schmidt, M. R.   209
Schmidt, R. A.   495
Schmidt-Relenberg, N.   131, 362
Schminke, C. W.   318
Schmitt, D. R.   119
Schmuck, P. A.   393
Schmuck, R.   131
Schnall, S.   498
Schneider, F.   489
Schneider, J.   330
Schneider, J. M.   251, 253, 254
Schneider, L.   168, 362
Schneier, C. E.   209
Schnepper, J. A.   439
Schnitzer, P. K.   235
Schockett, M. R.   544, 558
Schoenfeldt, L. F.   168
Schofield, L. F.   188
Scholz, J. P.   619
Scholz, N. T.   294, 362
Schomburg, T. E.   131, 188, 548
Schommer, D.   217
Schonberger, R. J.   439
Schoonover, J. W.   464
Schopler, J.   131
Schreiber, C.   464
Schreiber, K. J.   330
Schroeder, C. C.   131
Schroth, M. L.   569, 584, 598
Schuck, J. R.   21
Schuck, V.   330, 381
Schuell, H.   214
Schuldt, W. J.   131
Schuler, R. S.   439
Schulz, D.   569
Schumacher, D.   330
Schumacher, E. E.   362, 381
Schuman, H.   548
Schur, E. M.   24
Schussel, R. H.   278
Schwab, M. R.   183
Schwartz, A. J.   619
Schwartz, E. B.   464
Schwartz, F. N.   439
Schwartz, J.   131
Schwartz, J. L.   294
Schwartz, J. M.   264

Schwartz, M.   569
Schwartz, P.   330, 362
Schwartz, S. H.   191
Schwarzer, R.   209
Schwarzweller, H. K.   168, 219
Schwendiger, H.   381
Schwendiger, J.   381
Schwenn, M.   235
Schwindt, H. D.   489
Sciacco, A., Jr.   487
Sciara, F. J.   569
Scientific Manpower Commission   473
Sciortino, R.   188
Scott, A.   131, 362, 439, 440
Scott, A. F.   10, 31, 34, 37, 49, 68, 71, 277, 307, 330, 404
Scott, C. S.   131
Scott, D.   111, 423, 425, 459, 490, 496, 600
Scott, E.   370
Scott, E. L.   381
Scott, H.   71
Scott, M. V.   596, 621
Scott, O.   19, 155
Scott, P.   173, 294, 330, 540, 569, 598
Scott, R.   331, 569, 584
Scriven, A. L.   393
Scully, M.   331
Seaburg, D.   131
Seagull, A. A.   594
Sealy, J. R.   570
Seaman, B.   71
Seaman, J.   112
Sears, P. S.   362
Sears, R. R.   35, 71, 188
Seashore, E. W.   403
Seater, B. B.   32, 166
Seaver, J.   478
Seavey, C. A.   35
Seawell, W.   393
Sebald, M. L.   185, 205
Sedaka, J. B.   440, 464
Sedgwick, B. R.   294
Sedlacek, C. G.   209, 219, 514
Sedlacek, W. E.   58, 71, 271, 272, 316, 343, 354, 506, 545, 548, 569, 577, 588, 589, 590, 598, 623, 627

Sedney, M. A. 71, 294, 514
Seed, S. 440, 514
Seefeldt, V. 565
Seeman, J. 188, 209, 254
Seeman, M. V. 294
Segal, S. 519
Segal, S. J. 277
Segal, W. 30, 164, 251
Seiberling, B. 536
Seidel, H. 339
Seiden, A. M. 35, 131, 294
Seidenberg, F. A. 440
Seidenberg, R. 295
Seidner, C. J. 94, 254
Seifer, N. 440, 536
Selby, R. 363
Selcer, R. J. 35
Self, G. 440, 536
Self, P. A. P. 188, 219
Seligman, C. 261
Sell, J. M. 295
Sells, L. 71, 359, 363, 440, 548
Seltz, J. 381
Semler, V. 376
Senders, V. 35
Seni, C. 246
Senior, W. B. 627
Sepulveda, B. R. 615
Serbin, L. A. 35, 363
Sethney, B. J. 300, 335, 508
Setne, V. L. 295
Setzman, E. J. 131
Severance, L. J. 168
Severson, R. A. 584
Severy, L. J. 78
Seward, D. 35, 71
Seward, G. H. 35, 71, 132, 295
Sewel, C. 132
Sewell, T. 578
Sewell, T. E. 584
Sewell, W. H. 168, 331
Sexton, P. C. 35, 331, 381, 393
Sexton, V. S. 484
Seymour, W. R. 569
Shab, F. 514
Shack, S. 168, 331
Shade, B. J. 569, 584
Shafer, S. M. 465

Shaffer, D. R. 132
Shaffer, H. G. 331
Shaffer, J. P. 331
Shaffer, R. A. 570
Shah, V. P. 168
Shailer, T. 176
Shainess, N. 295
Shakeshaft, C. S. 391
Shaman, J. M. 363
Shanahan, E. 440, 490
Shank, J. K. 405
Shapira, A. 611
Shapiro, C. S. 478
Shapiro, E. 295
Shapiro, H. J. 440
Shapiro, J. 295
Shapiro, R. 41, 465
Shapley, D. 331, 363
Sharma, P. C. 71, 441, 623
Sharma, S. 627
Sharp, L. M. 363, 441, 514
Shauffer, C. B. 185
Shaughnessy, S. 465
Shaver, P. 168, 222, 232, 235, 238
Shaw, D. 295
Shaw, M. C. 132, 168, 188
Shaw, M. E. 78, 584, 598
Shaw, R. L. 584
Shaw, S. 437
Shaw-Hamilton, L. 70
Shaywitz, S. E. 536
Shea, D. 245
Shea, J. B. 254
Shea, J. R. 441, 532, 536
Shea, P. D. 168
Shearer, K. D. 404, 490
Sheehan, T. J. 132
Sheehy, G. 514
Sheikh, A. A. 576
Sheldon, E. B. 39, 441
Shell, L. G. 209
Shelley, H. P. 233
Shelly, A. C. 71
Sheldon, E. B. 445
Shelton, B. 485, 536
Shelton, P. B. 169, 254, 514
Shemberg, K. M. 114
Shepard, W. O. 132
Shepherd, J. 441
Sherman, J. A. 11, 16, 36, 45, 47, 98, 132, 198, 258, 295, 296, 348, 354, 398

Sherman, L. J.   487
Sherman, M. F.   188, 253
Sherman, R. C.   132, 231
Sherman, R. G.   514, 536
Shertzer, B.   377
Sherwood, E. B.   36, 169
Shiel, T. M.   21, 25, 322
Shields, P.   426
Shields, S. A.   3, 132
Shinar, E. H.   132
Shinn, M.   235, 331
Shipman, U. C.   157, 561
Shirk, E. J.   504, 523
Shishkoff, M. M.   296
Shively, M. G.   71
Shlomi, A.   171
Shockley, A. A.   570
Shore, M. F.   169, 350, 611
Short, J. A.   235
Short, J. C.   235
Shortridge, K.   381
Shotola, R.   119
Showalter, E.   381, 492
Showell, S.   477
Shrauger, J. S.   188
Shrigley, R. L.   132
Shuell, T. J.   79
Shutzer, F.   43, 80
Shuval, J. T.   36, 133, 169, 478
Shybut, J.   247, 545
Sidhu, N.   192
Sidlofsky, S.   473, 514
Siegel, A. E.   169, 363, 536
Siegel, A. I.   599
Siegel, C. L. F.   133
Siegel, J.   212
Sigall, H.   72
Sigel, I.   133
Siggin, L. D.   133
Siiter, R.   75, 548
Sikes, B. H.   486
Sikes, J. N.   350
Silber, J. W.   70
Silveira, J.   3
Silver, G. A.   478
Silver, P. F.   331
Silverstein, B.   558, 570, 599
Simmons, J.   536
Simmons, J. E.   473

Simmons, R. G.   187
Simmons, W. D.   189
Simon, B. D.   235
Simon, J. G.   97, 223, 240, 257, 258, 262
Simon, M. G.   189
Simon, R. J.   363, 381, 441
Simon, W. E.   187, 189
Simons, J. A.   296
Simons, R. H.   209
Simpson, E. J.   296
Simpson, I. H.   169, 441, 514
Simpson, L. A.   382
Simpson, R. L.   169, 441, 514
Simpson, W. A.   585
Simpson, W. E.   100
Sims, H. P., Jr.   242, 254
Singer, E.   169
Singer, J. N.   133
Singer, S. L.   133
Singh, K. P.   536
Singh, U. P.   55, 100
Singleton, D.   133, 353, 478
Sinha, S. P.   133, 209
Sinowitz, B. E.   382
Sistrunk, F.   83, 133
Sizemore, B. A.   393
Skinner, D. A.   191
Skotko, V.   133
Slaby, A. E.   570
Slaney, F. J.   189
Slaghter, D. T.   570
Slee, F. W.   133, 363
Sloan, M. E.   379, 473, 541
Slobodian, J.   345
Slocum, W. L.   133, 441
Slovie, P.   134
Small, A. W.   124, 189, 241
Smalley, D.   189
Smart, K. L.   153
Smart, M.   363
Smee, P. G.   131
Smelser, W. T.   169
Smith, A. D.   134
Smith, A. G.   599
Smith, B. D.   189, 235, 236
Smith, B. K.   536
Smith, C. H.   134
Smith, C. P.   40, 134, 198, 212, 235, 239
Smith, D.   36, 72, 485, 487
Smith, D. C.   492
Smith, D. G.   209

Smith, E. J.   570
Smith, F.   132, 466
Smith, G.   157, 441
Smith, G. M.   382
Smith, H. C.   514
Smith, H. M.   177, 189
Smith, H. P.   570
Smith, I.   138
Smith, J.   465
Smith, J. A.   296
Smith, J. B.   536
Smith, J. L.   536
Smith, K. S.   490, 514
Smith, L.   465
Smith, L. E.   570
Smith, L. M.   18, 110
Smith, M.   515, 599
Smith, M. A.   210, 549
Smith, M. E.   134, 219
Smith, M. L.   623
Smith, M. P.   332
Smith, N. S.   134
Smith, P.   615
Smith, P. C.   422
Smith, P. K.   36
Smith, R.   305
Smith, S.   493
Smith, S. A.   72
Smith, S. D.   72, 495
Smith, S. W.   216, 316
Smith, V. C., Jr.   545
Smith, W. S.   363
Smithells, J.   135
Smitherman, G.   570
Smokler, C. B.   189
Smothergill, D.   556
Smothergill, N. L.   90
Smouse, A. D.   163
Smutts, R. W.   442
Snider, A. J.   72
Snyder, C. A.   39
Snyder, D.   599
Snyder, E. E.   36, 134, 169, 189, 364
Snyder, F. A.   160
Snyder, H. N.   262
Snyder, W. D.   549
Snyder-Ott, J.   134
Soares, A. T.   189
Soares, L. M.   189
Sobel, R. S.   262
Sobieszek, B. I.   28
Sobol, M. G.   515, 537
Society of Women Engineers   364
Soehngen, S.   62
Sokeitous, J. F.   442
Sokoloff, N. J.   442
Solano, C. H.   364
Soldwedel, B.   382, 393
Solid, A. B.   457
Soliman, A. M.   214
Solmon, L. C.   364
Solomon, D.   169, 210, 585, 599
Solomon, L.   442
Solomon, L. D.   382, 515
Solomon, L. Z.   134, 235
Solomons, H. H.   364
Sommers, D.   442
Sommers, T.   134
Sommerville, R.   442, 571
Sontag, L. W.   210
Sorel, C.   493
Sorensen, A. B.   579
Sorenson, J.   169, 192, 213, 219
Sorenson, T. C.   134
Sorkin, A. L.   442, 549, 599
Sorotzkin, F.   364
Sorrentino, R.   235
Sostek, A. B.   169
Soto, D.   569
Soule, B.   36, 170, 515
Southard, H. F.   537, 615
Southern, M. L.   89, 126
Sowell, T.   599
Soysa, N.   72
Spain, J.   465
Spain, J. B.   490
Spaulding, J.   332
Spaulding, R.   189, 364
Specht, H.   129
Spence, B. A.   393
Spence, J. T.   72, 113, 134, 190, 236
Spencer, A. G.   36, 135
Spencer, L. M.   584
Spencer, P. A.   193
Sperry, D. L.   247
Spick, B.   135
Spiegel, D.   210
Spiegel, J.   72, 190, 332, 499, 537
Spiegler, M. D.   91
Spigel, I. M.   200

Spilerman, S. 94, 410, 445
Spilka, B. 608
Spitz, R. S. 435, 441, 532, 536
The Spocks 36
Spradley, J. P. 479
Sprague, M. S. 454
Spreitzer, E. 36, 134, 169, 364
Sprey, J. 571
Sprik, J. 382
Spuck, D. W. 621
Srull, T. K. 254
Staats, S. 254
Stabler, J. R. 262, 571, 600
Stacey, B. 170
Stacey, J. 36, 44, 135, 227, 298, 300, 316, 318, 319, 320, 328, 330, 332, 355, 362, 370, 373, 379, 380, 381
Stack, C. B. 571
Stack, J. J. 585
Staebler, B. K. 250
Stafford, F. P. 374
Stafford, M. P. 364
Stafford, R. L. 364, 515
Stafford, R. W. 172
Stahmann, R. F. 155
Staines, G. L. 427, 428, 442
Stake, J. E. 36, 135, 190, 236, 300
Stake, M. 135, 190
Staley, Y. 103, 225, 592
Stambler, S. 340, 341, 369
Standley, K. 36, 170, 515
Stanfiel, J. D. 571
Stanford, B. 135, 225, 497
Stanford Committee on the Education and Employment of Women in the University 364
Stanley, B. M. 73, 465
Stanley, J. C. 145, 215, 573, 599
Stanely, Y. 103
Stanwick, K. 488, 489
Stanwyck, D. J. 190, 210
Staples, R. 552, 567, 571
Stapp, J. 72, 134, 135, 190

Starer, R. 332, 442
Starker, L. 296
Starness, T. 595
Starr, R. R. 378
Stasz, C. 135, 382
Staszak, J. 461
Staten, B. J. 296
Statistics Committee 473
Stead, B. A. 465
Stebbins, C. A. 74
Stebbins, R. A. 515
Steckler, J. F. 298, 473
Stedman, J. M. 615
Stedman, L. A. 485
Steele, M. H. 332
Steele, R. S. 227
Steers, R. M. 465
Stefflre, B. 133
Stefic, E. C. 37
Stehbens, J. A. 170
Steichen, E. 465
Steigenga-Kouwe, S. E. 443
Steiger, J. M. 332
Stein, A. H. 37, 135, 242, 254
Stein, D. H. 513
Stein, L. 479
Stein, R. L. 443
Steinbacher, R. 135
Steinberg, B. 135
Steinberg, C. 228
Steinem, G. 73, 443
Steiner, J. W. 100, 199
Steiner, S. 605
Steinhart, F. 429
Steinke, B. K. 170
Steinmann, A. 37, 68, 73, 136, 187, 190, 296, 534, 537, 571, 572, 624
Stek, R. J. 242
Ste-Marie, L. 144
Stent, M. D. 542
Stephan, C. 190
Stephan, W. G. 190, 261
Stephens, M. W. 254
Stephenson, P. S. 297
Steppacher, R. C. 483
Stericker, A. B. 73, 136, 190, 236
Sterling, D. H. 572
Stern, R. N. 418
Stevens, B. 297
Stevens, H. A. 210

Stevenson, F. B. 394
Stevenson, G. 297
Stevenson, H. W. 100
Stevenson, M. H. 37, 229, 443
Stewart, A. J. 37, 136, 190, 210, 236, 539
Stewart, D. G. 599
Stewart, D. W. 210
Stewart, J. 623
Stewart, N. R. 298
Stewart, P. L. 412, 443, 475, 495
Stewart, R. A. 126, 166
Stewart, V. M. 236
Stiehm, J. 37, 318, 371, 410, 484, 490
Stiggins, R. J. 273
Stiles, L. J. 332
Still, E. 364
Stillion, J. M. 136
Stillwell, L. J. 190
Stimpson, C. 332, 443
Stimpson, C. R. 37
Stinger, L. A. 18
Stingle, S. F. 136
Stinnett, N. 37
Stivers, J. 365
Stivers, P. E. 376
Stix, D. L. 210
Stockard, A. J. 37
Stockburger, D. W. 300
Stodt, M. M. 210
Stoessel, J. 365
Stogdill, R. M. 91, 455
Stokes, G. 572
Stokes, S. 365
Stokowski, B. 236
Stoll, C. S. 382, 485
Stoller, R. J. 73
Stolz, L. 537
Stolzenberg, R. M. 538
Stone, B. 271
Stone, G. L. 254
Stone, L. A. 210
Stone, P. C. 615
Stone, S. 526
Stone, W. F. 253
Storandt, M. 213, 220
Stork, L. 15
Story, M. W. 382
Stout, E. 487
Stoyr, M. W. 537

Strache, L. K. 394
Strahan, R. F. 55
Strainchamps, E. 136, 493
Straub, W. F. 246
Straus, J. H. 170
Straus, M. A. 170
Strauss, M. D. 73
Strickland, B. R. 572, 586
Stringer, P. 136
Stroad, B. 283
Strober, H. M. 109
Strober, M. H. 412, 443, 454, 457, 465
Strodtbeck, F. L. 116
Stroink, P. L. 443
Stroller, R. J. 37
Strommer, D. W. 332, 333
Strong, C. R. 383
Strouf, J. 91
Strouse, J. 297
Strudler, B. 520
Stucker, J. J. 490
Sturm, S. G. 236
Sturtz, S. A. 365
Suarez, C. F. 615
Suber, C. J. 37
Suchner, R. W. 136, 365
Suddick, D. E. 184, 356, 429
Sue, E. 230
Suelzle, M. 443
Sugnet, C. J. 333
Suhr, J. M. 280
Sullerot, E. 38, 73
Sullivan, M. 479
Sullivan, W. J. 365
Suls, J. 136
Sumner, H. L. 443
Sundheim, B. J. M. 136, 190
Suniewick, N. 304, 398, 502
Surette, R. F. 297
Surman, M. B. 89
Suter, B. A. 136, 137
Suter, L. E. 443
Sutherland, E. 615
Sutker, P. B. 134
Sutton-Smith, B. 33, 137
Suziedelis, A. 73
Swaminathan, K. 210
Swanson, M. A. 137
Swanson, R. 627
Swartz, J. D. 618
Swartz, J. M. 549

688 / Index

Swartzbaugh, R. G. 615
Sweet, J. A. 444
Swerdloff, S. 444
Swidler, A. 495
Swinger, H. K. 585
Swisdak, B. 211
Sybouts, W. 38
Symonds, A. 38, 73
Symonds, J. D. 582
Symonds, Moulton R. 38, 73
Synge, J. 137
Syptak, F. M. 405
Szabo, M. 211
Szal, J. A. 38
Szilagyi, A. D. 242, 254
Szymanski, A. 444, 549

Tabak, M. N. 493
Taber, R. 70
Tabor, J. M. 327, 463
Tagiuri, R. 217
Taines, B. 365
Takata, G. 261
Takooshian, H. 549
Taleporos, E. 74
Tamir, P. 137, 365
Tangri, S. S. 2, 3, 8, 20, 28, 38, 48, 49, 57, 65, 85, 104, 120, 137, 170, 176, 194, 197, 211, 226, 227, 240, 258, 323, 402, 444, 510, 515, 537, 546
Tanner, N. 527
Tanney, M. F. 267, 280, 297, 340, 542
Targ, D. B. 31, 33, 43, 67, 472, 512, 560
Tarnoff, S. L. 545
Tarte, R. D. 134
Tatham, C. B. 572
Tatham, E. L. 572
Tatje, T. E. 572
Tautfest, P. B. 297
Tavris, C. 3, 25, 38, 57, 60, 74, 113, 137, 227, 236, 407, 428, 442, 444
Taylor, D. A. 549
Taylor, H. 333
Taylor, L. 495
Taylor, M. 609
Taylor, M. G. 537

Taylor, P. 537
Taylor, P. A. 505
Taylor, P. H. 191
Taylor, P. L. 137
Taylor, R. G. 191, 211
Taylor, S. E. 137
Taylor, S. P. 118, 137, 138
Taylor, S. S. 394
Taynor, J. 92, 138, 262, 462
Teahan, J. E. 170, 572
Technical Education Research Center 479
Tedeschi, J. T. 138
Teevan, R. C. 170, 189, 228, 235, 236
Teghtsoonian, M. 385
Teicher, J. 572
Templeton, J. F. 465
TenElshof, A. 138, 170
Tenhouten, W. D. 572, 591
Tennent, S. S. 124
Tennyson, W. W. 278
Tenrov, D. 74, 297, 515
Terborg, J. R. 259, 262, 444, 462, 464, 466
Terbovic, M. L. 188
Teri, L. 297
ter Laak, J. J. F. 157, 226
Terpstra, D. 409
Terrell, G. 138, 145, 219
Terrell, K. 445, 538
Terry, R. 549
Terstine, R. J. 398
Tessler, R. C. 191
Tessler, S. E. 394
Tetenbaum, T. B. 74
Thagaard, S. T. 138
Thalberg, I. 444
Tharp, R. G. 611
Theodore, A. 127, 143, 212, 226, 310, 366, 383, 405, 411, 418, 444, 469, 477, 484, 486, 499, 516, 519, 528, 529, 530, 533, 558, 591, 602
Thetford, M. L. 333, 383
Thistlethwaite, D. L. 365
Thomas, A. H. 298
Thomas, C. L. 573
Thomas, D. C. 196
Thomas, G. P. 138

Thomas, H. 138, 255
Thomas, J. L. 444, 490, 537
Thomas, K. A. 549, 563, 573
Thomas, L. E. 217
Thomas, M. H. 118
Thomas, P. 537
Thomas, P. J. 38, 498
Thomas, R. 529
Thomas, S. 587
Thomopoulos, E. H. 537, 538
Thompson, A. R. 549
Thompson, C. M. 74
Thompson, D. L. 246
Thompson, E. G. 138
Thompson, G. G. 357
Thompson, J. 311, 411, 599
Thompson, J. K. 298, 333
Thompson, M. H. 466
Thompson, M. L. 426, 494, 565
Thoresen, C. E. 298
Thornburg, K. R. 170
Thorne, B. 38, 343
Thorne, F. C. 74
Thornhill, G. J. 255
Thornhill, M. A. 255
Thornton, S. 47
Thrash, P. A. 336
Thurber, S. 138, 236, 255, 627
Thurnher, M. 38
Thurow, L. 549
Thurston, A. J. 394
Thurston, J. R. 211
Tibbetts, S. L. 74, 333, 573
Tickamyer, A. R. 376
Tidball, M. E. 170, 333, 383, 444
Tiedeman, D. V. 335, 510
Tiedt, I. M. 298
Tiffany, D. W. 302
Tifft, L. L. 381
Tilly, C. H. 333
Timmons, J. E. 394
Timpano, D. M. 394
Tinsley, A. 333
Tinsley, D. E. 211
Tipton, R. M. 219

Tittle, C. K. 138, 274, 298, 329, 333, 361, 473
Tjosvold, D. W. 137
Tobach, E. 295
Tobias, S. 138, 211, 298, 333, 334
Todd, F. J. 138, 211, 219
Toews, L. K. 74
Toffler, A. 44, 82
Tolbert-Stroud, S. 600
Tolchin, S. 487
Toldson, I. L. 600
Tolor, A. 74, 86, 243
Tomlinson-Keasey, C. 139, 236
Tompkins, P. 334
Tonesk, X. 74
Tonick, I. J. 363
Topa, V. 163
Toporoff, R. 444, 538
Tornabene, L. L. 444
Torney, J. V. 16
Torrance, E. P. 139, 243, 538
Torrance, P. 299, 383
Torres, D. C. 615
Torres-Matrullo, C. 616
Torrey, J. W. 299, 445
Touhey, J. C. 74, 139
Tovor, F. D. 616
Toyama, J. S. 38
Tracy, T. 446
Trask, A. 387
Treas, J. J. 445, 515, 538
Trecker, J. L. 334
Treiman, D. J. 445, 538
Tremaine, L. S. 75
Trembly, D. 139
Trent, I. M. 299
Trent, J. W. 139, 170, 211
Trent, S. J. 211
Tresemer, D. W. 75, 139, 228, 236, 237
Trewick, O. 445
Triandis, H. C. 573
Tribble, I. 600
Trickett, E. 365
Trickett, P. 365
Trigg, L. J. 39, 211
Trilling, B. A. 39, 140, 445
Trilling, D. 39
Trippot, L. 334
Trites, D. K. 171

Tritsch, C. 466
Trockel, J. F. 243
Troll, L. E. 39
Trow, J. J. 334
Truax, A. 383
Truex, D. 334
Trujillo, M. 616
Trumbo, S. S. 39
Tsong, P. Z. 549
Tsuchigane, R. 445
Tuck, M. G. 334
Tucker, B. Z. 139
Tudor, J. 277
Tuel, J. K. 212
Tukey, R. S. 139
Tulkin, S. 550
Turkat, D. 299
Turner, B. F. 191, 514, 573, 603
Turner, C. B. 573
Turner, E. M. 484
Turner, G. 230
Turner, M. B. 550
Turner, M. E. 237
Turner, R. H. 139, 516
Turner, S. A. 75
Turnipseed, D. 75
Turnure, C. 139
Tuska, S. 41
Tuttle, H. I. 394
'T Veld-Langeveld, H. M. 538
Tygart, C. E. 495
Tyler, B. B. 171
Tyler, F. B. 171
Tyler, L. E. 27, 28, 39, 139, 212, 287, 299, 394, 485
Tyree, A. 445, 538

Uesugi, T. T., and Vinacke, W. E. 140
Uhl, N. P. 584
Uhlig, G. E. 619
Ulbrich, H. H. 445
Ullian, D. Z. 39, 75
Ullrich, M. F. 445
Ulrich, C. 334
Unger, R. K. 33, 39, 75, 76, 107, 140, 157, 227, 237, 239, 371, 411, 481, 548
Unkel, E. 140, 171

Upchurch, W. H. 113
Useem, R. H. 334

Vacher, C. J. D. 191
Vaden, A. G. 477
Vaden, R. E. 477
Vail, A. F. 299, 550
Valdez, L. 605
Valentich, M. E. 485
Valentine, C. 395
Valentine, D. 140
Valenzuela-Crocker, E. 619
Valle, V. A. 140, 242, 258, 262
Valley, J. A. 299, 550
VanAken, C. G. 369, 463, 470, 471, 472, 473, 483
VanAlstyne, C. 334
Vance, J. J. 550
Van der Berghe, P. L. 372, 592
Van de Riet, H. K. 54
VanderWilt, R. B. 299, 365
Van Dijk-den Bandt, M. L. 39
Vane, J. R. 358
Van Egmond, E. 131
Vanek, J. 445
VanGelder, L. 76, 493
Vangie, M. 616, 623
VanHouten, D. R. 451
Vanik, V. 221
VanMeir, E. J. 395
VanSchoelandt, S. K. 114
VanVuuren, N. 76
Varenhorst, B. 298
Vasquez, A. G. 619
Vasquez, M. 616
Vatter, 438
Vaughan, R. P. 212
Vaught, G. M. 167, 191, 253
Vaughter, R. M. 140, 365, 445
Vedovato, S. 76
Vega, M. 252
Vega, S. 266
Vela, J. E. 619
Veldman, D. J. 140
Vener, A. M. 39
Venerable, W. R. 171
Verdesi, E. H. 495

Veres, H. C. 171, 191, 510
Verheyden-Hilliard, M. E. 39, 299, 334, 335, 366, 395, 445
Verma, M. R. 299
Vernon, C. R. 134
Veroff, J. 3, 40, 130, 140, 141, 171, 212, 237, 299, 538, 600
Vestin, M. 366
Vetter, B. M. 171, 366, 474, 485, 550, 600
Vetter, L. 141, 212, 219, 299, 300, 335, 508
Vetterling, M. 445
Vidal, M. 616
Viernstein, M. C., and Hogan, R. 171
Villareal, S. 526
Vinacke, W. E. 80, 85, 140, 141
Vincent, M. F. 191
Vincent, S. 114
Viola, M. T. 60
Vitola, B. M., Mullins, C. J., and Weeks, J. L. 498
Vogel, E. 446
Vogel, S. R. 40, 48, 69, 141, 187, 269, 516
Vogel, W. 9, 86, 124
Vollmer, F. 242
Vonder Lippe, A. 9
Vondracek, S. I. 563
Vontress, C. E. 157
Vos, C. 395
Voss, J. H. 191
Voss, V. 383
Vriend, T. J. 335
Vroegh, K. 40, 76, 366

Wachtler, J. 122
Waehrer, H. Y. 55, 57, 64, 65, 290, 315, 415, 416, 417, 418, 432, 446, 448, 480, 527, 558, 591, 602
Waetjen, W. B. 56, 179
Wagman, M. 141, 212, 219
Wagner, E. 76

Wagner, N. N. 608, 609
Wagstaff, L. 596
Wahba, M. A. 116
Wahrman, R. 141
Waite, L. J. 538
Wakefield, J. A., Jr. 76
Walberg, H. J. 141, 219
Waldman, E. 40, 446, 550
Walker, A. 574
Walker, B. 574
Walker, C. 241, 251
Walker, C. E. 226
Walker, E. F. 300
Walker, Y. K. 466
Wall, J. A., Jr. 446
Wallace, D. 208
Wallace, J. L. 171, 300
Wallace, M. J., Jr. 402
Wallace, M. R. 446
Wallace, P. A. 427
Wallace, W. L. 366
Wallach, A. 366
Wallston, B. S. 40, 141, 190, 520, 538
Walsh, D. K. 141
Walsh, M. 228
Walsh, M. R. 479
Walsh, P. A. 395, 516
Walstedt, J. J. 76, 300
Walster, E. 46, 51, 141, 343, 366, 550, 600
Walster, G. W. 246
Walt, D. E. 446, 499
Walters, J. 37, 55, 315, 417
Walters, P. A. 456, 504, 525
Walton, J. 237
Walton, R. G. 485
Wambach, H. S. 579
Wang, L. 446, 538
Ward, C. D. 27
Ward, M. M. 616
Ward, S. H. 574
Ward, W. D. 40, 76
Wardle, M. G. 446
Ware, C. 446, 574
Ware, C. K. 141
Warehime, R. G. 255
Wark, D. 103, 267, 345, 593
Warman, J. P. 466
Warnes, H. 76
Warren, N. T. 191

Warren, P. M. 271
Warren, V. L. 466
Warriner, C. C. 171
Warrior, B. 141
Wartofsky, M. W. 324, 377, 415, 433, 444, 445
Warwick, E. B. 395
Wasserman, C. 270
Wasserman, E. 308, 329, 335, 369, 374, 381, 383, 436, 468, 516, 547
Wasserman, L. 15
Waters, D. B. 156
Waters, E. B. 366
Waters, L. K. 239, 242
Watkins, B. 335
Watkins, J. F. 390
Watkins, M. 574
Watley, D. J. 171, 172, 516, 574
Watson, C. 45
Watson, D. 212, 255
Watson, J. 586
Watson, R. I., Jr. 228, 237
Watson, S. 437
Watson, V. 574
Watts, J. 335
Watts, W. A. 558
Wearer, F. J. 40
Weary, B. 27, 28, 287, 300
Weatherley, D. A. 145
Weaver, C. N. 505, 538
Webb, A. P. 76, 300
Webb, J. L. 206
Webb, S. C. 300
Webbink, P. 300
Webster, M. 578
Webster, S. W. 574
Wedel, C. C. 496
Weeks, J. L. 498
Weeks, M. O. 170
Wegley, C. 132
Weil, M. W. 516, 538
Weinbaum, S. 314
Weinberg, E. 141
Weinberg, J. R. 142
Weinberg, S. 135, 270, 382
Weiner, B. 142, 202, 212, 259, 262, 263
Weiner, G. P. 567, 597

Weiner, L. 263
Weiner, M. J., and Daughtry, T. 255
Weinfeld, F. D. 308, 577
Weir, T. 454, 521
Weis, S. J. F. 191
Weisbrod, B. A. 343
Weisenfelder, H. 533
Weisman, C. S. 142, 366, 577
Weiss, H. 529
Weiss, J. 61, 78
Weiss, J. A. 446
Weiss, P. 142
Weiss, S. D. 8
Weissman, E. I. 142, 516
Weissman, H. J. 2
Weisstein, N. 3, 40, 76, 142
Weitz, L. J. 264
Weitz, S. 40
Weitzel-O'Neill, P. A. 120
Weitzenkorn, S. D. 142
Weitzman, L. J. 40, 335
Welch, F. 550
Weldman, J. 496
Weldon, D. E. 18
Welds, K. 538
Wellens, G. J. 237
Weller, L. 171
Weller, R. H. 624
Welling, M. A. 46, 77
Welliver, T. J. 212
Wells, C. F. 154
Wells, J. 300, 335
Wells, R. A. 124, 359
Wells, T. 26, 117, 446, 460, 574
Welsh, G. S. 142, 195
Wen, S. S. 585
Wendt, D. T. 212
Werner, E. E. 17, 40, 193, 212, 544
Werner, J. E. 300
Werner, P. D. 300
Werner, S. 337
Wernick, W. 335
Werts, C. E. 142, 171, 172, 285, 366, 516
West, A. G. 77, 335
West, C. K. 191
West, S. D., Jr. 143, 301, 366, 383, 395
Westervelt, E. M. 40, 41,

77, 301, 335, 336, 447, 539
Westling, J. H. 458
Westoff, A. L. 539
Westoff, C. F. 424
Weston, M. 437
Weston, P. J. 585
Wetter, R. E. 46, 192
Wexford, M. E. 311, 411
Wexley, K. N. 143, 466, 591
Wheeler, L. 238
Wheeler, N. 365
Whinfield, R. W. 279
Whisenton, J. T. 585
Whitaker, S. V. 574
White, B. 395
White, B. C. 336
White, D. L. 168
White, J. J. 487
White, K. 143, 172, 516, 517, 574, 575, 585, 600
White, K. P. 575, 576, 586
White, L. 257
White, L. C. 539
White, M. S. 367, 383, 474, 517, 539
White, R. F. 143, 212
White, W. 301
White, W. F. 143
White, W. S. 447
Whited, C. 283
Whitehead, G. I. 201
Whitehurst, C. A. 89
Whitely, J. M. 280
Whitely, M. P. 212
Whitely, R. M. 301
Whiteman, M. 86, 150, 554, 575
Whitesel, L. S. 517
Whiteside, M. 143
Whiteside, W. 192
Whiting, B. B. 41
Whiting, F. S. 600
Whitman, A. 539
Whitman, L. 407
Whitmer, D. K. 539
Whitney, M. E. 395
Whitsitt, S. E. 197, 456, 488
Whittaker, E. W. 359, 434
Whitten, J. E. 395

Whitton, M. C. 301
Whyte, M. K. 77
Wiback, K. 93, 409
Wick, B. 50
Widdop, J. H. 213
Widdop, V. A. 213
Widick, C. C. 283
Widom, C. S. 89
Wiegers, R. M. 143
Wiesenfelder, H. 478, 512
Wiggins, J. W. 577
Wiggins, N. 367
Wiggins, R. G. 9, 84, 172, 192
Wigney, T. 336
Wigny, L. 447
Wilbourn, J. M. 498
Wilcox, P. 575
Wild, C. L. 336
Wilensky, H. L. 447
Wiley, J. W. 409
Wiley, M. G. 96, 143
Wilk, C. A. 301
Wilkerson, M. B. 336, 447
Wilkie, J. R. 485
Wilks, J. 447
Willerman, L. 172
Willett, R. S. 466
Williams, C. 143
Williams, D. 237
Williams, D. E. 213
Williams, D. L. 447
Williams, D. M. 21
Williams, H. 600
Williams, J. A. 143
Williams, J. E. 77, 600
Williams, J. G. 585
Williams, J. H. 41, 77, 172, 596
Williams, J. J. 479
Williams, J. M. 213
Williams, K. L. 336, 447
Williams, L. G. 400
Williams, M. 140, 145, 561, 575
Williams, O. 575, 600
Williams, P. A. 479
Williams, T. H. 143, 172
Williamson, J. B. 398, 552
Williamson, N. 496
Williamson, R. C. 35, 132
Williamson, S. Z. 172
Willie, C. V. 561, 567,

575, 583
Willis, C. H. 57
Willis, E. 77
Willis, K. 268
Willis, M. P. 301
Willoughby, R. H. 246, 579
Willows, D. M. 21
Wills, B. S. 144, 213
Willson, N. 336
Wilson, A. 41
Wilson, B. C. 144, 355, 367
Wilson, C. S. 555
Wilson, D. 383
Wilson, D. W. 144
Wilson, J. J. 492, 547
Wilson, K. M. 144, 367, 517, 600, 603
Wilson, M. 301, 474
Wilson, M. F. 479
Wilson, M. T. 575
Wilson, R. H. L. 29, 53, 57, 96, 104, 117, 119, 312, 322
Wilson, V. 144, 479
Winch, R. F. 336
Winchel, R. 238
Winfield, A. D. 301
Wingett, T. J. 301
Wingrove, C. R. 562
Winick, C. 77
Winkler, K. J. 395, 575
Winne, P. H. 582
Winsberg, S. 144
Winter, D. G. 37, 136, 144, 190, 539
Winter, R. 623
Winters, C. J. 192, 213, 219
Wirtenberg, T. J. 285, 336, 367
Wise, H. D. 550
Wisenthal, M. 144
Wish, C. W. 77
Wispe, L. G. 575
Withers, J. S. 334
Withey, S. 367, 384
Withycombe-Brocato, C. J. 172, 192, 220, 367
Witkin, M. H. 144
Witt, S. H. 628
Wittig, M. A. 144, 221, 485
Witty, P. A. 144, 172

Witwer, B. 322
Woelfel, J. 41
Wohl, J. 186
Wolf, W. C. 539
Wolfe, H. B. 301, 447, 517
Wolfe, J. L. 301, 302
Wolfgang, A. 255
Wolfgang, M. 144, 447
Wolfle, D. 474, 546
Wolfson, K. T. P. 517
Wolfson, M. 145, 263
Wolins, L. 356
Wolk, S. 245, 255, 577
Wolkon, G. H. 172
Wolkon, K. A. 172, 517
Woll, S. 302
Wolman, B. B. 77
Wolman, C. 144, 447
Wolpe, J. 302
Woman, C. S. 374
Women and Counselors 302
Women's Action Program 616, 623
Women's Bureau, Canada 448
Women's Bureau, U. S. Dept. of Labor 302, 337, 448, 449, 450, 517, 518, 539, 550, 551, 616, 628
Women's Caucus, Political Science Dept., University of Chicago 384
Women's Equity Action League 337
Wong, D. 17, 544
Wood, F. H. 585
Wood, L. E. 258
Wood, M. M. 238
Wood, M. W. 540
Woodhouse, W. 86
Woodman, W. F. 112, 354
Woodring, P. 337, 384, 396
Woods, E. M. 247
Woods, M. J. 597
Woods, M. M. 41, 467
Worell, J. 61, 78
Worell, L. 23, 41
Work, C. E. 367
Worthington, B. 467
Worthy, N. B. 453
Wortis, H. 4, 41, 78
Wortis, R. P. 4, 41, 78
Wortman, M. S. 82
Wozencraft, M. 145

Wrather, N. 145
Wright, B. 41
Wright, C. R. 368
Wright, L. 520
Wright, S. J. 601, 623, 628
Wrightsman, L. S., Jr. 213
Wukasch-Williamson, L. C. 451
Wursten, R. 212
Wurster, S. R. 110
Wyer, R. S., Jr. 145, 172, 213, 263
Wylie, R. C. 145, 173, 192, 551, 575
Wyly, M. V. 17
Wyman, C. 450
Wyne, M. D. 575, 576, 586
Wyse, L. 518
Wysocki, S. R. 302

Yackee, K. 181
Yancey, W. J. 567
Yarrow, M. 41, 173, 540
Yasinski, L. 145
Yates, B. 337
Yates, G. G. 78
Yawkey, T. D. 551
Yee, A. H. 337, 601
Yehia, M. A. 540
Yelsma, J. J. 356
Yeracaris, C. A. 116
Yerby, J. 145
Yockey, J. M. 78, 540
Yoesting, D. R. 128
Yohalem, A. M. 154, 426, 457, 505, 526
Yonge, G. D. 78, 145
Yorburg, B. 78, 302
York, R. L. 308, 577
Yorks, L. 465
Yoshida, T. 213
Young, A. 518
Young, D. M. 145
Young, F. A. 213
Young, L. R. 518
Young, R. K. 145
Young, V. H. 576
Youngman, M. B. 255
Yount, D. 368

Yudin, L. W. 368
Yudkin, S. 42, 173

Zaccaria, L. 265
Zalk, S. R. 35, 78
Zalkind, D. 460
Zalman, R. 238
Zanducci, R. 173
Zanna, M. P. 78, 108, 146, 223, 228, 238
Zapoleon, M. W. 302, 450, 518, 540
Zaro, J. S. 78, 238
Zatlin, C. E. 213, 220
Zecca, G. M., Muzio, N. R. 42
Zeldow, P. B. 56, 79
Zeller, F. A. 441, 532, 536
Zellman, G. L. 54, 146, 450
Zellner, H. 451
Zemon-Gass, G. 302
Ziebarth, C. A. 42
Ziegler, S. 192
Zigler, E. 61
Zikmund, W. G. 255
Zimmer, T. A. 337
Zimmerman, B. B. 337
Zimmerman, E. 376
Zimmerman, J. 146, 292, 474
Zimmerman, J. N. 396
Zimmermann, M. 246
Zimont, G. 171
Zinberg, D. 338, 368
Zinser, O. 81
Zissis, C. 173, 213, 220, 518, 540
Zito, R. J. 576
Zivotofsky, E. 275
Zubok, B. 89
Zuckerman, D. M. 146, 172, 192
Zuckerman, E. 68
Zuckerman, M. 238
Zung, B. 8
Zunich, M. 146
Zweig, M. 302
Zwerdling, D. 338
Zytkoskee, A. 586
Zytowski, D. C. 302

Ref
Z
7961
F38

MAY 7 1982